CALL US WITH YOUR O...

The Simplicity® DOLL HOUSE

Quality Miniature Houses
Real Good Toys

Doll House Family

HORSMAN

Basic Family #6001 $10.99
Grandparents #6006 $9.99
Boy, Girl & Dalmatian #6002 $8.25
Black Family #6003 $10.99
Twins #60160 $3.99
Victorian Family #6004 $19.99

#S700D $125.00
See other Real Good Toys Dollhouse models in this catalog pages 20-62.

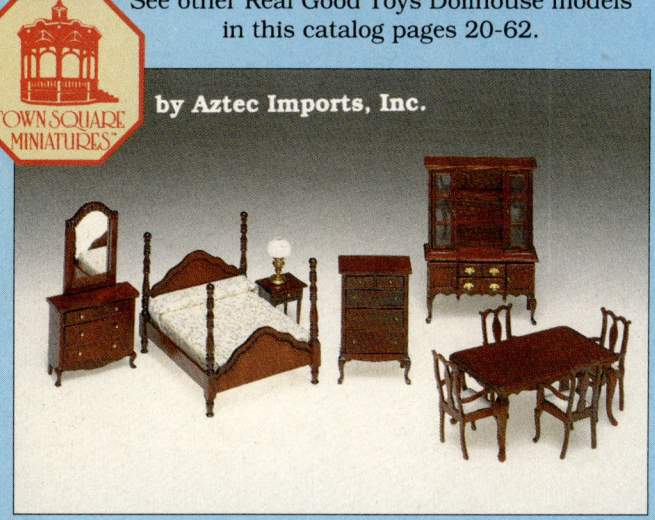

TOWN SQUARE MINIATURES
by Aztec Imports, Inc.

WALMER DOLL HOUSES

Bedroom Set T3128 $35.00
Dining Room Set T3057 $48.00
See their full page ad on the back cover of this catalog.

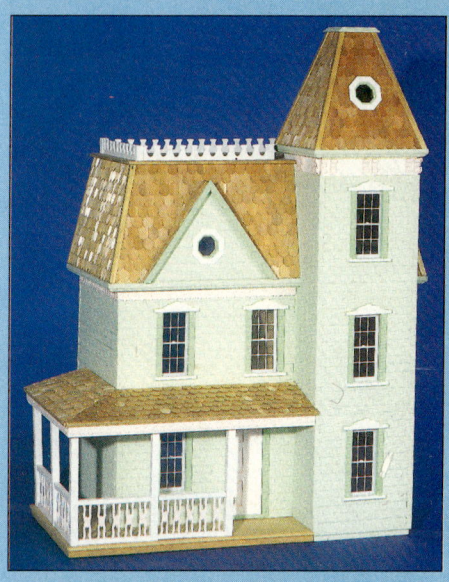

#457 APPLE BLOSSOM $99.00
See other Walmer Dollhouse models in this catalog pages 20-73.

Electrical Supplies

See pages 126-158 for more products.

Depot Dollhouse Shop, Inc.
215 Worcester Rd., Rt. 9
Framingham, MA 01701
1-800-882-1162

- Other catalogs available
- MC/Visa/Discover
- Low prices
- 15 years of excellent service

Binkee™

a
Division of
Pitty Pat Miniatures, Inc.
Presents

Binkee Bear

Binkee Bunny

High-Quality Imported Furniture At A Wonderful Price !!

For the dealer nearest you write:
Pitty Pat Miniatures, Inc.
1500 Old Deerfield Rd. • Highland Park, IL 60035

the miniatures catalog

Advertising Sales Manager
Sara Benz

Advertising Production Coordinator
Nadine Maas

Advertising Production Assistant
Sandra R. Johnson

Editorial Coordinator
Geraldine G. Willems

Staff Photographers
Chris Becker
Darla Gawelski
Bob Trimble

Publisher
Robert L. Hayden, Jr.

V.P. Sales/Marketing
Robert A. Maas

Product Manager
Kaye Broom

Advertising Director
Daniel Lance

Production Director
Karin Frederickson

Kalmbach Publishing Co.
Customer Service:
(800) 446-5489

THE MINIATURES CATALOG (ISBN 0-89024-129-5) is published annually by Kalmbach Miniatures, Inc., 21027 Crossroads Circle, Waukesha, WI 53187. Circulation: Available from Kalmbach Publishing Co., miniatures shops, book stores, craft, hobby, and gift shops in the United States and Canada. Product Listings: Address all inquiries and correspondence for listings to THE MINIATURES CATALOG, Advertising Sales Manager, 21027 Crossroads Circle, Waukesha, WI 53187. ©1991 by Kalmbach Miniatures, Inc. Printed in U.S.A. All rights reserved. Reproduction in part or in full is prohibited without the express, written permission of the publisher.

Note: THE MINIATURES CATALOG is not a mail order catalog. To obtain the products listed in this book, see your local miniatures dealer or write directly to the manufacturer or craftsperson. Additional ordering information and manufacturers' sales policies may be found in the Manufacturers Index in the back of the Catalog. Addresses of handcrafters and manufacturers shown in the color sections are available on request, please send LSASE.

Welcome to THE MINIATURES CATALOG

A dollhouse filled with charming miniatures awaits you!

"Hello" to all of our old friends who have been with us for years and a warm "welcome" to newcomers to THE MINIATURES CATALOG and the dollhouse miniatures hobby. As you page through this catalog an entire world of delightfully detailed miniatures will unfold, and hopefully, entice you into the wonderful world of miniature collecting.

THE MINIATURES CATALOG offers product information on miniatures that are handcrafted, manufactured, and imported and provides a variety of quality items and price ranges to choose from.

An all-new color section

The editorial sections have a brand new look, with original feature articles covering "how-to" projects and fun ideas on miniature decorating. An excellent article by Barbara Warner tells you everything you need to know to put together a dollhouse. For newcomers, Kathleen Zimmer of NUTSHELL NEWS tells you all about the miniatures hobby. Pam Henkel of MINIATURES SHOWCASE offers ideas on how to use accessories, and Jeanne Delgado of NUTSHELL NEWS explains kitbashing. For those without a dollhouse, we also include an article on how miniatures can be featured in displays. It all makes for enjoyable reading!

Support your local hobby store

This is not a mail order catalog, but a buyers guide. Most of the items you see in THE MINIATURES CATALOG can be found in your local miniatures store. You can depend on retailers to help get you started in miniatures. It's amazing how these experts can get you through a project that seems impossible to start!

For hobbyists who do not have a miniatures store in their area, look at the shop listings in this catalog for assistance. Readers can also use the Manufacturers Index in the back of this catalog to contact manufacturers directly. Please note that manufacturers who indicate "wholesale only" do not sell direct to the public, but they may be able to tell you where to find retailers in your area. Please include a self-addressed stamped envelope when requesting product information.

From novice to expert, everyone in your family can enjoy building dollhouses and miniature rooms with items from this catalog. Before you start, here are a few short instructions on how this catalog can help you create your dream house come true!

About the catalog

In addition to 3,000 miniature product listings, THE MINIATURES CATALOG also includes listings for Tools and Building Materials, Publications, Plans, Shops, Museums, and Miniatures Shows. Also included are a Manufacturers Index and a Product Index, which are cross-referenced for your convenience.

Product listings

In each product listing the following information is provided: product name, manufacturer's or handcrafter's name, a suggested retail price (prices are subject to change), and a brief product description. To insure accuracy, all product descriptions are written by the manufacturers and handcrafters. The catalog numbers refer to the manufacturers' catalog or price sheet numbers, and should be noted when ordering.

Show calendar and museums

The list of miniatures museums and retail shows are listed free of charge as a service to our readers. We encourage all of you to drop by your local miniatures shop and get started collecting today!

Geraldine
Geraldine Willems

THE MINIATURES CATALOG, *Fourteenth Edition* 3

IF YOU CAN'T VISIT OUR SHOWROOM, THEN LET OUR SHOWROOM VISIT YOU!

NEW 1991-'92

Send for The Dollhouse Factory™
CATALOGUE of DOLLHOUSES, SUPPLIES and MINIATURES

The Catalogue the Professionals Use!

DOLLHOUSES
NEEDLEWORK
WOOD
LIGHTING
DOLLS
COMPONENTS
BOOKS
ACCESSORIES

TOOLS
WALLPAPER
KITS
FURNITURE
MOLDINGS
PLANS
HARDWARE
MASONRY

Thousands of carefully selected products offered by one of the oldest and most experienced companies in the world of miniatures.

Send $5.50 for FIRST CLASS delivery or pick one up at our showroom.

Hrs: Tues - Sat. 11-6
Thurs. 11-9

(December–Open 7 days a week til Christmas.)

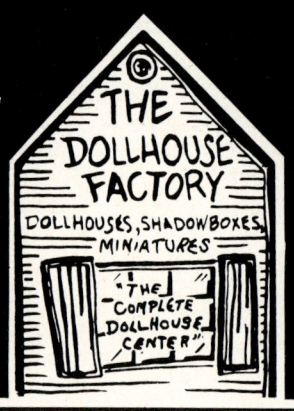

THE DOLLHOUSE FACTORY™
Box 456CM 157 Main St.
Lebanon, NJ 08833
(908) 236-6404

TABLE OF CONTENTS
The Miniatures Catalog, 14th Edition

Introduction 3
Cover Story 6
The World of Miniatures 8
A Bit Unusual 14

Houses and Buildings ... 17
Cape Cod 18
Castles and Forts 18
Children's Houses 19
Colonial 22
Contemporary 25
Cottage/Cabins 26
Farm 30
Federal 35
Greenhouses & Gazebos 36
Miscellaneous Buildings 38
Shop/Office 40
So. Colonial & Georgian 45
Townhouses 46
Tudor 48
Victorian 49

Displays 63
Display Cabinets, Boxes & Lamps 64
Dollhouse Turntables 66
Glass Domes & Showcase 66
Novelty Displays 67
Printer's Trays & Boxes 70
Room Boxes & Vignettes 70

Building Components ... 74
Architectural 75
Bay Windows 78
Brick & Stone Supplies 79
Door Kits & Parts 84
Doors, Working 86
Hardware & Metal Parts 93
Lumber Supplies 97
Millwork 98
Modeling Compounds 103
Molding 103
Roofing materials 106
Shutters 110
Siding Materials 111
Staircases 112
Windows, Non-Working 114
Window, Working 120
Window Parts & Kits 125

Electrical Systems 126
Ceiling Fixtures 127
Electrical Parts 137
Electrical Systems 145
Miscellaneous 147
Outdoor Lighting 148
Table & Floor Lamps 149
Wall Fixtures 157

Interior Decorating 160
Fabric & Trim 161
Fireplaces 161
Flooring 164
Panel & Trim Wall Ceiling 168
Rugs & Carpeting 169
Wall Covering 171
Window Treatments 173

How-to Section 178

Furniture 175
European 176
Colonial & Federal Kits 176
Colonial & Federal 195
Country Kits 197
Country 199
Victorian Kits 201
Victorian 202
20th Century Kits 205
Early 20th Century 206
l930-Contemporary 207
Outdoor Furniture & Landscaping Materials 213
Store & Office Furniture 218
Nursery 220
Bathroom 222
Kitchen 224
Miscellaneous 227
Wicker Furniture 228

Dollhouse Dolls 230
Accessories 231
Character Dolls 231
Clothing Patterns 232
Doll Clothing 232
Dollhouse Dolls 233
Doll Kits 236
Dollmaking Supplies 236

1" Scale Accessories 237
Contents for accessories 237

Smaller Scale 294
1/2" Accessories 295
1/2" Building Supplies 296
1/2" Furniture 301
1/2" Electrical & Interior Decorating 302
1/2" Houses, Plans & Displays 303
1/4" & Smaller Scale 305
Miscellaneous 309

Publications & Plans 310
Special Services 311
Magazines 311
How-to Books & Plans: Houses & Shops 312
How-to Books & Plans: Furniture 315
How-to Books & Plans: Decorative 316
How-to Books & Plans: Dolls 316
How-to Books & Plans: Miscellaneous 317
Books & Related Products 320
Books for Collectors 321
Ready-to-use Books 322

Tools & Supplies 323
Adhesives & Glues 324
Hand Tools 326
Paints & Finishes 329
Detailing 329
Power Tools 329

Miniatures Shops 332
Show Calendar 362
Museums 367
Index of Listers 369
Product Index 381

Cover Story:

The scene on this year's catalog cover is just one example of how you can turn the hobby of miniature collecting into a story-telling event and make it come to life, or death, as in this murder mystery. Many hobbyists are not content with the creation of a splendid miniature room; they take it one step further and make up a story about the people in the room and the events that are taking place.

Maggie Pernice of *Miniatures Showcase* magazine created the cover scene and wrote this fun "who-dun-it" caper. We'd like to thank the National Association of Miniature Enthusiasts (N.A.M.E.) for giving us the idea to create a murder mystery scene for the cover. "I Love A Mystery" was the theme for N.A.M.E.'s 1990 National Houseparty Convention.

Items in this scene were supplied by the following manufacturers:
Ron Benson: White umbrella stand, Staffordshire lions (in bookcase), English urns and Rockingham vase (on fireplace).
Bespaq Corporation: Upholstered love seat and armchair, small round Victorian table, corner chair, working grandfather clock, desk and desk chair.
Cir-Kit Concepts Inc.: Electrified wall sconces by Miniature House.
Clare-Bell Brass Works: Candlesticks, hour glass, brass bell, book ends, mortar and pestle, candle snuffer, fireplace tools and fender, spittoon.
Farrow Industries: Box of cigars.
Victor Franco: Ink well, magnifying glass, pocket watch, fountain pen (all on desk), knife (in dog's mouth), pipe (in man's hand), all walking sticks.
Gryphon's Den: Lace doily (on round table).
Houseworks Ltd.: Single bookcase units, all books, fireplace.
Innovative Photography: Portrait (on wall).
The Lawbre Company: Knife collection, mounted moose head.
Marilyn's Mini Studio: Tray of Cognac.
Mini Mansions: Electrified fireplace grate with logs.
Miniature Corner: Oriental carpets.
Miniature Manors: Faux marble floor tile.
MiniGraphics Inc.: "Fantastic Solid" wallpaper.
Gail Morey: Cocker spaniel.
Northeastern Scale Models Inc.: Baseboards and chair rail.
Omniarts of Colorado: Suit of armour.
Derek Perkins: Victorian windows.
Royce Piro: Party guests, including "The Body."
Robin's Roost: All potted plants.
Sir Thomas Thumb: Coil rope (behind desk), shotgun (in umbrella stand).
Small Accomplishments: Pearl-handled revolver.
Unique Miniatures: Wall panel frames.
Victoria's Garden: Flower arrangement (on desk) in Clare-Bell Brass Works' vase.

Who killed Sir Reginald K. Davver?

To celebrate an enormously successful financial year, British entrepreneur Sir Reginald K. Davver, CEO of Wee-Bend-It, Amalgamated; the leading manufacturer of paper clips and safety pins in the Northern Hemisphere, is hosting an intimate gathering of his closest friends and relatives. After an evening's repast of flummery and Welsh rarebit, Sir Reginald's guests retire to the drawing room for cognac and light conversation.

While awaiting the reappearance of the host, Lady Gwendelyn, Sir Reggie's step-sister and mother-in-law to the third cousin of the Fourth Earl of the Duke, frantically fumbles through Reginald's desk to find her pet cocker Corkie's chew-toy. She accidently comes across a revised version of her step-brother's Last Will and Testament.

"Why, what do we have here?" asks the somewhat absent-minded Lady Gwen as the inquisitive guests flock to her side.

Just then, Sir Reginald rejoins the group, and orders the butler, Robert, to serve the cognac, a special gift from Major Pitheous T. Myner. Major Myner, Sir Reginald's oldest and dearest friend, and Myner's young niece, fair Phoebe Fairfax, round out the roster of guests.

The cognac is served, Reggie toasts his guests; when suddenly there is a flash of lightning, a crash of thunder, and (as often happens in older homes), the electric system fails. When the lights come back on, the guests discover that Angus McDoogle, the Davver family chauffeur, has joined their group and that Sir Reginald has decided to lie down and take a nap on the floor in front of the fireplace. Since Reg is a diagnosed narcoleptic, no one thinks this behavior odd and the party continues.

Several hours later, there is a knock at the door. It is Constable Chausable responding to an anonymous phone call boding ill tidings for Sir Reginald. The guests lead the officer to the recumbent Reggie where, upon closer examination, all are forced to concede that the heretofore thought-to-be sleeping host is, in fact, dead.

But how did he die? Who made the phone call? Are there foul dealings afoot? Is there any significance to the discoloration around Sir Reginald's neck, or the unsightly swelling on his head? What of that peculiar nine millimeter blood-stained hole in the back of his smoking jacket? Which of the guests or employees could have performed this despicable act? Who planted the pistol in the potted palm? You'll find the incredible solution to this mystery hidden somewhere in this edition of *The Miniatures Catalog*! •

Dreams Can Come True!

That is, with the Lawbre expertise working for you. There is the assurance of true originality, and full attention to scale, detail and craftsmanship. Due to their artistic integrity, Lawbre custom creations are a part of some of the most discriminating collections in the world. Find out how reasonable it is to have a dream come true in the Lawbre tradition.

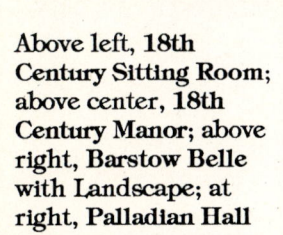

Above left, 18th Century Sitting Room; above center, 18th Century Manor; above right, Barstow Belle with Landscape; at right, Palladian Hall

For complete House & Accessories Catalog, send $4.00 to ...

The Lawbre Company
888 Tower Road, Mundelein, IL 60060

VISA and MasterCard accepted.

THE MINIATURES CATALOG, *Fourteenth Edition* 7

INTRODUCING!

The World of Dollhouse Miniatures

By Kathleen Zimmer
Production editor, Nutshell News

Welcome to miniatures! Maybe you've been searching for a new hobby to help you relax and to get those creative juices flowing; or perhaps you're looking for a different kind of hobby that will challenge you. Dollhouses and scale miniatures will certainly fit the bill! It offers something for everyone—builders can build, stitchers can stitch, artists can paint, and those of us with 10 thumbs can collect. Let's take a look at what this exciting hobby is all about...

To be quite literal, miniatures can be traced back to the pharoahs of Egypt, but the scale miniatures hobby that we're interested in actually started to organize itself in the early 1970s. It began with a relatively small group of enthusiasts who crafted most of their dollhouses, furniture, and dolls themselves. As their numbers grew, publications like *Nutshell News* and *The Miniatures Catalog* were started, and groups such as the National Association of Miniature Enthusiasts (N.A.M.E.) were founded. The hobby expanded quickly and, by the end of the decade, handcrafters and collectors had become more refined about what they made and bought.

In the 1980s the upward trend continued, as more people discovered miniatures, more shows and shops popped up across the country, and more clubs were formed. Miniaturists "discovered" smaller scales, especially half-inch and quarter-inch scale, and plunged into different decorating styles: Victorian, Country, Colonial, and Southwestern. The 1990s is certain to bring more innovations in crafting, new directions in collecting and decorating, and greater enthusiasm for our wonderful little world!

(Opposite) If you've already decided that half-inch scale is the way to go, you'll love this adorable half-inch scale dollhouse. Frank Moroz of Bauder Pine, Ltd., made it, based on a full-size home Sears and Roebuck offered via mail order from 1928 to 1937. Beverly Panas designed and constructed the landscaping. If you are interested in making this house, the instructions are in the April 1990 edition of *Nutshell News*.

(Opposite, below) Scale is everything in miniature: this is an example of the same item in three different scales. Handcrafters for these tables are Dean Jenson, quarter-inch scale; Bob and Nan Rankin, half-inch scale; and Don Ripley, one-inch scale.

(Above) The elegant Colonial bedroom features furniture by miniatures artisan Roger Gutheil. His work is sure to inspire collectors and crafters!

(Right) The tastefully decorated sitting room is done in English Country style. For more information on all types of Country decorating, see the Winter 1990 edition of *Miniatures Showcase*.

What is scale?

Now that you have an idea of where the hobby came from and where it might be headed, we need to discuss scale. And before we do that, I should mention the importance of consistency of scale. Nothing can look more awkward in an elegant room setting than a piece of furniture that is obviously too big or too small for the scale you've chosen to work with. When you're creating a one-inch scale scene, you need to add correctly proportioned one-inch scale furnishings in order to create a realistic look—a half-inch scale chair will be dwarfed when placed next to a one-inch scale sofa. There are, of course, exceptions; if you are putting together a child's nursery, that same half-inch scale chair might look perfectly appropriate as a toddler's chair. Just keep in mind the scale you are working with, and you should have no problems.

The most common scale in the hobby is one inch equals one foot (1" = 1'). Since it is considered the standard, just about anything is available in one-inch scale, from gorgeous Queen Anne furniture to 12-packs of Coke and bags of Doritos. More recently, half-inch, quarter-inch, and even smaller scales have gained popularity. Some hobbyists cite the fact that they're running out of room (one-inch scale takes up more space than you'd think!); other hobbyists are simply drawn to smaller dollhouses, furniture, and dolls. However, because this trend is still developing, the availability of different types of smaller scale furniture and accessories isn't as great as it is for one-inch scale. This lack of accessibility seems to stir up the creative juices in some smaller scale devotees—if they can't find what they want, they often try to make it themselves.

That urge to "make it myself" can easily be satisfied with miniatures. Plans and kits for dollhouses, dolls, furniture, and accessories, as well as do-it-yourself books are widely available in shops, through mail order, and at retail shows across the country. And once you become familiar with the material and techniques for whatever you choose to cre-

(Above) Suellen Blanton chose to craft the outside of a shop rather than the interior. Her "Red, White and Blue Shoppe" shows the front porch of an Americana store, featuring items she's collected over the years, both inexpensive and more valuable.

(Left) Barbara Conway of Wilmington, Delaware displayed her beautiful room box at the 1990 Delaware Antiques Show as part of a special exhibit demonstrating the art of reproducing antiques in miniature.

ate, there is nothing to stop you from developing your own plans and dreaming up your own projects. The bottom line is that whatever you can imagine, you can create.

An organized hobby

You might be wondering where to get new ideas and share information, and a club could be just the answer for you! Clubs provide an atmosphere of sharing and often prompt your creative side simply by providing communication with other miniaturists. N.A.M.E.'s clubs are good outlets for creativity and a great way to meet others interested in miniatures. Aside from club activity, this 12,000-member group sponsors miniatures shows and other miniatures-related events, and publishes *The Miniature Gazette*, a quarterly magazine.

There are also a number of well-organized independent clubs such as the Society of American Miniaturists (S.A.M.). Its 300 members are dedicated to sharing what they've learned with beginners through weekend workshop activities.

The International Guild of Miniature Artisans (I.G.M.A.) is yet another outlet. The Guild has a show in New York each spring, and a school in Maine each summer, which features classes by well-known artisans—a perfect way to hone your crafting skills!

Small groups of hobbyists, with no particular club affiliation, can be found all over the country. These groups gather together once or twice a month to chat, show their latest work, and come up with new ideas. They can sometimes be tracked down through miniatures shops.

Another way to learn more

The thrill of owning or creating a dollhouse and spending time filling it with furniture can't be beat! This customized version of the Chateau, a house offered by The Lawbre Company might be just the one you're looking for.

about miniatures and keep in touch with the hobby is through the various publications devoted to it. *Nutshell News* is a monthly magazine dedicated to both the crafter and collector. It features artisans and collections, do-it-yourself projects, various tips and reviews, and information on upcoming shows. *Nutshell News* also provides show coverage, highlighting new miniatures the editors and contributing writers find at shows across the country.

Each issue of *Miniatures Showcase,* a quarterly magazine, has a specific theme and features decorating ideas based on that particular theme. The staff creates miniature scenes with the many items sent to them by artisans and shops, as well as highlighting collections from around the country. Past themes have included Country, Victorian, and Southwestern decorating, landscaping, holiday decorating, international rooms, and much more. *Miniatures Showcase* also provides addresses for artisans, handcrafters, manufacturers, and shops whose miniatures appear in the magazine.

Miniatures shops, of course, provide access to the hobby in many ways. But don't despair if there isn't a shop nearby—the hobby also has a very healthy mail order business. Check the advertisements in *Miniatures Showcase* and *Nutshell News*—many of the shops and artisans who advertise will indicate whether or not they have cata-

> *" . . . Whatever you can imagine, you can create."*

logs available, and most ads include addresses. And by all means, use this catalog! It's a great way to get started in terms of finding companies and artisans whose work you're interested in. Addresses can be found in the Index of Manufacturers, Artisans, and Suppliers in the back of the catalog. One other thought—when you go on vacation, check the ads in all three publications for shops located in the area you're planning to visit. You never know what you might find!

Miniatures shows are yet another way to discover more about this hobby—they're an excellent way to find handcrafted and manufactured miniatures, and they provide wonderful opportunities to meet artisans and hobbyists. Many shows offer workshops as an added attraction, which gives you the chance to learn a new skill or perfect an old one. Quite a few also have exhibit areas near the sales room where local miniaturists and clubs display their work and share ideas. Be sure to pick up business cards and keep programs when you attend shows (the programs often have addresses in them), so that you can contact artisans and shops whose work you're interested in.

Keep your eyes open for local clubs presenting miniatures shows, as well as local non-profit organizations who often run shows as fund raisers. In addition, there are a number of promoters who put on fine miniatures shows across the country.

THE MINIATURES CATALOG, *Fourteenth Edition* 11

N.A.M.E. also presents what they call Houseparties, which are long weekends filled with workshops, demonstrations, brunches, dinners—and miniatures of course! You do have to be a member of N.A.M.E. to participate as a registered guest, but the general public is usually welcome on the last day of the show. Be sure to check *Nutshell News, The Miniatures Catalog* and local newspapers for information on upcoming shows.

Wait! There's another way to learn more about miniatures or to display your latest creation. Each October the Miniatures Industry Association of America (M.I.A.A.), a trade organization, sponsors National Dollhouse and Miniatures Month. This event gives you the chance to see special displays at local shops and malls. You can participate in this month-long celebration by entering special N.D.M.M. contests. The point of the entire month is to expose more people to the hobby and to give those already involved a chance to meet each other and to share.

There are dozens of other ways to become involved and enjoy miniatures—I just wanted to mention a few to get you started. But if you've bought a dollhouse kit or purchased an exquisite piece of furniture, you already know the feeling of excitement and happiness that miniatures can bring. It's so rewarding to build or buy a dollhouse, perhaps a copy of the home you grew up in or your dream house. The fun of filling it with items you've made or admired and bought really can't be beat. The one constant and maybe most attractive factor in miniatures is its flexibility. You can build, buy, decorate, and create anything you desire in any scale you want. The choice is up to you—have fun! •

(Above) If you discover that different types and styles of miniatures catch your eye and you can't decide on what to collect or make, why not incorporate all these items into an antiques store? Antiques shops and general stores are wonderful ways to display a variety of miniatures that might not fit together in a living room scene. This particular shop was designed by the *Miniatures Showcase* staff—see the Spring 1989 issue for more details.

(Opposite) Entire villages can be constructed using gatorboard kits. This International Village was created by the Wee "C" Club of Elk Grove Village, Illinois, and was featured in the Spring 1991 issue of *Miniatures Showcase*.

THE MINIATURES CATALOG, *Fourteenth Edition* 13

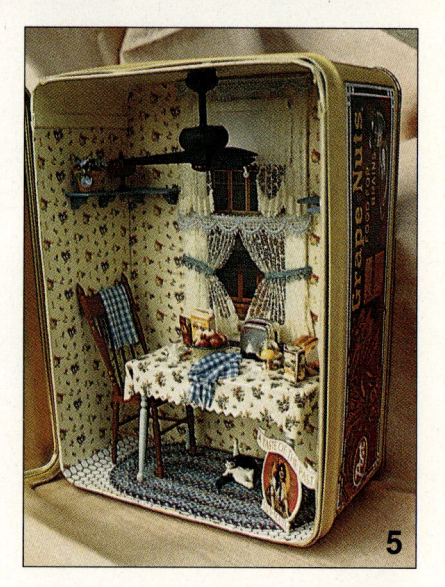

A Bit Unusual— You Bet!

By Geraldine Willems
Editor, Miniatures Showcase

"Recycle It" is the call of the 90s, and miniaturists are taking it to heart. At many club activities and weekend retail shows the displays hobbyists share range from gorgeous Victorian dollhouses and room boxes, decorated in all their finery, to cleverly thought-out unusual displays which bring smiles to those peeking into every entertaining "doorway."

Many of these light-hearted projects are done just for fun and can be put together quickly with a little scrounging and imagination. For those of you who love the challenge of searching through junk piles and flea markets to bring new life to otherwise hopeless pieces of clutter, here's your chance to recycle! This is also the opportunity to let your hair down and not worry about periods and historically correct pieces, but instead the fun comes when you find just the right container to feature your project's theme.

Choosing suitable containers

14

and subject matter can be quite the challenge for the apprentice scrounger. Start looking in basements, attics, flea markets, yard sales, and antique stores for your project's perfect "home."

Once you find your own unusual containers, you are well on the way to creating unique displays that stand out on their own! ●

Opposite and above:
1. Majorie Meyers of Wild Strawberries built a living room scene inside a gourd.
2. This railroading scene was made by Charles Tebelman.
3. Sandra M.A. Manring recycles lovely pocket watches!
4. Mary McGrath's birds found homes in an oval pin.
5. Eve Karoblis recreated her grandmother's kitchen in a box.
6. Minis in a nutshell were created by Martie Blackmon.
7. Shannon Moore built this book display that was arranged by Cindy Malon.
8. A laundry bottle becomes a display by Marti Duszynski.
9. Shirley Sitton created this nautical scene.
10. Cheryl Joines has a picnic in a candle sconce.

THE MINIATURES CATALOG, *Fourteenth Edition* **15**

From the publishers of
the miniatures catalog

Bring your dreams
to life

Spark your imagination and develop your crafting skills with *Nutshell News* and *Miniatures Showcase*. Whatever your miniatures project may be, these helpful publications give you the instruction and ideas to put it all together.

    Nutshell News' project articles teach you to make your own miniatures and decorate your dollhouse. Our how-to projects are easy to follow and tested by a staff craftsperson. We cover all aspects of the hobby, including news, product innovations, interviews with artisans and complete descriptions of collections.

    Miniatures Showcase is your quarterly source of miniatures ideas and inspiration. Each issue is devoted to a specific decorating theme or period in history. Our custom-made displays, created with an expert hand and discriminating eye, are presented to you in large, detailed color photographs.

    Whatever your dreams, *Nutshell News* and *Miniatures Showcase* help bring them to life.

NUTSHELL NEWS
1 year (12 issues) – $29.00 (Outside the U.S. $36.00, Canadians add 7% GST.)

MINIATURES SHOWCASE
1 year (4 issues) – $14.95 (Outside the U.S. $18.95, Canadians add 7% GST.)

    To subscribe, send in the attached reply cards. Or call (800) 446-5489 (weekdays 8:30 a.m. - 5:00 p.m. CST).

Kalmbach Publishing Co.
21027 Crossroads Circle
P.O. Box 1612
Waukesha, WI 53187-1612

Keep up-to-date on the latest in miniatures!

Subscribe to NUTSHELL NEWS!

Use the attached card.

Nutshell News

Stay informed about all the exciting happenings in the world of miniatures – and save money compared to single copy prices. Use this postpaid card to subscribe to NUTSHELL NEWS!

This is a ❑ new; ❑ renewal subscription.

❑ 1 year $29 (outside the U.S. $36)
❑ 2 years $55 (outside the U.S. $69)
Subscription payable in U.S. Funds.

❑ BILL ME
❑ Payment enclosed.
❑ Charge my credit card.

Name _____
Street _____
City, State, Zip _____
Charge to: ❑ Mastercard ❑ Visa
Card # _____ Exp. date _____
Signature _____

Canadian orders add 7% GST.

N1931

Treat yourself to the beautiful miniatures ideabook.

Subscribe to MINIATURES SHOWCASE.

Use the attached card.

MINIATURES SHOWCASE

Enjoy the colorful quarterly magazine featuring artisans and collections! Use this handy postpaid card to subscribe to MINIATURES SHOWCASE today!

This is a ❑ new ; ❑ renewal subscription.

❑ 1 year $14.95 (outside the U.S. $18.95)
❑ 2 years $27.95 (outside the U.S. $35.95)
❑ 3 years $39.95 (outside the U.S. $51.95)
Subscription payable in U.S. Funds.

❑ BILL ME
❑ Payment enclosed.
❑ Charge my credit card.

Name _____
Street _____
City, State, Zip _____
Charge to: ❑ Mastercard ❑ Visa
Card # _____ Exp. date _____
Signature _____

Canadian orders add 7% GST.

N1941

Give the enchanting world of miniatures.

Send a gift subscription today.

Use the attached card.

Please enter a gift subscription to:

❑ NUTSHELL NEWS
   1 Year $29 (outside the U.S. $36)

❑ MINIATURES SHOWCASE
   1 Year $14.95 (outside the U.S. $18.95)
   Subscription payable in U.S. Funds.

❑ Payment enclosed.
❑ Bill me.
❑ Charge my: ❑ Mastercard ❑ Visa
Exp. date _____
Card # _____

Gift from:

Name _____
Street _____
City, State, Zip _____

Gift to:

Name _____
Street _____
City, State, Zip _____

Canadian orders add 7% GST.

N1921

BUSINESS REPLY MAIL
FIRST CLASS MAIL   PERMIT NO. 16   WAUKESHA, WI

POSTAGE WILL BE PAID BY ADDRESSEE

NO POSTAGE NECESSARY IF MAILED IN THE UNITED STATES

Nutshell News
P.O. Box 1612
Waukesha, WI 53187-9950

BUSINESS REPLY MAIL
FIRST CLASS MAIL   PERMIT NO. 16   WAUKESHA, WI

POSTAGE WILL BE PAID BY ADDRESSEE

NO POSTAGE NECESSARY IF MAILED IN THE UNITED STATES

Miniatures Showcase
P.O. Box 1612
Waukesha, WI 53187-9950

BUSINESS REPLY MAIL
FIRST CLASS MAIL   PERMIT NO. 16   WAUKESHA, WI

POSTAGE WILL BE PAID BY ADDRESSEE

NO POSTAGE NECESSARY IF MAILED IN THE UNITED STATES

Kalmbach Miniatures, Inc.
P.O. Box 1612
Waukesha, WI 53187-9950

Houses & Buildings

THE MINIATURES CATALOG, *Fourteenth Edition* 17

Cape Cod

THE NANTUCKET

The Elfworks
Suggested Retail Price: $695 as shown, exterior finished with cedar shingled roof and all painting completed, your choice of colors
Dimensions: 24" x 36", eight rooms
Completely finished interior, $1950 includes your choice of wallpaper, paint, floor coverings including hardwood floors. Superb quality, extraordinary detailing. Also great Victorians, Farmhouse and 2-Story Colonial. We will also custom build any home or building.

Castles & Forts

CASTLE 101

Alessio Miniatures
Suggested Retail Price: $125
Catalog No. 101.
Specifications: 13-1/2"H x 22-1/2"W x 22-1/2"D
Material: Pine and plywood
Each castle is handmade, painted and grooved to provide you with a toy which will be realistic and sturdy. A very unique feature of our castles is the ability to separate their towers and walls, which provides for easy storage and hours of creative play and expansion. American made. Sold separately.

WESTERN FORT

Alessio Miniatures
Suggested Retail Price: No. 202—$154.50 (completely finished). No. 202A—$89.99 (kit form).
Specifications: 7"H x 23"W x 23"D
Material: All pine and cedar
The fort features cedar corners, pine posts and basswood ladders. It also has a four-hinge working gate. Extra ladders are also available. The fort is scaled for use with 1/32 Britains or any other 54mm miniature figure. American made.

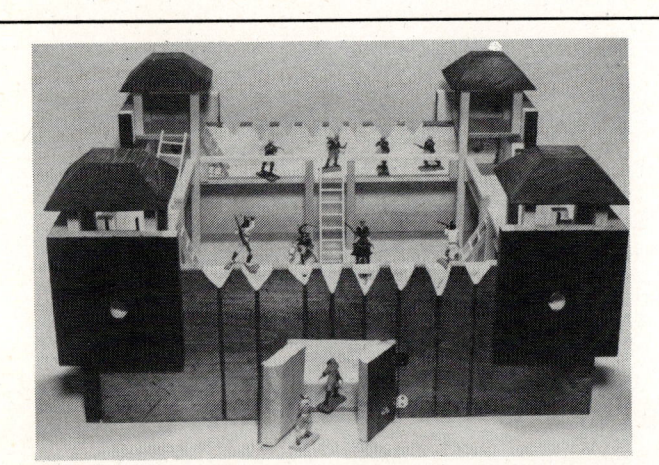

NEW WESTERN FORT

Alessio Miniatures
Catalog No. 220. Material: Pine
Suggested Retail Price: $154.50
Dimensions: 12"H x 25"W x 25"D
American Made. Each fort is handcrafted to last a lifetime. Seven ladders are included.

Prices are approximate and subject to change.

Children's Houses

Houses & Buildings

SIR EDWARD'S CASTLE

Alessio Miniatures
Suggested Retail Price: No. 301A—$60 (kit), No. 301—$94 (completely finished).
Specifications: 12"H x 14"W x 14"D
Material: 1/2" pine
Sir Edward's Castle is handmade and designed for hours of creative play. American made.

WELCOME HOME KIT

Celerity Miniature Homes
Specifications: 12" D x 24-1/2" L x 22-1/2" H
A quality little playhouse with easy access to rooms and well-designed for the younger child. The kit includes thirteen house pieces plus a ladder. Animal figures are sold seperately and add to the charm of this little house. See your local miniature shop for ordering.

PRISTINE COTTAGE
"Ready to Move-In Houses"
American Craft Products
Dimensions: 32"W x 21"D x 26"H, five rooms, 3/8" plywood, 1" scale
Completely assembled and finished inside and out. You will have to look twice to notice that the front door, siding, shutters, trim, foundation and shake roof are actually silkscreened. Inside, hardwood floors, paneled staircases and fireplace as well as "papered" walls are recreated using the same process. Working front door and non-working windows are comparable to the best on the market. Check with your dealer for color options available, as well as additional models in our Parade of Homes Collection. Made in America. Catalog No. 122.

RICHMOND MANOR
"Ready to Move-In Houses"
American Craft Products
Dimensions: 27"W x 13-1/2"D x 29-1/2"H, six rooms, 3/8" plywood, 1" scale
Completely assembled and finished inside and out. You will have to look twice to notice that the front door, siding, shutters, trim, foundation and shake roof are actually silkscreened. Inside, hardwood floors, paneled staircases and fireplace as well as "papered" walls are recreated using the same process. Working front door and non-working windows are comparable to the best on the market. Check with your dealer for color options available, as well as additional models in our Parade of Homes Collection. Made in America. Catalog No. 121.

THE MINIATURES CATALOG, *Fourteenth Edition* 19

PLAYSCALE FASHION DOLL DOLLHOUSES

Real Good Toys

When 2" scale is too big and 1" scale is too small - Playscale is just right! Playscale Doll House kits are designed for dolls 8 to 12 inches tall and their accessories. All models have precision pre-cut parts made of 3/8" cabinet grade plywood, grooved sidewalls, fancy octagonal wooden shingles, closets and storage drawer (or two) with divided compartments. They come with a complete set of pre-assembled components to finish the exterior of the house. All are very affordable and easy to assemble. The finest Fashion Doll Houses anywhere with durable construction for many years of play.

PLAYSCALE VICTORIAN TOWNHOUSE
Specifications: 26"W x 22-7/1"D x 58"H, four to seven rooms, three floors plus tower room and two sundecks, bay front, full length closet, a 560 cubic inch storage drawer with divided compartments in the foundation.

PLAYSCALE ESTATE
Specifications: 48"W x 24"D x 45-1/2"H, five huge rooms, two spacious full length closets and two storage drawers offering an amazing 1444 cubic inches of storage space with divided compartments.

PLAYSCALE COUNTRY FARMHOUSE
Specifications: 26"W x 23"D x 46"H, three to five rooms, three floors, gingerbread porch, detailed shutters, full length closet and a 740 cubic inch storage drawer with divided compartments in the foundation.

THE CHERRYDALE
Walmer Dollhouses
Suggested Retail Price: See your local dealer. Catalog No. 453.
Specifications: 29"W x 18-1/2"D x 25"H, two floors, four rooms plus attic.
Material: 1/4" exterior walls and partitions, 3/8" floors
Lilliput dollhouses are cute, easily assembled, sturdy and modestly priced. Third in the Lilliput series, the kit includes all gingerbread trims, wrap-around porch, pre-hung front door, plexiglass windows and interior staircase. A wing addition, siding and shingle packs are available for upgrading and expansion. The front gable extension provides extra interior space and interesting decorating possibilities.

THE CRANBERRY COVE
Walmer Dollhouses
Suggested Retail Price: See your local dealer. Catalog No. 452.
Specifications: 24"W x 17"D x 27-1/2"H Three floors, six rooms. Permanent nail and glue assembly. Material: 1/4" exterior walls and partitions, 3/8" floors
Lilliput dollhouses are cute, easily assembled, sturdy, and very affordable. The 6-room Cranberry Cove is the second kit in the Lilliput series. The kit includes all gingerbread trims, front porch, pre-hung front door, plexiglass window, and two interior staircases. Wing additions, siding, and shingles are available for upgrade and expansion.

THE LEMON TWIST
Walmer Dollhouses
Suggested Retail Price: See your local dealer. Catalog No. 449.
Specifications: 24"W x 12-1/2"D x 25"H, two floors, four rooms plus attic.
Material: 1/4" exterior walls and partitions, 3/8" floors
Lilliput dollhouses are cute, easily assembled, sturdy, and very affordable. The Lemon Twist is the fifth kit in the Lilliput series. The kit includes all gingerbread trims, window boxes with brightly colored flowers, pre-hung front door, plexiglass windows and interior staircase. Wing additions, siding and shingles are available as extras for upgrading and expansion.

Houses & Buildings

THE PEACHES 'N CREAM

Walmer Dollhouses
Suggested Retail Price: See your local dealer. Catalog No. 450
Specifications: 24" W x 16-1/2" D x 25" H
Two floors with four rooms and third floor attic. Permanent nail and glue assembly.
Material: 1/4" exterior walls and partitions, 3/8" floors
Lilliput dollhouses are cute, easily assembled, sturdy, and very affordable. The Peaches 'N Cream was the first kit in the Lilliput series. The kit includes all gingerbread trims, front porch, pre-hung front door, plexiglass windows, and interior staircase. Wing additions, siding and shingles are available for upgrading and expansion.

THE PLUM PUDDING

Walmer Dollhouses
Suggested Retail Price: See your local dealer. Catalog No. 454.
Specifications: 24"W x 17"D x 27-1/2"H, three floors, seven rooms. Permanent nail and glue assembly
Material: 1/4" exterior walls and partitions, 3/8" floors
Lilliput dollhouses are cute, easily assembled, sturdy and modestly priced. Fourth in the Lilliput series, the 7-room kit includes gingerbread trims, a 2-story porch, pre-hung french and front doors, plexiglass windows and two interior staircases. Wing additions, siding and shingle packs are available for upgrading and expansion.

THE APPLE BLOSSOM

Walmer Dollhouses
Suggested Retail Price: See your local dealer. Catalog No. 457
Specifications: 29" W x 18" D x 36" H
Material: Cabinet grade plywood, 1/4" and 3/8" and solid pine
A romantic Victorian, a quality kit, at a great price from your miniature dealer. The kit includes gingerbread, windows, prehung raised panel door, wrap-around porch, gable, four-story tower large enough to furnish (and a secret room in the top of the tower!), six interior rooms, two interior staircases and raised panel landing rails, three interior partitions. Available options are siding shingle pack and a two story wing addition. The house can also be ordered built up.

APPLE BLOSSOM WING ADDITION

Walmer Dollhouses
Suggested Retail Price: See your local dealer. Catalog No. 458
Specifications: 10-3/8" W x 17" H x 10-5/8" D
Two room addition designed specifically for the Apple Blossom dollhouse.

LILLIPUT WING ADDITION

Walmer Dollhouses
Suggested Retail Price: See your local dealer. Catalog No. 455.
Specifications: 1-1/2 stories 9"W x 16"H x 10"D
Lilliput wing for #449, #450 and #453 Lilliput Dollhouses.

Your Listings Belong Here!
Interested in advertising in the 15th Edition of
The Miniatures Catalog?

Contact Sara Benz at
1-800-558-1544,
Ext. 631
or write to;
The Miniatures Catalog
P.O. Box 1612
Waukesha, WI 53187

LILLIPUT WING ADDITION

Walmer Dollhouses
Suggested Retail Price: See your local dealer. Catalog No. 456.
Specifications: 10-3/8"W x 17"H x 10-5/8"D
Lilliput wing for #452 and #454 Lilliput Dollhouses.

STRAWBERRY PATCH WING ADDITION

Walmer Dollhouses
Suggested Retail Price: See your local dealer. Catalog No. 460
Specifications: 10-1/2" W x 11" D x 22-1/2" H
The Strawberry Patch dollhouse kit expands beautifully with the addition of the two story wing. Like the house, the wing opens in the front.

THE MINIATURES CATALOG, Fourteenth Edition

Colonial

THE STRAWBERRY PATCH

Walmer Dollhouses
Suggested Retail Price: See your local dealer. Catalog No. 459
Specifications: 25" W x 17" D x 33" H
Material: 1/4" and 3/8" cabinet grade plywood and solid pine
The Strawberry Patch opens in front and is another in the Lilliput kit series which means it assembles easily, is sturdy, playable and affordable. The kit includes the two-story front porch, first floor window boxes with flowers, gingerbread trims, shuttered windows, pre-hung raised panel door, six full rooms with partitions and two interior staircases with raised panel landing rails. Available as options are a two-story wing and a siding and shingle pack. The house is also available built-up.

THE COLONIAL

American Craft Products
Suggested Retail Price: See your local dealer. Catalog No. 101.
Specifications: 37"W x 18"D x 30"H, seven rooms plus full attic
Material: 3/8" birch plywood
Shell kit No. 101 includes all the precision cut materials necessary to build the basic house without windows, doors and trim. Optional component package No. 101-S is available providing all Carlson working windows, doors, interior stairs, and exterior trim. Fully open at rear, hinged attic back roof. Made in America.

WOODSTOCK GREENE

American Craft Products
Suggested Retail Price: See your local dealer. Catalog No. 110.
Specifications: 32"W x 20"D x 30"H. seven rooms plus attic, two-story, wire-ready pre-grooved panels for solid wire
Material: 3/8" cabinet grade birch plywood
House kit No. 110 is of the Wire-Ready Series. It includes all the precision cut materials necessary to build the basic house and also includes Carlson windows, doors, interior staircase and railing, complete exterior trim package, pre-assembled foundation and steps. Optional room addition No. 115 available for one or both sides. Exceptional value! Fully enclosed with two piece hinged front, full attic with large dormer and hinged front. Made in America.

THE WILLIAMSBURG

Afton Classics
Suggested Retail Price: Wholesale only. See your local dealer. Catalog No. KT1003
Specifications: 28" H x 31-1/2" W x 17-1/2" D
Seven rooms include two hallways, bathroom plus full attic, pre-assembled raised panel door and windows plus stairs. 3/8" cabinet grade wood and unbelievable price. Additions available.

RICHMOND MANOR

"Ready to Move-In Houses"
American Craft Products
Dimensions: 27"W x 13-1/2"D x 29-1/2"H, six rooms, 3/8" plywood, 1" scale
Completely assembled and finished inside and out. You will have to look twice to notice that the front door, siding, shutters, trim, foundation and shake roof are actually silkscreened. Inside, hardwood floors, paneled staircases and fireplace as well as "papered" walls are recreated using the same process. Working front door and non-working windows are comparable to the best on the market. Check with your dealer for color options available, as well as additional models in our Parade of Homes Collection. Made in America. Catalog No. 121.

22 Prices are approximate and subject to change.

Houses & Buildings

THE WORTHINGTON

Artply, Inc.
Suggested Retail Price: See your dealer
Model No. APL136
Dimensions: 31"H x 49"W x 19"D
1150 shingles required to cover roof
This authentic three-story center hall Georgian colonial exemplifies the beauty of Georgian architecture. Its ten spacious rooms offer infinite decorating possibilities. Bay windows, a balcony, stately columns and a detailed portico entrance with side lights add to the elegance of this estate. Also included are two staircases and a chimney. Easy tab and slot assembly. All parts are pre-cut plywood. No nails or tools needed.

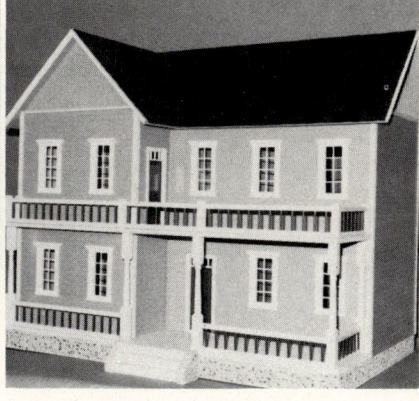

ENGELSON HOME

Celerity Miniature Homes
See your local miniatures dealer for retail price
Specifications: 32"H x 40"W x 24"D (includes porch), three floors, nine rooms. Top quality 3/8" plywood. Dado joint construction.
Beautiful farm house with a large front offset an full length front porch and steps. Large rooms plus two stairways, movable partitions, chimney and all on a firm foundation. Decorated exterior as shown is a special order. Catalog #1501 kit, #1502 assembled.

COLONIAL MINIATURE HOUSE KIT

Dura-Craft, Inc.
Catalog No. CH300
Dimensions: 32"H x 28"W x 15"D, eight rooms, one stairway, three floors
Material: Tongue and groove clapboard siding
Split shake roofs, hardwood flooring. Complete pre-cut kit including hardware (hinges) and plastic windows. Outstanding detail including windows, shutters, etc. See your dealer.

CINDY'S HOUSE

Celerity Miniature Homes
Wholesale only. See your local dealer. Catalog Nos. 1701 (kit) and 1702 (assembled).
Specifications: 28"H x 23"W x 19"D. 3 floors, 6 rooms. 3/8" plywood throughout. Dado joint construction.
A charming dollhouse for "Cindy". Kit includes 9 main pieces plus railings, corner posts, and turned posts, 2 stairways, chimney, and moveable room partitions. Great little house! Now available with room addition. Six main parts to create a charming kitchen! Size: 16"H x 11-3/4"W x 9-3/4"D.

October National Dollhouse & Miniatures Month

1/12TH SCALE COLONIAL SHELL

Houseworks
Suggested Retail Price: $180
Catalog No. 4101
Specifications: 33"H x 16"D x 33-1/4"L
Kit includes 3/8" cabinet grade plywood, front opening designs, step-by-step instructions, and a 3-in-1 Dollhouse Planbook for your reference. Write to Houseworks for information on the Houseworks Component Sets.

THE MINIATURES CATALOG, *Fourteenth Edition* 23

THE JEFFERSON

Greenleaf Products, Inc.
Suggested Retail Price: $96.25
Catalog No. 8014
Specifications: 29"H x 28"W x 16"D, two floors, four rooms, 1/8" di-cut plywood
The Jefferson replicates the handsome simplicity of colonial American "saltbox" architecture. A paneled front door opens into a gracious hallway flanked by two large rooms, one of which includes a fireplace and built-in bookcase wall. The center stairs lead to another wide hallway and two big rooms, while a large third floor attic partitions in two. Realistic window sashes add to the overall appearance of the house, as do windows silkscreened into divided panes. Rectangular shingles and durable clapboard siding are included in the kit and further enhances this affordable and authentic dollhouse.

NEW CONCEPT MONTPELIER

Real Good Toys
Suggested Retail Price: See your dealer.
Catalog No. NC-1001.
Specifications: 30-1/4"H x 31-7/8"W x 18"D, 3 floors, 10 rooms.
Material: 3/8" and 1/4" cabinet grade plywood.
A simple, lovely colonial home that is sturdy and spacious. The New Concept Montpelier is preassembled Houseworks windows and door, foundation and steps, bannisters and railings for interior stairs. It also includes precut clapboard and trim, and wooden shingles. This is proof that "simple" can be beautiful.

Interested in Becoming a Miniatures Manufacturer?

Join the Miniatures Industry Association of America and sell products to retailers across the country.

MIAA
1100-H Brandywine Blvd.
P.O. Box 2188
Zanesville, OH 43702-3288

BETHEL/BETHEL DELUXE

Russell Crafts
Suggested Retail Price: Kit, $113/$179.80; assembled unfinished, $136.50/$203.30; exterior finished, $246.50/$368.50
Material: 3/8" birch plywood
Dimensions: 24"L x 28"H x 15"D
This house is available either as a Standard or Deluxe model. The Deluxe model has louvered shutters, dormers and foundation. Both houses come with a chimney, stairs, windows, front door and hardware.

THE BROOKSHIRE

Walmer Dollhouses
Suggested Retail Price: See your local dealer. Catalog No. 501
Specifications: 30-1/2" H x 34-1/2" W x 18-1/2" D, three floors, five rooms
Material: 3/8" plywood exterior walls, 1/4" partitions, nail assembly with glue
The basic kit has five rooms, separate bathroom interconnecting upstairs hallway, plus a full-width attic. Kit complete with front steps, framed plexiglas windows and trim, staircase, and railing. Start with basic kit. Grow with Brookshire options: wing additions, various porches, dormer and working windows, siding, and shingles. Slowly create your own dream dollhouse.

BROOKFIELD COLONIAL WITH TWO ADDITIONS

Russell Crafts
Suggested Retail Price: Kit, $243/$417.25; assembled unfinished, $272.50/$498.75; exterior finished, $542.50/$828.25
Material: 3/8" birch plywood
Dimensions: 56"L x 28"H x 15"D
This house is available either as a Standard or Deluxe model. The Deluxe model includes dormers, bay windows, louvered shutters, french doors, a colonial front door and foundation. All houses include windows, doors and shutters.

Prices are approximate and subject to change.

Contemporary

THE HIGHLAND

Artply, Inc.
Suggested Retail Price: See your dealer
Model No. APL148
Dimensions: 24"H x 47"W x 19"D
1000 shingles required to cover roof
A sprawling, sophisticated six-room contemporary house featuring recessed double-panel entrance doors, suspended staircase, cathedral family room in this elegant interior. Other features include a twelve-piece set of outdoor furniture, a wrap-around sun deck, a balcony porch with a wood-beamed canopy and a garage door that actually works. Easy tab and slot assembly. All parts are pre-cut plywood. No nails or tools needed.

NEW BRUNSWICK

Compass Miniatures Industries
Suggested Retail Price: See your dealer
Dimensions: 33"W x 18"D x 34"H
Material: Cabinet grade 3/8" plywood
This modern design adapts to many areas from mountain lodge to beach house. It features a large, well-detailed deck area and walk out lower level. Available in kit form, assembled shell or as a decorated model. The kit includes all deck plank and railing parts, skylights, interior stairs and moveable partitions. Door and windows are available in a components package. Openings are sized to fit standard components.

BLAKELY

Compass Miniatures Industries
Suggested Retail Price: See your dealer
Dimensions: 65"W x 22"D x 30"H
Material: Cabinet grade 3/8" plywood
12 rooms of contemporary elegance. The open foyer creates interesting decorating opportunities. Available in kit form, assembled shell or the all-brick decorated model (shown). The kit includes chimney, moveable partitions, foundation parts, front steps and interior stairs. Doors and windows are available in components packages. Openings are sized to fit standard components.

MINIATURES SHOWCASE

Published quarterly, each issue explores a particular decorating period or popular theme. Miniatures Showcase is printed in a 8-1/2 X 11 inch format, in full color. Available from your miniatures shop, or by subscription.

THORNHILL

Houseworks
Suggested Retail Price: $420, shell only
Catalog No. 9001
Specifications: 46"L x 28"D x 36"H
A classic dollhouse designed with the most prestigious and spacious interior on the market. Kit includes all plywood parts precut to fit, 14 spacious rooms, quoin (precut, mitered corner blocks), dentil trim on front gable, chimneys, front steps, hinges, and magnets.

Houses & Buildings

THE MINIATURES CATALOG, *Fourteenth Edition* 25

Cottages & Cabins

THE BROOKWOOD

Greenleaf Products, Inc.
Suggested Retail Price: $86 Catalog No. 8017
Specifications: 24" H x 32" W x 18" D, three floors, six rooms, solarium, shingles included
This is a house that dreams are made of - your chalet in the mountains, your gateway at the beach, your home on a quiet cul-de-sac. A redwood deck leads to magnificent greatroom where an adjoining solarium provides an airy showcase for miniature plants and greenery. There's a kitchen and bath and three multi-tiered loft bedrooms, two accessible by staircase, the top one by ladder. Rectangular shingles are included and we've added beautifully realistic wood planters, a picnic set, removable kitchen cabinets, two platform beds, and a set of bunks. With three fireplaces, 10 skylights, two decks and a hot tub, you'll wish you could have this fabulous house in life size.

CUSTOM CREATIONS

Itsy-Bitsy Realty
Whether you desire a simple basic shell or an elaborate, move-in condition for your dollhouse family, we specialize in custom made dollhouses to your specifications (1/2" to 1" scale). It may be a replica of your home or a dream house of your own creation. Your choice of material, color, style, lighting and furnishings (if desired) makes your structure a unique masterpiece. All homes are furnished with an Itsy-Bitsy Deed and Itsy-Bitsy Mortgages are available. We also specialize in professional, commercial, public and historical buildings, churches, farm structures and room boxes. No order too big or too small!

COTTAGE

Celerity Miniature Homes
Retail Price: See your local dealer
Specifications: 18"H x 24"W x 19"D (includes porch), two floors, four rooms. Top quality 3/8" plywood.
Our very popular Cottage now available in front opening. The front roof hinges up and the front of the house simply slides out. Catalog #1103 kit, #1104 assembled.

THE ALLISON

Artply, Inc.
Suggested Retail Price: See your dealer
Dimensions: 25"H x 21"W x 13"D
450 shingles required to cover roof
Model No. APL77
This popular-priced charming Victorian is ideal for beginners. Its features include a staircase and five spacious rooms. Elegant gingerbread trim, a full 1/4" thick porch rail, "cathedral" French balcony with canopy and bay window complement the exterior decor. Easy tab and slot assembly. All parts are pre-cut plywood. No nails or tools needed.

THE BOBBIE

Artply, Inc.
Suggested Retail Price: See your dealer
Dimensions: 18"H x 18"W x 12"D
415 shingles required to cover roof
Model No. APL66
This popular-priced delightful beginner cottage has true Victorian charm. Its features include four spacious rooms, a staircase and twelve pieces of furniture. Elegant gingerbread trim and flower boxes add to the exterior charm. Easy tab and slot assembly. All parts are pre-cut plywood. No nails or tools needed.

Prices are approximate and subject to change.

See if you can pick up a couple of porcelain thimbles because they make superb hanging lamp shades. Carroll found some, took them to her local glass shop, and had the glazier drill a hole in the top of each, through which she threaded miniature electrical wires connected to tiny screw-in light bulbs. Since the thimbles were decorated with painted-on flowers they looked very beautiful when the light was turned on.

CARROLL MEEK
PULLMAN, WA

HAND PAINTED COTTAGE

Celerity Miniature Homes
Catalog No. 1102
Dimensions: 18" H x 24" W x 19" D, two floors, four rooms, made of 3/8" quality plywood
This beautiful handpainted Garden Cottage is truly unique. Each house is numbered and signed by our artist, a collector house. Must be seen to be appreciated. See your local miniature dealer.

THE COTTAGE

Celerity Miniature Homes
Suggested Retail Price: See your dealer
Specifications: 18"H x 24"W x 19"D, two floors, four rooms. Top quality 3/8" plywood. Dado joint construction.
Small pioneers! The log cabin has four rooms with two moveable partitions plus a stairway to sleeping loft for your North woods get-away. Logs sold separately. The thatch roof accessory kit, #1101AK contains a full-height chimney and window box to complete this model (thatched roofing not included). Logs available. Catalog #1101 kit, #1102 assembled, #1103 decorated.

THE CHALET

Celerity Miniature Homes
See your local miniatures dealer for retail price
Specifications: 29-1/2"H x 32"W x 16"D (includes base), three floors, six rooms. Top quality 3/8" plywood. Dado joint construction. Plenty of fun for the mini-family that owns this home with front porch and patio deck. Details include stairway, movable partitions, shutters and flower boxes. Kit contains 10 main pieces plus scroll trim, railings and turned posts. A charming dollhouse for a beginning miniaturist. Decorated exterior as shown is a special order. Catalog #203 kit, #204 assembled.

CHALET

CHALET DELUXE

LITTLE MOLLY

Celerity Miniature Homes
See your local miniatures dealer for retail price
Specifications: 30"H x 17"W x 32"L. Top quality 3/8" plywood.
Little Molly enjoys her playtime with this charming house. The living room, dining room and kitchen of this seven room house are all on the first floor. Plus an outside deck to play in the sunshine! The kit contains 14 main house parts plus railings, shutters, turned posts, moveable partitions and interior stairway. Excellent children's house. Catalog #3901 kit, #3902 assembled.

Houses & Buildings

ALBANY

Compass Miniatures Industries
Suggested Retail Price: See your dealer
Dimensions: 30"W x 20"D x 20"H
Material: Cabinet grade 3/8" plywood
The Albany cottage has 4 spacious rooms under its distinctive gambrel roof. Available in kit form, assembled shell or as a hand decorated display model. The kit includes chimney, moveable partitions and interior stairs. Door and windows are not included in the kit. Openings are sized to fit standard components.

AMANDA'S HOUSE

Compass Miniatures Industries
Suggested Retail Price: See your dealer
Dimensions: 34"W x 18"D x 27"H
Material: Cabinet grade 3/8" plywood
This seven room cottage has a large deck over the addition. There is a door opening on the second floor for the deck area. Available in kit form, assembled shell or as a hand decorated display model. The kit includes porch posts, deck railing parts,, moveable partitions and interior stairs. Door and windows are available in a component package. Openings are sized to fit standard components.

NEW JERSEY COTTAGE

The Dollhouse Factory™
Suggested Retail Price: $1780 completely finished including shipping
Catalog No. RVD89
Specifications: 30" H x 26" W x 20" D, two and one half floors, four rooms
Material: Plywood and pine construction with screws, nails, and glue
A truly charming cottage indeed! Four spacious rooms, clapboard siding, asphalt shingles, and hand-turned porch columns. See our catalog for other models.

THE BAVARIAN

Compass Miniatures Industries
Suggested Retail Price: See your dealer
Dimensions: 42"W x 20"D x 32"H
Material: Cabinet grade 3/8" plywood
The Bavarian is an interesting variation of traditional Alpine styling featuring two balconies and a recessed front entry. Available in kit form, assembled shell or as a hand decorated display model with authentic stucco and beam treatment. The kit includes moveable partitions and interior stairs. Door and windows are available in a component package.

PIONEER LOG CABINS

Homestead Homes
Dimensions: 10" x 12"
Material: Recycled wood
1" scale reproductions of one-room log cabins with shingled, slatted or corrugated aluminum roofs. Furnishings include table, two benches, bed, mattress, tied quilt and matching curtain. Cabins sold furnished or unfurnished.

COLUMBIAN MINIATURE HOUSE KIT

Dura-Craft, Inc.
Catalog No. CB150
Dimensions: 23"H x 20"W x 13"D, four rooms, two floors, pine frame, 1/8" plywood, knock-down construction
Material: Tongue and groove clapboard siding
This delightful chalet style house has all the gingerbread charm of the real thing. Kit includes pine frame construction, silk screened windows, stairway and real split shakes.

Prices are approximate and subject to change.

Houses & Buildings

THE SWEETHEART MINIATURE HOUSE KIT

Dura-Craft, Inc.
Catalog No. SW125
Dimensions: 16"H x 17"W x 11"D, four rooms, two floors
Material: KD lauan plywood, silk screened windows, roof panels are scored with shingle pattern
Charming Tudor style dollhouse kit will delight little girls everywhere. The cute little hearts, real stairs and flower boxes make it a sure favorite. Sturdy pine frame construction. See your dealer.

THE COVENTRY COTTAGE

Greenleaf Products, Inc.
Suggested Retail Price: $47.25
Catalog No. 8023
Specifications: 20" H x 17" W x 17" D, two rooms, large attic, tab and slot assembly
The Coventry snaps together with glue needed only for reinforcement and trim. It comes complete with shingles and 16 pieces of furniture. It has two rooms downstairs and a full "L" shaped attic plus a hanging swing for the front porch, two bay windows, flowerbox, gingerbread...it's all there in this charming dollhouse.

THE STORYBOOK COTTAGE

Greenleaf Products Inc.
Suggested Retail Price: $38.50
Catalog No. 8021
Specifications: 19-1/2" H x 19" W x 13" D, two floors, one room, attic, tab and slot assembly
Shingles and nine pieces of die-cut furniture are included with this appealing dollhouse and you'll find plenty of space to arrange it in the one large room and attic nook. You'll also find the customary Greenleaf charm - two bay windows, a flowerbox, sign, and of course, plenty of gingerbread trim. For ease of assembly, our designers have constructed the house to snap together into place, with glue needed only for reinforcement, shingles, trim and furniture.

LOG CABIN KIT

Jan's Small World
Suggested Retail Price: $114.95
Specifications: 24"W x 13"D x 18-1/2"H, 1-1/2 floors, two rooms, made of pine.
This log cabin kit is authentic in its styling...perfect for your collection of "country" or "primitive" miniatures. Kit includes windows, door, shingles, chimney, and rocks to cover chimney as well as wood for walls and floor. The pine cabin features one room on bottom floor and a half-loft (reached by ladder) on the second floor.

LOG CABIN ADDITION

Jan's Small World
Suggested Retail Price: $34.95
Specifications: 12" x 13"
This addition can be made to fit on either side of your cabin - or for a large cabin, put one on each end.

SHADY GROVE

Real Good Toys
Suggested Retail Price: See your dealer
Catalog No. NC-S-8100 Shady Grove with NC-45D Dormers and S-711 Porch
Specifications: 26"L x 18"D x 22-1/2"H, two floors, seven rooms
Ease of assembly makes this classic house very popular. Featuring pre-grooved parts for a guaranteed fit, all components are pre-assembled including the foundation and staircase. Gingerbread and fancy porch columns are included in the porch kit. Handcrafted pre-cut parts include clapboard siding and wooden shingles. Optional additional features include working windows, #5025 shutters by Houseworks, #1125 shingle dye and #SC copper flashing.

THE MINIATURES CATALOG, Fourteenth Edition 29

Farmhouses

THE NEBRASKA FARMHOUSE

American Craft Products
Suggested Retail Price: See your local dealer. Catalog No. 102.
Specifications" 36"W x 20"D x 30"H, 7 rooms plus large second floor landing, upstairs and downstairs hall, two full attics.
Material: 3/8" birch plywood
Shell kit No. 102 includes all the precision cut materials necessary to build the basic house without windows, doors, and trim. Optional component package No. 102-S is available providing all Carlson working windows, doors, interior stairs, and exterior trim. Fully open at rear, separately hinged roof on each attic, hinged side openings. Made in America.

THE GREENFIELD FARMHOUSE

Afton Classics
Suggested Retail Price: Wholesale only. See your local dealer. Catalog No. KT1004
Specifications: 28" H x 36-3/8" W x 22-1/2" D
Material: 3/8" cabinet grade plywood and pine.
Seven rooms include two hallways, bathroom plus full attic, beautiful balustered wrap-around porch, pre-assembled raised panel door and windows plus stairs. Reasonably priced - additions available.

NEW ENGLAND FARMHOUSE

Architecturally Designed Dollhouses
Specifications: Three floors, nine rooms
Material: Cabinet grade plywood
This is a partial front opening with back open. The house can be completely enclosed. It has two entry doors onto the porch. The house done in clapboard with cedar shingles has five dormers.

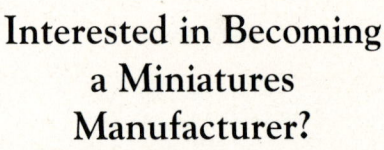

Interested in Becoming a Miniatures Manufacturer?

Join the Miniatures Industry Association of America and sell products to retailers across the country.

MIAA
1100-H Brandywine Blvd.
P.O. Box 2188
Zanesville, OH 43702-3288

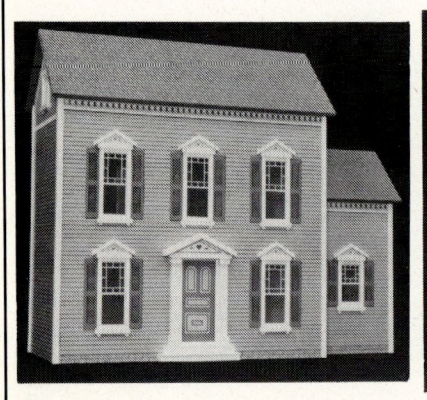

WINFIELD MANOR

"Ready to Move-In Houses"
American Craft Products
Dimensions: 37"W x 13"D x 29"H, eight rooms, 3/8" plywood. Catalog No. 120
Completely assembled and finished inside and out. Our finishing process meticulously reproduces architectural details and interior designs created by Leroy Carlson. The front door, siding, shutters, trim, foundation and shake roof are actually silkscreened. Inside, hardwood floors, paneled staircases and fireplace as well as "papered" walls are recreated using the same process. Check with your dealer for color options, as well as additional models in our Parade of Homes Collection. Made in America.

Houses & Buildings

THE FRANKLIN

Artply, Inc.
Suggested Retail Price: See your dealer
Model No. APL124
Specifications: 30"H x 34"W x 19"D
This classic farmhouse exemplifies the grace and beauty of the Victorian era. Its nine spacious rooms, three floors and two curved staircases complement the interior. A balcony with French doors, full wrap-around porch with detailed railings and gingerbread trim add to its authenticity and charm. Easy tab and slot assembly. All parts are pre-cut plywood. No nails or tools needed.

THE LITTLE FARMSTEAD

Celerity Miniature Homes
See your local miniatures dealer for retail price
Specifications: 18"H x 24"W x 19"D (includes porch), two floors, four rooms. Top quality 3/8" plywood. Dado joint construction.
The Little Farmstead is a quaint old place with its' own special charm. The kit contains eight main pieces plus dormers, shutters, flower boxes, railings, posts, stairway and moveable partitions. Decorated exterior as shown is a special order. Catalog #2501 kit, #2502 assembled.

CHRISTY'S HOUSE

Compass Miniatures Industries
Suggested Retail Price: See your dealer
Dimensions: 36"W x 18"D x 28"H
Material: Cabinet grade 3/8" plywood
This seven room farmhouse features extra space above the addition. Available in kit form, assembled shell or as a decorated display model. The kit includes porch posts, railings and spindles, chimney, moveable partitions and interior stairs. Door and windows are available in a component package. Openings are sized to fit standard components.

THE OLD HOMESTEAD

Celerity Miniature Homes
See your local miniatures dealer for retail price
Specifications: 28-1/4"H x 15"W x 29"L (includes 6" porch), three floors, six rooms. Top quality 3/8" plywood.
The Old Homestead is the perfect spot to sit and swing awhile! This side-opening house does not require a turntable to enjoy the front and inside of this unique Old Country flavor house. Kit contains seven main house parts, front porch, turned posts, foundation, stairways, full-height chimney and moveable partitions. Catalog #2801 kit, #2802 assembled.

DOLLHOUSE KITS

G.E.L. Products
Suggested Retail Price: Shown is the Ava Louise #A-123, see your local dealer
Specifications: 25-1/2"H x 45"W x 20-1/2"D
Materials: Quality cabinet wood, 3/8" plywood front, sides and floor
Easy assembly. Precut routed wood parts. Nail holes started. Assembled stairways, window and door units and outside railings. Dovetailing. Seven-room starter house expands with one or two-room extensions. Porches. Standard openings. Kits come complete with working windows, special clapboard surfacing, foundations, all trim and hardware. Video-taped and printed instructions in kits. Brochure.

Clapboard surface cut into 3/8" plywood by our exclusive process.

THE MINIATURES CATALOG, *Fourteenth Edition*

"ARCHITECT'S CHOICE" DOLLHOUSES

Design Tecnics Miniatures
Suggested Retail Price: See your local dealer or write direct
Specifications: 31-5/8"W x 19-1/2"D x 31"H
Material: 3/8" Medex wood
Design Number One is one of six Architect's Choice houses shown in the Publications and Plans section of this catalog. All six designs are available as assembled but unfinished shells or with the exterior completely finished. Completed houses are furnished with windows by Miniature Lumber Shoppe as shown.

THE PONDEROSA

Dura-Craft, Inc.
Catalog No. PD175
Dimensions: 23"H x 25"W x 14"D, five rooms, two floors, pine frame, 1/8" plywood, knock-down construction
This charming farm house kit is loaded with gingerbread and comes complete with pine frame, real split shakes, silk screened windows, flower boxes and stairway. Very easy assembly.

FARMHOUSE MINIATURE HOUSE KIT

Dura-Craft, Inc.
Catalog No. FH500
Dimensions: 30"H x 40"W x 21"D, eight rooms, three floors plus stairway
Material: Tongue and groove construction, authentic clapboard siding, split shake roofs, hardwood flooring (one floor).

THE FARMHOUSE

The Lawbre Company
Suggested Retail Prices: Assembled and unfinished $195 plus options. Exterior finished as shown $670. Crating and shipping extra.
Specifications: 27"H x 39"W x 18"D. Two floors plus attic, seven room. 3/8" 7-ply solid birch plywood throughout
Characteristic of the Midwest just before the turn of the century, the Farmhouse is suitable for Early American or Victorian decorations. Trim parts and staircase are included. Finished as shown.

THE GALENA FARMHOUSE

The Lawbre Company
Suggested Retail Price: Assembled and unfinished $375 plus options. Exterior finished as shown $2085. Crating and shipping extra.
Specifications: 32"H x 47"W x 21"D. Two floors plus attic, seven rooms. 3/8" 7-ply birch plywood
Another Lawbre miniature house of great distinction, the all-time favorite farmhouse. We have used wonderful new original details and as always great attention to craftsmanship. Available as an assembled shell or with completely finished exterior. Various options, too.

WALTON PRE-CUT FINISHING KIT NEW CONCEPT WALTON

Real Good Toys
Suggested Retail Price: See your dealer.
Catalog No. NC-1003 New Concept Walton
Specifications: 30-1/4" H x 32-3/4" W x 23" D three floors, 10 rooms. Material: All wood construction with 3/8" cabinet grade plywood walls and floors
Full-length porch and dormers highlight this pleasant country home. 3/8" and 1/4" plywood precision-cut by Vermont artisans for easy and sturdy construction. The New Concept Walton includes pre-assembled Houseworks windows, door, foundation, steps, fancy porch posts, gingerbread trim and it comes complete with wooden shingles. Extensions are available if you want this house with more room.

Prices are approximate and subject to change.

NEW CONCEPT VERMONT FARMHOUSE

Real Good Toys
Suggested Retail Price: See your dealer
Catalog No. NC1401
Specifications: 30-1/4"H x 32-3/4"W x 23"D, three floors, 10 rooms
The New Concept Vermont Farmhouse with its full-length gingerbread trimmed porch reflects the pleasant country living of Vermont. The kit includes pre-assembled windows and doors, foundation, front steps, stairways with bannisters and landing rails and fancy columns for the porch. The finishing kit is included with Northeastern clapboard siding precision pre-cut for exact fit on this dollhouse and wood shingles. One of the most complete and easily finished collector's dollhouse kits available.

NEW CONCEPT GREENACRES

Real Good Toys
Suggested Retail Price: See your dealer.
Catalog No. NC-1700 or NC-1700 (FO).
Specifications: 3 floors, 11 rooms, knock-down construction
Material: All wood 3/8" and 1/4" plywood; precut clapboard siding; wooden shingles
Available front opening or rear open. An L-shaped farmhouse with spacious interior, the kit includes everything you need for a finished dollhouse. Easy construction with sturdy 3/8" plywood wall and floor panels, pre-assembled Houseworks windows and door, precut clapboard siding and trim that you simply glue on to the basic house, fancy gingerbread trim and porch posts, foundation and wooden shingles.

THE SIMPLICITY DOLLHOUSE

Real Good Toys
Suggested Retail Price: See your dealer.
Dimensions: 18" D x 26" L x 30" H
Features the simplest assembly ever with its fully pre-grooved parts. Optional porches and extensions shown here.

THE SIMPLICITY DOLLHOUSE

Real Good Toys
Suggested Retail Price: See your dealer.
Dimensions: 25" D x 46" L x 30" H
Shown above with S-711 gingerbread porch and S-722 extensions.

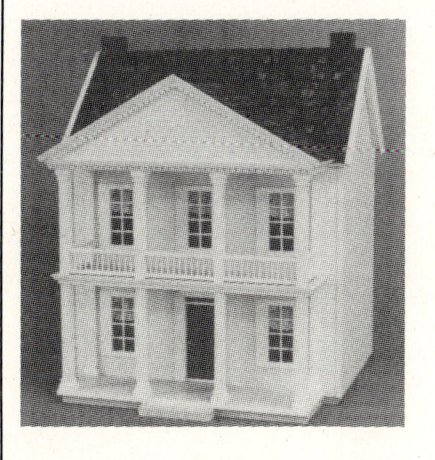

THE SIMPLICITY DOLLHOUSE

Real Good Toys
Suggested Retail Price: See your dealer.
Dimensions: 18" D x 26" L x 30" H
Shown above with the new S714 plantation porch.

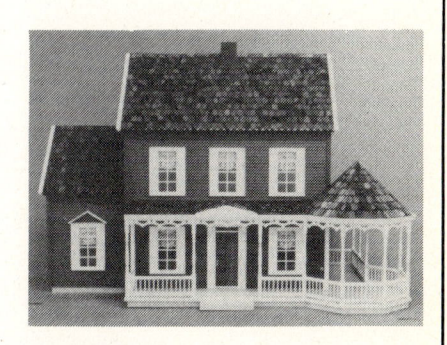

THE SIMPLICITY DOLLHOUSE

Real Good Toys
Suggested Retail Price: See your dealer.
Dimensions: 25-1/2" D x 44" L x 30" H
Shown above with the model S-722 extension and the new S-717 Victorian gazebo porch.

Houses & Buildings

NEW CONCEPT SHELBURNE (OUR CLASSIC FARMHOUSE)
Real Good Toys
Suggested Retail Price: See your dealer. Catalog No. NC-1010.
Specifications: 56"L x 22"D x 32"H, 3 floors, 14 rooms, knockdown construction Material: All wood 3/8" and 1/4" plywood; precut clapboard siding; wooden shingles Classic Colonial simplicity with front porch as they're found on many farms in Vermont and across the country, this dollhouse is Real Good Toys' epitome of a farmhouse. The kit comes complete from foundation and steps to wooden shingles, with pre-assembled Houseworks windows and door, fancy porch posts and gingerbread trim, and pre-cut clapboard and trim that simply needs to be glued on (shutters are optional). The quality of materials makes for easy construction, and combined with the size of this farmhouse provides a setting appropriate for the finest miniatures collection.

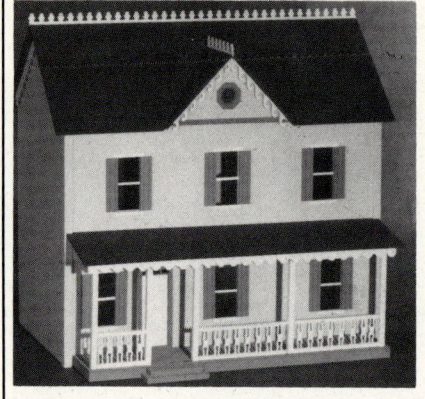

THE BEECHWOOD
Walmer Dollhouses
Suggested Retail Price: See your local dealer. Catalog No. 405
Specifications: 34" W x 24" D x 31" H, three floors, 10 rooms. Permanent nail and glue assembly. Material: 1/2" plywood exterior walls and partitions and 3/8" plywood floors
The Beechwood is spacious (10 rooms to decorate), attractive, and budget priced! The kit includes all gingerbread trims, front porch, exterior front steps, pre-hung front door, plexiglass windows, and interior staircase. Wing additions, siding, and shingles are available for upgrading and expansion.

THE EVERGREEN
Walmer Dollhouses
Suggested Retail Price: See your local dealer. Catalog No. 406
Specifications: 40" W x 31" H x 24" D, three floors, nine to ten rooms. Permanent nail and glue assembly. Material: 1/4" plywood exterior walls and partitions, 3/8" plywood floors
The Evergreen is a lot of house at a budget price. The kit includes the wrap-around porch, pine clapboard siding, all gingerbread trims, exterior steps, pre-hung front door, plexiglass windows, and interior staircase. The twin gable roof and front extension offer fun and interesting interior decorating possibilities. A wing addition is available for expansion.

DANVILLE & BRISTOL MANOR
Real Good Toys
Suggested Retail Price: See your dealer Catalog No. NC1707 Danville/NC1717 Bristol Manor
This farmhouse is enhanced by a wrap-around side porch to become the elegant "Danville". It adds yet another dimension as the "Bristol Manor" with RGT's two-story extension. Both kits have a hinged left front. All components are pre-assembled and include front steps, foundation, stairways with bannisters and landing rails, gingerbread and fancy porch columns. Optional features include #5025 shutters by Houseworks, #A-20 hinged rear roof panel, #1125 shingle dye and #SC copper flashing.

THE HERITAGE HOUSE
Walmer Dollhouses
Suggested Retail Price: See your local dealer. Catalog No. 404
Specifications: 39" W x 24" D x 31-1/2" H, three floors, 10 rooms. Permanent nail and glue assembly
Material: 1/4" plywood exterior walls and partitions, 3/8" plywood floors
The Heritage is a large house with a spacious 10-room interior at a budget price. The kit includes all gingerbread trims, wrap-around porch, pine clapboard siding, exterior front steps, pre-hung front door, plexiglass windows, and interior staircase. Wing additions, shingles, and dormer windows are available for upgrading and expansion.

LOOKING FOR SOMETHING SPECIAL? CHECK WITH YOUR LOCAL MINIATURES SHOP!

Prices are approximate and subject to change.

Federal

Houses & Buildings

NEWTOWN WITH MANSARD ADDITION

Russell Crafts
Suggested Retail Price: Kit, $255/$343.25; assembled unfinished, $315/$408.25; exterior finished, $515/$663.75
Material: 3/8" birch plywood
Dimensions: 43"L x 28"H x 15"D
This house is available either as a Standard or Deluxe model. The Deluxe model has a bay window, louvered shutters, foundation and a deluxe front door. All of the houses include windows, doors and shutters.

THE LEXINGTON

Afton Classics
Suggested Retail Price: Wholesale only. See your local dealer. Catalog No. KT1008
Dimensions: 40-1/2" H x 31-7/8" W x 17-1/4" D. 3/8" cabinet grade plywood and pine.
Large and beautiful. Featuring: three dormers, fine widows walk, nine lower windows and pre-assembled fine raised panel door. Finely trimmed throughout. Inside features two stairways. Additions available.

THE CHATEAU

The Lawbre Company
Suggested Retail Price: Assembled and unfinished $525 plus options. Exterior finished as shown $1305. Crating and shipping extra.
Specifications: 36"H x 57"W x 22"D. Three floors, 12 rooms. 3/8" 7-ply solid birch plywood throughout
A French inspired country house of genteel proportion and detail, the Chateau is an ideal setting for a truly fine collection. Room sizes are generous, elegant architectural detail inside and out, even a curved staircase in the foyer, and French doors in both wings.

FEDERAL "CIRCA 1740"

The Lawbre Company
Suggested Retail Price: Assembled and unfinished $265 plus options. Finished as shown $710. Crating and shipping charges extra.
Specifications: 31"H x 38"W x 18"D. Three floors, nine rooms. 3/8" 7-ply solid birch plywood throughout
An example of the classic refinement and balance found in our Colonial period. The Federal is available with additional wings attached to either or both sides.

CHATEAU CHARMAINE

Architecturally Designed Dollhouses
Specifications: Three floors, 11 rooms
Material: Cabinet grade plywood
This is front opening. The back is closed with appropriate fenestration and with the porch repeated. The house as shown has one extension, another may be added. It is under construction being done in brick and slate.

THE MINIATURES CATALOG, *Fourteenth Edition* 35

THE MONTEREY AND THE SOMERDALE

Real Good Toys
Suggested Retail Price: See your dealer
Catalog No. NC2009 Monterey/NC2019 Somerdale

The hinged front panel on large front opening dollhouses can be awkward. With a little "Magnet Magic" RGT eliminates the problem, you take it all off! With an uncompromising fit, the entire front and front roof panels are easily removed from the Federal style "Monterey". When extensions are added with the same features, this kit becomes the "Somerdale". Optional features include #5025 shutters by Houseworks, #1125 shingle dye and #SC copper flashing.

THE THORNHILL

Real Good Toys
Suggested Retail Price: See your dealer
Specifications: 46"L x 28"W x 36"T, three floors, 14 spacious rooms

The Thornhill is a unique dollhouse that opens on all sides and has a spacious interior. The shell and the components can be purchased separately or together. The shell includes all pre-cut plywood, dentil trim, chimneys, front steps, hinges and magnets. The component pack includes Houseworks doors, windows, shingles, hardware, staircases and trim. This dollhouse kit is the result of Real Good Toys and Houseworks teamwork.

WILLIAMSBURG AND WILLIAMSBURG IN BRICK

Real Good Toys
Suggested Retail Price: See your dealer
Catalog No. DH86K
Specifications: 34"H x 32"W x 24"D, three floors, nine rooms

One of our customer's favorite designs, the Williamsburg comes with pre-cut clapboard or with pre-painted, "distressed" brick panels. These complete kits, clapboard or brick, also include wooden shingles, pre-assembled windows and door, porch and roof rails and interior stairs with railings. Cabinet grade plywood.

Greenhouses/ Gazebos/Garden

TINY TURNINGS KITS GAZEBO

Quad Company
Suggested Retail Price: $15
Catalog No. 3050

Finely detailed hardwood turnings with a unique interlocking design. Each kit contains "tiny turnings", instructions and cutting diagrams.

36   Prices are approximate and subject to change.

Houses & Buildings

VICTORIAN GAZEBO

Aztec Imports, Inc.
Catalog No. RC0300
Specifications: 15"D x 22"H
This Gazebo is eight-sided wood construction. The kit includes: precut pieces, fancy posts and spindles and roofing kit. The roof lifts off for additional access. Perfect for any garden. Available in kit, assembled and finished. Handcrafted by Russell Crafts, exclusively distributed by Aztec Imports, Inc.

VICTORIAN GAZEBO

Betty's Wooden Miniatures
Specifications: Now available in two sizes; 15-1/2"H x 10-1/2"W or 16-1/2"H x 11"W
Available four ways: as a complete kit, assembled and unpainted, assembled and painted sparkling white with a light blue or a terra cotta roof or painted white with light blue and decorated for a wedding as shown. Furnishings are not included but are made and sold by us. All pieces in the kit are pre-drilled and pre-cut, easy to assemble. Beautifully authentic Victorian gazebo. Handcrafted by us in the USA.

GAZEBO KIT

The Lawbre Company
Suggested Retail Price: $44.50 kit, $88.50 assembled and unfinished. Shipping extra
Specifications: 18"H x 9-1/2"W x 9-1/2"D, one room. Material: Wood
To create a garden fantasy or furnish as a separate display, this quality made kit has most parts cut to size, templates and full instructions included.

DECK WITH HOT TUB KIT

Betty's Wooden Miniatures
This lovely contemporary deck kit is also available without the hot tub. All wood material needed to construct steps, deck, hot tub, privacy screens and plant brackets included. Easy to assemble. Can also be ordered fully- assembled and stained. Finished size: 11" D x 14" W x 8-1/2" H. Chairs, table, hanging basket chair and portable TV are also available. Hot tub is also available by itself. American made by us.

ARBOR KITS

Greenleaf Products
Suggested Retail Price: $5.50
Catalog No. 9017 (Heart shaped arbor with settles, 8"H x 8"W x 5-1/4"D) and 9018 (Sunrise arbor, 7-1/4"H x 8"W x 4"D)
On a hot summer day imagine sipping a cool drink and enjoying a breeze under your arbor. These delightful arbor kits will add realism and charm to any dollhouse setting. 1" to 1' scale.

THE MINIATURES CATALOG, *Fourteenth Edition*

GREENHOUSE KIT

The Lawbre Company
Suggested Retail Price: Greenhouse kit $65.50 plus shipping, greenhouse kit with potting shed kit $88.50 plus shipping.
Specifications: Greenhouse: 12" H x 10" W x 13-1/4" D Potting shed: 14-3/4" H x 12-1/4" W x 7" D
This is the ultimate greenhouse kit! It is generous in size and materials are high quality with all parts precision-cut to size. Easy-to-assemble with templates and complete instructions included. Basic kit is shown in example on the left.

GAZEBO

Russell Crafts
Suggested Retail Price: Kit, $89.95; assembled unfinished, $195.95; completely finished, $395.95
Material: 3/8" birch plywood
Dimensions: 22"H x 15"D
Our Gazebo includes pre-cut pieces, fancy posts and spindles and a roofing kit. The roof also lifts off for additional access.

Miscellaneous Buildings

THE GAZEBO

Real Good Toys
Suggested Retail Price: See your dealer
Catalog No. G-12
Specifications: 13-1/2"D x 16"H
Let your imagination run with miniature wicker furniture, bench seats, swings, planters or foundations. Use flowers, dolls or stuffed animals to create your own style. The Gazebo kit includes pre-cut gingerbread trim, octagonal wooden shingles, foundation and front step. Step-by-step instructions are simple and easy to follow.

RUSSELL CRAFTS SCHOOL HOUSE

Aztec Imports, Inc.
Catalog No. RC0200
Specifications: 20"L x 15"W x 18H
Wholesale only. This one-room School House with an upstairs room for the teacher is hand-crafted by Russell Crafts and exclusively distributed by Aztec Imports, Inc.

THE BARN

Jan's Small World
Suggested Retail Price: $130
Dimensions: 30"L x 18"W x 21"H
Material: 3/8" and 1/4" mahogany plywood
Your dream house, and we've begun the remodeling for you. One large room 18" x 18" and two smaller rooms on ground floor, large loft and room for two bedrooms on second story. Two sides and one roof piece hinge open. Shingles included. Openings are standard sizes. Windows and siding not included.

Prices are approximate and subject to change.

Houses & Buildings

THE FIFTH AVENUE

Architecturally Designed Dollhouses
Specifications: 47"H x 19-1/2"W x 19-1/2"D; four floors, four rooms
Material: Cabinet grade plywood
Scale: 1" - 1'
Available as shell or completed.
Rooms in your dollhouse too small? This is the answer to a decorator's prayer. A cabinet that looks like a house, a house that is a cabinet. It is completely enclosed and front opening. Floor size of the first three rooms is a spacious 15-3/4" x 17-1/2". Top floor is 15-1/2" x 17". First three floors are 10" high, fourth floor is 12" high.

THE HAUNTED HOUSE

Artply, Inc.
Suggested Retail Price: See your dealer
Model No. APL90090
Dimensions: 18"H x 18"W x 12"D
For a real treat and tons of fun, this haunted house kit is just the answer. Creativity has no bounds and as you can see from our made-up sample, the possibilities provided by this exciting kit are endless. Let your imagination go wild. Bonus: 12 piece furniture kit is included. Shingles, fence and railings are all included with this four room house.

CARRIAGE HOUSE & STABLE

Jan's Small World
Suggested Retail Price: $105.95
Specifications: 20"H x 24-1/2"W x 14"D, one floor with hayloft, 1/4" mahogany plywood This carriage house is an authentic reproduction of those seen in the 1850's-1880's. The kit includes doors, windows, shingles, battens, and cupola.

THE SQUATTER

Homestead Homes
Dimensions: 3" x 3-1/2"
Material: Recycled wood
1" scale replica of the typical one-holer, complete with a Sears catalogue.

COUNTRY CHURCH

Jan's Small World
Suggested Retail Price: $209.95
Specifications: 30"L x 20"W x 32"H, one floor, one room
This church is a model of the St. Paul's church in Forest Grove, Montana. The church was built in the Fall of 1907 and still stands today. Kit includes door, siding, shingles, windows, and trim pieces, entryway and bell tower. This is a very small church, so is perfect for a dollhouse town.

COUNTRY SCHOOL

Jan's Small World
Suggested Retail Price: $199.95
Specifications: 30"L x 14"W x 29"H, one floor
Material: 3/8" plywood
This school is designed from one built around 1905 here in Montana. Kit includes windows, door, siding, shingles and trim. Entryway and bell tower also included. A perfect addition to any town.

THE MINIATURES CATALOG, *Fourteenth Edition*

JAPANESE ROOM

Mini Minerals
New, larger Japanese room kit designed by Darlene Guerry for the Sakura line of Mini-Minerals.

DELUXE ROADSIDE STAND
"Precious Little Things"
by the Fieldwood Company, Inc.
Dimensions: 15-1/2"W x 9"D x 9-1/4"H
Handmade of wood with asphalt roof. Shown with store furnishings. Color catalog $3.50 or ask your local dealer.

THE DOLL'S HORSE STABLE

Wilshire Miniatures
Suggested Retail Price: $200
Dimensions: 25-1/2"L x 17-1/2"H x 14"D
Material: cabinet birch 1/4" to 3/4" plywood
Assembled and finished turn-of-the-century in-town stable includes two straight stalls, a tack room and a loft. Horse sold separately.

DOLLHOUSE OF A DOLLHOUSE

Northeastern Scale Models, Inc.
Suggested Retail Price: $11.95 Kit, plus shipping
Catalog No. 1003
Specifications: 1-1/8"x1-3/4", 4 rooms, 2 floors. Material: Basswood
Kit contains all wooden walls, flooring, roofing, plus snap-in plastic windows and doors. Please see our insert between pages 80 and 81 for more information.

GARAGE KIT

Timberbrook Wood Products
Suggested Retail Price: $73.50
Specifications: 11-3/4" W x 9-3/8" H x 15-3/4" D
With working overhead garage door. Door and windows shown are not included and may be purchased seperately. See your dealer or write for information.

ONE-ROOM BRICK SCHOOLHOUSE KIT

Rossco Products, Inc.
Suggested Retail Price: Kit $99.95
Specifications: 17-1/2" H x 10" W x 13" D (16" including steps). One floor, one room. Made of rigid polyurethane foam. Interlocking brick corners construction.
One side open for room box use. Second side available on optional four-sided version. All detail is pre-molded. Simply glue and paint. Interlocking brick corners. Slate roof. Flooring and door included.

Shop/Office

40 Prices are approximate and subject to change.

THE GENERAL STORE
American Craft Products
Suggested Retail Price: See your local dealer. Catalog No. 105.
Specifications: 24"W x 22"D x 36"H. Full width "store" area on first floor, 4 extra large rooms on the second and third floors
Material: 3/8" birch plywood
Shell kit No. 105 includes all the precision cut material necessary to build basic house without windows, doors, and trim. Optional component package No 105-S is available providing all Carlson working windows, doors, interior stairs, and exterior trim. Fully open at rear. Floor plan is equally suited for post office, sheriffs office, hotel, etc. Made in America.

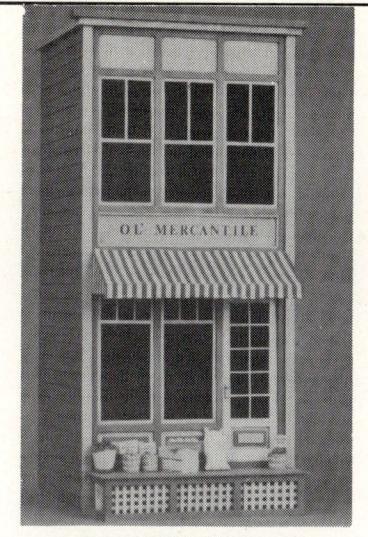

OL' MERCANTILE
American Craft Products
Suggested Retail Price: See your local dealer. Catalog No. 8506.
Specifications: 12-1/2"W x 25"H x 14"D. 2 rooms, new simplified construction. Outer walls presided.
Material: Precision machine pine and solid plywood
Complete kit with no extras to buy. Precision machined pine - no sanding. Plastic for door and windows included. Easy to paint and light. Foremost in quality and design. Typical 1800's small town store front. Fully open back. Made in America.

THE NORWOOD
Ballhagen Woodcraft
Suggested Retail Price: See your local dealer. Assembled unfinished.
Catalog No. SF904
Specifications: 13" H x 14" W x 11" D, 14" x 14" base, one room. Material: Finland birch and sugar pine, glass in bay windows
Small store with small bay window (Village Crafter No. SC801), one Houseworks door in front. Access to interior is by sliding up front and slide out roof. Exterior has lots of victorian trim. Kit No. 904K comes precut, bay window is assembled. Houseworks door is not included in kit.

THREE LITTLE SHOPS
Architecturally Designed Dollhouses
Dimensions: 21"H x 48"W x 23"D; two floors, five rooms
Material: Cabinet grade plywood
These three shops come with a balcony, exterior stairs and an upper level for living quarters. For variety, there's one Victorian, one Georgian and one Colonial. They can easily be added to.

THREE LITTLE SHOPS
Architecturally Designed Doll Houses
Rear view of "Three Little Shops." It is now being done with additional roofs. Base is approximately 72" long for walks and landscaping.

Houses & Buildings

THE MINIATURES CATALOG, *Fourteenth Edition*

THE CLAIRMORE

Ballhagen Woodcraft
Suggested Retail Price: See your local dealer. Assembled unfinished.
Catalog No. SF901
Specifications: 13" H x 17-1/2" W x 11" D 14" x 20" base, one room. Material: Finland birch and sugar pine, glass in bay windows Small corner store with small bay window on one side and large bay window and Houseworks door on front. Access to interior is by removal of slide-up front and slide-out roof. Kit No. 901K comes precut, bay window is assembled. Houseworks door is not included in kit.

OAKLANE SHOPPE

Ballhagen Woodcraft
Suggested Retail Price: See your local dealer. Assembled unfinished.
Catalog No. SF9097
Specifications: 20"H x 17-1/2"W x 12"D, one room downstairs with large wrap-around bay window and attic.
Material: Finland birch and sugar pine, glass in bay window.
Small shop with attic room. Bay window is removable. Comes with Houseworks door. Second story has two Houseworks dormer windows and an octagonal window on one side. Kit No. 907K comes with all pieces pre-cut. Bay window is assembled. Houseworks door and windows are not included with kit.

GENERAL STORE

Celerity Miniature Homes
See your local miniatures dealer for retail price
Specifications: 19"H x 24"W x 15"D; base, 28"L x 19"W, two floors, three rooms. Top quality 3/8" plywood. Tongue and groove construction.
The General Store sells a variety of wares! This kit contains six main store parts plus posts, store sign-board and outside stairway. Here's the chance to be in business for yourself - in miniature! Catalog #2701 kit, #2702 assembled.

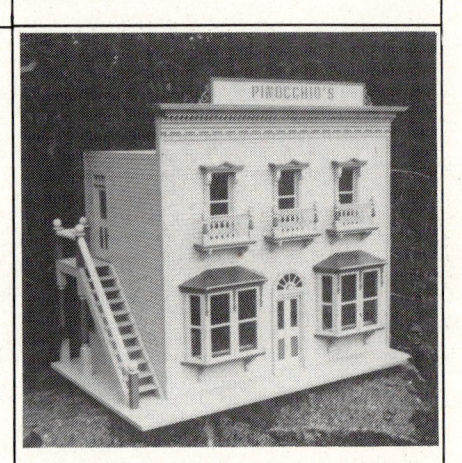

OLD TIME GAS STATION

Ballhagen Woodcraft
Suggested Retail Price: See your local dealer. Assembled unfinished.
Catalog No. GS906
Specifications: Base size 14" x 23", one room/office. Material: Finland birch and sugar pine, pumps are metal
Old time two-pump gas station with office. Office has four Houseworks windows and one Houseworks door. Assembled. Includes building, two pumps, four windows, one door. Kit No. GS906K comes partially assembled. Houseworks door and windows and pumps are not included in kit.

THE RIDGEMONT

Ballhagen Woodcraft
Suggested Retail Price: See your local dealer. Assembled unfinished.
Catalog No. SF905
Specifications: 13" H x 22" W x 12" D, 15" x 22" base, one room
Material: Finland birch and sugar pine, glass in bay windows
A long store front with one small bay window on each side of a Houseworks door. Access to interior is by sliding front up and out and slide out roof.
Kit No. 905K comes with all pieces precut, bay windows are assembled. Houseworks door does NOT come with kit.

VICTORIAN ANTIQUE SHOP

Celerity Miniature Homes
See your local miniatures dealer for retail price
Specifications: Store; 19"H x 15"W x 24"L, base; 28"L x 19"W, store front; 25"H. Top quality 3/8" plywood.
The Antique Shop sells many exclusive items! The kit contains six main store parts plus sign board and outside stairway with posts and balls to complete. Decorative moldings and trims are listed in the instructions and are found in your local miniature shops. Catalog #3801 kit, #3802 assembled.

THE CORNER STORE

Celerity Miniature Homes
See your local miniatures dealer for retail price
Specifications: 27-1/2"H x 24"W x 15"D, three floors, five rooms. Top quality 3/8" plywood. Dado joint construction.
The Corner Store kit contains 10 main house pieces plus moveable partitions, interior stairway, exterior stairway with railing, two window boxes (plexiglass not included) and turned posts. A unique design for two-side display in the Corner Store. The corner entrance is enhanced by three turned posts. The store is on the first level with living quarters for the seamstress, florists or baker above. Decorated exterior as shown is a special order. Catalog #601 kit, #602 assembled.

October National Dollhouse & Miniatures Month

SHINBONE

Compass Miniatures Industries
Suggested Retail Price: See your dealer
Dimensions: 30"W x 16"D x 34"H
Material: Cabinet grade 3/8" plywood
Capture the Old West in this storefront/saloon with six rooms above. The upper floors have a separate enclosed stairway. Available in kit form, assembled shell and decorated model. The kit includes sidewalk planks, building sign boards, posts, hitching rails and moveable partitions. Door and windows are available in a component package. Openings are sized to fit standard components.

WILD WEST SALOON

Itty Bitty Builder
Suggested Retail Price: Write for brochure
Specifications: 24"H x 16"W x 15-1/2"D; base 16" x 20", two floors, two rooms. Constructed of quality 3/8" and 1/4" plywood.
Other sizes available on special order.

TWO-STORY STORE BUILDING

Design Tecnics Miniatures
Suggested Retail Price: $290/kit
Product No.: 102
Specifications: 16"W x 14-3/4"D x 27-5/8"H
Material: wood, cast resin brackets
Kit includes 3/8" wood shell parts, windows, door, brackets and all trim parts shown. Complete instructions. Entire front removable for access to interiors.

THE MILLWOOD COUNTRY STORE

The Lawbre Company
Suggested Retail Price: See your dealer
Specifications: 38"H x 28"W x 24"D, one large room with stair and large balcony
Material: 3/8" cabinet grade birch plywood
Intended as a store, the large first floor is perfect for a variety of merchandise displays. The stair leads to a balcony that could be used as an office or additional display of goods. The Millwood is front opening, two doors and 1/2 of the roof is hinged for additional access. There are many exterior details and textures making this a very exciting little building. It is available as an unfinished shell with a separate components pack or with a completely finished exterior.

Houses & Buildings

THE MINIATURES CATALOG, Fourteenth Edition

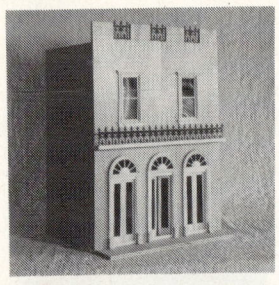

BLUEBERRY PIE

Walmer Dollhouses
Suggested Retail Price: See your local dealer. Catalog No. 461
Specifications: 18"W x 17-1/2"D x 32"H
Material: 3/8" cabinet grade plywood
The Blueberry Pie is a front-opening shop with 2-1/2 stories above for proprietor's living space, including separate bath. The ideal dollhouse for small spaces and big imaginations. Kit includes gingerbread trims, front porch, pre-hung front door, windows and three interior staircases. Wing addition, siding, shingles and other components are available for customizing and expansion.

GENERAL STORE

Real Good Toys
Suggested Retail Price: Less than $30/kit
Catalog No. GS1
Specifications: 11-1/4"H x 15-1/4"W x 10-3/4"D, one floor, one room
A complete general store with two walls of shelves, a counter, a ladder, Plexiglas windows, pine door, hinges, a sliding Plexiglas top and Victorian molding. Includes an assortment of miniatures: barrel, butter churn, bottles, orange crates, old-time signs, checkerboard and more. The best low-end value we've ever made!

CLASSIC SHOPS

Itty Bitty Builder
Suggested Retail Price: Write for brochure
Specifications:
Orleans; 22"H x 16"W x 12"D; base 16" x 15" (top)
Ferndale; 24"H x 20"W x 12"D; base 20" x 16" (middle)
Comstock 23"H x 16"W x 12"D; base 16" x 15" (bottom)
Constructed of quality 3/8" and 1/4" plywood with lift-off fronts. Let your imagination run wild with these classic shops. Orleans and Comstock are available with brick facing. Other sizes available on special order.

BRIMBLE'S MERCANTILE

Greenleaf Products
Suggested Retail Price: $72.50
Catalog No. 8022
Specifications: 21-1/2"H x 18-1/2"W x 25"D, two floors, two large rooms, 1/8" di-cut plywood
Your imagination will take over with the Brimble's Mercantile - we've seen it decorated as every kind of enterprise, from bakery to saloon. The kit has one huge room on each floor which allows for a variety of shop or shop/apartment designs, and it comes equipped with counters, display island, a whole wall of built-in shelves, and extra wide window ledges to serve as display areas. A little ingenuity and you're in business.

BLUEBERRY PIE

Walmer Dollhouses
Suggested Retail Price: See your local dealer. Catalog No. 461
Specifications: 18"W x 17-1/2"D x 32"H
Material: 3/8" cabinet grade plywood
The Blueberry Pie Townhouse is identical to the Blueberry Pie Shop. The front-opening kit may be built with or without the porch which is included in the kit. The 3-1/2 story kit is perfect for those miniaturists with limited space and unlimited imaginations. The kit includes all trims, windows, pre-hung door and front porch (not shown). Wing addition, siding, shingles and other components available for expansion.

Prices are approximate and subject to change.

Southern Colonial & Georgian

Houses & Buildings

THE OLDE FIREHOUSE

Walmer Dollhouses
Specifications: 18" W x 17" D x 36" H
Material: 1/2" and 3/8" plywood and solid pine
What little (and big!) boys' dreams are made of. This collector quality kit includes windows, pre-hung entrance and garage doors, firetruck ramp, a blank sign over the door for personalization, interior stairs, railings and firepole. The firemen share the three-story firehouse with sleeping quarters and a bath upstairs, mess hall on the second floor, office and firetruck barn on the first floor. Two sets of stairs, bathroom partitions, firepole railings and, of course, a three-story firepole for quick exit are all included. Furnishings are not included.

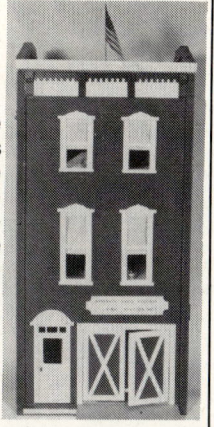

SOUTHERN MANSION MINIATURE HOUSE KIT

Dura-Craft, Inc.
Catalog No. SM700
Dimensions: 31"H x 55"W x 27"D, ten rooms, three floors
Material: Tongue and groove construction, 1/4" pine, authentic clapboard siding, split shake roof, hardwood flooring (one floor).

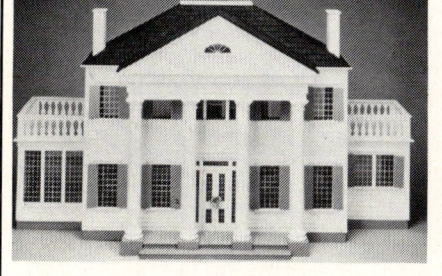

THE BEAUMONT

Greenleaf Products
New Southern Colonial, Greek Revival Style
Suggested Retail Price: $161.25
Catalog No. 8003
Specifications: 26-1/4"H x 48-3/8"W x 20-1/2"D, 1/8" di-cut plywood
Serene and elegant, the Beaumont evokes the romance and refinement of the Greek Revival style in American architecture. With its grand portico, authentically proportioned turned wooden columns and airy sunroom, it's truly a masterpiece. Six room interior with large attic, elegant staircase and four fireplaces. Sundecks off the second floor bedrooms with traditional balustrades all around are the picture perfect spot for white wicker and iced tea. Shingles and siding included.

ROSEDAWN PLANTATION

The Lawbre Company
Suggested Retail Price: Assembled and unfinished $990 plus options. Completely finished, $3150. Crating and shipping extra
Specifications: 37"H x 55"W x 26"D, three floors, 12 rooms, 3/8" 7-ply solid birch plywood throughout
Rosedawn Plantation is a bold and beautiful statement of the Southern Classical Greek Revival in all its elegant glory!

THE MOUNT VERNON

Afton Classics
Suggested Retail Price: Wholesale only. See your local dealer. Catalog No. KT1002
Dimensions: 28" H x 31-1/2" W x 22-5/8" D
Seven rooms including two hallways, bathroom plus full attic, beautiful portico with round pillars, pre-assembled raised panel door and windows plus stairs. 3/8" cabinet grade plywood at a very reasonable price. Additions available.

THE PLANTATION

The Lawbre Company
Suggested Retail Price: Assembled and unfinished $635 plus options. Exterior finished as shown $1670. Crating and shipping extra
Specifications: 31"H x 60"W x 22"D, three floors, 11 rooms, 3/8" 7-ply solid birch plywood throughout
The Plantation is an example of the classical line, proportion and balance that was the pride of the Antebellum South. Photo and prices include the two optional wings that may be eliminated. Many options are available.

ASHLEY'S MANOR

Compass Miniatures Industries
Suggested Retail Price: See your dealer
Dimensions: 51"W x 24"D x 32"H
Material: Cabinet grade 3/8" plywood
A majestic 12 room Southern Colonial with a large upper balcony. Available in kit form, assembled shell and decorated display model. The kit includes foundation pieces, columns, railings and spindles, chimney, and interior and exterior stairs. Doors, windows and trims are available in component packages. Openings are sized to fit standard components.

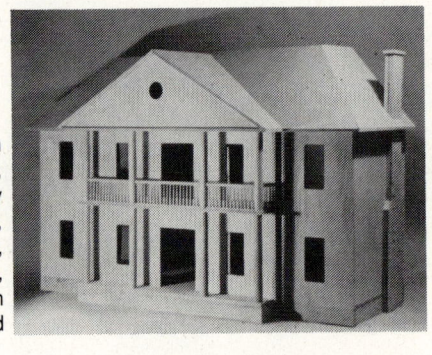

THE MULBERRY AND TWELVE OAKS

Real Good Toys
Suggested Retail Price: See your dealer
Catalog No. NC1201 Mulberry/NC1210 Twelve Oaks
The gracious "Mulberry" features a two-story porch with Southern style columns accessed by french doors. The unique extensions make the "Twelve Oaks" a true mansion for the discriminating collector. Comes with front steps, a full foundation, stairways with bannisters and landing rails. Gingerbread trim and fancy porch columns are included. Optional features include windows, #5025 shutters by Houseworks, #1125 shingle dye and #SC copper flashing.

1/12TH SCALE GEORGIAN SHELL

Houseworks
Suggested Retail Price: $200
Catalog No. 4202
Specifications: 33"H x 21-1/2"D x 33-1/4"L
Kit includes 3/8" cabinet grade plywood, front opening designs, step-by-step instructions, and a 3-in-1 Dollhouse Planbook for your reference. Write to Houseworks for information on the Houseworks Component Sets.

Townhouses

46 Prices are approximate and subject to change.

Houses & Buildings

GOLDEN GATE VIEW

American Craft Products
Catalog No. 8507
Dimensions: 14"W x 12"D x 10-3/4"H
Two rooms, new simplified construction. Outer walls presided. Complete kit with no extras to buy. Precision machined pine. Plastic for door and windows included. Easy to paint and light. Foremost in quality and design. An accurately detailed reproduction of Victorian architecture. Fully open back. Made in America.

DEBORAH'S TOWNHOUSE

Celerity Miniature Homes
See your local miniatures dealer for retail price
Specifications: 31-1/2"H x 23-1/2"W x 19-1/2"D (includes porch), three floors, five rooms. Top quality 3/8" plywood. Dado joint construction.
Welcome to Deborah's townhouse! Kit contains 10 main pieces plus two stairways, two porches, shutters, flower boxes, railings, corner posts, turned posts and scroll trim. Exterior beams not included in kit. Decorated model as shown is a special order. Catalog #2401 kit, #2402 assembled.

CHESSINGTON PLAZA

The Lawbre Company
Suggested Retail Price: $5950 finished as shown with variations (crating and shipping extra).
Specifications: 60"H x 30"W x 28"D, five floors, 20 rooms.
Material: 3/8" 7-ply solid birch plywood.
First floor shops, two 3-floor apartments with studio gardens. Building is front and side opening. Quite an elegant limited edition building for the creative serious collector.

BROWNSTONE COMPLEX

Compass Miniatures Industries
Suggested Retail Price: See your dealer
Dimensions: 60"W x 20"D x 37"H
Material: Cabinet grade 3/8" plywood
The Main Street units are available as the whole complex or as four individual units. They are offered in kit form, assembled shell or decorated model. Each includes interior stairs and front steps and various components to personalize each unit. Doors, windows and trim pieces, including a real cloth awning are available. Openings are sized to fit standard components.

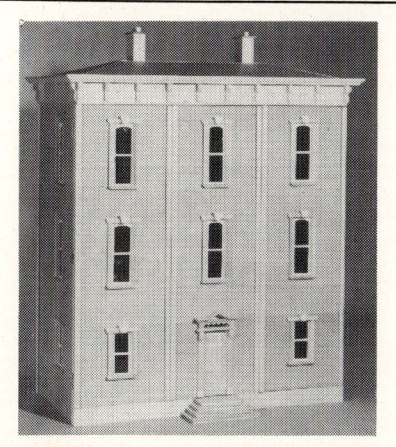

THE TIFFANY HOUSE

Walmer Dollhouses
Suggested Retail Price: See your local dealer. Catalog No. 503
Specifications: 41-1/2"H x 35"W x 19"D
Three floors, seven rooms, center halls and bath
Material: 3/8" plywood exterior walls and floors, 1/4" partitions, solid pine
Front opening kit has seven rooms, separate bathroom, and two connecting hallways on upper levels. Kit complete with front steps, exterior door, framed plexiglas windows and trim, two staircases and railings. Start with basic kit, grow with one or more Tiffany options: a two-story wing, two-story bay windows or a front porch, all with our classic hip-roof design.

THE MINIATURES CATALOG, Fourteenth Edition

THE ARLINGTON

Walmer Dollhouses
Suggested Retail Price: See your local dealer. Catalog No. 502
Specifications: 37-1/2" H x 34" W x 17-1/2" D, three floors, seven rooms
Material: 3/8" plywood exterior walls, 1/4" partitions, 1/2" floors and solid pine. Nail-and-glue assembly
The basic kit has seven rooms, separate bathroom, and interconnecting upstairs hallway. Kit complete with front steps, exterior door, framed plexiglas windows and trim, two staircases, and railings. Start with basic kit. Grow with Arlington options: Wing additions, various porches, dormer and working windows, balconies, siding, shingles, french door, and wide stairs. Slowly create your dream dollhouse.

THE BUNGALOW

The Lawbre Company
Suggested Retail Price: $795 (finished as shown), $375 (assembled/unfinished). Shipping/crating costs are extra.
Dimensions: 32"H x 23"W x 35"D
Floors: Two, plus attic. Rooms: Nine
Material: Birch plywood
Construction: Assembled
This Bungalow-style house was popular in the cities and suburbs of the 1920's. It is fully enclosed on all four sides.

THE OLD VILLAGE SHOP

Walmer Dollhouses
Suggested Retail Price: See your local dealer. Catalog No. 519
Specifications: 36" H x 16" W x 17" D, three floors, four rooms
Material: 3/8" cabinet grade plywood. 1/2" floors, sugar pine. Nail-and-glue assembly
This front-opening house features store window for display of miniature goodies and an exterior side staircase to the proprietor's quarters. A most popular choice. Kit includes exterior and interior staircases, top landing rail, doors, windows, and porch steps. Easy illustrated instructions.

Tudor

OLD WESTBURY HALL

The Lawbre Company
Suggested Retail Price: Exterior completely finished as shown $3850. Limited edition. Only available with exterior finished. Crating and shipping extra.
Specifications: 36"H x 61"W x 26"D, three floors, 15 rooms, 3/8" 7-ply solid birch plywood
This Elizabethan half-timber, fully constructed with exterior finished is truly a collector's house. Old Westbury Hall is a limited edition, completely handfinished house with slight variations in each edition to make it individual. An engraved brass plate is supplied with each house stating its number, date of manufacturer and owner.

TUDOR

Dura-Craft, Inc.
Suggested Retail Price: See your dealer. Catalog No. TD200 Specifications: 20" H x 19" W x 12" D, four rooms, pine frame, 1/8" plywood, knock-down construction
This tudor house has an elegant bay window, real stairs, spacious rooms and delightful trim. Silkscreened windows and roof panels are scored with shingle pattern. This house will assemble easily and will delight the young ones. See our catalog for other models.

Prices are approximate and subject to change.

Houses & Buildings

THE HARRISON
Greenleaf Products
Suggested Retail Price: $129
Catalog No. 8006
Specifications: 31"H x 37-1/4"W x 21-1/8"D, three floors, nine large rooms, tab and slot assembly
Material: 1/8" di-cut plywood
Big rooms in this Tudor mansion! The Harrison uses movable partitions to creat up to nine large rooms with six, count 'em, six bay windows to make the interior wonderfully bright and spacious. There's a hidden roof panel leading into a secret third floor studio room with French doors opening onto an elegant terrace. Window boxes and diamond patterned "leaded" windows complete the regal picture.

THE GLENCROFT
Greenleaf Products
Suggested Retail Price: $86
Catalog No. 8001
Specifications: 21"H x 25-1/4"W x 17"D, two floors, four rooms
Material: 1/8" di-cut plywood
Our cozy Tudor cottage reflects the designers' research into authentic English architecture. With its' picket fence and half-timbered exterior, the house is a visual delight; it has silkscreened windows to simulate leaded glass and a flower box too. There are four spacious rooms, beamed ceilings, built-in bookcases, two window seats and two fireplaces. A winding staircase completes the mood of this wonderful English Tudor. Shingles included.

TUDOR DOLLHOUSE
Hill's Dollhouse Workshop
Suggested Retail Price: Wholesale only, see your local dealer
Dimensions: 27"H x 30"W x 14"D. Two floors plus attic, seven rooms. Made of 3/8", 5-ply birch type plywood. Dadoed partitions and center floor removable after assembly, 1-1/2" foundation
Eye-catching English Tudor, finished in white stucco with dark brown wood trim, roof and front door. Windows are silk-screened brown to simulate leaded windows. Kit includes everything for finished exterior, plus stairs, railings, attic and bathroom partitions. Porch railings, interior stairs and stairwell hole railings are Timberbrooks'. Available without bays or addition. Front door will take some of Houseworks and Carlsons doors. Basic assembly time is two hours.

Victorian

Interested in a Club?
Contact the National Association of Miniature Enthusiasts for a club in your area.

N.A.M.E.
130 N. Rangeline Rd.
Carmel, IN 46032

THE ROSEHILL VICTORIAN
Afton Classics
Suggested Retail Price: Wholesale only. See your local dealer. Catalog No. KT4008
Dimensions: 39" H x 31-1/2" W x 17 1/2" D
Material: 3/8" cabinet grade plywood
A fine, towered Victorian with seven rooms including two hallways and a bathroom plus a full attic area with additional living area with tower and gable openings. Also includes windows and a pre-assembled raised panel door with frosted glass transom. Wow! What a price!!

THE MINIATURES CATALOG, Fourteenth Edition

THE BRIARHILL VICTORIAN

Afton Classics
Suggested Retail Price: Wholesale only. See your local dealer.
Dimensions: 36" H x 25-3/4" W x 15 3/16" D
Material: 3/8" cabinet grade plywood
A beautiful Victorian with mansard roof, two dormers, widows walk, gingerbread, two stairways, windows plus a pre-assembled raised panel door with frosted glass transom. Again, unbelievable pricing. Porch and addition available.

FOX POINT

American Craft Products
Suggested Retail Price: See your local dealer. Catalog No. 112.
Specifications: 32"W x 21"D x 30"H. 8 rooms plus full attic, 2 story, Wire-Ready pre-grooved panels for solid wire
Material: 3/8" cabinet grade birch plywood
House kit No. 112 is of the Wire-Ready Series. It contains all the precision cut materials necessary to build the basic house and also includes Carlson windows, doors, interior staircase and railing, complete exterior trim package, pre-assembled foundation. Optional room addition No. 115, wrap around porch No. 113, and Victorian tower No. 114 available to customize this house. Partial front opening and fully open back, hinged attic back roof. Made in America.

THE COUNTRY LADY

American Craft Products
Suggested Retail Price: See your local dealer. Catalog No. 109-C.
Specifications: 33"W x 23"D x 32"H. 6 large rooms plus dormer and tower area. Large 2nd floor landing and hall
Material: 3/8" birch plywood
House kit No. 109-C includes precision cut materials necessary to build the basic house and also includes all the Carlson working windows, doors, interior stairs, and exterior trim to finish the house. Optional tower unit No. 114 is also available. Fully open at rear, hinged wing front with bay Made in America.

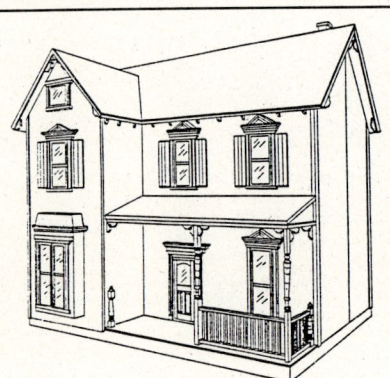

MAPLE HILL

American Craft Products
Suggested Retail Price: See your local dealer. Catalog No. 111.
Specifications: 32"W x 21"D x 30"H. 7 rooms, plus full attic, 2 story, Wire-Ready pre-grooved panels for solid wire
Material: 3/8" cabinet grade birch plywood
House kit No. 111 is of the Wire-Ready Series. It includes all the precision cut materials necessary to build the basic house and also includes Carlson windows, doors, interior staircase and railings, complete exterior trim package, pre-assembled foundation. Optional room addition No. 115, wrap around porch No. 113, and Victorian tower No. 114 available to customize this house. Partial front opening and fully open back, hinged back attic roof. Made in America.

THE QUEEN ANNE ROWHOUSE

American Craft Products
Suggested Retail Price: See your local dealer. Catalog No. 106.
Specifications: 24"W x 29"D x 37"H. 8 rooms including spacious front/entry parlor plus room sized 2nd floor landing and hall area. Divided full-sized attic
Material: 3/8" birch plywood
Shell kit No. 106 includes all the precision cut material necessary to build the basic house without windows, doors, and trim. Optional component package No. 106-S is available providing all Carlson working windows, doors, interior stairs, and exterior trim. Hinged, fully opening rear wall. Hinged attic, side roof and two hinged side openings. Made in America.

THE VICTORIAN HOUSE

American Craft Products
Suggested Retail Price: See your local dealer. Catalog No. 104.
Specifications: 35"W x 27"D x 41"H. 7 large rooms on 1st and 2nd floors plus dormer and tower areas on divided 3rd floor. Large lower entry hall, 2nd floor landing and hall
Material: 3/8" birch plywood
Shell kit No. 104 includes all the precision cut material necessary to build the basic house without windows, doors, and trim. Optional component package No. 104-S is available providing all Carlson working windows, doors, interior stairs, and exterior trim. Fully open at rear, hinged attic back roof, two hinged side openings. Guaranteed best seller. Made in America.

Prices are approximate and subject to change.

Houses & Buildings

WINFIELD MANOR
"Ready to Move-In Houses"
American Craft Products
Dimensions: 37"W x 13"D x 29"H, eight rooms, 3/8" plywood. Catalog No. 120
Completely assembled and finished inside and out. Our finishing process meticulously reproduces architectural details and interior designs created by Leroy Carlson. The front door, siding, shutters, trim, foundation and shake roof are actually silkscreened. Inside, hardwood floors, paneled staircases and fireplace as well as "papered" walls are recreated using the same process. Check with your dealer for color options, as well as additional models in our Parade of Homes Collection. Made in America.

VICTORIA PLACE
"Ready to Move-In Houses"
American Craft Products
Dimensions: 18"W x 15"D x 44"H, five rooms, 3/8" plywood, 1" scale
The Victoria Place is completely assembled and finished inside and out. Our unique finishing process meticulously reproduces original architectural details and interior designs by Leroy Carlson. You will have to look twice to notice that the front door, siding, shutters, trim, foundation and shake roof are actually silkscreened. Inside, floors, staircases, fireplace and "papered" walls are created using the same process. Check with your dealer for color options, as well as other models in our Parade of Homes Collection. Made in America. Catalog No. 123.

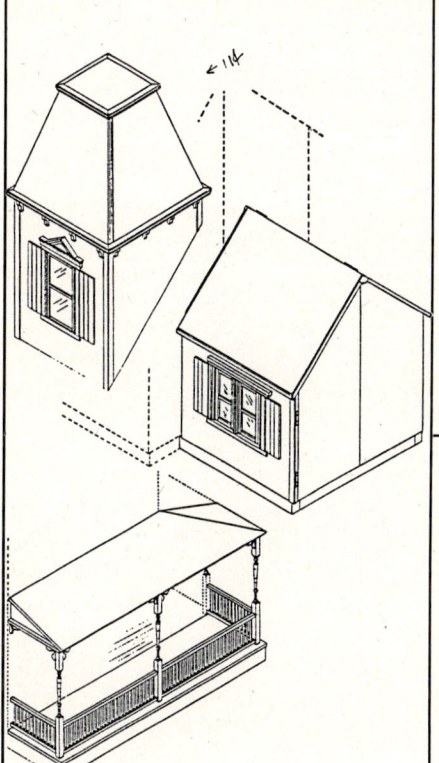

"WIRE READY" SERIES ADD-ONS

American Craft Products
Suggested Retail Price: See your dealer.
Material: 3/8" birch plywood
The three additions shown have been designed to fit perfectly with "wire ready" series model Nos. 110, 111, and 112. Each kit is complete with components and trim. Victorian Tower kit No. 114, 7"W x 7"D x 14"H. Room Addition No. 115, 12"W x 12"D x 17"H fully enclosed with hinged front roof (for right or left). Wrap-Around Porch kit No. 113, 21"L x 5-1/2"W x 13"H makes left or right porch addition. Made in America.

JOSIAH GOLDEN HOUSE

American Victorians by Clell Boyce
Suggested Retail Price: $310 assembled unfinished, $4000 with exterior finished. All prices plus shipping.
Dimensions: 46" W x 28" D x 51" H
Material: Multi-ply solid core 3/8" thick
This beautiful Victorian house designed and built by Clell Boyce has 15 generous rooms, front and back porches, removable tower and interior partitions. This house shell offers superior construction as well as ease in finishing. Each house is numbered, signed and comes with instructions to finish as shown in photograph.

JOSEPH ANGEL HOUSE

American Victorians by Clell Boyce
Suggested Retail Price: $310 assembled unfinished, $4000 with exterior finished. All prices plus shipping.
Dimensions: 48" W x 26" D x 51" H
Material: Multi-ply solid core 3/8" thick
Another gracious Victorian designed and built by Clell Boyce. This house offers 16 rooms, open tower and front and back porches. Interior partitions and tower are removable for easier finishing. As always, the same high quality construction we are known for, with instructions to simplify finishing. Each house is numbered and signed.

THE MINIATURES CATALOG, Fourteenth Edition 51

PRISTINE COTTAGE
"Ready to Move-In Houses"
American Craft Products
Dimensions: 32"W x 21"D x 26"H, five rooms, 3/8" plywood, 1" scale
Completely assembled and finished inside and out. You will have to look twice to notice that the front door, siding, shutters, trim, foundation and shake roof are actually silkscreened. Inside, hardwood floors, paneled staircases and fireplace as well as "papered" walls are recreated using the same process. Working front door and non-working windows are comparable to the best on the market. Check with your dealer for color options available, as well as additional models in our Parade of Homes Collection. Made in America. Catalog No. 122.

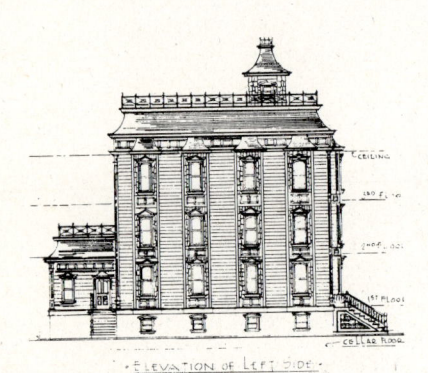

BAYVIEW
Architecturally Designed Dollhouses
Specifications: 54"H x 24"W x 48"D; four floors, 10 rooms plus attic and basement
Material: Cabinet grade plywood with tongue and groove shiplap
Architect's rendering of a Victorian design carefully constructed with attention to architectural details. All working windows and interior doors, staircases. Custom designs.

THE RUTHERFORD
Artply, Inc.
Suggested Retail Price: See your dealer
Model No. APL112
Dimensions: 38"H x 30"W x 17"D
800 shingles required to cover roof
An intricately detailed American Victorian house inspired by the decorative architecture of the Second Empire in France. This three-story, ten room house features a hideaway tower room, elegant porch, fireplace, ornate chimney, two curved staircases and gingerbread trim. Easy tab and slot assembly. All parts are pre-cut plywood. No nails or tools needed.

THE EMPORIUM
Compass Miniatures Industries
Suggested Retail Price: See your dealer
Dimensions: 31"W x 18"D x 45"H
Material: Cabinet grade 3/8" plywood
The Emporium kit includes moveable interior partitions and interior stairs to arrange three floors of flexible decorating space. Available in kit form, assembled shell and as a striking decorated display model which is highlighted by real cloth awnings. Doors, windows and trim pieces are available in optional component packages. Openings are sized to fit standard components.

SALEM HOUSE
Architecturally Designed Dollhouses
Specifications: Three floors, 11 rooms
Material: Cabinet grade plywood
This is a stunning Victorian with turned railings, four dormers and a graceful curved interior staircase. The house can be completely enclosed. It is being done in vertical cedar siding.

Prices are approximate and subject to change.

Houses & Buildings

THE BARRINGTON

Artply, Inc.
Suggested Retail Price: See your dealer
Model No. APL236
Dimensions: 41"H x 35"W x 26"D
1200 shingles required to cover roof
A house which inspires fantasy, this exact replica of a Queen Anne style Victorian house is an aesthetic delight. Its many features include a full wrap-around porch, an exciting three-story turret spire, and ten spacious rooms with a full staircase and elegant high ceilings. This unique use of space allows full access to all rooms and extensive wall space permits decorators infinite possibilities. Easy tab and slot assembly. All parts are pre-cut plywood. No nails or tools needed.

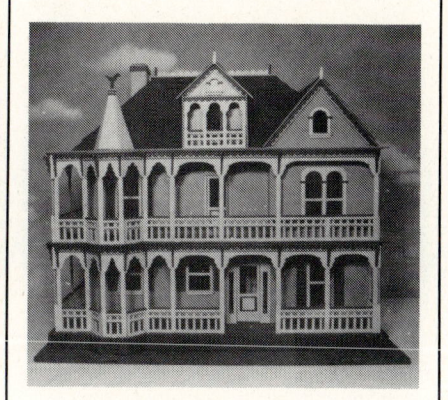

THE GRANVILLE

Artply, Inc.
Suggested Retail Price: See your dealer
Model No. APL510
Dimensions: 31"H x 34"W x 22"D
1100 shingles required to cover roof
A majestic house with exceptional attention to detail. Nine spacious rooms feature a full separate kitchen and formal dining room, living room, dropped-floor staircase, balcony, two staircases and six bedrooms. Double wrap-around porches and authentic door and window treatments add to the grandeur of this dollhouse. Easy tab and slot assembly. All parts are pre-cut plywood. No nails or tools needed.

THE TENNYSON

Artply, Inc.
Suggested Retail Price: See your dealer
Model No APL99
Dimensions: 32"H x 23"W x 15"D
700 shingles required to cover roof
A truly beautiful depiction of Victorian elegance, this special house exemplifies the architectural style of 19th century Gothic. Noted for its fine detail, this three story, five room house features two elaborate full bay windows, wrap around porches with finely-shaped dimensional railings, windows trim and gingerbread trim. Also included are a fireplace and a floor-to-ceiling planter. Easy tab and slot assembly. All parts are pre-cut plywood. No nails or tools needed.

CEEWEED MANOR

Architecturally Designed Dollhouses
Specifications: 81"L x 36"H x 27"D; three floors, 14 rooms
Material: Cabinet grade plywood
Construction: Knockdown, glue/nail
This 14 room Victorian can have as many as seven dormers. The house is fully enclosed with back opening. This is a gracious and stunning country home.

LADY KATHLEEN

Celerity Miniature Homes
See your local miniatures dealer for retail price
Specifications: 47"H x 58"W x 24"D. Top quality 3/8" plywood. Dado joint construction. Truly a Victorian lady's beautiful dwelling in miniature! Three level Victorian roofline is accented with a six-sided tower, front projection and attached kitchen and nanny's quarters. This house features two porches with turned posts, moveable partitions, two stairways, nine rooms, 10" ceilings and 8" attic. Kit includes house shell, railings, dowels, corner posts, turned porch posts and front steps. Catalog #1801 kits only.

THE MINIATURES CATALOG, *Fourteenth Edition* 53

BARROW CASTLE

Betty's Hobbies
Dimensions: 68"L x 26"H x 40"D
One floor, 11 rooms (two round), drawbridge and moat porch. Material: cabinet grade plywood 3/8", 3/4" floor base Barrow Castle, assembled unfinished. Custom finished, room sizes can be adjusted.

THE QUEEN ANNE

Betty's Hobbies
Specifications: 52"L x 42"H x 30"D, three floors, 13 rooms.
Material: Cabinet grade plywood 3/8", 3/4" floor base.
The Queen Anne, assembled, unfinished and custom finished, additions available.

LADY KRISTINE

Celerity Miniature Homes
See your local miniatures dealer for retail price
Specifications: 36-1/2"H x 22"W x 32-3/4"L. Top quality 3/8" plywood.
The Victorian Lady Kristine is a beautiful old home enhanced with three charming bay areas. The kit contains all main house parts plus moveable partitions with door openings, two interior stairways, turned porch posts, front steps, bay roof top moldings, tower, attic knee walls and foundation. Decorative trims are not in kit, but are found in most local miniature shops. Catalog #4001 kit, #4002 assembled.

LADY JILL MARIE

Celerity Miniature Homes
See your local miniatures dealer for retail price
Specifications: 34-1/2"H x 22"W x 32-3/4"L. Top quality 3/8" plywood.
The Victorian Lady Jill Marie is a beautiful old historic house in Prescott, noted for its' charming parlors. The kit contains all main house parts plus moveable partitions with door openings, two interior stairways, turned porch posts, front steps, charming bays with roof top moldings, tower, attic knee walls and foundation. Decorative trims are not in kit, but are found in most local miniature shops. Catalog #4301 kit, #4302 assembled.

LADY EMILY

Celerity Miniature Homes
See your local miniatures dealer for retail price
Specifications: 34-1/2"H x 22"W x 23"L. Top quality 3/8" plywood.
Lady Emily would sit and write her poetry in the parlor of her beautiful old Victorian home. The kit contains all main house parts plus moveable partitions with door openings, two interior stairways, turned porch posts, front steps, bay area in parlor, tower, attic knee walls and foundation. Decorative trims are listed in the instructions, but are not in the kit. Catalog #4201 kit, #4202 assembled.

LADY MELISSA

Celerity Miniature Homes
See your local miniatures dealer for retail price
Specifications: 36-1/2"H x 22"W x 23"L. Top quality 3/8" plywood.
The Victorian Lady Melissa is a charming old home found on Main Street. The kit contains all main house parts plus moveable partitions with door openings, two interior stairways, turned porch posts, front steps, bay area in parlor, tower, attic knee walls and foundation. Decorative trims are listed in the instructions, but are not in the kit. Catalog #4101 kit, #4102 assembled.

SECOND EMPIRE VICTORIAN
Celerity Miniature Homes
See your local miniatures dealer for retail price
Specifications: 40"H x 52"W x 23-1/2"D, three floors, 11 rooms. Top quality 3/8" plywood. Dado joint construction.
This huge Victorian mansion is a majestic dwelling in miniature. The three level mansard roofline is enhanced by the cubical central tower. The kit contains all main house parts plus railings, corner posts, turned porch posts, front steps, two stairways, moveable partitions and firm foundation pieces. The house features 10" ceilings and 8-3/4" attic height. Model available without addition. Catalog #2601 kit.

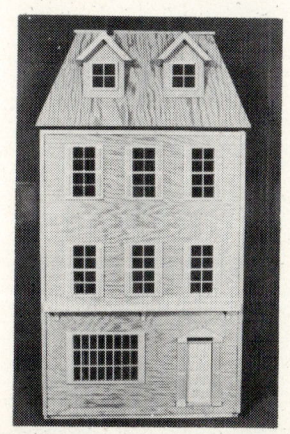

THE HOUSE THAT JACK BUILT
Dee's Delights, Inc.
Suggested Retail Price: See your dealer. Shown are just two of the houses made by the House That Jack Built and distributed by Dee's Delights, Inc. Each house is built to last of 3/8" fir plywood. Available completely constructed with siding installed, and includes all windows, doors, and stairways (removable for easy painting). Also available as kits. See your local dealer for prices.

THE VICTORIAN DOLL MANSION
The Dollhouse Factory™
Suggested Retail Price: $5750 completely finished including shipping. Catalog No. RVD5.
Specifications: 51" H x 56" W x 21" D, four floors, eight rooms Material: 1/4" plywood and 3/4" pine construction with screws, nails, and glue
For the doll that has everything! Eight large rooms, electric elevator, stained glass solarium, hand-turned columns, spiral staircases, door buzzer, and secret compartments. See our catalog for other models.

ALPINE
Dura-Craft, Inc.
Catalog No. AL200
Dimensions: 24"H x 23"W x 19"D, four rooms, one stairway, two floors
Material: Tongue and groove clapboard siding
This charming design is full of character. It includes working windows, chimney, fireplace, under-stairway closet and balcony door plus realistic brickwork, gutters and downspouts, one floor hardwood flooring, split redwood shakes, stairway, silkscreened windows and molded pine corner posts and trim. The open interior allows for maximum interior design flexibility. Precision die-cut parts.

CAMBRIDGE
Dura-Craft, Inc.
Catalog No. CA750
Dimensions: 43"H x 33"W x 22"D, nine rooms, three floors, two stairways
Material: Tongue and groove clapboard siding
This classic curved mansard roof house features all the amenities including working windows and doors, split redwood shakes, brickwork, gutters and downspouts, one floor hardwood flooring, silkscreened windows, a sliding French door and molded pine corner posts. Precision die-cut parts.

Houses & Buildings

THE MINIATURES CATALOG, Fourteenth Edition   55

POMEROY HOUSE

Compass Miniatures Industries
Suggested Retail Price: See your dealer
Dimensions: 24"W x 17"D x 44"H
Material: Cabinet grade 3/8" plywood
Large rooms spread over three floors highlight this West Coast style Victorian. The unique octagon tower roof is removable for interior decoration. Available in kit form, assembled shell and beautifully finished as a display model. Doors and windows are available as options. Openings are sized to fit standard components. Trim pieces are available in an optional package.

THE QUEEN ANNE

Dura-Craft, Inc.
Suggested Retail Price: See your dealer.
Catalog No. QA575
Specifications: 42" H x 33" W x 21" D
This beautiful Victorian house kit has the authentic look that collectors and young ladies will adore. Its sturdy pine frame construction and pre-cut pieces make assembly easy. Three floors, seven rooms, two stairways, silkscreened windows with sailing ship on front door window and real hand-split redwood shingles for all roof sections.

HERITAGE

Dura-Craft, Inc.
Catalog No. HR560
Dimensions: 29"H x 27"W x 20"D, seven rooms, three floors
Material: Tongue and groove clapboard siding
This Victorian Gothic style house radiates elegance and grace. It features working windows and doors, fancy redwood shakes for the gables and roof, working attic access ladder, inside staircase with landing along with realistic brickwork gutters and downspouts, one floor hardwood flooring, silkscreened windows and molded pine corner posts and trim. Precision die-cut parts.

"ARCHITECT'S CHOICE" DOLLHOUSES

Design Tecnics Miniatures
Suggested Retail Price: See your local dealer or write direct
Specifications: 23-1/8"W x 20-3/4"D x 31-7/8"H
Material: 3/8" Medex wood
Design Number Four is one of six Architect's Choice houses shown in the Publications and Plans section of this catalog. All six designs are available as assembled but unfinished shells or with the exterior completely finished. Completed houses are furnished with windows by Miniature Lumber Shoppe as shown.

THE HEATHER

G.E.L. Products
Suggested Retail Price: See your dealer
Specifications: 38"H x 30"W x 24"D
Materials: Quality cabinet wood, 3/8" front, sides and floor, 1/4" interior walls
This nine room Victorian features G.E.L. Products' exclusive clapboard surfacing actually cut into 3/8" plywood by our own process. Eliminates gluing and warping. Has 9-1/2" Victorian ceilings, front opening bay window ell, louvered shutters, pre-assembled window/door units and railings, dovetailing and elegant Victorian trim. Each A & H series kit has video-taped as well as printed instructions. #H-67.

Prices are approximate and subject to change.

Houses & Buildings

THE CRESTVIEW

Dura-Craft, Inc.
Catalog No. CR250
Dimensions: 43"H x 22"W x 18"D
This elegant three-story dollhouse kit with seven rooms features a tower and peaked tower roof with finial. Comes with a large porch, bay window in the second level, three floors, two stairways and silk screened windows with a sailing ship on the front door window. It features a sturdy molded pine frame and pre-cut pieces to make assembly easy. Includes real hand-split redwood shingles for all roof sections. Fish scale shakes for the perfect look included.

THE NEWBERG

Dura-Craft, Inc.
Catalog No. NB180
Dimensions: 24"H x 22"W x 18"D
This beautiful dollhouse kit has the authentic look that collectors and young ladies love. It features a sturdy molded pine frame and pre-cut pieces for easy assembly. Two floors, four rooms, one stairway and a garden window. Silk screened windows with sailing ship on the front door window and real hand-split redwood shingles for all roof sections. Fish scale shakes for that special look included. The main level includes a bay window.

SAN FRANCISCAN

Dura-Craft, Inc.
Catalog No. SF550
Dimensions: 43"H x 22"W x 18"D, four floors, seven rooms, two stairways. Made of wood, tongue and groove construction. Authentic clapboard siding, split shake roof, hardwood flooring. Complete pre-cut kit including hardware hinges and plastic windows. Outstanding detail including windows and shutters. See your dealer.

VICTORIAN MINIATURE HOUSE KIT

Dura-Craft, Inc.
Catalog No. VH600
Dimensions: 40"H x 47"W x 21"D, three floors, ten rooms, two stairways. Tongue and groove construction
Material: Authentic clapboard siding, split shake roof, hardwood flooring
Complete pre-cut kit including hardware, hinges and plastic windows. Outstanding detail including windows and shutters. See your dealer.

THE MCKINLEY

Greenleaf Products, Inc.
Suggested Retail Price $95.25 Specifications: 33" W x 9" D x 31" H, three floors, 6 rooms, tab and slot assembly
Material: Pre-cut plywood
Any collector looking to display miniatures at eye level or in limited space will find his answer in the McKinley. This unique wall-hanging model is just 9" deep, yet with five large rooms, an attic cubby, and a tower chamber. It has all the potential of a full-size house. Three latticed storage drawers beneath enhance the design and are perfect for storing accessories or hiding electrical components. Decorated in your taste, the McKinley is truly a piece of art which will be the focal point of any room.

THE WESTVILLE

Greenleaf Products
Suggested Retail Price: $85
Catalog No. 8013
Specifications: 22"H x 25"W x 17-1/4"D, two floors, four rooms
Materials: 1/8" di-cut plywood
Look familiar? You've probably seen this house in real life someplace in your travels! Our Westville is a replica of a home sold by mail order catalog at the turn of the century; we spotted this one in the little hamlet of Westville, New York. Designed in the style of "Carpenter Gothic," the house features long pointed gables with elaborate decorative trim around the porch, balconies, and roof. There are four large rooms and a spacious attic, as well as two bay windows and two balconies. We've included shingles and clapboard siding to fully capture the look of that "little house by the side of the road" for your trip down memory lane.

THE MINIATURES CATALOG, Fourteenth Edition

VICTORIAN MANSION

Dura-Craft, Inc.
Suggested Retail Price: See your dealer.
Catalog No. VM800 Specifications: 45" H x 52" W x 25" D, four floors, 13 rooms, 1/4" pine. Tongue and groove construction. Authentic clapboard siding, split shake roof, hardwood flooring, two stairways. Complete pre-cut kit including hardware, hinges and plastic windows. New bay window construction. Outstanding detail. See your dealer.

EMERSON ROW

Greenleaf Products
Suggested Retail Price: $74.25
Catalog No. 8007
Specifications: 32-1/2"H x 23"W x 20"D
Materials: 1/8" di-cut plywood
The Emerson Row, a stately and elegant Victorian as much at home in Back Bay Boston or Baltimore as it would be among the "painted ladies" of San Francisco. Features include full, seperate entrance, basement living quarters that could be apartment or servant's space. Up above, four large rooms all with bay windows, and a full-sized attic comprise the main house. You'll love decorating all this space! The Emerson Row, a wonderfully charming and well-designed row home! Shingles included.

THE ARTHUR

Greenleaf Products, Inc.
Suggested Retail Price: $43
Catalog No. 8012
Specifications: 23-1/2" H x 18" W x 13" D, two floors, four rooms
Material: Pre-cut plywood, shingles included
A long-time favorite of our customers, the Arthur is a wonderful little house for the new collector. Features include silk-screened windows, a quaint front porch, and four ample rooms. Gingerbread on ridge and roof make this cottage especially appealing to young and old.

THE BEACON HILL

Greenleaf Products
Suggested Retail Price: $182.75
Catalog No. 8002
Specifications: 40"H x 32"W x 17"D, three floors, seven rooms
Material: Pre-cut plywood
Dignified and grand, the Beacon Hill has become the "flagship" of the Greenleaf line. Its sophisticated exterior is enhanced by a curved Mansard roof, and no detail has been omitted, including even a little window in the cellar! The Beacon Hill has seven rooms, and it has two hallways that are large enough to be finished as rooms. Three fireplaces, three bay windows, and winding staircase add to the elegance of this outstanding dollhouse. Shingles and siding included.

THE PIERCE

Greenleaf Products, Inc.
Suggested Retail Price: $120
Catalog No. 8011
Specifications: 33" H x 35-1/2" W x 25" D, three floors, six rooms, tab and slot assembly
Material: Pre-cut plywood
The Pierce is a "Grande Dame" in its own right. One of our most popular models, the Pierce offers tremendous value at a most reasonable price, with lots of gingerbread, and lots of Victorian charm. The house has six large rooms, an attic, and a secret tower chamber along with an elegant curved staircase, silkscreened windows, two fireplaces, and a wrap veranda. There's a fine open feeling to this stately home, and you're sure to be impressed by its grandeur.

Houses & Buildings

THE GARFIELD

Greenleaf Products
Suggested Retail Price: $242
Catalog No. 8010
Specifications: 40"H x 41-1/2"W x 29-1/2"D, three floors, 10 rooms, tab and slot assembly
Material: 1/8" di-cut plywood
The Garfield is the largest model Greenleaf makes and one of the most impressive dollhouses to be found. Nathaniel Hawthorne hadn't seen it when he wrote *The House of the Seven Gables*, but indeed our mansion has seven peaks as well as a wrap-around porch, two balconies and two bay windows. You'll find easy access to the large rooms. In addition to the corner opening is a removable roof section and a lift-off turret atop the tower chamber. the secret tower chamber. With its wonderful gingerbread trim and lovely detail, the Garfield is magnificent!

TELEGRAPH HILL

Compass Miniatures Industries
Suggested Retail Price: See your dealer
Dimensions: 57"W x 21"D x 41"H
Material: Cabinet grade 3/8" plywood
An opulent 12 room Victorian. The decorated model (shown) features a copper and batten tern roof and extremely detailed, hand painted trim pieces. Available in kit form, assembled shell and decorated model. The kit includes foundation parts, porch posts, bay and porch roofs, interior and exterior stairs and moveable partitions. Doors, windows and trim pieces, as well as a detailed decorating guide are available. Openings are sized to fit standard components.

THE WILLOWCREST

Greenleaf Products
Suggested Retail Price: $106.50
Catalog No. 8005
Specifications: 34"H x 25-1/2"W x 21-1/2"D
Materials: 1/8" di-cut plywood
A beautiful Victorian in the rich Mansard style with windows framed in ornate Second Empire moulding. the Willowcrest features two bay windows, a third-story garret with curved front gable, balcony and two dormer windows. A front hall with winding staircase and three fireplaces complete the touches. In addition to the ample garret space, the Willowcrest rooms include a kitchen, living/dining room, bath and master bedroom. Shingles and siding included.

NEW ENGLAND VICTORIAN

Hill's Dollhouse Workshop
Suggested Retail Price: Wholesale only, see your local dealer
Dimensions: 32-1/2"H x 30"W x 14"D. Three floors plus attic, eight rooms. Made of 3/8", 5-ply birch type plywood. Dadoed, pre-hinged roof 1-1/2" foundation
Charming Victorian with a two-windowed tower, topped by a widow's walk railing and trimmed with post braces. The front section opens on hinges, the back is open with a hinged roof. The attic has a window in front dormer section. The peak and house front are trimmed with dentil molding. A front porch is in the recessed section. Also available with a wrap-around porch, with or without addition. Porch railings, interior stairs and stairwell hole railings are Timberbrooks'.

SHADOW CLIFF VICTORIAN HOUSE

The Lawbre Company
Suggested Retail Price: Assembled and unfinished $750 plus options. Exterior finished as shown $3150. Crating and shipping extra.
Specifications: 43"H x 32"W x 32"D, 3 floors, 10 rooms, 3/8" 7-ply solid birch plywood throughout
An outstanding Victorian house in the Queen Anne style, Shadow Cliff's rooms are arranged as they would be in a real house and are easily accessible from three sides. Options including full enclosure walls are available.

THE MINIATURES CATALOG, Fourteenth Edition 59

VANESSA

Compass Miniatures Industries
Suggested Retail Price: See your dealer
Dimensions: 35"W x 24"D x 47"H
Material: Cabinet grade 3/8" plywood
A beautiful, nine room house plus the tower area. Available in kit form, assembled shell and as a decorated display model. The kit includes all foundation parts, piazza posts, railings and spindles, tapered bay roof trim, moveable partitions and interior and exterior stairs. Openings are sized to fit standard components. Door, windows and trim are available in packages.

1/12TH SCALE VICTORIAN SHELL

Houseworks
Suggested Retail Price: $220
Catalog No. 4303
Specifications: 33"H x 22-1/2"D x 33-1/4"L
Kit includes 3/8" cabinet grade plywood, front opening designs, step-by-step instructions, and a 3-in-1 Dollhouse Planbook for your reference. Write to Houseworks for information on the Houseworks Component Sets.

CUSTOM 3-STORY TOWNHOUSE WITH TOWER ROOM

The Lawbre Company
Suggested Retail Price: $7000 as shown with slight variations. Crating and shipping extra.
Specifications: 55" H x 40" W x 25" D, four floors, 12 rooms
Material: 3/8" 7-ply solid birch plywood
New England Victorian Townhouse with a great deal of flexibility in interior room layout. Exquisite detail and workmanship throughout. Each house has slight variations to make it individual.

RAVEN'S CROFT – CIRCA 1840

The Lawbre Company
Suggested Retail Price: $845 assembled and unfinished, plus options. Exterior finished as shown (excluding greenhouse) $3350. Crating and shipping extra.
Specifications: 45"W x 29"D x 35"H, 3 floors, 13 rooms, 7-ply solid birch plywood used throughout
American Gothic Revival—a forthright expression of the picturesque and romantic. Features large rooms, beautiful 2-story entry stairhall with balcony and unique "stained glass" window sections.

FRENCH COUNTRY HOUSE

The Lawbre Company
Suggested Retail Price: See your dealer
Specifications: 39"H x 64"W x 26"D, three floors, 11 rooms, plus two rooms above wings
This splendid miniature house was inspired by the great manor farmhouses of Ile-de-France. The time period is the late 17th Century. The detail is elegant and authentic, complete with oeil-de-boeuf dormers. The much requested large rooms are perfect for an elegant yet casual country decor. The first floor ceilings are 12" and the second floor 11". There is a broad forecourt, perfect for a party. The windows and doors were designed especially for this house and are beautifully crafted.

Prices are approximate and subject to change.

Houses & Buildings

Barstow Belle

BARSTOW BELLE "PAINTED LADIES" VICTORIAN HOUSE

The Lawbre Company
Suggested Retail Price: $1595 unfinished, $3895 finished. Crating and shipping extra.
Specifications: 28"W x 33"D x 60"H, three floors plus tower, 13 rooms
Material: 3/8" 7-ply birch
This is one of four new "San Francisco Stick/Eastlake" style houses with new Lawbre brackets, oriel windows, verge board, stick style windows, and newel posts.

GLENN COVE VILLA – CIRCA 1880

The Lawbre Company
Suggested Retail Price: $950 assembled and unfinished, plus options. Exterior finished as shown (excluding greenhouse) $3350. Crating and shipping extra.
Specifications: 48"W x 26"D x 41"H, 4 floors, 11 rooms, 3/8" 7-ply solid birch plywood throughout except for mansard roofs
A mansard "turreted" villa boldly detailed in the late Victorian manner. Impressive two-story entry stairhall with split staircase and railings plus many interesting rooms make this house a decorator's delight.

MARIPOSA "PAINTED LADIES" VICTORIAN HOUSE

The Lawbre Company
Suggested Retail Price: $1145 unfinished, $3195 finished. Crating and shipping extra.
Specifications: 28"W x 33"D x 47"H, two floors plus tower, nine rooms
Material: 3/8" 7-ply birch
This is one of four new "San Francisco Stick/Eastlake" style houses with new Lawbre brackets, oriel windows, verge board, stick style windows, and newel posts.

Morley House

Winchester

MORLEY HOUSE "PAINTED LADIES" VICTORIAN HOUSE

The Lawbre Company
Suggested Retail Price: $1020 unfinished, $2995 finished. Crating and shipping extra.
Specifications: 28"W x 33"D x 34"H, two floors plus attic, nine rooms
Material: 3/8" 7-ply birch
This is one of four new "San Francisco Stick/Eastlake" style houses with new Lawbre brackets, oriel windows, verge board, stick style windows, and newel posts.

WINCHESTER "PAINTED LADIES" VICTORIAN HOUSE

The Lawbre Company
Suggested Retail Price: $1455 unfinished, $3695 finished. Crating and shipping extra.
Specifications: 28"W x 33"D x 47"H, three floors plus attic, 13 rooms
Material: 3/8" 7-ply birch
This is one of four new "San Francisco Stick/Eastlake" style houses with new Lawbre brackets, oriel windows, verge board, stick style windows, and newel posts.

NEW CONCEPT CHESAPEAKE

Real Good Toys
Suggested Retail Price: See your dealer
Catalog No. NC1710
Specifications: 30-3/4"L x 54'L x 21"D, three floors, 15 rooms
The New Concept Chesapeake is an expanded L-shaped farmhouse with two additions. All windows and door, including the bay window, are Houseworks pre-assembled components that come with the kit. The kit also features fancy porch posts, gingerbread trim, full foundation and steps, clapboard siding and wooden shingles. Everything you need is in this kit.

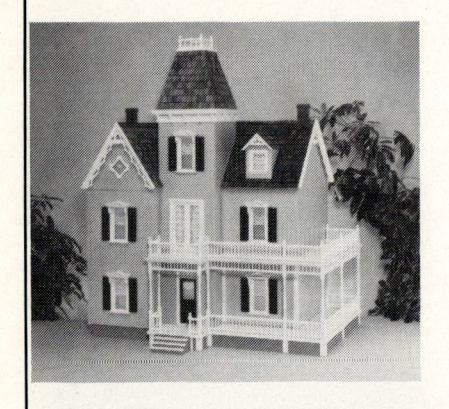

THE HAWTHORNE AND THE WOODSTOCK

Real Good Toys
Catalog No. NC3205 Hawthorne/NC3215 Woodstock
This beautiful Victorian, the "Hawthorne", has a tower and widow's walk. With the addition of an elegant extension, it becomes the "Woodstock" for that million dollar look! All components are pre-assembled. They come with front steps, a full foundation, stairways with bannisters and landing rails. Gingerbread trim and fancy porch columns are included. Optional features include #5025 shutters by Houseworks, #A-20 hinged rear roof panel, #1125 shingle dye and #SC copper flashing.

NEW CONCEPT ALTAMONT

Real Good Toys
Suggested Retail Price: See your dealer
Catalog No. NC3200
Specifications: 41-1/4"H x 32-3/4"W x 26"D, three floors, 11 rooms
The New Concept Altamont includes the complete basic kit plus deluxe features: foundation and steps, pre-assembled Houseworks windows and door, fancy porch posts and gingerbread trim. The kit also includes a finishing kit with pre-cut clapboard and trim and wooden shingles. Classic Victorian elements come together in the Altamont.

THE APPLE BLOSSOM

Walmer Dollhouses
Suggested Retail Price: See your local dealer. Catalog No. 457
Specifications: 29" W x 18" D x 36" H
Material: Cabinet grade plywood, 1/4" and 3/8" and solid pine
A romantic Victorian, a quality kit, at a great price from your miniature dealer. The kit includes gingerbread, windows, prehung raised panel door, wrap-around porch, gable, four-story tower large enough to furnish (and a secret room in the top of the tower!), six interior rooms, two interior staircases and raised-panel landing rails, three interior partitions. Available options are siding shingle pack and a two-story wing addition. The house can also be ordered built-up.

THE NOB HILL

Walmer Dollhouses
Dimensions: 38"W x 26"D x 36"H
Every aspect of this detailed home has "collector appeal", inside and out. The exterior window and door treatments, wrap-around porch, trims and rails are typically Victorian. The interior features eight spacious rooms, entry hall, two upstairs halls with stairs and a second floor front hall. The kit includes all windows and trim, exterior doors, decorative rails and trim, wrap-around porch, outside steps and interior stairs. It is available with working or non-working windows. Pictured with asphalt shingles and pine siding, sold separately.

HARLINGEN HOUSE

Woodcraft Specialties
Suggested Retail Price: $700 complete kit; $850 assembled shell with doors, windows and siding kit included; $1500 completely finished as pictured
A limited edition and truly majestic Victorian house. Reaching over 4'H and 3'W, this 30"D house boasts the following: 11 large rooms with high ceilings, two room-size landings and a grand foyer, two intermediate stair landings with four sets of removable stairs and two long halls. Accessible from both front and back, 3/8" plywood throughout. Superior workmanship with meticulous attention to every detail.

Want to list your products in the catalog next year?

To receive information on the 15th Edition of *The Miniatures Catalog*, send your name and address to: Sara Benz, *The Miniatures Catalog*, 21027 Crossroads Circle, P.O. Box 1612, Waukesha, WI 53187.

62   Prices are approximate and subject to change.

Displays for Miniatures

Display Cabinets, Boxes & Lamps

COACHMAN CLOCK BOX

American Craft Products
Suggested Retail Price: $29.95 - kit, $44.95 - assembled and unfinished
Catalog No. 203
Dimensions: 12"H x 10-1/2"W x 6"D
The Coachman Clock Box kit comes complete with a 110-volt light assembly, antique bronze handle and removable glass front. Easily assembled with precision cut parts. This kit is furniture quality, made of high quality select hardwood. Made in America.

THE INCREDIBLE KIT

American Craft Products
Suggested Retail Price: $22.95
Catalog No. 8452
Dimensions: 6-1/2" across, 14" high flats

With it's precision machined parts, this kit will easily assemble in less than one hour. Hang it - light it - or make two bay windows. Not cutting necessary. All pine. Made in America.

VICTORIAN BAY KIT

American Craft Products
Suggested Retail Price: $23.95
Catalog No. 8451
Dimensions: 10"W x 5"D x 11-1/2"H
Material: pine, masonite and mahogany
This charming bay window kit will add a decorator touch to any room. Features include pre-cut parts for fast assembly. So versatile you can create practically any scene or setting you wish. Made in America.

OLD-TIME STORE KIT

American Craft Products
Suggested Retail Price: $23.95
Catalog No. 8448
Dimensions: 6"D x 12-1/2"W x 12"H
Material: pine, masonite and mahogany
Everyone will enjoy creating a unique store from yesteryear with this kit. No special tools required. Pre-cut parts, quick assembly. Designed to be Santa's Workshop, tavern, antique store, flower shop, etc. Extension kit no. 8450 is available to add 6" depth to kit if desired. Made in America.

HOUSE OF HIDDEN TREASURES

American Craft Products
Suggested Retail Price: $99.95 - kit
Catalog No. 204
Dimensions: 13"H x 11"W x 13"D
Not just another little house, it has the look of a completed house inside and out. But swing it around on it's swivel and there are two drawers and a hinged access to the attic. The kit includes the basic house shell and all the trim to complete the house including all hardware, siding, shingles, windows, door spindles, fretwork and gingerbread. Made in America.

Prices are approximate and subject to change.

Displays for Miniatures

LARGE SHOWCASE UNLIMITED KIT

American Craft Products
Suggested Retail Price: $21.95
Catalog No. 8500
Dimensions: 13-1/2"H x 5-3/8"Sq.
A truly unique kit for displaying miniatures. Very versatile and quick and easy to assemble. Can be hung up or set in any area for a special decorator touch. Easy to light. All pine. Made in America.

OUR TOWN

American Craft Products
Suggested Retail Price: $21.95
Catalog No. 8502
Dimensions: 7" x 6-1/4" x 4", total height is 20-1/4"
No cutting. Create your own little craft village - perfect for a wedding gift. Displays a setting or your favorite collector's piece. All pine. Made in America.

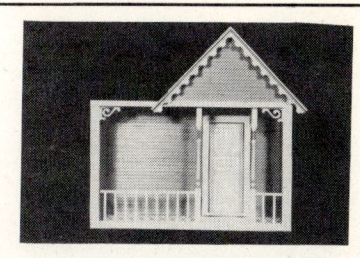

PORCH BOX KIT

Celerity Miniature Homes
Specifications: 14" L x 8-3/4" W x 3-1/2" D, (excluding roof section). Each kit complete in one box; no decorating material in kit, may be found in your local miniature shop.

ROOM OR WALL BOXES

Celerity Miniature Homes
See your local dealer for retail price.
Specifications:
8-3/4"W x 3-1/2"D x 19"L, (small box)
8-3/4"W x 5-1/4"D x 27-1/4"L, (large box)

October National Dollhouse & Miniatures Month

VICTORIA PLACE
"Ready to Move-In Houses"
American Craft Products
Dimensions: 18"W x 15"D x 44"H, five rooms, 3/8" plywood, 1" scale
Victoria Place is more than a dollhouse. Completely assembled and finished inside and out, each room can be used a storage compartment. You will have to look twice to notice the exterior and interior details of siding, shingles, trim, flooring and "papered" walls are actually silkscreened. Fully enclosed with front and attic hinged openings. Check with your dealer for color options available, as well as additional models in our Parade of Homes Collection. Made in America. Catalog No. 123.

CABINET RENOVATION

The Dollhouse Factory™
Suggested Retail Price: Depends on size and detail. Each is done to order.
Dimensions: 14-1/2" H x 14" W x 20" D
Material: Pine, cherry, or basswood
A custom renovation of an antique cabinet done by "Mr. Dollhouse." The techniques and materials used are available at his showroom or through the catalog, which contains thousands of products plus "Helpful Hints" on how the professionals do it.

PLASTIC BOXES

Gary Plastic Packaging
Gary Plastic manufactures over 350 stock sizes of clear rigid plastic boxes, ranging in size from 1"x1" to 8"x6". Assorted styles come in hinged, unhinged, round and vertical display boxes. Cut-to-size foam is available for nesting your miniatures.

THE MINIATURES CATALOG, Fourteenth Edition

DISPLAY BOX

Handcraft Designs, Inc.
Suggested Retail Price: See your dealer
Dimensions: Catalog #8002 (shown) 9-3/8" x 7-3/8" inside floor, height is 11"
Also available is #8003 with 9-3/8" x 9-3/8" inside floor. Knockdown design makes for easy storing and shipping. End-user buys glass needed for front, two side and top. Finely machined corner posts, top and bottom make for excellent fit. Assembles without tools. Quality wood construction with red oak random flooring.

IDEA BOX

d. Anne Ruff Miniatures
This 1" scale Hat Box kit (5-1/2" x 8" x 7") is designed to display your favorite dolls or miniatures. Folding screen kit adds an architectural interest. Idea Box kit, $16.95, curved or straight screen kit, $9.95, skirted table kit $4.95, packaged fabric/trim kit, $14.95.

1/2" HAT BOX VIGNETTE KIT

d. Anne Ruff Miniatures
Now in kit form, our enchanting 1/2" hat box vignette has die-cut parts, fusing material, complete illustrated instructions, $15.95 each. Also available are two companion kits: 1/2" furniture kit (12 pieces), $16.95 each and coordinated fabric/trim kit, $19.95 each. Group piece for all three kits, $49.95.

Dollhouse Turntables

ELECTRIC COLLECTOR'S TURNTABLE

Paul's Specialties
Suggested Retail Price: $36-$40
Dimensions: 16" W x 16" D, 12" W x 12" D, 8" W x 8" D. Material: Plywood (birch)
Turntable complete with wiring. Connect to electrical system of any 12-volt dollhouse. Designed by a collector. Rotates 360° with no tangled wires. Non-electric collector's turntable also available. Suggested Retail Price: $17-$20. Same dimensions and material.

Glass Domes & Showcases

TAOS PUEBLOS

Maison des Maisons
Dimensions: 6" x 8" to 10" x 18"
Taos Pueblos by Jeri Track, for displaying American Indian arts and crafts.

Prices are approximate and subject to change.

Novelty Displays

KIVA SCENES

Maison des Maisons
Suggested Retail Price: $110 and up
Dimensions: Various sizes available from 9" x 6" x 10" H to 30" x 18" x 14"
Kiva scenes hand-cut of native stones and various materials. Made by an American Indian - complete with dust cover.

GLASS DOMES

Paul's Specialties
Dimensions: 5-1/2" W x 11" H or 8" W x 12" H
Glass domes with lazy Susan base. It is a hardwood base made of either oak or walnut. The lazy Susan rotates easily, allowing viewing from all angles.

CHRISTMAS TREE DISPLAY

Aunt Ginny's
Suggested Retail Price: $23.95 plus $3 shipping
Completely finished, ready to fill. Pine with plexiglass sides, brass screws. Unique wood shape shows off your favorite minis. May be hung on wall or displayed on shelf or table. Perfect Christmas gift, filled or unfilled. 9"W x 12"H x 2"D.

COUNTRY COTTAGE

Aunt Ginny's
Suggested Retail Price: $21.95 plus $3 shipping
Completely finished, ready to fill. Pine with plexiglass sides, brass screws. Display those special minis safely in our little cottage. Ideal for 1" or 1/2" scale items. Change with the seasons. Teddy bear, ark, barn, cat and bunny also available.

PETITE COLLECTOR SHELVES

Betty's Wooden Miniatures
Our teddy bear wall shelf is perfect for displaying miniatures. It is 11" H x 9" W. It is just one of over 20 different styles of display shelves we offer. They're all handmade by us in the U.S.A.

YOUR LOCAL MINIATURES SHOP
WILL BE HAPPY TO SPECIAL ORDER FOR YOU!

Displays for Miniatures

THE MINIATURES CATALOG, Fourteenth Edition   67

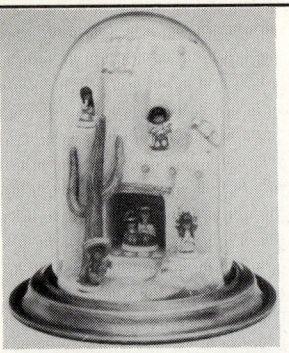

THE ADOBE DISPLAY
Goebel Miniatures
Designed exclusively for the DeGrazia Collection. Issued in '88. Total height 4-5/8".

AMERICANA DISPLAY
Goebel Miniatures
A display case for the Americana collection. Issued in 1989. Dimensions: Height 4-7/8", Width 8", Depth 4-1/4".

CHILDREN'S DISPLAY
Goebel Miniatures
A delightful way to display the Children's Series. Issued in '88. Total height 4-5/8".

COUNTRY DISPLAY
Goebel Miniatures
An appropriate setting designed by Robert Olszewski to showcase the Wildlife Series. Issued in '87. Total height 4-5/8".

ENGLISH COUNTRY GARDEN
Goebel Miniatures
Show off your Historical Series figurines in this beautiful display.

FANTASIA
Goebel Miniatures
Produced to commemorate the 50th anniversary of Disney's Fantasia, the Fantasia living brooms display and Mickey Mouse as the sorcerer's apprentice. Dimensions: 4-3/4"H x 4-1/2"W x 4-1/2"D.

FRONTIER MUSEUM DISPLAY
Goebel Miniatures
A handsome case to display the bronze collection. Issued in '87. Dimensions 13-3/4" x 5" x 4-1/2". American made.

HISTORICAL DISPLAY
Goebel Miniatures
Designed exclusively for the Historical Series. Issued in '88. Total height 4-5/8".

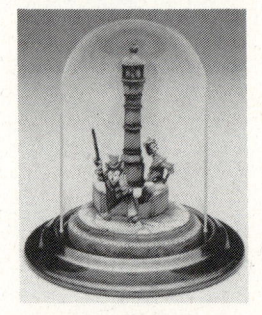

LITTLE STREET LAMP
Goebel Miniatures
To go with the Pinocchio Series. Released in 1991. Dimensions: 4-3/4"H x 4-1/2"W x 4-1/2"D.

MARKET SQUARE FLOWER STAND
Goebel Miniatures
The market square flower stand can be displayed under a dome as shown here or in the Bavarian market square in place of the market square hotel. Issued in 1990. Dimensions: 1-3/4"H x 2"W x 2"D.

ORIENTAL DISPLAY
Goebel Miniatures
This miniature sculpture attractively displays the Oriental Series. Issued in 1987. Total height 4-5/8".

ROCKWELL DISPLAY
Goebel Miniatures
A handsome case to display the 1988 Norman Rockwell collection. Issued in 1989. Dimensions: Height 5-3/4", Width 11", Depth 4-1/2".

SOLITAIRE DISPLAY

Goebel Miniatures
Designed to spotlight individual miniatures. Comes with two different size platforms. Issued in 1988. Total height 4-5/8". American made.

THE THREE LITTLE PIGS' HOUSE DISPLAY

Goebel Miniatures
This display completes the story of the Three Little Pigs. Issued in 1989. Total height 4-5/8".

WISHING WELL

Goebel Miniatures
From the Snow White Series with dome and base. Dimensions: 4-3/4"H x 4-1/2"W x 4-1/2"D.

WOMEN'S DISPLAY

Goebel Miniatures
Arrange your Women's Series collection on this simply elegant sculpture of gift boxes. Issued in 1989. Total height 2-11/16".

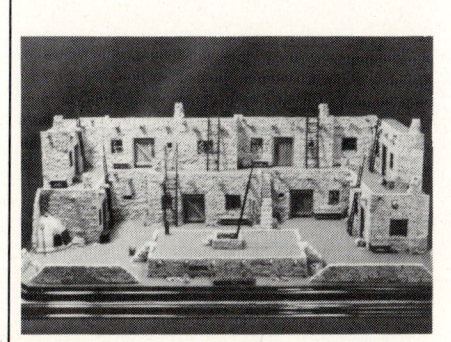

PLAZA SCENES

Maison des Maisons
Suggested Retail Price: $110 - $4000
Full plaza scenes for displaying Native American pottery and Kachinas. Made of hand-cut stones and other natural materials, complete with glass cover. One, two, and three stories, various designs.

DISNEY'S CINDERELLA

Goebel Miniatures
Cinderella's dream castle, now available, captures the mood of Cinderella's dream ball. Cinderella's coach will be available at a later date. Not all figurines are available at this time.

KINDERWAY

Goebel Miniatures
1991 brings growth in the M.I. Hummel Village. Joined with the Bavarian Village and Bavarian Market Square is the Bavarian Country School with the Wayside Shrine. Issued in 1991.

Displays for Miniatures

THE MINIATURES CATALOG, *Fourteenth Edition* 69

Printer's Trays & Collector's Boxes

ORIGINAL PRINTER'S TYPE CASES & REPRODUCTION SHADOW BOXES

Joshuas Wholesale
Suggested Retail Price: $15-$29
Specifications: 16" x 32" x 1-1/2"
Original printer's type cases 25-100 years old. Many different styles made of wood and masonite. Perfect for miniature collectibles. $5 for color catalog, refundable with first order.

YARDSTICK SHADOWBOX

Betty's Wooden Miniatures
Specifications: 36"H x 10-3/4"W x 1-3/8"D
Two high-quality heavy-duty varnished yardsticks with pine shelves and back. Complete with clear plexiglass front that slides in place and hanging hole. It has black numbers and the words "Little Things Mean A Lot" in red. The perfect gift for the collector. Holds 18 miniatures or thimbles. Miniatures shown are not included. Completely assembled and finished. Handcrafted in the USA.

Room Boxes & Vignettes

"VIEW-180" DISPLAY BOX

B. H. Miniatures
Catalog No. 403
Dimensions: 9-1/2"H x 10-3/4"D x 13-1/2"W
Display box with curved lucite front provides a 180° view of the interior. Top opening with lucite adds additional viewing and light. Made of quality birch plywood, the box is available as a kit or assembled unfinished. Also available with a solid top.

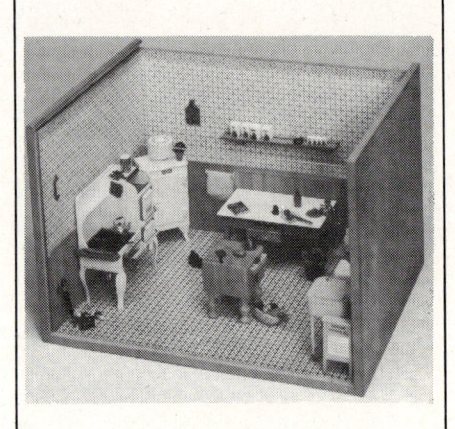

ROOM BOX KIT

Betty's Wooden Miniatures
Material: 3/8" Baltic birch plywood with clear plexiglass top and front
Now in three sizes! The best idea in room boxes yet. The clear plexiglass top and front allows your room to always be lit and completely visible. All pre-grooved for easy assembly. Takes 10 minutes to assemble. Made by us in the USA. Porcelain top table, butcher block, washboard and shelf shown are ours. Sizes available:
  10"H x 15"W x 12"D
  10"H x 20"W x 12"D
  10"H x 25"W x 12"D

Displays for Miniatures

ROUND SHADOW BOX DISPLAY KIT

Betty's Wooden Miniatures
Sizes: Small: 10" o.d., 8-1/2" i.d., 3-1/4"D; Medium: 12-1/2" o.d., 10-1/2" i.d., 3-3/4"D
Furniture finished hardwood frame in choice of fruitwood or antique white. Unfinished wood back, floor and floor front. Walls are white posterboard. A great new display for your wall or shelf. We used the medium size to make the vignette shown here. All furnishings shown are handmade by us in the USA.

ROOM BOXES

Philip E. Bugosh
Sug: Retail Price: See your local dealer
Material: Oak plywood, birch plywood or basswood, depending on model
Boxes feature mitered corners, no nails and no visible end grain. Fully assembled from select materials. Slide-in fronts eliminate hinges or frames. Available in 1/2", 1/4" and 1/44 scale, plus several sizes in 1" scale.

CORRI ROOM BOXES

Corri Products
Suggested Retail Price: $4.95 kit #302; $5.95 kit #301 - wholesale only
Dimensions: #302 - 8-1/2"H x 11"W x 8"D; #301 - 9-1/2"H x 14"W x 10"D
All Corri products are die cut from snowy white corrugated fiberboard. Corri rooms are sold flat and need simple assembly to form the room box. When they are assembled they give you a white interior and exterior and are sturdy and strong. The material will take paint, wallpaper, stenciling, fabric and most craft finishes. Our protective plastic fronts provide an ideal showcase for all your miniatures. Send $2 for catalog of our complete line and local dealers.

"HOUSEBOX"

Design Tecnics Miniatures
Suggested Retail Price: $325/kit
Specifications: 19-3/4"W x 10-3/8"D x 28-1/8"H
Product No.: 101
Material: wood, cast resin brackets
More than a roombox yet not quite a house, the "Housebox" kit includes 3/8" shell parts, windows, door, wall surfacing, brackets, brick strips and all exterior treatments except roof shingles, which are omitted to allow individual selection of shingle style. Interior treatment not included. Complete illustrated instructions.

Interested in a Club?
Contact the National Association of Miniature Enthusiasts for a club in your area.

N.A.M.E.
130 N. Rangeline Rd.
Carmel, IN 46032

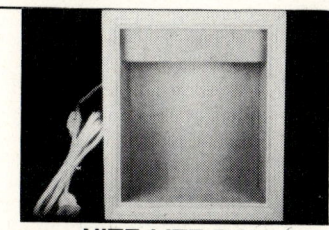

NITE-LITE BOX

Diminutive Specialties
Suggested Retail Price: $30 plus shipping, assembled and unfinished
Unfinished nite-lite box made of fine grain plywood and a pine frame with clear lexan front comes completely assembled and wired. Uses standard 4 watt nite-lite bulb. 9" x 8" x 5".

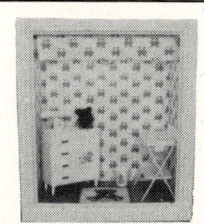

NURSERY NITE-LITE BOX

Diminutive Specialties
Suggested Retail Price: $70 plus shipping, finished
The nursery box comes with choice of two sets of furniture, personalized or character petit point rug and a personalized birth certificate. Choice of colors. 9" x 8" x 5".

THEATRE BOX

J. Hermes
Suggested Retail Price: $8 plus shipping
Dimensions: 8"H x 9-1/2"W x 4"D
Material: Art and foam core board
Theatre box is ideal for one's favorite stage setting, holiday vignette or just a miniature roombox! Very easy to assemble. Full instructions included.

THE MINIATURES CATALOG, *Fourteenth Edition*

HANG UP ROOM BOXES

Itty Bitty Builder
Suggested Retail Price:
#1012; 8"H x 11-1/2"W x 8"D; $34.95, finishing kit $28.15 (top)
#1016; 9"H x 15-1/2"W x 8"D; $44.95, finishing kit $33.10 (middle)
#1016-D; 9"H x 15-1/2"W x 8"D; $39.95, finishing kit $47.20 (bottom)
A room box that doesn't look like a box and it can hang on the wall. Constructed of quality 1/4" plywood, comes assembled and complete with acrylic front cover. Finishing kit includes pre-cut siding, brick foundation and chimney, wood shingles, trim and moldings. Prices do not include shipping.

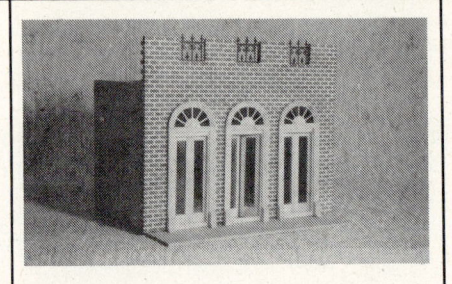

DISPLAY SHOPS

Itty Bitty Builder
Suggested Retail Price: Write for brochure
Specifications:
Lafayette; 13"H x 16"W x 10"D; base 16" x 14" (top)
Arcata; 12"H x 20"W x 10"D; base 20" x 14" (middle)
Fairmont; 14"H x 16"W x 10"D; base 16" x 14" (bottom)
Constructed of quality 3/8" and 1/4" plywood. Front and clear acrylic roof removable. Ideal for antique, boutique, art gallery or bank. Lafayette and Fairmont are available with brick facing. Other sizes available on special order.

Reach the heart of the miniatures industry - with your ad in MINIATURES DEALER!

MINIATURES DEALER

The Business News Magazine Serving The Miniatures Trade

CUSTOM DESIGN ROOM BOXES: THE BLUE DRAWING ROOM AT CHATSWORTH DERBYSHIRE, ENGLAND

The Lawbre Company
Suggested Retail Price: Contact the Lawbre Company for further details and price information.
Custom room reproductions in 1" and 1/2" scale. Historical rooms in any period or a room in your own home. Custom furnishings and accessories also available.

BOOKSHELF DISPLAY CASE KIT

The Lawbre Company
Suggested Retail Price: $48.50 and $88.50 plus shipping. Catalog Nos. 1200/1201
Specifications: 10" H x 19-1/2" W x 10-1/2" D, made of plywood, pine and plexiglass
Display box that takes little space, is easy-to-build, and looks great. Front and top removable, shelves in bay window, also removable. Ideal for bookcase shelf or tabletop. Includes two bay windows and door. Basic kit is shown in the example on the left.

Prices are approximate and subject to change.

October National Dollhouse & Miniatures Month

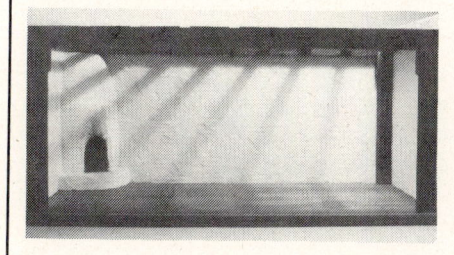

CASA PEQUENA ROOM BOX

Olde Mountain Miniatures
Suggested Retail Price: $64.50, kit; $225 finished
Dimensions: 22-1/2" W x 11-1/2" D X 10-1/4" H. Material: pine, stucco, plywood and acrylic.
Imagine your favorite Southwestern setting in this innovative room box with thick adobe walls. It includes a post and beam insert, acrylic top and front. There is an optional hardwood random width flooring package priced at $19.50 (included in finished model). No special tools are required for assembly.

"WABI" ORIENTAL ROOM BOX

Olde Mountain Miniatures
Suggested Retail Price: $159.50, kit; $385, finished
Dimensions: 23-1/2" x 11-1/2" including exterior deck. Material: Rough pine timbers, hardwood decking, inside and out, sliding framed shoji panels, moon gate, thatched "grass" or split shake roof (your option)
Let yourself be seduced by the delicacy of cherry blossoms and basic oriental simplicity. This precut kit assembles in a manner like no other, giving you a decidedly distinctive setting for your mini-Ming treasures.

PORCH FOR ALL SEASONS
Walmer Dollhouses
Suggested Retail Price: See your local dealer. Catalog No. 440
Specifications: 19"H x 18"W x 7"D
Make our porch a centerpiece for miniature fun in your home. Change accessories and furnishings with the holidays and seasons. Even the house interior can be decorated, giving a hint of the season indoors. The Porch For All Seasons may be hung on a wall or placed on a table or shelf. The kit is complete as shown with siding, shingles, unitized shuttered window, turned posts and rails, pre-hung Victorian oval-light door, trims and removeable back. The kit is available with or without interior curio light.

PUEBLO ROOM

Taos Sun Miniatures
Suggested Retail Price: $149 with oak floor, $175 with tile floor. Prices Ppd.
Dimensions: 19-1/2" W x 12" H x 10" D
Material: Pine and plexiglass
Room comes with carved Kiva fireplace, oak or tile floors, vigas, plexiglass top and front. Walls have "stucco" look finish.

ROOM BOX
Walmer Dollhouses
Suggested Retail Price: See your dealer
Catalog No. 117S/117D/117L/117CD/117CL
Material: 1/4" plywood and pine mouldings
Our room boxes are the perfect showcase for special displays and themes. They are available in three sizes. Three of our five models feature a plexiglas front which slides out as shown in photo. Two models have a plexiglas front and top. Choose the design and size best suited to your space and miniature collection.

I wish you could have seen the photos of this stylish coffee table. The top is a slice of highly polished, petrified wood which is now virtually stone. The irregularly shaped base is cut from a short stick of mesquite and whittled down to size and shape before sanding smooth and varnishing. Set with a decorative candle holder and small potted fern, the effect is stunning.

Displays for Miniatures

THE MINIATURES CATALOG, Fourteenth Edition

Building Components & Supplies

Architectural Components

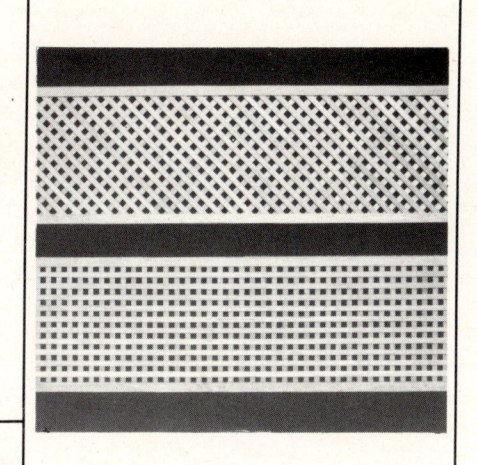

LATTICE

American Victorians by Clell Boyce
Suggested Retail Price: From $6 - $7.50 plus shipping. Catalog No. L1. Dimensions: 12" lengths, various widths.
Our handmade lattice is accurately crafted of clear pine to exact scale. We make diamond and square styles which come in a variety of widths. Each piece is fully glued so it can be cut if necessary to fit your projects perfectly. The finest available, an exact duplication of Victorian lattice.

CUPOLA

Betty's Wooden Miniatures
Specifications: 2-3/4"square x 4-1/2"tall from point of house roof to peak of cupola roof. Unfinished basswood with wooden top decoration.
The perfect finishing touch for any dollhouse. Fits 45° roof. Top decoration can be removed to accommodate weather vane. Square base available for other roof angles. A high-quality product. Handcrafted in the USA.

CHIMNEYS

American Victorians by Clell Boyce
Suggested Retail Price: From $5 plus shipping. Catalog No. C1. Dimensions: Universal fit
At last! A properly scaled brick chimney adaptable to all houses. Our chimneys were developed because of the need for a Victorian style chimney system that is architecturally correct yet does not require painstaking brick by brick construction. Made from actual masonry materials and is available in authentic Victorian red color.

LATTICE WORK

Handley House
Suggested Retail Price: $8.95
Catalog No. HH322, No. HH513; 1/2" scale
Dimensions: 6" x 8", 5" x 6" respectively
Made of walnut veneer, each panel contains over 270 glue joints. Easy to cut, fit and paint. Great for gazebos, room dividers, flower trellises and foundation lattice. Handmade in the USA.

ARCHITECTURAL DETAILS

The Lawbre Company
The Lawbre collection of difficult to find architectural details made specifically for 1" scale projects. A variety of styles; Victorian, 18th Century, English/American and French are represented in this ever growing collection. A custom service is also available for making your original and reproducing them for your project. Lawbre products always mean integrity. Send $2 for Architectural Components Catalog.

Building Components & Supplies

THE MINIATURES CATALOG, *Fourteenth Edition*

LARGE DORMER UNIT

Houseworks
Suggested Retail Price: $13.95
Catalog No. 7017
This dormer was designed to accept Houseworks single glazed windows #5038, #5039 and #5040. Your dormers can now have a much more varied and attractive look. Size: 4-1/8" W x 6-29/32" H x 7-9/16" D. Covers roof area: 4-1/8" W x 6-29/32" H x 9-3/4" D with a 45• pitch.

SCROLL WORK

The Fretworker, Kirk Ratajesak
Suggested Retail Price: $.55 - $3
Material: birch plywood
Now you can get the quality finished dollhouse you've always wanted with authentic scroll trim from The Fretworker. These styles of porch and eave brackets are also available in 1/2" scale.

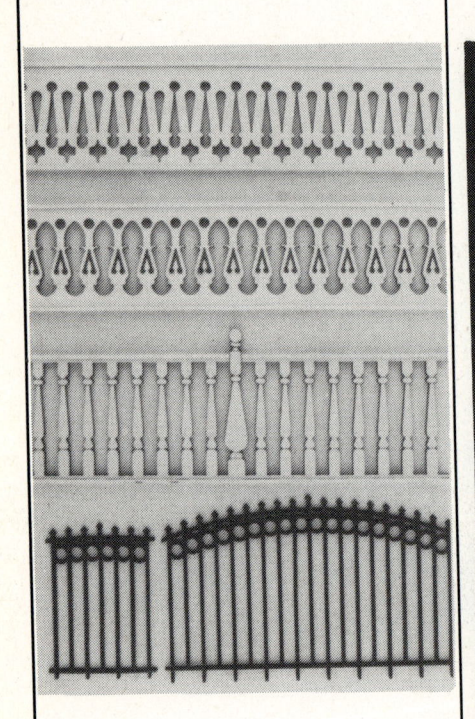

PORCH RAILINGS AND FENCING

Laser Tech
Suggested Retail Price: (top to bottom) #PR-045 (12") $14.95; #PR-040 (12") $14.95; #PR-041 (8-3/4") $10.95; #GF-038 (gate) $4.95; #F-038 (6") 12.95 (2)
Made of 3/32 basswood with intricate detailing to add a welcoming accent to your Victorian dollhouse. Railings come with top and bottom handrail.

LASER CUT APEX TRIMS

Laser Tech
Suggested Retail Price: (top to bottom) #AT-001 $6.95; #AT-002 $6.75; #AT-003 $6.85
Made of 3/32 basswood with intricate detailing to add a welcoming accent to your Victorian dollhouse. Intended for use on a 45° slope roof.

CHIMNEY

Houseworks
Suggested Retail Price: $6.95
Catalog No. 2404
Specifications: 4-1/16"H x 1-15/16" sq.
This solid wood chimney is topped with a detailed ornamental chimney hood. 45° pitch at base. Two per package.

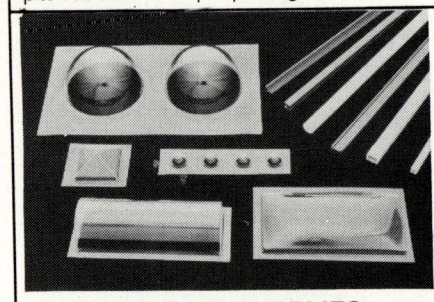

BUILDING SUPPLIES

Model Builders Supply
MBS manufactures and distributes several thousand items for building construction. See our listing under index of manufacturers.

Prices are approximate and subject to change.

DORMER WITH WORKING WINDOW

Miniature House
Suggested Retail Price: $12.49
Catalog No. MH219
Dimensions: 3-5/8"W x 6-3/8"H x 6-7/8"D
This traditional dormer creates a classic look to any doll house. The working window adds an authentic touch.

APEX TRIM

Miniature House
Suggested Retail Price: $1.59
Catalog No. MH224, one per package
Dimensions: 4-5/8"W x 2-3/4"H
Made of unfinished wood with intricate detailing to add a great aura of style to your Victorian doll house. For 45° slope.

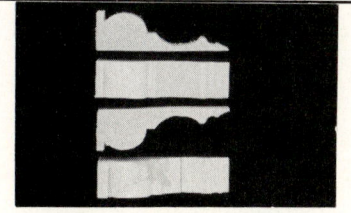

FANCY BRACKETS

Miniature House
Suggested Retail Price: $2.10
Catalog No. MH261
Dimensions: 3/8"D x 1-3/8"H
These wood brackets add a special touch to eaves, bookshelves, and other areas of your miniature creation. Four to a package.

HANGING STORE SIGN

Miniature House
Suggested Retail Price: $3.98
Catalog No. MH234
Dimensions: 2-1/2"W x 3-1/2"H
This sign is perfect for a country store or shop. Has gold-tone chains to hang sign. Sign made of unfinished wood.

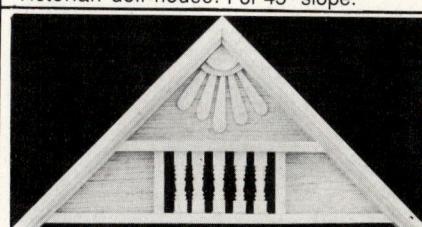

LARGE APEX TRIM, SUN DESIGN

Miniature House
Suggested Retail Price: $8.98
Catalog No. MH245
Dimensions: 7-5/8"W x 4"H
This sun designed apex trim is a welcoming accent. It is intended for use with a 45° slope roof. Trim made of unfinished wood.

PORCH LATTICE

Miniature House
Suggested Retail Price: $10.39
Catalog No. MH250
Dimensions: 1-1/2"H x 12"L
These wood lattice panels come fully assembled and are proportioned for exactly 1" scale. Three panels per package.

PORCH TRIM

Miniature House
Suggested Retail Price: $2.39
Catalog No. MH223
Dimensions: 1-1/16"D x 1-5/8"L
This wood trim reflects the beauty and grace of the Victorian Age. Four per package.

SMALL APEX TRIM, FAN DESIGN

Miniature House
Suggested Retail Price: $5.29
Catalog No. MH243
Dimensions: 5-1/4"W x 2-3/4"H
This lovely trim adds flair to any dollhouse. Designed for a 45° slope roof.

VICTORIAN BRACKETS

Miniature House
Suggested Retail Price: $2.05
Catalog No. MH217
Dimensions: 9/16"W x 1"L
These wood brackets add a special touch to eaves, bookshelves and other areas of your miniature creation. Six per package.

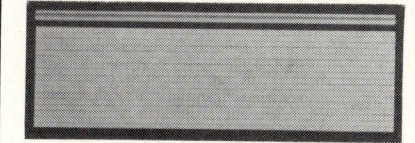

WAINSCOTTING AND CHAIR RAIL TRIM

Miniature House
Suggested Retail Price: $10.49 3-1/4"H x 12"L, catalog no. MH239. $1.25 24"L, catalog no. MH240.
This lovely wainscotting and matching chair rail give an elegant, distinguished look to any miniature room. No. MH239 has four panels per package.

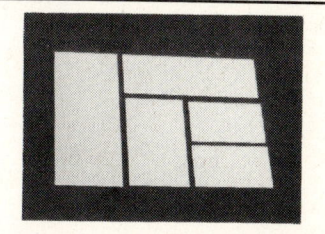

THIN GLASS MIRROR STOCK

Noonmark
Suggested Retail Price: 60¢ each piece, plus 20¢ per square inch, plus shipping Hand-silvered and backed on real 3/64" thick micro-glass. Custom cut to order or bulk sheets.

Building Components & Supplies

ARCHITECTURAL COMPONENTS

Derek Perkins
Suggested Retail Price: $1 - $3.95
Finely detailed, high quality moldings. I will also custom mold your originals. Other moldings included in my catalog.

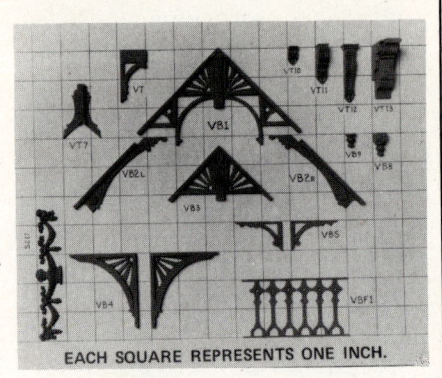

DEFINITIVE ARCH FRAME

Derek Perkins
Suggested Retail Price: $29.50
Specifications: 9"H, o.d. x 6"W, i.d. Made of molded resin.
Arch has fine detailing on all faces. Wraps around wall edges. Template provided. Columns available separately for archways of different widths. The details are worth looking at!

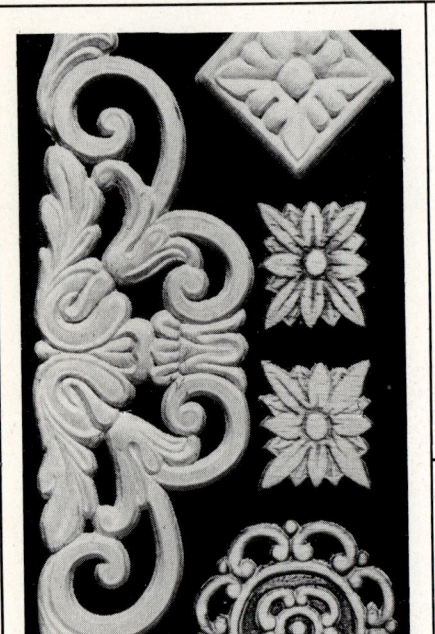

ARCHITECTURAL SHAPES CATALOG

Plastruct
Suggested Retail Price: $7 plus shipping
Plastruct catalog and New Product Supplement containing over 2500 plastic shapes for model building. Sheet, profiles, strips, tubing and bric-a-brac.

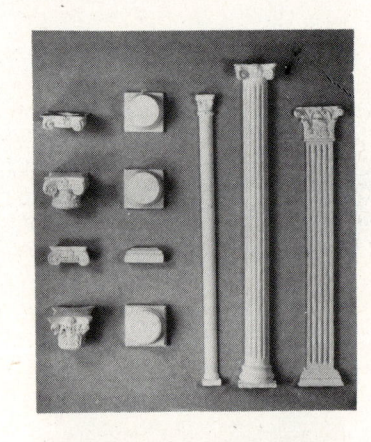

CARVED AND EMBOSSED ORNAMENTS

Miniature Manors
These ornaments are made of wood and can be used as ceiling medallions, gable trim or other period architecture. Many styles and sizes are available.

HALF COLUMNS

Unique Miniatures
These polyester resin cast column halves can be cut down and fitted together to construct any size column. Use alongside a door opening or frame out an archway. Adds the ornate trim needed to doll up a miniature room. Available in three styles: No. CO-1, 11" x 1/2", No. CO-2, 12" x 1-1/2" and No. CO-3, 11" x 2". All are sold in pairs. The CS-1 and CS-2 are three-dimensional and can easily form a column by using a 1" dowel. The CS-3 is a half column top (pilaster) and base. Send $2 for catalog. Made in the U.S.A.

Bay Windows

VICTORIAN BAY WINDOW

Houseworks
Suggested Retail Price: $22.95.
Catalog No. 5035.
Highly detailed bay window includes trim and mullions. Size: 4-5/8"W x 10-1/4"H. Fits opening: 3-9/16"W x 5-3/8"H.

ASSORTED BAY WINDOWS

Houseworks
#5008-Nonworking Bay Window-Features three 8-light windows. Size: 9-1/2"W x 6-3/4"H. Fits opening: 6-15/16"W x 5"H $16.50.

#5020-Working Bay Window-Features three double hung, fully functional windows with mullions. Size: 9-1/2"W x 6-3/4"H. Fits opening: 6-15/16"W x 5"H. $28.50.

BAY WINDOW

Timberbrook Wood Products
Suggested Retail Price: $33.80.
Fits opening 6-15/16" wide x 5-1/2" high. Shown with tudor casement windows. Also available with working or non-working windows. Roof is sold separate. Retail cost $3.20. See your dealer or write for information.

CARLSON BAY WINDOWS

American Craft Products
Suggested Retail Price: No. 8441 - $23.95; No. 8442 - $21.95; No. 8443 - $19.95
These charming bay windows add that decorator touch to most dollhouses. Also great for hanging or standing vignettes. Three styles: No. 8441 Tall Victorian Bay Window, perfect for long Victorian windows 11"H x 8-1/4"W x 2-1/4"D (inside depth 1-1/2"); No. 8442 General Purpose Bay Window, floor model 9"H x 8-1/4"W x 2-1/4"D (inside depth 1-1/2"); No. 8443 Our Most Popular Bay Window, looks great on any house 6-3/4"H x 8-1/4"W x 2-1/4"D (inside depth 1-1/2"). Made in America.

Brick & Stone Supplies

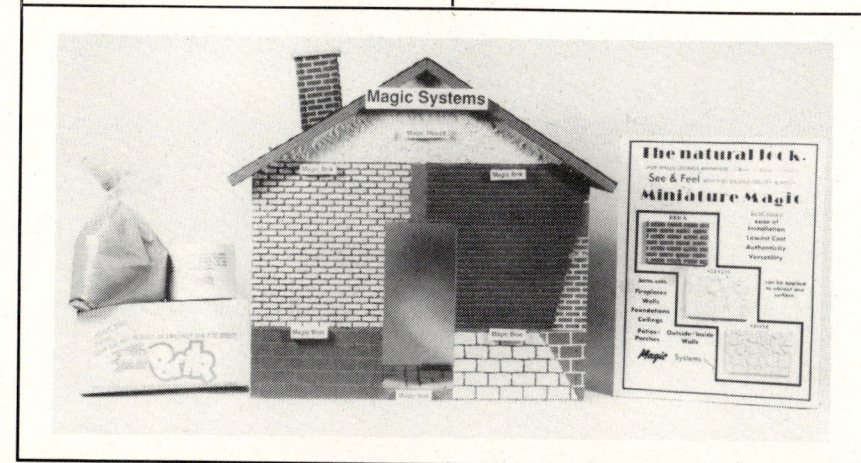

MAGIC SYSTEMS® TEXTURED SURFACE KITS

Dee's Delights
Lets you create realistic walls, patios, foundations, fireplaces, ceilings - anywhere! Each kit contains dry mix, self-adhesive patterned tape and complete instructions. Very easy to install. Available in different patterns and kits to cover 2-8 square feet.
   Magic Brik® in white and red
   Magic Slat®
   Magic Stucco® in white and red
   Magic Ston®
   Magic Bloc® in white and red
See your local dealer.

Building Components & Supplies

THE MINIATURES CATALOG, Fourteenth Edition

MINI BRICK MORTAR

Handley House
Suggested Retail Price: $4.95
Catalog No. OR599 (gray), OR599W (white)
For applying all types of miniature brick (both sheet and bulk) as well as stone, slate. Color can be changed by adding a good latex paint to OR599W. 18 oz.

STUCCO/ADOBE MIX

Handley House
Suggested Retail Price: $5.98 2-1/2" sq. ft., catalog no. HH340. $9.49 5 sq. ft., catalog no. HH341
Handley House Stucco Mix is our own formulation blended to achieve the correct scale pattern and grain for the miniaturist. Easy-to-work (complete instructions included), long-lasting and economical.

KIMBERLY FLAGSTONE KITS

Kimberly House Miniatures
Suggested Retail Price: $16.48
Catalog #: KIT8 Grey Flagstone, KIT9 Buff Flagstone, KIT10 Brown Flagstone.
Dimensions: 65 sq. in. coverage.
Kits come complete with premixed mortar, sealer, mastic and instructions. Individual, realistic warmth and feel of real masonry. Easy to cut, shape and apply. Available in three soft earth-tone colors with accent stones for a touch of contrast. Loose stock is also available. See your dealer or write to Kimberly House.

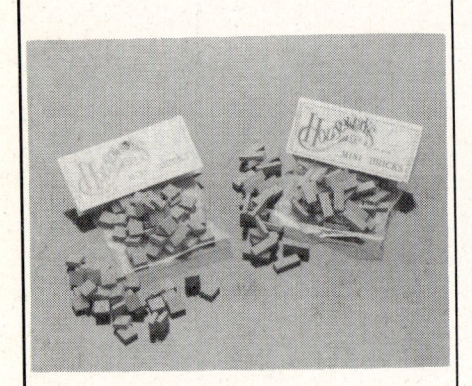

PATIO BRICKS AND COMMON BRICKS

Houseworks
Suggested Retail Price: $1.25.
#8204-Common Bricks. 50 pieces of genuine clay bricks. All pieces are loose and polybagged.
#8205-Patio Bricks. 50 pieces of genuine square clay bricks. All pieces are loose and polybagged.

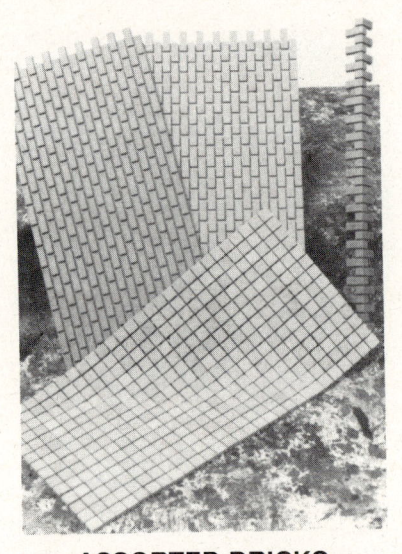

ASSORTED BRICKS

Houseworks
#8206-1/12" Scale Joint Common Brick Sheets. Approximately 63 square inches. Styrene plastic. $4.95.
#8201-Common Bricks. Genuine clay, mesh mounted. Each sheet covers approximately 72 square inches. $7.25.
#8202-Patio Bricks. Genuine clay, mesh mounted. Each sheet covers approximately 72 square inches. $7.25.
#8207-1/12" Scale Common Joint Brick Corner. 11-1/2" Long. Styrene plastic. $4.75.

KIMBERLY BROWNSTONE

Kimberly House
Suggested Retail Price: $3.55/35 sq. in. or; $6.30/70 sq. in.
Catalog #. BR-35 or BR-70.
Individual, realistic warmth and feel of real masonry. Easy to cut, shape and apply with our premixed mortar. Beautiful compliment to Kimberly Premixed Stucco. Easy to create sculptured appearance. Makes great "cobblestone" walkways. Compatible sealer, $4.05 (4 oz. jar), compatible Premixed Mortar, $2.19 (4 oz. net wt. jar). See your dealer or write to Kimberly House.

KIMBERLY USED BRICK MASONRY KIT

Kimberly House Miniatures
Suggested Retail Price: $16.48
Catalog #. KIT3 Used Brick
Dimensions: 75 sq. in. coverage
Kit comes with premixed mortar, sealer, mastic and instructions. Individual, realistic look and feel of real masonry. Easy to cut, fit and apply. Ideal for interior walls, fireplaces, exteriors, etc. Loose stock also available. See your dealer or write to Kimberly House.

Prices are approximate and subject to change.

NORTHEASTERN SCALE MODELS INC.

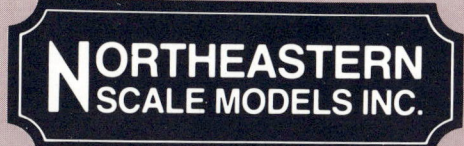

H O M E
IMPROVEMENTS

A collection of essential accessories for dollhouses and room boxes.

Select Wood ■ **Precision Crafted** ■ **Laser Cut**

DOLLHOUSE
DOLLHOUSES

Give your house a home. Our miniature dollhouse kits are superbly detailed, easy to assemble and come complete with windows and doors. Both are cut open in the back. Assembly instructions included. Just add paint, wall paper and a little imagination.

DH1-1003 Dollhouse
2 3/16"W x 2 11/16"D x 2 3/8"H

DH2-1006 Dollhouse
4 9/16"W x 3 1/2"D x 3 5/8"H

SCREEN
STARS

Our three and four panel screens will dress up any scene. Solid cherry. Our lasers have allowed us to replicate the intricate hand carved patterns of these screens' full sized counterparts. Brass hardware included.

1440 - Three Panel Screen   1441 - Four Panel Screen

CHILD'S
PLAY

Our children's toy kits are child's play to assemble and decorate. You'll appreciate the quality and detail that our laser cutting provides. Perfect for miniature playrooms or whenever the setting calls for a toddler's touch. Assembly instructions included.

1450 - Rocking Horse

1452 - Mouse on Wheels

1451 - Rocking Swan

Halloween - RGT 1404
Halloween - TWP 1424

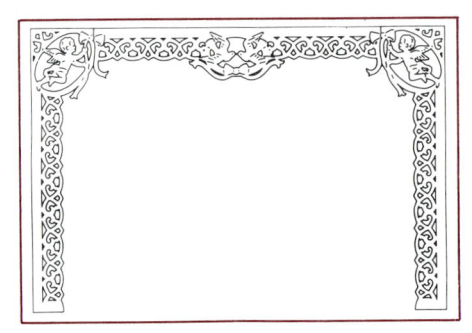

Victorian - RGT 1401
Victorian - TWP 1421

Easter - RGT 1402
Easter - TWP 1422

Christmas - RGT 1403
Christmas - TWP 1423

PROPER
PERSPECTIVE

Turn your labor of love into a work of art with our laser cut fascia trim for room boxes. We offer seven designs in two popular sizes. Crafted in cherry. Finish with stain, leave natural or paint to complement the scene.

Sizes available: Code "RGT", 14⅛" x 9¼", fits "Real Good Toys" room boxes. Code "TWP", 17" x 9⅜", fits "Timberbrook Wood Products" room boxes.

Americana - RGT 1406
Americana - TWP 1426

Colonial - RGT 1405
Colonial - TWP 1425

Hanukkah - RGT 1407
Hanukkah - TWP 1427

NORTHEASTERN SCALE MODELS INC.

Innovation, quality and precision for close to a half a century.

P.O. Box 727 • Methuen, MA 01844
Tel. 508-688-6019

KIMBERLY BRICK AND CUT-STONE KITS

Kimberly House Miniatures
Kits come complete with premixed mortar, sealer, mastic and instructions. Individual, realistic warmth and feel of real masonry. Cuts easily with knife or razor saw. Can sand to fit.
KIT1 Red Brick (75 sq.in.) $16.48
KIT2 White Brick (75 sq.in.) $16.48
KIT3 Used Brick (75 sq.in.) $16.48
KIT4 Grey Cut-Stone (75 sq.in.) $18.68
KIT5 Pink Cut-Stone (75 sq.in.) $18.68
Loose stock is also available. See your dealer or write to Kimberly House.

KIMBERLY NEW YORK BROWNSTONE

Kimberly House Miniatures
Suggested Retail Price: $6.15 (45 sq. in.) $11.55 (90 sq. in.)
Catalog No. NYB-45 or NYB-90
Dimensions: 45 sq. in. or 90 sq. in.; trim stone 45 sq. in. $6.15
Individual, realistic warmth and feel of real masonry. Easy to cut, fit and apply with our premixed mortar. Companionable accent stones available for trim, sills, corners, etc. Compatible sealer, $4.05 (4 oz. jar); compatible Premixed Mortar, $2.19 (4 oz. net wt. jar). See your dealer or write to Kimberly House.

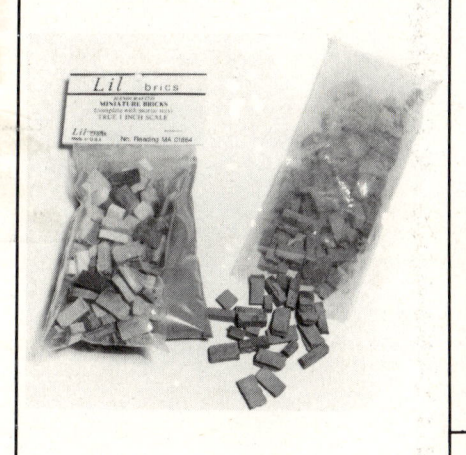

KIMBERLY REGULAR, DARK, AND WHITE MORTAR

Kimberly House Miniatures
Premixed, ready to use. Easy to apply, clean with wet sponge. Works well on all manufactured masonry 4 oz. net wt. jar covers 3 regular bags Kimberly Masonry.
MR-5 Regular   4 oz. net wt. $2.19
MD-5 Dark   4 oz. net wt. $2.19
MW-5 White   4 oz. net wt. $2.19

KIMBERLY SANDSTONE KIT

Kimberly House Miniatures
Suggested Retail Price: $20.34
Catalog #. KIT7 Sandstone
Dimensions: 100 sq. in. coverage
Kit comes complete with premixed mortar, sealer, mastic and instructions. Individual, realistic warmth and feel of real masonry. Easy to cut, fit and apply. Ideal for interior or exterior decor; fireplaces, chimney stacks, planters, etc. Loose stock is also available. See your dealer or write to Kimberly House.

LIL BRICS

Lil Crafts
Suggested Retail Price: $4.95 per 100 with mortar, $2.95 without mortar
Dimensions: 3/4" x 3/8" x 3/16" each
These handcrafted scale bricks are available in nine colors plus six color blends, including used assortment. First choice of many professional builders.

CHIMNEY STRUCTURAL FORM KIT

Lil Crafts
Suggested Retail Price: $1.70
Kit includes form, copper flashing and instructions. Roof slope versions also available. Designed for use with Lil Brics miniature bricks. Requires approximately 175 bricks (not included). Cat. #203 peak, Cat. #204 slope narrow, Cat. #205 slope square. 3" x 3" x 3".

MASTIC

Lil Crafts
Suggested Retail Price: $2.80
Pre-mixed, ready-to-use wherever cement is appropriate. 6oz. jar is adequate for three packs of Lil Brics miniature bricks. Superior to mortar or grout in all respects. Cat. #440.

Building Components & Supplies

BRICK AND STONE SUPPLIES

The Lawbre Company
All Lawbre brick, stones, and slate are cast in Hydrocal cement, and all except the slate are supplied in natural white that can be easily colored with acrylic tints and paints. Slate is tinted medium gray when it is cast but can also be colored with acrylics. Package includes instructions and finishing suggestions.

From left to right: No. 1026 Slate Flooring Kit, covers 36 sq. in., $8.95. No. 1001 Rusticated Stone Blocks (small) covers 25 sq. in., $5.95 (54 pieces). No. 1000 Rusticated Stone Blocks (large) covers 25 sq. in., $5.95 (29 pieces). No. 1002 Field Stones, covers 35 sq. in., $5.95. No. 1016 Lannon Stone, 6 pieces covers 54 sq. in., $8.95 (also No. 1017, 26 pieces covers 234 sq. in., $32.95). No. 1011 Lawbre Brick, 6 pieces covers 66 sq. in., $8.95 (also No. 1012, 26 pieces covers 286 sq. in., $32.95).

"IRON AND BRICK" GATES AND FENCING

The Lawbre Company
Suggested Retail Price: $12-$120
Catalog Nos. 0450/0465
Material: Resin and metal castings
For the complete landscape. These components can be used in many ways and combinations. Available finished or in kit form.

POLYSTYRENE RED BRICK PANEL

Miniature House
Suggested Retail Price: $5.25
Catalog No. MH5320
Dimensions: 10-3/4"W x 16-3/4"L
Three-dimensional Polystyrene Red Brick Panel is completely finished, with gray mortar color. Accurately scaled 1"=1'. Easy-to-use and apply. Cut with scissors or razor.

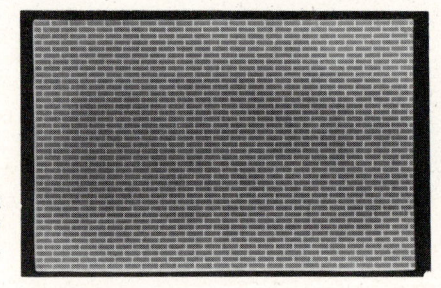

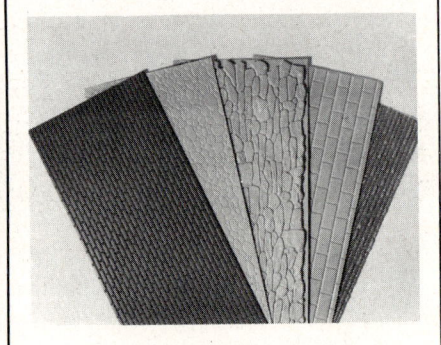

PLASTIC PATTERNED SHEETS

Plastruct
Suggested Retail Price: $3.50 - $7 plus shipping
Plastic patterned sheets in various scales and patterns including brick, random coursed stone, random field stone, dressed stone, coursed and field stone. Roofing, siding and flooring sheets also available.

FOUNDATION BRICK STRIPS

Rossco Products
Suggested Retail Price: $9.95
Four strips per package results in 37-1/2 length for the easiest foundation availalbe. Simply score and bend for either outside or inside corners. Interlocking ends fit perfectly.

Prices are approximate and subject to change.

CHECKERBOARD BRICKS ON MESH

Miniature House
Suggested Retail Price: 8.49
Catalog No. MH5421, MH5423
Dimensions: 72 square inches
Kiln-fired ceramic bricks are available in black-and-white (MH5421) or red-and-white (MH5423). Pre-mounted on mesh backing, each covers 72 square inches.

PORCH AND STAIRS STRUCTURAL FORM KIT

Lil Crafts
Suggested Retail Price: $1.70
Dimensions: 4-1/2"W x 5"D x 2-1/4"H
Kit includes structural form and assembly instructions. Designed for use with Lil Brics miniature bricks (not included). Cat. #207.

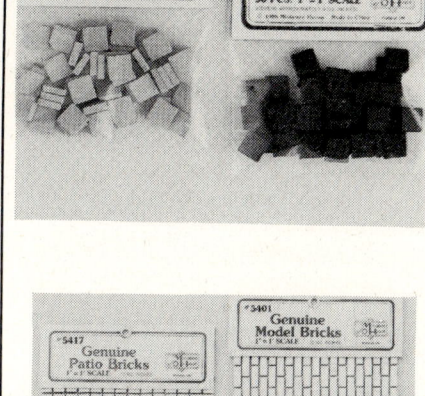

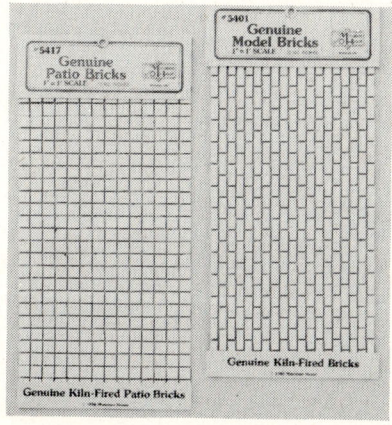

KILN-FIRED CERAMIC BRICKS

Miniature House
Both patio and standard common brick shapes are available in 1" scale, on 72 sq.in. mesh-mounted sheets or as loose brick (50 per package).
MH5400 mesh mounted standard red-$7.25
MH5401 mesh mounted standard white-$7.25
MH5415 mesh mounted patio red-$7.25
MH5417 mesh mounted patio white-$8.25
MH5405 50/bag standard red-$1.30
MH5406 50/bag standard white-$1.69
MH5425 50/bag patio red-$1.30
MH5426 50/bag patio white-$1.69
MH5427 50/bag patio block-$1.69

CHIMNEY KITS

Rossco Products
Suggested Retail Price: $8.95 each
Hollow basswood core and 3-D elastomer brick components already cut to size, simply glue and paint. Available in ridge model or 45° model.

PLASTIC FORMED SHEETS

Model Builder Supply
MBS's popular 3-D plastic sheets look more real than actual materials when painted with acrylic paints and mortar filled for masonry designs. Fieldstone, sandy grey, Clapboard, white, Dressed stone, sandy grey, Brick red, sandy grey. Split cedar shakes in grey. 7" x 24" - $6.75 Canadian. 7" x 12" - $3.95 Canadian. U.S. customers, see "Plastruct".

PLASTIC FORMED SHEETS

Model Builder Supply
Our decorative accent brick sheet features framing surrounds for Palladian window and door plus two styles of corner brick detail and four sets of sills or eyebrow headers. Available in sandy grey on brick red. Ask your local dealer or order direct. 7" x 24" - $8.95 Canadian. U.S. customers, see "Plastruct".

Building Components & Supplies

THE MINIATURES CATALOG, Fourteenth Edition   83

FLOOR AND PATIO BRICK

Rossco Products
Suggested Retail Price: $9.95 each
Specifications: 1/16" x 10" x 10"
Material: Elastomer
Thin enough to be used as inside floors such as kitchens, family rooms and foyers as well as patios, drives, streets and paths. Specify basketweave or herringbone pattern.

WALL OR STREET BRICK

Rossco Products
Suggested Retail Price: $9.95 each
Specifications: 1/16" x 10" x 10"
Material: Elastomer
Thin enough to be used as inside floors such as kitchens, family rooms and foyers as well as patios, drives, streets and paths. There are 472-1/2 completely different 3-D bricks already mounted. Multiple sheets can be combined with no visible butt joints. Easily cut to any size using scissors or an X-Acto knife. Simply score and bend for either outside or inside corners. Specify new or used.

Door Kits & Parts

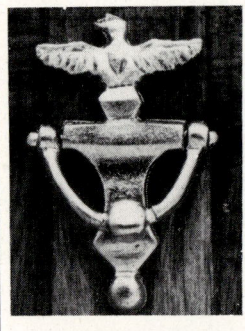

DOOR KNOCKER

Clare-Bell Brass Works
Suggested Retail Price: $4.50
Catalog No. 1763100
Solid brass door knocker.

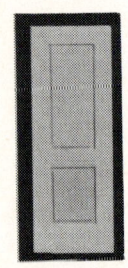

CARLSON TWO PANEL DOOR

American Craft Products
Suggested Retail Price: $4.95
Catalog No. 8421
Dimensions: 2-3/16" x 6-5/8"
Made of clear pine. Foremost in quality and design. No jamb. Made in America.

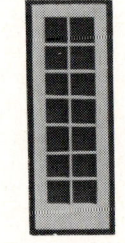

CARLSON SINGLE FRENCH DOOR

American Craft Products
Suggested Retail Price: $6.95
Catalog No. 8420
Dimensions: 2-3/16" x 6-5/8"
Made of clear pine with removable mullion for easy painting. No jamb. Made in America.

DOOR PLATES AND KNOB

Clare-Bell Brass Works
Suggested Retail Price: $5.25
Catalog No. 1762100
Threaded two-piece assembly. Fits 1/8" to 1/4" door. Solid brass.

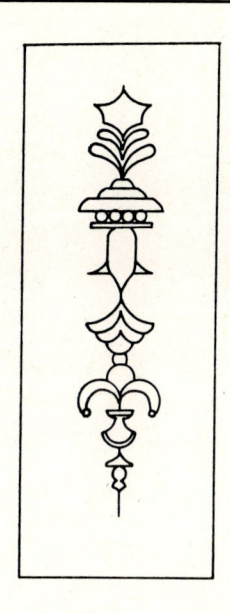

CROWNED ELEGANCE DOOR PANE

Houseworks
Suggested Retail Price: $6.95.
Catalog No. 7085 fits #6002
Laseretch® plexiglass inserts either replace or snap in over existing panes. They are a wonderfully unique and inexpensive way to add elegant style to your dollhouse.

VICTORIAN CIRCLE GRID DOOR PANE

Houseworks
Suggested Retail Price: $6.95.
Catalog No. 7086 fits #6002
Laseretch® plexiglass inserts either replace or snap in over existing panes. They are a wonderfully unique and inexpensive way to add elegant style to your dollhouse.

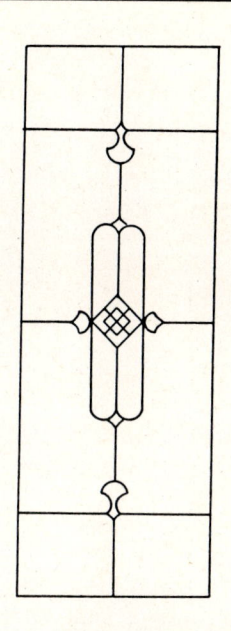

VICTORIAN DIAMOND CENTER GRID DOOR PANE

Houseworks
Suggested Retail Price: $6.95.
Catalog No. 7088 fits #6002
Laseretch® plexiglass inserts either replace or snap in over existing panes. They are a wonderfully unique and inexpensive way to add elegant style to your dollhouse.

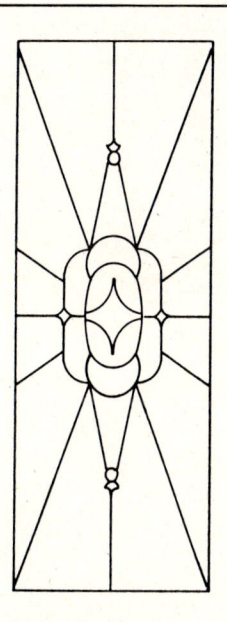

VICTORIAN SHINING FLOWER DOOR PANE

Houseworks
Suggested Retail Price: $6.95.
Catalog No. 7087 fits #6002
Laseretch® plexiglass inserts either replace or snap in over existing panes. They are a wonderfully unique and inexpensive way to add elegant style to your dollhouse.

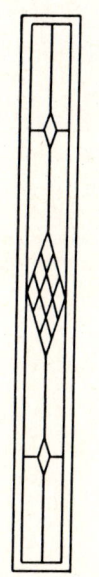

VICTORIAN SIDELIGHTS

Houseworks
Suggested Retail Price: $4.95.
Catalog No. 7095 fits #6010, 7096 fits #6027
Laseretch® plexiglass inserts either replace or snap in over existing panes. They are a wonderfully unique and inexpensive way to add elegant style to your dollhouse.

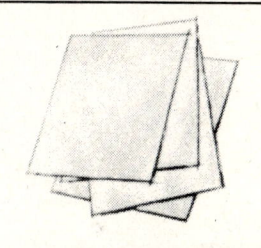

BUTYRATE SHEETS

K & S Engineering
Hard clear plastic sheets, 8" x 10" for forming windows, doors, etc. Four sizes: .010 - Cat. No. 301, $ .40; .0075 - Cat. No. 302, $ .30; .015 - Catalog No. 304, $ .60; .030 - Catalog No. 306, $1.

Your Listings Belong Here!
Interested in advertising in the
15th Edition of
The Miniatures Catalog?

Contact Sara Benz at
1-800-558-1544,
Ext. 631
or write to;
The Miniatures Catalog
P.O. Box 1612
Waukesha, WI 53187

Building Components & Supplies

THE MINIATURES CATALOG, Fourteenth Edition

LASER ENGRAVED DOOR INSERTS AND SIDELIGHTS

Laser Tech
Suggested Retail Price: (left to right) #VO-095 $6.95; #VD-096S $6.50; #VS-102S $8.50
Made of 1/16" plexiglass, our laser engraved and sandblasted door and sidelight inserts are made to fit in Houseworks door #6002, #6010 or #6033 and will add elegance to any entry.

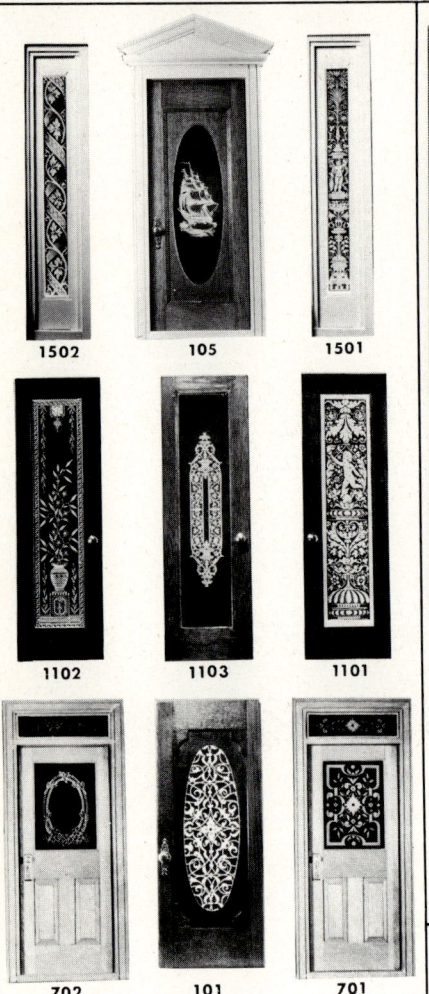

Doors, Working

APPLIQUES

Unique Miniatures
Made of polyester resin, these uniquely styled appliques have unlimited uses to accent your room decor. Apply to wood to decorate doors, wainscots, walls or even furniture and see them become handsome ornate creations. Each bag contains between two and four appliques. Send $2 for complete catalog. Made in the USA. Many other styles to choose from.

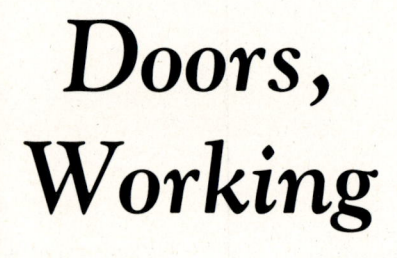

ETCHED DOOR GLASS

Noonmark
Suggested Retail Price: $2.50-$17.50 per pair, plus shipping
Our doorlights are beautifully etched on real 3/64" micro-glass. The designs are sized to fit popular door components and are also suitable for scratchbuilding. Other designs are available. Numbers shown refer to glass only.

CARLSON DOUBLE WORKING DOOR

American Craft Products
Suggested Retail Price: $22.95
Catalog No. 8423
Dimensions: 6-1/8" x 7-7/16" opening size for standard 3/8" wall
Made of clear pine. Foremost in quality and design. Made in America.

CARLSON WORKING DOOR

American Craft Products
Suggested Retail Price: $11.95
Catalog No. 8402
Dimensions: 3-5/16" x 7-7/16" opening size for standard 3/8" wall
Made of clear pine. Foremost in quality and design. Made in America.

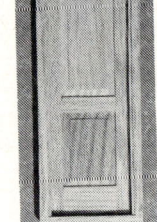

CARLSON OAK INTERIOR DOOR

American Craft Products
Suggested Retail Price: $8.95
Catalog No. 8635
Dimensions: Standard 3" x 7" opening
Made of solid oak. Foremost in quality and design. Made in America. Also available without jamb No. 8621 (2-3/8" x 6-1/2").

Prices are approximate and subject to change.

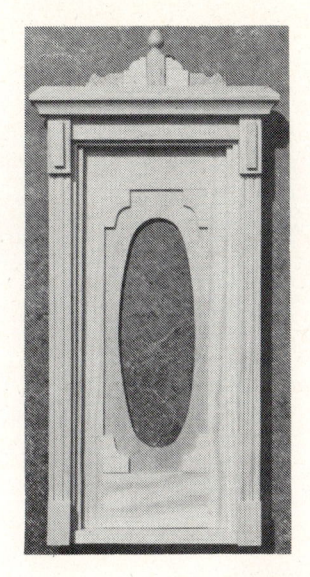

CARLSON WORKING DOOR

American Craft Products
Suggested Retail Price: $13.95
Catalog No. 8463
Dimensions: 3-5/16" x 7-7/16" opening size for standard 3/8" wall
From the Victorian Profile series. Accurately detailed architecture. Made of clear pine and made in America.

CARLSON WORKING DOUBLE DOOR

American Craft Products
Suggested Retail Price: $24.95
Catalog No. 8464
Dimensions: 6-1/8" x 7-7/16" opening size for standard 3/8" wall
Made of clear pine from the Victorian Profile series. Accurately detailed architecture. Made in America.

CARLSON WORKING COLONIAL SIDELIGHT DOOR

American Craft Products
Suggested Retail Price: $26.95
Catalog No. 8424
Dimensions: 6-5/16" x 7-7/16" opening size for standard 3/8" wall
Made of clear pine. Truly a masterpiece for the serious collector. Made in America.

CARLSON WORKING DOOR

American Craft Products
Suggested Retail Price: $11.95
Catalog No. 8401
Dimensions: 3-5/16" x 7-7/16" opening size for standard 3/8" wall
Made of clear pine. Foremost in quality and design. Made in America.

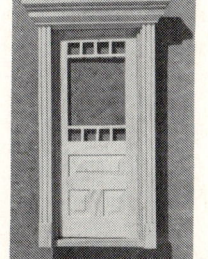

CARLSON WORKING DOOR

American Craft Products
Suggested Retail Price: $11.95
Catalog No. 8436
Dimensions: 3-5/16" x 7-7/16" opening size for standard 3/8" wall
Made of clear pine. Foremost in quality and design. Made in America.

CARLSON WORKING DOOR

American Craft Products
Suggested Retail Price: $12.95
Catalog No. 8400
Dimensions: 3-5/16" x 7-7/16" opening size for standard 3/8" wall
Made of clear pine. Foremost in quality and design. Made in America.

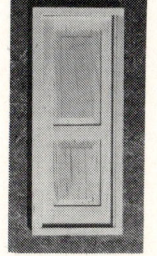

CARLSON WORKING INTERIOR DOOR

American Craft Products
Suggested Retail Price: $6.95
Catalog No. 8435
Dimensions: 2-7/8" x 7-7/16" opening size for standard 3/8" wall
Made of clear pine. A beautiful finishing touch to your interior walls. Made in America.

CARLSON WORKING DOUBLE DOOR

American Craft Products
Suggested Retail Price: $22.95
Catalog No. 8422
Dimensions: 6-1/8" x 7-7/16" opening size for standard 3/8" wall
Made of clear pine. Foremost in quality and design. Made in America.

CARLSON WORKING DOOR

American Craft Products
Suggested Retail Price: $12.95
Catalog No. 8413
Dimensions: 3-5/16" x 7-7/16" opening size for standard 3/8" wall
Made of clear pine. Foremost in quality and design. Made in America.

Building Components & Supplies

THE MINIATURES CATALOG, Fourteenth Edition

CARLSON WORKING FRENCH DOORS

American Craft Products
Suggested Retail Price: $15.95
Catalog No. 8425
Dimensions: 5" x 7-7/16" opening size for standard 3/8" wall
Made of clear pine. Removable mullion. Foremost in quality and design. Made in America.

CARLSON WORKING DOOR

American Craft Products
Suggested Retail Price: $12.95
Catalog No. 8412
Dimensions: 3-5/16" x 7-7/16" opening size for standard 3/8" wall
Made of clear pine. Foremost in quality and design. Made in America.

CARLSON WORKING DOOR

American Craft Products
Suggested Retail Price: $12.95
Catalog No. 8411
Dimensions: 3-5/16" x 7-7/16" opening size for standard 3/8" wall
Made of clear pine. Foremost in quality and design. Made in America.

SLIDING FRENCH DOORS

Houseworks
Suggested Retail Price: $16.95
Catalog No. 6030
This contemporary version of the classic French Door has two separate door panels that slide side to side and the frame includes spring loaded tracks to allow easy removal of each door. Fits opening 5-3/16" W x 7-9/16" H.

ASSORTED EXTERIOR DOORS

Houseworks
#6012-Crossbuck Door-Exterior door with "crossbuck" panel, acrylic window and four section transom. Size: 3-1/2"W x 7-3/4"H. Fits opening: 3-1/16"W x 7-9/16"H. $10.25
#6018-Traditional Door-Exterior door with two panel lower half, acrylic window upper half and four section transom. Size: 3-1/2"W x 7-3/4"H. Fits opening: 3-1/16"W x 7-9/16"H. $9.50
#6009-Crossbuck Dutch Door. Exterior door with lower "crossbuck" panel, upper acrylic window hinged to operate separately and four section transom. Size: 3-1/2"W x 7-3/4"H. Fits opening: 3-1/16"W x 7-9/16"H. $10.95

EXTERIOR SIX PANEL DOORS

Houseworks
#6010-The Jamestown Door-Exterior six panel door with twin sidelights and detailed dentil moulding. Size: 8-5/8"W x 8-3/16"H. Fits opening: 6-5/16"W x 7-7/16"H. $22.50
#6014-Yorktown Door-Exterior six panel door with sculpted doorcap and complimenting dentil moulding. Size: 5-5/8"W x 8-1/8"H. Fits opening: 3-3/8"W x 7-7/16"H. $14.75

ASSORTED EXTERIOR DOORS

Houseworks
#6013-Victorian Door-Exterior six panel door with low pitch hooded doorcap, scalloped transom and fluted moulding. Size: 5"W x 8-7/16"H. Fits opening: 3-3/8"W x 8-5/16"H. $14.75.
#6004-Traditional "Americana" Door-Exterior door with eight raised door panels and four raised side panels. Size: 4-3/4"W x 8-7/8"H. Fits opening: 3-1/16"W x 7-9/16"H. $10.50.

INTERIOR PANEL DOORS

Houseworks
#6007-Traditional Door-This interior six panel door is effective for all of your interior door uses. Size: 3-9/16"W x 7-1/8"H. Fits opening: 3"W x 7"H. $8.95.
#6021-Traditional Door-Interior five panel door with detailed horizontal panels. Size: 3-7/16"W x 7-3/16"H. Fits opening: 3"W x 7"H. $8.95.
#6008-Classic Door-Interior five panel door is a stylish alternative for your interior door uses. Size: 3-7/16"W x 7-3/16"H. Fits opening: 3"W x 7"H. $8.95.

PALLADIAN DOORS

Houseworks
#6015-Palladian Door-Two panel lower half, acrylic window upper half and fan transom with acrylic pane. For exterior use. Size: 3-3/4"W x 8-7/8"H. Fits opening: 3-5/16"W x 8-11/16"H. $23.50.
#6016-Palladian Double Entry Door-Two panel lower half, acrylic windows upper half and fan transom with acrylic pane. Hinged to operate separately. For exterior use. Size: 3-3/4"W x 8-7/8"H. Fits opening: 3-5/16"W x 8-11/16"H. $23.50.

FRENCH DOORS

Houseworks
#6011-Classic French Doors-Double entry french doors with preassembled grids and acrylic panes. Hinged to operate separately. For interior and exterior use. Size: 5-3/8"W x 7-11/16"H. Fits opening: 3-1/16"W x 7-9/16"H. $14.50.
#6022-Single French Door-French door with preassembled grids and acrylic pane. For interior and exterior use. Size: 3-7/16"W x 7-5/8"H. Fits opening: 3-1/16"W x 7-9/16"H. $8.95.

TRADITIONAL PANEL DOORS

Houseworks
#6001-Traditional 4 Panel Door-Exterior door with four raised door panels and four section transom. Size: 3-1/2"W x 7-3/4"H. Fits opening: 3-1/16"W x 7-9/16"H. $8.75.
#6000-Traditional 6 Panel Door-Exterior door with four section transom. Size: 3-1/2"W x 7-3/4"H. Fits opening: 3-1/16"W x 7-9/16"H. $10.95.

ASSORTED PANEL DOORS

Houseworks
#6025-Traditional Block and Trim Door-Interior six panel door with detailed corner blocks and trim. Size: 3-3/4"W x 7-15/16"H. Fits opening: 2-15/16"W x 6-15/16"H. $12.95.
#6026-Double Entry Doors-Interior six panel doors hinged to operate perfectly together. Size: 6-1/16"W x 7-1/8"H. Fits opening: 5-5/8"W x 6-15/16"H. $17.95.
#6023-Carolina Door-Exterior six panel door with lavish circlehead and removable acrylic pane. Size: 3-3/8"W x 7-3/4"H. Fits opening: 2-15/16"W x 7-1/2"H. $10.95.

EXTERIOR SIX PANEL DOORS

Houseworks
#6028-Deerfield Door-Exterior six panel door with sidelights and intricate scroll pediment. Size: 7-3/16"W x 9-3/16"H. Fits opening: 5-1/2"W x 7-3/8"H. $23.95.
#6027-Sunburst Door-Exterior six panel door with sidelights and detailed sunburst pediment. Size: 6-3/16"W x 8-5/8"H. Fits opening: 5-1/2"W x 7-3/8"H. $23.95.

Building Components & Supplies

VICTORIAN OVAL DOOR

Houseworks
Suggested Retail Price: $10.95.
Catalog No. 6002.
Detailed Victorian hood tops this exterior door with oval window. Removable acrylic pane. Size: 4-1/4"W x 8-1/2"H. Fits opening: 3-1/16"W x 7-7/16"H.

FOR FAST SERVICE, VISIT YOUR LOCAL MINIATURES SHOP

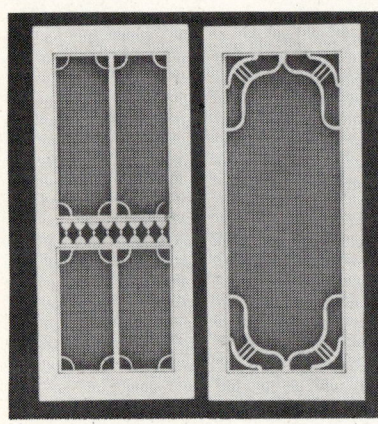

LASER CUT VICTORIAN SCREEN DOORS

Laser Tech
Suggested Retail Price: (left to right) #SD-066 $9.95; #SD-065 $9.85; #SD-061 $9.85; #SD-070 $9.95
All screen doors are made slightly oversized (2-7/8" x 6-11/16") to fit all doors and can be easily trimmed to fit your door openings perfectly.

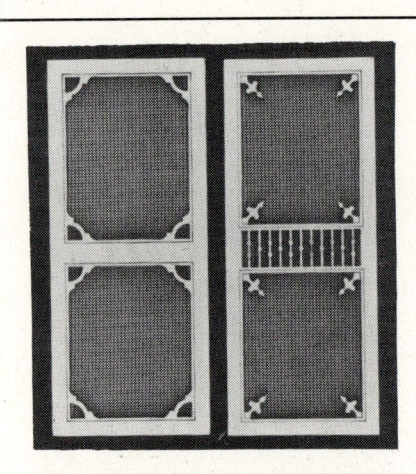

CLASSIC FRENCH DOOR

Miniature House
Suggested Retail Price: $13.50
Catalog No. MH1011
Dimensions: Fits opening 5-1/16"W x 7-9/16"H
Classic French door with removable mullions.

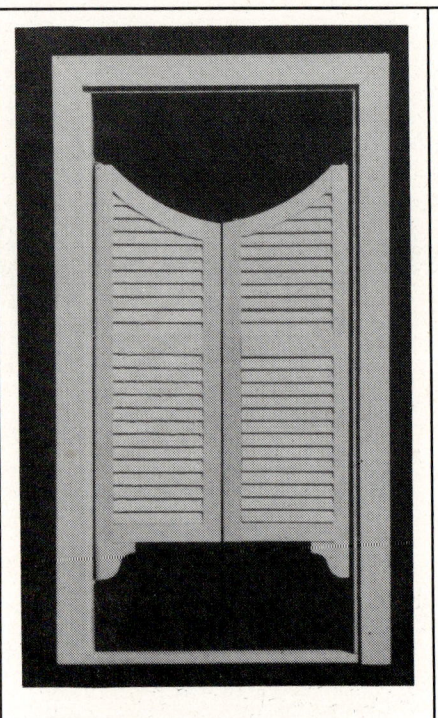

DOUBLE SWINGING DOOR

Miniature House
Suggested Retail Price: $8.95
Catalog No. MH134
Dimensions: Fits opening 3-1/2"W x 6-3/4"H
Classic swinging door, perfect for kitchen, bathroom, saloon, or use your imagination.

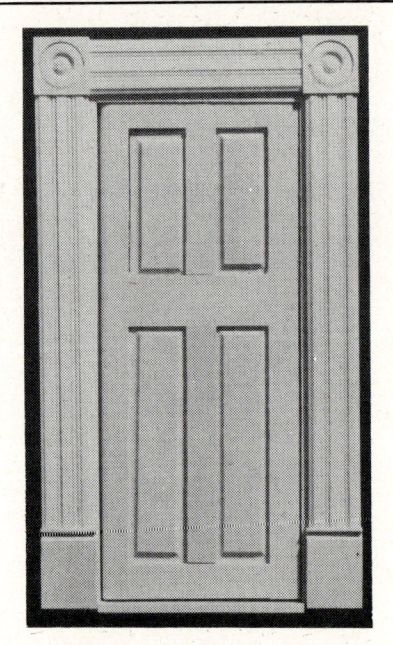

FANCY INSIDE DOOR

Miniature House
Suggested Retail Price: $10.98
Catalog No. MH120
Dimensions: Fits opening 3-1/16"W x 6-15/16"H
This attractive door has assembled interior trim to match exterior trim. Corner blocks add a special touch.

Prices are approximate and subject to change.

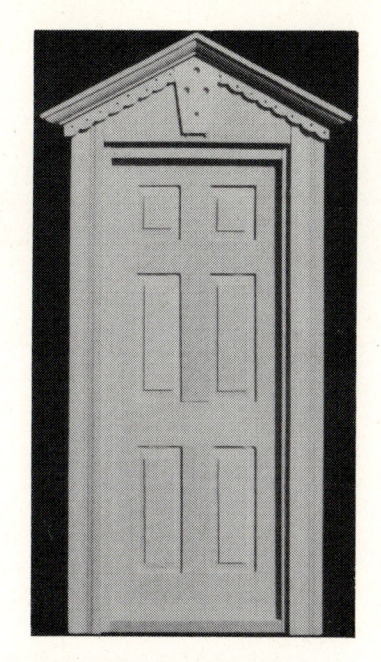

FANCY VICTORIAN OUTSIDE DOOR
Miniature House
Suggested Retail Price: $11.98
Catalog No. MH1020
Dimensions: Fits opening 3"W x 7-3/16"H
This delightful door enhances the Fancy Victorian series with the dainty, scalloped upper trimwork. It also has interior molding.

FANCY VICTORIAN OUTSIDE DOOR
Miniature House
Suggested Retail Price: $14.98
Catalog No. MH132B basket, MH132R rose, MH132U urn
Dimensions: Fits opening 3-1/2"W x 7-9/16"H
The dainty scalloped trim completes the Victorian look with the lovely etched glass pane. Door has interior molding.

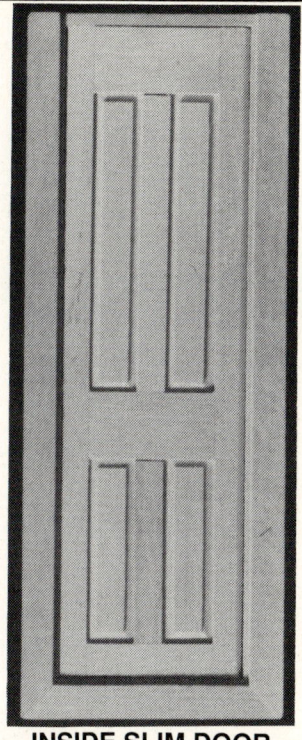

INSIDE SLIM DOOR
Miniature House
Suggested Retail Price: $6.70
Catalog No. MH133
Dimensions: Fits opening 2-5/16"W x 7"H
This four-panel door is ideal for those narrow walls between rooms. Door has interior trim.

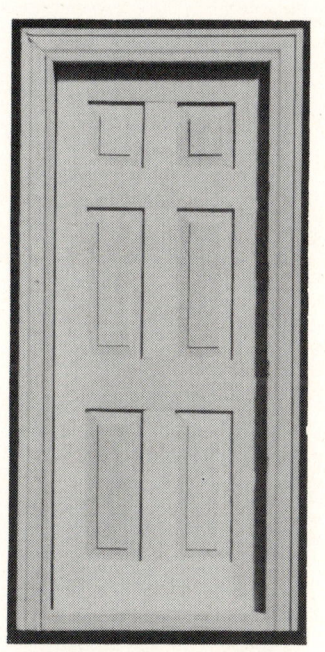

STANDARD 6-PANEL INTERIOR DOOR
Miniature House
Suggested Retail Price: $7.98
Catalog No. MH1382
Dimensions: Fits opening 3"W x 7"H
This ever-popular, traditional door has grooved exterior trim. Door has interior molding to match exterior.

TRADITIONAL ETCHED GLASS DOOR
Miniature House
Suggested Retail Price: $14.98
Catalog No. MH131C compote, MH131D deer, MH131SH ship
Dimensions: Fits opening 3-1/16"W x 7-9/16"H
Beautiful etched glass adds the finishing touch to this traditional door. Door has interior molding.

VICTORIAN OUTSIDE DOOR
Miniature House
Suggested Retail Price: $12.40
Catalog No. MH1040
Dimensions: Fits opening 3-1/16"W x 7-3/16"H
This Victorian door, with matching molded interior trim, is a beautiful style exemplifying the Victorian era.

Building Components & Supplies

THE MINIATURES CATALOG, *Fourteenth Edition*

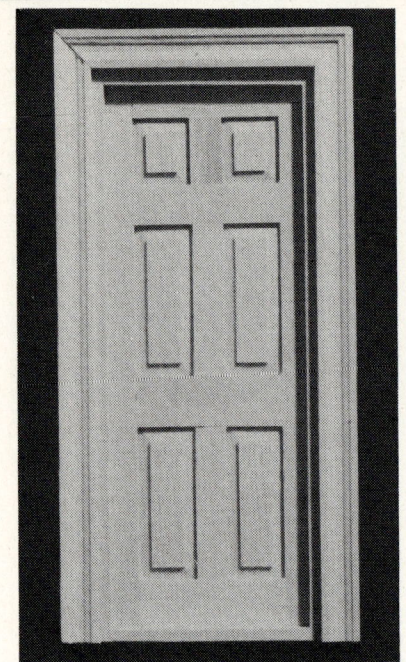

TRADITIONAL 6-PANEL DOOR

Miniature House
Suggested Retail Price: $7.98
Catalog No. MH1380
Dimensions: Fits opening 3"W x 7"H
This door has the same special molded side trim as No. MH1040 Victorian door. Door comes with matching interior trim.

VICTORIAN DOOR

Miniature House
Suggested Retail Price: $13.95
Catalog No. MH1013
Dimensions: Fits 3-3/8"W x 8-5/16"H
Six panel highly detailed door with transom molding.

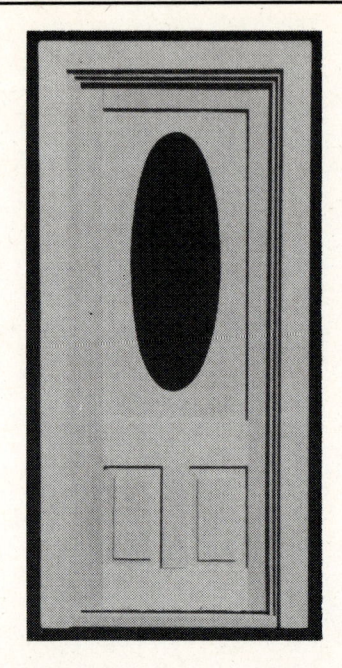

VICTORIAN OVAL GLASS DOOR

Miniature House
Suggested Retail Price: $10.39
Catalog No. MH137
Dimensions: 3-1/8"W X 7-9/16"H
Graceful Victorian door has a removable pane for easy painting or staining. Door comes with interior trim.

YORKTOWN DOOR

Miniature House
Suggested Retail Price: $13.95
Catalog No. MH1014
Dimensions: Fits opening 3-3/8" W x 7-7/16" H
Six panel door with detailed doorcap and dentil molding.

YORKTOWN EXTERIOR DOOR

Miniature House
Suggested Retail Price: $13.98
Catalog No. MH117
Dimensions: Fits opening 3-5/16"W x 7-3/16"H
This lovely door, with interior trim, has 1/2 light windows and is highly detailed in the Yorktown tradition.

DEFINITIVE EXTERIOR DOORS

Derek Perkins
Suggested Retail Price: $29.50
One of three exterior doors well illustrated in my catalog.

92 Prices are approximate and subject to change.

Hardware & Metal Parts

WALNUT DOORS WITH ETCHED GLASS

Noonmark
Suggested Retail Price: $26 for Ship; $29 for Peacock
Door and frame are solid walnut with exquisite mortise and tenon joinery, fully assembled with brass hinges. Includes interior trim. Doorlights are beautifully etched on real glass and are removable for finishing wood. Doorknob is not included. Other designs are available. Doors are also available with clear glass doorlights.

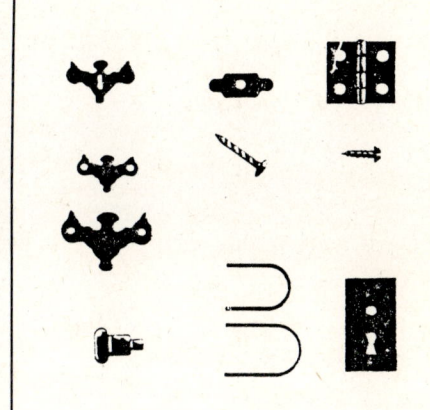

HARDWARE ASSORTMENT

Craftmark House of Miniatures
Solid brass hardware in perfect 1" to 1' scale. From the period 1740-1775. No. 43101 - small Chippendale brass with bail, (set of 12) $2.45. No. 43102 - large Chippendale brass with bail, (set of 12) $2.45. No. 43103, brass door hinges (6 hinges, 24 screws) $3.50. No. 43104, Chippendale brass complete with brass door pull (set of 12) $2.45. No. 43105, Chippendale brass key plate (12 pieces) $1.95. No. 43106, brass door knob and door key plate (4 sets) $2.45.

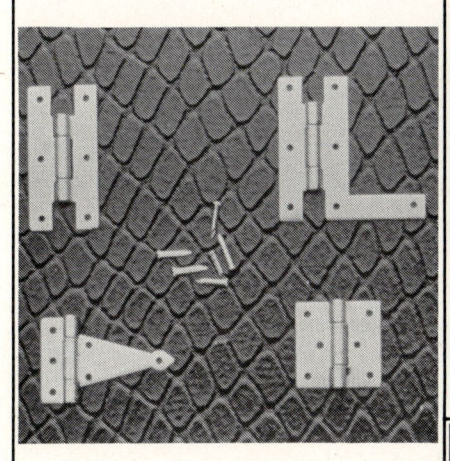

CRYSTAL HARDWARE

Houseworks
#1140, Crystal Provincial Knob, $1.95. #1143, Crystal Opryland Knob with key, $1.95. #1142, Crystal Classic Knob with key, $1.95. #1144 Crystal Door Knob, $3.50. #1141, Crystal Medallion Knob, $1.95. All come two to a package except for #1144 which has six included..

MINIATURE BRASS HINGES

Greenleaf Products
Suggested Retail Price: $3.35
The doors in your dollhouse can be hinged to open with these perfectly scaled hinges, four to a package complete with brass nails. Four styles, butt, H, HL, and T. Catalog Nos. 9009H, 9009HL, 9009T, 9009.

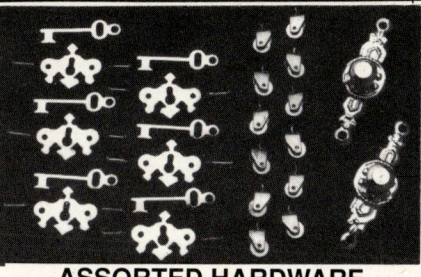

ASSORTED HARDWARE

Houseworks
#1103-Gold Plated Brass Chippendale Keyplate w/key-6 sets/pkg., $1.95. #1104-Brass Furniture Casters-12 pcs./pkg., $3.75. #1105-Gold Plated Brass Round Doorknob-2 pcs./pkg., $1.95.

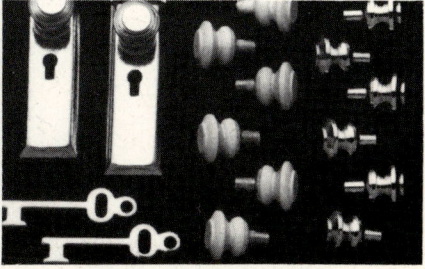

ASSORTED KNOBS

Houseworks
#1114-Gold Plated Brass Knob & Keyplate w/key-2 pcs./pkg., $1.95. #1115-White Enameled Brass Knob-6 pcs./pkg., $1.95. #1116-Gold Plated Brass Knob-6 pcs./pkg., $1.95.

Building Components & Supplies

THE MINIATURES CATALOG, Fourteenth Edition 93

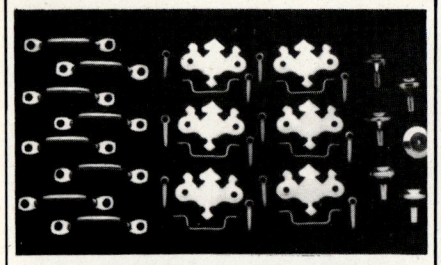

ASSORTED PULLS

Houseworks
#1123-Gold Plated Brass Window Handle Pull-6 pcs./pkg., $2.50. #1124-Gold Plated Brass Chippendale Drawer Pull-6 pcs./pkg., $1.95. #1127-Gold Plated Brass Round Cabinet Pull-6 pcs./pkg., $1.95.

BRASS POINTED NAILS

Houseworks
#1128-Brass Pointed Pin-Nails-6mm long, 100 pcs./pkg., $2.25. #1129-Brass Pointed Nails-4mm long, 100 pcs./pkg., $2.25.

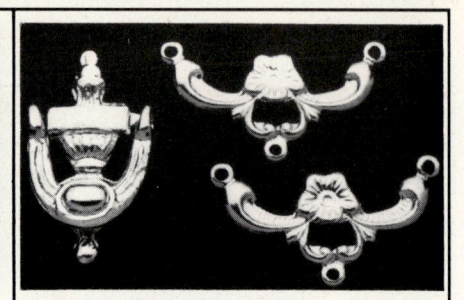

DOOR KNOCKER & BELL PULLS

Houseworks
#1107-Gold Plated Door Knocker-1 pc./pkg., $1.95. #1108-Gold Plated Brass Bell Pull-2 pcs./pkg., $1.50.

DOOR PULL & KNOB

Houseworks
#1110-Gold Plated Brass Door Pull-2 pcs./pkg., $1.50. #1111-Gold Plated Brass Medallion Knob-2 pcs./pkg., $1.75.

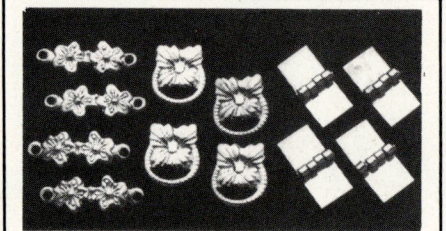

DRAWER PULLS & HINGE

Houseworks
#1117-Gold Plated Brass Double Flower Drawer Pull-4 pcs./pkg., $1.50. #1119-Gold Plated Brass Square Drawer Pull-4 pcs./pkg., $1.50. #1120-Gold Plated Brass Square Hinge-4 pcs./pkg., $1.75.

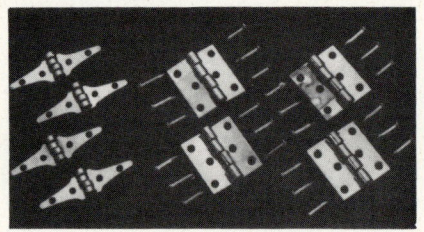

GOLD PLATED BRASS HINGES

Houseworks
#1121-Gold Plated Brass Triangle Hinge-4 pcs./pkg., $1.75. #1122-Gold Plated Brass Butt Hinge-4 pcs. w/24 nails, $2.25.

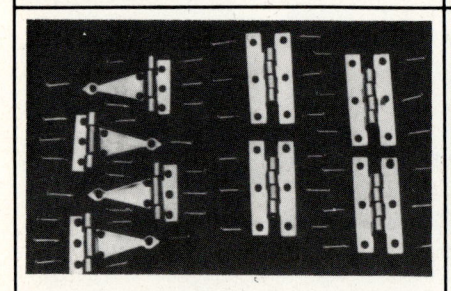

GOLD PLATED BRASS HINGES

Houseworks
#1130-Gold Plated Brass "T" Hinge-4 pcs. w/24 nails, $2.25. #1131-Gold Plated Brass "H" Hinge, 4 pcs. w/24 nails, $2.25.

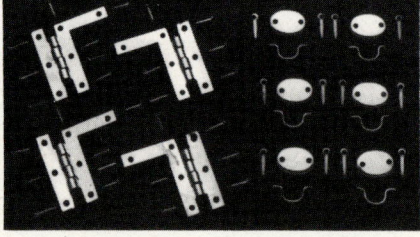

HINGE & DRAWER PULL

Houseworks
#1132-Gold Plated Brass "HL" Hinge-4 pcs. w/28 nails, $2.50. #1133-Gold Plated Brass Hepplewhite Drawer Pull-12 pcs./pkg., $1.95.

LOCK & DOOR HANDLE

Houseworks
#1134-Gold Plated Brass "Americana" Lock-1 pc./pkg., $2.25. #1139-Gold Plated Brass "Opryland" Door Handle w/key-2 pcs./pkg., $1.75.

S-HOOKS

Houseworks
#1101-Black Enameled Brass "S" Hook-4 pcs./pkg., $1.50. #1102-Gold Plated Brass "S" Hook-4 pcs./pkg., $1.50.

UNITED STATES FLAG

Miniature House
Suggested Retail Price: $2.89
Catalog No. MH5670
Dimensions: 3" x 5"
The perfect touch for your miniature home on July 4th or other patriotic holidays. This 3" x 5" U.S. flag includes mounting brackets.

Interested in Becoming a Professional Miniatures Handcrafter? Contact the Cottage Industry Miniaturists Trade Association

CIMTA
P.O. Box 5071
New Haven, CT 06525

Prices are approximate and subject to change.

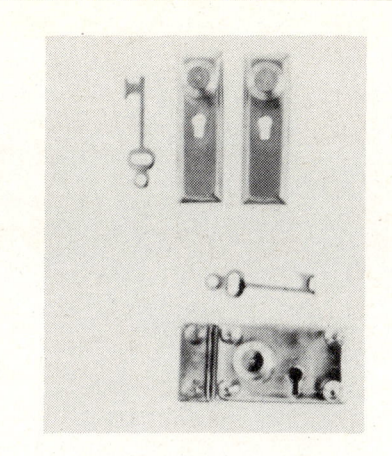

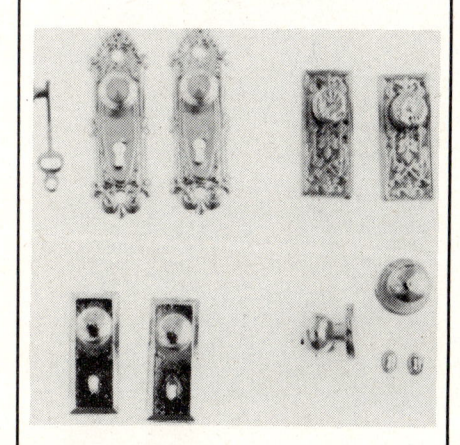

MINIATURE BRASS DOOR KNOBS AND LOCKS

Miniature House
Door knobs with keyplates and keys, 2/pk., gold-plated brass. MH5528 $1.80
Victorian door knobs with keys, 2/pk., gold-plated brass. MH5578 $1.70
Ornate door knobs, 4/pk., polished brass. MH5612 $2.80
Box lock with key, 1/pk., gold-plated brass. MH5568 $1.98
Door knobs with plates, 4/pk., polished brass. MH5606 $2.69
Door knobs with keyholes, 4/pk., polished brass. MH5608 $2.49

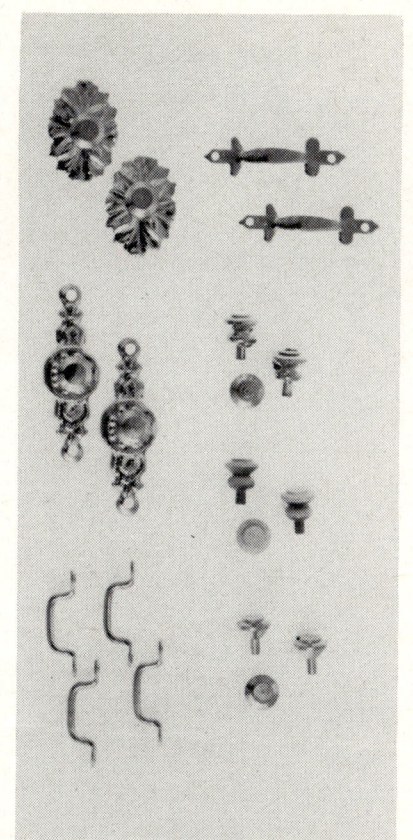

MINIATURE BRASS DOOR KNOBS AND PULLS

Miniature House
Window pull handles, 6/pk., gold-plated brass. MH5546 $2.39
Colonial door knobs, 2/pk., gold-plated brass. MH5510 $1.79
Medallion door knobs, 2/pk., gold-plated brass. MH5522 $1.59
Round cabinet pulls, 6/pk., polished brass. MH5554 $1.80
White enameled round knobs, 6/pk. MH5530 $1.80
Round knobs, 6/pk., gold-plated brass. MH5532 $1.80
Door pulls, 2/pk., gold-plated brass. MH5520 $1.40

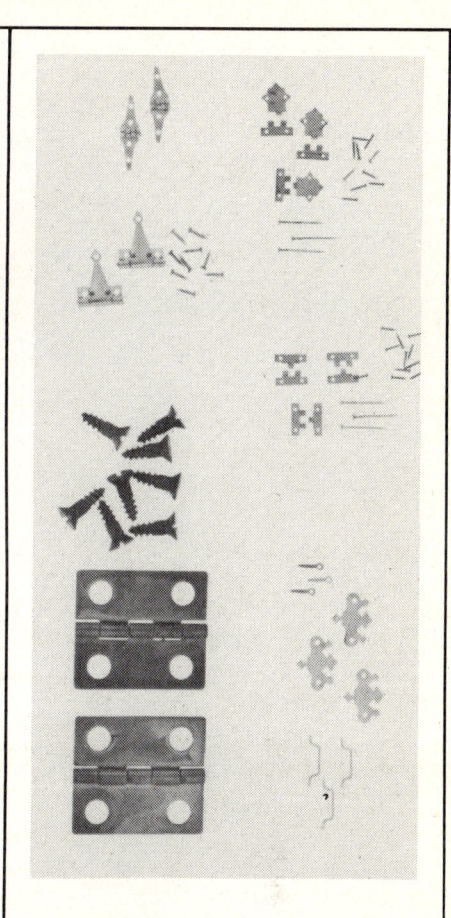

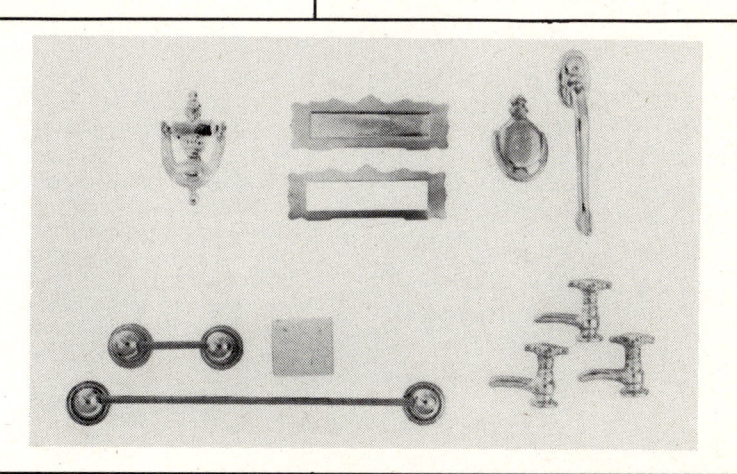

MINIATURE BRASS HINGES AND PULLS

Miniature House
Offset hinges with nails, 6/pk., polished brass. MH5646 $2.89
Flush hinges with nails, 4/pk., polished brass. MH5644 $2.89
Chippendale drawer pulls, 6/pk., gold-plated brass. MH5548 $1.69
Triangle hinges, 4/pk., gold-plated brass. MH5542 $1.59
Strap hinges with nails, 4/pk., polished brass. MH5560 $2.10
Doll house roof hinges with screws, 2/pk., satin-finished brass. MH5672 $2.39

MINIATURE BRASS HARDWARE

Miniature House
Door knocker, 1/pk., polished brass. MH5514 $1.80
Mail slot, 1 set, polished brass. MH5676 $2.79
Door handle and knocker, polished brass. MH5602 $2.49
Towel rod and tissue holder, polished brass. MH5674 $2.98
Faucets, 4/pk., polished brass. MH5668 $2.49

Building Components & Supplies

MINIATURE BRASS HINGES

Miniature House
Square Hinges, 4/pk., gold-plated brass. MH5540 $1.69
Butt hinges with nails, 4/pk., polished brass. MH5544 $2
"H" hinges with nails, 4/pk., satin-finished brass. MH 5666 $2.98
"H" hinges with nails, 4/pk., polished brass. MH5562 $1.98
"HL" hinges with nails, 4/pk., polished brass. MH5564 $2.39
"Butt hinges with nails, 4/pk., satin-finished brass. MH5640 $2.89

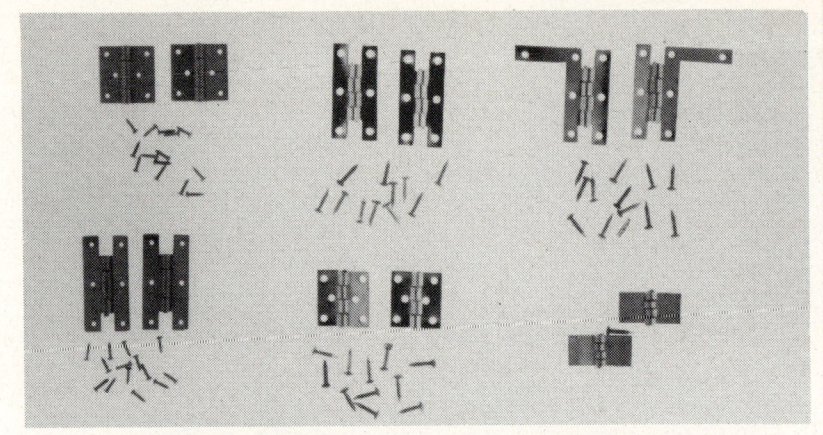

MINIATURE BRASS NAILS

Miniature House
Mini nails, 3/8" long, 100/pk. MH5680 $2.10
Mini nails, 3/32" long, 100/pk. MH5678 $2.10
Mini nails, 1/8" long, 100/pk. MH5558 $2.10
Mini nails, 1/4" long, 100/pk. MH5556 $2.10

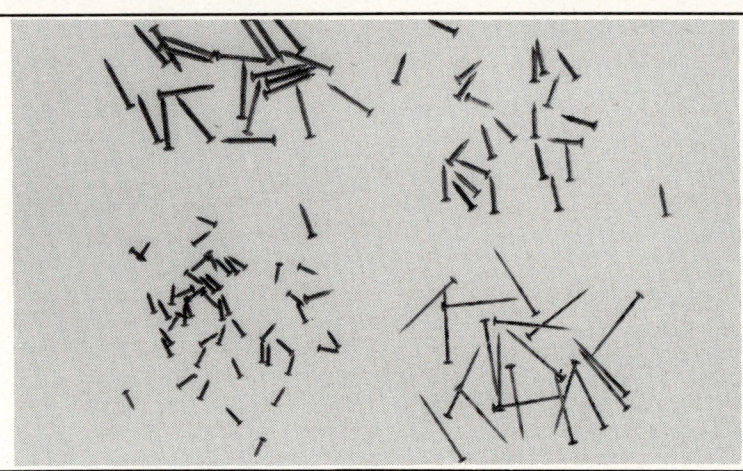

DESCRIPTION	NO.
Butt Hinges — doz.	HWA-10
Piano Hinge — ea.	HWA-250
Door Knob/Dummy Brass	HWC-1
Door Knob/Working	HWC-2
Door Knob Template	HWC-3

HARDWARE

Northeastern Scale Models, Inc.
Suggested Retail Price: $2.50-$8.50
Catalog No. HWA10 $5, No. HWA250 $7.95, No.HWC-1 $3.20, No. HWC-2 $8.50, No. HWC-3 $2.50.

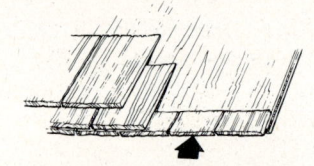

This lady has an eye for detail! She noticed that the first row of shingles on any house is always sloped the same as the remainder, because under the first row of shingles lay shorter ones. So, when you start shingling, cut the shingles in the first row about half their usual length, then glue these along the edge of the eave. The shingles glued on top of these short ones are full size — so too are the succeeding shingles. If you study my sketch, I am sure you will see what I mean.

JANIS ERNST
SILVER SPRING, MD

HARMONY FORGE HARDWARE

Olde Mountain Miniatures
We proudly present over 100 items in 1/12 scale collector quality reproductions of early American hardware, fireplace accessories and lighting devices. "Forged" Britannia alloy pieces duplicate the rough surface created by the blacksmith's hammer. Finished in a burnished satin black that will not chip or peel but may be painted over if desired. Dealer inquiries welcome.

Prices are approximate and subject to change.

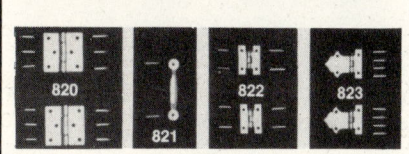

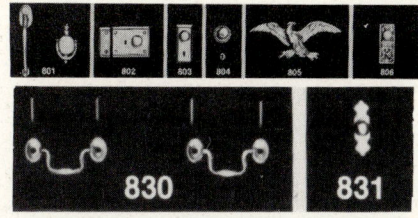

REALIFE MINIATURES® HARDWARE

Scientific Models, Inc.
Suggested Retail Price: $1.98-$2.79.
Catalog No. 801-856.
A wide range of brass finishing hardware and accessories authentically reproduced in 1" scale. These items will add that special touch to your dollhouses and furniture.

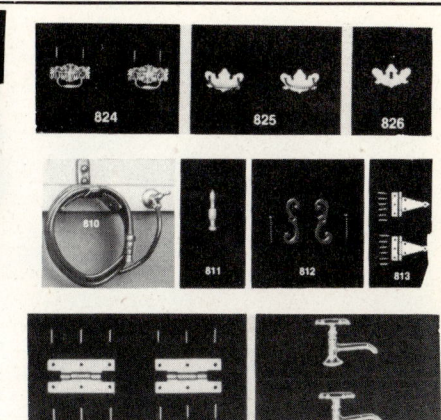

Lumber Supplies

WOOD STORAGE SYSTEM

The Dollhouse Factory™
Suggested Retail Price: $1.95 small, $4.95 large. Catalog No. DHT-2 small, DHT-4 large.
Dimensions: 2"W x 2"H x 25-1/2"L small, 4-1/2"W x 8"H x 25-1/2"L large
Materials: Rigid kraftboard
Wood storage system features rigid rectangular tubing that keeps wood flat and does not contribute to warpage. Small tubes nest into large tube. Economical and practical way to keep your wood neat, clean, and in order. See our catalog for many other unique products.

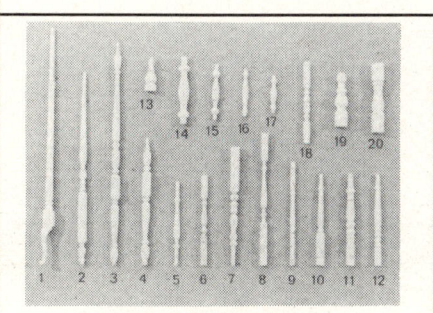

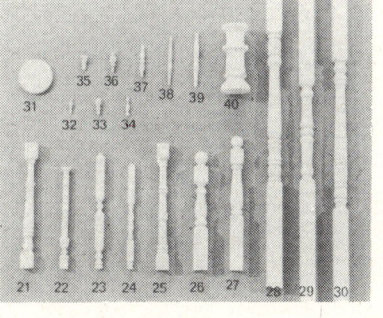

WOOD TURNINGS

The Dollhouse Factory™
Suggested Retail Price: 20¢-$2.50. Catalog Nos. T1 through T40.
Dimensions: 3/8" to 12"

The finest of turnings for use in every facet of construction. Made from maple, basswood, pine, mahogany, or walnut. Medium run custom work done to order. See our catalog for more.

LASER CUT TRIM

Northeastern Scale Models, Inc.
Material: Basswood
The laser allows us to manufacture intricate wood trims for dollhouse and miniature projects. All items are in 1" scale, except as noted. One piece per package except as noted.
GBC-1 1250 Gingerbread Trim $5.20
GBD-1 1251 Gingerbread Trim $5.20
APX-4 1233 Apex Trim $4.50
APX-3 1232 Apex Trim $5.20
APX-5 1235 Apex Trim $4.50
RFA-1 1260 Roof Finial $1.60
RFB-1 1261 Roof Finial $1.60

AGC-1 1270 Gingerbread/Apex Combination. (2 per pkg.) $12.60
Also available in 1/2" scale as follows:
GBC-1A 1252 Gingerbread Trim $2.85
GBD-1A 1253 Gingerbread Trim $2.85
APX-4A 1234 Apex Trim $2.85
APX-5A 1236 Apex Trim $2.85
RFA-1A 1262 Roof Finial $1.15
RFB-1A 1263 Roof Finial $1.15
AGC-1A 1271 Gingerbread/Apex Combination. (2 per pkg.) $8.00
Please see our insert between pages 80 and 81 for more information.

Building Components & Supplies

THE MINIATURES CATALOG, Fourteenth Edition

LASER CUT TRIM

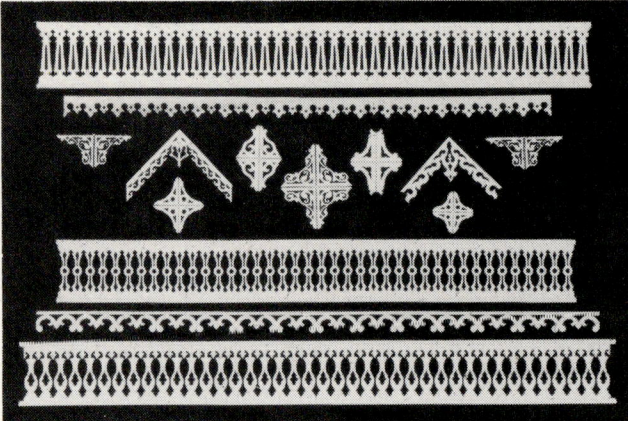

Northeastern Scale Models, Inc.
PBL - 1 1201 Porch Baluster - Assembled with top and bottom rails - $18.95
PBL - 2 1202 Porch Baluster - Assembled with top and bottom rails - $18.95
PBL - 3 1203 Porch Baluster - Assembled with top and bottom rails - $18.95
GBA - 1 1210 Gingerbread Trim - $3.45 (1)
GBB - 1 1211 Gingerbread Trim - $3.45 (1)
BRA - 1 1220 Bracket - $2.95 (4)
BRB - 1 1221 Bracket - $2.05 (4)
BRC - 1 1222 Bracket - $2.05 (4)
BRD - 1 1223 Bracket - $2.05 (4)
BRE - 1 1223 Bracket - $2.05 (4)
APX - 1 1230 Apex Trim - $3.30
APX - 2 1231 Apex Trim - $3.30
Please see our insert between pages 80 and 81 for more information.

WOOD STRIPS AND SHEETS

Northeastern Scale Models, Inc.
Shaded spaces indicate sizes that are available in basswood or mahogany.
Tolerances: Wood strips up to 1" wide are cut to precise dimensions. Sheets 2" wide or more are cut to a close tolerance of 1/8" (3mm.) plus or minus. All strips, sheets, and structural shapes are 22" long or more.
Finish: Because of the inherent character of wood and the tooling employed in cutting, most strips and sheets have one surface smoother than the other. Modelers are advised to inspect stock to take advantage of this.

MM		.75	1.0		1.5	2.0		3.0	4.0		5.0	6.0	8.0		10.0	12.5		25.0	50.0	
▼	IN	1 32	.040	3 64	1 16	5 64	3 32	1 8	5 32	3 16	.200	1 4	5 16	3 8	.400	1 2	3 4	1	2	3	4
	.012	.14	.14	.14	.14	.17	.17	.17													
.5	.020	.14	.14	.14	.14	.17	.17	.17	.19												
.75	1 32	.14	.14	.14	.14	.17	.17	.17	.20	.20		.20	.24	.27		.39	.44	.44	.50	.94	1.26	1.65
1.0	.040		.18	.18	.18	.18	.18	.18	.22	.22		.26	.30	.39		.44	.44	.44	.50	.99	1.26	1.65
	3 64			.20	.20	.20	.20	.20	.24	.24		.31	.35	.39		.44	.44	.44	.55	1.21	1.48	1.92
1.5	1 16				.20	.20	.20	.24	.24	.27		.35	.35	.44		.50	.50	.60	.72	1.21	1.48	1.92
2.0	5 64					.20	.24	.24	.24	.27		.35	.35	.44		.50	.50	.60	.72	1.26	1.60	2.25
	3 32						.24	.24	.24	.27		.27	.35	.50		.50	.55	.60	.72	1.26	1.60	2.25
3.0	1 8							.24	.31	.33	.33	.39	.39	.50		.50	.66	.77	.82	1.38	1.76	2.53
4.0	5 32								.31	.33	.33	.39	.44	.50		.50	.66	.77	.82	1.54	1.82	2.53
	3 16									.39	.39	.44	.50	.64	.66	.72	.81	.88	1.54	1.98	2.80
5.0	.200									.39	.44	.50	.64	.66		.72	.81	.94	1.76	2.25	3.30
6.0	1 4											.50	.50	.70	.70	.82	.88	1.10	1.76	2.25	3.30
8.0	5 16												.72	.82	.82	.88	.96	1.10	1.92	2.64	3.68
	3 8													.82	.82	.88	.96	1.10	1.92	2.64	3.68
10.0	.400														.82	.88	.96	1.10	2.04	2.92	4.12
12.5	1 2															.88	.96	1.15	2.20	3.02	4.24
	3 4																1.10	1.20	2.20	3.35	4.40
25	1																	1.38	2.75	3.80	4.78
50	2																		5.50	7.48	9.24

Millwork

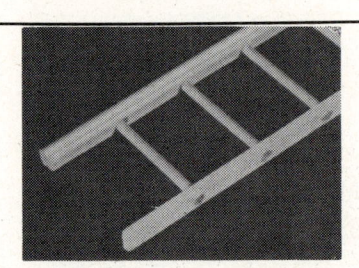

PINE HAND RAILING

Alessio Miniatures
Suggested Retail Price: $2.20
Specifications: 10"L x 2"H. Made of pine.
Railing to be used around tops of staircases.
Also available 10"L x 3"H, 10"L x 2-1/4"H, 4"L x 2"H, and 4"L x 2-1/4"H. $.50 retail.

PINE PORCH RAILINGS

Alessio Miniatures
Suggested Retail Price: $5.50
Material: 1/2" pine on top, 1/4" x 1/4" on the bottom
Dimensions: 24" lengths. Posts 1" apart
Railings to be used on porches, roofs, etc.
American Made.

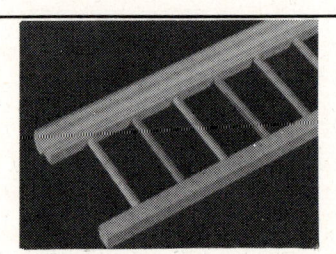

PINE PORCH RAILINGS

Alessio Miniatures
Suggested Retail Price: $5.50
Material: 1/2" pine on top, 1/4" x 1/4" on the bottom
Dimensions: 24" lengths. Posts 3/4" apart
Railings to be used on porches, roofs, etc.
American Made.

Interested in Becoming a Miniatures Manufacturer?

Join the Miniatures Industry Association of America and sell products to retailers across the country.

MIAA
1100-H Brandywine Blvd.
P.O. Box 2188
Zanesville, OH 43702-3288

Prices are approximate and subject to change.

FIMO® MODELING MATERIAL
Eberhard Faber GmbH
Suggested Retail Price: See your dealer.
Catalog No. 8000
Specifications: 55 x 55 x 15 mm/65 g small block, 165 x 55 x 30 mm/350 g large block. FIMO®, the fantastic and most popular modeling material, is the leading product of its kind in Europe. It's versatile and easy to handle, and hardens in the oven at 265°F. (20 to 30 minutes). Available in 42 brilliant colors, it's ideal to create the finest decorative accessories for your dollhouse and to make exciting and imaginative objects (miniatures, figures, fashion jewelry, decorations, pictures, nameplates and a lot more).

APEX TRIM
Houseworks
Suggested Retail Price: $2.95. Catalog No. 7058
Specifications: 3-5/16"L x 3-5/16"L x 4-3/4"W
With elaborate waves of detail, this 45 pitch trim fits perfectly into most roof apexes (the point at which both halves of the roof meet). 2 per package.

ASSORTED BRACKETS
Houseworks
#7028-Post Bracket-Exterior decorative brackets for Victorian detailing. 4 per pkg. 11/16"W x 1-11/16"H x 1-5/16"D. $3.95.
#7027-Eaves Bracket-Smaller exterior decorative brackets for Victorian styling. 4 per pkg. 11/16"W x 1-3/16"H x 1"D. $3.60.

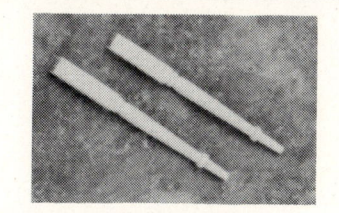

BALUSTERS
Houseworks
Suggested Retail Price: $3.50. Catalog No. 7025.
Specifications: 3/16"W x 2-1/2"L
Most commonly used as spindles on stairs and railings. The square base of the baluster gives it many other potential uses. 12 per package.

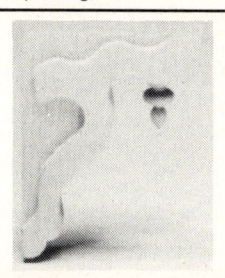

CORBEL BRACKET
Houseworks
Suggested Retail Price: $5.95. Catalog No. 7026.
Specifications: 3/16"W x 1-1/4"H x 1"D
Ornate bracket used side-by-side in the top corners of open interior doorways. Also excellent for exterior detailing. 4 per pkg.

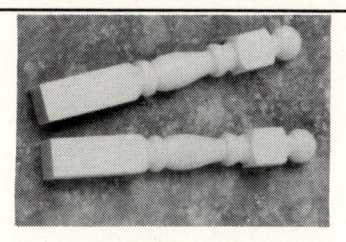

NEWEL POST
Houseworks
Suggested Retail Price: $3.50. Catalog No. 7012.
Specifications: 3-1/2"L x 7/16"W
Handcrafted, turned posts to complete the look of your porch. 6 per package.

PORCH RAILING SET
Houseworks
Suggested Retail Price: $4.50. Catalog No. 7011.
Specifications: Rails measure 18"L
Includes curved top rail and squared bottom rail. Both grooved to accept #7025 and #7009 spindles easily. 2 sets per package.

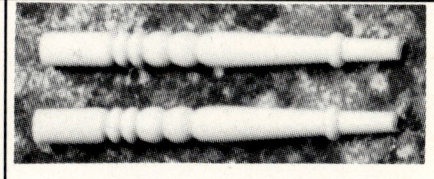

PORCH SPINDLES
Houseworks
Suggested Retail Price: $2.25. Catalog No. 7009.
Specifications: 2-5/8"L x 1/4"W
These multi-purpose spindles can be used on the interior or exterior of the house and even in the yard or walkway as fence spindles. 12 per package.

PORCH TRIM
Houseworks
Suggested Retail Price: $1.50. Catalog No. 7059.
Specifications: 1/8"W x 1-5/8"H x 1"D.
This subtly ornate trim works well on any part of your dollhouse exterior. 2 per pkg.

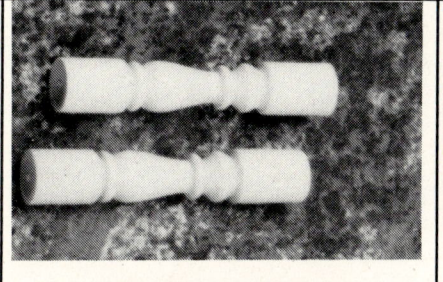

VERANDA SPINDLE
Houseworks
Sug. Retail Price: $3.50. Catalog No. 7029.
Specifications: 2"L x 3/8"W
Completes your front porch or stairway. 12 per package.

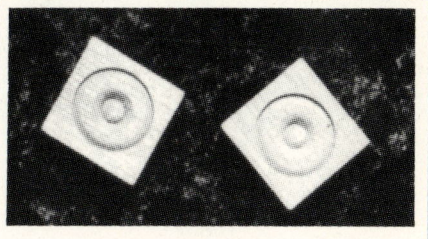

WOOD HEAD BLOCKS
Houseworks
Suggested Retail Price: $2.95. Catalog No. 7064.
Specifications: 9/16" square
Decorative square trim used most commonly on the corners of door frames. 12 per pkg.

Building Components & Supplies

THE MINIATURES CATALOG, Fourteenth Edition

ASSORTED POSTS

Houseworks
#7010-Porch Post-4 per pkg.
Size: 12"L x 7/16"W. $4.25

#7030-Veranda Corner Post-Though the decorative posts are excellent for your veranda, they are most commonly used on the porch from floor to ceiling. 4 per pkg. Size: 1/2"W x 12"L. $5.50

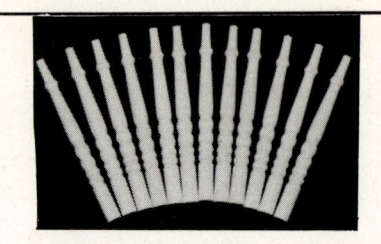

BALUSTERS

Miniature House
Suggested Retail Price: $2.35
Catalog No. MH201
Dimensions: 1/4"W x 2-5/8"L
These detailed spindles create a very distinctive front porch or staircase. Total of 12 per package.

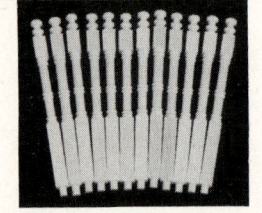

BALUSTERS

Miniature House
Suggested Retail Price: $3.98
Catalog No. MH202
Dimensions: 1/4"W x 3-1/8"L
Highly detailed balusters with dowel stub to stabilize installation. Rounded cap makes spindles work well as newel posts. Total of 12 per package.

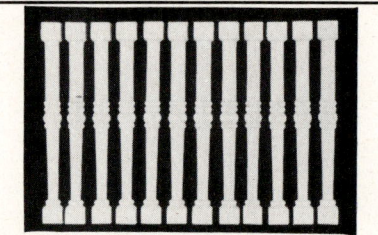

BALUSTERS

Miniature House
Suggested Retail Price: $3.69
Catalog No. MH206A
Dimensions: 3/16"W x 2-5/8"L
Fine detailing and square bases on these spindles finish a staircase or railing. Total of 12 unfinished wood spindles per package.

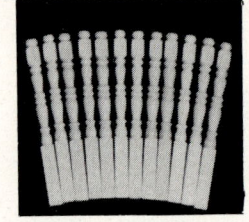

BALUSTERS

Miniature House
Suggested Retail Price: $3.69
Catalog No. MH207
Dimensions: 3/16"W x 2-7/16"L
Unusual rounded cap and high detail make these balusters a good choice. Could be used as a small newel post. Total of 12 unfinished wood balusters per package.

BALUSTERS

Miniature House
Suggested Retail Price: $3.69
Catalog No. MH209
Dimensions: 3/16"W x 2-9/16"L
Detailing and symmetrical style add charm to these balusters. Total of 12 per package.

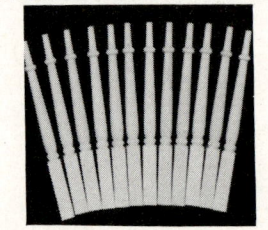

BALUSTERS

Miniature House
Suggested Retail Price: $3.89
Catalog No. MH229
Dimensions: 3/16"W x 2-1/2"L
Fine detailing and square bases on these spindles finish a staircase or railing. Total of 12 unfinished wood balusters per package.

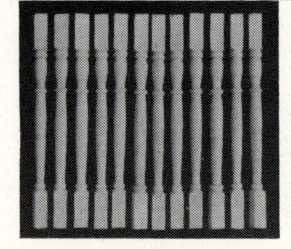

BALUSTERS

Miniature House
Suggested Retail Price: $4.10
Catalog No. MH235
Dimensions: 3/16"W x 2-1/2"L
These spindles have dainty, finely turned detailing. 12 per package.

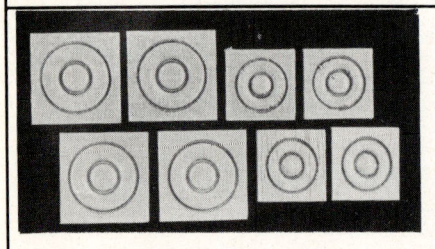

CORNER BLOCKS

Miniature House
Suggested Retail Price: $1.45, 3/4" sq., $1.35, 5/8" sq.
Catalog No. MH236 - 3/4", MH265 - 5/8"
A distinctive addition to trim work on many projects. Four unfinished blocks per package.

NEWEL POSTS

Miniature House
Suggested Retail Price: $3.10
Catalog No. MH200
Dimensions: 7/16"W x 3-11/16"L
Distinctive styling. Posts match the Newel Posts on No. MH252 Stair Kit. Four posts per package.

PORCH FENCE

Miniature House
Suggested Retail Price: $6.98
Catalog No. MH241
Dimensions: 2-1/2"H x 11-3/8"L
Porch fence is assembled and ready to use. Made of unfinished wood. Three per package.

Prices are approximate and subject to change.

PORCH POSTS

Miniature House
Suggested Retail Price: $4.40
Catalog No. MH269
Dimensions: 1/2"W x 11"L
These wood posts have finely turned detail work. Four posts per package.

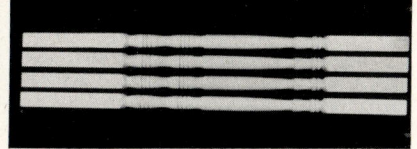

PORCH POSTS

Miniature House
Suggested Retail Price: $4.19
Catalog No. MH290
Dimensions: 7/16"W x 12"L
These wood porch posts are designed in a casual style. Four posts per package.

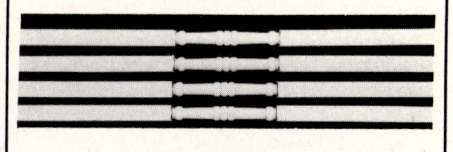

PORCH POSTS

Miniature House
Suggested Retail Price: $3.99
Catalog No. MH210
Dimensions: 7/16"W x 9"L
These wood posts are great to use with a lower porch roof. Four posts per package.

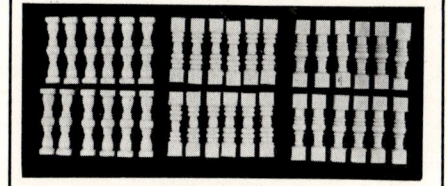

SPINDLES

Miniature House
Suggested Retail Price: $4.10
Catalog No. MH226, MH227, MH228
Dimensions: 1/4"W x 1-1/8"H
A perfect touch of Victorian detailing, to finish your dollhouse or miniature construction. Total of 12 unfinished wood spindles per package.

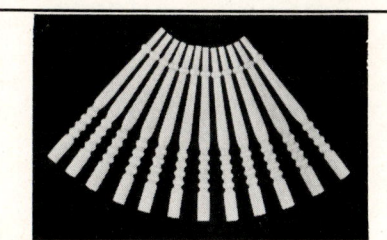

STAIRCASE SPINDLES

Miniature House
Suggested Retail Price: $3.59
Catalog No. MH246.
Dimensions: 3/16"W x 2-5/8"L
Lovely spindles enhance a formal staircase or can create an outstanding porch. Total of 12 unfinished spindles per package.

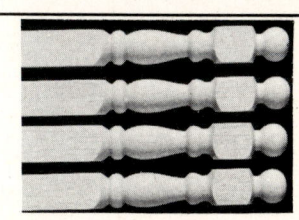

TRADITIONAL NEWEL POSTS

Miniature House
Suggested Retail Price: $2.49
Catalog No. MH204
Dimensions: 7/16" W x 3-7/16" L
These traditional wood newel posts are finely turned and highly detailed. Four per package.

October National Dollhouse & Miniatures Month

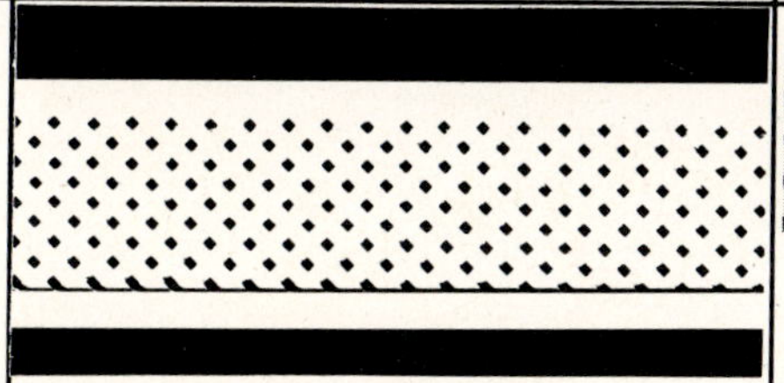

LATTICE

Miniature Lumber Shoppe
Suggested Retail Price: See your dealer
Dimensions: 2" x 12" or 2" x 24"
Scale lattice with adjustable height of 2" or less. #982 is 12" length, #983 is 24" length.

VERANDA CORNER POSTS

Miniature House
Suggested Retail Price: $4.98
Catalog No. MH292
Dimensions: 7/16"W x 12"L
The perfect way to beautifully finish your porch. Four posts per package.

TINY TURNINGS

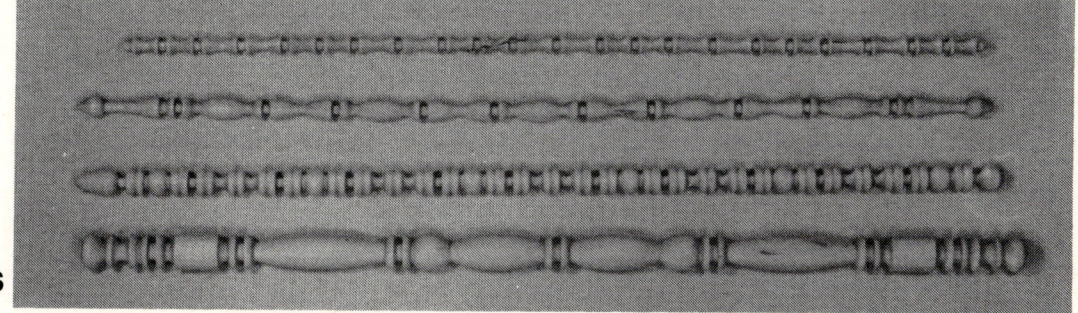

Quad Company
Suggested Retail Price: $6/package
Catalog No. 2000, 4000, 1000, and 3000 top to bottom

Specifications: 1/8" to 1/4" in diameter, 6-1/4" to 6-3/4" long
Finely detailed hardwood turnings. The unique interlocking design of "tiny turnings" enables them to fit together neatly and hold with just a dab of glue. Use for porch posts, chair and table legs, fences, gingerbread and more!

Building Components & Supplies

THE MINIATURES CATALOG, *Fourteenth Edition* 101

NORTHEASTERN SCALE MODELS
MOULDING AND PANELS (All moulding are 24" long)

Description	Number	Size	Price
QUARTER ROUND	364QRD	3/64	.60
	116QRD	1/16	.65
	564QRD	5/64	.65
	332QRD	3/32	.65
	18QRD	1/8	.80
HALF ROUND	364HRD	3/64	.60
	116HRD	1/16	.65
	564HRD	5/64	.65
	332HRD	3/32	.65
	18HRD	1/8	.80
	532HRD	5/32	.85
	316HRD	3/16	.85
	14HRD	1/4	.90
ROUNDS	364RND	3/64	.60
	116RND	1/16	.65
	564RND	5/64	.65
	332RND	3/32	.65
	18RND	1/8	.80
COVE	116COV	1/16	.65
	564COV	5/64	.65
	332COV	3/32	.65
	18COV	1/8	.80
	532COV	5/32	.85
	316COV	3/16	.85
	14COV	1/4	.90
DOUBLE BEAD	364DBL	3/64	.60
	116DBL	1/16	.65
	564DBL	5/64	.65
	332DBL	3/32	.65
	18DBL	1/8	.80
PICTURE FRAMES	PFA-3	3/32	.65
	PFA-4	1/8	.80
	PFA-6	3/16	.85
	PFA-8	1/4	.90
	PFB-4	1/8	.80
	PFB-6	3/16	.85
	PFB-8	1/4	.90
	PFC-6	3/16	.85
	PFC-8	1/4	.90
	PFD-4	1/8	.80
	PFD-6	3/16	.85
	PFE-5	5/32	.85
	PFE-6	3/16	.85
CROWN/ CORNICE	COA-10	5/16	.94
	COA-16	1/2	1.20
	COB-8 (1/2" scale)	1/4	.77
CORNER ANGLE	TRA-12	3/8	1.80
	TRA-16	1/2	1.92
CORNER BLOCK	CBA-18	9/16	2.15
	CBB-18	9/16	2.15

Description	Number	Size	Price
BASEBOARD	BBA-8 (1/2" scale)	1/4	.85
	BBA-16	1/2	1.20
	BBB-16	1/2	1.20
	BBC-16	1/2	1.20
	BBD-16	1/2	1.20
CHAIR RAIL	CRA-6	3/16	.80
	CRA-8	1/4	.85
	CRB-8	1/4	.85
SUB-RAIL	HRC-10	5/16	.90
HAND RAIL	HRA-8	1/4	.96
	HRA-12	3/8	1.20
	HRA-16	1/2	1.55
HAND RAIL	HRB-10	5/16	1.30
PORCH RAIL TOP	PRA-9	9/32	1.20
PORCH RAIL BOTTOM	PRB-8	1/4	.82
DOOR & WINDOW CASING	DCA-8 (1/2" scale)	1/4	.85
	DCA-16	1/2	1.20
	DCB-8	1/4	.85
	DCB-12	3/8	1.10
	DCC-16	1/2	1.20
	DCD-16	1/2	1.20
	DCE-12	3/8	1.10
	DCF-12	3/8	1.10
	DCG-16	1/2	1.20
DOOR JAMB	DJA-16	1/2	1.20
	DJB-16	1/2	1.20
THRESHOLD	THA-24	3/4	1.75
DOOR FRAMES	DFA-14	7/16	1.38
	DFA-20	5/8	1.55
	DFA-24	3/4	1.65
	DFA-14G	7/16	1.38
	DFA-20G	5/8	1.55
	DFA-24G	3/4	1.65
DOOR PANELS Raised on both sides	DPA-32-3	2 3/16 x 3	1.10
	DPA-32-6	2x3	1.10
	DPA-48-2	2 3/16 x 3	1.10
	DPA-70-1	2 3/16 x 2 3/16	.88
WINDOW HEADER	WHA-11	.335	1.05
	WHA-15	.460	1.38
	WHA-16	1/2	1.00
WINDOW JAMB	WJA-11	.335	1.00
	WJA-15	.460	1.25
	WJA-16	1/2	1.25
WINDOW SILL	WSA-16	1/2	1.25
	WSA-20	5/8	1.38

Description	Number	Size	Price
WINDOW SASH	SFA-4	1/8	.80
	SFA-5	5/32	.85
	SFA-5G	5/32G	.85
	SFA-6	3/16	.85
	SFA-8	1/4	.90
WINDOW OUTSIDE CASING	WCA-12	.335	1.05
	WCA-16	1/2	1.38

HARDWARE pg. 6 in catalog

Description	Number	Size	Price
BUTT HINGES —doz.	HWA-10	5/16 x 3/8	5.00 per doz.
PIANO HINGE —ea.	HWA-250		7.95
DOOR KNOB/ DUMMY BRASS	HWC-1		3.20 ea.
DOOR KNOB WORKING	HWC-2		8.50 ea.
DOOR KNOB TEMPLATE	HWC-3		2.50 ea.
FLATWIRE		.010x1/16	.40 per ft.

MISCELLANEOUS Available in 24" lengths pg. 6 in catalog

Description	Number	Size	Price
SHUTTER FRAME	SFC-5	5/32	.85
	SFC-6	3/16	.85
SHUTTER STOCK	CLC-5	3 1/2 x 24	3.68
STAIR STRINGER	SRA-14	3/4 x 14	1.10
	SRA-22	3/4 x 22	1.38
STAIR RISER	SRB-20	5/8	.65
STAIR TREAD	SRC-28	7/8	.82
GUTTER	GA-12	3/8	1.38
WAINSCOT TRIM	MMA-6		.90
	MMB-6		.90
	MMC-6		.90
WAINSCOT PANELS (Raised on one side only)	DPB-32-3	2 3/16 x 3	1.10
	DPB-32-6	2 x 3	1.10
	DPB-48-2	2 3/16 x 3	1.10
	DPB-70-1	2 3/16 x 2 3/16	.88
FLOORING (RANDOM)		1/16 x 3 1/2 x 24	2.45

Prices are approximate and subject to change.

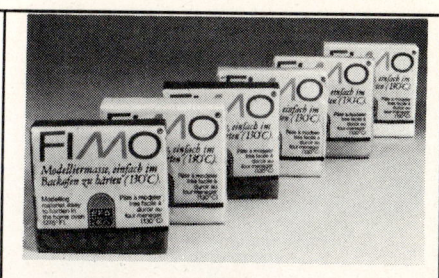

Modeling Compounds

FIMO®
Dee's Delights
We import FIMO® and sell through dealers only. Offering three sizes of blocks, kits and lacquer. We have 42 colors and three sizes available. The miniaturist's first choice. Send for a list of dealers in your area.

CERNIT NO. 1 MODELING COMPOUND
Handcraft Designs, Inc.
Suggested Retail Price: See your dealer.
Catalog Nos. KC510 -KC529
Dimensions: 65 grams (2.3 ozs.) and larger blocks
Superior modeling medium, able to be cured in home oven. Known for its translucence and superior elasticity, Cernit is the choice of professional miniaturists making foods, flowers and dolls. 18 standard colors in 65-gram blocks plus larger blocks in white, black, flesh and bisque. 12 pearlescent colors and six neon/day-glo colors for jewelry and crafts. Doll by Kit Cropper.

MODELING COMPOUNDS
Model Builders Supply
Vinamold - flexible reusable molding compound. Three consistencies. Cernit - Alumilite casting plastic, liquid to solid in three minutes - specialty casting plasters - clear casting resins - color pastes - R.T.V. molding compound.

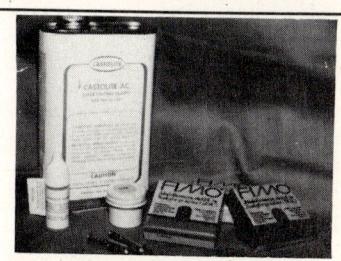

FIMO AND RESIN
"Pannikins" by M.E.
Suggested Retail Price: $1.89 to $10.79
Catalog/Project Booklet: $4.50
Full line of Fimo, resins and dyes plus all related supplies such as cutters, instruction books and empties for miniature foods and beverages. Retail only.

Moldings

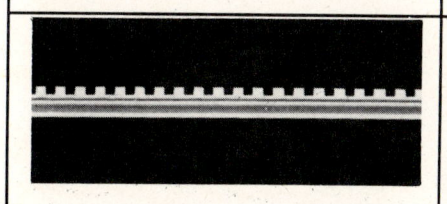

COVE DENTIL MOLDING
Alessio Miniatures
Suggested Retail Price: $2
Dimensions: 3/32" x 1/4", 22" long
Catalog No. 23A
This molding provides the perfect finishing touch for the top of your room, porch or roofline.

DENTIL MOLDING
Alessio Miniatures
Suggested Retail Price: $1.10
Dimensions: 3/32" x 1/4", 22 long
Catalog No. 23.
This dentil molding is to be used on roof eaves and around the tops of rooms.

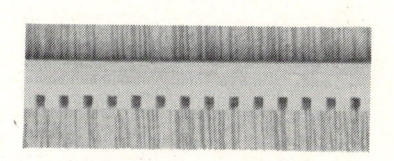

DENTIL MOLDINGS
Alessio Miniatures
Suggested Retail Price: $ 1.10 per length
Dimensions: 24" lengths. Made of pine. 1/8" x 3/8". Catalog no. 19.
Dentil moldings to be used on roof eaves, around top of rooms, etc. American made.

Building Components & Supplies

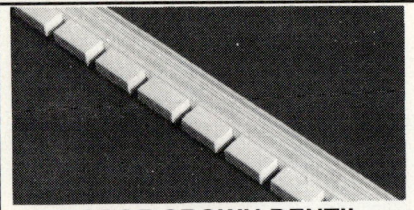

LARGE CROWN DENTIL MOLDING

Alessio Miniatures
Suggested Retail Price: $2/length
Dimensions: 1/8" x 3/8", 22" long. Made of pine.
Dentil moldings to be used on roof eaves, around top of rooms, etc. American made.

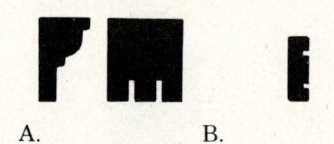

A. B. C. D.

MOLDINGS

Houseworks
A. #7008-Dentil Crown Molding. Size: 18"L. $1.75.
B. #7041-Door & Window Casing. Size: 18"L. 80¢.

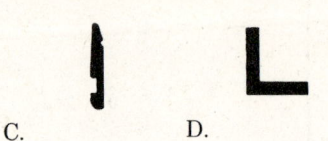

MOLDINGS

Houseworks
C. #7042-Baseboard. Size: 18"L- 95¢
D. #7045-Corner Molding. Size 3/8" x 3/8" x 24"- $1.20.

PEDIMENTS

Houseworks
#7071- Federal Circle Pediment-This original design will give your windows a look never seen before. Style matches any Federal dollhouse design. 2 per pkg. Size: 1-3/8"H x 3-1/8"W. $4.95.
#7070-Federal Hooded Pediment-Sleek, intricate detailing in this pediment will give you an easy way to enhance your dollhouse exterior. 2 per pkg. Size: 1-3/16"H x 3-1/2"W. $4.95.
#7072-Deerfield Pediment-Now all of your windows can match your Deerfield door. This pediment boasts a delicately scrolled design with the most intricate detail ever seen in a pediment. 2 per pkg. Size: 1-1/8"H x 3-1/2"W. $9.50.

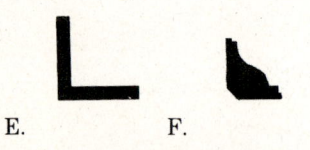

E. F. G. H. I. J.

MOLDINGS

Houseworks
E. #7046-Corner Molding. Size: 1/2" x 1/2" x 24". $1.50.
F. #7047-Crown Molding. Size: 3/8" x 18". $.85.

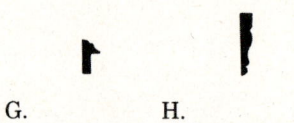

MOLDINGS

Houseworks
G. #7048-Chair Rail Molding. Size: 1/4" x 18". $.75.
H. #7056-3 Stepped Door & Window Casing. Size: 18"L. $.85.

MOLDINGS

Houseworks
I. #7060-Roof Ridge Molding. Size: 22"L. $2.99.
J. #7061-Roof Ridge Molding. Small picket. Size: 22"L. $4.99.

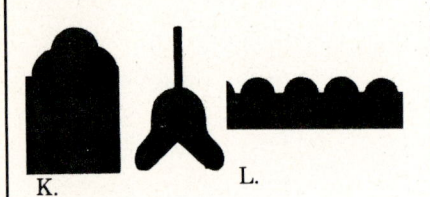

K. L. M. N.

MOLDINGS

Houseworks
K. #7062-Roof Ridge Molding. Large picket. Size: 22"L. $4.99.
L. #7063- Small Gingerbread Trim. Size: 55"L. $3.25.

MOLDINGS

Houseworks
M. #7065-Large Gingerbread Trim. Size: 44"L. $3.25.
N. #7069-Small Crown Molding. Size: 18"L. $.75

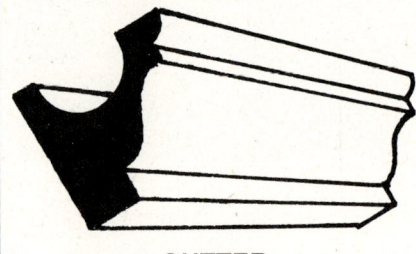

GUTTER

Miniature Lumber Shoppe
Suggested Retail Price: See your dealer
Finishing trim that is beautiful as well as functional. 32" length minimizes splicing #890.

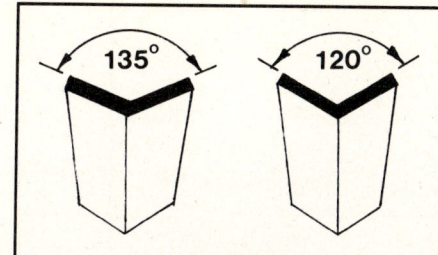

CHEVRON

Miniature Lumber Shoppe
Suggested Retail Price: See your dealer
Basswood trim for octagon and hexagon bays. Available with a 1/4" face or a 3/8" face. Thickness is 1/16" and length is 24".

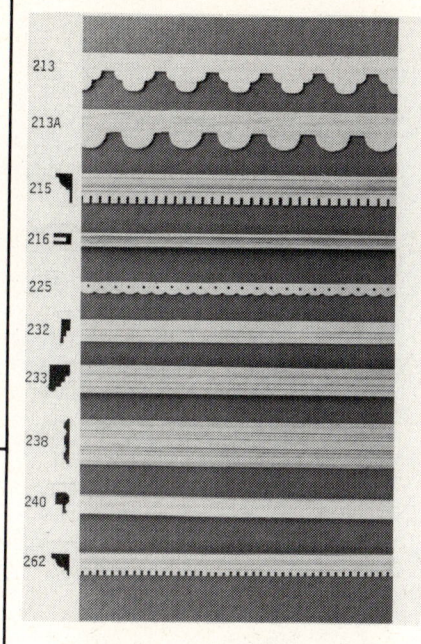

DECORATIVE WOOD TRIM

Miniature House
Suggested Retail Price: $1.98 - $2.98
Catalog No. MH213 - MH262
Dimensions: 24"L
Lovely trims are carved, die-cut and/or embossed and are authentically designed for exterior and interior uses.

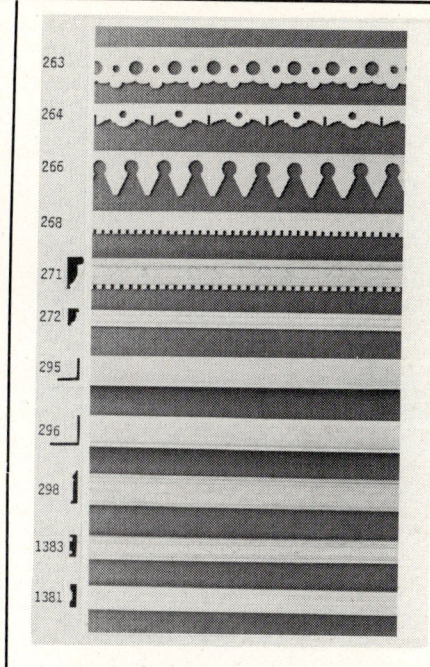

DECORATIVE WOOD TRIM

Miniature House
Suggested Retail Price: $.75 - $2.98
Catalog No. MH263 - MH1383
Dimensions: 24"L
Variety of gingerbreads, cornices and other trims. Uses are limited only by one's imagination.

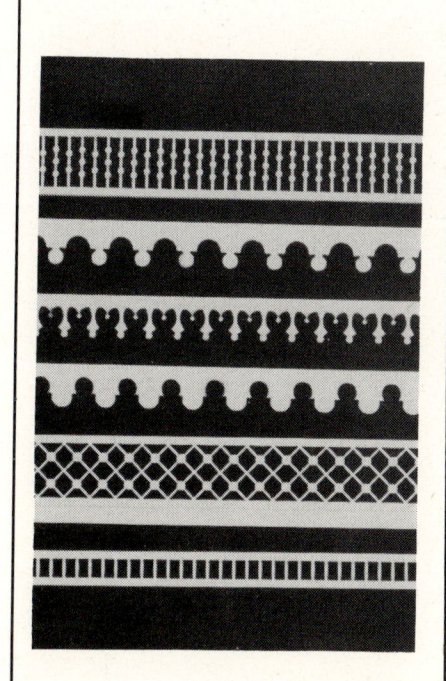

LASER CUT TRIMS

Laser Tech
Suggested Retail Price: (top to bottom) #ET-120 $6.95; #RT-130 $2.95; #RT-121 $5.95; #RT-131 $2.95; #GEX-029 $4.95; #GEX-028 $2.50
Made of 3/32 basswood. A variety of trims which uses are limited only by ones' imagination. They range in length from 5-3/4" to 12"L.

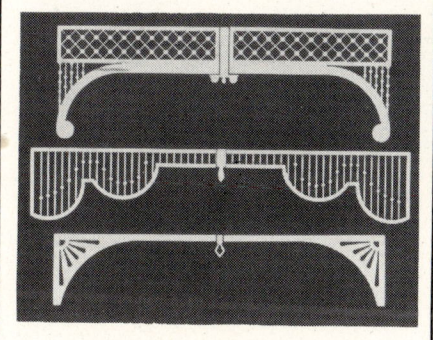

LASER CUT GRILLES

Laser Tech
Suggested Retail Price: (top to bottom) #G-031 $9.95; #G-030 $8.95; #SA-035 $7.25
Elegant grilles that are made in three pieces to be easily trimmed to fit any porch or room opening. SA-035 is also available in 1/2" scale.

MOLDINGS

Unique Miniatures
Cast in polyester resin. Can be painted or stained. All moldings are 18" in length. The widths of the moldings vary from 3/8" on the narrowest to 1" on the widest. Moldings can be used as cornices and in conjunction with ceiling appliques. Moldings are ideal for edge trim around a table or cabinet. Many styles to choose from. Send $2 for a complete catalog. Made in U.S.A.

Building Components & Supplies

THE MINIATURES CATALOG, Fourteenth Edition 105

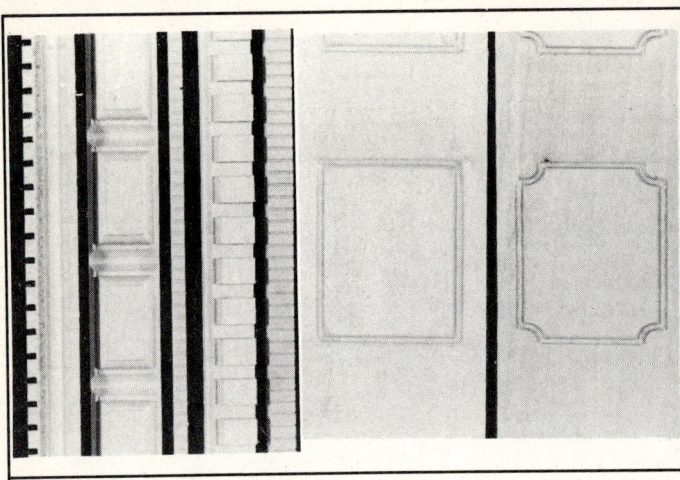

DECORATIVE TRIMS

Miniature Manors
Suggested Retail Price: $1-$10.95. Catalog Nos. 501-710.
Specifications: Most styles 22" to 24" long
Material: 500 series carved basswood, 700 series embossed, carved and die-cut in various types of wood
Authentically designed miniature trims for exterior and interior uses. Many styles and sizes perfect for use in Colonial, Victorian, and other period miniatures as cornice, chair-rail, and wainscoting. Other styles can be used as exterior gingerbread around eaves, gables, porches, bays, windows, and doors. Great for San Francisco Victorians.

Roofing Materials

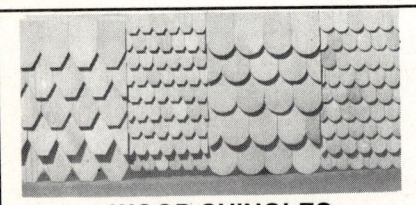

WOOD SHINGLES

Betty's Wooden Miniatures
Dimensions: Four 1" styles, three 1/2" styles
We have two sizes each of the hexagon and fishscale and three sizes of shakes. The shakes are tapered from top to bottom for a great look. We make them all in the USA. All our shingles are precise and smoothly machined of clear pine.

DEER WEATHERVANE
Clare-Bell Brass Works
Suggested Retail Price: $20.50
Catalog No. 1913100

SHINGLES

Alessio Miniatures
Suggested Retail Price: $2.50 - $3.30/sq. ft. (approximately).
Dimensions: approximately 1" x 3/4"
American made pine, redwood, cedar and hardwood shingles. All shingles are processed by hand to insure our high quality standards. Also available, our cedar fish scale and cedar hexagon shingles, as shown in photo. No one makes a higher quality shingle! American made.

EAGLE WEATHERVANE
Clare-Bell Brass Works
Suggested Retail Price: $20.50
Catalog No. 1916100

GABRIEL WEATHERVANE
Clare-Bell Brass Works
Suggested Retail Price: $20.50
Catalog No. 1915100

Prices are approximate and subject to change.

ROOSTER WEATHERVANE
Clare-Bell Brass Works
Suggested Retail Price: $20.50
Catalog No. 1910100
Striking brass weathervanes. All have exquisite details and turn.

SCHOONER WEATHERVANE
Clare-Bell Brass Works
Suggested Retail Price: $20.50
Catalog No. 1918100

TRAIN WEATHERVANE
Clare-Bell Brass Works
Suggested Retail Price: $20.50
Catalog No. 1912100

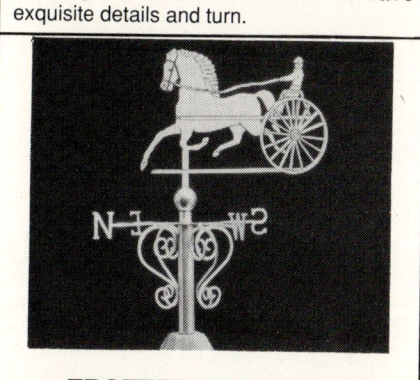

TROTTER WEATHERVANE
Clare-Bell Brass Works
Suggested Retail Price: $20.50
Catalog No. 1911100

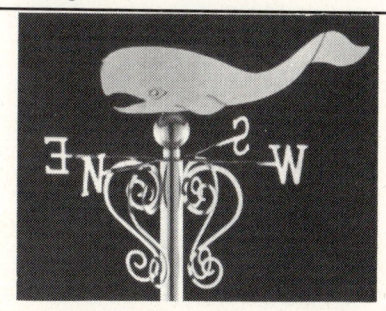

WHALE WEATHERVANE
Clare-Bell Brass Works
Suggested Retail Price: $20.50
Catalog No. 1917100

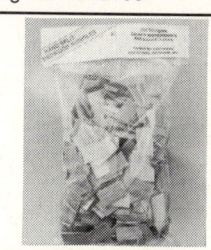

PLAIN SHINGLES
Dura-Craft, Inc.
Suggested Retail Price: See your local dealer
Catalog No. SH70
Split redwood shingles with hand-cut look. 350/bag with header. Covers approximately 260 sq.in. per bag.

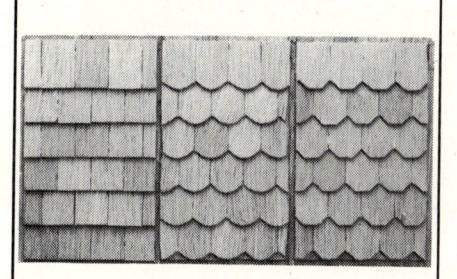

WOOD SHINGLES
Greenleaf Products, Inc.
Suggested Retail Price: $4.50 and up.
Catalog No. 9002 rectangular, No. 9005 fishscale, No. 9006 octagonal.
Greenleaf's wood veneer shingles come in three shapes - rectangular, fishscale and octagonal. They paint and stain beautifully - choose the style that suits your taste. There are 300 shingles per package covering 170 square inches; amounts required for Greenleaf houses are printed on the package headers.

CORRUGATED ALUMINUM ROOFING
Homestead Homes
Dimensions: 2" x 7"
Usable as roofing or siding. Eight sheets per package. Will cover 112 sq. in., 1" scale.

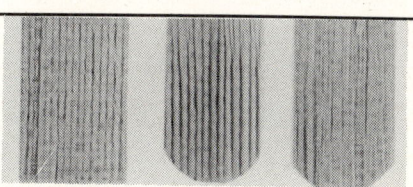

SPLIT CEDAR SHINGLES
Jan's Small World
Suggested Retail Price: $5 - $6.95, $10 - $11.95. Catalog No. CN105.
Dimensions: 1000 pieces covers approximately four sq. feet - 1-1/4" x 3/4"
High quality authentic split shingles. Choose from standard, octagon, or fishscale style. Available in 1/2" scale also. Most orders shipped within two weeks.

TRADITIONAL DORMER
Houseworks
Suggested Retail Price: $10.95
Catalog No. 7002
Specifications: 4"W x 5-1/4"H x 6-3/16"D
Assembled and ready-to-be-dressed out with your choice of windows. Designed for 45° pitch roof.

Building Components & Supplies

THE MINIATURES CATALOG, *Fourteenth Edition* 107

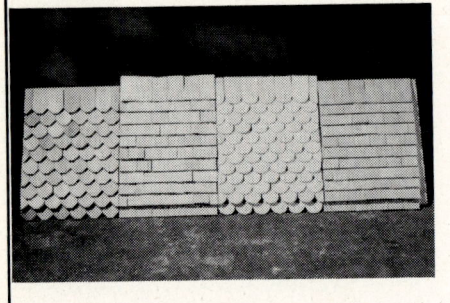

SHINGLES

Houseworks
Suggested Retail Price: $23.50
($18 for #7106)
Catalog No. 7103: Octagon Butt Shingles. Hand split cedar shakes. 1000 pcs. per pkg. Covers 760 square inches. Can be reversed for use as square butts. Catalog No. 7104: Square Butt Shingles. Classic hand split cedar shakes. 1000 pcs. per pkg. Covers 760 square inches. Catalog No. 7105: Fishscale Shingles. Half circle wooden butts. 1000 pcs. per pkg. Covers 760 square inches. Catalog No. 7106: Square Butt Shingles. Douglas Fir Shingles taken from the hearts of U.S. forests. 1000 pcs. per pkg. Covers 760 square inches.

SHINGLES

Houseworks
Suggested Retail Price: $2.50
Pictured left to right, Catalog No. 7003: Octagon Butt Shingles are made of handsplit cedar. 100 per bag, covers approximately 76 sq. inches. Catalog No. 7004: 3/4" W x 1-1/4" L wooden shingles can be used to create the traditional Early American Shaker roof. 100 pieces per bag. Catalog No. 7005: 3/4" W x 1-1/4" L Fishscale roofing shingles are made of high quality wood and will add Victorian styling to your dollhouse. Over 100 pieces per bag, covers 76 sq. inches. Mounting instructions included.

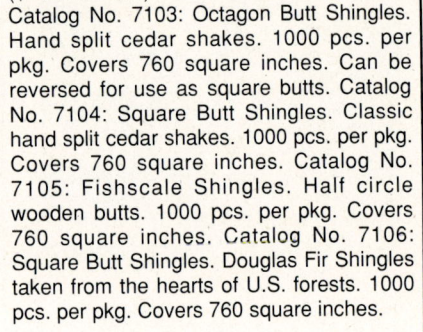

CHIMNEYS

Lil Crafts
Suggested Retail Price: $5.50
Dimensions: 2" x 2" x 2-3/4"H
Ready to install on roof peak or slope. Extension for increasing height of chimneys or for flat roof applications. Available in brick red. Cat. #405 peak, Cat. #406 slope, Cat. #407 extension.

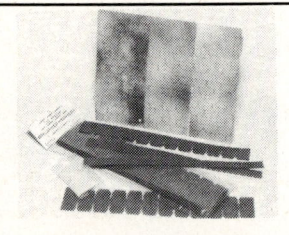

STRIP SHINGLES

Lil Crafts
Suggested Retail Price: $2.20
Chipboard strips go on fast, stay flat. Paint to suit and sprinkle with grit included. Separate starter and capping strips means shingles cover full 144 sq. in. Cat. #601.

CEDAR SHINGLES

Miniature House
Suggested Retail Price: $19.50
Catalog No. MH259
Dimensions: 3/4"W x 1-1/4"H
These square-built shingles add the perfect finishing touch to a dollhouse roof. 1000 pieces per bag. Covers approximately 760 square inches.

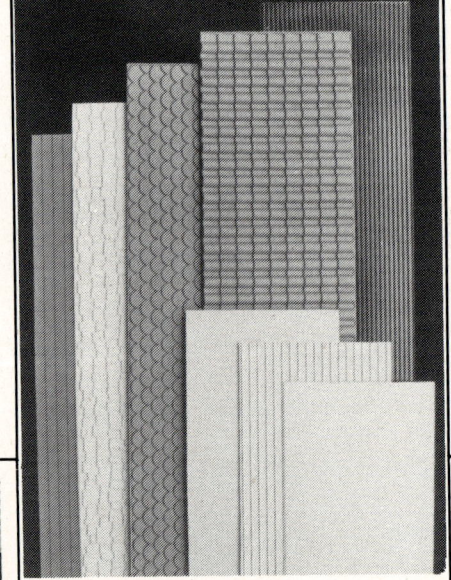

PLASTIC FORMED SHEETS

Model Builders Supply
Some of MBS's 112 designs of formed plastic sheets, all 7" x 24" at $6.75 Canadian. Round tile, brick red or slate gray. Regular shingle, brick red or slate gray. Spanish roof tile, brick red or slate gray. Wood shakes, sandy gray. Ribbed metal, sandy gray or slate gray. Clear corrugated panelling. U.S. customers, see "Plastruct".

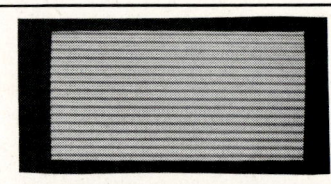

3-D POLYSTYRENE TIN ROOF PANEL

Miniature House
Suggested Retail Price: $4.75
Catalog No. MH5335
Dimensions: 4" x 8"
Prepainted to look like galvanized tin roofing, this realistic replica has many possible applications. Three panels per package.

FOR FAST SERVICE, VISIT YOUR LOCAL MINIATURES SHOP

3-D POLYSTYRENE ADOBE ROOF PANEL

Miniature House
Suggested Retail Price: $6.25
Catalog No. MH5330
Dimensions: 10-3/4"W x 16-3/4"L
This Spanish type roof panel is pre-painted red adobe clay color. Easily cut with scissors or razor and amazingly realistic.

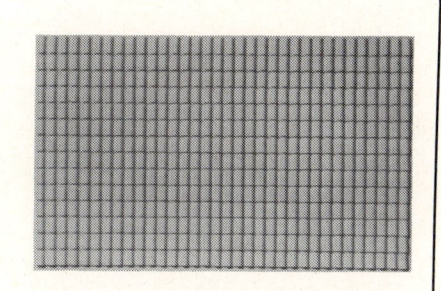

GENUINE SLATE SHINGLES

Mini Treasure House
Suggested Retail Price: $13.50 for 75 pieces, 40 sq. in. , $21.95 for 125 pieces, 72 sq.in. $39.95 for 250 pieces, 144 sq.in. $74.95 for 500 pieces, 288 sq. in.
Material: Natural dark grey slate
Handsplit, easy to apply, texture and thickness will vary just like full size slate. Shingles are approximately 7/8" wide and can be trimmed to add extra variation. The exposed edge is smooth and can be worked to give it a unique treatment. The ultimate in custom roofing.

PLASTIC PATTERNED SHEETS

Plastruct
Suggested Retail Price: $3.50 - $7 plus shipping
Plastic patterned sheets in various scales and patterns including asphalt shingle, Spanish roof tile, scalloped tile, wood shake shingles and ribbed roof. Brick, stone, siding and flooring sheets also available.

SPLIT CEDAR SHINGLES
Miniature Manors
Suggested Retail Price: *Economy Squares - $3.60/250 pieces, $6.50/500 pieces, $11.50/1000 pieces; 1" Scale Styles - $3.70/250 pieces, $6.95/500 pieces, $12.95/1000 pieces
Our shingles have exceptional quality, authenticity and in-scale cut and texture. A must for roofing and siding Colonial, Victorian and other period architecture. 1/2" scale shingles are also available. Write for more information and samples. *Economy Squares are 3/4"W x 1-1/2"H x 1/24" thick and 1000 pieces cover up to 1000 sq.in. The 1" scale styles include squares, octagons, fishscale and decorative Victorian styles.

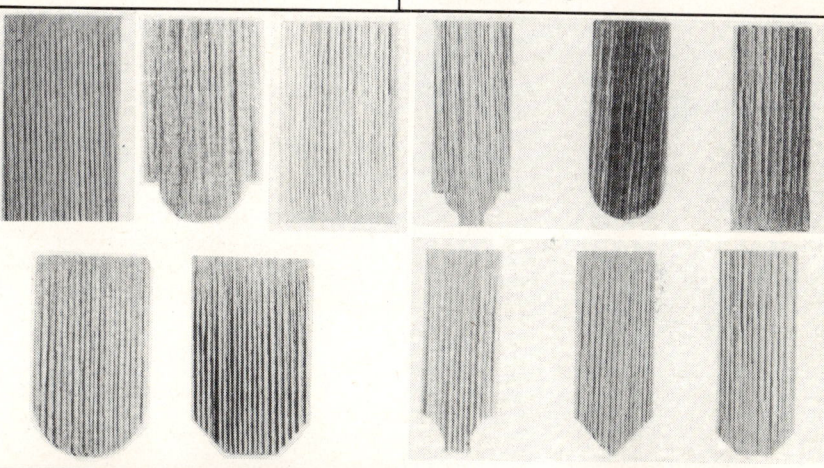

SLATE ROOFS

Rossco Products
Suggested Retail Price: $51.95 for 13" x 33", $61.95 for 17" x 42"
Made of rigid polyurethane foam. Approximately 3/16" thickness. Larger dimensions easily achieved without visible joints using multiple sheets. Easily cut or formed with any woodworking tool. Apply over plywood roof. Also now available in rubber 1/16" x 10" x 10" approximately. Make larger with interlocks. $9.95 ea.

ASPHALT ROOFING SHINGLES
What's Next?
Suggested Retail Price: $7 per sq. ft.
New museum quality Granular Asphalt Shingles. Real multi-colored granules are imbedded into the asphalt, just like real shingles. They come in a continuous belt that pulls directly out of the box. Six colors - desert tan, canyon red, spruce green, slate gray/white and black. Rectangular and hexagonal styles. Also available in a simulated slate finish.

Building Components & Supplies

THE MINIATURES CATALOG, *Fourteenth Edition*

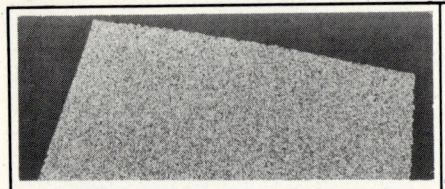

ROLL ROOFING - ASPHALT
What's Next?
Suggested Retail Price: $2 - $4.99
Material: Asphalt with multi-colored granules imbedded in the asphalt.
Same material and colors as our Museum Shingle except it comes in a 6" x 24" sheet. Use for widows walks, mansard roofs, flat roofs on stores and houses. Also use plain black for tar paper roofs.

CEDAR SHAKES
What's Next?
Suggested Retail Price: $2. Covers 76 sq. in. Over 100 pieces.
Real Western Red Cedar Shakes. Wood is weathered by our special process, making staining unnecessary. Each shake precision cut in exact scale. Color and grain variations run through each package to enhance beauty of finished roof.

Shutters

CARLSON RAISED BAND SHUTTER
American Craft Products
Suggested Retail Price: $6 for 2 pair
Catalog No. 8428
Dimensions: 1-1/4" x 4-13/16"
Made of clear pine for standard size component. Foremost in quality and design. American made.

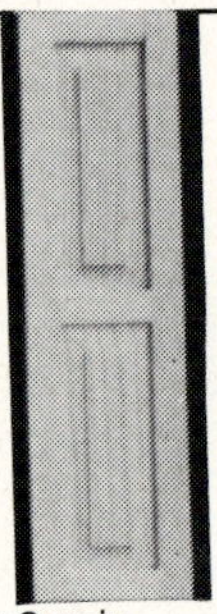

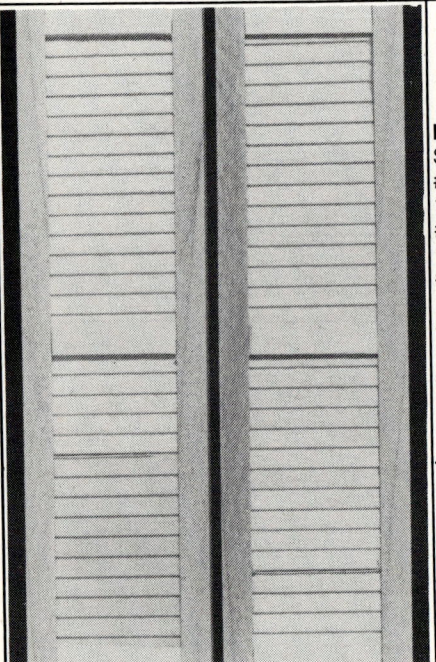

ASSORTED SHUTTERS
Houseworks
Suggested Retail Price: $2.95.
#5018-Louvered Shutters-2 pcs./pkg. Size: 1-1/2"W x 5-5/8"H.
#5019-Louvered Shutters-2 pcs./pkg. Size: 1-7/16"W x 5-3/16"H.
#5025-Louvered Shutters-2 pcs./pkg. Size: 1-1/4"W x 44-5/8"H.
#5022-3 Panel "Americana" Shutter-2 pcs./pkg. Size: 1-1/4"W x 4-11/16"H.
#5017-2 Panel Jamestown Shutter-2 per pkg. Size: 1-1/4"W x 4-11/16"H.

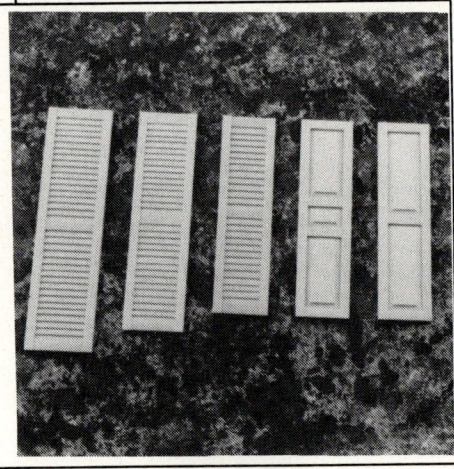

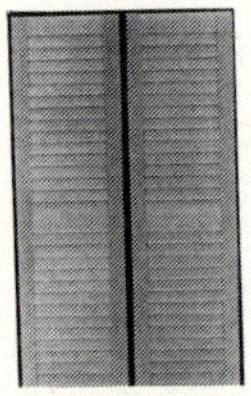

CUSTOM MADE SHUTTERS
Alessio Miniatures
Suggested Retail Price: $ 3/pair
Dimensions: made to order
These shutters are available in widths of 1", 1-1/4", and 1-1/2", and custom made lengths.

LOUVERED SHUTTERS
Miniature House
Suggested Retail Price: $2.95
Catalog No. MH293
Dimensions: 5-3/16"H x 1-3/8"W
These louvered shutters fit standard working and non-working windows. Two per package.

LOUVERED SHUTTERS
Miniature House
Suggested Retail Price: $2.95
Catalog No. MH294
Dimensions: 4-5/8"H x 1/5/16"W
These louvered shutters are precisely detailed and add an additional touch of realism to your dollhouse. Two per package.

Prices are approximate and subject to change.

Siding Materials

CLAPBOARD SIDING

Houseworks
#7035-1/4" Lap width Clapboard Siding. Each sheet is 24" long and 3-1/2" wide. $26.95
#7036-3/8" Lap width Clapboard Siding. Each sheet is 24" long and 3-1/2" wide. $26.95
#7037-1/2" Lap width Clapboard Siding. Each sheet is 24" long and 3-1/2" wide. $26.95
#7038-1/4" Lap Clapboard Siding. Each sheet is 12" long and 3-1/2" wide. $13.50
#7039-3/8" Lap Clapboard Siding. Each sheet is 12" long and 3-1/2" wide. $13.50
#7040-1/2" Lap Clapboard Siding. Each sheet is 12" long and 3-1/2" wide. $13.50
All standard packs include 10 sheets.

PLASTIC FORMED SHEETS

Model Builders Supply
More of MBS's easy-to-use formed plastic sheets. Three spacings of clapboard, two per inch and three per inch, both 7" x 24" $6.75. Four per inch 7" x 12" $3.95. Board and batten at three per inch and four per inch 7" x 12" $3.95. Planking at 3/16" spacing and 1/4" spacing $3.95. All available either white or sandy gray. New 12" x 24" stucco in two textures in white or adobe $10.95 each Canadian. U.S. customers, see "Plastruct".

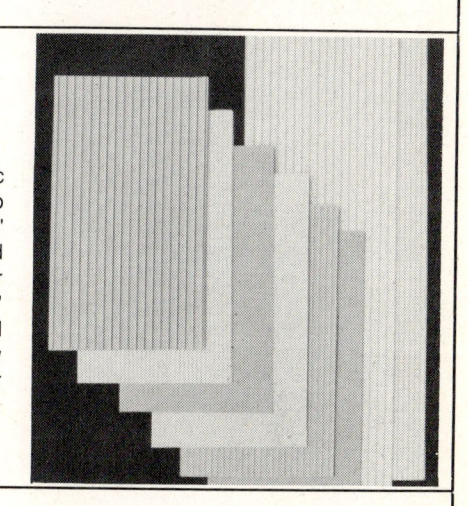

CLAPBOARD SIDING

Miniature House
Catalog No. MH5450, MH5455, MH5460; 3-1/2" x 24"L - $23.95. MH5465, MH5470 and MH5475; 3-1/2" x 12"L - $12.98. Unfinished wood siding is available in 24" and 12" lengths and comes 10 pieces per pack. 24" sidings are MH5450–1/4" lap; MH5455–3/8" lap; MH5460–1/2" lap. 12" sidings are MH5465–1/4" lap; MH5470–3/8" lap; MH5475–1/2" lap.

PLASTIC PATTERNED SHEETS

Plastruct
Suggested Retail Price: $3.50 - $7 plus shipping
Plastic patterned sheets in various scales and patterns including corrugated, planking, clapboard, stucco, brick, block and wood shake shingle. Roofing and flooring sheets also available.

Clapboard

Sheet size .080" × 3½" × 22"

CLB-8	1/4	2.45
CLB-12	3/8	2.45
CLB-16	1/2	2.45

Sheet size .080" × 3½" × 36"

CLB-8-36	1/4	3.95
CLB-12-36	3/8	3.95
CLB-16-36	1/2	3.95

Beaded Clapboard

CLE-12	3/8	2.45
CLE-16	1/2	2.45

SIDING

Northeastern Scale Models, Inc.
Specifications: 1/16" thick, 3-1/2" W x 22" L (with the exception of 35" clapboard)
Clapboard CLB-8, 36" L/1/4" lap - $3.95 ea.
Clapboard CLB-12, 36" L/3/8" lap - $3.95 ea.
Clapboard CLB-16, 36"L/1/2" - $3.95 ea.
Beaded Clapboard CLE-12, 3/8" lap - $2.45
Beaded Clapboard CLE-16, 1/2" lap - $2.45
Bead and Board SIG-8 - $2.45. Bead and Board Hollow SIH-4 - $2.45.

THE MINIATURES CATALOG, *Fourteenth Edition*

Staircases

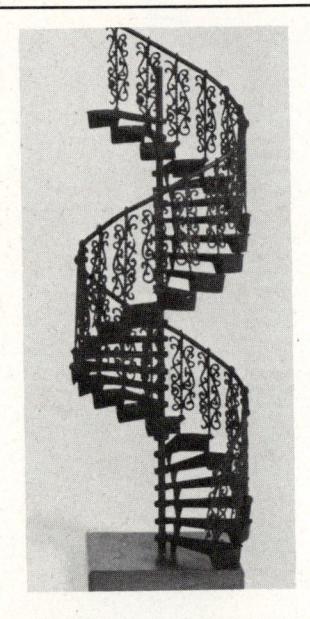

AMSI ORNATE 'CAST IRON' SPIRAL STAIR KIT

AMSI Scale Model Supplies
Suggested Retail Price: $59.95
Catalog #AMS-15
Dimensions: 10"H, 5"Dia.
Material: cast metal
Same design as AMS-10, but with ornate Victorian balusters. Available in 12" height for $71.95 per kit, catalog #AMS-16.

AMSI 'CAST IRON' SPIRAL STAIR KIT

AMSI Scale Model Supplies
Suggested Retail Price: $47.95
Catalog #AMS-10
Dimensions: 10"H, 5"Dia.
Material: cast metal
Easy to assemble as each tread slides over the center pole and keys into the tread below. Available in 12" height for $59.95 per kit, catalog #AMS-12.

CARLSON STAIRCASES

American Craft Products
Fits up to 10-1/2" height or can be adjusted for a shorter height (right or left rail). Includes treads, turned newel posts, spindles, scrolled end trim and railing. No. 8470 kit (right or left) $13.95, No. 8471 assembled (right-hand rail) $21.95, No. 8472 assembled (left-hand rail) $21.95, No. 8478 90° landing stair kit (right or left) $17.95, No. 8473 stairwell railing set $6.95. Made in America.

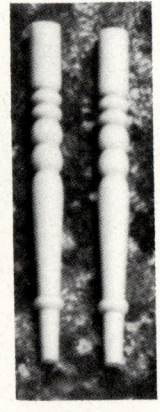

STAIR ACCESSORIES

Houseworks
#7019-Staircase Spindles-Delicately sculpted spindles to rise between your stair treads and handrail. 12 per pkg. Size: 3/16"W x 2-5/8"L. $3.
#7020-Stair and Landing Handrail-Notched on underside to accommodate #7019 spindles. Each rail measures 18"L. $1.50.

ASSEMBLED NARROW STAIRS

Miniature House
Suggested Retail Price: $4.89
Catalog No. MH251
Dimensions: 2"W x 11-1/8"L
Wood stairs created to fit in that space too small for a full-sized staircase.

STRAIGHT STAIRCASE KIT
Houseworks
Suggested Retail Price: $19.95
Catalog No. 7000
14"L X 3-3/16"W riser/stringer. All wood. Detailed kit contains riser/stringer assembly, 13 treads, 13 balusters, two newel posts and one handrail. Can be adjusted to varying floor to ceiling heights 9" - 10".

"Right Turn Shown"

KIMBERLY DELUXE STAIRCASE KIT WITH CURVED LANDING

Kimberly House Miniatures
Deluxe staircase kit (right or left).
Suggested Retail Price: $36.25
Kits fit 10" ceilings or less. Kits for higher ceilings available upon request. Must specify right or left turn when ordering. Does not include upper landing. Also available: Special Deluxe Staircase Kit designed for Greenleaf Harrison Dollhouse. Includes two staircases with second and third floor landings. Entire kit $86.85. See your dealer or write to Kimberly House.

CURVED STAIRCASE

Miniature House
Suggested Retail Price: $39.95
Catalog No. MH221 left curve or MH222 right curve.
Dimensions: 3"W of riser/stringer, 9"H
This wood staircase has a highly detailed, elegant Victorian look. Fully assembled. For use with 9" or 10" ceiling.

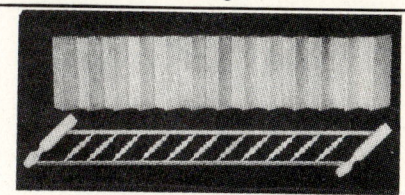

STRAIGHTSTAIR KIT

Miniature House
Suggested Retail Price: $17.98
Catalog No. MH220
Dimensions: 3"W x 12-1/2"L
Stair kit with components can be adjusted for 9" or 10" ceilings. Kit includes riser/stringer assembly, two newel posts, 10 balusters, and separate landing step.

STAIRCASES AND RAILINGS

The Lawbre Company
All Lawbre staircases are completely assembled in clear pine stock and ready to finish. Stock staircases are 10"H and 2-7/8"W with smooth birch spindles. They can have rails on the left, right or both sides, and curve or turn left or right. Decorative turned spindles are also available as well as any custom size or configuration to fit your needs. Rail sets complement the staircases in smooth birch spindles or decorative turned spindles. Lattice work and widow's walk are also available. All are fully assembled and ready to finish.

From left to right: No. 1147 $26.95, No. 1101 $21.95, No. 1106 $25.95, No. 1122 $32.95, No. 1126 $38.95, No. 1127 $38.95, No. 1117 $32.95, No. 1111 $27.95, No. 1136 $48.95.
In front: No. 1141, 10" x 2-1/2" railing with smooth birch spindles and two posts $8.95. No. 1186, 10" x 2-1/2" railing with decorative turned spindles and two posts $17.95.
No. 1191 10-3/4" x 2-1/2" fully assembled lattice, work section $9.95. No. 1192 20" x 2-1/8" widows' walk section $8.95.

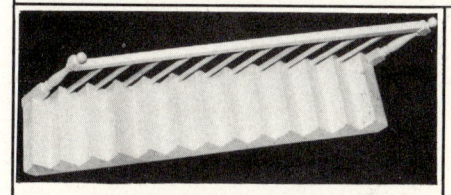

PREASSEMBLED STAIR WITH HANDRAIL

Miniature House
Suggested Retail Price: $13.98
Catalog No. MH283. Assembled stair, right or left interchangeable rail.
Dimensions: 3"W
Unfinished wood staircase, ready to stain or paint. Square balusters and handrail. Assembled railing separate.

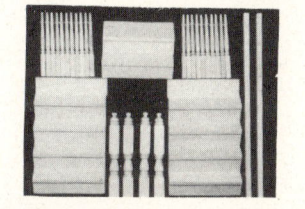

STAIRS WITH LANDING KIT

Miniature House
Suggested Retail Price: $17.50
Catalog No. MH252
Dimensions: 2-7/8"W
This unfinished wood kit has a number of possibilities for assembly. Includes all necessary spindles and newel posts.

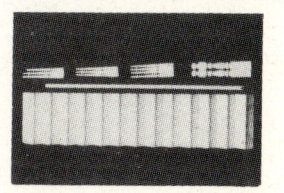

FANCY STAIR KIT

Miniature House
Suggested Retail Price: $15.50
Catalog No. MH280
Dimensions: 3"W
This wood kit has a dainty, graceful Victorian look. Preassembled railing. For 10" ceilings.

Building Components & Supplies

THE MINIATURES CATALOG, *Fourteenth Edition* 113

Windows, Non-working

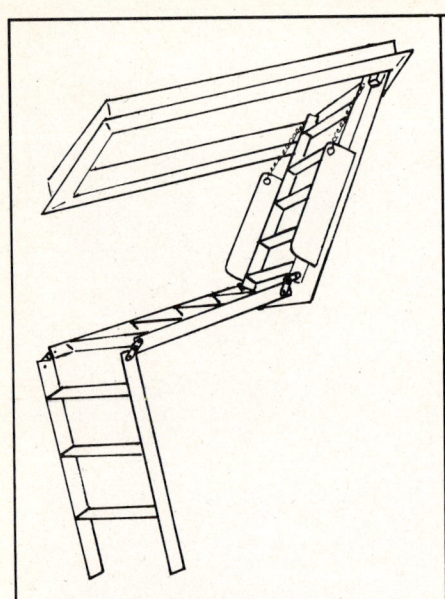

DISAPPEARING ATTIC STAIRS

Timberbrook Wood Products
Suggested Retail Price: $23.10
Dimensions: 2-3/8"W x 5-5/16"L
These stairs accommodate a ceiling height of up to 10" and can be trimmed to suit the need. They have a spring closure, solid brass hinges and 3/8" insets. See your dealer or write for more information. Order No. 4001.

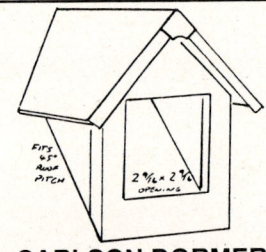

CARLSON DORMER

American Craft Products
Suggested Retail Price: $7.95
Catalog No. 8475
Dimensions: fits 45° roof pitch
Standard dormer made of clear pine. Holds No. 8477 square 2-9/16" window. Made in America.

CARLSON DOUBLE NON-WORKING WINDOW

American Craft Products
Suggested Retail Price: $11
Catalog No. 8405
Dimensions: 5-1/16" x 5-1/16"
Made of clear pine. Removable plexiglass for easy painting. Made in America. Also available working, No. 8406 $13.50.

CARLSON NON-WORKING WINDOW

American Craft Products
Suggested Retail Price: $4.75
Catalog No. 8410
Dimensions: 3-1/16" x 5-1/16"
Carlson's wide window style. Made of clear pine. Removable plexiglass for easy painting. Made in America.

CARLSON NON-WORKING WINDOW

American Craft Products
Suggested Retail Price: $7.95
Catalog No. 8430
Dimensions: 2-9/16" x 7-1/16"
Long Victorian window is made of clear pine with removable plexiglass for easy painting. Made in America.

CARLSON NON-WORKING WINDOW

American Craft Products
Suggested Retail Price: $6.95
Catalog No. 8437
Dimensions: 2-9/16" x 5-1/16"
Single French window is made of clear pine with removable mullion for easy painting. Made in America.

CARLSON NON-WORKING WINDOW

American Craft Products
Suggested Retail Price: $4.50
Catalog No. 8404
Dimensions: 2-9/16" x 5-1/16"
Made of clear pine. Removable plexiglass for easy painting. Made in America.

CARLSON NON-WORKING WINDOW

American Craft Products
Suggested Retail Price: $14.95
Catalog No. 8433
Dimensions: 5-1/16" x 7-1/16"
Long double Victorian window is made of clear pine with removable plexiglass for easy painting. Made in America.

CARLSON NON-WORKING WINDOW

American Craft Products
Suggested Retail Price: $12.95
Catalog No. 8438
Dimensions: 5-1/16" x 5-1/16"
Double French window is made of clear pine with removable mullion for easy painting. Made in America.

Prices are approximate and subject to change.

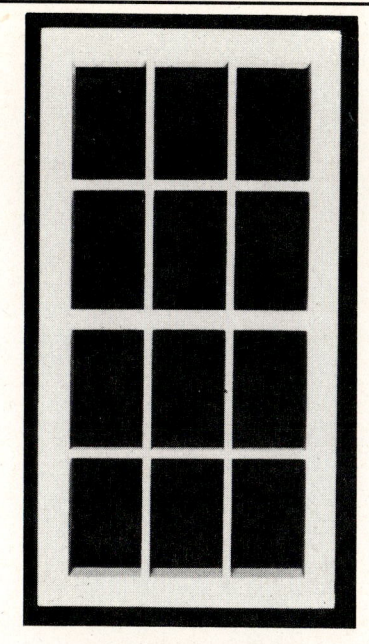

12-LIGHT WINDOW

Miniature House
Suggested Retail Price: $3.59
Catalog No. MH1062
Dimensions: Fits opening 2-9/16"W x 5-1/16"H
Classic 12-light window without panes - class without expenses. Fits standard window openings.

YORKTOWN NON-WORKING DOUBLE WINDOW

Miniature House
Suggested Retail Price: $10.89
Catalog No. MH102
Dimensions: Fits opening 4-9/16"W x 5-15/16"H
Perfect for that large space. Same appealing design as MH101 single window and MH117 door.

VICTORIAN NON-WORKING DOUBLE WINDOW

Miniature House
Suggested Retail Price: $13.39
Catalog No. MH1046
Dimensions: Fits opening 2-9/16"W x 5-1/16"H
Top-of-the-line non-working Deluxe Standard Window with removable panes has molded exterior and interior trim. Separate mullions included.

YORKTOWN NON-WORKING SINGLE WINDOW

Miniature House
Suggested Retail Price: $6.59
Catalog No. MH101
Dimensions: Fits opening 2-5/16"W x 5-13/16"H
This attractive window has rounded upper sash and dentil molding to add a special distinction. It has interior trim.

VICTORIAN NON-WORKING SINGLE WINDOW

Miniature House
Suggested Retail Price: $7.19
Catalog No. MH1042
Dimensions: Fits opening 2-9/16"W x 5-1/16"H
This elegant window has removable panes and molded exterior and interior trim. Separate mullions included.

YORKTOWN NON-WORKING WINDOW

Miniature House
Suggested Retail Price: $7.49
Catalog No. MH1041
Dimensions: Fits opening 2-9/16"W x 5-1/16"H
Traditional Yorktown Non-working window with removable panes.

Building Components & Supplies

SMALL YORKTOWN NON-WORKING WINDOW

Miniature House
Suggested Retail Price: $5.69
Catalog No. MH116
Dimensions: Fits opening 2-1/16"W x 4-1/16"H
This window has the same elegant design as MH101, MH102 and MH104. It also has interior trim.

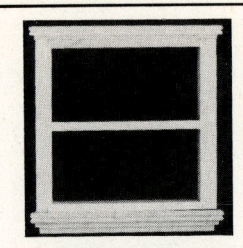

2-LIGHT WINDOW

Miniature House
Suggested Retail Price: $4.10
Catalog No. MH105
Dimensions: Fits opening 2-9/16"W x 2-9/16"H
2-light window, without panes, works well in attics or bathrooms. Two windows per card.

24 PANEL PICTURE WINDOW

Miniature House
Suggested Retail Price: $5.25
Catalog No. MH1080
Dimensions: Fits opening 6-11/16"W x 5-1/16"H
This picture window is perfect for a room box. Storefronts and libraries often have this window.

STAINED GLASS WINDOWS

Plastruct
Suggested Retail Price: $2.95 - $3.95 plus shipping
1:12 unfinished stained glass windows in standard and custom sizes. Easy do-it-yourself finishing allows you to match your decor. Screen material also available.

DEFINITIVE WINDOWS

Derek Perkins
Two of 17 different size windows well illustrated in my catalog. #PVW1 and #PVW4.

2-LIGHT WINDOW

Miniature House
Suggested Retail Price: $3.98
Catalog No. MH107
Dimensions: Fits opening 2-9/16"W x 5-1/16"H
This window without panes matches No. MH105 and No. MH108.

Windows, Working

Prices are approximate and subject to change.

CARLSON WORKING WINDOW

American Craft Products
Suggested Retail Price: $17.95
Catalog No. 8461
Dimensions: 5-1/16" x 5-1/16" opening size for standard 3/8" wall
Victorian Profile series double window is made of clear pine. Accurately detailed reproduction of Victorian architecture. Made in America.

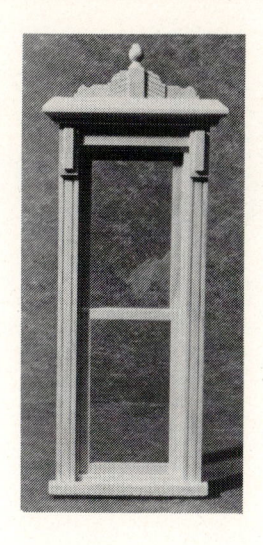

CARLSON WORKING WINDOW

American Craft Products
Suggested Retail Price: $9.95
Catalog No. 8462
Dimensions: 2-9/16" x 7-1/16" opening size for standard 3/8" wall
Victorian Profile series long window is made of clear pine. Accurately detailed reproduction of Victorian architecture. Made in America.

CARLSON WORKING WINDOW

American Craft Products
Suggested Retail Price: $9.95
Catalog No. 8460
Dimensions: 2-9/16" x 5-1/16" opening size for standard 3/8" wall
Victorian Profile series window is made of clear pine. Accurately detailed reproduction of Victorian architecture. Made in America.

CARLSON WORKING WINDOW

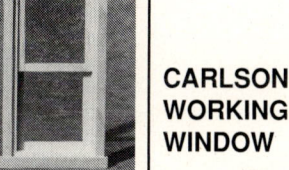

American Craft Products
Suggested Retail Price: $8.95
Catalog No. 8414
Dimensions: 2-9/16" x 5-1/16" opening size for standard 3/8" wall
Made of clear pine. Foremost in quality and design. Made in America.

CARLSON WORKING WINDOW

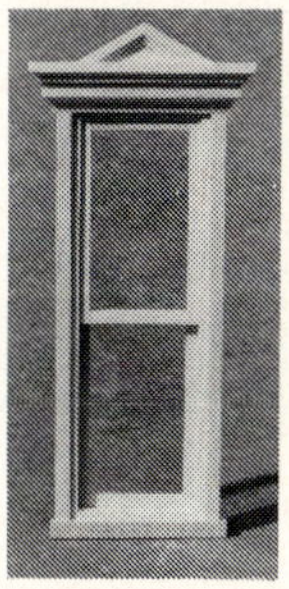

American Craft Products
Suggested Retail Price: $8.95
Catalog No. 8429
Dimensions: 2-9/16" x 7-1/16" opening size for standard 3/8" wall
Long Victorian working window is made of clear pine. Made in America.

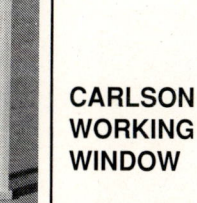

CARLSON WORKING WINDOW

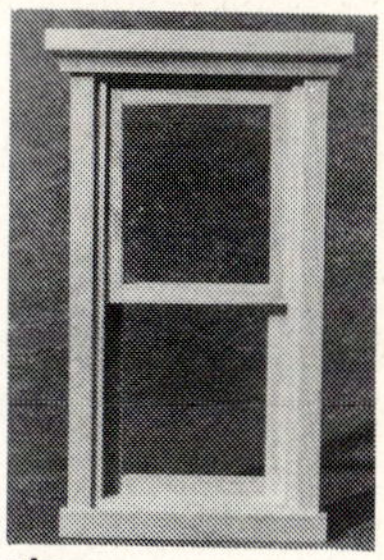

American Craft Products
Suggested Retail Price: $6.50
Catalog No. 8403
Dimensions: 2-9/16" x 5-1/16" opening size for standard 3/8" wall
Made of clear pine. Foremost in quality and design. Made in America.

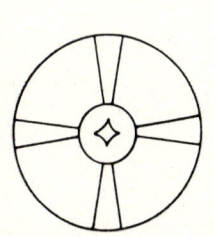

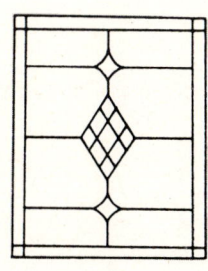

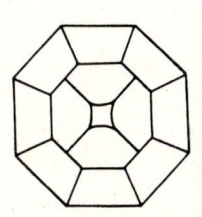

WINDOW PANE INSERTS

Houseworks
Suggested Retail Price: $2.50 each
Laseretch® plexiglass inserts, either replace or snap in over existing panes. A wonderfully unique and inexpensive way to add style to your dollhouse.
#7090 Victorian Octagon pane fits #5045
#7092 Victorian pane fits #5038, 5039, 5040
#7091 Tudor pane fits #5038, 5039, 5040
#7089 Victorian Circle pane fits #5052

Building Components & Supplies

THE MINIATURES CATALOG, Fourteenth Edition   121

DOUBLE WINDOWS

Houseworks
Suggested Retail Price: Catalog No. 5058, Double Casement Window is $16.25. No. 5054, Double Sliding Window is $14.95. #5058 fits opening 5-6/16" W x 4-27/32" H and has two removable outer panes and the two inner panes are hinged to open separately. #5054 fits opening 5-3/32" W x 5-1/16" H and is a very simple contemporary window with sill and includes spring loaded tracks for easy removal of panes.

PALLADIAN WINDOWS

Houseworks
#5049-Circlehead Double Casement Window-Palladian-styled window complete with working inner vertical panes and outer removable acrylic panes. Size: 5-7/8"W x 7"H. Fits opening: 5-5/8"W x 6-7/16"H. $21.
#5014-Palladian Working Window-Double hung, fully functional formal French window. Includes removable acrylic pane for fan light and mullions. Size: 4-1/8"W x 7-1/16"H. Fits opening: 3-1/16"W x 6-13/16"H. $13.95.

SLIM WINDOWS

Houseworks
#5030-Victorian Slim Window-Double hung and fully functional window has rounded top sash and includes back frame moldings and mullions. Size: 3-7/8"W x 7-1/4"H. Fits opening: 2-3/4"W x 7-1/16"H. $10.95
#5031-Traditional Slim Window-Double hung and fully functional. Includes back frame moldings and mullions. Size: 3-1/16"W x 7-5/16"H. Fits opening: 2-3/4"W x 7-1/16"H. $8.95.

SIDE BY SIDE WINDOWS

Houseworks
#5037-Yorktown Side by Side Window-Double hung, fully functional windows with detailed cap and dentil moulding. Size: 6-3/8"W x 5-7/8"H. Fits opening: 5-1/16"W x 5-1/16"H. $18.25.
#5015-Victorian Side by Side Window-Double hung and fully functional windows with low pitch hooded caps and sculpted brackets. Includes mullions. Size: 6-5/16"W x 6-3/16"H. Fits opening: 5-1/16"W x 5-1/16"H. $19.25.

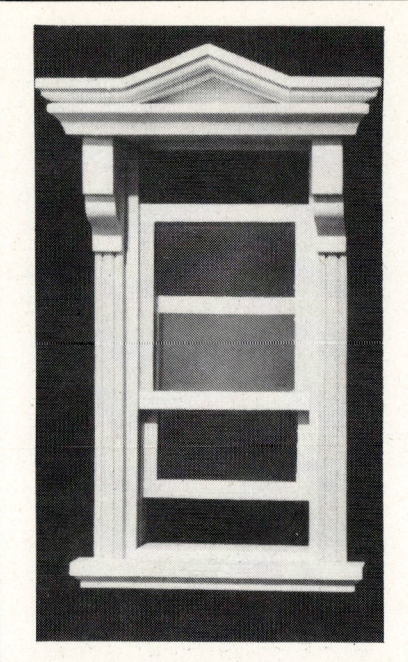

ELEGANT VICTORIAN WINDOW

Miniature House
Suggested Retail Price: $8.25
Catalog No. MH1002
Dimensions: Fits opening 2-9/16"W x 5-1/16"H
Elegant Victorian non-working window with removable panes.

FANCY VICTORIAN DOUBLE WORKING WINDOW

Miniature House
Suggested Retail Price: $13.98
Catalog No. MH1028
Dimensions: Fits opening 5-1/16"W x 5-1/16"H
This double window with the dainty scalloped trim has molded side trim and matching interior trim. The panes are removable for easy finishing. Separate mullions are included.

TRADITIONAL WORKING WINDOWS

Houseworks
#5000-Traditional Working Window-Double hung and fully functional. Mitered corners, self framing exterior and six mullions. Size: 2-3/4"W x 5-1/4"H. Fits opening: 2-9/16"W x 5-1/16"H. $7.25.
#5044-Traditional Side by Side Window-Double hung and fully functional windows are self framing and include mullions. Size: 5-5/16"W x 5-5/16"H. Fits opening: 5-1/16"W x 5-1/16"H. $13.95.

WORKING WINDOWS

Houseworks
#5046-Traditional Working Attic Window-Smaller double hung, fully functional window. Size: 2-11/32"W x 4-5/16"H. Fits opening: 2"W x 4"H. $6.95.
#5050-Working Casement Window-Great for kitchens, bathrooms, or attics. Includes acrylic panes and outer sill. Size: 3-5/8"W x 2-7/8"H. Fits opening: 3-3/8"W x 2-5/8"H. $7.95.

WORKING WINDOWS

Houseworks
#5001-Yorktown Working Window-Double hung and fully functional. Sculpted pediment accented by dentil moulding. Includes six mullions. Size: 3-7/8"W x 5-3/4"H. Fits opening: 2-9/16"W x 5-1/16"H. $8.95.
#5002-Victorian Working Window-Double hung and fully functional. Features low pitch, hooded window cap with sculpted brackets and six mullions. Size: 3-13/16"W x 6-3/16"H. Fits opening: 2-9/16"W x 5-1/16"H. $8.95.

October National Dollhouse & Miniatures Month

ATTIC WINDOW
Miniature House
Suggested Retail Price: $6.19
Catalog No. MH119
Dimensions: Fits opening 2-1/8"W x 2-1/4"H
The perfect attic window for the charming scalloped-trimmed Victorian series.

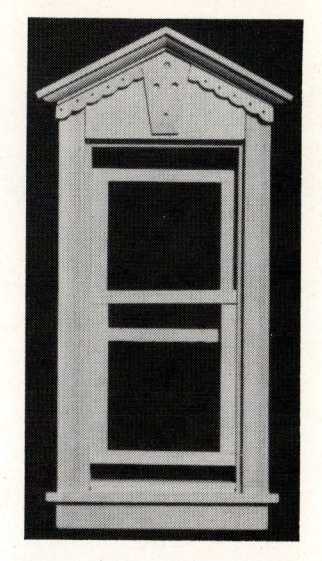

FANCY VICTORIAN SINGLE WORKING WINDOW

Miniature House
Suggested Retail Price: $7.75
Catalog No. MH1022 (old MH122)
Dimensions: Fits opening 2-9/16"W x 5-1/16"H
This working window adds dainty charm to a Victorian home. It has removable panes for easy painting and molded exterior and interior trim. Separate mullions included.

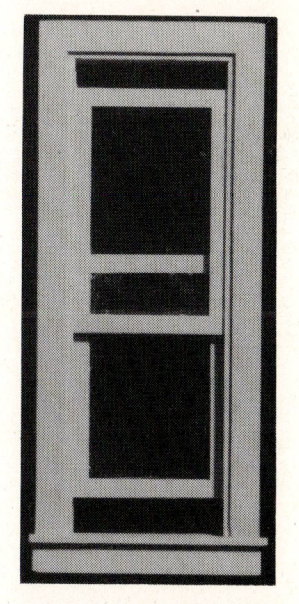

NARROW DOUBLE HUNG WORKING WINDOW

Miniature House
Suggested Retail Price: $6.49
Catalog No. MH109
Dimensions: Fits opening 2-5/16"W x 5-13/16"H
This working window has interior trim and is ideal for a narrow space.

Building Components & Supplies

THE MINIATURES CATALOG, *Fourteenth Edition* 123

SLIM DOUBLE WORKING WINDOW

Miniature House
Suggested Retail Price: $12.49
Catalog No. MH124
Dimensions: 4-1/2"W x 5-7/8"H
This working window has removable panes and interior trim.

STANDARD DOUBLE-HUNG WINDOW

Miniature House
Suggested Retail Price: $6.49
Catalog No. MH1000
Dimensions: 2-9/16"W x 5-1/16"H
Working standard double-hung window with removable panes and interior trim has separate mullions included.

STANDARD WINDOW

Miniature House
Suggested Retail Price: MH1010, Working - $6.49. MH1032, Non working - $5.15.
Dimensions: Fits opening: 2-9/16" W x 5-1/16" H.
Versatile Standard Window with removable panes. Interior trim included with MH1010.

VICTORIAN DOUBLE WORKING WINDOW

Miniature House
Suggested Retail Price: $14.98
Catalog No. MH1048
Dimensions: Fits opening 5-1/16"W x 5-1/16"H
A distinctive addition to the Victorian series, this window has removable panes and interior trim. Separate mullions included.

VICTORIAN SINGLE WORKING WINDOW

Miniature House
Suggested Retail Price: $8.25
Catalog No. MH1044
Dimensions: Fits opening 2-9/16"W x 5-1/16"H
This elegant window has removable panes and molded exterior trim. Interior trim matches. Separate mullions are included.

WORKING DELUXE STANDARD WINDOW

Miniature House
Suggested Retail Price: $6.69
Catalog No. MH1045
Dimensions: Fits opening 2-9/16"W x 5-1/16"H
Working Deluxe Standard window with removable panes and interior trim. This top-of-the-line window has molded exterior trim and compliments the new Victorian series. Separate mullions are included.

Prices are approximate and subject to change.

Are you in the miniatures business?

If you sell retail at shows or have a miniatures shop you should be reading *Miniatures Dealer*! For more information on the only trade magazine for the miniatures industry, write to: Kalmbach Publishing Co., Subscriptions Dept., 21027 Crossroads Circle, PO Box 1612, Waukesha, WI 53187.

DOUBLE SWING-OUT WINDOW
Miniature House
Suggested Retail Price: $6.49
Catalog No. MH112
Dimensions: Fits opening 3-7/16"W x 2-5/8"H
This unusual window swings out from the sides. It includes panes and interior trim.

SMALL WORKING WINDOW
Miniature House
Suggested Retail Price: $4.65
Catalog No. MH110
Dimensions: Fits opening 2-1/16"W x 3-15/16"H
This operating double-hung window is ideal for small spaces such as attics or bathrooms. Window has interior trim.

Window Stock, Parts & Kits

STAIN GLASS WINDOW COMPONENTS
J. Hermes
Suggested Retail Price: $1 - $5.99
J. Hermes distributes everything one needs to make beautiful miniature stained glass windows. The Emboss-Art tool syringe with two sizes of points is used to apply the liquid lead to the glass. Stains are used to tint the window. Also available is Dover's book on stain glass window designs, liquid lead and mylar.

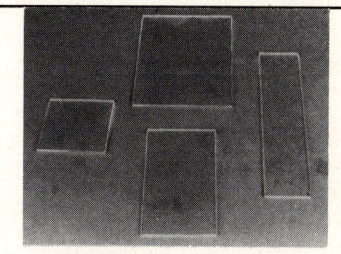

EXTRA THIN GLASS
Noonmark
Suggested Retail Price: 60¢ each piece, plus 6¢ per square inch, plus shipping
Made of real 3/64" thick micro-glass. Imparts a brilliance and clarity to your window which is not obtainable with plastic. Custom cut to order or bulk sheets.

Nutshell News
The monthly miniatures magazine, covering all aspects of miniatures for collectors and hobbyists. Available at your local miniatures shop or by subscription.

LEADED, STAINED WINDOWS
Olde Mountain Miniatures
Suggested Retail Price: $6.50 to $11.50, kits; $15 to $50, finished
These are some designs, shapes and sizes we have in our unique leaded windows. We do custom sizes and designs to fit your windows or doors. All are available in kits (glass stain not included), or already leaded and stained on acrylic or micro-glass ($10 extra). Ask your local miniatures dealer for our kits and finished pieces or custom sizes.

Building Components & Supplies

THE MINIATURES CATALOG, *Fourteenth Edition* 125

Electrical Systems & Accessories

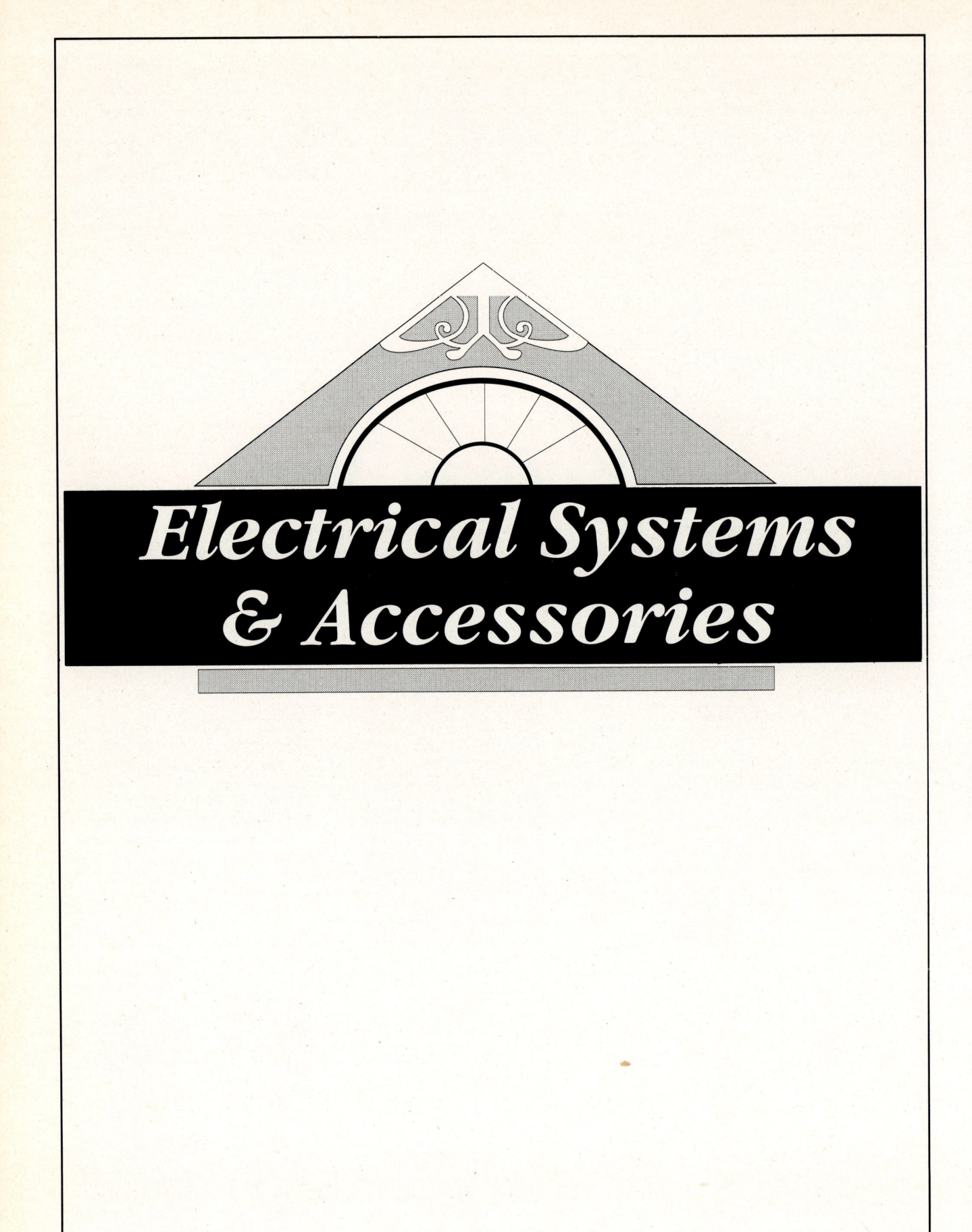

Ceiling Fixtures

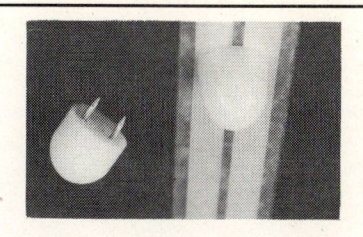

SMALL PIN-IN CEILING GLOBE

Cir-Kit Concepts, Inc.
Suggested Retail Price: $3.49
Catalog No. CK842
A smaller version of the CK841; measuring 3/8" in diameter. 12 volt bulb enclosed. Approximately 60 ma current drain.

ROYAL MAJESTIC CHANDELIER

Chrysolite, Inc.
Suggested Retail Price: $35
Catalog No. 151-E
Truly worthy of the most exclusive miniature homes! Includes • 24 scale prisms • white etched flowers in hand-blown glass shade • frosted glass hand-blown chimney • our famous canopy for easy ceiling attachment • use with any 12V lighting system • it really lights!. There are 37 other Chrysolite products available to you.

"WEDDING CAKE" PRISM CHANDELIER

Chrysolite, Inc.
Suggested Retail Price: $21 kit, $28 assembled
Catalog No. 135C kit, 145C assembled
Dimensions: 1-3/4"H x 1-1/2"W
This is an authentic treasure! Seen in antique European palaces and manors, it's also in today's traditional settings. 12V system. True-scale prisms.

PATTERNED CEILING SHADE

Cir-Kit Concepts, Inc.
Suggested Retail Price: $7.49
Catalog No. CK509
Completely transparent and embellished with distinctive cut glass pattern. Comes with 12-volt bulb and instructions. Solid brass mounting rim. Diameter 1", 1/2" H.

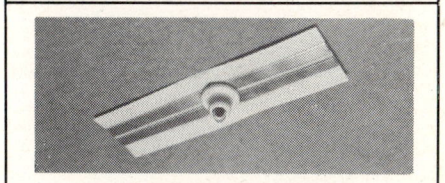

PORCELAIN TYPE CEILING FIXTURE

Cir-Kit Concepts, Inc.
Suggested Retail Price: $4.98, Cat.# CK501
This fixture may be taped directly into a tape run and brass bradded in place. Perfect for those hard-to-reach areas. Consists of 1-1/2" segment of tape with bulb and base plate attached. Diameter of base 3/8", height 1/4".

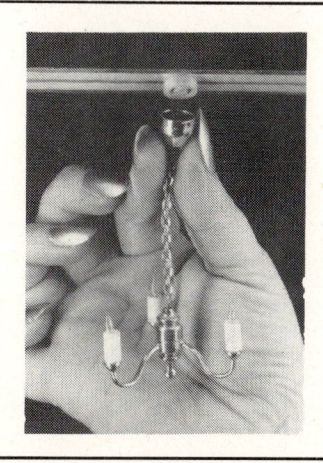

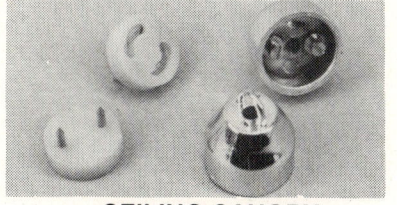

CEILING CANOPY

Cir-Kit Concepts, Inc.
Suggested Retail Price: $3.98, Cat.# CK800
A dramatic new way of making any chandelier removable. Unique design allows quick "twist-on/twist-off" operation. Beautiful brass plating complements any hanging chandelier. Also available in gold-plated version (CK800-1, $4.98).

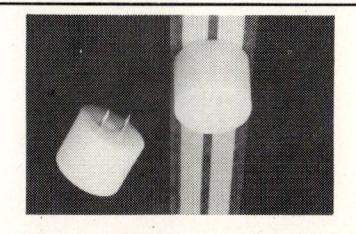

LARGE PIN-IN CEILING GLOBE

Cir-Kit Concepts, Inc.
Suggested Retail Price: $4.49
Catalog No. CK841
The easiest to install ceiling light yet! Simply place over tape run and pound in. Constructed of tough Lucite plastic. May also be used as tester.

Electrical Systems & Accessories

THE MINIATURES CATALOG, *Fourteenth Edition*

6-ARM CHANDELIER

Cir-Kit Concepts, Inc.
Suggested Retail Price: $36.95
Catalog No. CK833
All brass construction with fluted shades. Screw-in bulbs. Works on any 12-volt lighting system. Overall diameter 2-1/8". Shades 3/8" in diameter. Hangs approximately 2" from ceiling.

AMERICANA SWAG

Elect-a-Lite
Suggested Retail Price: $6.20
Catalog No. 9815
Authentic reproduction detail makes this a great looking fixture with a white globe. 12 volt bulb.

CEILING FAN WITH LIGHT

Elect-a-Lite
Suggested Retail Price: $10.70
Catalog No. 9813
Beautiful wood grain look on the blades with a globe light mounted underneath. The blades do not turn. Hangs 2" and is 4" across. 12 volt bulb.

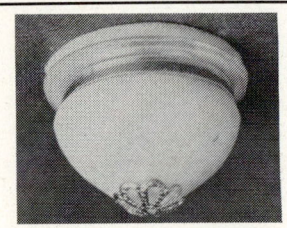

GENERAL STORE LAMP

Cir-Kit Concepts, Inc.
Suggested Retail Price: $9.95
Catalog No. CK320
This ceiling fixture may be used for lighting a general store or as a period setting. Incorporates a 12V bulb and hand-blown glass chimney. Dimensions: 3"H with 1-1/2" diameter shade. Bright brass plated.

CEILING FIXTURE WITH SMALL GLOBE

Elect-a-Lite
Suggested Retail Price: $6
Catalog No. 9820
Ornamental brass look trim on our ceiling fixture is right at home in any room of your miniature project. 1" in diameter.

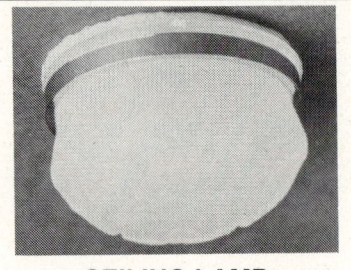

CEILING LAMP

Elect-a-Lite
Catalog No. 9816, clear globe - $6.50 and 9817, frosted globe - $6.90
The starburst pattern on our ceiling globes gives the look of "cut glass". 12 volt bulb. 1" in diameter.

CEILING LAMP WITH LARGE TULIP SHADE

Elect-a-Lite
Suggested Retail Price: $5.50
Catalog No. 9818
A large frosted tulip shade adorns our ceiling fixture with brass look base. Complete with a 12 volt candleflame replaceable bulb. 1-1/16" long.

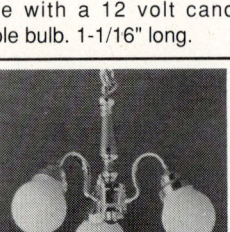

CEILING LAMP WITH SMALL TULIP SHADE

Elect-a-Lite
Suggested Retail Price: $5.50
Catalog No. 9819
Ceiling fixture with small frosted tulip and brass look base comes complete with a 12 volt replaceable candleflame bulb 1" length.

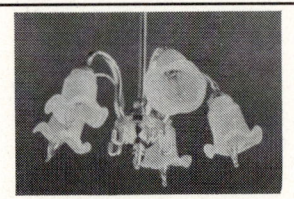

FROSTED 5-LIGHT CHANDELIER

Elect-a-Lite
Suggested Retail Price: $38.98
Catalog No. 9812
An elegant Victorian chandelier with five frosted tulip shades. Candleflame 12 volt replaceable bulbs included. 2-5/8" from ceiling.

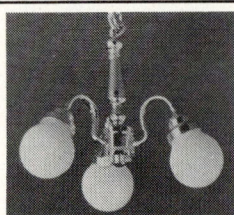

3-LIGHT CHANDELIER

Elect-a-Lite
Catalog No. 9807 amber globes - $18.98; 9808 frosted globes - $19.50; 9809 white globes - $18.98
Three handblown globes with candleflame 12 volt bulbs and brass look base complete our lovely chandelier. 2-1/4" from ceiling.

Prices are approximate and subject to change.

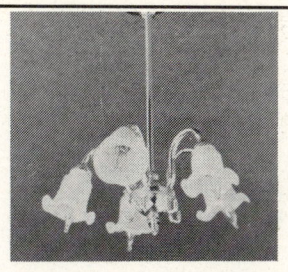

TULIP 5-LIGHT CHANDELIER
Elect-a-Lite
Suggested Retail Price: $31.98
Catalog No. 9810
This elegant five arm chandelier has white tulip shades and replaceable 12 volt candleflame bulbs.

TULIP 4-LIGHT CHANDELIER
Elect-a-Lite
Suggested Retail Price: $28.80
Catalog No. 9811
Our four arm chandelier has clear glass shades and replaceable 12 volt candleflame bulbs.

AMERICANA SWAG LANTERN
Houseworks
Suggested Retail Price: $5.75
Catalog No. 2002
Authentic in reproduction detail, solid brass with white translucent shade. 12 volt only.

PALACE FIVE ARM CHANDELIER
Houseworks
Suggested Retail Price: $29.95
Catalog No. 2009
Palace Five Arm chandelier of solid brass is 12 volt with replaceable bulbs. The perfect addition to any miniature house.

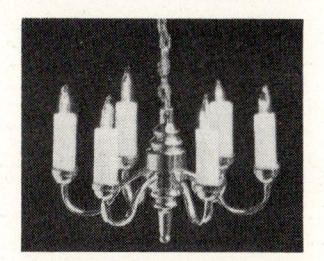

SIX ARM COLONIAL CHANDELIER
Houseworks
Suggested Retail Price: $34
Catalog No. 2010

TIFFANY CHANDELIER
Houseworks
Suggested Retail Price: $5.50
Catalog No. 2008
Swag style with hand-painted amber shade. 18" of swag chain and spare bulb. 65 m.a. for use with 12-volt systems.

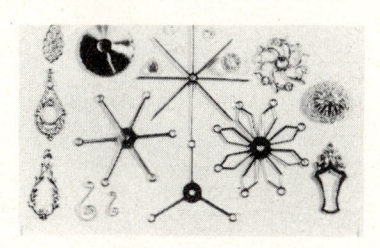

JEWELRY FINDINGS
JAF Miniatures
Jewelry Findings selected especially for the miniaturist. Components to make lamps, chandeliers and accessories. Solid brass findings, Austrian lead crystals, European lustres and glass chimneys.

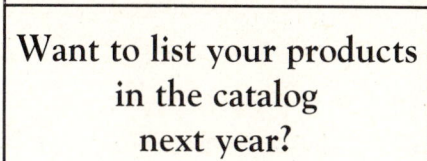

BOHEMIAN LUSTRE CHANDELIER KIT
JAF Miniatures
Suggested Retail Price: $59.95 plus S&H
Clear illustrated directions and all materials. Opulent solid brass chandelier with European lustres. Electrical option uses three central bulbs, purchased separately. Selection of 16 Kadeli kits, priced from $8.95 includes lamps, accessories, easy to build crystal chandeliers like the one pictured, built in tiers then simply stacked onto a central rod. Catalog #KB-502.

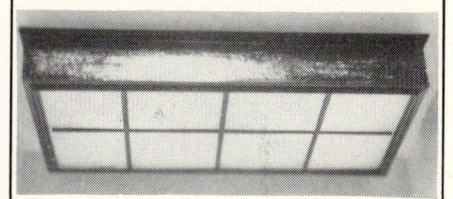

CONTEMPORARY CEILING LIGHTBOX
Le´ Petite Architect
Suggested Retail Price: $29.95
Designed to enhance any kitchen or bathroom. 12V with replaceable fluorette bulbs. Available in various finishes.

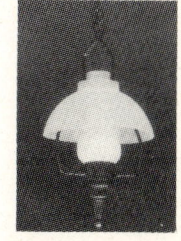

AMERICANA SWAG LANTERN
Miniature House
Suggested Retail Price: $5.75
Catalog No. MH704
This lantern, authentic in reproduction detail, has an antiqued-brass look and a white translucent shade. Use in a 12-volt system.

Want to list your products in the catalog next year?

To receive information on the 15th Edition of *The Miniatures Catalog*, send your name and address to: Sara Benz, *The Miniatures Catalog*, 21027 Crossroads Circle, P.O. Box 1612, Waukesha, WI 53187.

Electrical Systems & Accessories

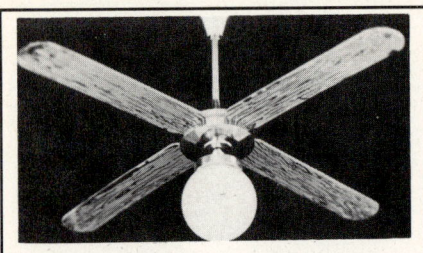

CEILING FAN WITH LIGHT
Miniature House
Suggested Retail Price: $10.98
Catalog No. MH630 (for 12V system)
Perfect for any room in the house, this ceiling fan has a globe light mounted directly under the blades. It hangs 2" from the ceiling and is 4" across.

CEILING LIGHT GLOBE
Miniature House
Suggested Retail Price: $5.98
Catalog No. MH652
Classic white globe ceiling fixture has many applications in your doll house (for use in a 12-volt system). Metal work is gold-tint plating.

CEILING LIGHT WITH LARGE TULIP SHADE
Miniature House
Suggested Retail Price: $5.79
Catalog No. MH650
This ceiling fixture has a large frosted tulip shade. The 12-volt bulb is replaceable. The metal work is gold-tint plating.

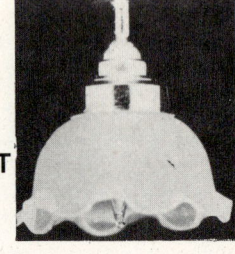

CEILING LIGHT WITH SMALL TULIP SHADE
Miniature House
Suggested Retail Price: $5.79
Catalog No. MH651
Ceiling fixture has small frosted tulip shade and replaceable 12-volt bulb. Metal work is gold-tint plating.

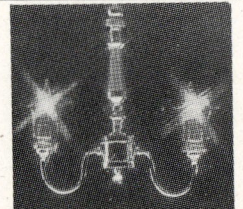

CHANDELIER WITH AMBER TULIP SHADES
Miniature House
Suggested Retail Price: $12.39
Catalog No. MH724
This attractive two-light chandelier has amber colored glass tulip shades and replaceable 12-volt candleflame bulbs. The metal work is gold-tint plating.

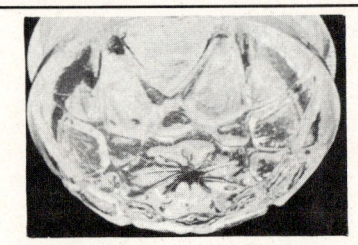

CLEAR CEILING LIGHT
Miniature House
Suggested Retail Price: $6.79
Catalog No. MH669
Dimensions: 1" diameter
This versatile ceiling fixture has a clear shade with a star pattern which causes the light to dance. The 12-volt bulb is replaceable.

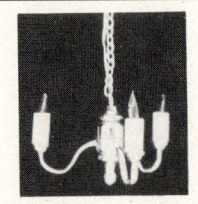

COLONIAL THREE-LIGHT CHANDELIER
Miniature House
Suggested Retail Price: $18.59
Catalog No. MH624
This authentic solid brass 12-volt chandelier comes complete with three replaceable candleflame bulbs.

CONTEMPORARY CEILING FIXTURE
Miniature House
Suggested Retail Price: $6.39
Catalog No. MH682
Just the fixture for your contemporary setting. Nursery decals are separate in package. For use in a 12-volt system.

DELUXE THREE-TULIP CEILING FAN
Miniature House
Suggested Retail Price: $27.95
Catalog No. MH720
Exquisitely detailed ceiling fan with simulated wood grain paddles and three elegant tulip shades. Even the detailed gold-plated base captures the elegance of the Victorian era.

DESK/CEILING LAMP
Miniature House
Suggested Retail Price: $7.69
Catalog No. MH697 (white glass with rose print) and MH698 (clear glass with rose print).

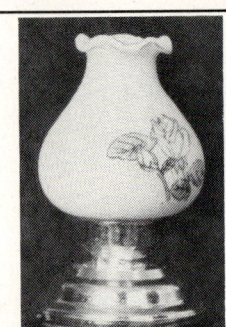

EXTRA FANCY CHANDELIER
Miniature House
Suggested Retail Price: $31.79
Catalog No. MH637
This unusual swag-type fixture has two 12-volt screw-in candleflame bulbs. Decorations painted on white shade are black.

FOR THE FASTEST SERVICE VISIT YOUR LOCAL MINIATURES SHOP

130   Prices are approximate and subject to change.

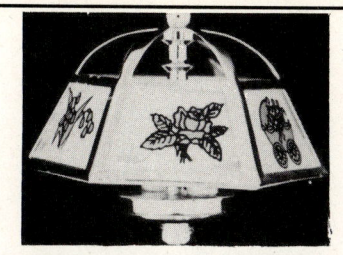

EXTRA FANCY CHANDELIER
Miniature House
Suggested Retail Price: $32.98
Catalog No. MH648
This swag-type chandelier has multi-colored designs applied on a white shade. The two 12-volt candleflame bulbs are replaceable.

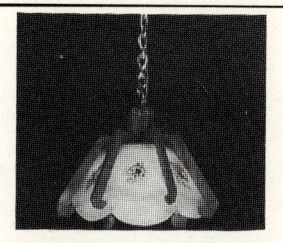

FANCY HANGING LAMP
Miniature House
Suggested Retail Price: $15.69
Catalog No. MH680
An attractive hanging swag-type lamp with an Oriental flavor. Wood trim is stained a medium finish. The screw-in bulb is 12-volt.

FIVE-ARM CHANDELIER
Miniature House
Suggested Retail Price: $42.50
Catalog No. MH676
A truly Victorian look in a fancy chandelier. Frosted fluted tulip shades are enhanced by the 12-volt replaceable candleflame bulbs. The metal work is gold-tint plating.

FIVE-LIGHT CHANDELIER
Miniature House
Suggested Retail Price: $31.49
Catalog No. MH623
This lovely solid brass chandelier adds elegance to any room and has replaceable 12-volt candleflame bulbs that are screw-in for easy replacement.

FIVE-LIGHT PALACE CHANDELIER
Miniature House
Suggested Retail Price: $30.75
Catalog No. MH788
This lovely brass chandelier is perfect to formalize any miniature setting. The 12-volt candleflame bulbs are replaceable. Two extra white glass tubes are included.

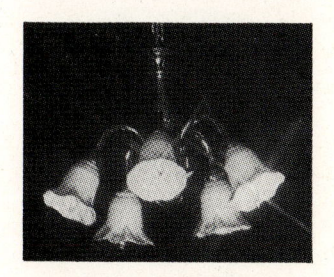

FIVE-LIGHT TULIP CHANDELIER
Miniature House
Suggested Retail Price: $32.98
Catalog No. MH634

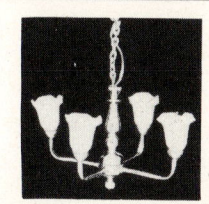

FOUR-ARM CHANDELIER WITH TULIP SHADES
Miniature House
Suggested Retail Price: $29.79
Catalog No. MH633
Solid brass construction with individual clear tulip shades. 12-volt screw-in candleflame bulbs for easy replacement.

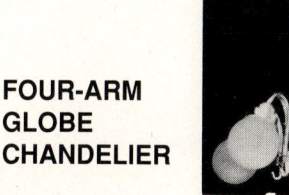

FOUR-ARM GLOBE CHANDELIER
Miniature House
Suggested Retail Price: $34.49 (frosted globes), $32.95 (white globes)
Catalog No. MH674 (white) and MH675 (frosted)
Dramatic copy of a gasolier with hand-blown globes. Replaceable 12-volt bulbs and gold-tint plating are standard. Hangs 2-7/8" from ceiling.

FOUR-LIGHT FROSTED CHANDELIER
Miniature House
Suggested Retail Price: $28.98
Catalog No. MH756
This elegant chandelier has hand-blown frosted glass tulip shades and replaceable 12-volt candleflame bulbs. Metal work is gold-tint plating.

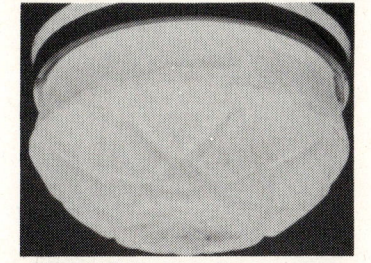

FROSTED CEILING LIGHT
Miniature House
Suggested Retail Price: $6.98
Catalog No. MH671
For a more muted effect, this fixture with the cut-glass look has a frosted shade. It has a 12-volt screw-in bulb. 1" in diameter.

HANGING LIGHT
Miniature House
Suggested Retail Price: $6.25
Catalog No. MH632
Unique hanging light has a half-globe chimney. An economical way to dress up any room. For use in 12-volt systems.

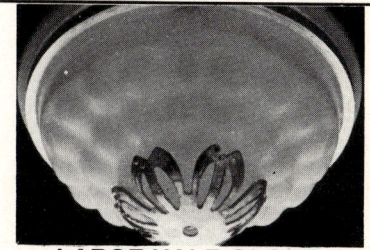

LARGE HALF-GLOBE CEILING FIXTURE
Miniature House
Suggested Retail Price: $6.69
Catalog No. MH684
Frosted half-globe shade has a hob-nail look and fancy treatment in center. Use with a 12-volt system. 1-1/2" diameter.

Electrical Systems & Accessories

PLASTIC CHANDELIER
Miniature House
Suggested Retail Price: $4.79
Catalog No. MH612
This crystal-look chandelier has a 12-volt replaceable bulb in the center, surrounded by five candles. An economical fancy look.

PLASTIC CHANDELIER
Miniature House
Suggested Retail Price: $6.19
Catalog No. MH758
Attractive inexpensive chandelier has brass down-rod and a replaceable 12-volt screw-in bulb.

Your Listings Belong Here!
Interested in advertising in the
15th Edition of
The Miniatures Catalog?

Contact Sara Benz at
1-800-558-1544,
Ext. 631
or write to;
The Miniatures Catalog
P.O. Box 1612
Waukesha, WI 53187

RATTAN HANGING LIGHT
Miniature House
Suggested Retail Price: $17.95
Catalog No. MH678
This rattan hanging light has a handblown globe. Perfect for that garden room or other special room. Use with a 12-volt system.

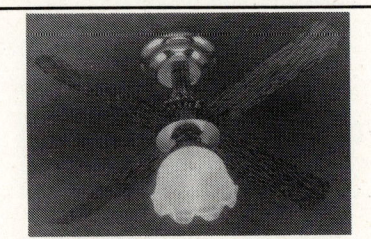

SINGLE TULIP CEILING FAN
Miniature House
Suggested Retail Price: $13.50
Catalog No. MH719
Elegant ceiling fan. Detailed design enhanced by the tulip shade makes it a must for the miniature enthusiast.

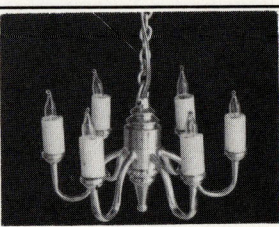

SIX-LIGHT COLONIAL CHANDELIER
Miniature House
Suggested Retail Price: $32.50
Catalog No. MH789
Elegance in miniature is the phrase to describe this 12-volt brass chandelier. It has replaceable candleflame bulbs and two extra white glass tubes.

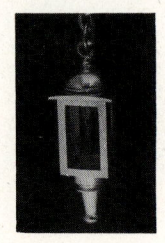

SMALL BRASS HANGING COACH LAMP
Miniature House
Suggested Retail Price: $12.49
Catalog No. MH764
Dainty brass hanging coach lamp has a 3" chain. Ideal for an entranceway. Lamp has a replaceable 12-volt bulb.

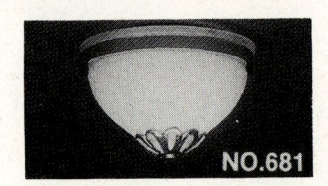

SMALL HALF-GLOBE CEILING FIXTURE
Miniature House
Suggested Retail Price: $6.19
Catalog No. MH681
Elaborately trimmed ceiling fixture with a white half-globe. For use with 12-volt systems. Metal work is gold-tint plating. 1" diameter.

SMALL HANGING RATTAN LAMP
Miniature House
Suggested Retail Price: $14.98
Catalog No. MH679
This unique swag-type hanging lamp is perfect for that garden room, or other special place. The 12-volt screw-in bulb is replaceable.

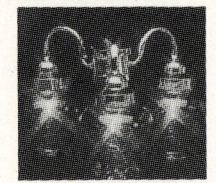

THREE-LIGHT AMBER CHANDELIER
Miniature House
Suggested Retail Price: $22.49
Catalog No. MH746, MH688 replacement chimneys
This unique chandelier has quaint handblown amber chimneys. It comes with replaceable 12-volt bulbs and gold-tint plating.

THREE-LIGHT CHANDELIER
Miniature House
Suggested Retail Price: Catalog No. MH728 (frosted globes) - $20.49, Catalog No. MH730 (clear globes), MH732 (amber globes) - $19.69.
This beautiful chandelier has handblown globes and replaceable 12-volt bulbs. The metal work is gold-tint plating.

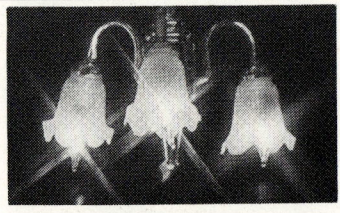

THREE-LIGHT FROSTED CHANDELIER
Miniature House
Suggested Retail Price: $19.29
Catalog No. MH748
Dainty frosted tulip shades set off this unique chandelier. 12-volt bulbs are replaceable. Metal work is gold-tint plating.

Prices are approximate and subject to change.

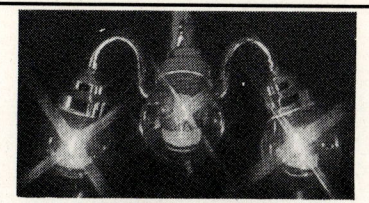

THREE-LIGHT GLOBE CHANDELIER
Miniature House
Suggested Retail Price: $19.69
Catalog No. MH740 (white globes), MJHH742 (frosted globes), MH744 (amber globes)
Reproduction of a gasolier has handblown globes. Replaceable 12-volt candleflame bulbs and gold-tint plating.

THREE-LIGHT ROSEBUD CHANDELIER
Miniature House
Suggested Retail Price: $19.69
Catalog No. MH738
This distinctive chandelier has white rosebud shades and replaceable 12-volt candleflame bulbs. Metal work is gold-tint plating.

THREE-LIGHT TULIP CHANDELIER
Miniature House
Suggested Retail Price: $20.49
Catalog No. MH734 frosted shades, MH736 clear shades - $19.69
Tulip shades add elegance to this chandelier. 12-volt replaceable bulbs.

THREE-TULIP CEILING FAN
Miniature House
Suggested Retail Price: $22.95
Catalog No. MH721
The same exquisite detail you've come to expect from Miniature House. Three elegant tulip shades with simple gold-plated base.

TIFFANY HANGING LAMP
Miniature House
Suggested Retail Price: $5.49
Catalog No. MH600 white, MH601 colored
This swag-type hanging Tiffany chandelier is equipped with a replaceable 12-volt, screw-in bulb. Metal work is gold-tint plating.

TIFFANY HANGING LAMP
Miniature House
Suggested Retail Price: $1.98
Catalog No. MH617, MH617W (white)
This non-electric hanging swag-type lamp has a multi-colored shade. An inexpensive way to dress up a dollhouse. Also available in white.

TIFFANY HANGING LAMP
Miniature House
Suggested Retail Price: $4.39
Catalog No. MH700
This bright, multi-colored swag-type hanging lamp has a replaceable 12-volt screw-in bulb. Metal work is gold-tint plating.

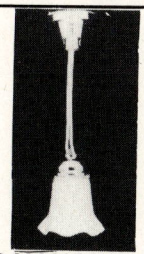

TULIP HANGING LAMP
Miniature House
Suggested Retail Price: $4.79
Catalog No. MH635
Hanging light has white fluted tulip shade and 12-volt bulb. Metal work is gold-tint plating.

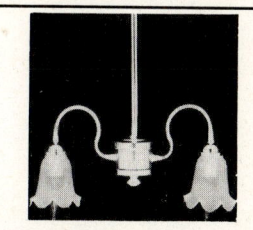

TWO-ARM CHANDELIER
Miniature House
Suggested Retail Price: $10.98
Catalog No. MH660
This authentic reproduction of a gasolier adds a unique touch to any room. The 12-volt screw-in bulbs are surrounded by frosted shades. Metal work is gold-tint plated.

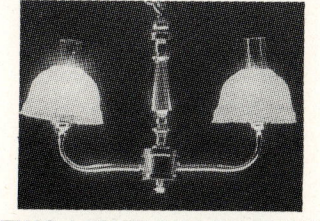

TWO-LIGHT CHANDELIER
Miniature House
Suggested Retail Price: $11.39
Catalog No. MH722
This quaint two-light chandelier has clear glass chimneys and frosted shades. The 12-volt candleflame bulbs are replaceable. The metal work is gold-tint plating.

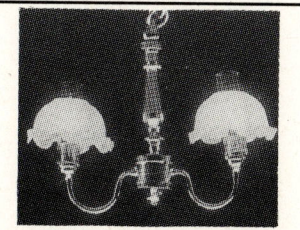

TWO-LIGHT CHANDELIER WITH FLUTED SHADES
Miniature House
Suggested Retail Price: $12.39
Catalog No. MH726
Frosted shades enhance this chandelier which has clear chimneys. 12-volt screw-in bulbs and gold-tint plating.

WHITE HANGING GLOBE LIGHT
Miniature House
Suggested Retail Price: $5.69
Catalog No. MH615
Ideal for a high ceiling in an entranceway, or shorten the chain and use in kitchen or bath. For use with 12-volt systems.

Electrical Systems & Accessories

THE MINIATURES CATALOG, Fourteenth Edition

The Happy Unicorn
Crystal Chandeliers & Sconces—Only the finest imported Austrian and Czechoslovakian crystals are used in these assembled chandeliers, wall sconces and chandelier kits. Also made with brass with 22K color English gold gilt. Fixtures furnished with 1-1/2" of chain, jump ring and matching ceiling plate. Most styles are available electrified or non-electrified. Items shown are available at miniatures shops, or send for catalog, $4.50. Suggested retail price: $30.00-$250.00.

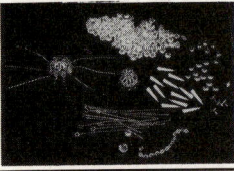

Kit Components

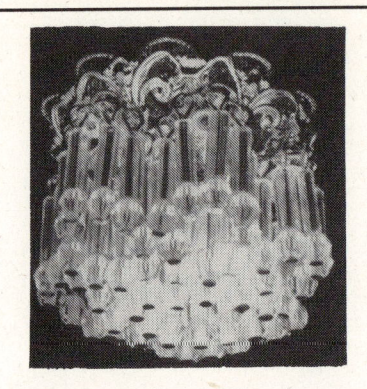

Merry Mary

Maureen

Kit A

Serena with prisms, 6 lights, electrified

Twinkle Bell

Kit B

Girandole Sconce

Sybil

Kit C

Serena

Wisteria

134   Prices are approximate and subject to change.

FOUR-LITE BRASS CHANDELIER
The Lighting Bug
Brass. Frosted shades with raised design. Order #B.

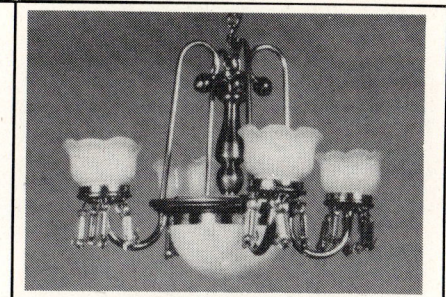

FOUR-ARM, SIX-LITE CHANDELIER
The Lighting Bug
Glass and brass - - much class. Glass, crystal and delicate brasswork. Order #623.

FIVE-LITE FLORAL CHANDELIER
The Lighting Bug
Green, white or gold leaves with either pink, white or yellow flowers. Regular or replaceable flame bulbs. Order #N.

FOUR-ARM CHANDELIER
The Lighting Bug
Frosted shades. Polished brass or yellow or white filigrees with green accent. Order #633.

FIVE-LITE CHANDELIER
The Lighting Bug
Almond or matte black finish. Floral designs with Almond. Regular or replaceable flame bulbs. Order #311.

SIX-LITE CRYSTAL CHANDELIER
The Lighting Bug
Made with replaceable flame bulbs. Order #LBO.

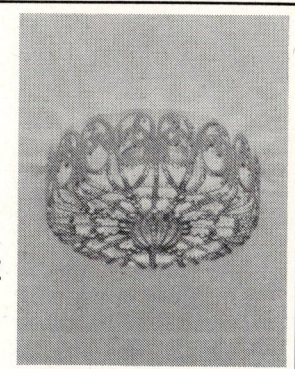

FILIGREE CEILING LAMP
Miniaturelite
One light filigree ceiling lamp. Brass. Order #204.

DROPPED FROSTED CEILING LAMP
Miniaturelite
One light, dropped ball-like frosted shade with ribs. Pleasant. Order #229.

CLEAR FACETED CEILING LAMP
Miniaturelite
One light, attractively faceted clear shade with brass mount and trim. Order #235.

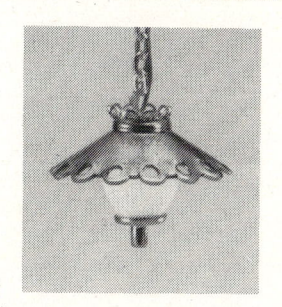

BRASS HANGING LAMP
Miniaturelite
One light, brass top with white shade, very brassy. Order #250.

VERTICAL PATTERN CEILING LAMP
Miniaturelite
One light, clear and round shade with vertical pattern. Brass mount. Order #227.

WHITE OPAQUE CEILING LAMP
Miniaturelite
One light, white opaque shade. Order #214.

Electrical Systems & Accessories

THE MINIATURES CATALOG, Fourteenth Edition

D'LIGHTFUL MINIATURES

Small Time Operators
Handcrafted by Dawn and Bob McKay with Aloha from Hawaii. See your local dealer.

PRINCESS KAIULANI

ROSE CHANDELIER (WHITE BASE)

PRINCESS ABIGAIL

FLORAL FANTASY

ROSETTE (ALSO AVAILABLE IN GOLD)

COLONIAL

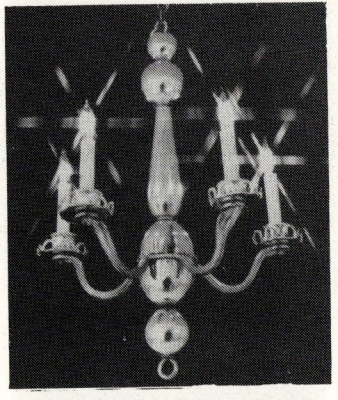

HERITAGE FIVE-LIGHT

HAPA HAWAIIAN

QUEEN EMMA

VERSAILLES

VICTORIA

136   Prices are approximate and subject to change.

Electrical Parts & Accessories

12-VOLT TRANSFORMERS

Cir-Kit Concepts, Inc.
CK1009A, 10W, 1A, powers 16-23 GOW bulbs $16.95
CK1009B, 5W, 0.5A, powers up to 10 GOW bulbs $12.95
CK1009C, 20W, 2A, powers 32-46 GOW bulbs $20.95
CK1009D, 40W, 4A, powers 64-100 GOW bulbs $27.95
Each transformer from the inexpensive 5 watt unit to our 40 watt powerhouse is circuit-breaker protected. These built-in circuit breakers eliminate any possibility of transformer burn out. Screw lugs on back provide easy access to 12-volt output. Use for smallest room box to largest dollhouse.

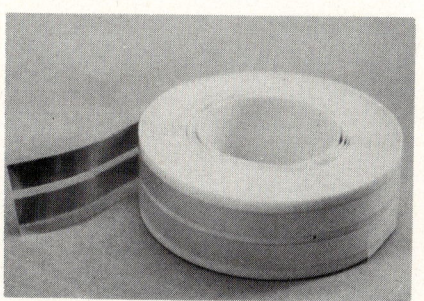

TAPEWIRE, 5' ROLL

Cir-Kit Concepts, Inc.
Suggested Retail Price: $2.95, 5' roll
Catalog No. CK1002
Since 1976, the most popular method of wiring a dollhouse. Completely eliminates the "rats nest" of wiring involved in conventional wiring. Super adhesion allows installation on any surface, even metal. No possibility of overlap shorts with new "sandwich-type" construction. 5/8" wide adhesive tape has 3/16" wide copper foils imbedded between .001" layers of Mylar. Also available in 15' (CK1001 $7.95) and 50' (CK1017 $23.95) rolls.

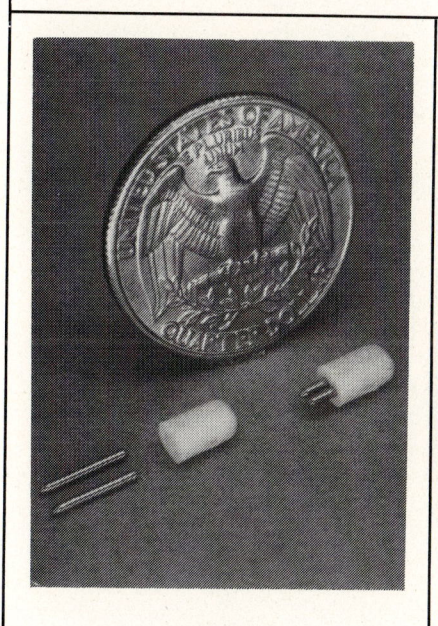

PLUG

Cir-Kit Concepts, Inc.
Suggested Retail Price: $1.98
Catalog No. CK1004
The smallest electrical plug made! May be connected to any miniature lamp with household pliers and used over and over again. Mates with CK1003 outlet. Instructions included.

OUTLET

Cir-Kit Concepts, Inc.
Suggested Retail Price: $1.98
Catalog No. CK1003
First "to scale" and operational outlet ever made. Built with offset nails to allow mounting on vertical or horizontal tape runs. Mates with CK1004 and CK1004-2 plugs. Measures .25" x .42".

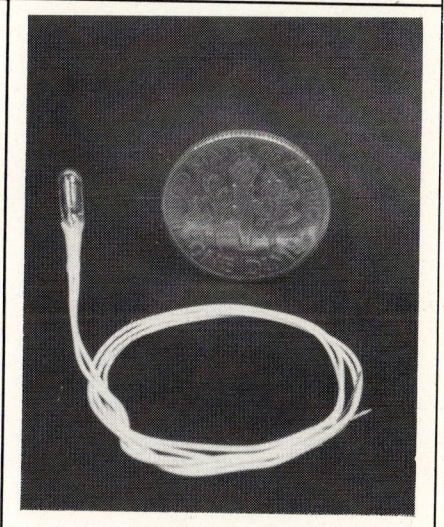

GOR BULBS

Cir-Kit Concepts, Inc.
CK1010-6A 12V (w/8" black wires) $1.15
CK1010-6B 12V (w/8" white wires) $1.15
CK1010-6C 16V (w/8" black wires) $1.15
CK1010-6D 16V (w/8" white wires) $1.15
CK1010-20 12V (w/12" brown wires) $1.25
CK1010-23 12V (w/8" brown wires) $1.20

GOR bulbs measure approximately 3/32" in diameter. 12-volt bulbs draw approximately 55 ma. and 16-volt bulbs approximately 35 ma. Other characteristics same as GOW bulbs.

1.5-VOLT TRANSFORMER
Cir-Kit Concepts, Inc.
Suggested Retail Price: $10.95
Catalog No. CK1009G
The perfect power source for any 1.5-volt bulb. Three watts of power will light up to 130 micro bulbs or 65 1.5-volt GOR bulbs.

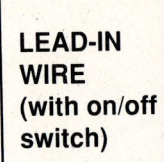

LEAD-IN WIRE (with on/off switch)
Cir-Kit Concepts, Inc.
Suggested Retail Price: $5.50
Catalog No. CK1008-1
This 6' long lead-in wire is great for connecting 12V from any screw-lug type transformer to a tape wired house. Allows for control of dollhouse power at the lead wire. Available with fuseholder (CK1008-2, $6.75).

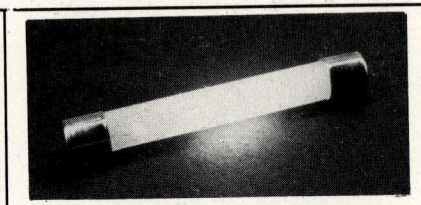

12V FLUORETTE BULB (FROSTED GLASS)
Cir-Kit Concepts, Inc.
Suggested Retail Price: $1.39
Cat. No. CK1018-2, measures 1/4" x 1-1/2" Ideal for backlighting or indirect miniature illumination. Snaps into CK1019 holder for easy installation. Consumes 80 ma. Also available in clear glass (CK1018-1).

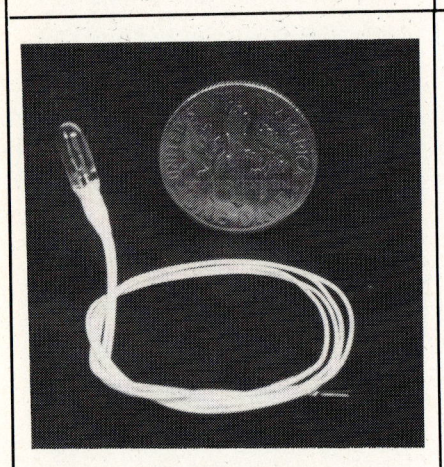

GOW BULBS
Cir-Kit Concepts, Inc.
CK1010-1 12V (w/8" black wires) $1.15
CK1010-1A 12V (w/8" white wires) $1.15
CK1010-2 16V (w/8" white wires) $1.15
CK1010-2A 16V (w/8" black wires) $1.15
CK1010-21 12V (w/12" brown wires) $1.05
CK1010-22 12V (w/18" brown wires) $1.15

GOW bulbs measure approximately 1/8" in diameter and are guaranteed for 10,000 operational hours. 12-volt bulbs draw approximately 60 ma. and 16-volt bulbs approximately 40 ma. Use 16-volt bulbs where soft, non-glaring light is preferred and 12-volt bulbs in locations where brighter illumination is necessary.

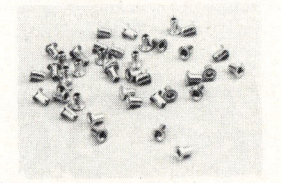

LARGE HOLLOW EYELETS
Cir-Kit Concepts, Inc.
Suggested Retail Price: $1.29 (pkg. of 20)
Catalog No. CK1023-2
Dimensions: 3/16" L, .054" I.D., .068" O.D.
These brass eyelets allow insertion of large lamp plugs at any point along tape run. Simply make starter holes and install with CK1044 awl. Illustrated instructions included.

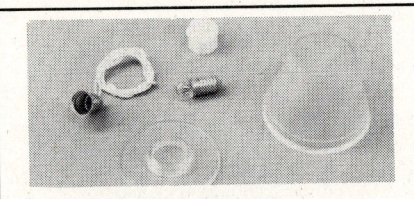

LAMP SHADE KIT, PLAIN
Cir-Kit Concepts, Inc.
Suggested Retail Price: $5.95, Cat.# CK5009
Now you can make your own lamp shades with this handy kit. Cover with fabric of your choice to match interior decor. 1-3/16" at base, 11/16" at top, 7/8" high. Materials: 12 volt screw-base bulb and socket with 8" white wires. Also available with pleated shade (CK5009-1, $7.95).

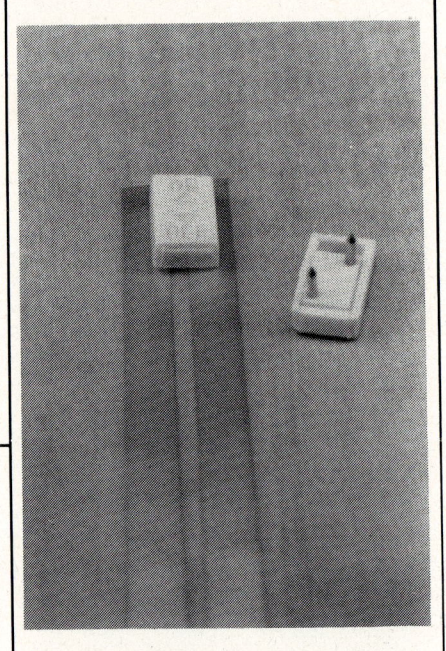

MINIATURE SLIDE SWITCH
Cir-Kit Concepts, Inc.
Suggested Retail Price: $2.98
Catalog No. CK1011
Most remarkable switch yet invented. Entire outer body slides for ON/OFF operation. Only hammer required for installation. Molded in nails, no loose parts.

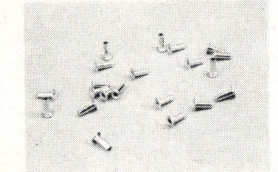

SMALL HOLLOW EYELETS
Cir-Kit Concepts, Inc.
Suggested Retail Price: $.98 (pkg. of 20)
Catalog No. CK1023
These brass eyelets are a substitution for 1/8" brads in making electrical connections. Their larger size simplifies electrical installation. Just use the CK1044 awl. Dimensions: 1/8" L, .044" I.D., .062" O.D. Available in 110 paks (CK1023-1, $4.98).

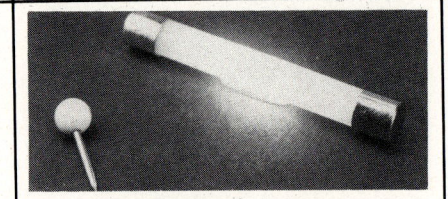

SHOWCASE BULB (FROSTED GLASS)
Cir-Kit Concepts, Inc.
Suggested Retail Price: $1.49
Catalog No. CK1018-3
Provides up to 50% more light than ordinary fluorette bulb. Excellent for perimeter lighting or indirect room box illumination. Draws 240 ma at 12 volts.

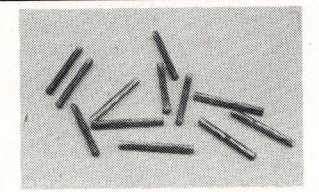

GREEN HEAT SHRINK TUBES
Cir-Kit Concepts, Inc.
Suggested Retail Price: $1.89 (pkg. of 12)
Catalog No. CK1033
Use for interconnecting green bulb wires. Measure 1/2" long. Made of green polyethylene heat shrink plastic. Also available in clear tubes (CK1033-3).

Prices are approximate and subject to change.

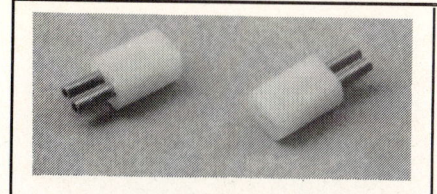

HOLLOW TUBE PLUG

Cir-Kit Concepts, Inc.
Suggested Retail Price: $2.49
Catalog No. CK1004-2
An adaptation of our regular CK1004 plug. Wires are fed into hollow tubes. Creates an extremely real and authentic looking plug.

12-VOLT "FLAME TIP" BULB

Cir-Kit Concepts, Inc.
Suggested Retail Price: $1.29
Catalog No. CK1010-4
Use where a candle-flame look is required. Consumes approximately 50 ma. GOW bulb, 1/8" diameter with 8" white wires.

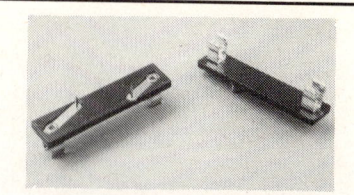

FLUORETTE SOCKET

Cir-Kit Concepts, Inc.
Suggested Retail Price: $2.25 plus shipping
Catalog No. CK1019
Specially constructed holder for fluorette bulbs. Imbedded nails automatically make electrical contact when pounded into tape. Also available with tabs for soldering (CK1019-1, $1.89).

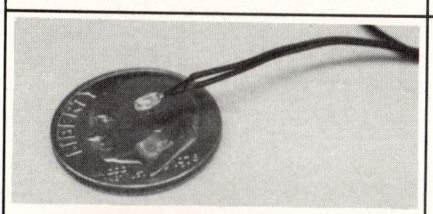

1.5-VOLT MICRO BULB WITH 8" BLACK OR WHITE WIRES

Cir-Kit Concepts, Inc.
Suggested Retail Price: $1.25. Catalog No. CK1010-13 black, CK1010-14 white.
To our knowledge, the smallest bulb in the world. Only .055" in diameter. Use with any 1.5-volt battery or our CK1009G 1.5-volt transformer. Current drain 15 ma.

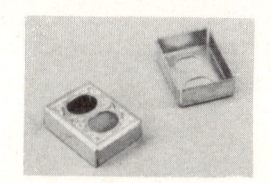

OUTLET COVER

By **Cir-Kit Concepts, Inc.**
Suggested Retail Price: $1.98. Catalog No. CK1003A.
The finishing touch for any CK1003 outlet. Engraved brass trim makes this the perfect complement to any room decor. Simply snaps on.

SCREW-BASE SOCKET

Cir-Kit Concepts, Inc.
Suggested Retail Price: $1.10
Catalog No. CK1010-8
Use with CK1010-7 series bulbs for making "screw-in bulb" type fixtures. 8" black leads. Also available with white wires (CK1010-8A).

SPOTLIGHT BULB WITH 24" WHITE WIRES

Cir-Kit Concepts, Inc.
Suggested Retail Price: $2.98
Catalog No. CK1010-10
Bulb contains built-in lens and rotates 360 degrees, plus front to back for complete maneuverability. Consumes approximately 200 ma. at 12 volts.

SWITCH COVER

Cir-Kit Concepts, Inc.
Suggested Retail Price: $1.98
Catalog No. CK1011A
The finishing touch for all CK1011 switches. Engraved brass. "Snap-on" fit. Protruding toggle for added feel of realism.

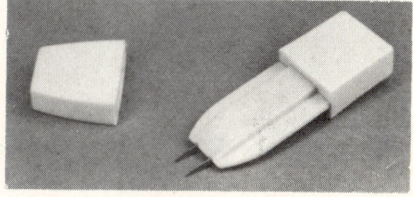

TEST PROBE

Cir-Kit Concepts, Inc.
Suggested Retail Price: $3.95
Catalog No. CK204
Use this handy tool for checking power along any tape run, even under wallpaper. Constructed with two sharp pins, a self-contained light bulb and safety cap. Overall length: 2" with .175" pin spacing.

THREE-WATT TRANSFORMER

Cir-Kit Concepts, Inc.
Suggested Retail Price: $10.95
Catalog No. CK1009F
Perfect for any installation requiring five or less bulbs. Plugs into wall. Provides 12 volts out across screw-lug terminals. Lowest price anywhere!

TWO-POLE TERMINAL BLOCK

Cir-Kit Concepts, Inc.
Suggested Retail Price: $1.49
Catalog No. CK1049
Use for interconnecting wires of all sizes. One or more wires may be attached to each screw lug. Measures 1-1/2" long. Also available in 4-pole (CK1049-1 $1.98) and 6-pole (CK1049-2 $2.49).

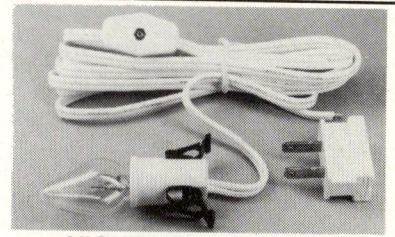

VIGNETTE LIGHT SET

Cir-Kit Concepts, Inc.
Suggested Retail Price: $7.95
Catalog No. CK1047
Use for 115-volt backlighting any vignette box or miniature room. Contains removable switch and plug for easy cord threading. No transformer necessary. Includes 4W bulb.

Electrical Systems & Accessories

THE MINIATURES CATALOG, *Fourteenth Edition*

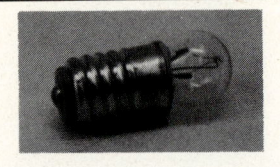

12-VOLT SCREW-BASE BULB

Cir-Kit Concepts, Inc.
Suggested Retail Price: $1.10
Catalog No. CK1010-7
Use with socket CK1010-8 to make lamps where easy bulb replacement is desirable. 60 ma at 12 volts. Also available in 16 volt (CK1010-7A) and 8 volt (CK1010-7C) versions.

COPPER FOIL TAPE

Elect-a-Lite
Suggested Retail Price: $4.50 for 675", #EP219; $5.50 for 1100", #EP240.
Single copper foil tape 1 mm thick and 3/16" wide has a long-aging pressure-sensitive adhesive protected by easily removable peel-off interliner. Easily installed in two parallel runs. No nailing, drilling, grooving or cutting. No tools required. Made in the USA.

COPPER FOIL DOUBLE TAPE

Elect-a-Lite
Suggested Retail Price: $10.90 for 25', #EP209; $19.90 for 50', #EP217
Wire your dollhouse with a single run of adhesive backed, mylar encasing two 3/16" copper foil tapes. The run in 5/8" wide and the mylar protection eliminates shorts caused by tape to tape contact. Also an option in our E120 electrical kit, available Fall 1991.

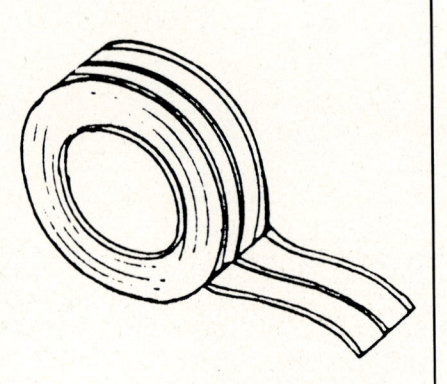

ELECTRIFIED CHRISTMAS WREATH KIT

Elect-a-Lite
Suggested Retail Price: $22.70
Catalog No. EAW10
This wreath is prewired with 10-light emitting diodes (LED's) in molded plastic and ready-to-decorate with greenery, ribbon and beads, which are included. Our patented plug included is also included to easily install on any double tape run. Made in the USA.

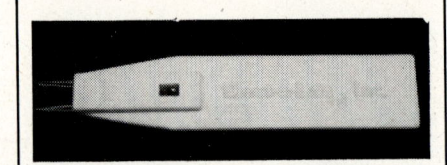

BI-PRONG TEST TOOL

Elect-a-Lite
Suggested Retail Price: $4.50
Catalog No. EP450
Used during installation, for locating tape runs after decorating, finding a break, or testing the transformer. Universal 12-volt, two-pronged tester. Made in the USA.

FLICKERING FIRE UNIT

Elect-a-Lite
Suggested Retail Price: $27.90
Catalog No. EAFF60
American-made solid state electronic control unit with three bulbs contains three separate circuits to allow the bulbs to flicker at random or different rates creating a most realistic illusion of a burning fire. This miniaturized unit will operate two sets of three bulbs or two different fireplaces.

MULTI-PURPOSE 21-LIGHT CHRISTMAS STRING

Elect-a-Lite
Suggested Retail Price: $31.90
Catalog No. EAS20
String of mixed color light emitting diodes (LED's). Perfect for decorating miniature trees. American designed and made, these lights can be used with any 12-volt system for thousands of hours without the inconvenience of bulbs burning out. Preassembled, pretested, ready-to-use.

TEST BULB

Elect-a-Lite
Suggested Retail Price: $2.40
Catalog No. EP490
Used for testing electrical installations or electrifying new or existing lamps or fixtures. 12" pigtail leads may be cut to desired length. 80 MA. Two per package.

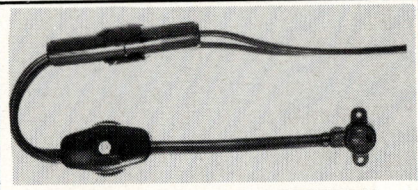

USFPC™ CORD ASSEMBLY

Elect-a-Lite
Suggested Retail Price: $9.40
Catalog No. EP460
Used with screw terminal transformer. Provides any transformer with a preassembled cord with in-line fuse, switch, and patented end plug. Comes without fuse. Made in the USA.

CANDLEFLAME REPLACEMENT BULBS

Elect-a-Lite
Suggested Retail Price: $4.30
Catalog No. EP530
These 12 volt screw base bulbs are for replacement in miniature lamps and lighting fixtures using candleflame bulbs. Four per package.

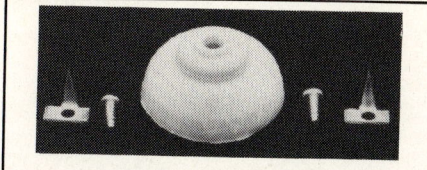

CEILING PLUG

Elect-a-Lite
Suggested Retail Price: $3.50
Catalog No. EP430
1" scale. The ceiling plug is used for attaching chandeliers directly into the copper tape run. Can be painted to match color scheme. 100% reliable and easily removed. Made in the USA.

12-VOLT LIGHTING TRANSFORMER

Elect-a-Lite
Suggested Retail Price: $35.10
Catalog No. EP119
American-made transformer with USFPC™ cord assembly. In-line fuse, switch, and patented two-pronged end plug. All one unit, ready-to-use. 21-bulb capacity. 12 volts, 15 watts.

12-VOLT LIGHTING TRANSFORMER

Elect-a-Lite
Suggested Retail Price: $39.90
Catalog No. EP140
American-made transformer with USFPC™ cord assembly. In-line fuse, switch, and patented two-pronged end plug. All one unit, ready-to-use. 42-bulb capacity. 12 volts, 40 watts.

RECTANGLE PLUG

Elect-a-Lite
Suggested Retail Price: $3.90
Catalog No. EP420
1" scale. This one-piece plug is for attaching table and floor lamps directly into the copper tape run. Can be used for two lamps at one time. 100% reliable and easily removed for redecorating. Made in the USA.

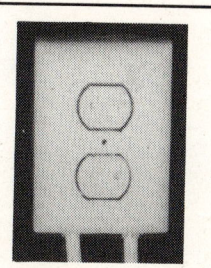

SCONCE ATTACHMENT

Elect-a-Lite
Suggested Retail Price: $2.20
Catalog No. EP400
1" scale sconce attachment is used to attach wall sconces and fixtures directly to copper tape runs through wallpaper and paint. Sconce wires attach to prongs (lamp not included). Easily removed for redecorating or bulb changing. Made in the USA.

SPLICING/ INSULATING TAPE

Elect-a-Lite
Suggested Retail Price: $1.50
Catalog No. EP480
Used to hold in-line splices and right angle splices tightly together and as an insulated separator between copper tape cross-overs so they cannot touch. Precut for easy handling and color coded. Two sheets of 32 pieces per package. Made in the USA.

STANDARD REPLACEMENT BULBS

Elect-a-Lite
Suggested Retail Price: $2.30
Catalog No. EP531
Extend the life of your miniature electrical fixtures using our screw base 12 volt replacement bulbs. For lamps and lighting fixtures using standard bulbs. Four per package.

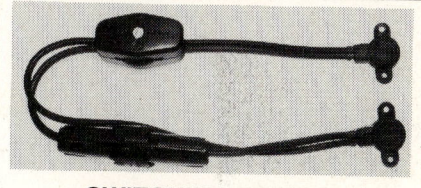

SWITCHING BRIDGE

Elect-a-Lite
Suggested Retail Price: $10.70
Catalog No. EP470
Used to attach a series of room boxes using only one transformer. 18" bridge has USFPC™ with in-line fuse, switch, and two patented end plugs. Completely assembled and ready-to-use. Made in the USA.

October National Dollhouse & Miniatures Month

WALL SWITCH

Elect-a-Lite
Suggested Retail Price: $3.70
Catalog No. EP410
1" scale. Wall switch allows lights to be turned on and off just like your own home. One-piece unit plugs directly into the copper tape runs. Made in the USA.

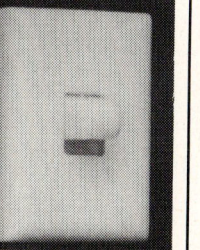

WHITE SHRINK TUBE

Elect-a-Lite
Suggested Retail Price: $1.90
Catalog No. EP440
Used to join lamps and fixtures to plug wires by heat shrinking without solder or tools. Provides insulation against bare wires touching. Comes in 2-1/2" lengths, two per package. Made in the USA.

Electrical Systems & Accessories

THE MINIATURES CATALOG, Fourteenth Edition 141

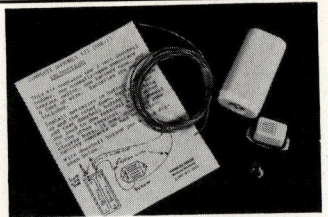

COMPLETE DOORBELL KIT
Handley House
Suggested Retail Price: $10.95
Catalog No. HH304
The complete doorbell kit comes with solid state doorbell buzzer, wiring and pushbutton doorbell switch. Complete instructions included. Easy to install in a finished house. 12-volt AC.

ASSORTED BULBS
Houseworks Ltd.
Suggested Retail Price: $ .79 each
#8100-Candle Flame Bulb. 16-volt, white 8" wires.
#8101-Grain of Wheat Bulb. 1.5-volt, green 8" wires.
#8102-Grain of Wheat Bulb. 16-volt, white 8" wires.

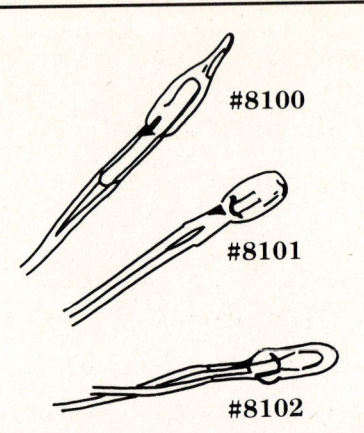

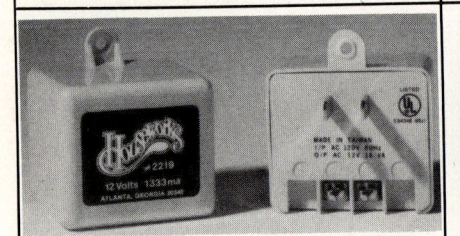

12-VOLT LIGHTING TRANSFORMER
Houseworks Ltd.
Suggested Retail Price: $16.50
Catalog No. 2219
U.L. approved. Features automatic circuit breaker. Output of 1333 milliamps. Illuminates up to 26, 12-volt 50 milliamp bulbs.

3 VOLT REPLACEMENT SCREW BASE BULBS
Houseworks
Suggested Retail Price: $2. Catalog No. 2213. 65 m.a. Four pieces.

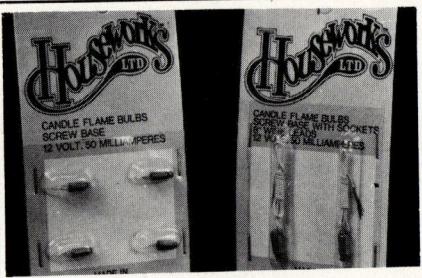

ASSORTED BULBS
Houseworks
#2103-Screw Base Candle Flame Bulbs with socket. Two sets. $4.95.
#2101-Screw Base Candle Flame Bulbs. Four pieces. $5.50.

BATTERY CONSOLE
Houseworks
Suggested Retail Price: $2.25. Catalog No. 2212.
For use with 3 volt systems. Requires two "C" cell 1.5 volt batteries. Batteries not included.

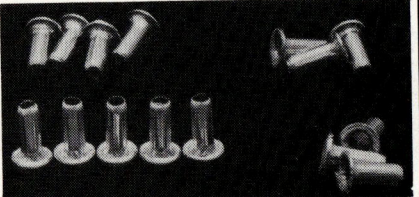

BRASS GROMMET
Houseworks
Suggested Retail Price: 95¢. Catalog No. 2205.
For electric receptacle (plugs). 1/8" deep and fits Housework plugs. To be used with tap wire systems. 20 pieces per package.

BULBS
Houseworks
#2215 - 12 volt, 65 m.a. bulbs with sockets. 24" conductor wire and male plugs $2.30
#2214 - 12 volt, 65 m.a. Bulbs, 4 pcs. $2.40

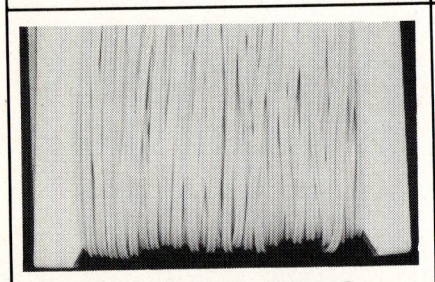

ELECTRICAL WIRING
Houseworks
Suggested Retail Price: $3.95
Catalog No. 2217
For miniature wiring projects. 50 feet per package, two conductor, 32 gauge.

FLICKER FLAME UNIT
Houseworks 
Suggested Retail Price: $3.75. Catalog No. 2019. 12 volt, 150 m.a. for fireplaces. Includes plug and 2 spare bulbs. Use with separate transformer.

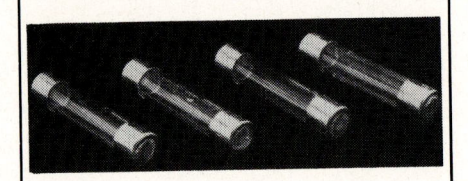

FUSES
Houseworks
Suggested Retail Price: $1.75
Catalog No. 2216
1500 m.a. Four pieces.

LIGHTING CONTROL PANEL
Houseworks
Suggested Retail Price: $14.50
Catalog No. 2200
12 volt lighting control panel for tape and hardwire systems. Controls up to eight separate circuits with on/off operation. Includes diode for dimming operation.

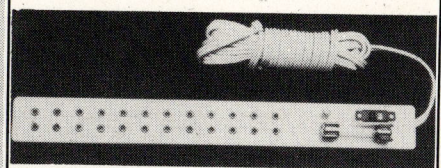

POWER STRIP
Houseworks
Suggested Retail Price: $6.95. Catalog No. 2203.
With on/off switch. One piece.

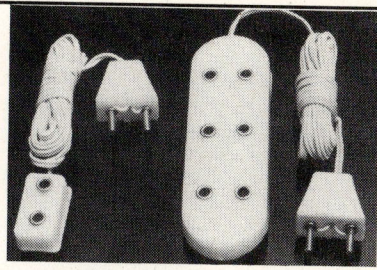

RECEPTACLE EXTENSION CORDS
Houseworks
#2201-Triple Receptacle Extension Cord with plug. Two pieces. $2.30
#2202-Single Receptacle Extension Cord with plug. Four pieces. $2.95

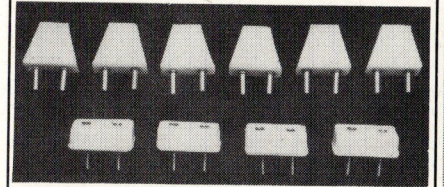

SINGLE WALL RECEPTACLES
Houseworks
#2218 - Plug-in single wall receptacles. For use with tape wiring systems. Plugs into tape. Accepts #2204 plug. Four pieces, $3.95. #2204 - Male plugs. Six pieces, $1.35

FLICKERING FIRE UNIT
Mini Mansions
Suggested Retail Price: $40
Catalog No. III
Hi-tech electronic unit creating the flicker of real fire. Simple to integrate into 12 volt system. Three bulb leads, 3/4" or 6" for installation. Suitable grates or ranges.

AMBER GLASS CHIMNEYS
Miniature House
Suggested Retail Price: $5.79
Catalog No. MH688
Handblown amber glass chimneys to change the color emphasis of an existing light or create a new one. Four per card.

DOLLHOUSE TRANSFORMERS
Miniature House
Suggested Retail Price: MH770-$12.95, MH772-$16.95, MH774-$25.95
These economical 12-volt transformers are all UL approved and circuit breaker protected. MH770, 5 watts, lights 10 bulbs; MH772, 10 watts, lights 23 bulbs; MH774, 30 watts, lights 75 bulbs.

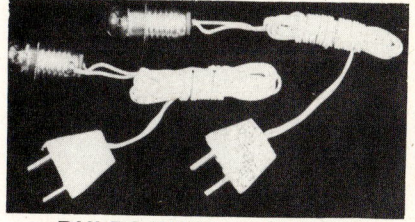

BULBS WITH SOCKETS
Miniature House
Suggested Retail Price: $2.30
Catalog No. MH622
Create your own lighting fixtures with these bulbs with sockets. There are two 12-volt sets per package.

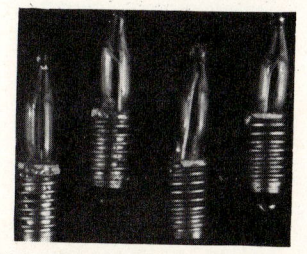

CANDLEFLAME SCREW BULBS
Miniature House
Suggested Retail Price: $5.29 12-volt, $5.49 3-volt
Catalog No. MH611 12-volt, MH639 3-volt
Candleflame screw bulbs come four to a package.

CHANDELIER MODIFICATION KITS
Miniature House
Suggested Retail Price: $4.99 each
Catalog No. MH783-MH786
Completely change the look and style of chandeliers with these unique chimneys and shades. Available in four colors: White (MH783), clear (MH784), amber (MH785), blue (MH786).

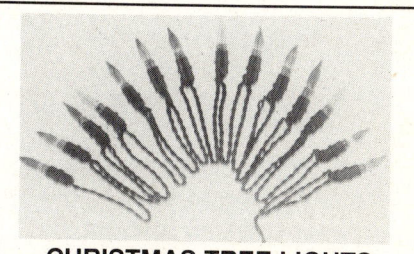

CHRISTMAS TREE LIGHTS
Miniature House
Suggested Retail Price: $24.79
Catalog No. MH638, No. MH690 replacement bulbs
Bright and beautiful Christmas tree lights have 14 replaceable 12-volt bulbs, with two extra. Replacement bulbs are available.

Electrical Systems & Accessories

THE MINIATURES CATALOG, Fourteenth Edition

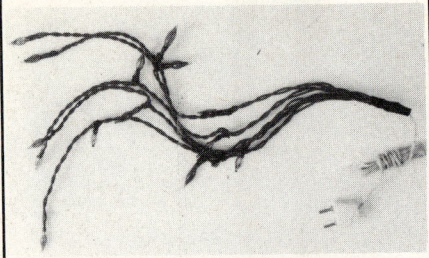

CHRISTMAS TREE LIGHTS

Miniature House
Suggested Retail Price: $32.95
Catalog No. MH782
These multi-colored lights cascade from a central point. The set has 15 12-volt bulbs.

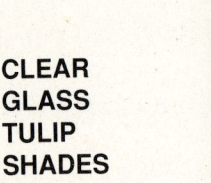

CLEAR GLASS TULIP SHADES

Miniature House
Suggested Retail Price: $4.95
Catalog No. MH667
Replacement shades for lamps and light fixtures, or create your own. There are four per card. 1/2" high.

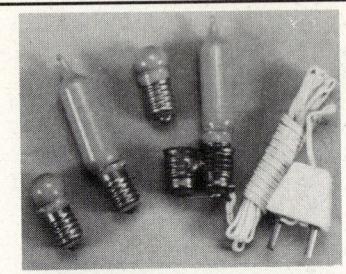

FLICKERING LIGHT UNIT

Miniature House
Suggested Retail Price: $3.89
Catalog No. MH714
Flickering light unit for fireplaces has flame-colored bulbs and comes with a plug and two spare 12-volt bulbs.

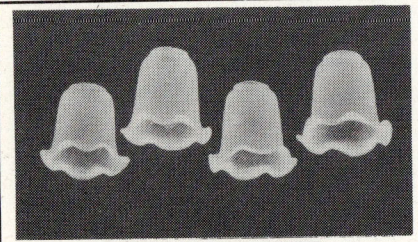

FROSTED GLASS TULIP SHADES

Miniature House
Suggested Retail Price: $5.15
Catalog No. MH668
Frosted glass tulip shades to create your own lighting fixtures or replace shades in existing ones. Four per card. 1/2" high.

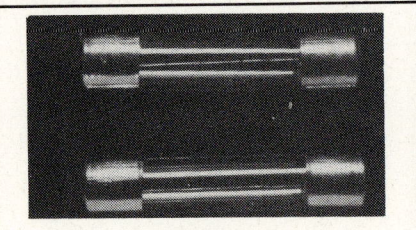

FUSES

Miniature House
Suggested Retail Price: $1.79
Catalog No. MH778, MH779, MH780
Use these fuses to protect both transformer and lighting fixtures. MH778 is 1500 ma., MH779 is 2000 ma., MH780 is 4000 ma. All are four per package.

GLASS CHIMNEYS

Miniature House
Suggested Retail Price: $3.98, clear, $4.19 frosted
Catalog No. MH665 clear, MH666 frosted
Glass replacement chimneys for lamps and light fixtures come four per card 11/16" high.

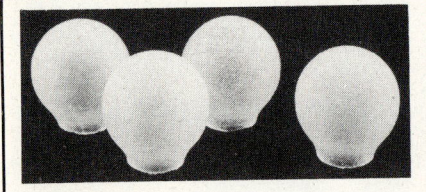

HANDBLOWN GLASS GLOBES

Miniature House
Suggested Retail Price: $3.89 white, $4.79 clear, $4.98 frosted
Catalog No. MH685 white, MH693 clear, MH686 frosted
Four handblown replacement globes per card.

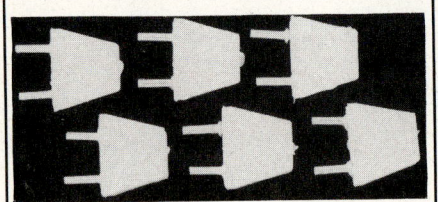

MALE PLUGS

Miniature House
Suggested Retail Price: $1.15
Catalog No. MH658
Package contains six male plugs.

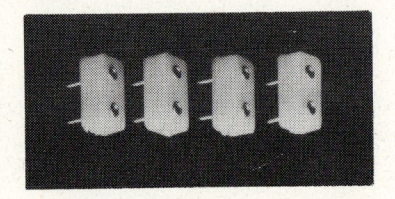

PLUG-IN SINGLE WALL OUTLET

Miniature House
Suggested Retail Price: $6.19
Catalog No. MH776
No fuss, no bother, just plug directly into tape wire for an "instant" outlet. Four per package.

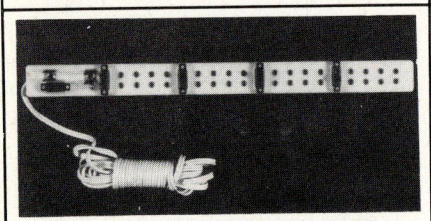

POWER STRIP WITH FIVE SWITCHES AND FUSE

Miniature House
Suggested Retail Price: $7.59
Catalog No. MH777
12-volt power strip has a fuse and five off/on switches. The strip holds 16 male plugs.

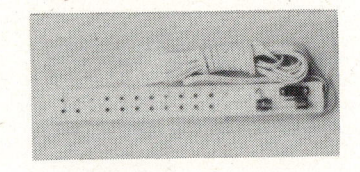

POWER STRIP WITH SWITCH AND FUSE

Miniature House
Suggested Retail Price: $6.95
Catalog No. MH653
12-volt power strip has a fuse and an off/on switch. Holds 12 male plugs.

ROUND SCREW BASE BULBS

Miniature House
Suggested Retail Price: $3
Catalog No. MH621
Each package has four round screw-base, 12-volt bulbs to serve as replacements for lamps and lighting fixtures.

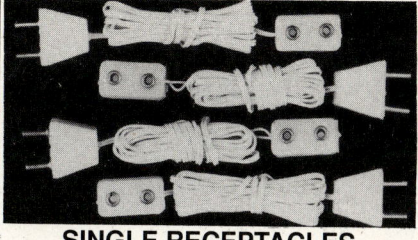

SINGLE RECEPTACLES

Miniature House
Suggested Retail Price: $2.95
Catalog No. MH655
These single receptacles have a male and female plug and extension cord included. Four per package. For use with 12-volt systems.

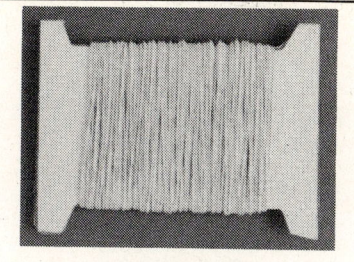

SUPERFINE TWO-STRAND WIRE

Miniature House
Suggested Retail Price: $6.19
Catalog No. MH691
Superfine two-strand white wire is 50' long.

THREE-VOLT BATTERY BOX

Miniature House
Suggested Retail Price: $3.49
Catalog No. MH610
This economical dresser is actually a battery box which holds two size C batteries to power your 3-volt system. Holds up to three lights. 2-1/2"W x 2-1/4"H x 1-1/4"D.

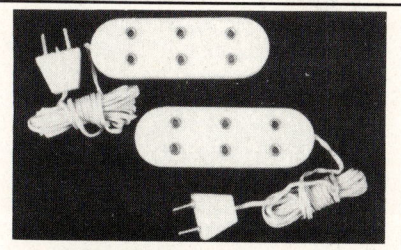

TRIPLE RECEPTACLES

Miniature House
Suggested Retail Price: $2.30
Catalog No. MH656
Triple receptacles have three female plugs and one male plug each. Also extension cord. For use with 12-volt systems. Two per package.

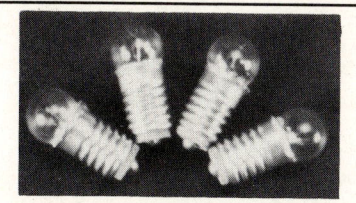

3-VOLT ROUND SCREW-BASE BULBS

Miniature House
Suggested Retail Price: $4
Catalog No. MH687
These 3-volt round screw-base bulbs are for replacement in 3-volt lamps and light fixtures, and come four per card.

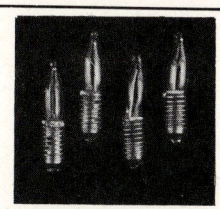

12-VOLT CHRISTMAS TREE BULBS

Miniature House
Suggested Retail Price: $5.69
Catalog No. MH690
The package contains four 12-volt colored bulbs, assorted colors, to replace bulbs in MH638 Christmas tree lights or to add color in a light fixture or lamp.

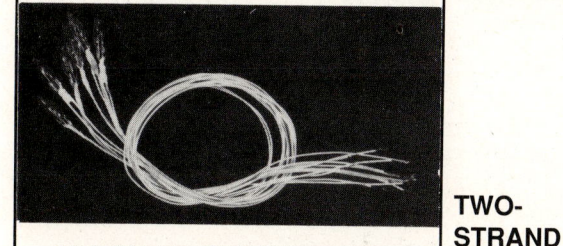

12-VOLT FLAME TIP BULBS

Miniature House
Suggested Retail Price: $6.90
Catalog No. MH692
These 12-volt candleflame tip bulbs are on 8" white wires. There are six bulbs per package.

TWO-STRAND WIRE

Miniature House
Suggested Retail Price: $3.95
Catalog No. MH654
This two-strand wire is 50' long and is perfect for wiring a doll house.

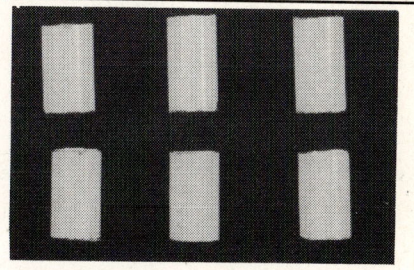

WHITE REPLACEMENT TUBES

Miniature House
Suggested Retail Price: $5.69
Catalog No. MH694
White glass tubes for chandeliers and other lighting fixtures. Six per package.

Want to list your products in the catalog next year?

To receive information on the 15th Edition of *The Miniatures Catalog*, send your name and address to: Sara Benz, *The Miniatures Catalog*, 21027 Crossroads Circle, P.O. Box 1612, Waukesha, WI 53187.

Electrical Systems

Electrical Systems & Accessories

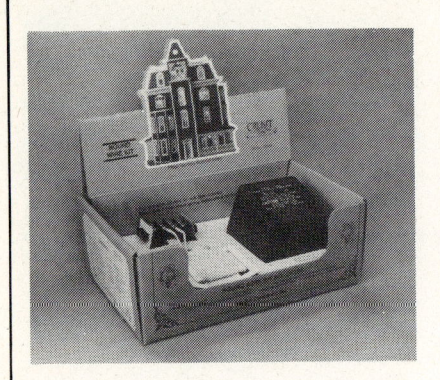

ROUND WIRE KIT

Cir-Kit Concepts, Inc.
Suggested Retail Price: $48.95
Catalog No. CK104
The ideal kit for round wiring enthusiasts. Contains the most comprehensive round wiring instructions ever written. Instructions cover groove wiring, surface wiring and proper installation procedures for all types of lighting fixtures. Contains powerful 20W transformer for lighting 32 to 46 bulbs and sufficient hookup wire for a 6 to 8 room dollhouse.

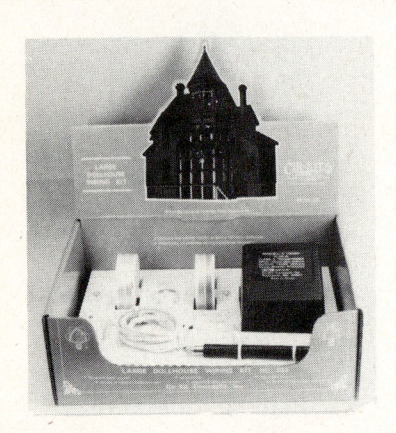

LARGE DOLLHOUSE WIRING KIT

Cir-Kit Concepts, Inc.
Suggested Retail Price: $58.95
Catalog No. CK103
This kit has all the basic Starter Kit items plus a double quantity of brads and tapewire. Large enough to wire a 10 or 11-room dollhouse. Contains a high-power transformer with automatic circuit breaker capable of lighting 32 to 46 bulbs. Lead wire contains built-in on/off switch. No special tools necessary.

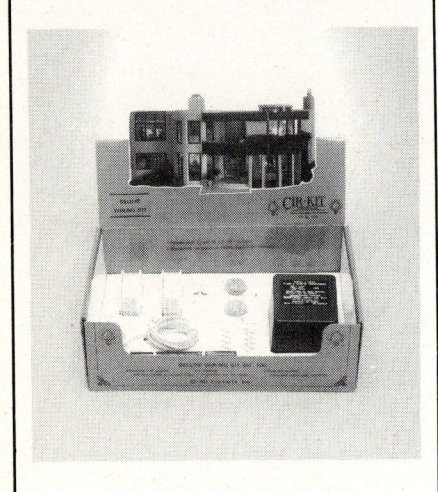

BATTERY HOLDERS

Cir-Kit Concepts, Inc.
CK211, "AA" Size, 2 Cell, 3.0 Volts $1.25
CK211-1, "C" Size, 2 Cell, 3.0 Volts $1.75
CK211-2, "D" Size, 2 Cell, 3.0 Volts $1.98
CK211-3, "AAA" Size, 2 Cell, 3.0 Volts $1.19
CK211-4, "D" Size, 1 Cell, 1.5 Volts $1.39
CK211-5, "C" Size, 1 Cell, 1.5 Volts $1.19
CK211-6, "AA" Size, 1 Cell, 1.5 Volts $.98
CK211-7, "AA" Size, 8 Cell, 12 Volts $1.98
CK211-8, 9-Volt Battery Clips (2 pak) $.98
These battery holders accomodate a wide range of battery sizes and provide numerous output voltage and current options. Special design locks each battery in place. 18" lead wires.

DELUXE WIRING KIT

Cir-Kit Concepts, Inc.
Suggested Retail Price: $89.95
Catalog No. CK100
The ultimate wiring kit. Enough tape and transformer power to wire a 10 or 11 room dollhouse. Includes eight each of our famous Cir-Kit outlets and plugs as well as two sparkling, cut-glass ceiling shades. No previous electrical experience necessary. Extremely thorough and well illustrated instructions. 10% savings over buying parts separately.

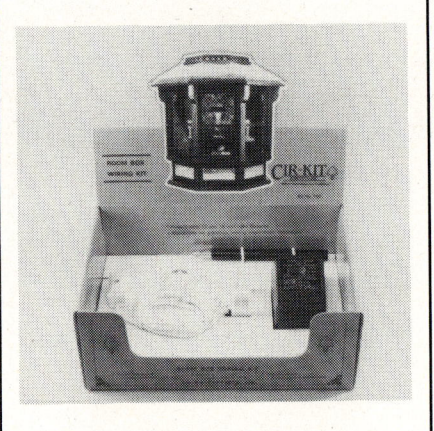

ROOM BOX WIRING KIT

Cir-Kit Concepts, Inc.
Suggested Retail Price: $32.95
Catalog No. CK102
The perfect size kit for any small wiring project. Circuit breaker transformer will power up to ten miniature bulbs. Features 5' of easy-to-use tapewire.

MINIATURE LITE SETS

J. Hermes
Suggested Retail Price: $2.50-$10
Flora lites run on two AA batteries. Various wire lengths and bulbs. Musical flashing lights play various holiday tunes while colored lights flash. Requires two AA batteries.

Prices are approximate and subject to change.

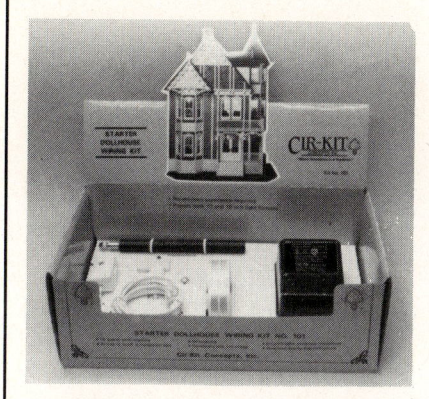

STARTER DOLLHOUSE WIRING KIT

Cir-Kit Concepts, Inc.
Suggested Retail Price: $44.95
Catalog No. CK101
The most popular wiring kit in the industry today. Uses easy-to-apply two-conductor tapewire with embedded copper foils. Wires a five or six-room dollhouse. The 10-watt circuit-breaker protected transformer has a capacity for 16 to 23 bulbs. Lead wire includes on/off switch. Complete instructions included. No previous electrical experience required.

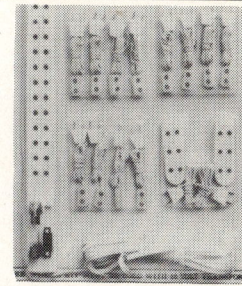

WIRING SET

Miniature House
Suggested Retail Price: $16.98
Catalog No. MH657
Everything needed to wire a dollhouse except a transformer. Contains power strip with fuse and switch, 12 single receptacles, two triple receptacles and an extra fuse.

SAFE AND EASY MINIATURE LIGHTING KITS

Elect-a-Lite
Suggested Retail Price: $37.90, $47.60, $78.80   Catalog Nos. E110, E120, E142
American-made kits contain all materials needed to electrify any miniature house or room box. Capacities to light 12 to 42 bulbs. No electrical knowledge is required. Easy to install, safe to operate and 100% reliable. Also used for model train boards and theatrical stage design. You get plenty of our copper tape, splicing and insulating tape, shrink tubing and our USA fuse-type transformers—the easiest for you to use. Plus, our easy-to-follow instructions. In addition: our E110 contains one of our patented plugs with shrink tube, a test bulb and practice sheet. Our E120 for 21 bulbs has a full 675" of copper tape, three of our patented plugs, one of our popular ceiling plugs, a test bulb, shrink tubing, splicing and insulating, a Tiffany lampshade and a practice sheet. Our E142, the best value in miniature electrification, has a larger transformer, 1350" of copper tape, six of our patented easy-to-use plugs, two of our own ceiling plugs, our EAL bi-prong test tool, two packages of our splicing and insulating tapes, a test bulb, a tiffany lampshade for ceiling installation, a full tiffany lamp and a full-sized practice board.

Miscellaneous Electrification

24-BULB COLORED CHRISTMAS STRING

Cir-Kit Concepts, Inc.
Suggested Retail Price: $29.95
Catalog No. CK1020-5
The first of its kind. String wound around tree in concentric circles from top to bottom. 1" between bulbs. 24" lighted length. 12" green lead wire. Also available with clear bulbs (CK1020-6, $27.95).

YOUR LOCAL MINIATURES SHOP WILL BE HAPPY TO SPECIAL ORDER FOR YOU!

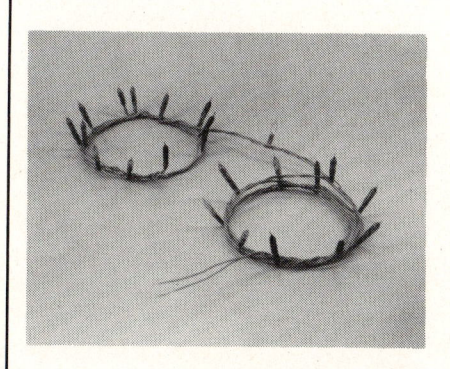

24-BULB COLORED FLAME-TIP CHRISTMAS STRING

Cir-Kit Concepts, Inc.
Suggested Retail Price: $33.95
Catalog No. CK1020-7
This string is constructed with the smallest "flame-shape" bulbs made (.079" in dia.), making them a perfect "to scale" light source for any Christmas tree. Same length as CK1020-5. Also available with clear bulbs (CK1020-8, $31.95).

Electrical Systems & Accessories

THE MINIATURES CATALOG, Fourteenth Edition   147

Outdoor Lighting

BRASS COACH LAMPS

Clare-Bell Brass Works
Suggested Retail Price: #1790120 (solid brass); #1790320 (black finish) $33.70
Sold in pairs, replaceable bulbs available.

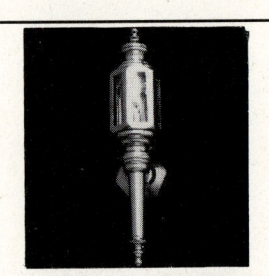

ELEGANT COLONIAL COACH LAMPS

Clare-Bell Brass Works
Suggested Retail Price: $47.65
Catalog No. 1791130
Sold in pairs. Solid brass, gold plated. 1" to 1' scale. Replaceable bulbs.

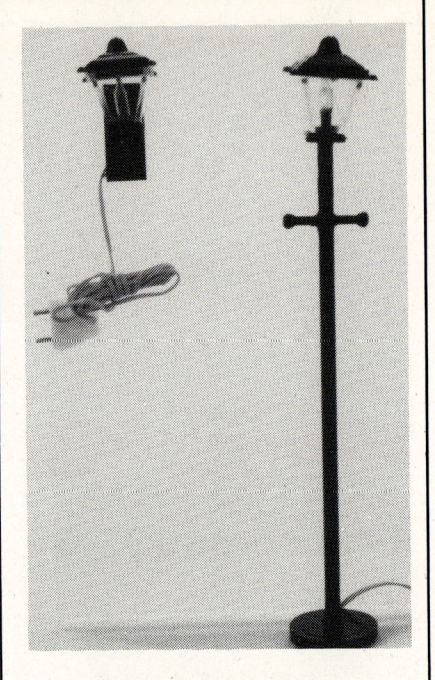

OUTDOOR LIGHTING

Aztec Imports, Inc.
Catalog No. M1754 and M1706
Wholesale only. Add that special touch to the outside of your house with our 6" street lamp (M1754) or coach lamp (M1706). Both are for use in a 12-volt system.

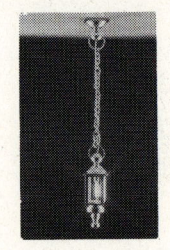

HANGING COACH LAMP

Clare-Bell Brass Works
Suggested Retail Price: $14
Catalog No. 1792120
Solid brass. Ceiling plate and 2" of chain included. Replaceable bulbs also available.

BRASS CARRIAGE LAMP

Elect-a-Lite
Suggested Retail Price: $11.98
Catalog No. 9801
Our authentic reproduction of a carriage lamp will enhance any entry way. Complete with a 12 volt replaceable candleflame bulb. 1-7/8" long.

BLACK COACH LAMP

Miniature House
Suggested Retail Price: $3.40
Catalog No. MH609 3-volt, No. MH628 12-volt - $3.39. MH609 is especially made for 3-volt electrification systems. MH628 is a 12-volt lamp. Both are finished in black.

BRASS CARRIAGE LAMP

Miniature House
Suggested Retail Price: $12.39
Catalog No. MH614
This lovely solid brass carriage lamp has a replaceable candleflame, 12-volt bulb. An authentic reproduction with a hexagonal base.

OUTDOOR LIGHTING FIXTURES

The Lawbre Company
Suggested Retail Price: $20 to $70
Catalog Nos. 0501/0505
Dimensions: Bishops Crook 15" H, Street Lamp 7-3/4" H, Gallery Lamp Post 4-1/2" H, Gallery Lamp Post 3-1/4" H
Beautifully hand-finished lamp posts with screw-in type replaceable bulbs. Wall sconce available (No. 0505, see inset photograph).

Prices are approximate and subject to change.

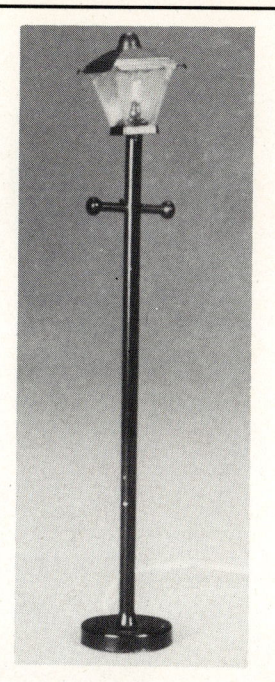

BLACK PLASTIC POST LAMP

Miniature House
Suggested Retail Price: $6.19
Catalog No. MH706
This post lamp is an economical way to add authenticity to the outside around your dollhouse. For use with a 12-volt system. 5" high.

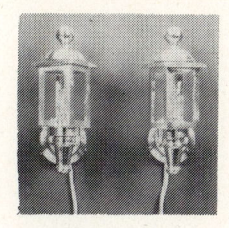

SMALL BRASS COACH LAMPS

Miniature House
Suggested Retail Price: $23.89
Catalog No. MH760
Dimensions: 1-1/2" H x 5/8" D
Pair of solid brass coach lamps are smaller than MH614. Have screw-in 12-volt candleflame bulbs. Sold by the pair.

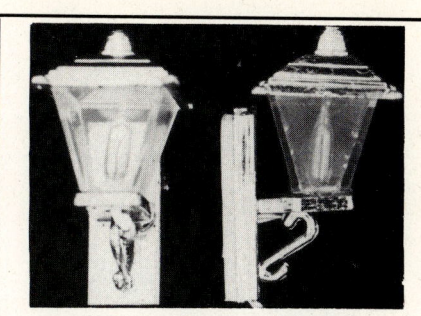

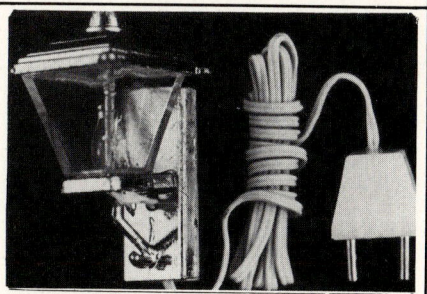

GOLD COACH LAMP

Miniature House
Suggested Retail Price: $3.49
Catalog No. MH629
Inexpensive 12-volt coach lamp, with gold-painted plastic trim.

GOLD COACH LIGHT

Miniature House
Suggested Retail Price: $6.29
Catalog No. MH625
There are two economical coach lights per box. For use in 12-volt systems.

Interested in Becoming a Professional Miniatures Handcrafter? Contact the Cottage Industry Miniaturists Trade Association

CIMTA
P.O. Box 5071
New Haven, CT 06525

Table & Floor Lamps

FLOOR AND TABLE LAMP

Aztec Imports, Inc.
Catalog No. M1768 and G8858
Wholesale only. For the table (M1768) or the floor (G8858). Beautiful brass lamps with plastic shades. Both are for use in a 12-volt system.

ELECTRIC LAMPS

Betty's Wooden Miniatures
All of our lamps are designed and handmade by us. Football helmet available in four colors. Teddy Bear lamp has light blue or pink shade and bow. Clown lamp is white with pastel or bright clown. All are electrified except our Harlow lamp with crystal base. Brass desk lamp has green shade.

CONTEMPORARY BEDROOM LAMP

Clare-Bell Brass Works
Suggested Retail Price: $17.30
Catalog No. 2022-130
Solid brass and gold plated base with contemporary floral or plain cloth shade. Replaceable 12-volt bulb.

Electrical Systems & Accessories

THE MINIATURES CATALOG, Fourteenth Edition

FLOOR LAMP

Cir-Kit Concepts, Inc.
Suggested Retail Price: $8.95
Catalog No. CK808
All-metal base and stand, bronze in color. Removable Tiffany-style lamp shade. 18" power cord with plug. Equipped with replaceable, 12-volt screw-in bulb. Overall height 5", shade diameter 1-1/2".

CANDLESTICKS, ROUND BASE

Clare-Bell Brass Works
Suggested Retail Price: $6.80
Catalog No. 1800111
Available in solid brass.

CONTEMPORARY TABLE LAMP

Clare-Bell Brass Works
Suggested Retail Price: $19.45
Catalog No. 2021-130
Solid brass and gold plated base with contemporary floral or plain cloth shade. Replaceable 12-volt bulb.

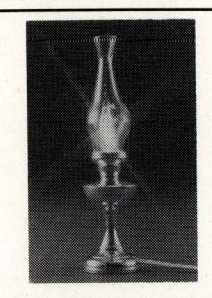

HURRICANE LAMP

Clare-Bell Brass Works
Suggested Retail Price: $11.95
Catalog No. 1750120
Solid brass. Available replaceable bulbs. Handblown glass chimney.

ORIENT EXPRESS LAMP

Clare-Bell Brass Works
Suggested Retail Price: $33.90
Catalog No. 1986120
Solid brass, gold plated, handblown glass and electrified. Replica of Orient Express gas lamp. Replaceable bulbs available.

ORIENTAL TABLE LAMPS

Dollhouse Doll-ups
Suggested Retail Price: $18 - $40
Oriental designs in cloisonne and porcelain. Cloisonne lamps are rust, blue, gold, white and yellow. Porcelain are white, hand-painted with pink, rust and green designs. Electric or non-electric with replaceable 12 volt bulb. Special orders available.

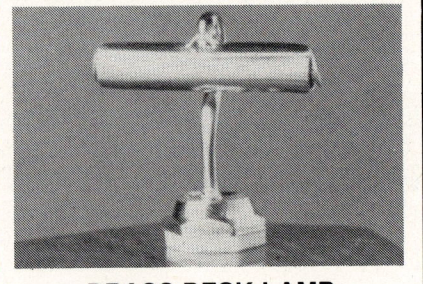

BRASS DESK LAMP

Elect-a-Lite
Suggested Retail Price: $6.98
Catalog No. 9814
Our brass lamp will enhance any desk or secretary. 12 volt bulb. 1-1/8" high.

HURRICANE LAMP WITH WHITE SHADE

Elect-a-Lite
Suggested Retail Price: $4.70
Catalog No. 9822
Our table lamp is complete with white shade and globe and 12 volt bulb.

TABLE LAMP WITH SCALLOPED SHADE

Elect-a-Lite
Suggested Retail Price: $4.60
Catalog No. 9823
This table lamp comes with a white scalloped shade, brass color base and trim and 12 volt replaceable bulb. 2-3/8" high.

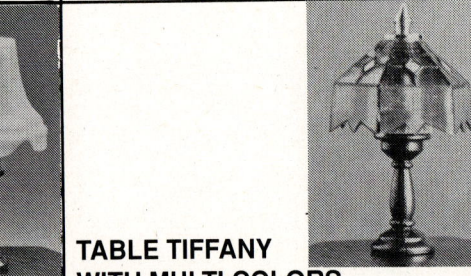

TABLE TIFFANY WITH MULTI COLORS

Elect-a-Lite
Suggested Retail Price: $4.60
Catalog No. 9821
Multi-colored Tiffany table lamp has an antiqued brass look base. Complete with a 12 volt standard replaceable bulb. 2" high.

AS/IS OR DECORATE TABLE LAMP

Miniaturelite
One light table lamp. Decorate base for a custom look or use as/is. Order #526.

150   Prices are approximate and subject to change.

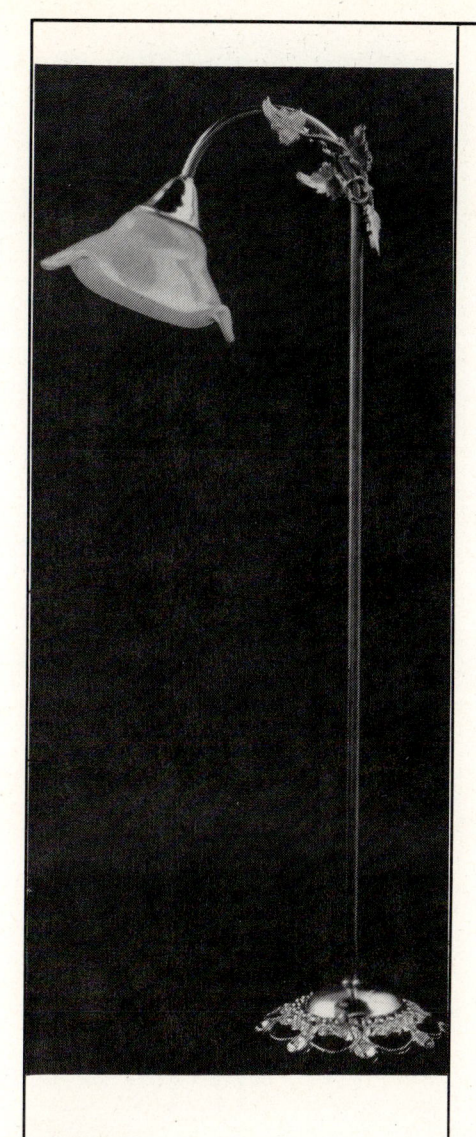

ONE-LITE BRASS FLOOR LAMP

The Lighting Bug
All brass with white hand-blown glass shade. Order #VVV.

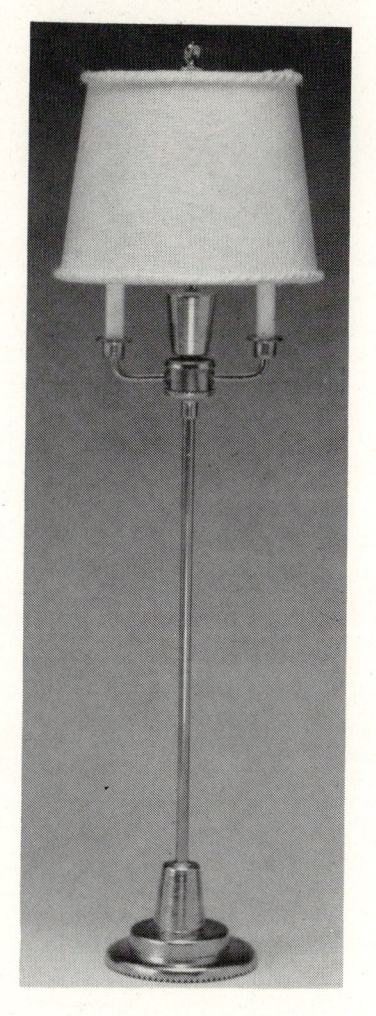

TWO-LITE FLOOR LAMP

The Lighting Bug
Two-lite floor lamp with two candle holders. Silk shade. Order #609.

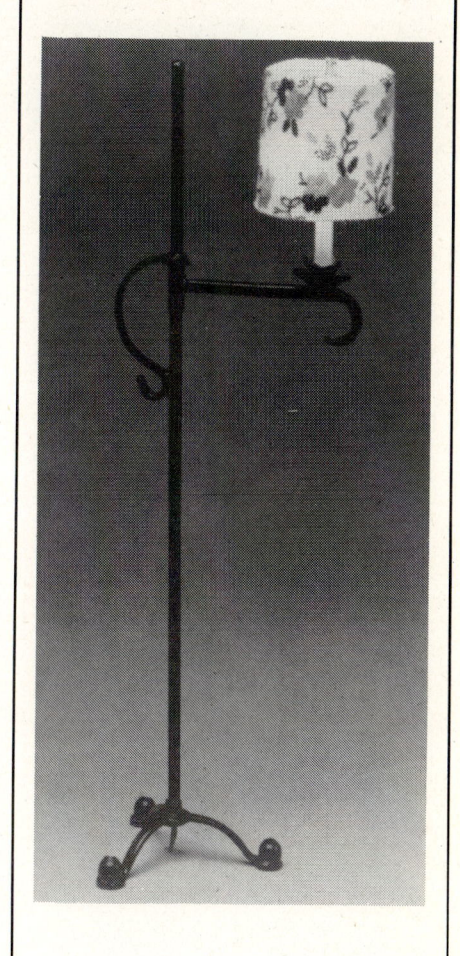

"WROUGHT IRON"-LOOK FLOOR LAMP

The Lighting Bug
Flat black finish with multi-colored print shade. Order #202.

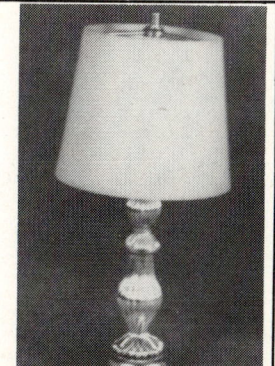

FANCY TABLE LAMP

Miniaturelite
One light, designer type - fancy appearance. Brass. Order #534.

SHINY BRASS TABLE LAMP

Miniaturelite
One light brass table lamp. Very polished, shiny appearance. Order #530.

TABLE LAMP WITH WHITE SHADE

Miniature House
Suggested Retail Price: $9.49
Catalog No. MH757
Electric lamp with modern white shade and gold-plated base. Supplied with a 12-volt bulb.

Electrical Systems & Accessories

THE MINIATURES CATALOG, *Fourteenth Edition* 151

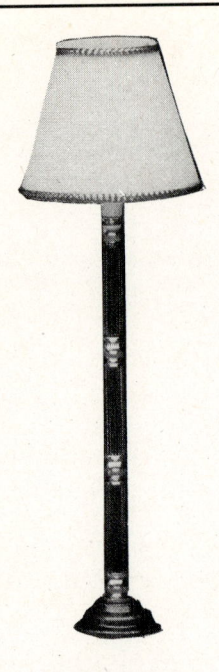

FLOOR LAMP

Miniature House
Suggested Retail Price: $7.19
Catalog No. MH716
Floor lamp with white plastic shade trimmed with gold braid. It is equipped with a replaceable screw-in, 12-volt bulb and stands 4-3/4" high.

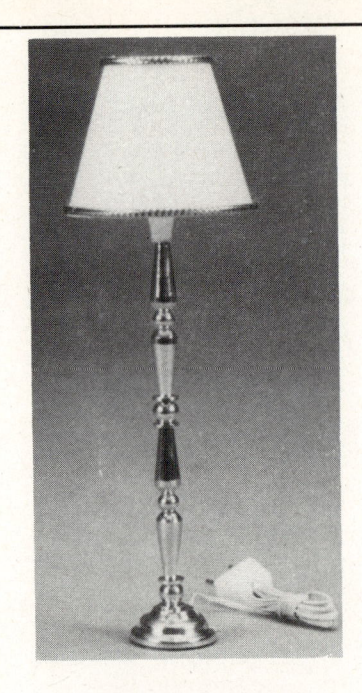

FLOOR LAMP

Miniature House
Suggested Retail Price: $7.19
Catalog No. MH718
Lovely floor lamp has a gold-tone base and white plastic shade trimmed with gold braid. It is equipped with a replaceable screw-in, 12-volt bulb and stands 4-1/2" high.

THREE TULIP ARCHED FLOOR LAMP

Miniature House
Suggested Retail Price: $12.39
Catalog No. MH712
This elegant floor lamp creates an exquisite atmosphere. The unusual base and arched posts are gold-tint plating. Lamp stands 4-1/8" high. Metal work is gold-tint plating.

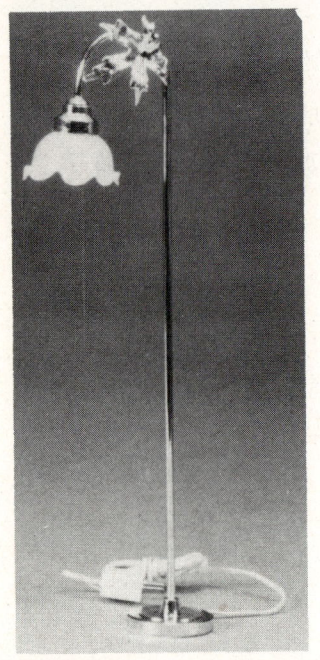

VICTORIAN FLOOR LAMP

Miniature House
Suggested Retail Price: $10.29
Catalog No. MH762
This graceful Victorian floor lamp has a large fluted tulip shade and a gold-tone maple leaf on the arch of the post. It comes with a replaceable screw-in 12-volt bulb.

VICTORIAN FLOOR LAMP

Miniature House
Suggested Retail Price: $6.10
Catalog No. MH647
This lovely floor lamp has a white half-globe shade. Metal work is gold-tint plating. An economical way to dress up your Victorian home. For use in a 12-volt system. 4-1/4" high.

Miniatures Showcase

Published quarterly, each issue explores a particular decorating period or popular theme. Miniatures Showcase is printed in a 8-1/2 X 11 inch format, in full color. Available from your miniatures shop, or by subscription.

TABLE LAMP WITH CLEAR GLOBE

Miniature House
Suggested Retail Price: $11.50
Catalog No. MH759
The ball globe with tulip design makes an attractive addition to your dollhouse. The simple gold-plated base will enhance any decor. 12-volt.

Prices are approximate and subject to change.

BALLERINA TABLE LAMP

Miniature House
Suggested Retail Price: $6.39
Catalog No. MH670
Perfect for the little girl's room, this charming lamp has a white shade trimmed in gold paint. The metal work is gold-tint plating. For use in a 12-volt system. 2-3/8" high.

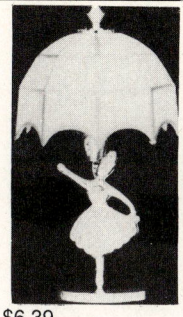

BEDROOM TABLE LAMP

Miniature House
Suggested Retail Price: $5.98
Catalog No. MH662
Dimensions: 1-1/4" high
This mini-boudoir lamp has a graceful base and a white cloth shade. The 12-volt screw-in bulb is replaceable. The metal work is gold-tint plating.

Your Listings Belong Here!
Interested in advertising in the
15th Edition of
The Miniatures Catalog?

Contact Sara Benz at
1-800-558-1544,
Ext. 631
or write to;
The Miniatures Catalog
P.O. Box 1612
Waukesha, WI 53187

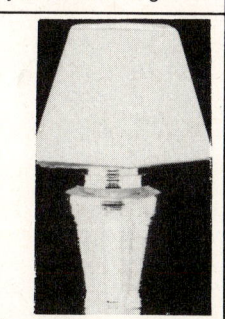

BEDROOM TABLE LAMP

Miniature House
Suggested Retail Price: $6.29
Catalog No. MH664
Small table lamp has a ginger jar-shaped base and a removable white cloth shade. 12-volt bulb is replaceable. Metal work is gold-tint plating.

BRASS DESK LAMP

Miniature House
Suggested Retail Price: $8.25
Catalog No. MH708
Brass desk lamp is ideal for the office or teen's desk. Use with a 12-volt system.

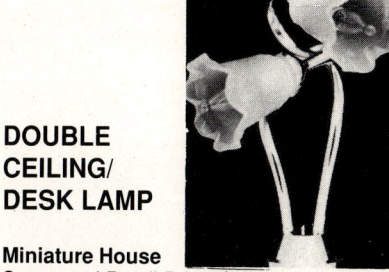

DOUBLE CEILING/ DESK LAMP

Miniature House
Suggested Retail Price: $11.19
Catalog No. MH672
The entwined necks of this double light enhance the beauty of the frosted, fluted shades. For use in a 12-volt system. It has screw-in replaceable bulbs. Metal work is gold-tint plating.

ELECTRIC CANDLES

Miniature House
Suggested Retail Price: $11.98
Catalog No. MH768
Dainty solid brass candlestands have 12-volt candles. Sold in pairs.

GLAZED CERAMIC TABLE LAMP

Miniature House
Suggested Retail Price: $6.98
Catalog No. MH711
Glazed ceramic table lamp, pastel blue.

GOLD FRINGED TABLE LAMP

Miniature House
Suggested Retail Price: $4.75
Catalog No. MH602
Removable white shade with gold braid and fringe accents this lamp. It has a replaceable screw-in bulb. The base is gold-tint plating. Use with 12-volt systems only. 3" high.

HANGING TABLE LANTERN

Miniature House
Suggested Retail Price: See below
MH713-Hanging table lantern, white-$10.65
MH715-Hanging table lantern, frosted-$10.85
MH717-Hanging table lantern, clear-$10.85

HURRICANE LAMP

Miniature House
Suggested Retail Price: $8.25
Catalog No. MH766
Solid brass replica with hand-blown chimney is 12-volt and is a lovely addition to any miniature project.

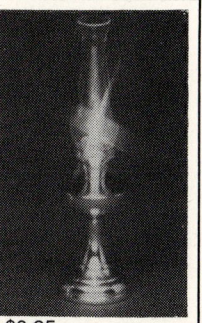

HURRICANE LAMPS

Miniature House
Suggested Retail Price: $16.95
Catalog No. MH695 and MH696
MH695 - Hurricane table lamp, blown white glass with rose print. MH696 - Hurricane lamp, blown white glass with rose print.

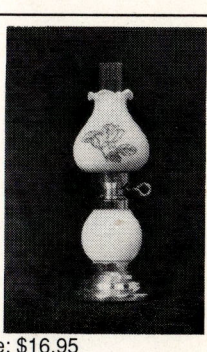

Electrical Systems & Accessories

KARO STYLE TABLE LAMP

Miniature House
Suggested Retail Price: $4.19
Catalog No. MH604
This lovely reproduction has a white chimney and antiqued brass-look finish on the base. For use in 12-volt systems, it's 2-1/8" high.

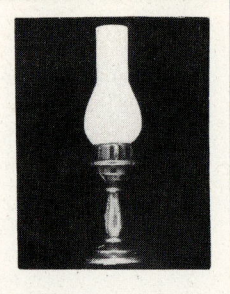

KARO TABLE LAMP WITH SHADE

Miniature House
Suggested Retail Price: $5.50
Catalog No. MH702
This karo table lamp has a white translucent shade and antiqued brass-look base. It is 2-1/8" high. For use in a 12-volt system.

TABLE/DESK LAMP

Miniature House
Suggested Retail Price: $10.79
Catalog No. MH703
Table/desk lamp, large frosted tulip.

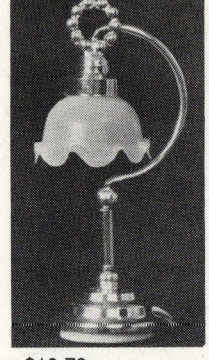

TABLE/DESK LAMP

Miniature House
Suggested Retail Price: $10.39
Catalog No. MH705
Table/desk lamp, fringed, rose decal.

TABLE LAMP

Miniature House
Suggested Retail Price: Catalog No. MH618 gold-tone base - $6.20, No. MH618A dark stained base - $5.89
Lamp has a white shade trimmed in gold braid. It has a replaceable screw-in 12-volt bulb. 2-3/8" high.

TABLE LAMP

Miniature House
Suggested Retail Price: $4.79
Catalog No. MH642.
Lamp has scalloped plastic shade and dark base. The 12 volt bulb is replaceable and an extra bulb is included. Available in white or peach. 2-3/8" high.

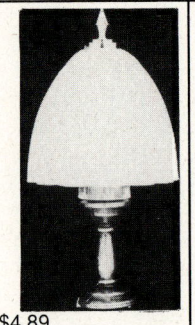

TABLE LAMP

Miniature House
Suggested Retail Price: $4.89
Catalog No. MH643
Lamp has plastic removable shade and replaceable 12-volt bulb. Extra bulb included. Dark base. Available in white or peach. 2-1/2" high.

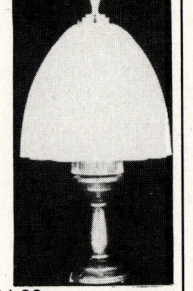

TABLE LAMP

Miniature House
Suggested Retail Price: $4.75
Catalog No. MH644
Shade is trimmed top and bottom with dark peach braid. Base is antiqued-brass look. 12-volt bulb is replaceable and an extra bulb is included. Available in white or peach. 2" high.

TABLE LAMP

Miniature House
Suggested Retail Price: $4.89
Catalog No. MH645
Attractive lamp has dark peach braid along bottom edge of shade. 12-volt bulb is screw-in and an extra one is included. Available in white or peach. 2-1/4" high.

TABLE LAMP

Miniature House
Suggested Retail Price: $4.75
Catalog No. MH646
Lamp has plastic removable shade with dark peach braid trimming. 12-volt bulb is replaceable and an extra one is included. Available in white or peach. 2-3/8" high.

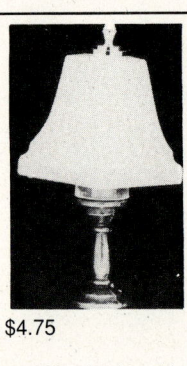

October National Dollhouse & Miniatures Month

Prices are approximate and subject to change.

FREE-HAND CHINA PAINTED LAMPS
Ni-Glo® Lamps
Catalog No.: L7, L20, L30 and L43 (left to right)
Accent lamp with brass filigree base or trimmed with 24K gold. Bird or floral design of your choice. Replaceable 12V light. Made in the USA.

NI-GLO® LAMP COLLECTION
Just A Shade Better

STUDENT LAMP
Ni-Glo® Lamps
Catalog No.: L51
Solid brass student lamps with dark green or cranberry shade. Replaceable 12V light. Made in the USA.

VICTORIAN LAMPS
Ni-Glo® Lamps
Catalog No.: L32 and L33 (left to right)
Classic Victorian all porcelain lamp. Hand decorated dome shade with rose magnolia with hummingbird or pink multi roses. With or without hanging tubular crystals.

TAM O'SHANTOR SHADES
Ni-Glo® Lamps
Catalog No.: L24, L34, L45 and L41 (left to right)
Tam O'Shantor shades decorated with your favorite floral or bird design. Plain or handing crystal facet beads. Replaceable 12V light. Made in the USA.

MANTEL LAMP
Ni-Glo® Lamps
Catalog No.: L46
Mantel or piano with tubular hanging crystals. Black onyx base with brass stand. Tiny pink roses enhances this timeless design. Replaceable 12V light. Made in the USA.

TIFFANY ANTIQUE BRONZE LAMPS
Ni-Glo® Lamps
Catalog No.: L21, L26, L36 and L36 (left to right)
Lamps designed in the tradition of Tiffany. Handpainted dome shade is trimmed with filigree band. Plain band or tubular hanging crystals. Replaceable 12V light. Made in the USA.

VICTORIAN TABLE LAMPS
Ni-Glo® Lamps
Catalog No.: L23, L31, L17 and L18 (left to right)
Exquisitely handcrafted and decorated translucent porcelain with brass components. Replaceable 12V light. Made in the USA.

CHINA TABLE LAMPS
Ni-Glo® Lamps
Catalog No.: L2, L4, and L3 (left to right)
Contemporary porcelain base - 1" or 1/2" scale. Free hand china painted design on an off-white base, trimmed with 24K gold. Silk fabric over vinyl shade.

HANDEL STYLE LAMPS
Ni-Glo® Lamps
Catalog No.: L44, L44 and L50 (left to right)
Authentic handel-style lamp from the 20's era. Dome shade can be designed to match your decor. Replaceable 12V light. Made in the USA.

BRASS CHANDELIERS
Ni-Glo® Lamps
Catalog No.: L40 and L42 (left to right)
Three branch brass chandelier by Clare-Bell Brass Works. Complemented with #40 round globe and #42 Colonial. Not shown; #10 Tam O'Shantor shade with tiny pink roses. This particular fixture is a finished product by Ni-Glo®.

BRASS TABLE LAMPS
Ni-Glo® Lamps
Catalog No.: L13, L16, L15 and L27 (left to right)
Brass lamp base with round globe or Tam O'Shantor shade with plain filigree band or hanging crystal facet beads.

HANGING CEILING FIXTURE
Ni-Glo® Lamps
Catalog No.: L25 and L28 (left to right)
Brass lamps with fanciful turn of the century styling. Hand decorated design of your choice. Replaceable 12V light.

Electrical Systems & Accessories

THE MINIATURES CATALOG, Fourteenth Edition

TABLE LAMP

Miniature House
Suggested Retail Price: $9.98
Catalog No. MH699
Elegant table lamp, clear blown glass with rose print.

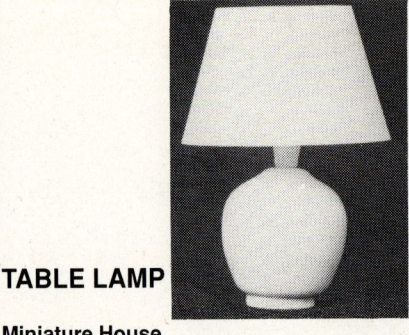

TABLE LAMP

Miniature House
Suggested Retail Price: $6.98
Catalog No. MH707, glazed ceramic table lamp, pastel pink; MH709, glazed ceramic table lamp, ivory.

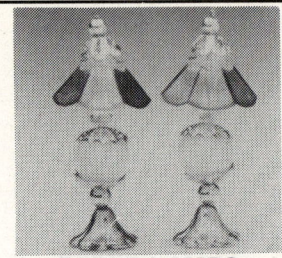

TABLE LAMPS

Miniature House
Suggested Retail Price: $3.10
Catalog No. MH613
These cute non-electric lamps come in assorted colors and styles. Two per package.

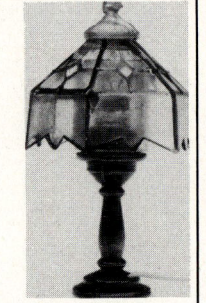

TIFFANY TABLE LAMP

Miniature House
Suggested Retail Price: $4.89
Catalog No. MH607
Lamp is multi-colored with an antiqued brass-look base. It has a replacement screw-in, 12-volt bulb. An extra bulb is included. 2" high.

TIFFANY TABLE LAMP

Miniature House
Suggested Retail Price: $4.75
Catalog No. MH608
This lamp has a multi-colored shade and an antiqued brass-look base. It has a replaceable screw-in, 12-volt bulb. An extra bulb is included. 2" high.

TIFFANY TABLE LAMPS

Miniature House
Suggested Retail Price: $8.79
Catalog No. MH620
Lamps come two per box, with multi-colored shades. Replaceable 12-volt bulbs and two extra per box. Styles are assorted. 1-7/8"H.

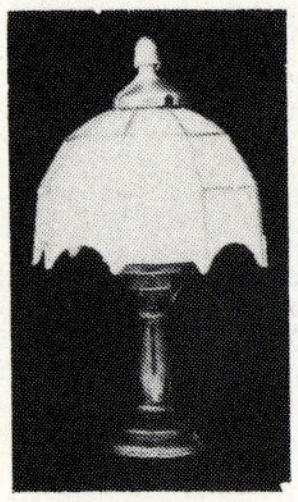

TIFFANY TABLE LAMP

Miniature House
Suggested Retail Price: $4.79
Catalog No. MH627
Dimensions: 1-7/8" high
Lamp has a white removable shade, trimmed in gold. Bulb is screw-in and an extra bulb is included. For use in 12-volt system.

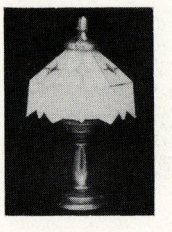

TIFFANY TABLE LAMP

Miniature House
Suggested Retail Price: $4.79
Catalog No. MH631
Dimensions: 1-7/8" high
An attractive lamp with a white diamond-patterned shade. It has a screw-in, 12-volt bulb, and an extra bulb is included in package.

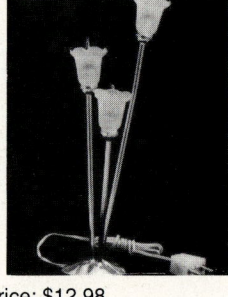

3-TULIP STRAIGHT FLOOR LAMP

Miniature House
Suggested Retail Price: $12.98
Catalog No. MH710
This eclectic mixture of the Victorian and contemporary eras creates a unique floor lamp. The three 12-volt candleflame bulbs are replaceable. Gold-tint plating.

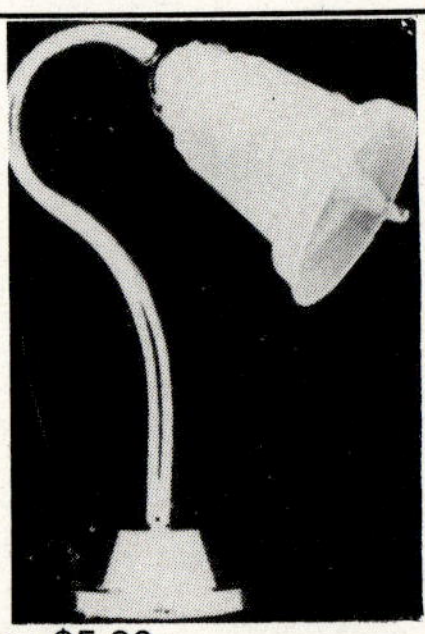

WALL/DESK LAMP

Miniature House
Suggested Retail Price: $5.39
Catalog No. MH661
This curve-necked lamp is very versatile, useful both as a wall light or a desk lamp. The 12-volt bulb is replaceable. Metal work is gold-tint plating.

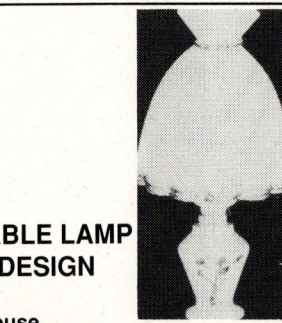

WHITE TABLE LAMP PAINTED DESIGN

Miniature House
Suggested Retail Price: $6.59
Catalog No. MH663
Ceramic look base has a painted design. Shade is white, trimmed in gold braid. 12-volt, screw-in bulb. 2-1/2" high.

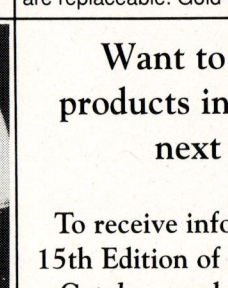

Want to list your products in the catalog next year?

To receive information on the 15th Edition of *The Miniatures Catalog*, send your name and address to: Sara Benz, *The Miniatures Catalog*, 21027 Crossroads Circle, P.O. Box 1612, Waukesha, WI 53187.

LOOKING FOR SOMETHING SPECIAL? CHECK WITH YOUR LOCAL MINIATURES SHOP!

Wall Fixtures

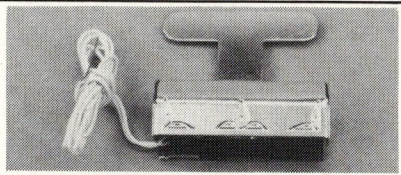

BRASS PICTURE LAMP

Cir-Kit Concepts, Inc.
Suggested Retail Price: $9.98
Catalog No. CK5003
Dimensions: 7/8" W x 1/4" D x 5/16" H
Material: Solid brass
Decorative brass picture lamp for lighting miniature pictures and paintings. Mounts on top of frame. Connects to any 12-volt electrical system. 8" wires. Draws 60 ma.

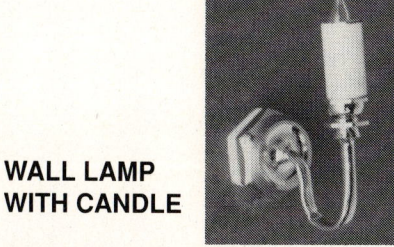

WALL LAMP WITH CANDLE

Elect-a-Lite
Suggested Retail Price: $5.30
Catalog No. 9803
One arm candle sconce with brass look base comes with a replaceable 12 volt candleflame bulb. 1" long.

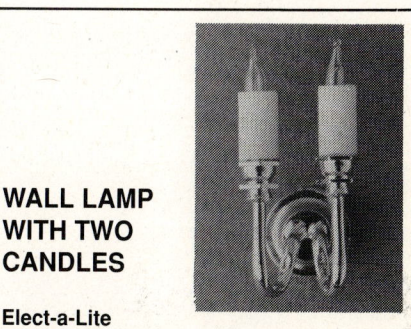

WALL LAMP WITH TWO CANDLES

Elect-a-Lite
Suggested Retail Price: $9.50
Catalog No. 9802
This wall sconce with two arms and brass look base comes with two replaceable 12 volt candleflame bulbs. 1" long.

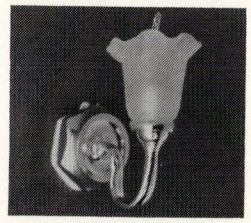

WALL SCONCE WITH FROSTED CANTED TULIP

Elect-a-Lite
Suggested Retail Price: $5.40
Catalog No. 9804
One arm canted wall sconce with frosted tulip shade. Comes with 12 volt replaceable candleflame bulb. 1" long.

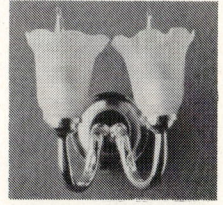

WALL SCONCE WITH TWO TULIPS

Elect-a-Lite
Suggested Retail Price: $9.98
Catalog No. 9806
Two arm wall sconce with dainty frosted tulip shades and brass look base. Replaceable candleflame 12 volt bulb included. 1" long.

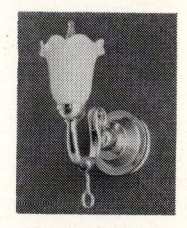

WALL SCONCE WITH WHITE TULIP AND LOOP

Elect-a-Lite
Suggested Retail Price: $5.96
Catalog No. 9805
One arm wall sconce with loop and white tulip shade. Complete with 12 volt candleflame replaceable bulb. 1-1/4" long.

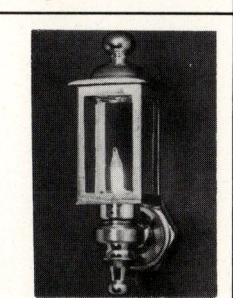

COLONIAL COACH LAMP

Houseworks
Suggested Retail Price: $13.50
Catalog No. 2014
This lovely Colonial Coach Lamp is solid brass with 12-volt lamp and replaceable bulbs.

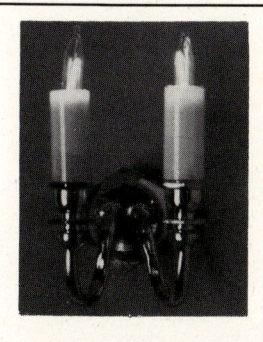

COLONIAL TWO-ARM SCONCE

Houseworks
Suggested Retail Price: $12.75
Catalog No. 2013
Solid brass, 12-volt with replaceable bulbs.

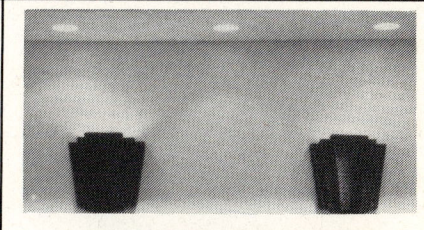

WALL SCONCES AND RECESSED LIGHTING UNIT

Le' Petite Architect
Suggested Retail Price: $12.95 sconces, from $23.95 recessed lighting units
Designed to lighten up any room. 12V replaceable bulbs. Available in a variety of colors.

Electrical Systems & Accessories

THE MINIATURES CATALOG, **Fourteenth Edition** 157

CANTED WALL SCONCE WITH GLOBE

Miniature House
Suggested Retail Price: $5.79
Catalog No. MH641
Lovely canted wall sconce has a white globe shade. Metal work is gold-tint plating. Bulb is 12-volt.

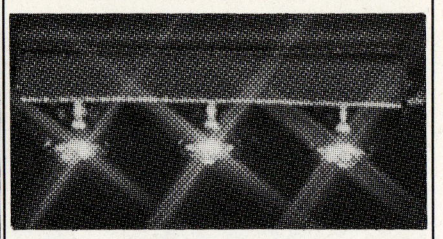

BAR LIGHT

Miniature House
Suggested Retail Price: $11.39
Catalog No. MH659
This bar light has many uses: make-up area, bar display boxes, contemporary settings. It has three 12-volt bulbs. Metal work is gold-tint plating.

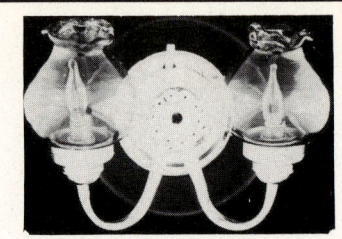

TWO-GLOBE AMBER WALL SCONCE

Miniature House
Suggested Retail Price: $16.25
Catalog No. MH683
Victorian style with clear amber globes and fluted caps. Candleflame bulbs and gold-tint plating. Replacement globes available.

WALL SCONCE

Miniature House
Suggested Retail Price: $12.98
Catalog No. MH761
Medallion wall sconce with clear globe and gold-plated base and medallion. Comes with a 12-volt bulb.

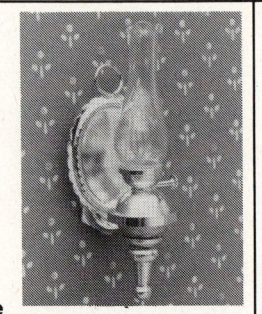

WALL LAMP WITH TWO CANDLES

Miniature House
Suggested Retail Price: $9.98
Catalog No. MH606
This two-arm wall sconce works with any 12-volt electrification system. Metal work is gold-tint plating.

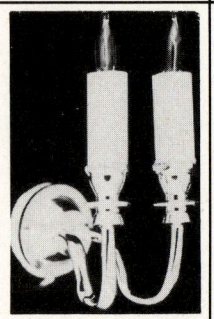

DOUBLE TULIP WALL SCONCE

Miniature House
Suggested Retail Price: $10.79
Catalog No. MH673
The lovely frosted tulip shades add elegance to your miniature creation. The 12-volt candleflame bulbs are replaceable. Metal work is gold-tint plating.

WALL SCONCE

Miniature House
Suggested Retail Price: $8.98
Catalog No. MH701
Wall sconce with backplate reflector.

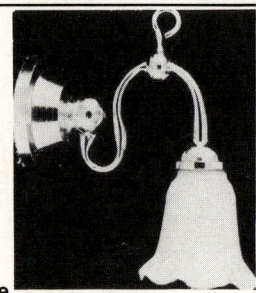

WALL SCONCE

Miniature House
Suggested Retail Price: $6.19
Catalog No. MH636
A lovely addition to any hallway, bedroom or bathroom. Scone has a white fluted tulip shade and a 12-volt screw-in candleflame bulb. Metal work is gold-tint plating.

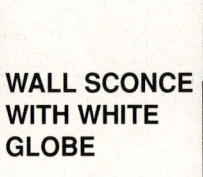

WALL SCONCE WITH WHITE GLOBE

Miniature House
Suggested Retail Price: $6.20
Catalog No. MH603
A classic sconce perfect for lighting stairs, hallways, or porches. Metal work is gold-tint plating. 12-volt only.

CANTED WALL SCONCE

Miniature House
Suggested Retail Price: $5.50
Catalog No. MH640
This canted wall sconce has a frosted tulip shade. Metal work is gold-tint plating. For use in a 12-volt system.

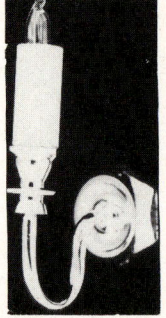

WALL LAMP WITH CANDLE

Miniature House
Suggested Retail Price: $5.49
Catalog No. MH605
This brass-tone sconce has a hexagonal back and a 12-volt candleflame bulb.

October National Dollhouse & Miniatures Month

Prices are approximate and subject to change.

D'LIGHTFUL MINIATURES

Small Time Operators
Handcrafted by Dawn and Bob McKay with Aloha from Hawaii. See your local dealer.

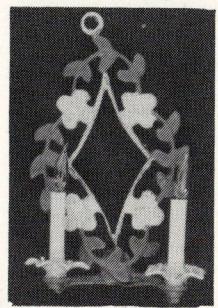

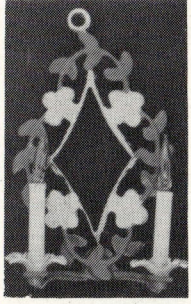

LEILANI SCONCES

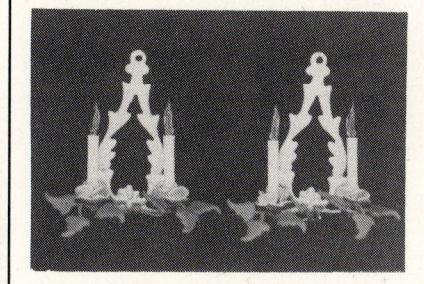

ROSE SCONCE

PRINCESS ABIGAIL

FLORAL FANTASY

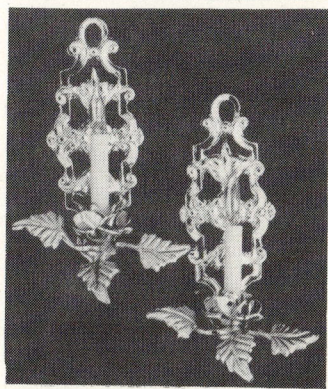

SINGLE ROSE (GOLD)

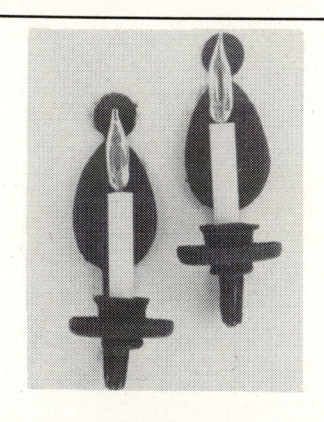

COLONIAL

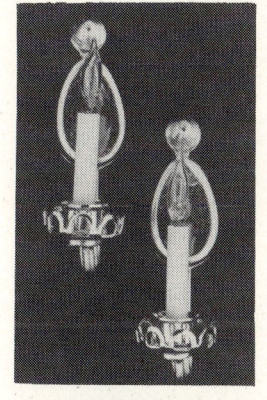

HERITAGE

LIMOGE ROSE

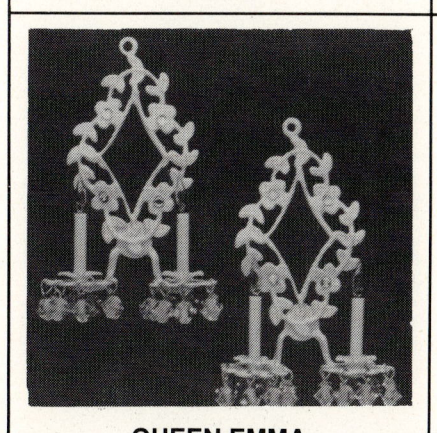

QUEEN EMMA

VERSAILLES

VICTORIA

Electrical Systems & Accessories

THE MINIATURES CATALOG, *Fourteenth Edition* 159

Interior Decorating Materials

Interior Decorating Materials

Fabric & Trim

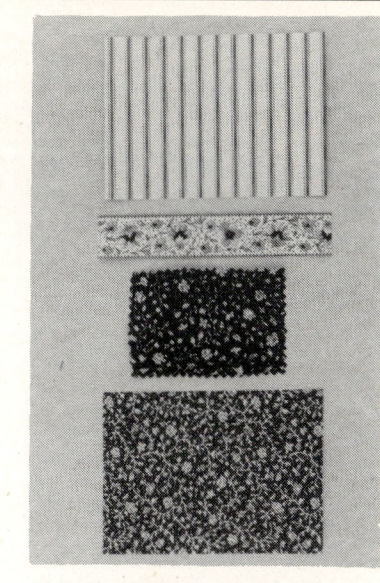

"ROSE" FABRIC, WALLPAPER AND BORDER

KriStan Prepasted Wallpaper & Floor Covering
Suggested Retail Price: wholesale only
Our fabrics match and/or coordinate with our wallpaper selections. Our borders also match or coordinate with both the wallpaper and fabric. The fabric measures 12" x 20" and includes moires. The borders are 18". Product #819-237F-230B & 821.

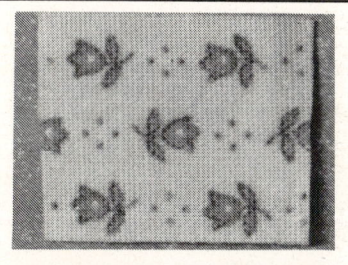

CALICO PRINT COTTONS

Dollhouse Doll-ups
Suggested Retail Price: $3.50 - $10
Calico print cottons with special adhesive backing makes upholstering cushions and covering walls an easy task. 14" x 30" small prints and plain in 31 patterns.

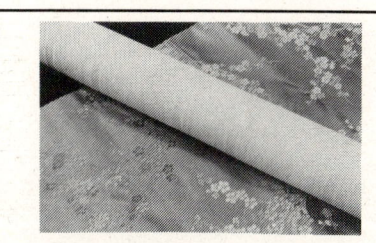

SILK BROCADE FABRIC

Dollhouse Doll-ups
Suggested Retail Price: $10 - $20
Chinese silk brocade fabric with coordinated plain colors for use as wallpaper, upholstery, curtains, bedspreads and canopies. Also lace curtain material, ribbons and trims.

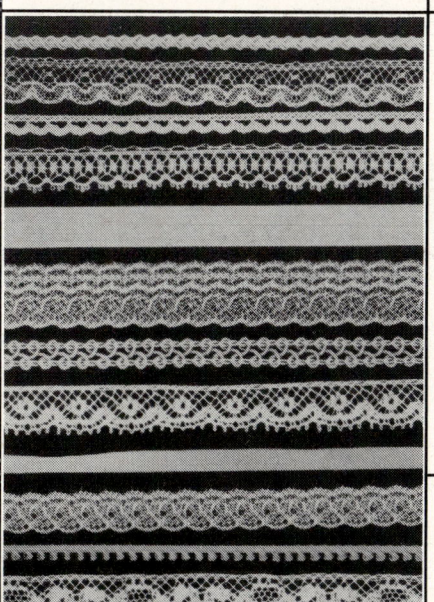

RIBBONS

YLI Corporation
Catalog No. 100-1
Kanagawa silk ribbon: 1/16" - 63 colors. 1/8" -185 colors. 1/4" - 29 colors in stock. Applications: Egg decorating, miniatures, dolls, knitting. Spark Organdy ribbon: 5mm and 9mm—30 colors. 13mm and 18mm—10 colors. Most unique. Also, Feather touch ribbon, synthetic silk ribbon, fancy ribbon, synthetic suede knit. Catalog, $2.50. Immediate shipping. Imported.

RIBBONS AND LACE

Viv's Ribbons & Lace
Our large selection of trims includes six sizes of silk ribbon, 1/16" - 1-1/4", bunka dyed to match the silk ribbon, small braids, cotton laces, 20 colors of tiny picot and 32 colors of soutache. We also carry fabric glue.

Fireplaces

THE MINIATURES CATALOG, *Fourteenth Edition*

FIREPLACE

Aztec Imports, Inc.
Catalog No. T5001
Wholesale only. Contemporary white wooden fireplace with a black-painted interior. The sleek lines add to any contemporary look.

FIREPLACE

Aztec Imports, Inc.
Catalog No. T6014
Wholesale only. This walnut wood fireplace features an inter-white trim. The combination of colors makes this piece perfect for your federal home.

FIREPLACE WITH FLICKERING LIGHTS

Cir-Kit Concepts, Inc.
Suggested Retail Price: $18.95, Cat.# CK866
Dimensions: 3-3/4" H x 4-15/16 " W x 1-5/16" D
All-wood construction with brass fire box. Includes a two-bulb flickering unit, wood logs and decorative brass trim. Use with separate CK1009F 12-volt transformer.

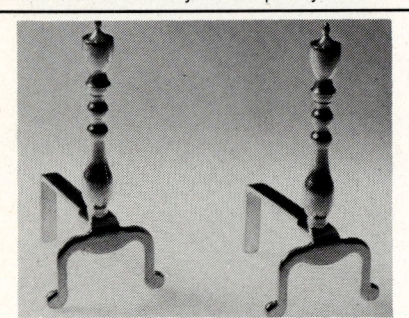

ANDIRONS

Clare-Bell Brass Works
Suggested Retail Price: $21.75
Catalog No. 1781100
Solid brass, gold plated andirons. 1" to 1'.

FIREPLACE FAN SCREEN

Clare-Bell Brass Works
Suggested Retail Price: $9.85
Catalog No. 1783100
Beautiful brass fan screen. Superb quality. All Clare-Bell items are American made.

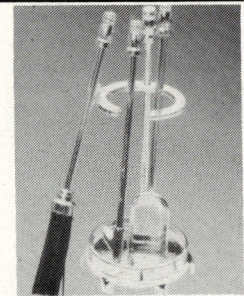

FIREPLACE TOOL SET

Clare-Bell Brass Works
Suggested Retail Price: $47.45
Catalog No. 1985100
Solid brass, gold plated tool set. The finest quality found. 1" to 1' scale.

FIREPLACES

Handcraft Designs, Inc.
Catalog No: Left to Right: 3902W, 3925, 3910S
Dimensions: No. 3902 is 4-3/4" H x 5-3/8" W.
Material: Wood with marble, simulated brick, and paper "tile" decoration.
No. 3902 is available in white paint or walnut-stain finish (3902S). No. 3925 is faced with green marble. No. 3910 is available in walnut-stain or white paint finish (3910W). A complete line of fireplace accessories and tools is also available.

ASSORTED FIREPLACES

Houseworks
#2403-Jamestown Fireplace. This fireplace boasts handcrafted moulding and refined beveled edges. Size: 4-3/16" H x 5-15/16" W x 1-9/16" D, $13.75
#2401-Monticello fireplace. Traditional colonial style with detailed moldings and turned, sculpted posts. Size: 5-1/8" H x 6-1/8" W x 1-1/2" D, $15.50

CORNER FIREPLACE

Exclusive Products
Have the warmth of a fireplace and free up the floor plan for other furnishings. A novel solution finished in mahogany. #B-9920.

Interior Decorating Materials

VICTORIAN MIRRORED FIREPLACE

The Lawbre Company
Suggested Retail Price: $18.95
Catalog No. 1085
Cast in hydrocal cement. Available in white only. Shown painted with acrylic paints and stains. 5" W x 6" H x 1" D

ASSORTED FIREPLACES

Houseworks
#2022-"Americana" fireplace. Electric fireplace includes brass fire box, two bulb flickering unit, natural logs and two spare bulbs. Use with separate 12-volt transformer, $18.50
#2402-Orleans fireplace features gracefully sculpted front rising to a beautiful beveled mantle. Size: 3-3/4" H x 4-5/16" W x 1-1/2" D, $16.50

PERIOD FIREPLACES

The Lawbre Company
Suggested Retail Price: Early American Kitchen No. 1061 white (crane included) $21.95, No. 1062 finished, brick red (shelf and crane included) $35.95. French Console No. 1066 white $13.95, No. 1067 black marbled $18.95, No. 1068 rose marbled $18.95.
Cast in hydrocal cement, available in white, black marbled, rose marbled or finished.

PERIOD FIREPLACES

The Lawbre Company
Suggested Retail Price: Federal No. 1050 white $13.95, No. 1051 black marbled $18.95. Victorian No. 1056 white $13.95, No. 1057 black marbled $18.95.
Fireplaces cast in hydrocal cement are available in natural white, black marbled, rose marbled or finished.

FIREPLACE SET

Miniature House
Suggested Retail Price: $8.98
Catalog No. MH2400
Dimensions: 4-3/4"W x 3"H x 1-1/2"D
Material: Painted wood and metal
Economical stained wood fireplace with black base. Set also has mantel clock, bellows, tool set, wood logs and andirons.

PERIOD FIREPLACES

The Lawbre Company
Suggested Retail Price: Victorian Columned No. 1071 white $13.95, No. 1072 black marbled $18.95. Salem Corner No. 1076 white only (beveled wall section included) $18.95.

FIREPLACE

Lil Crafts
Suggested Retail Price: $16.50
Dimensions: 6-1/4"W x 4-3/8"H x 2-1/2"D
Available in brick red. Features a raised hearth and wood mantel. Cat. #403 red.

THE MINIATURES CATALOG, *Fourteenth Edition* 163

TRUE ELEGANCE SAWTOOTH SPECIALTY FLOOR
Handley House
Suggested Retail Price: $8.95
Catalog No. HH154
Material: U.S. hardwood veneers
An unusual distinctive sawtooth pattern of alternating light and dark woods sets this floor apart. Hand-laid on a flexible backing, ready-to-install and finish to your specifications. 6" x 8".

PARQUET FLOORING
Houseworks Ltd.
Suggested Retail Price: $12.95
Catalog No. 7007 Size: 2" W x 6" L
Genuine wood parquet pattern. Six sheets per package. Covers 72 sq. in.

SOUTHERN PINE RANDOM PLANK FLOORING
Houseworks Ltd.
Suggested Retail Price: $10.95
Catalog No. 7123
Made of genuine wood veneers laminated to a special paper to ensure easy staining, varnishing and installation. One sheet per package. Covers 187 sq. in. Size 11" x 17".

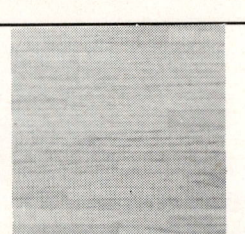

RED OAK RANDOM PLANK FLOORING
Houseworks
Suggested Retail Price: $10.95
Catalog No. 7122
Made of genuine wood veneers laminated to a special paper to ensure easy staining, varnishing and installation. One sheet per package. Covers 187 sq. in. Size 11" x 17".

HINOKI RANDOM PLANK FLOORING
Houseworks Ltd.
Suggested Retail Price: $10.95
Catalog No. 7024
Made of genuine wood veneers laminated to a special paper to ensure easy staining, varnishing and installation. One sheet per package. Covers 187 sq. in. Size 11" x 17".

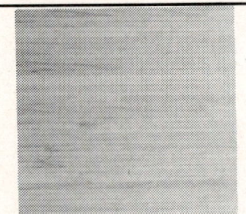

SOUTHERN PINE FLOORING
Houseworks Ltd.
Suggested Retail Price: $10.95
Catalog No. 7023
Made of genuine wood veneers laminated to a special paper to ensure easy staining, varnishing and installation. One sheet per package. Covers 187 sq. in. Size 11" x 17".

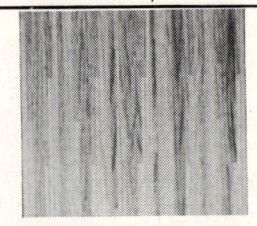

RED OAK FLOORING
Houseworks Ltd.
Suggested Retail Price: $10.95
Catalog No. 7022
Made of genuine wood veneers laminated to a special paper to ensure easy staining, varnishing and installation. One sheet per package. Covers 187 sq. in. Size 11" x 17".

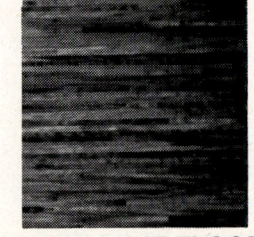

BLACK WALNUT FLOORING
Houseworks
Suggested Retail Price: $13.25
Catalog No. 7021
Made of genuine wood veneers laminated to a special paper to ensure easy staining, varnishing, and installation. One sheet per package. Covers 187 sq. in. Size 11" x 17"

PAPER FLOORING
J. Hermes
Suggested Retail Price: $1.25/sheet
Dimensions: 11" x 17", made of paper
Paper wood flooring, easy to lay, inexpensive, finishes beautifully with varnish or lacquer. Can even be stained. Many other flooring patterns available. Catalog #413.

THREE-DIMENSIONAL POLYSTYRENE TILE PANELS
Miniature House
Suggested Retail Price: $5.25
Catalog No. MH5301 black/white, MH5302 red/white, MH5303 blue/white, and new MH5315 pastel pink
Dimensions: 10-3/4" W x 16-3/4" L
This economical tile is perfect for kitchens, bathrooms, ice cream parlors . . . or use your imagination.

Interior Decorating Materials

Kitchen Patio Tile:
KP-35, 35 sq. in, $6
KP-70, 70 sq. in., $10.85

Black and Red Italian Tile:
IBT-50 (Black, 50 tiles), $3
ITR-100 (Red, 100 tiles), $5.45

Black and Red Slate:
RS-35 (Red, 35 sq. in.), $5.45
BS-35 (Black, 35 sq. in.), $5.45
Compatible sealer, $4.05 (4 oz. can)
Premixed mortar, $2.19 (4 oz. net wt. jar)
See your dealer or
write to Kimberly House

KIMBERLY MASONRY TILES

Kimberly House Miniatures
Individual, realistic-looking tiles. Cut easily with knife or razor saw; can sand to fit. Ideal for entries, baths, kitchens, porches, patios, hearths. Create your own design.

CONTEMPORARY FLOORING TILES

Le´ Petite Architect
Suggested Retail Price: $11.95-$14.95
Available in marble finishes, black and white finish and granite stone finishes. Each package contains 72 tiles, covers approximately 42 square inches.

FLOORING TILES

The Lawbre Company
Suggested Retail Price: $8.95, package of 64 pieces. Catalog No. 1022, black-veined marble; No. 1023 Quarry tile; No. 1021 white.
These flooring tiles, cast in hydrocal cement are extremely versatile. Each package covers 36 sq. inches. Can be painted with acrylic paints or stains.

HARDWOOD FLOORING

Miniature House
Suggested Retail Price: $9.98
Catalog No. MH511, MH512, MH513, MH516, MH518, MH519
Size: 11" W x 17" L
MH511 - Tan oak flooring, 1/4" strips with random joints.
MH512 - Very light pine/ash flooring, 1/4" strips with random joints
MH513 - American walnut flooring, 1/4" strips with random joints
MH516 - Tan oak flooring, mixed widths with random joints
MH518 - Mixed dark and light flooring. 1/4" strips with random joints
MH519 - American walnut flooring, mixed widths with random joints

FORMED PLASTIC SHEETS

Model Builders Supply
MBS shows more of its versatile floor surfaces, all 7" x 12". Cut stone, pebble stone, small or medium. Strip flooring, scale 2" planks, scale 3" planks. Square tiles in brick red, grey, white, slate grey, also transparent can be back painted any color or pattern. These make effective glass block walls also used as lighting panels. Available sizes, per inch are: 2, 4, 5, 10, 13 and 16. All are $3.95 Canadian. Ask dealer for MBS "How to Use" tips sheet. U.S. customers, see "Plastruct".

THREE-DIMENSIONAL POLYSTYRENE TILE PANELS

Miniature House
Suggested Retail Price: $5.25
Catalog No. MH5300 white, MH5305 pastel yellow, MH5310 pastel blue, MH5315 pastel pink.
Dimensions: 10-3/4" W x 16-3/4" L
These polystyrene tile panels are accurately scaled 1" to 1'. Easily cut with scissors or razor. Applies quickly, cleanly with double-faced tape.

FLOOR TILES

Miniature Manors
These individual 1" square tiles are available in 42 colors/styles. Textured, marbled, speckled, swirled and plain are among the choices. They fit together easily to instantly create the beautiful floor your dollhouse deserves.

TILE FLOORING

What's Next?
Suggested Retail Price: $2.50 per 9" x 12" sheet
Smooth, polished look, printed on varnished card stock. Available in green and white, yellow and black, black and white, 1/2" squares, white hexagon, terra cotta quarry tile and black and white 3/4" square tiles.

PLASTIC PATTERNED SHEETS

Plastruct
Suggested Retail Price: $3.50 - $7 plus shipping
Plastic patterned sheets in various scales and patterns including hardwood, square tile, pebble, random stone, random field stone, dressed stone and block. Brick, roofing and siding sheets also available.

Paneling & Trim for Walls & Ceiling

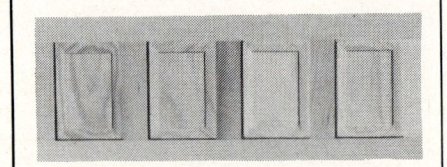

CARLSON RAISED PANEL WAINSCOTING

American Craft Products
Suggested Retail Price: $4.95
Catalog No. 8426
Dimensions: 3" x 8-5/16"
Accurately detailed wainscoting to add richness and depth to your decor. Made of clear pine. American made.

FIMO® MODELING MATERIAL

Eberhard Faber GmbH
Suggested Retail Price: See your dealer.
Catalog No. 8000
Specifications: 55 x 55 x 15 mm/65 g small block, 165 x 55 x 30 mm/350 g large block. FIMO®, the fantastic and most popular modeling material, is the leading product of its kind in Europe. It's versatile and easy to handle, and hardens in the oven at 265°F. (20 to 30 minutes). Available in 42 brilliant colors, it's ideal to create the finest decorative accessories for your dollhouse and to make exciting and imaginative objects (miniatures, figures, fashion jewelry, decorations, pictures, nameplates and a lot more).

BELL STENCIL SETS

New England Hobby Supply, Inc.
Suggested Retail Price: $10.95 plus $1.50 shipping
Catalog No. BE1110, BE1115, BE1120
Reusable high quality brass stencil patterns for scale stenciling of walls, floors and ceilings. Complete with brushes and instructions. Three styles: Moses Eaton (1110), Hospitality (1115), Victorian (1120).

Prices are approximate and subject to change.

Rugs & Carpeting

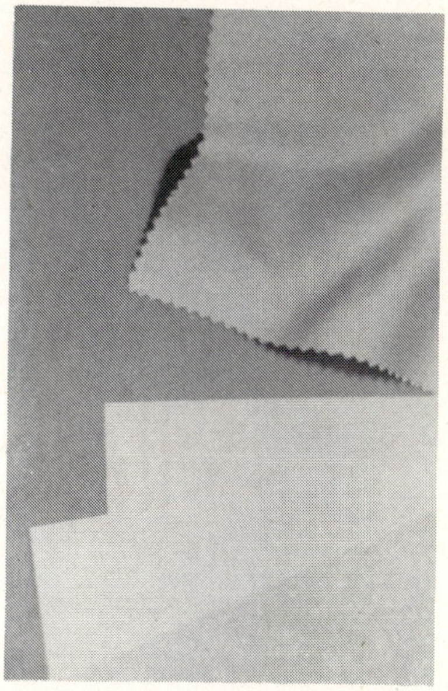

Interior Decorating Materials

VELVET CARPETING
B. H. Miniatures
Luxurious velvet carpeting in 16 gorgeous colors. Selected to provide an appropriate coordinate for our line of prepasted wallpapers. Available in two sizes: 12" x 16" (regular) and 16" x 24" (large). Special order sizes available.

ORIENTAL RUGS
Dollhouse Doll-ups
Suggested Retail Price $35 - $65
Authentic Oriental rugs have 200 hand-knotted threads to an inch. Bokhara designs include Tree of Lift, Kazak, Sarooq, Keshan, Kirman or a camel, a horse or a peacock pattern. Many one-of-a-kind.

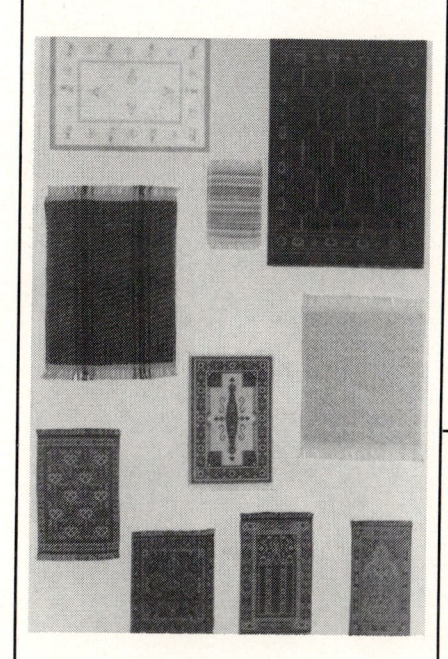

STAIR RUNNER KITS
J. Hermes
Suggested Retail Price: $12.95-$14.95 plus shipping
Material: Imported tapestry, brass rods (solid), fringe
Beautiful tapestry stair/hall runners add a touch of elegance to any 1" (or 1/2") vignette or dollhouse. Made of the finest materials. Assorted colors. Catalog #618.

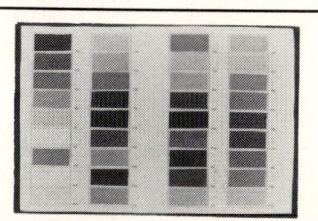

KRISTAN FLOOR COVERING
KriStan Prepasted Wallpaper & Floor Covering
Suggested Retail Price: $2.50-$3.50 plus shipping
Our 35 color selections are scratch proof, moisture resistant, can be sponged clean, easy to cut and laminate, totally inert and non-toxic, non-slip surface. 14" x 18".

RUGS
Handcraft Designs, Inc.
Suggested Retail Price: See your dealer
Catalog No.: (top-left, clockwise) #1075Y, #1064, #1070B, #1112, #1111, #1109, #1103, #1092; center-top #1086; center-bottom #1069
A selection from our broad range of rugs. Offerings range from transfer printed nursery rugs to hand-loomed and machine-loomed rugs and from simple to intricate patterns and designs. All woven rugs are thin, with fringe made from the warp of the loom, which is thinner than the rug body. The 1100 series of woven silks make throw rugs for 1/12th scale and full room rugs for 1/24th scale. Poly, machine-loomed and poly-cotton, hand-loomed rugs are 1":1' scale, but the throw rugs fit 1/24th scale rooms. Colors for every taste.

BRAIDED RUGS
Little Things by Jody
Suggested Retail Price: From $5 plus shipping and handling
Material: Braided, assorted yarns with muslin for stability
These rugs are handmade. They are available in hundreds of color combinations including "Country", "Victorian", "Modern", "Nursery", etc. Rugs can also be custom crafted to compliment your unique decor and/or room size.

THE MINIATURES CATALOG, Fourteenth Edition

HERIZ MOHTASHEM SAVONNERIE

The Keshishian Collection
Charm, elegance, sophistication. All of these plus the magic of Keshishian rug. $45 at better shops everywhere. Brochure $3.

RUGS AND CARPETS

The Keshishian Collection
Recognized miniaturists who know specify carpets from the Keshishian Collection. At better shops worldwide. Brochure $3.

THE KESHISHIAN COLLECTION

The Keshishian Collection
A bouquet of flowers for your floor. No imagination needed with a Keshishian. Seen at better shops. Runner $31, carpet $45. Brochure $3.

TAPESTRIES

The Keshishian Collection
No imagination needed. Bring the magic of a Keshishian tapestry into your home. Left, clockwise; March To The Castle $43, Lady With the Unicorn $43, The Boar Hunt $43, English Tapestry $25.

Interior Decorating Materials

NAVAJO INDIAN RUGS

Maison des Maisons
Navajo Indian rugs by various weavers from the Southwest. Hand-spun natural wool and dyes.

RUGS

Nanco Distributors
Suggest Retail Price: From $27
Handwoven, vibrant Mideast patterns and colors. Color sheets available.

CARPETS BY HAEL

Miniature Corner
Suggested Retail Price: See your dealer
Material: Ultra-thin velour with special stay flat backing
Oriental carpets and stair runners in authentic Victorian designs and colors. Large variety of sizes and shapes. Also available are brass stair rods in 2" and 2-3/8" width. Special 1/2" scale designs available. Send $1 and LSASE for full-color carpet literature.

SHEARED PUNCHNEEDLE RUGS

Miniature Rugs by Joan Adams
1/12th sheared punchneedle rug catalog of over 40 designs. Graphs, transparency graphs, completed rugs, canvas, punchneedles and embroidery scissors available. Kits for needlepoint are in the process of being developed. Price for catalog: $2.75.

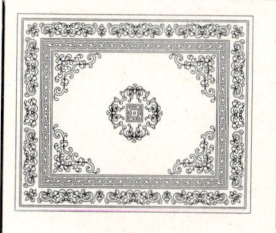

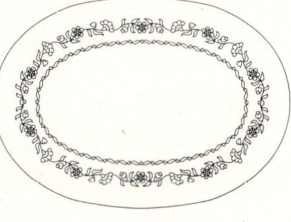

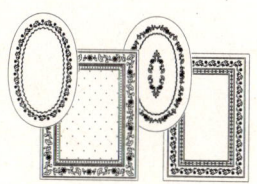

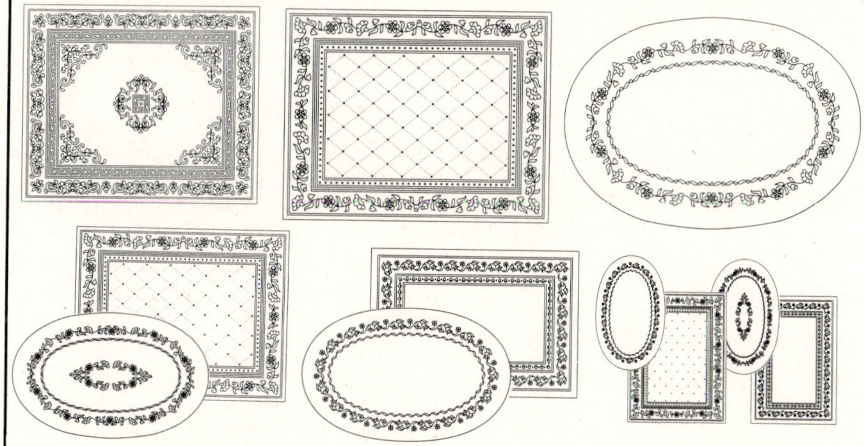

PRETTI POINT RUG KITS

d. Anne Ruff Miniatures
Suggested Retail Price: $10.95
There are now six new Pretti Point rug kits to add to those you've enjoyed for years. Classic, Victorian and Country designs for both 1" and smaller scales. Kit #1212 is perfect for 1/2" settings. These lovely designs are silk screened onto a cream colored napped fabric and can be quickly and easily colored with felt tip pens to coordinate with your decorating needs. Pretti Point pen sets with 20 colors also available, $4.95.

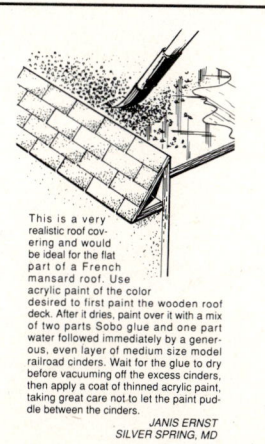

This is a very realistic roof covering and would be ideal for the flat part of a French mansard roof. Use acrylic paint of the color desired to first paint the wooden roof deck. After it dries, paint over it with a mix of two parts Sobo glue and one part water followed immediately by a generous, even layer of medium size model railroad cinders. Wait for the glue to dry before vacuuming off the excess cinders, then apply a coat of thinned acrylic paint, taking great care not to let the paint puddle between the cinders.
JANIS ERNST
SILVER SPRING, MD

Wall Coverings

THE MINIATURES CATALOG, Fourteenth Edition

MINIATURE WALLPAPER

J. Hermes
Suggested Retail Price: $1.25-$1.50/sheet
Dimensions: 11"x17"
Material: Printed paper
Miniature wallpapers are both original and researched designs. Patterns for every room in the house: living room, bed and bath, kitchen and nursery. Papers available for wood and the floors and ceilings. Exterior papers in brick, clapboard, stone and roofing shingle and shake patterns.

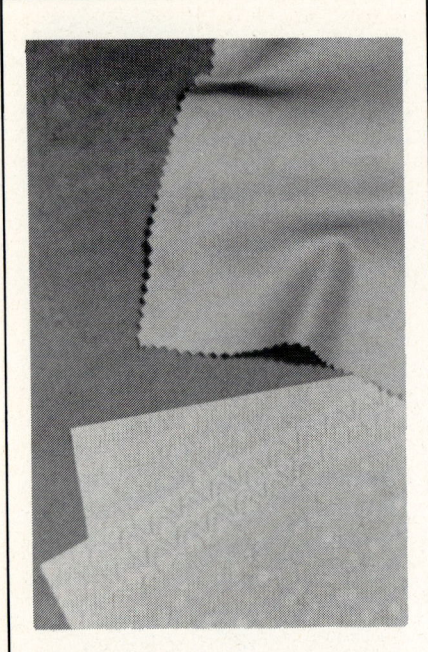

PREPASTED WALLPAPER AND COORDINATING FABRICS

B. H. Miniatures
Sheet Size: 11" x 20-1/2"
High quality prepasted wallpaper carefully selected for design, scale and color. Easy to apply. Some patterns have coordinating fabrics.

FLOCKED WALLPAPER

J. Hermes
Suggested Retail Price: $.75-$3/sheet
Dimensions: 5"x8" and 11"x17"
Material: Paper with flocking
This wallpaper is available in many designs and color combinations. You can add a touch of elegance to a boudoir, living room, parlor or saloon. Catalog #1100.

TILE PAPERS

J. Hermes
Suggested Retail Price: $2/sheet
Dimensions: 11"x17"
Material: Printed heavy stock paper
Authentic style, multi-color printed tile papers. With the Southwestern influence so popular, this paper will be a beautiful addition to one's Spanish adobe or casa. Catalog #481 and 482.

KIMBERLY PREMIXED STUCCO

Kimberly House Miniatures
Suggested Retail Price: $7.85 per pint
Material: Latex-base
White pre-mixed ready-to-use.
Ideal for ceilings, bays, interior walls, or exterior. May be painted with choice of color. Covers tape wiring, wood grain, and a multitude of sins. Easy to create swirls and designs. Attractive alone, with wainscotting, and ceiling appliques. See your dealer or write to Kimberly House.

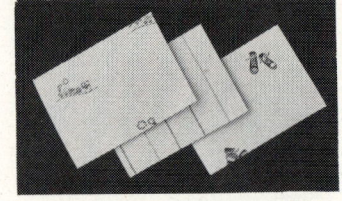

KRISTAN PREPASTED WALLPAPER

KriStan Prepasted Wallpaper & Floor Covering
Suggested Retail Price: $2 ppd.
Over 230 selections of the most reasonably priced prepasted wallpaper. Packaged flat or one to a tube. Matching fabrics and borders also available. 10-1/2" x 20".

Your Listings Belong Here!

Interested in advertising in the 15th Edition of The Miniatures Catalog?

Contact Sara Benz at 1-800-558-1544, Extension 631, or write to:
The Miniatures Catalog
P.O. Box 1612
Waukesha, WI 53187

Window Treatments

BARBARA O'BRIEN CURTAINS

New England Hobby Supply, Inc.
Suggested Retail Price: See your dealer
Barbara O'Brien curtains are available in over 40 colors and styles. Please see the New England Hobby Supply insert between pages 288 and 289 for more information.

CURTAINS AND DRAPERIES

Delicate Draperies by Donna Smith
Specializing in elegant, handcrafted curtains and draperies at moderate prices. Made in synthetic silks and fine laces. Custom-made curtains are also available. Available at your local miniatures shop.

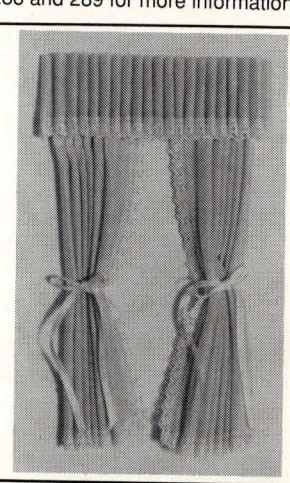

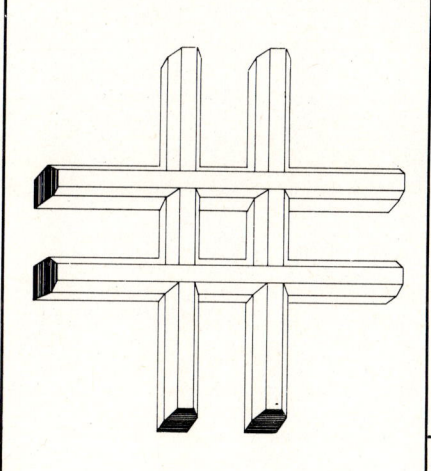

MULLIONS

Houseworks Ltd.
Suggested Retail Price: $1.50
Catalog No. 7043
Pre-assembled molded window grid mullions made of white ABS. Easily trimmed to fit sash with knife or nail clippers. Four grids per package.

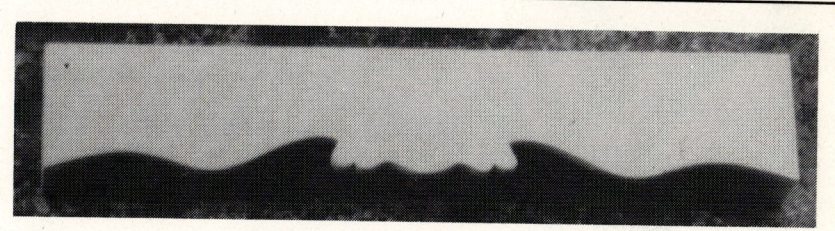

WOODEN CORNICES WITH DRAPERY ROD AND SHADES

Houseworks
#3005-Chippendale-Double. Size: 6-3/16" L x 1-1/16" H. Two per package, $3.50

WOODEN MATCHSTICK AND VENETIAN BLINDS

Houseworks
#3300-Size: 1-15/16" W. Two per package, $4
#3301-Size: 2-3/16" W. Two per package, $4
#3200-Size: 1-15/16" W. Two per package, $5

Interior Decorating Materials

THE MINIATURES CATALOG, Fourteenth Edition

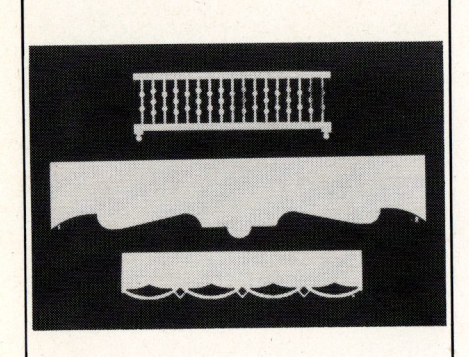

October National Dollhouse & Miniatures Month

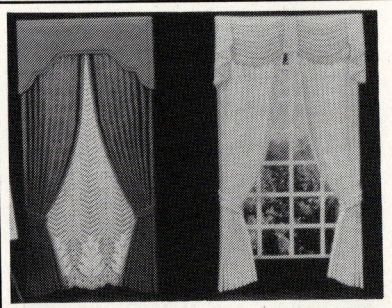

CORNICES AND PLANTER BOXES

Laser Tech
Suggested Retail Price: (top to bottom) #C-052 Cornice (3" x 1/16") $4.95; #C-053 Double Cornice (6-3/16" x 1-1/16") $3.95; #WPB-050 Window Planter Box (3-7/8" x 3/4") $4.10
Made of 3/32 basswood in 1" scale.

PRETTY PLEATERS

d. Anne Ruff Miniatures
Suggested Retail Price: $13.95 to $21.95 plus shipping
The Pretty Pleater, an easy-to-use pleating tool in three scales, simplifies the pleating of draperies, doll clothes and accessories.

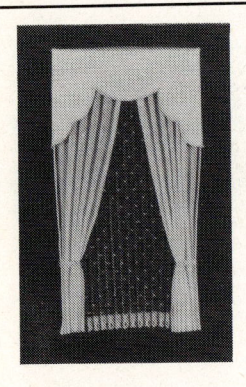

CURTAINS AND DRAPERIES

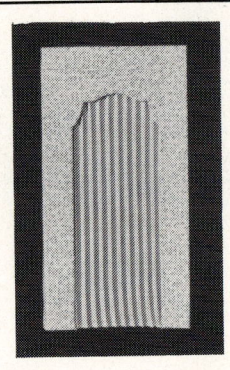

Little Linens
Material: Cotton
Ready-to-hang custom-look drapes. Available in a variety of colors. Each Victorian set includes valence, drape and sheer panel. Other styles available.

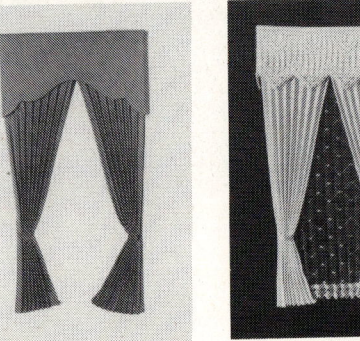

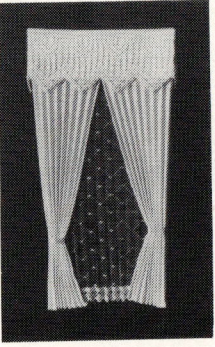

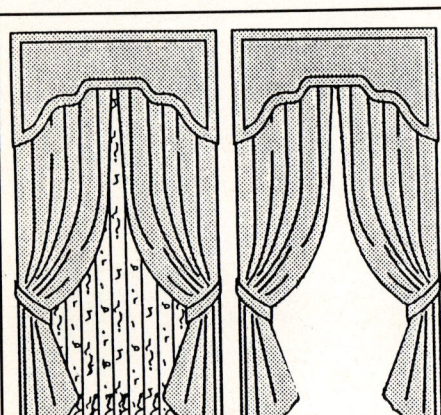

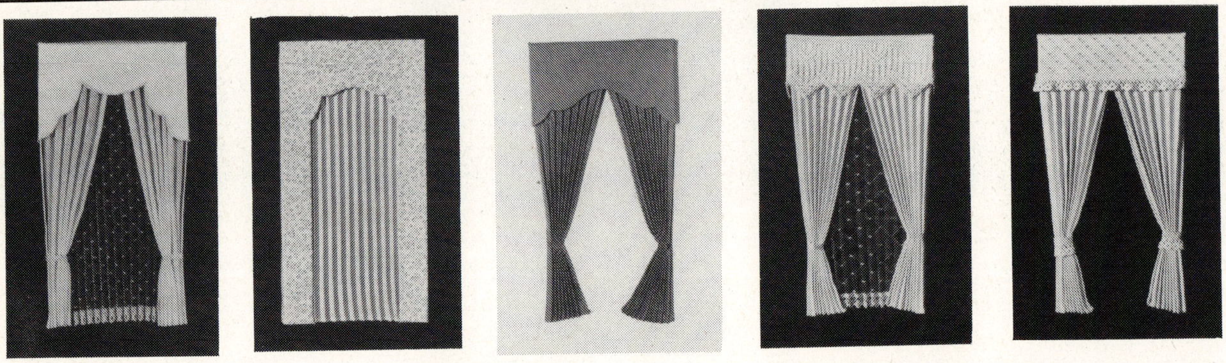

THE WINDOW COLLECTION

d. Anne Ruff Miniatures
Suggested Retail Price: $8 to $20
Draperies, cornices and curtains in coordinating colors and fabrics. Each beautiful piece is packaged separately to be mixed or matched to fit standard width windows. Lengths are adjustable. Available in lace curtains, cornices, tie-back draperies, sheer curtains and matching skirted tables.

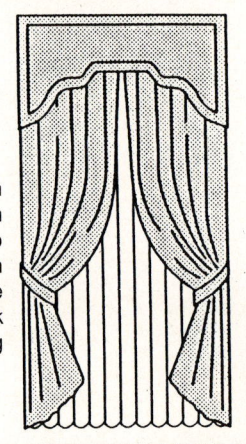

Prices are approximate and subject to change.

Furniture

European Colonial & Federal Kits

GILT FURNITURE
Omniarts of Colorado
Suggested Retail Price: $100-$300 finished 16th Century furniture, cast by lost wax process and gold plated. Some with marble tops. By John Hodgson of England. Tables, chairs, mirrors and torchieres.

CASE CLOCK & BREAKFRONT
By Craftmark House of Miniatures
Furniture kits. All wood parts machined, brass hardware, detailed instructions.
Breakfront - Chipppendale circa 1760. When finished 7-7/8" H x 6 -1/2" W x 7/8" D. Catalog No. 40048, $21.95/kit.
Willard Tall Case Clock - circa 1790. When finished 7-1/4" H x 2" W x 1-1/8" D. Catalog No. 40046. $12.95/kit.

CHIPPENDALE FURNITURE KITS
By Craftmark House of Miniatures
Suggested Retail Price: $18.95 kit. Authentic reproductions. All made of mahogany. Solid brass hardware included. Straight-Top Highboy, circa 1750. When finished measures 6-1/2" H x 3-1/2" W x 2" D. Catalog No. 40022.

CABRIOLE LEG CHIPPENDALE CHAIR KITS
Craftmark House of Miniatures
Authentic reproductions. Made of mahogany. Cabriole Leg Chair - circa 1760. When finished measures 3-3/16" H x 2" W x 1-7/8" D. Kit $10.95 (set of two). Catalog No. 40026.
Cabriole Leg Arm Chair - circa 1760. When finished measures 3-3/16" H x 2-3/8" W x 1-7/8" D. Kit $11.95 (set of two). Catalog No. 40027.

FURNITURE KITS
Craftmark House of Miniatures
Suggested Retail Price: $3.50 - $21.95 Total of 88 furniture kits, 1/12 scale, all machined solid wood parts, solid brass hardware, detailed instructions. See your local dealer.

THE HOUSE OF MINIATURES · CRAFTMARK INC. · COLLECTORS SERIES

Prices are approximate and subject to change.

From the publishers of
the miniatures catalog

Julian Roman Gregorian Chinese Miniatures

#68063/ $9.95

Throughout time, only the *Miniatures Calendar* has measured time in small proportions. So celebrate 1992 with thirteen 11" x 14" color photographs detailing life scaled down. Descriptions of each month's finely crafted display reveal tricks of the trade. To order this legendary calendar, call today **(800) 446-5489** (weekdays 8:30a.m. - 5:00p.m. CST).

**The Miniatures Calendar
Changing the way you look at time.**

Or send your order to: Kalmbach Publishing Co., Dept. 0390, 21027 Crossroads Circle, P.O. Box 1612, Waukesha, WI 53187-1612. Include for postage and handling: U.S. $3.00, Canada and foreign add 18% (min. $4.00). Wisconsin residents add 5% sales tax. Canadian orders add 7% GST to total.

Dept. 0390

GET IT TOGETHER!

A professional dollhouse builder explains how to finish your new dollhouse.

By Barbara Warner

(Left) Hobbyist Jeanne Delgado of *Nutshell News* puts the finishing touches on a Real Good Toys' 1776 model. Dollhouse kits come in all styles and sizes to fit your price range.

(Top) Shared from *Miniatures Showcase's* Spring 1990 issue, a *real* miniature hobbyist, created by Cathy Ellis-O'Brien, is busy getting her quarter-inch scale dollhouse finished.

(Opposite) The Victorian model, *Melissa*, from Celerity Miniature Homes is easy to assemble, like most of the dollhouses shown in this catalog.

When beginners open a dollhouse kit, sometimes the excitement that was generated with the purchase quickly disappears as reality sets in and the challenge of putting it together is faced. Courage! We will tell you how to breeze through construction and completely finish your dream house.

First of all, pull out the instruction sheets from the box. Decorating decisions need to be made before you start so that an efficient plan of action for assembling the house is formulated early. This applies to those finishing a pre-assembled shell as well.

Most of the exceptionally well decorated dollhouses you've seen have owners who "lived with the house" for a while. This gave them time to design a total "look" for the house, using its features and rooms to their best advantage.

Collectors approach the finishing of houses from several different angles and sometimes utilize all approaches at the same time. Most like to set a time period for the house, present or past, with a definite year when it was completed. A favorite color can be the unifying element. Sometimes furnishings that you collected previous to the purchase of the house will be the starting point. The architectural design of the house can suggest its own scheme. A decision must be made as to the function of each room, too. You may be most comfortable with selecting the furnishings for the house and setting them throughout the rooms before making a decision concerning wallpaper, flooring, and lighting. Use these aids to help you visualize your finished dollhouse.

The most efficient sequence of steps for finishing a house are as follows:

1. Assemble the basic shell with room partitions permanently in place. Do not install doors, windows, moldings, staircase, porch railings, or house trim at this time. Any hinged wall or roof flap should be left unattached for the present.

2. Apply clapboard, brick, or stucco finishes to exterior walls and paint where needed.

3. Wire the dollhouse for lighting, both interior and exterior.

4. Finish the interior walls, ceilings, and floors.

5. Glue doors, windows, moldings, staircases, porch railings, and exterior trim permanently in place. Attach hinged walls and roof flaps now.

6. Shingle the roof.

Let's get started!

With the house kit and all the

(Above) This detailed 1910 back porch shows part of the model Robert Barnes built for his daughter Alma Kiss of Huntsville, Alabama. It was featured in *Miniatures Showcase,* Fall 1990.

components you will use on it, always, and I can't emphasize this enough, read the directions first! Then think of ways you can make the various steps go faster or more efficiently.

There are three basic types of dollhouses available: plywood, die-cut plywood, and tongue and groove wood with masonite floors, roofs, and partitions.

The plywood kits are usually the easiest to assemble since pieces are large and can easily be identified. The die-cut houses generally have more trims and frills. There will be sheets of pre-cut pieces that must be punched out before assembling. The tongue and groove houses have bundles of pre-cut wood slats that must be glued together and left to dry flat before house assembly can begin.

With any kit, identify each piece with help from the instructions and mark them by name with pencil. Sort pieces into like bundles—porch assemblies, window pieces, stair parts, walls, roof, etc., and set aside.

Begin with the main house pieces—floors, walls, bases, and roofs. Paint the interior walls with a coat of white-pigmented shellac or white acrylic paint to seal the wood and provide a white base for wallpaper. Avoid putting paint on the edges of the wood, which will be glued together later. Give the ceilings two to three coats of white paint. It is much easier to paint them while they're lying flat instead of upside down inside a dollhouse. The recommended way to final finish with acrylic paint is to paint one coat of white-pigmented shellac. When dry, sand with 220 garnet paper and wipe off the dust. Finish with two coats of brush-on semi-gloss acrylic.

If you are using the kit's bare wood as flooring, finish that now with stain and several coats of a clear wood finish. Use a brush-on, water base satin varnish (acrylic). It dries quickly and requires only soap and water clean-up.

Paint the exterior of the tongue and groove style houses with the final finish now. This is also true if you are going to give any kit a plain painted exterior finish.

The preliminary work is now completed; the next step is to follow assembly directions to build the basic kit. For easier construction, do not put on the back roof piece until after doing the wiring and wallpapering on the top floor.

Glue and nail the house together. The best glues to use are yellow carpenter's glue or Quick Grab. Never use a hot glue gun. It's not durable enough for this job.

When directions require you to nail walls together, it's helpful to mark and drill holes for the nails. Then the nails will go straight into the edge of the attaching floor or wall without any unsightly misses.

If siding is desired, there will be corner trim which may be necessary to install before the siding. If so, glue it in place and give it finishing coats of paint before attaching the sides.

Exterior Finishes

Clapboard siding comes in 3" x 24" and 3" x 36" sheets that have 1/4", 3/8", or 1/2" strips milled into the wood. Some dollhouse manufacturers pre-cut these to fit your kit.

Start the clapboard on the most plain wall first, usually a side wall. Work from the bottom up. Cut the siding with a straight edge and utility knife. Tape the pieces to the wall temporarily so you can cut the next piece to fit. Siding has a little lip that must sit over the top of the preceding piece. Be sure to align this before cutting the new piece. In the gable area, make a paper pattern to guide you in cutting the angles.

When working the front side, which usually has windows and doors, a strip of siding to fit the whole width must be used when only part of the siding is cut into for the door and window openings. Never piece this siding since the seam which will cross several milled strips and look very unprofessional. A real house would never have all the seams in a line.

Siding requires careful gluing. Work with Quick Grab or contact cement. The whole surface must be covered with a thin coat of glue. Tape pieces in place until the glue is dry. Clean any excess glue off before it dries.

Alternatives to clapboard siding are brick, stucco, or paint. Brick comes in sheets (plastic and clay), individual clay bricks, or the "Magic Brik" plaster system. The sheets are glued in place like siding using the manufacturer's recommended adhesive. That's important since some glues will "eat" the sheets. Individual clay bricks work best on dollhouse exteriors when just a few are needed.

The "Magic Brik" system is easiest to use when a lot of house must be covered. Apply per directions in the kit. The brick plaster can be reactivated after it is dry by adding water. This means you can reuse wasted plaster. It's necessary to coat the dried brick on the house with a brush-on clear acrylic finish to make the brick plaster permanent. The alternative is to add thin white glue, like Elmer's, or acrylic paint to the wet plaster mix before you apply it to the house. This makes a permanent finish but the leftover plaster will not be reuseable.

A stucco finish can be achieved with "Hyplar" modeling paste or the "Magic Stucco" system which are effective when shell flaws must be hidden or a patterned texture is desired. The easiest way to create a stucco look is to add painter's sand to the appropriate color acrylic paint. Apply the paint with a swirling brush motion. For a Tudor style house, glue the already finished wood trim over the dried paint stucco.

Another simple method for a stucco look is to apply textured wallpaper to the shell or spray paint pre-colored Flex-Stone®. If the color of the textured wallpaper is not appropriate, you can paint it, and then apply the wood trim.

Wiring

In general, when planning your wiring scheme, try to keep your wiring runs as long as possible without splicing. If using tape wiring, make folded corners and burnish them down so they are as flat as possible. With round wire runs, have no splices in the wires that are under wallpaper, flooring, and moldings. When you have completed your wiring, make templates of each room from tracing paper. Mark where splices and tape runs are. When wallpaper is in place, it's a simple thing to lay the template against the wall and know exactly where to tap in with outlets and additional lights.

Do not attach the lights now. They will only hinder you when installing wallpaper and flooring. The exception is porch lights since their wires join the system on the interior wall and will be under wallpaper. At each location, drill a hole through the wall. Insert the wires through the wall and glue the fixture in place with Quick Grab. Attach the wires using the appropriate method.

The most successful way to install lights that have a little white foam piece on the mounting plate is to remove the foam. Apply Quick Grab glue directly to the mounting plate and attach it to the house.

Paint all tape wiring white to match the wall primer and camouflage it under the wallpaper.

Wallpaper and floor finishings

The sequence to finishing a room is determined by the choice of flooring. If installing a wood floor, final finish it before the walls. If using tile or carpeting, finish this type of floor after wallpapering. Wallpaper paste easily wipes off of finished wood floors, but varnish will not come off of wallpapered walls.

Before you begin wallpapering, the ceilings should be finished and the walls primed. Always use wallpaper paste to adhere wallpaper, even pre-pasted, to the walls. The cellulose-type paste, which is non-staining, mixed to a gel consistency, works well.

Spray the front side of the wallpaper with a matte clear acrylic finish. This protects the paper from smudges and color lifting. Paint the walls of the house with a thin coat of wallpaper paste to size them; let the paste dry completely.

Paper the back wall, the one at the deepest point in the room, first. Then do the side walls. Cut the back wall piece the height less a bit for stretching and the width plus half inch on each side to go around the corners. Lay the wallpaper piece face down on a clean washable surface and apply the paste with a 1-1/2" paint brush. Put the wallpaper piece on the back wall, patting it into place with a clean damp rag. To get it into the corners, smooth it gently in place with a small plastic putty knife or a credit card. Roll the edges of the paper with a small wallpaper seam roller. Wipe up excess paste with a clean damp cloth. With a single edge razor blade trim all window and door openings while the paper is damp.

Next, finish the side walls. Butt the paper at the seams and match your patterns. Side wall seams allow for plumbing the pattern and hiding the seamline.

(Above) "The day after Christmas" features a front door by Houseworks, Ltd. It has been finished in four different colors of paint to accent its Victorian details.

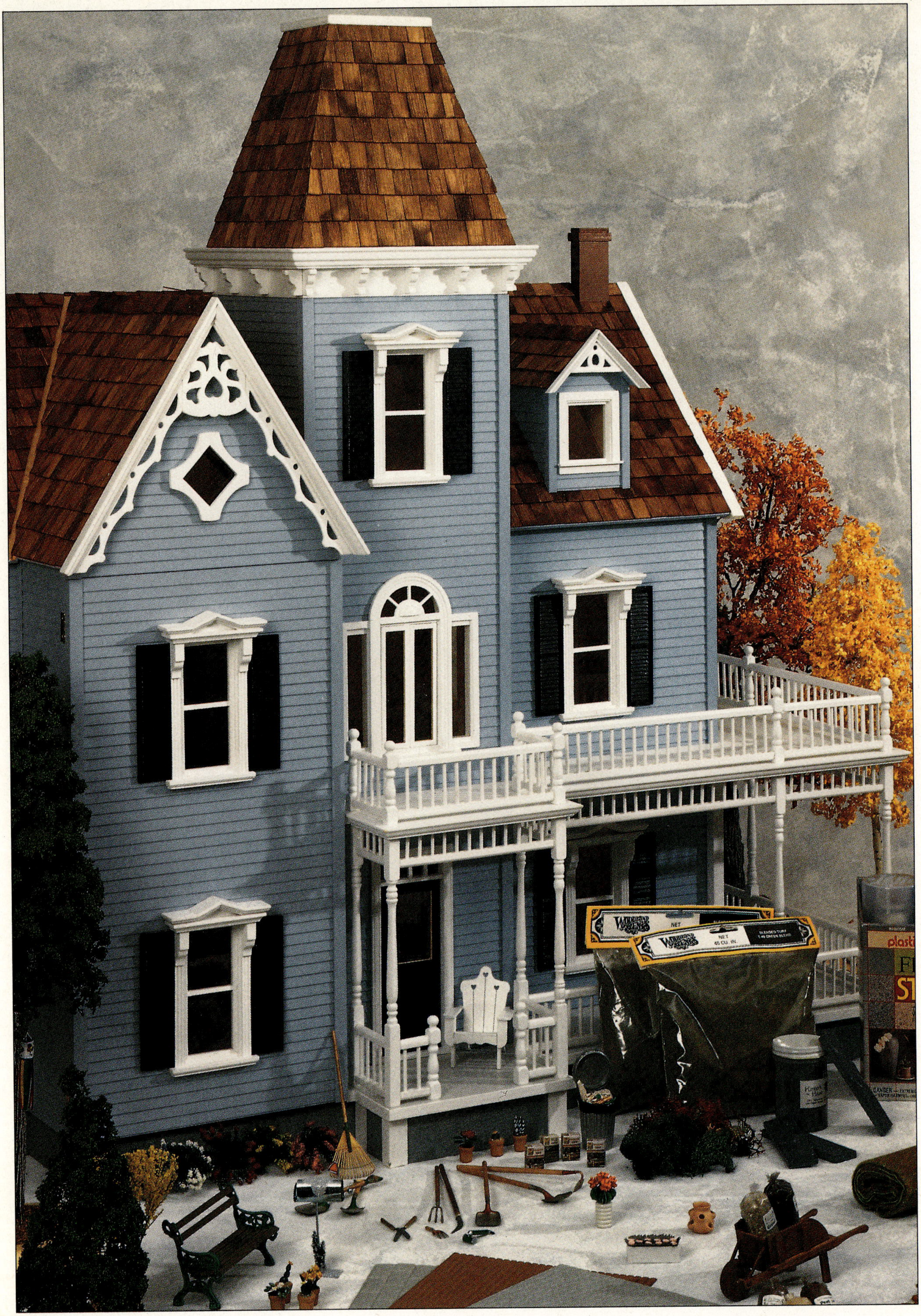

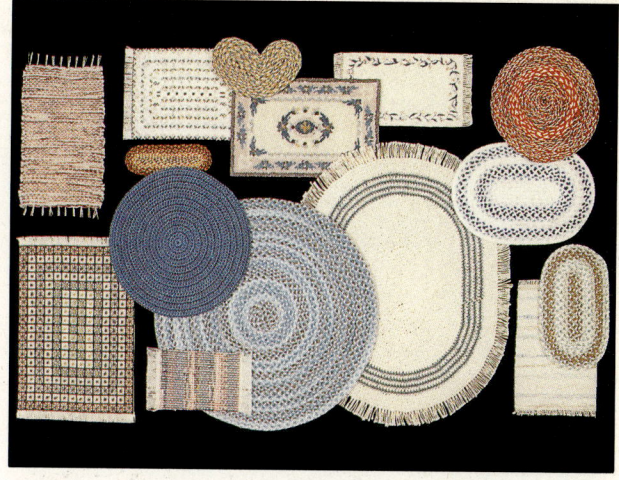

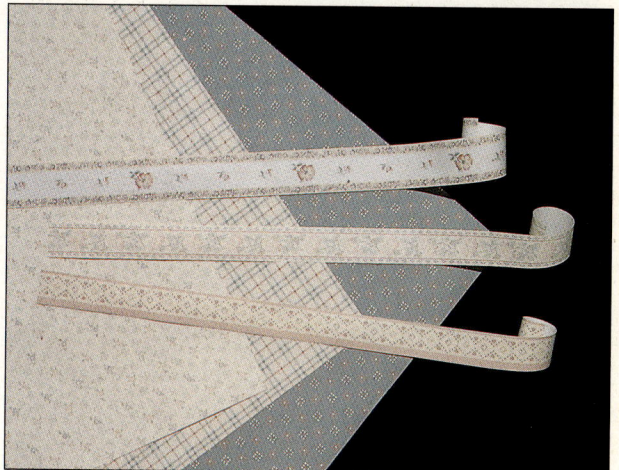

Floors

Flooring may be wood, tile, or carpet. Wood flooring comes in room-size sheets of strips on a paper backing, scribed 3" x 24" pieces, or in strip wood, 1/16" thick by 1/4, 3/8, or 1/2" wide by 24" long. Stain the wood, if needed, before laying the floor.

Measure the area to be covered and cut the flooring to fit. Measure the front and back of the room since partitions can make the room wider at one point than the other. If there are construction details to be skirted, it's easier to make a paper pattern and transcribe that to the flooring.

Start laying the floor from the open edge of the house. Carpenter's glue, Quick Grab, or the glue recommended by the flooring manufacturer is best. Be sure to apply a thin, even coat of glue all the way to the edges. Cover the floor with wax paper and weigh it down with books, flat irons, or whatever is heavy and will fit in the space. Let it dry this way for 24 hours.

Finish the floor with water-base satin varnish (acrylic). Apply the first coat. Let it dry and lightly sand the floor with 220 garnet sandpaper. Wipe off sanding dust. Brush on two more coats of varnish. Apply a coat of paste wax to fill any remaining small gaps.

Tile sheet flooring is best cut to a paper pattern. Glue in place per manufacturer's recommendation for glue. This flooring is made of plastic and will "melt" with certain glues. To insure good adhesion, follow the same method mentioned for wood floors.

Velveteen carpeting is also cut to a paper pattern of the area to be covered. If you're experienced with fabric you may find it easier to "snip and fit." In cutting velveteen, a rotary cutter, mat, and straight edge is the easiest way to cut a straight line. Piecing may be done along the back edge if necessary but only if the nap of the fabric may be run in the same direction. After piecing, lightly brush the nap together with a toothbrush.

To lay the carpeting, it can just be glued around the edges using a thin coat of white glue. Do not weigh it down as you will flatten the pile.

Moldings

Final finish the molding strips with paint or stain before cutting and installing them. Ceiling moldings are mitered at the corners and straight cut at the open edge of the room. Use an X-Acto saw and miter box to get 45 degree angles. Glue the ceiling moldings in place. Custom fit the molding where a staircase interrupts the wall.

Baseboard moldings are treated the same way for ease of installa-

---

(Opposite) *The Hawthorne* dollhouse from Real Good Toys is a front-opening model and is all set to be landscaped.

(Above) Wallpaper patterns, matching borders, and area rugs are just a few of the items available to make your dollhouse everything you want it to be.

Above: Here's what dollhouse miniatures is all about—whether it's a hobby for a child or an adult, the most important part is to have fun! The Apple Blossom model shown here is part of Walmer Doll Houses' Lilliput line.

tion. If you want to be authentic, inside corners on baseboard are butted with the molding contour cut out for a close fit. Butting the inside corners is definitely used when the molding is a plain wood strip. However, outside corners are always mitered. At doorways, the door molding goes to the floor and the baseboard butts against it. Glue the baseboard moldings in place as you are installing the doors and staircases.

Doors, windows and the rest

Doors and windows come as assembled components or else must be constructed from designated pieces in the kit. Final finish them before gluing them on the house.

Assembled windows usually have Plexiglas® panels in them that may be slipped out a slot for easier painting. Working windows have a spring release to all the sashes, so they also may be removed for ease in painting.

Assembled doors have pins that may be removed with a needle-nose pliers so the door can be separated from the frame for painting.

For windows and doors which have to be constructed, final finish the parts, then glue them together. With some kits the windows may be partially assembled before painting and the paint helps hold them together. Follow individual kit directions for the best method. Paint the window before the "glass" is inserted in the frame. Now you can glue the doors and windows on the house.

Final finish the rest of the exterior trims and glue them to the house. Porch railings are easier to paint if the balusters are glued in place between the handrail and the bottom rail.

Before you assemble the staircase, decide on its finish. If you want a stained wood finish, stain before assembling it and varnish after it's glued together. If you want stained treads and handrails and painted risers and balusters, stain and varnish first and paint second. Paint wipes off a varnished surface, but stain does not cover paint splashes. A painted staircase may be done when it's assembled as paint adds strength to the glue bonds.

Install light fixtures and chandeliers at this point. Attach the staircases as the very last step.

Put a roof over your head

The two most popular roofing materials are rolls of asphalt shingles or individual shingles made of wood. For both styles, guidelines need to be drawn on the shell roof. Draw these on before attaching the roof to the house. To have a very even roof, it pays to mark each line fully in pencil. Also mark a center line.

Glue the chimney in place. Attach any roof flap connected with hinges now. Custom trim shingles to go around or cover hinges as you reach them with the roofing.

Start the roofing at the bottom edge of the shell roof and work to the peak. Have roofing overhang the edges less than 1/16". This prevents shingle breakage. Center the first row of shingles on the width so that the amount of shingle on each end is equal. If a gable or opening interferes, measure the first row out at the peak and transfer the pattern to the beginning row. The second row of shingles is centered over the spaces in the first row.

There are two ways to start the roof. Either paint the first row space on the shell a matching color to the roof or lay a row of shingles the depth of the overlap that will be on the rest of the roof. The second method is more realistic.

Use thick white glue, like Tacky, to install wooden shingles. Run a line of glue along the pencil guideline and along the top edge of the preceding row. On the first row, run two lines of glue on the shell, one at the guideline and one along the edge. Remember to center the second row shingles over the spaces or cracks in the first row.

Asphalt shingles are best attached with a staple gun. The smallest one available with 1/4" staples works on houses with shell roofs 3/16" or more thick. If you must use glue, Quick Grab holds best. Run a line of glue along the marked line and a line along the top edge of the preceding row.

Use single shingles to finish the peaks. Fold the shingles in half, overlap them slightly, and lay them in one direction along the ridge line. Presto, you've put a roof over your head!

Enjoy your new hobby

The most difficult step in dollhouse building is getting the house out of its box! Too many dollhouses are hidden in closets and under beds because would-be hobbyists never get started. If this article doesn't answer all your questions, take your kit to a retailer who specializes in dollhouse miniatures and you will quickly be headed along the right track! A finished dollhouse kit is just the beginning to many hours of rewarding miniature collecting. •

Barbara Warner is a frequent contributing writer to Miniatures Showcase *and* Miniatures Dealer. *She is presently living in London, England, with her husband, but will be returning to her business in the United States next year.*

Fine needle work, and hand pieced quilts to fit the iron wire wicker.

Iron Wire Wicker & Software

design by
Alice Lacy

Alice Lacy, Ltd.
411 Front Street, Bath, Maine 04530
Telephone (207) 443-2319

Your Products Belong in the Miniatures Catalog!

For information on advertising in the 15th edition, please write:

Sara Benz, Adv. Sales Manager
The Miniatures Catalog
P.O. Box 1612
Waukesha, WI 53187

Call toll free **1-800-558-1544, ext. 631**

#1 Interior Decorator for Your Dollhouse

HOT
NEW 64 PAGE ALL COLOR CATALOG

MiniGraphics
Wallpaper
Matching Fabric
Coordinated Fabric
Upholstered Furniture

SAVE NOW!

Merchandise rebate in catalog.
Catalog $5.00
Save with coupon $1.00
$4.00

$$$$$$$$$$$$ **Valuable Coupon** $$$$$$$$$$$$

Save $1.00

Mini Graphics Complete Catalog

Send name, address & check to:
Mini Graphics
2975 Exon Avenue
Cincinnati, Ohio 45241   MC91

Accessories Can Make The Difference

By Pamela Henkel
Editorial Assistant, Miniatures Showcase

Character and personality are as much a part of a dollhouse as its richly panelled walls, oak parquet floors, and stained glass windows. After completing your dream house, there are many ways you can turn it into a distinctive home with carefully selected miniature accessories. Your dollhouse family will come to life as you create the members' personalities with bits and pieces of their past, present, and future. Accessories are available in abundance; all you need is a good imagination.

Just one peek into a dollhouse window and the personalities of its occupants are discovered by the scattered clues throughout the house. A "woman's touch" is established with fresh bouquets on the piano or dining room table, baskets of blooms in the living room, or a dozen roses in the master bedroom. Plants about the house also reflect the owner's love of gardening.

When a family is home together, activity usually centers around meal times. A meal in progress in the kitchen or popcorn in the family room are realistic scenes that can fill your home. Other homey scenarios could be a snack time set up for the kids after school, or morning coffee and croissants in a breakfast nook. Miniature food makers have so skillfully prepared foods that you might catch the aroma of baked bread, fried fish, or a turkey roasting in the oven!

Simple accessories like candy dishes in the living room hint of an upcoming party, or champagne and glasses in the dining room tell of a planned celebration. Accessories help establish the lifestyle, time period, and social level of your family.

Photographs tell the family's history. What the members look like and who is important to them can be established with photographs. Family pictures on the walls in the hallways, a portrait above the fireplace, or an ensemble of framed pictures on top of the piano tell the members' ages,

Scenes created by the *Miniatures Showcase* staff include these photos from previous issues.

(Opposite, top) This room filled with toys and holiday decorations is a colorful example of how you can decorate your house for the holidays.
(Bottom) Accessories say, "Country!"

(Top) Food is often the center of family activity; and here, mom picks up leftover pizza and popcorn after her teens' "study group" leaves. The "lived-in" look finds a comfortable place in this house's family room.

(Left) These masculine accessories clearly set the scene for the man of the house. In his rec room, he is safe to relax with his buddies in a room filled with games and drinks.

the family's size, and what important events and locations have influenced their lives.

Accessories can also be used to establish the importance of hobbies and recreation. If the owner of the house is an artist, an easel, paints, and paper can be positioned in an attic room. A weight room filled with exercise equipment for the muscle-building teenager, a sewing machine and fabric in the corner of a room for the budget-minded homemaker, or the star athlete's sports equipment lying in the hallway can be used to show what family members do in their spare time.

Personal items offer hints about each family member, and sometimes their darkest secrets. For instance, a razor and shaving cream hidden in an adolescent boy's closet could suggest he's shaving but doesn't want his parents to know.

Spilled lotion and perfume on mom's vanity suggests a culprit in the house. A pipe and tobacco on dad's nightstand, or an abundance of jewelry on mom's dresser, tells what "extras" they indulge themselves in.

Families with young children can utilize toys in various ways. Dolls, toy trains, guns, coloring

THE MINIATURES CATALOG, Fourteenth Edition   187

books, and crayons can all be blended into areas of the home and feature their active lives. Fill a teenage girl's room with make-up, hair products, and posters of movie stars. A stereo and albums strewn around the family room may accurately depict the lifestyle of the adolescent boy or girl of the house.

Pets add a new dimension to the family. It's been said that pets take on the personality of their owners, or is that vice versa? You can decide by choosing a particular dog for your family. Or do they prefer a bird? Are goldfish and gerbils the chosen pets? Can you create a scene with a young boy chasing his sister around the kitchen with his pet snake, or an elderly woman swatting her cat away from the bird cage? House pets provide an opportunity for humor, action, and plenty of mischievous "disasters."

Because the family in action is not always beautiful, clean, and organized, some accessories need to be appropriately placed for the "lived-in" look of the home. A desk piled high with papers, books, and a computer emphasizes the busy, hectic lifestyle of today's average family. Some of those flowers in vases can be wilted and dying. Garbage cans filled to the brim, piles of toys waiting to be straightened, after-dinner dishes in the sink, and a messy laundry room are scenes which add reality to your house.

Holidays afford you the opportunity to add accessories in yet another fashion. A Christmas tree and eggnog set up in the family room, or a full Hannukah meal in tempting array on the dining room table are festive ways to incorporate special occasions. By including holiday decorations throughout the house, you are opening the doors to a variety of ways to constantly change your dollhouse; celebrate Easter with baskets and bunnies in the kids' bedrooms, the Fourth of July with flags on the porch and in the yard, and Halloween with goblins and ghouls sneaking candy from the kitchen. Holiday accessories can show your family's religious beliefs, party preferences, or wilder side. And you can decorate your dollhouse with festive accessories while you embellish your full-size house with holiday ornamentation!

(Above) A back room of this dollhouse is the perfect setting for the local vet's shop! Dogs, cats, fish, and birds come together in one scene to create mischief.

The outside of your dollhouse needs a family's presence, too. What is found on the exterior can set the tone for what's inside. A bike precariously placed on the front steps, a skateboard in the driveway, and a headless doll lying in the grass offer great insight to younger families. A creaky porch, peeling paint, growing weeds, and an aging rocking chair surrounded by potted plants could be appropriate if your family was older and not able to get around anymore.

Whether your dollhouse family is young or old, busy or retired, you can get to know them by the accessories you place in their residence. A dollhouse doesn't have to be just a "cute little house"— give it a style and flair of its own. The accessories you lace throughout the rooms of your house can transform it into a home with striking character and a one-of-a-kind personality.

FROM C TO SHINING C
CIR-KIT CONCEPTS

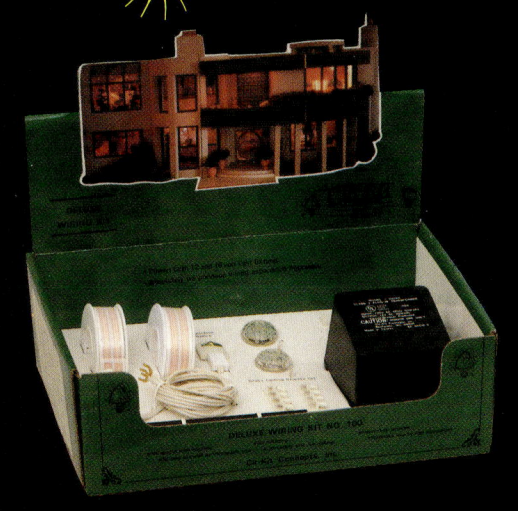

CK100 Deluxe Kit

CK101 Starter Kit

CK102 Room Box Kit

CK103 Large House Kit

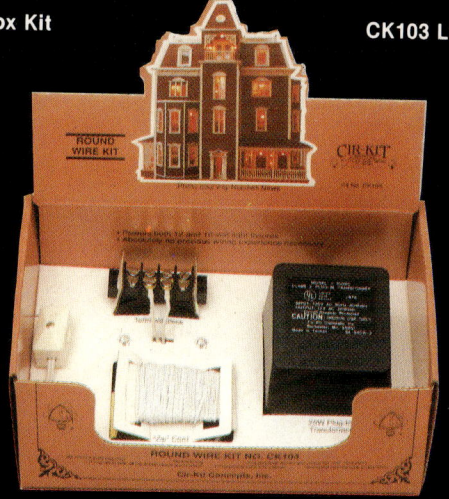

CK104 Round Wire Kit

CIR-KIT
CONCEPTS · INC ·
407 14th St. N.W. • Rochester, MN 55901
(507) 288-0860
"Where Innovation is a Tradition"
FAX (507) 288-9181
Send $4.00 for Cir-Kit Catalog #8

For more than 15 years Cir-Kit Concepts has been instrumental in developing, pioneering and popularizing the art of dollhouse lighting. Today, with five levels of wiring kits, we offer the widest range of lighting options available anywhere. We're proud to be the company who has been in the forefront of miniature lighting technology for more than a decade. We care about quality. We care about realism. We care about miniatures. And should you have a question, should you ever need service of any kind, rest assured we'll be here.

Do It Yourself!

By Jeanne Delgado
Associate Editor, Nutshell News

If your hobby is stamp collecting, you don't make your own stamps. If it's golf, you can't find kits to build your own cart or patterns to make new clubs, and if it's knitting or needlepoint, you wouldn't dream of buying someone else's sweater or sampler just so you could make it over. But in miniatures, this most versatile of all hobbies, we can and we do. Not only does our miniatures hobby fit everyone, there's always room—and unlimited ways—to grow.

Thank heavens it is possible to buy virtually everything we need—and a lot we never thought of—to finish and furnish our miniature projects. (That's what makes shows, shops, and catalogs so much fun!) But making something wonderful out of nothing is the miniaturist's special talent and joy. You can "scratch-build" a room, a cottage, or a mansion, a tiny shop or a whole mall. And you can handcraft everything in it. *Nutshell News* has had "how-to's" for them all, and there are many other plans and how-to books available. Or you can design your own.

A wide range of kits and ready-

(Opposite, top) Chrysnbon's new blue furniture kits invite you to paint a posy or a whole bouquet for a new "country-look." This set was hand-painted by Norma Smithers of Apopka, Florida, for Jerry Hacker of Dee's Delights.

(Opposite, left) Dee Snyder designed this whimsical harvest wreath as a how-to project for *NN* readers in September 1983 and it is just as popular today.

(Opposite, right) Louise Hedrick created a "wearable" wardrobe for Gretchen, a Roz doll, and shared her how-to skills with *NN* readers in March 1991.

(Top) Shirley Cox combined the best of kitbashing and scratch-building to create her Polo/Ralph Lauren shop. Starting with an inexpensive Dura Craft Tudor kit, she added bricks made from coffee stirrers, timbers and flooring made from wooden blind slats, and a poster board roof to the exterior, then made a "stone" doorway, steps, foundation, and flagstones made from matboard textured with grouting and painted. Shirley made most of the interior furnishings and accessories (copies of actual Ralph Lauren rooms and designs) from found items as well.

(Center) A do-it-yourself project doesn't have to be a house or a room box. Joann Swanson designed this county fair "Winners Booth" (and all the veggies) as a how-to project for *NN* readers in September 1990.

(Right) Madelyn Cook's "Hilltop" mansion began life as Miniature Lumber Shoppe's quarter-inch scale "Mallory" kit. In the past year Madelyn has shared with *NN* readers her how-to plans for quarter-inch scale furniture she designed for the house, using parts from model railroading kits.

THE MINIATURES CATALOG, *Fourteenth Edition*

(Above) Ron Benson, known for creating miniature porcelain figurines and dishes, is also *NN's* kitcrafting expert. Carving the lovely ball and claw feet on a Chippendale armchair was one of the modifications he taught in an August 1990 *NN* article on turning a Craftmark kit chair into "an extremely accurate antique."

made components for buildings, and kits for furnishings and accessories offer miniaturists the advantages of economy, professional design, time-saving, and above all, versatility. You can build a kit exactly as shown and it probably won't look just like your neighbor's, but you'll both be pleased as punch with your results. One of *Nutshell News* readers' all-time favorites was a kit-built house, modified and furnished with nearly 100 kits!

Probably the most popular issue of *Nutshell News* is the annual customizing issue. Kitcrafting or "kitbashing" (not as violent as it sounds!) is the way in which miniaturists have the best of both worlds. Begin with a kit and customize it to fit your taste and your needs. *Nutshell News* readers have changed two-and-a-half-story frame Colonials into a built-into-a-hillside stone Cape Cod with a basement, or into an adobe hacienda, and turned Greenleaf's modest "Arthur" into a glamorous Oriental. They've converted countless inexpensive cottages to an incredible variety of shops, tea rooms, gnome homes, and bordellos.

Furniture kits, whether wood or molded styrene, offer unlimited possibilities for personalization. Ron Benson's "Kit Renderings," a regular feature in *Nutshell News*, will show you how to make the Hepplewhite chest you've been seeking, using a readily available Chippendale kit version or how to turn a Hepplewhite side table kit into a Sheraton game table with a fold-up leaf. You can paint instead of staining and add decorative stenciling or freehand designs to Chrysnbon pieces for a custom country look, or combine two kits to make entirely new pieces.

You wouldn't tamper with an artisan's collector-quality piece of course, but refinishing and reupholstering inexpensive manufactured furniture is both an economical and a thoroughly enjoyable way to have the quality and the color scheme you want.

You *can* have it all. Collect, craft your own miniatures, build from a kit, customize—the choices are infinite. Remember, this is *your* world. There are no rules but one— Have Fun! •

YLI

YLI Corporation

YLI Corporation is the silk ribbon source. Same day shipping, in most instances, makes for quick delivery.

Rush $2.50 for sample catalog to:

YLI CORPORATION
P.O. Box 109
Provo, Utah 84603-0109
800-854-1932
FAX: 801-375-2879

YLI CORPORATION offers: 100% Silk Ribbon, Spark Organdy Ribbon, Synthetic Silk Ribbon, Fancy Ribbon. YLI also has silk thread in 215 colors and many more unique, hard to find products.

Attention Retailers!

Subscribe to the only trade magazine dedicated to dollhouses and miniatures –

MINIATURES DEALER

MINIATURES DEALER is now, more than ever, your connection to the miniatures trade. We've tailored our editorial content to include articles from retailers who know how to solve the challenges you're facing everyday. We've also increased the number of feature articles per issue, so you'll be more informed on trends in the field.

MINIATURES DEALER
keeps you up-to-date on:
- what products are selling
- how to make the most of a good opportunity
- news on national trade shows
- information on new products.

Plus, the publishers of **MINIATURES DEALER** also produce **NUTSHELL NEWS**, **MINIATURES SHOWCASE** and **THE MINIATURES CATALOG**. We're a leader in the miniatures field and we're in touch with your concerns and needs.

Subscribe today!
12 issues a year - only $24.00

(Foreign $32.00 surface mail; $72.00 air mail)Canada orders add 7% GST. Send your subscription request on your company's letterhead to MINIATURES DEALER, Dept. A41062, 21027 Crossroads Circle, P.O. Box 1612, Waukesha, WI 53187-1612. We will be happy to bill you, or you may include a check or money order. All subscriptions payable in U.S. funds.
Dept. A41062

For immediate service call
1-800-558-1544, ext. 579

CHIPPENDALE DESK

Craftmark House of Miniatures
Suggested Retail Price: $10.95
Catalog No. 40042
Slant front desk, circa 1750. Finished size measures 3-1/4"H x 3-1/4"W x 1-7/8"D. No. 55042, finished, $27.95.

COLONIAL FURNITURE KITS

By Craftmark House of Miniatures
Authentic reproductions of American Colonial pieces. Each kit includes machined mahogany wood parts and detailed instructions:
Hooded Cradle-circa 1750. When finished measures 2-1/8" H x 2-7/8" L x 2-1/8" D. Kit, $7.95. Catalog No. 40035.
Dower Chest - circa 1790. When finished measures 1-3/4" H x 3" W x 1-3/4" D. Kit $8.95. Catalog No. 40034.
Corner Cupboard-circa 1730-1750. When finished measures 7-3/8" H x 3-1/2" W x 2" D. Kit $15.50. Catalog No. 40041.

CHIPPENDALE FURNITURE KITS

By Craftmark House of Miniatures
Suggested Retail Price: $21.95 kit.
Authentic reproductions. All made of mahogany. Solid brass hardware included. Broken-Bonnet Highboy, circa 1750. When finished measures 7-1/16" H x 3-1/2" W x 2" D. Catalog No. 40023.

COLONIAL KITS

By Craftmark House of Miniatures
Hepplewhite Serving Table - circa 1780-1800, 3" W x 1 -1/2" D x 2 -7/8" H. Catalog No. 40065. $7.95/kit.
Tavern Table - circa 1700-1725, 3" W x 3" D x 2 -1/2" H. Catalog No. 40069, $8.95/kit.
Chippendale Chest of Drawers - circa 1760-1780, 3- 3/8" W x 1 -3/8" D x 4- 3/4" H. Catalog No. 40066, $11.95/kit.
Bagnail Tall Case Clock - circa 1730, 2" W x 1" D x 8-3/4" H. Catalog No. 40068, $14.50/kit.
Chippendale Desk on Frame - circa 1770, 3" W x 1-7/8" D x 3-5/8" H. Catalog No. 40067. $10.95/kit.
Chippendale Double Chest - circa 1780, 5" W x 1-7/8" D x 2-3/4" H. Catalog No. 40064. $16.95/kit.

CHIPPENDALE FURNITURE KITS

Craftmark House of Miniatures
Suggested Retail Price: $11.95 kit
Catalog No. 40025
Authentic reproductions. All made of mahogany. Solid brass hardware included. Sideboard, circa 1750. Finished size measures 2-7/8"H x 4-1/2"W x 2"D.

PERIOD FURNITURE

Sonia Messer Co., Inc.
Suggested Retail Price: $1.50-$90 completely finished
Exquisite 1" scale hardwood furniture in eight periods. Some kitchen, bathroom. Retail price list, $1.

Interested in Becoming a Miniatures Manufacturer?

Join the Miniatures Industry Association of America and sell products to retailers across the country.

MIAA
1100-H Brandywine Blvd.
P.O. Box 2188
Zanesville, OH 43702-3288

Prices are approximate and subject to change.

COLONIAL FURNITURE KITS

Olde Mountain Miniatures
Build with the best and most unique line of 14th to 18th Century Colonial furniture kits on the market. All precision cut, including hardware and full instructions. Also available custom finished in your choice of stain or paint. Ask your local miniatures dealer for our kits or finished pieces.

THE COLONIAL COLLECTION

Shenandoah Designs, Inc.
Suggested Retail Price: $8.49 - $16.49 (kit), $11.49 - $24.99 (assembled/sanded), and $16.99 - $24.99 (finished).
The furniture will add a touch of country to any collection. The designs were adapted from the finest of the country craftsmen who made this style so popular. The ten designs of this collection are now available in 1/2" scale assembled and ready to finish.

THE CHIPPENDALE COLLECTION

Shenandoah Designs, Inc.
Suggested Retail Price: $8.49 - $32.99 (kit)
Material: Mahogany
The Chippendale Collection contains some of the finest wood miniature furniture kits available. All parts are pre-cut and some are even pre-carved to enable you to construct 1/12 scale versions of some of Chippendale's finest designs. The pieces pictured are only a few of the many designs available.

Colonial & Federal

COLONIAL BED

Aztec Imports, Inc.
Catalog No. T3036
Wholesale only. Mahogany colonial bed with curved head board. Fine detail on the footboard makes this a unique piece.

DRESSER WITH MIRROR

Aztec Imports, Inc.
Catalog No. M2017
Wholesale only. Mahogany nine-drawer dresser with attached mirror. Fine detail for a unique colonial look.

FOUR POSTER BED

Aztec Imports, Inc.
Catalog No. D9074 mahogany, D9073 oak
Wholesale only. This four poster bed is available in mahogany with white fabric or oak with printed fabric. A wonderful addition to your colonial collection.

Furniture

THE MINIATURES CATALOG, *Fourteenth Edition* 195

COLONIAL ELEGANCE

By Grace
Suggested Retail Price: $50 #176 bed ; $59 #212 bed; $38 #BYGRQC chair
Whether you are creating with the elegance of colonial today or its charm of yesteryear, customize your decor with our beds and designer linens. Upholstered furniture to match or coordinate. Large selection of styles and variety of fabrics. Wholesale/retail. Price list with photocopies. $1.50 plus LSASE, refundable. Completely finished.

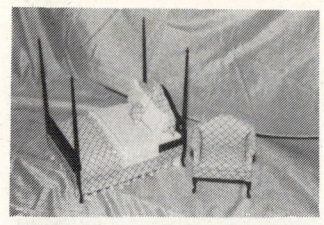

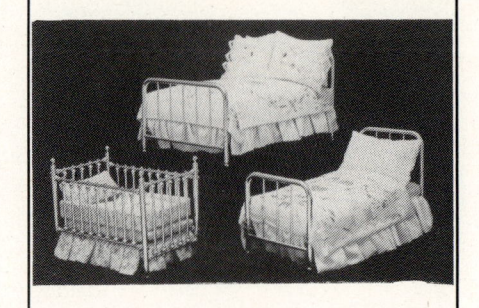

HANDCRAFTED COLONIAL FURNITURE

Dan-Dy Crafts
Suggested Retail Price: See your dealer
Shown is a fine sampling of our line of country pine precision miniatures. All are handcrafted in New England from select pine with working doors and drawers. All pieces are finished inside and out and are available in light and dark stains as well as uniform blue, gloss white, unfinished or select pieces in richtone black. Selections that are not pictured include kitchen cabinets, trestle table and benches, half-round table, canopy and twin beds, mirror, dresser, cradle and many more.

DRESSED BRASS BEDS

Clare-Bell Brass Works
Brass crib, catalog no. 1701-DOO, $120.95; plain brass bed, catalog 1703-DOO, $96.60; twin brass bed, catalog no. 1704-DOO, $76.65. All beds are solid brass with a gold-plated finish. Beds are dressed by Tiny Touch & Co. Also available undressed.

HANDCRAFTED COLONIAL FURNITURE

Dan-Dy Crafts
Suggested Retail Price: See your dealer
Shown is a fine sampling of our line of country pine precision miniatures. All are handcrafted in New England from select pine with working doors and drawers. All pieces are finished inside and out and are available in light and dark stains as well as uniform blue, gloss white, unfinished or select pieces in richtone black. Selections that are not pictured include kitchen cabinets, trestle table and benches, half-round table, canopy and twin beds, mirror, dresser, cradle and many more.

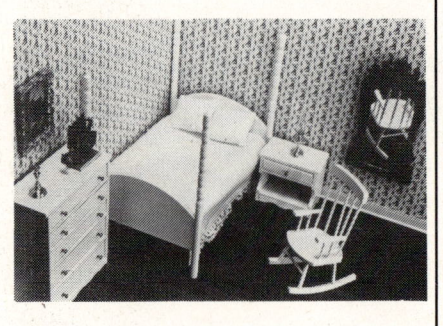

MAHOGANY DOUBLE BED

Exclusive Products
The elegance of mahogany frames this festive floral bed cover with twin pillows. A stunning piece to plan a bedroom around. #B-9847.

FEDERAL DINING ROOM

Handcraft Designs, Inc.
Suggested Retail Price: See your dealer
Catalog No. (top row, left to right) #3003M, #3404M knife boxes on #3410M, #3405M, (bottom row) #3409M, #3408M, #3411M
A Federal period dining room grouping including designs in Queen Anne and Hepplewhite styles. The urn-shaped knife boxes each contain a four-piece pewter place setting of flatware. The corner cupboard has clamshell carved top. The Queen Anne dining table is gate-legged and usefully small with its drop leafs down.

YOUR LOCAL
MINIATURES SHOP
WILL BE HAPPY TO
SPECIAL ORDER
FOR YOU!

DOUBLE BED
Miniature House
Suggested Retail Price: $10.79
Catalog No. MH411
Material: All wood, fabric covered mattress
Finish: Early American oak
A lovely, inexpensive way to furnish a bedroom.

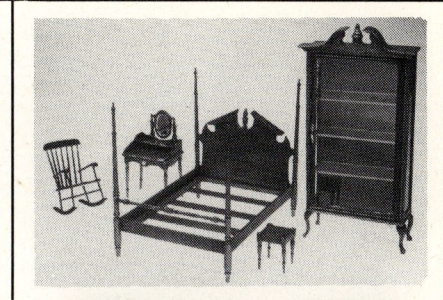

COLONIAL HERITAGE
Don Perkins Miniatures
How can the rich furniture heritage of our Colonial past be better exemplified than by a Carver chair, a Brewster chair and a graceful hutch. Each piece is handcrafted from select birch and cherry woods and signed by Don Perkins. 1" scale.

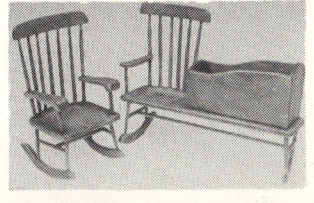

HANDCRAFTED FURNITURE
Nellie Originals
Suggested Retail Price: $25 - $110
Designed and made by Nelson Lewis. All dated and signed, choose your finish. Some pieces available unfinished. Distinctive, affordable furnishings. Beds dressed, towels and pillows by Louise. Custom designs in linens and furniture.

NANNY BENCH & ROCKING CHAIR
Nellie Originals
Suggested Retail Price: $42 and $40 ppd plus shipping. Completely finished.
Nanny bench designed with rockers and cradle by Nelson Lewis. Basswood with mahogany finish or choice of finishes. Fits any decor or your porch. His rocking chair is small enough to fit in any corner.

Country Kits

COUNTRY COLLECTION II
B. H. Miniatures
Precut, ready-to-assemble basswood kits.
No. 611K Hoosier Cabinet (5-3/4"H x 3-7/8"W x 2-3/8"D). Includes brass hardware, tooling aluminum and lucite. Photo on left.
No. 606K Pie Safe (5-5/8"H x 3-7/8"W x 1-3/4"D). Includes brass hardware and tooling aluminum.
No. 605K Work Table (5-1/4"L x 2-5/8"H x 2-1/2"W). Includes brass hardware and tooling aluminum. Photo on right.
No. 607K Dry Sink (4"W x 2-7/8"H x 1-5/8"D). Includes brass hardware and tooling aluminum.

Furniture

THE MINIATURES CATALOG, Fourteenth Edition 197

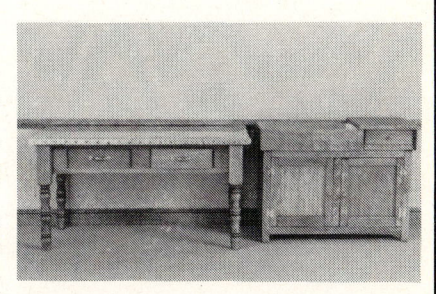

COUNTRY COLLECTION II

B. H. Miniatures
Precut, ready-to-assemble basswood kits.
No. 622K Dresser with Mirror (5-3/4"H x 3-1/2"W x 1-5/8"D). Includes brass hardware and mirror.
No. 620K Double Bed (6-3/4"L x 5-1/4"W x 3-7/8"H). Includes foam mattress.
No. 621K Wardrobe (6-3/4"H x 4-1/2"W x 1-7/8"D). Includes brass hardware.
No. 623K Day Bed (6-3/4"L x 3-7/8"H x 2-7/8"W). Includes foam mattress.

KITCHEN FURNITURE KIT

Dura-Craft, Inc.
Suggested Retail Price: See your dealer
Catalog No. KR30
This beautifully crafted country furniture is something to really please the collector or young ladies. The kits are die-cut 1/8" plywood that is easily assembled. Can be painted or stained to the color scheme of your home. Nine pieces: kitchen cabinet, stove, table and four chairs, refrigerator and picture frame.

BEDROOM FURNITURE KIT

Dura-Craft, Inc.
Suggested Retail Price: See your dealer
Catalog No. BR40
This beautifully crafted country furniture is something to really please the collector or young ladies. The kits are die-cut 1/8" plywood that is easily assembled. Can be painted or stained to the color scheme of your home. Twelve pieces: bed, linen chest, dresser, baby cradle, wall mirror, two nightstands, chest of drawers, vanity and stool, full length mirror and picture frame. Foil mirrors included. Mattresses, chair pad and doilies not included.

DINING ROOM FURNITURE KIT

Dura-Craft, Inc.
Suggested Retail Price: See your dealer
Catalog No. DR10
This beautifully crafted country furniture is something to really please the collector or young ladies. The kits are die-cut 1/8" plywood that is easily assembled. Can be painted or stained to the color scheme of your home. Thirteen pieces: table with four chairs, china cupboard, serving card, desk and chair, four picture frames.

LIVING ROOM FURNITURE KIT

Dura-Craft, Inc.
Suggested Retail Price: See your dealer.
Catalog No. LR20
This beautifully crafted country furniture is something to really please the collector or young ladies. The kits are die-cut 1/8" plywood that is easily assembled. Can be painted or stained to the color scheme of your home. Twelve pieces: Sofa, three end tables, piano and bench, two armchairs, coffee table, entry table, two picture frames. Cushions and doilies not included.

COUNTRY FURNITURE KITS

Inch/Foot
Suggested Retail Price: kits; $6-$18 ppd completely finished; write for prices
Material: Cherry, walnut and pine
Easy-to-assemble kits of friendly country furniture in natural and painted finishes. Kits guaranteed. Send LSASE for price list, descriptions and photos. Retail only.

October National Dollhouse & Miniatures Month

Country

REALIFE MINIATURES® COUNTRY BEDROOM

Scientific Models, Inc.
Suggested Retail Price: $32.95
Made of basswood and brass. Recreate the country's most popular home decor with these authentic reproductions. Add that warm country atmosphere to your dollhouse or miniature collection with our easy-to-assemble kits at 1/5 the cost of assembled pieces. Complete instructions included. No special tools are required. Country Bedroom Kit No. 207 includes four poster bed with mattress, blanket chest, pre-decorated dower chest, wash stand and hooded cradle. Approximately 12 cotton balls required for pillow stuffing not included. Bed 5" W x 6-1/8" H. American made.

COUNTRY COLLECTION II

B. H. Miniatures
Basswood, finished in a warm maple stain.
No. 622F Dresser with Mirror (5-3/4"H x 3-1/2"W x 1-5/8"D). Includes brass hardware and mirror.
No. 620F Double Bed (6-3/4"L x 5-1/4"W x 3-7/8"H). With foam mattress, undressed.
No. 621F Wardrobe (6-3/4"H x 4-1/2"W x 1-7/8"D). With brass hardware.
No. 623F Day Bed (6-3/4"L x 3-7/8"H x 2-7/8"W). With foam mattress, undressed.
Walnut stain also available, please specify.

COUNTRY COLLECTION II

B. H. Miniatures
Basswood, finished in a warm maple stain.
No. 611F Hoosier Cabinet (5-3/4"H x 3-7/8"W x 2-3/8"D). Includes brass hardware, metal bins and top, lucite doors.
No. 606F Pie Safe (5-5/8"H x 3-7/8"W x 1-3/4"D). Includes brass hardware and pierced tin doors and sides.
No. 605F Work Table (5-1/4"L x 2-5/8"H x 2-1/2"W). Includes brass hardware and metal top.
No. 607F Dry Sink (4"W x 2-7/8"H x 1-5/8"D). Includes brass hardware and metal sink.
Walnut stain also available, please specify.

SHAKER AND AMERICAN COUNTRY

Renee Bowen Miniaturist
Complete line of Shaker and American Country furniture, accessories, toys and games. All handmade and always adding new items. Wholesale or retail inquiries invited. Brochure available.

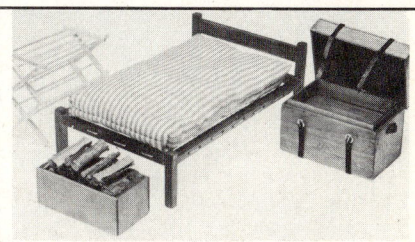

CABIN FURNITURE

Jan's Small World
Suggested Retail Price: $4 and up
Material: Wood construction
Rustic American made furniture and accessories are available for your log cabin, summer home or Pilgrim cottages. 1"-1' scale. Write for catalog.

COZY COUNTRY

By Grace
Suggested Retail Price: $50 #202 bed; $52 #BYGRQLS loveseat
Home is where the heart is. Create a special feeling with our custom designed bed linens on walnut, oak, mahogany, brass or wire beds. Skirted loveseats and chairs to match or coordinate. Wholesale/retail. Price list with photo-copies. $1.50 plus LSASE, refundable. Completely finished.

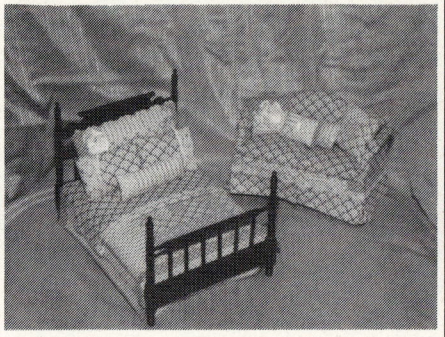

REALIFE MINIATURES® COUNTRY KITCHEN

Scientific Models, Inc.
Suggested Retail Price: $32.95
Catalog No. 194
Kit includes all materials necessary to make four pieces shown (stove, sink, ice box and hoosier cabinet). Materials include precut basswood parts, brass hardware, metal castings, stain, gloss coat, brush, sandpaper, glue, and instructions. American made.

ENGLISH GARDEN BEDROOM

Concord Miniatures
Suggested Retail Price: See your dealer
This oak bedroom is an inviting ensemble for collectors everywhere. Meticulous oak craftsmanship. Handrubbed finish. Handpainted floral design. #M718 - chest; #M620 - armoire; #M621 - bed; #M623 - dresser/mirror; #M622 - night table.

COLONIAL AND SHAKER FURNITURE

The Tree Trunk Studio
Suggested Retail Price: $5.50 - $94
Historic 1" and 1/2" Colonial and Shaker reproductions, handmade for you by Jenifer K. Johnson. Accurate scale, beautiful detailing and finish. Shown: Colonial high chair with rush-woven seat, birch and maple frame; $38 in 1", $31 in 1/2" Can't find a special piece? Send description for custom order quote.

BEDROOM FURNITURE

Miniature Towne, USA
Suggested Retail Price: $105 bed, $94 dresser, $50 nightstand. All plus shipping
Also available are chest-on-chest and vanity with bench. Natural myrtlewood. Exclusive offering of Mr. Ken Kenyon. Exquisitely crafted bedroom furniture signed and dated.

PAINTED COUNTRY FURNITURE

Sir Thomas Thumb
Our tastefully antiqued country kitchen furniture will take you back to the warm hearths of yesteryear. Beautifully finished wood in red, blue, green or antique pine. Catalog available.

REALIFE MINIATURES® COUNTRY LIVING ROOM

Scientific Models, Inc.
Suggested Retail Price: $32.95
Made of basswood, brass and cotton fabric. Recreate the country's most popular home decor with these authentic reproductions. Add that warm country atmosphere to your dollhouse or miniature collection with our easy-to-assemble kits at 1/5 the cost of assembled pieces. Complete instructions included. No special tools are required. Country living room kit 206 includes settle bench, sofa, tavern table, sea chest and shaker candle stand. (Approximately 24 cotton balls required for pillow stuffing not included). Settle bench 4-1/2" W x 4" H.

Victorian Kits

THE VICTORIANA COLLECTION

B.H. Miniatures
Precut, ready-to-assemble basswood kits.
No. 702K Leaded-glass cupboard with two doors. (4-1/4 H x 3-5/8" W x 1-1/8" D) Includes brass hardware, micro-thin glass and lead foil tape.
No. 707K Base Unit with two doors (3" H x 3-1/2" W x 1-3/4" D). Includes brass hardware.
No. 709K China Closet (7-1/2" H x 4-7/8" W x 1-3/4" D) Includes brass hardware and micro-thin glass.
No. 710K Two Kitchen Chairs (3-7/8" H x 1-1/2" W x 1-1/2" D)
No. 711K Round Kitchen Table (4" Round x 2-1/2" H)

THE VICTORIANA COLLECTION

B.H. Miniatures
Precut, ready-to-assemble basswood kits.
No. 712K Double Bed (7-1/8" H x 6-7/8" L x 5-1/2" W) Includes foam mattress.
No. 713K Dresser (7" H x 4-3/4" W x 1-3/4" D) Includes brass hardware, marble tops and mirror.
No. 714K Nightstand (2-1/4" H x 2-3/8" W x 1-5/8" D) Includes brass hardware and marble top.
No. 715K Wardrobe (7-3/4" H x 5-7/8" W x 2" D) Includes brass hardware and mirror.

DOLLHOUSE FURNITURE KITS

Greenleaf Products, Inc.
Suggested Retail Price: Catalog No. 9010 $38.25, and 9030 $21.50.
Material: Precut plywood
There's terrific value in these kits - Greenleaf's best selling items. Available in 56-piece or 30-piece version. In addition to the die-cut wooden pieces (1" to 1' scale), we've added plastic mirrors and "glass" for frames along with foam batting for upholstering. Paint or stain the pieces to the color scheme of your choice, and let your decorating abilities come to the fore!

VICTORIAN HAT SALON

Miniature Corner
Suggested Retail Price: See your dealer
Available as a set or individual kits. Furniture kits of high quality wood, cut for easy assembly. All furniture pieces available as kits as well as hat making kit. Shelf and counter kits can be used in other shops or as library shelves and credenza. Dolls not included.

Furniture

THE MINIATURES CATALOG, *Fourteenth Edition* 201

REALIFE MINIATURES® VICTORIAN BEDROOM KIT

Scientific Models, Inc.
Suggested Retail Price: $29.95
Catalog No. 200
Museum quality detailing makes this furniture comparable to replicas that cost up to $75 assembled. Kit includes bed, night table and dresser. Bed is seven inches high. No sewing or special tools required to build kit. Kit also includes precut and numbered basswood parts, foam upholstery materials, metal hardware, simulated marble table tops, a sandpaper and craft glue, brush, wood stain, gloss coat and complete instructions. American made.

REALIFE MINIATURES® BATHROOM

Scientific Models, Inc.
Suggested Retail Price: $29.95
Catalog No. 197
Authentic reproductions in basswood. Kit includes all materials to make five pieces shown plus two rugs and three towels. Materials include precut basswood parts, brass hardware, tub, sink, bowl, stain, gloss coat, brush, sandpaper, glue and instructions.

WICKER DOLL CARRIAGE KIT

Smallworks
Suggested Retail Price: $16 ppd., kit
Dimensions: 3"H x 3"L x 1-1/4"W
Childsize carriage holds 1-1/2" doll. Includes wire, thread, wheels plus specs for larger carriage. Uses common tools. Illustrated instructions for average skill levels.

Contact Sara Benz at 1-800-558-1544, Ext. 631 or write to;

The Miniatures Catalog P.O. Box 1612 Waukesha, WI 53187

Victorian

THE VICTORIANA COLLECTION

B.H. Miniatures
Basswood, finished in a deep walnut stain.
No. 712F Double Bed (7-1/8" H x 6-7/8" L x 5-1/2" W) Undressed but includes foam mattress.
No. 713F Dresser (7" H x 4-3/4" W x 1-3/4" D) With brass hardware, marble tops, and mirror.
No. 714F Nightstand (2-1/4" H x 2-3/8" W x 1-5/8" D) With brass hardware and marble top.
No. 715F Wardrobe (7-3/4" H x 5-7/8" W x 2" D) With mirror and brass hardware. Center section has three shelves and three drawers. Maple stain also available (please specify).

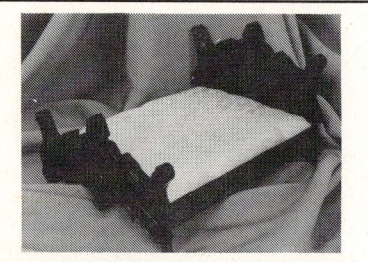

VICTORIAN BED

Aztec Imports, Inc.
Catalog No. T3180
Wholesale only. This unique mahogany victorian bed with white satin bed covering will be the perfect centerpiece for your victorian bedroom.

VICTORIAN SOFA

Aztec Imports, Inc.
Catalog No. T3018
Wholesale only. This unusual mahogany sofa with white satin fabric is perfect for your Victorian home. The unique look adds a special grace to any formal living room.

THE VICTORIANA COLLECTION

B.H. Miniatures
Basswood, finished in a deep walnut stain.
No. 702F Leaded-glass cupboard with two doors. (4-1/4" H x 3-5/8" W x 1-1/8" D) Includes brass hardware and micro-thin glass.
No. 707F Base unit with two doors. (3" H x 3-1/2" W x 1-3/4" D) Brass hardware included.
No. 709F China closet (7-1/2" H x 4-7/8" W x 1-3/4" D) With brass hardware and micro-thin glass.
No. 710F Two Kitchen Chairs (3-7/8" H x 1-1/2" W x 1-1/2" D)
No. 711F Round Kitchen Table (4" Round X 2-1/2" H) Maple stain or painted white also available. Please specify.

DRESSED BRASS BEDS

Clare-Bell Brass Works
Canopy bed, catalog no. 1702-DOO, $187.95; fancy dressed bed, catalog 1700-DOO, $156.45; wagon wheel bed (with or without footboard), catalog no. 1706-DOO, $115.50 (with footboard), catalog no. 1707-DOO, $94.50 (without footboard). All beds are solid brass with a gold-plated finish. Beds are dressed by Tiny Touch & Co. Also available undressed.

VICTORIAN DELIGHTS

By Grace
Suggested Retail Price: $80 #166 bed; $28 #BYGRCC chair
Unique designs suited for today or the charm of yesteryear are created with a large selection of fabrics and trims to suit your special desires. Deluxe quality at collectable prices. Bedroom suites are our specialty.. Wholesale/retail. Price list with photo-copies. $1.50 plus LSASE, refundable. Completely finished.

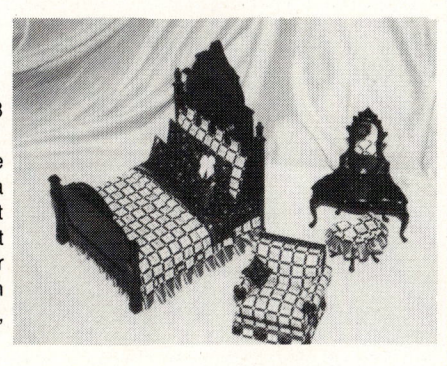

VICTORIAN PARLOR

Concord Miniatures
Suggested Retail Price: See your dealer
Delicately carved in mahogany finish and upholstered in our exclusive pink brocade fabric. #M584 - sofa; #M585 - gent's chair; #M586 - rocker; #M045 - coffee table.

QUEEN ANNE LIVING ROOM

Concord Miniatures
Suggested Retail Price: See your dealer
This Queen Anne living room features Concord's new cabbage rose fabric. Mahogany finish. #M733 - four piece living room set; #M042 - coffee table.

VICTORIAN PARLOR

Concord Miniatures
Suggested Retail Price: See your dealer
This elegant Victorian parlor is richly upholstered in our new exclusive floral print corduroy fabric. Mahogany finish. #M764 - three piece parlor set; #M673 - drum table; #M765 - marble fireplace.

Furniture

THE MINIATURES CATALOG, Fourteenth Edition

VICTORIAN GROUPING

The Dollhouse Factory™
Suggested Retail Price: $40-$500 completely finished
Materials: Walnut, mahogany and maple. Bisque doll

This is just a small sampling of some of the finest miniatures you will see. Some are one-of-a-kind pieces, others are made in limited editions, all are impeccably crafted. See our catalog for more.

CHEVAL MIRROR

Exclusive Products
A full length mirror mounted on swivels in a frame. Just the right touch for the bedroom, in walnut. #K-6514

HYDE PARK BEDROOM

Handcraft Designs, Inc.
Catalog Nos. from left to right: 3502, Hyde Park Dresser; 3503, Hyde Park Nightstand; 3504, Hyde Park Bed (dressings not included); 3508, Hyde Park Wardrobe; 3526, Brass Clothes Pole.
Material: Wood in walnut stain, white marble, brass. This late Victorian Bedroom grouping was inspired by furnishings in the Blue Room at Hyde Park. All four case pieces are based on the originals in FDR's boyhood room. There are common architectural motifs indicating a "set" of furniture.

HAND-CARVED VICTORIAN FURNITURE

Mary's Miniature Mansions
Suggested Retail Price: $175 cradle, $140 wardrobe, $90 pier table (all completely finished).
Material: Cherry or mahogany hardwoods
Finish: Satin or gloss
This elegant handcrafted Victorian furniture is available in signed, limited editions in 1" and 1/2" scale. The carving and detail are truly exquisite. Made by Dennis Spirek, IGMA artisan. Pieces are available for the dining room, hall, library and bedroom. Custom work welcomed.

SPINNING WHEEL

Exclusive Products
This old time spinning wheel with cotton feeding spool is crafted in quality walnut. A nice accent for a den or sewing room. #M-265.

VICTORIAN COOKSTOVE

Miniature Corner
Suggested Retail Price: $49
Catalog No. BH6600
Finish: Brass and lacquer
Victorian era cookstove with our exclusive curved stovepipe. All metal construction. The finest quality stove in the miniature world. Drawers and doors open. Copper accessories also available. Send $3 for catalog of all Bodo Hennig products. At miniature shops everywhere.

Prices are approximate and subject to change.

20th Century Kits

VICTORIAN PARLOR STOVE

Miniature Corner
Catalog No. BH942.
Material: Metal
Finish: Black with nickel trim, brass accents
Ornate Victorian parlor stove in exquisite detailed metal. Working door and ash drawer. Authentic design even includes brass "scent vase" on top. Can be electrified.

BEDROOM SET KIT

Artply, Inc.
Suggested Retail Price: See your dealer
Catalog No. APLF102
1" scale kit with four pieces. Easy-to-follow instructions for assembly and finishing. All parts are pre-cut plywood for easy construction and durability.

DINING ROOM KIT

Artply, Inc.
Suggested Retail Price: See your dealer
Catalog No. APLF101
1" scale kit with six pieces. Easy-to-follow instructions for assembly and finishing. All parts are pre-cut plywood for easy construction and durability.

LIVING ROOM KIT

Artply, Inc.
Suggested Retail Price: See your dealer
Catalog No. APLF100
1" scale kit with six pieces. Easy-to-follow instructions for assembly and finishing. All parts are pre-cut plywood for easy construction and durability.

DOLLHOUSE FURNITURE KIT

Artply, Inc.
Suggested Retail Price: See your dealer
1" scale kit with 19 pieces. Easy-to-follow instructions for assembly and finishing. All parts are pre-cut plywood for easy construction and durability.

CHRYSNBON® KITS

Chrysnbon
Chrysnbon® kits are easy to assemble, easy to customize, authentically detailed. Over 40 different kits of home furniture and accessories - all accurately scaled in wood-grained polystyrene for a realistic look.

Pictured Left:
CHR2112 Cook Stove Kit. Authentic replica of a cook stove, complete with lid lifter, two trivets, match safe, two sad irons, grate shaker, large and small cast iron skillets and stove board with decal. No painting necessary.

Pictured Middle:
CHR2111 Victorian Bathroom Kit. With a claw-footed bathtub, tank-top commode with pull-chain, radiator, mirrored medicine cabinet, stool and swan decals.

Pictured Right:
CHR2114 Round Table Kit. Features a beautiful replica of a claw-foot round oak table, expandable with two leaves and accented with two cane seat chairs.

Furniture

THE MINIATURES CATALOG, *Fourteenth Edition* 205

TINY TURNINGS KITS "CANOPY BED"
Quad Company
Suggested Retail Price: $13.50
Catalog No. 3030
Finely detailed hardwood turnings with a unique interlocking design. Each kit contains "tiny turnings", instructions and everything necessary for completion. Towel bar kit #1040, $3.

TINY TURNINGS KITS "NURSERY"
Quad Company
Suggested Retail Price: $6.50 each kit
Catalog No. 3010-cradle, 2010-playpen, 2020-crib
Finely detailed hardwood turnings with a unique interlocking design. Each kit contains "tiny turnings", instructions and everything necessary for completion.

TINY TURNINGS KITS "TABLE AND CHAIRS"
Quad Company
Suggested Retail Price: $4.50 each
Catalog No. 1010-two chairs, 1020 table
Finely detailed hardwood turnings with a unique interlocking design. Each kit contains "tiny turnings", instructions and everything necessary for completion.

TINY TURNINGS KITS
Quad Company
Finely detailed hardwood turnings with a unique interlocking design. Each kit contains "tiny turnings", instructions, cutting diagrams and wood or foam components necessary for completion. Easel kit #1060-$3.50, bed kit #1030-$6.50, hall tree kit #3040-$3.

TINY TURNINGS KITS "SCREEN AND PLANT STANDS"
Quad Company
Finely detailed hardwood turnings with a unique interlocking design. Each kit contains "tiny turnings", instructions, cutting diagrams and wood or foam components necessary for completion. Screen kit #2030-$6.50, plant stands kit #2040-$3.50.

TINY TURNINGS KITS "LIVING ROOM"
Quad Company
Suggested Retail Price: $18
Catalog No. 3060
The "tiny turnings" living room furniture kit contains all the components needed to complete an entire living room ensemble consisting of everything shown. All materials and instructions included.

REALIFE MINIATURES® KITCHEN
Scientific Models, Inc.
Suggested Retail Price: $32.95
Catalog No. 191
Original design. Kit includes all materials to make five furniture pieces shown (shelf, refrigerator, upper cabinet, lower cabinet, stove, sink and stove hood also included). Materials include precut basswood parts, brass hardware, stain, gloss coat, brush, sandpaper, glue and instructions. American made.

TINY TURNINGS KITS "RAILINGS"
Quad Company
Suggested Retail Price: $3.50
Catalog No. 1050
Finely detailed hardwood turnings with a unique interlocking design. Each kit contains "tiny turnings", instructions and cutting diagrams.

Nutshell News
The monthly miniatures magazine, covering all aspects of miniatures for collectors and hobbyists. Available at your local miniatures shop or by subscription.

Early 20th Century

Prices are approximate and subject to change.

ANGELA CANOPY

Amoroso Originals
Suggested Retail Price: $231 Ppd.
Finish: Walnut, almond, Early American and oak. An elegant wood canopy dressed lavishly. Made by Mike, dressed by Ann.

ANN MARIE

Amoroso Originals
Suggested Retail Price: $251 Ppd.
Designed by Ann-Marie and manufactured by Clare-Bell exclusively for us in the same quality they are known for.

DRESSING TABLE SET

Amoroso Originals
Suggested Retail Price: Kit, $48 Ppd. Finished, $73 Ppd. Three piece set, real mirrors and wood bench.

COLLECTORS EDITION SEWING MACHINE

Miniature Corner
Suggested Retail Price: See your dealer
Working treadle moves needle up and down. Pressure foot holds fabric. Oak finish work surface. Highly detailed metal parts. Shown with doll from Bodo Hennig. Portable table model also available. Imported from Germany. At better shops.

DAY BEDS

Amoroso Originals
Suggested Retail Price: $104 Ppd.
Country series - country prints in a variety of colors with lace or ribbon ruffle trim. Romance series - frilly feminine laces and materials in a variety of colors. Also available are brass daybeds made by Mike from Clare-Bell just for us.

STICKLEY DINING ROOM

Norm's Originals
Suggested Retail Price: $65 kit, $200 finished, plus shipping
Handcrafted replica of Stickley's 1912 furniture. Available as kits or completely finished. Made of fine hardwood (walnut, cherry, maple, mahogany). Other pieces available.

1930 - Contemporary

Furniture

1930's LIVING ROOM SET

Aztec Imports, Inc.
Catalog No. T6165
Wholesale only. A five piece living room set circa 1930. The couch, loveseat, chair and ottoman have a classic mauve and white fabric. The walnut coffee table will accent any decor.

TOMMY'S ROOM

B. H. Miniatures
Basswood, finished in a warm maple stain. No. 501F Trundle Bed, No. 508F Student's Desk, No. 509F Desk Chair, No. 504F Chest of Drawers, No. 512F Nightstand, No. 510F Toy Chest. Walnut stain also available, please specify. Items also available as furniture kits.

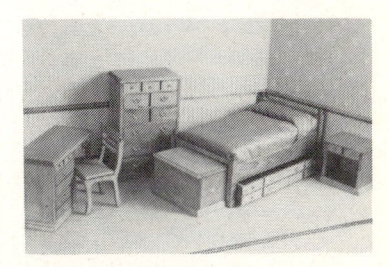

THE MINIATURES CATALOG, *Fourteenth Edition*

ELECTRONIC EQUIPMENT

Betty's Wooden Miniatures
Suggested Retail Price: See your dealer. These are all 1" scale, original, handmade miniatures. Shown are our Starshoot game that lights up and flashes, console TV, video game TV, walnut clock radio, boom box radio, 3-piece walnut stereo and speakers, computer, portable TV in five cabinet colors, and our Walkman. All are handmade by us in the USA.

COUNTRY BEDROOM COLLECTION

Betty's Wooden Miniatures
This handmade collection has a lovely honey colored finish, delicate brass hardware, beveled drawers that open and fat bun feet. The fabric comes in soft rose or country blue. The bed skirt is ivory. Made of clear pine. Completely finished. All pieces sold separately. Handcrafted by us in the USA.

THE PRINCESS COLLECTION

Betty's Wooden Miniatures
Completely finished. See your local dealer for price.
All pieces sold separately.
Pretty enough for a princess, the white "quilted" coverlet is strewn with the loveliest multi-colored rose buds, as are the rounded padded headboard, the slipper chair, and the top of the vanity stool. The classic shaped vanity has a glossy white non-scratch surface with a lovely white eyelet skirt. Truly lovely! All handcrafted by us in the USA.

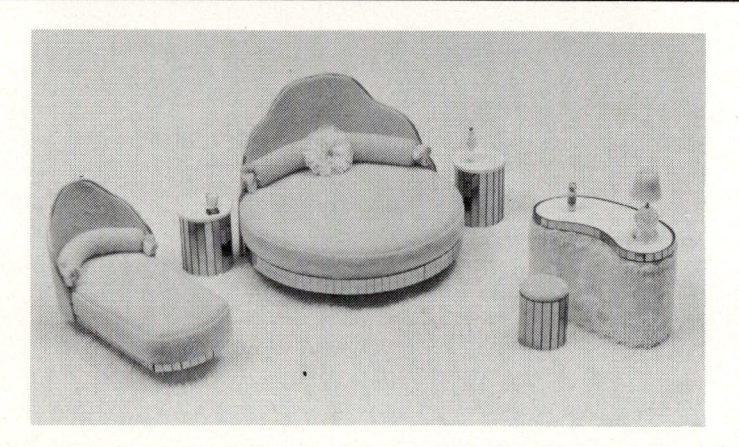

THE HARLOW COLLECTION

Betty's Wooden Miniatures
Our gorgeous round bed features a sculptured headboard in the softest, prettiest pink with a deep rose mirrored frame. The sculptured vanity has a crystal pleated overskirt with deep rose mirrored edging. The nightstands and stool are also mirrored. Our lovely soft chaise lounge completes the collection. This is a truly luxurious boudoir ensemble. All pieces sold separately, completely finished. All handcrafted in the USA.

LITTLE VILLAGE BEDROOM COLLECTION

Betty's Wooden Miniatures
A beautiful collection for a young girl's room. All pieces are painted a sparkling satin white. The fronts are designed to look like houses. The clapboard drawer fronts are painted in a contrasting color; the general store is terra cotta, the Victorian house is country blue, the nightstand is a soft green and the sliding doors of the headboard are a pretty yellow. The roofing is stained wood tone. All drawers open (mini furniture and accessories shown are not included). All pieces are sold separately. All are handmade by us in the USA.

CAR BED AND CRAYON FURNITURE

Betty's Wooden Miniatures
Our boys' bed is a Pontiac banshee "dream machine" painted bright red. The quilt and pillow are covered in a colorful car print. Our crayon furniture is bright and colorful with shiny white tops. Each crayon leg is painted a bright primary color. All are handmade by us in the USA.

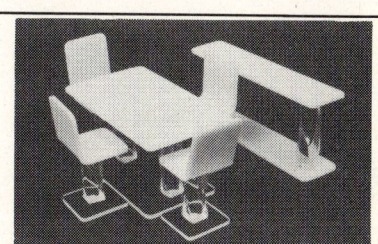

CONTEMPORARY LUCITE FURNITURE

By Barb
Material: Lucite
Lucite tables, chairs and sideboard. Available in a large variety of colors. Made in the U.S.A.

CORDUROY RECLINING CHAIR AND WALNUT STEREO WITH SPEAKERS

Betty's Wooden Miniatures
Material: Cabinet and speakers are genuine walnut wood, recliner is corduroy or ultra-suede.
Our recliner is the perfect touch for a contemporary room. It is fully adjustable. The walnut stereo unit features "stacked" components with smoked plastic dust cover and separate speakers. Record albums are not included. All handmade by us in the U.S.A.

CONTEMPORARY GLASS, BRASS AND WOOD CABINETS

Maison des Maison
Suggested Retail Price: $300
Executed by master craftsman Noral Olson exclusively for Maison des Maison, these beautiful contemporary cabinets of glass, brass and wood are perfect for displaying your treasured miniatures plates, silver, sculpture and other fine pieces. It measures 7-1/4"H x 3-1/4"W x 1-1/2"D.

FOR FAST SERVICE, VISIT YOUR LOCAL MINIATURES SHOP

CUSTOMIZED CONTEMPORARY

By Grace
Suggested Retail Price: $59 #147 bed; $41 #BYGRTLS loveseat
We create custom designer bed linens on a wide variety of period wooden and brass beds with upholstered furniture to match or coordinate to your decor. Wholesale/retail. Price list with photo-copies. $1.50 plus LSASE, refundable. Completely finished. Prices vary according to selection and details.

Furniture

THE MINIATURES CATALOG, Fourteenth Edition

APPLIANCES

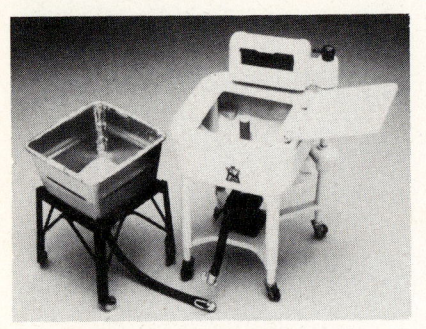

Dee's Delights
Authentic, die-cast metal reproductions of "old faithful" appliances. Designed in miniature by Jacqueline Kerr Deiber, these high-quality metal replicas recreate the memories of your childhood.
Suggested Retail Prices: DDL7516, wringer washer, $40; TIN50-20, metal tub, $14; DDL7510, roper range, $40; DDL7512, monitor top refrigerator, $40; DDL7514, porcelain kitchen sink, $20.
All are quality made with movable parts. See your local dealer.

CLASSIC LIVING ROOM

Handcraft Designs, Inc.
Suggested Retail Price: See your dealer.
Catalog No. 2031C, Chinese Garden Seat, used as a side table; 3831P, Upholstered Side Chair; 3833, Brass/Lucite Side Table; 3830P, Upholstered Sofa; 3832 Brass/Lucite Coffee Table; 6714, Umbrella Stand w/two umbrellas.
The Chinese Garden Seat in modern times is a plant stand or side table indoors. The upholstered chair and sofa pictured here are timeless in style and are appropriate in a Victorian sitting room or 1990's living room. The brass and lucite tables are a modern look, the brass cylinder umbrella stand is as timeless as the upholstered pieces.

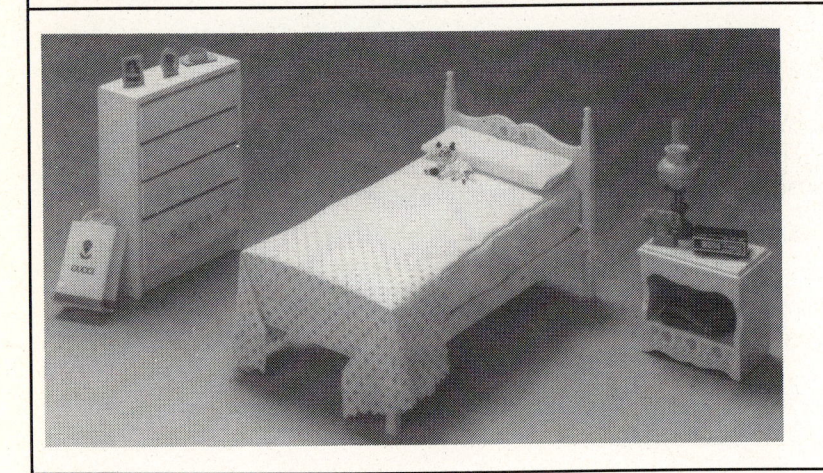

BETH'S ROOM

Handcraft Designs, Inc.
Suggested Retail Price: See your dealer.
Three pieces that together make the perfect room for pre-teen or teenage girl. Dresser drawers open via undercuts on bottom side of the drawers. Bed comes with mattress and pillow, not spread. Each piece is hand stenciled using a brass stencil.

HANDCRAFTED FURNITURE

Little Linens
Handcrafted bedroom furniture in both Classic and Contemporary design. Each style consists of a custom look dressed bed, chaise lounge, chair, hassock and skirted table. Various colors and fabrics available. All items proudly made in the USA.

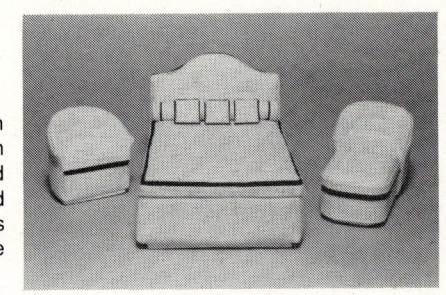

CLASSIC   CONTEMPORARY

STEREO TURNTABLE AND TUNER KITS

Martha's Miniatures

Suggested Retail Price: $14.95; tuner, $10.95, Ppd. (Kits only.)
Superior quality cast pewter components and walnut veneer. Easy-to-follow assembly instructions. Accurately detailed models. Turntable has prefinished, moveable disc. Speaker kits available. Guaranteed.

SINGLE BED

Miniature House

Suggested Retail Price: $7.98 finished
Catalog No. MH410
Material: All wood, fabric covered mattress
This oak finished, single bed is perfect for the child's room in your dollhouse. The mattress is fabric covered.

DAPPER DUCK SET

Mini Graphics

This charming set will be available in the pieces shown: the bed $45, bedside table $14, toy chest $18, table with two chairs $35 and the rocker $28. It comes in white with pink and blue (pictured), blue (a darker shade of blue and yellow) and cream (with peach and seafoam.

FANTASY DOT BOW BEDROOM SET

Mini Graphics

The pieces available are as follows: single bed only $45, dressing table with stool and mirror $19, bedside table $12 and a slipper chair $28. It comes in light blue, pink, aqua and peach. This is also available with a heart bed, which also comes in lilac and yellow.

2" SCALE BEDROOM SET

Mini Graphics

This adorable set includes a bed $54, bedside table $17, bench $14, slipper chair $34, dressing table and stool $25. These pieces are available in pink and aqua polka dot and lilac solid. Fashion dollhouse wallpaper and carpeting coming soon!

2" SCALE LIVING ROOM FURNITURE

Mini Graphics

A three-seat sofa (not shown) $48, two-seat sofa $44, chair $35 and ottoman (not shown) $15 are all of the finest quality. These pieces are available in pink, blue, aqua, lilac and white chintz. Fashion dollhouse wallpaper and carpeting coming soon!

2" SCALE SECTIONAL SOFA

Mini Graphics

Suggested Retail Price: $78
An outstanding three-piece sectional sofa, beautifully curved, is available in pink, blue, aqua, lilac and white moire or chintz. Fashion dollhouse wallpaper and carpeting coming soon!

Furniture

THE MINIATURES CATALOG, *Fourteenth Edition* 211

BOOKCASE UNITS

Miniature House
Suggested Retail Price: Assembled unfinished: MH1072, $7.25; MH1074, $11.49
Material: All wood
These bookcase units are ideal for your dollhouse or miniature store. MH1072, single, is 3-3/8"W x 7-3/8"H x 1-1/4"D. MH1074, double, is 6-3/8"W x 7-3/8"H x 1-1/4"D.

CORNER SOFA

Miniatures by Carol
Suggested Retail Price: $30 to $40
Contemporary furniture, several styles available. Solid color velvets, cotton prints, choice of colors. Measures 7" x 7" x 2-1/2".

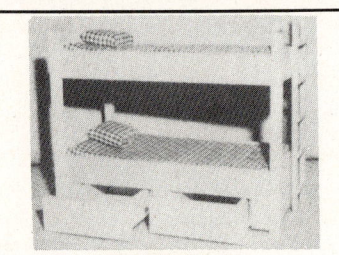

BUNK BED

Miniatures Unlimited
Material: Basswood
Bunk beds are available in natural, white or brown finish. Choice of linen colors are red, navy, blue, pink or yellow gingham. American made. Bed available with or without drawers.

CORNER DESK/BOOKCASE

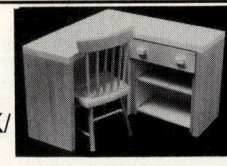

Miniatures Unlimited
Material: Basswood
Finish: Natural, white or brown
Limited for space? Well, this corner desk is perfect for either a bedroom, study, library or that area where not too much seems to work. Can also be used for a computer station (computer available separately). Handcrafted, made in the USA. Chair sold separately. Wholesale only.

STUDY AND STORAGE UNITS

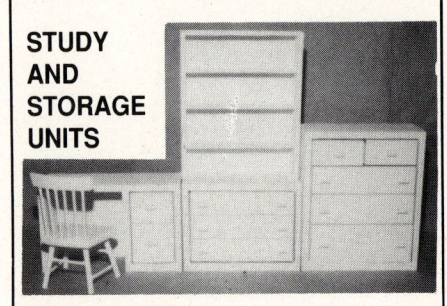

Miniatures Unlimited
Material: Basswood or walnut
Finish: Natural, white or brown
All pieces are available in white, brown or natural. American made.

CONTEMPORARY COUNTRY KITCHEN

Don Perkins Miniatures
These contemporary kitchen pieces are new additions to the Perkins line of furniture and accessories from America's past. Each piece is a pleasing blend of natural cherry and white painted maple. The kitchen group includes a dining table, chairs, side table, buffet/hutch and butcher block. 1" scale.

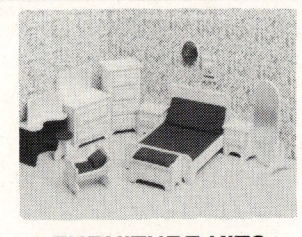

FURNITURE KITS

Ross' Treasure House
Suggested Retail Price: $4.98 - $6.50
Children's pre-cut furniture kits. Very nice for the price. Tab and slot construction, cabinet grade white plywood on both sides, hinged doors. Great for children's dollhouses. Five kits to choose from.

THE DISNEY COLLECTION

Pitty Pat Miniatures, Inc.
Your favorite Disney characters: Mickey Mouse, Minnie Mouse, Baby Minnie, Baby Mickey with Pluto, and Baby Donald are available in two-poster bedroom or nursery groupings. The two-poster twin bedroom consists of bed, armoire, toy chest, bookcase, table and chairs, settle, wallpaper, electrified lamps, clothes pole with hanger, wall shelf, skirted table or wooden nightstand, club chair and cornice with drapes. The nursery groups consist of crib, chest of drawers, wall shelf, clothes pole with hanger, toy chest, bookcase, rocking chair, play table and chairs, wallpaper, electrified lamps and cornice with drapes. Wholesale only. See your local dealer.

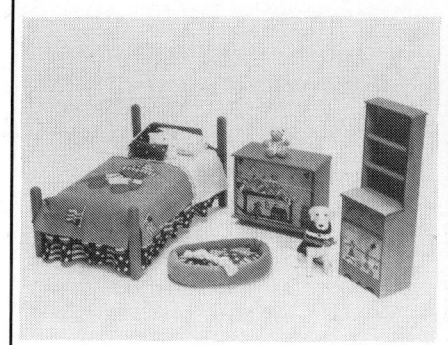

BEDROOM SET

Pat Russo Miniatures
Suggested Retail Price: See your local miniatures dealer
This unique collection includes a single bed, dresser, hutch, sailor bear, dog with coat and a dog bed. These handmade items are sold wholesale only by Pat Russo. For color sheets with prices send $1 and LSASE.

BRASS FURNITURE

Royal Miniatures
Suggested Retail Price: $8.50 - $20
Material: brass
Shown is a small selection from our large line of brassware. Many pieces are 14K gold plated. Other styles available.

Outdoor Furniture & Landscaping Materials

12-PIECE OUTDOOR FURNITURE KIT

Artply, Inc.
Suggested Retail Price: See your dealer
1" scale kit. Easy to follow instructions for assembly and finishing. All parts are pre-cut plywood for easy construction and durability.

CLASSIC PARK BENCH

AMSI Scale Model Supplies
Suggested Retail Price: Catalog No. AMS-500 1" scale, $10.30; Catalog No. AMS-502 1/2" scale, $9.95; Catalog No. AMS-504 1/4" scale, $9.65.
Material: Basswood (ready-to-stain) and cast metal (ready-to-paint).
American made.
The timeless design fits any decor. It's ready to paint and stain . 4" L, 2-3/4" H, 2" D. Simple assembly instructions are included.

AMSI BIG TREE KIT

AMSI Scale Model Supplies
Suggested Retail Price: $22.50 (kit)
American made.
This kit includes everything required to make a handsome "Big Tree" (19"H with 12" spread). The kit also includes full instructions and all incidental material.
Catalog No. AMSK-50.

AMSI LANDSCAPE MATERIALS

AMSI Scale Model Supplies
A wide selection of metal tree structures, finished trees, hedge material and packaged foams in several grades. All American-made. All foliage, ground, and floral colors available in convenient packages. Everything landscapers need for color, texture, and natural effects. Ask your dealer for full description and prices.

THE MINIATURES CATALOG, *Fourteenth Edition* 213

KIMBERLY STREET OR GARDEN LAMP

Kimberly House Miniatures
Suggested Retail Price: $20.85
Catalog #: LAMP500
Dimensions: 1" to 1' scale
Street lamp is finished in flat black ready to place in garden or in front of your dollhouse. Equipped with a 12V light and can be wired from your dollhouse wiring. See your dealer or write to Kimberly House.

KIMBERLY PARK BENCH KIT

Kimberly House Miniatures
Suggested Retail Price: $8.75
Catalog #: PBK-501
Dimensions: 1" to 1' scale
Molded metal bench ends with precut redwood slats. Ends may be painted green or black. Slats either stained or painted. Easy to assemble. See your dealer or write to Kimberly House.

KIMBERLY SHADE TREE KIT

Kimberly House Miniatures
Suggested Retail Price: $23.70 plus shipping. Catalog No. KST-101
Dimensions: Up to 18" high
Create realistic, attractive landscaping. Kit includes all materials for tree shown including instructions. Flexible, may be contoured to fit any desired setting. Sturdy enough to hang a swing from your favorite branch. Perfect accent for your dollhouses, park scene, or local squirrels and birds. Shown in *Dollhouses to Dream Houses, Book 2*, in landscaping chapter. See your dealer or write to Kimberly House.

KIMBERLY SHRUBBERY KITS

Kimberly House Miniatures
Suggested Retail Price: $11.22 plus shipping. Catalog No. KSK-201
Size: Makes three shrubs.
Create realistic, attractive landscaping. Kit includes all materials for three bushy shrubs including instructions. Flexible, may be contoured to fit any desired setting. Multiple flower colors in every kit to create varied flowering shrubs. "Plant" individually or in row to create a hedge. Shown in *Dollhouses to Dream Houses, Book 2*, in landscaping chapter. See your dealer or write to Kimberly House.

KIMBERLY ITALIAN CYPRESS TREE KIT

Kimberly House Miniatures
Suggested Retail Price: $11.94 plus shipping. Catalog No. KIC-101
Dimensions: Up to 18" high
Create realistic, attractive landscaping. Kit includes all materials for tree shown including instructions. Create any size up to 18" high. Use as accent between windows. "Plant" in row and create windbreak for your house. Shown in *Dollhouses to Dream Houses, Book 2*, in landscaping chapter. See your dealer or write to Kimberly House.

KIMBERLY TOPIARY TREE KIT

Kimberly House Miniatures
Suggested Retail Price: $14.40, plus shipping.
Catalog No. TTK-101
Creative realistic, attractive landscaping. Kit includes materials and instructions to make two Topiary trees of either style shown. Two precut redwood planters, materials for planting your Topiary trees and decorative gravel for planters are also included. Lovely for entryway, garden, store fronts, anywhere. Shown in *Dollhouses to Dream Houses, Book 2*, in landscaping chapter. See your dealer or write to Kimberly House.

KIMBERLY ORNAMENTAL FLOWERING TREE KIT

Kimberly House Miniatures
Suggested Retail Price: $19.74 plus shipping. Catalog No. KFT-101
Dimensions: Up to 14" high.
Create realistic attractive landscaping. Kit includes all materials for tree shown including instructions. Flexible, may be contoured to fit any desired setting. Multiple flower colors in every kit to create flowering tree of your choice. Ideal for vignette, room box, garden or perfect accent for your dollhouse. Shown in Dollhouses to Dream Houses, Book 2, in landscaping chapter. See your dealer or write to Kimberly House.

BUILDERS CHOICE LANDSCAPES

New England Hobby Supply Inc.
Preformed and decorated landscaping system for dollhouses. Products include bark and timber landscaping beds, paths and planting beds, round tree planting beds and sandboxes, small evergreens, flower buds, wood chips, decorative stone, mulch, foundation shrubs and more. Send SASE for brochure and complete product price list.

PORCH SWING

Miniature House
Suggested Retail Price: MH408 (walnut) $9.39, MH408A (oak) $10.29, MH408B (white) $12.30
Size: 4-1/2" W x 1-3/4" H
Material: Swing is all wood, chain is metal. Traditional porch swing to be suspended from the ceiling with chains. Available stained, varnished or painted.

October National Dollhouse & Miniatures Month

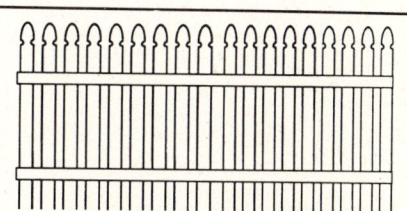

BUILDER'S CHOICE LANDSCAPING FENCES

New England Hobby Supply, Inc.
Suggested Retail Price: See your dealer
We are the source for all your landscaping needs. Fences are available in a variety of styles. Please see the New England Hobby Supply insert between pages 288 and 289 for more information.

THE MINIATURES CATALOG, Fourteenth Edition   217

LANDSCAPING

Plastruct
Over 200 different landscaping products in various scales and price ranges. Included are ready-made trees, ground cover, flexible grass mat, rocks, hedges, shrubs, flowers and vines.

THE PORCH AND PATIO COLLECTION

Shenandoah Designs, Inc.
Suggested Retail Price: $5.99 to $12.99 kit; $6.49 to $18.99 assembled unfinished.
Catalog No. 3600 Series kit, No. 4600 series assembled unfinished.
Material: Mahogany
1/12 scale versions of the ever-popular "Adirondack" or "Country Craftsman" style.

Store & Office Furniture

LAWYER'S BOOKCASES

Aztec Imports, Inc.
Wholesale only. Lawyer's Bookcases are available in two sizes: two or four shelves. Each size is available in four colors: white (T5298,99), walnut (T6298,99), mahogany (T3298,99) and oak (T4298,99). Perfect for office, den or stores!

SINGLE OPEN-SHELF UNIT

B B Fine, Inc.
Suggested Retail Price: $7
This unit comes with adjustable shelves and can be used as a bookcase, room divider, store shelf, entertainment center, pantry shelf and more.

STORE FURNITURE

Aztec Imports Inc.
Wholesale only. Fine store furniture available in walnut and white. The shelves are perfect for displaying a variety of products including food, paper and novelties. The bottom picture shows the storage space available behind the counter.

PRODUCE UNIT

B B Fine, Inc.
Suggested Retail Price: $10
Comes with a back mirror and can be used for fruits, vegetables, meat, poultry and fish. Also, it makes a great salad bar, ice cream or hot buffet server.

DESK CHAIR

Exclusive Products
A needed compliment for any desk, that fits everyone's budget. Crafted with a walnut finish. #B-9091.

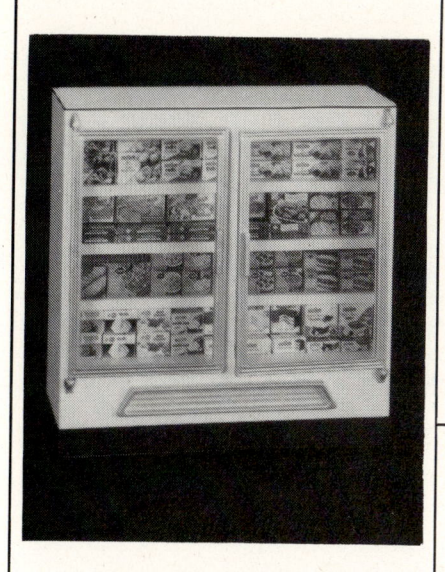

FREEZER/COOLER UNIT

B B Fine, Inc.
Suggested Retail Price: $10
Comes with clear plastic doors and three adjustable shelves. Can be used as a freezer or cooler for flowers, deli or restaurant, or as a side by side refrigerator/freezer.

OFFICE DESK AND FILE CABINET

Miniatures Unlimited
Material: Basswood
Finish: Gray, natural or white
Handcrafted office desk and file cabinet. Complete with accessories or plain. Chair is also available. Each piece sold separately.

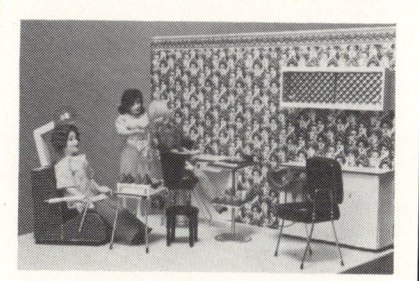

BEAUTY PARLOR

Teri's Mini Workshop
Furniture and accessories for a miniature beauty parlor. Many color choices available.

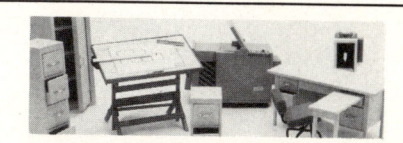

This beautiful cake cover is simply made from a 4" circle of fine lace heavily sprayed with starch before stretching it, wet, over a suitable size dowel and securing with a rubber band. Let it dry thoroughly before gently peeling off the dowel and trimming away the excess lace.

JOY RAMSEY
KINGSPORT, TN

1" SCALE OFFICE FURNITURE AND SUPPLIES

Three Blind Mice
Suggested Retail Price: Same price for finished or unfinished (we supply hardware for unfinished). $30, desk w/typing stand; $25, desk without stand; $12, two-drawer file, $14.00, four-drawer file; $17, drafting table; $35, Xerox machine; $20, water cooler, $20, storage cabinet; $12, desk chair. Made of wood.

MULTI-PURPOSE DISPLAY UNIT

B B Fine, Inc.
Suggested Retail Price: $10
Comes with back mirror and three shelves. Shelves may go in straight or at an angle. Excellent for a display case, bakery, home cupboard, collectibles or clothing rack.

KIMBERLY BAKERY AND CANDY CASE KITS

Kimberly House Miniatures
Suggested Retail Price: $10.85 and $14.45
Materials and finish: Plexiglass with wood base
Kit easy to assemble and finish. Shelf and plexiglass remove for easy cleaning. Style fits any era.
BK-1 5" W x 2" D x 3-1/4" H, $10.85
BK-2 5" W x 3" D x 6-1/2" H, $14.45
See your dealer or write to Kimberly House.

BK-1 Candy Case Kit

BK-2 Bakery Case Kit

Furniture

Nursery

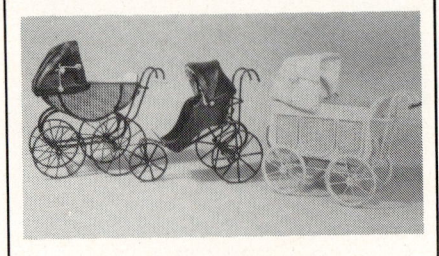

KIMBERLY SHOWCASE KITS

Kimberly House Miniatures
This kit is easy-to-assemble and finish. The shelf and Plexiglass removes for easy cleaning. The style fits any era. All sizes are 3-1/2" high. Sizes available:

LD-1K 6" x 2" $7.85
LS-1K 6" x 1-1/2" $7.25
MD-1K 4" x 2" $7.25
MS-1K 4" x 1-1/2" $6.85
SD-1K 2" x 2" $6.85
SS-1K 2" x 1-1/2" $6.30

See your dealer or write to Kimberly House.

BABY CARRIAGES

Omniarts of Colorado
Suggested Retail Price: $100-$200 finished
Baby carriages and prams handcrafted in England of metal, fabric and leather by the Robersons. Several styles available.

BABY AND CHILDREN'S FURNITURE

Betty's Wooden Miniatures
Suggested Retail Price: See your dealer. Our wicker bassinet and changing table are sparkling white with pink, blue, or yellow rosebuds and under-skirting. Our nursery lamp and clothespole feature a hand-painted pastel or bright clown. The rockers are hand-painted too. Also shown are our new children's bench and children's table and chairs. The stork is handpainted for "boy" or "girl." The teddy in the wagon is really cute. All are handmade by us in the USA.

SWEET DREAMS

By Grace
Suggested Retail Price: $45 #167A crib; $32 #167B changing table; $45 #213 crib; $28 #213A changing chest; $28 BYGRCC chair
Create the ultimate customized nursery. Contemporary, victorian, country, canopy crib or brass cradles. Wide selection of styles with a large variety of fabrics and trims. Wholesale/retail. Price list with photocopies. $1.50 plus LSASE, refundable. Completely finished.

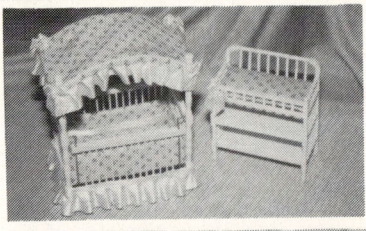

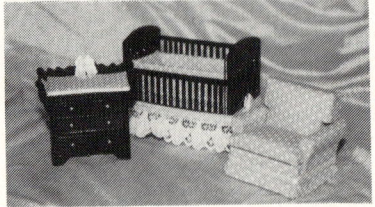

LOOKING FOR SOMETHING SPECIAL? CHECK WITH YOUR LOCAL MINIATURES SHOP!

ALICE LACY'S ROSETTE CRIB, INFANT QUILT AND "SWEETIE"

Alice Lacy, Ltd.
Catalog No. 52, S32A, S38
The Rosette Crib epitomizes the scrolly delicate look of our handcrafted iron wire designs. Belying the look, it is tough. The quilt is also handmade. The mutt, "Sweetie", is soft and flexible.

NURSERY FURNITURE KIT

Dura-Craft, Inc.
Catalog No. NR70
A home is not a home without a nursery. This beautifully crafted country nursery is die-cut 1/8" plywood that is easily assembled. Can be painted or stained to the color scheme of your home. 12 pieces; crib, changing table, dresser, rocking chair, pram, child's swing chair, rocking horse chair, scooter, toy box and three picture frames.

CHAIR FOR BABY'S ROOM

Miniature House
Suggested Retail Price: $1.35 completely finished
Catalog No. MH892
Material: Wood
Finish: Painted white and yellow
White chair with yellow trim and checked material on seat. Also ideal for kitchens.

OAK POTTY CHAIR WITH POT

Miniature House
Suggested Retail Price: $8.98 completely finished
Catalog No. MH887
Material: Wood with metal pot
Finish: Stained and varnished
Cute potty chair has door in front and metal pot. Chair is oak stained.

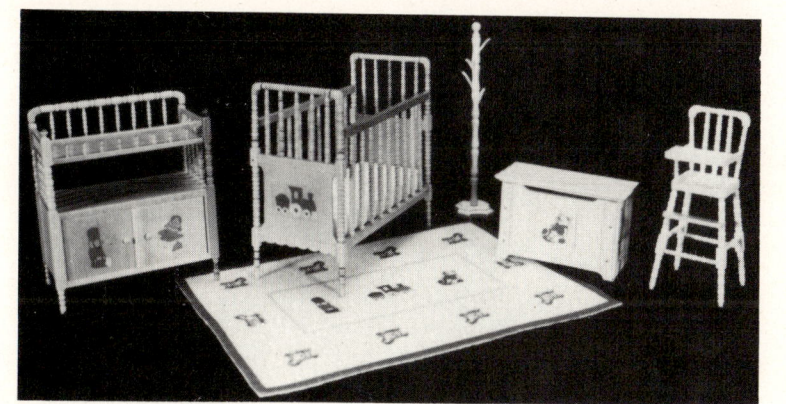

ROYAL NURSERY

Handcraft Designs, Inc.
Suggested Retail Price: See your dealer
Catalog #3760/3770 crib; #3761/3771, changing table; #3762/3772, toy box; #3763/3773, clothes pole; #3764/3774, high chair
Material: Wood, oak stained or painted white
#3760-3764 denote white-painted pieces; #3770-3774 are light oak finish. As modern as today, this luxurious nursery grouping is available in the two finishes most popular in the juvenile furniture stores and is enhanced by charming figures in the currently popular primary colors of blue, red and yellow. Intricate turnings and fine details make this "fit for royalty"

BABY ROCKING CHAIR

Miniature House
Suggested Retail Price: $2.60 completely finished
Catalog No. MH894
Material: Wood
Finish: White and yellow paint
Baby rocking chair is white with yellow trim.

BABY PLAY PEN

Miniature House
Suggested Retail Price: $6.10 finished
Catalog No. MH896
Material: Wood and fabric
Finish: White and yellow paint
This attractive play pen has a white and yellow checked pad.

BABY HIGH CHAIR

Miniature House
Suggested Retail Price: $5.20
Catalog No. MH897
Material: Wood
Finish: White and yellow paint
White baby high chair with yellow trim. Tray is moveable.

Furniture

THE MINIATURES CATALOG, *Fourteenth Edition*

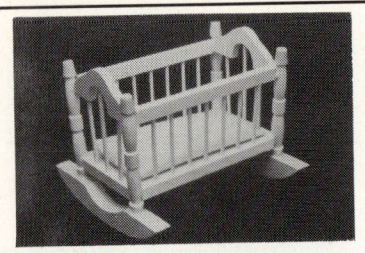

BABY CRADLE

Miniature House
Suggested Retail Price: $5.15 finished
Catalog No. MH893
Material: Wood and fabric
Finish: Painted white and yellow
This rocking cradle has a yellow checked covered pad.

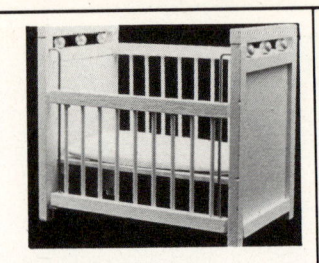

BABY CRIB

Miniature House
Suggested Retail Price: $6.20
Catalog No. MH895
Material: Wood
Finish: Painted white and yellow
White baby crib with yellow trim and checked material on mattress.

BABY DRESSER

Miniature House
Suggested Retail Price: $6.20 finished
Catalog No. MH898
Material: Wood
Finish: Painted white and yellow
This inexpensive baby dresser is painted white with yellow trim. Drawers and doors open.

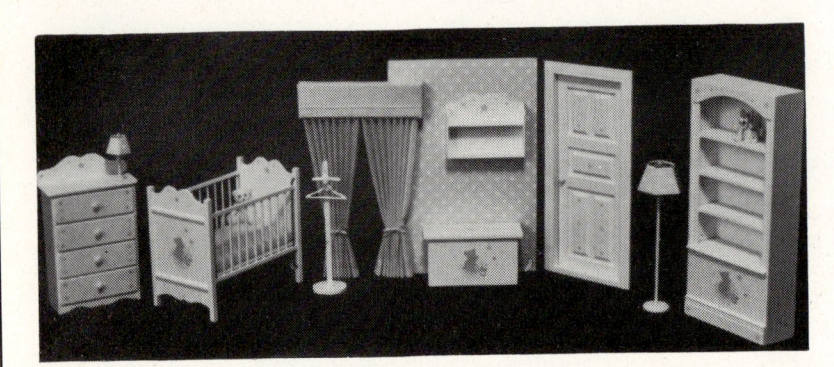

ADORABLE NURSERY GROUPINGS

Pitty Pat Miniatures, Inc.
Five completely coordinated nursery groups. Each grouping consists of a crib with working rail, chest of drawers, clothes pole with hanger, toy chest, bookcase, cornice with drapes, electrified light for chest and floor lamps, wallshelf, wallpaper, rocking chair and nursery play table with chairs. Wholesale only. See your local dealer.

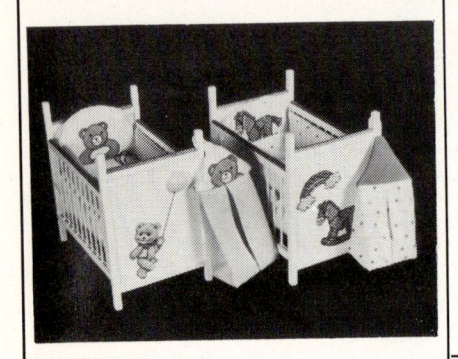

Bathroom

MUSICAL CRIB

By Teri's Mini Workshop
Suggested Retail Price: Completely finished — $50, plus $2 shipping.
Material: Wood
Many designs are available in the crib sets. (Includes musical crib, mattress, bumpers, quilt and diaper bags). Canopy crib — $100, also includes a mobile.

BATHROOM SINK

Aztec Imports, Inc.
Catalog No. T5019
Wholesale only. Oak and white! The newest color combination! This unique piece will accent your miniature bathroom. The color combination will allow you to use this item with either oak or white bathroom furniture.

DELFT BATHROOM SETS

J. Hermes
Suggested Retail Price: 1" $15.95-1/2" $13.95, complete finished
Material: Porcelain
Finish: Glazed
Dutch import. Handpainted Blue Delft style porcelain bathroom sets. Available in both 1" and 1/2" scales.

Prices are approximate and subject to change.

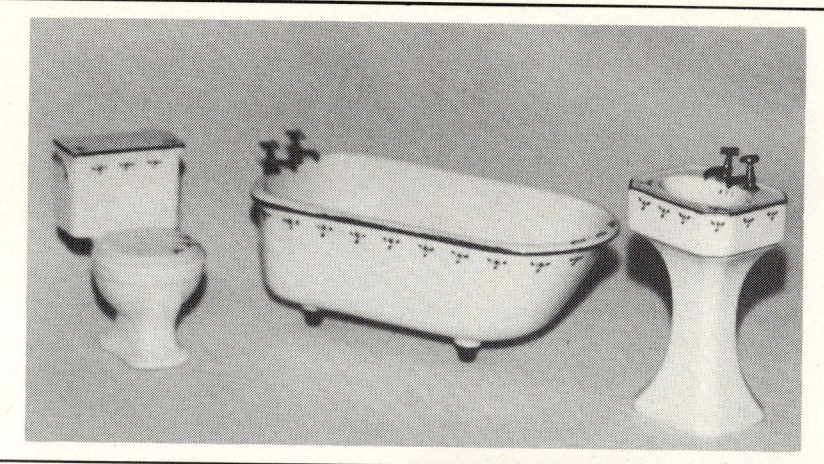

HANDPAINTED CERAMIC BATH SET

By Dollhouse Miniatures by Flo
Suggested Retail Price: $24/set
Material: Ceramic
Handpainted three-piece bathroom set with brass faucets. Available in white with pink, rose, yellow, light blue or dark blue flowers. Also available in solid colors. American made.

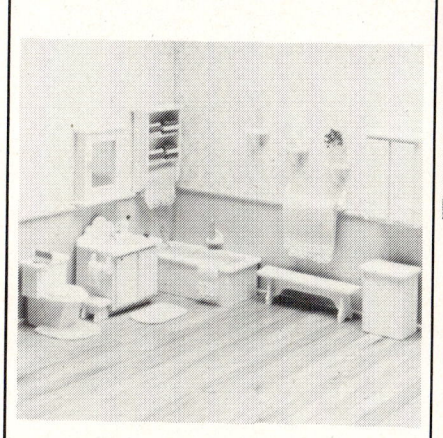

CONTEMPORARY BATHROOM SET

Le´ Petite Architect
Suggested Retail Price: $26.95-$48.95
Easy-to-assemble kits available in marble finishes. All fixtures and paints included. Shower comes with pre-laid ceramic tile walls to compliment the marble finishes.

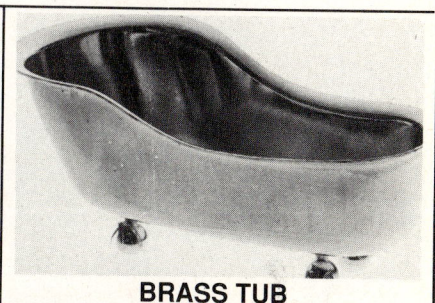

BRASS TUB

Miniature House
Suggested Retail Price: $10
Catalog No. MH404
This Early American tub is ideal for a small bath or to go in a bedroom. The finish is brass-tone.

BATHROOM FURNITURE KIT

Dura-Craft, Inc.
Catalog No. BT60
No house is complete without this beautifully crafted country bathroom furniture set. The kit is die-cut from 1/8" plywood that is easily assembled. Can be painted or stained to the color scheme of your home. 15 pieces; bathtub, commode, sink with cabinet, toilet paper holder, stepstool, medicine cabinet with mirror, towel shelf, towel rack, bench, hanging cabinet, clothes hamper, soap dish, three knick-knack shelves (rugs, etc. not included).

VICTORIAN BATHROOM

Miniature Corner
Finished baked white enamel with rose garland decoration on all pieces. Commode has working brass flush chain and movable wood seat. Bathtub has gilded feet and brass faucets that turn. French lava bowl sink. Available without decoration. Matching rose/pattern wallpaper also available.

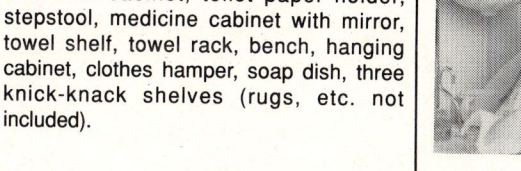

ROYAL VICTORIAN BATHROOM SET

Falcon Collectible Miniatures
Suggested Retail Price: See your dealer
Introducing . . . the most delightfully luxurious miniature bath ensemble in the history of the art! Our three-piece Royal Victorian Bathroom set is crafted of genuine porcelain, highly polished wood and highlighted with 24K gold plated hardware. Set includes tub with claw feet, commode with pull-chain, sink and authentic plumbing hardware. 1" scale.

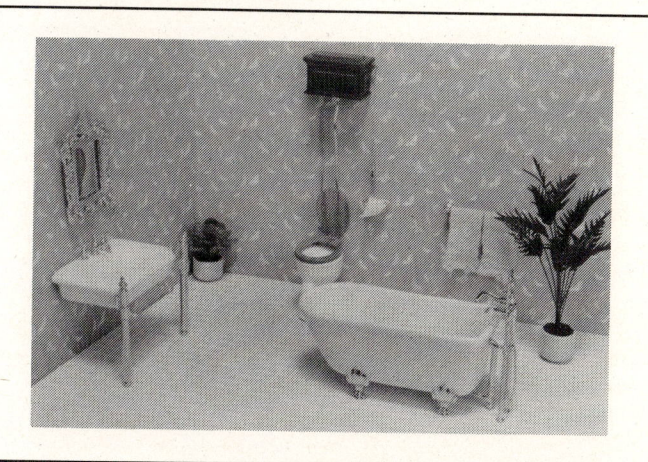

Furniture

THE MINIATURES CATALOG, *Fourteenth Edition*

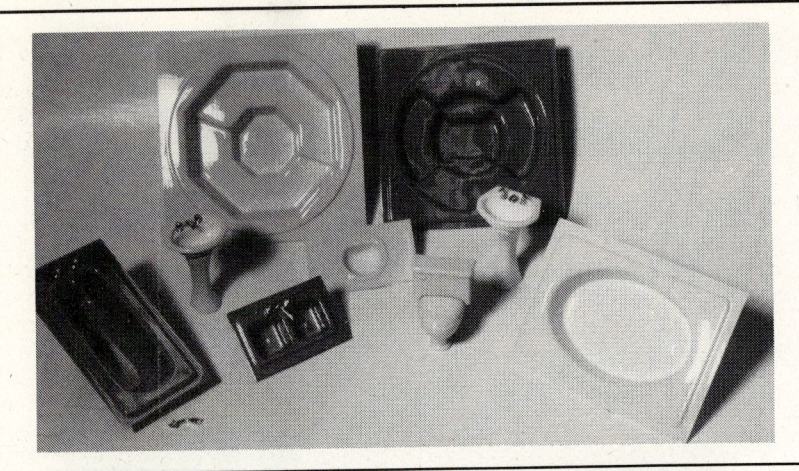

BATHROOM ITEMS

Model Builders Supply
Octagonal hot tub $9.95. Round hot tub $8.95. Oval tub $5.95. Regular tub $4.95. Pedestal sink $6.25. Vanity sink $2.95. Toilet $6.25. Available in almond, white, grey, hot tubs also in red and black. Regular chrome on gold tub taps and shower head $9.60 per set. Regular chrome sink set $7. Fancy gold sink set $7.50. All prices are Canadian. Ask your favorite dealer for MBS products. U.S. customers, see "Plastruct".

PORCELAIN BATHROOM SET

What's Next?
Suggested Retail Price: $175 finished
Catalog No. 50
Exquisite three-piece bathroom set is exact 1" scale. Made of the finest porcelain slip imported from England and hand-polished with diamond dust. Brass fixtures are 24K gold-plated. Eleven coats of hand-rubbed lacquer on wood parts. All sets signed and numbered. Also available as early 20th century style with porcelain tank on toilet. Most elegant set offered in the miniatures business.

Kitchen

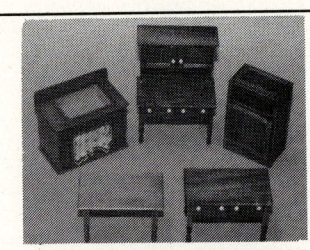

VICTORIAN KITCHEN FURNITURE

A-Dora-Bill Miniatures
Suggested Retail Price: $20.95 No. FK-1, bin cabinet kit; $15.95 No. FK-2, ice box kit; $13.95 No. FK-3, dry sink kit; $15.95 No. FK-4, kitchen work table; $13.95 FK-7, kitchen breakfast table.

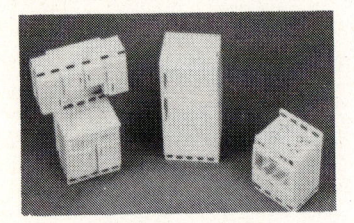

FOUR-PIECE KITCHEN KIT

Artply, Inc.
Suggested Retail Price: See your dealer 1" scale kit. Easy-to-follow instructions for assembly and finishing. All parts are pre-cut plywood for easy construction and durability.

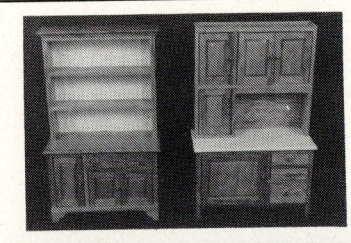

COUNTRY KITCHEN

Aztec Imports, Inc.
Wholesale only. The oak and white kitchen furniture will complement your country kitchen. Town Square Miniatures offers a full line of oak and white furniture. The pieces featured here include: hutch with white backboard (T4099); oak cupboard hutch with white counter (T4100); oak table with white tiles and legs (T5113); oak chair with white seat (T4100) and white chair with oak seat (T5143).

Prices are approximate and subject to change.

FOR THE KITCHEN

Betty's Wooden Miniatures
Suggested Retail Price: See your dealer.
For the older kitchen, we have our porcelain-top work table and tin top tables in two sizes with divided silverware drawers, a chair to accompany them, a washboard with a metal scrub surface, and our butcher block. For the contemporary kitchen, we have our butcher block with rack, our kitchen work center, and our portable TV. All our handcrafted by us. Accessories shown are not included.

CONTEMPORARY KITCHEN

Concord Miniatures
Suggested Retail Price: See your dealer
Concord introduces a new kitchen in contemporary design featuring double wall oven, countertop stove, sink, refrigerator/freezer, glass doors and working drawers. Also available in white.. Upper cabinet set: #M731 - oak; #M745 - white; Lower cabinet set: #M730 - oak; #M746 - white.

COLLECTOR FRIDGE AND STOVE

Model Builders Supply
Acrylic and molded styrene. Opening units. Color: almond. Lighted option add $10. Frost-free fridge $98. Self-cleaning stove $95.70. Canadian prices. U.S. customers, see "Plastruct".

HANDCRAFTED COLONIAL FURNITURE

Dan-Dy Crafts
Suggested Retail Price: See your dealer
Shown is a fine sampling of our line of country pine precision miniatures. All are handcrafted in New England from select pine with working doors and drawers. All pieces are finished inside and out and are available in light and dark stains as well as uniform blue, gloss white, unfinished or select pieces in richtone black. Selections that are not pictured include kitchen cabinets, trestle table and benches, half-round table, canopy and twin beds, mirror, dresser, cradle and many more.

VICTORIAN KITCHEN

Handcraft Designs, Inc.
Catalog No.: (top left, clockwise) #3314, #3315, #3305D, #3303D, #3301D, #3316, #3310D, #3306, #3311D, #3312D
Material: Beechwood stained walnut or painted black; cast zinc alloy painted.
Victorian kitchen, circa 1899. Single oven range based on "perfect" model by Richardson and Boynton Co. Refrigerator modeled after Belding-Hall Co. design at Henry Ford Museum. Die cast sink (white also available) simulates cast-iron sinks of the period. #3303 shelves, mounted on #3301 cabinet base, sold separately and can be wall shelves or be used to make a hutch with the base cabinet. #3305, #3310, #3311, #3312 also available in oak, plus #3302, dry sink.

THE MINIATURES CATALOG, Fourteenth Edition

APPLIANCES

Model Builders Supply
Acrylic and molded styrene, enamelled finishes. Fridge and stove are almond with black acrylic doors. Washer and dryer are white. Non-opening. Fridge $17.50, stove $18.95, washer $14.25, dryer $14.25, dishwasher with wood top (not shown) $16.50. Fridge $11.50, stove $11.95, washer and dryer $9.25 each, microwave $8.95. Fridge and stove also now available in 1/2" scale, $11.95 and $13.95. Canadian prices. U.S. customers, see "Plastruct".

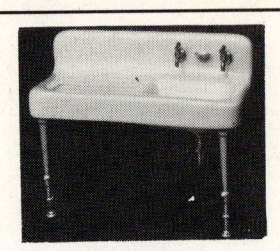

SINK

Handley House
Suggested Retail Price: $19.95
Catalog No. HH8000
Material: Kiln-fired glazing
A kiln-fired glazing process is used for this 1" scale two-legged kitchen sink.

DOUBLE KITCHEN SINK

Model Builders Supply
Silver metallic $3.95, single sink $3.50. Chrome faucet and tap set $9.60 Canadian. Setting not included. Single and double sinks also available in 1/2" scale. U.S. customers, see "Plastruct".

REFRIGERATORS AND STOVES

Miniatures by Carol
Suggested Retail Price: $25.95 to $39.95
Contemporary kitchen refrigerators and stoves with working doors and drawers. Black or white doors.

COMPLETE MODERN KITCHEN

Pitty Pat Miniatures, Inc.
Modern kitchen grouping complete with all major appliances: refrigerator, stove with oven, dishwasher, sink cabinet with porcelain sink in a choice of red, country blue, navy blue or white porcelain. Our large variety of upper, base and corner cabinets will accommodate any arrangement in the dollhouse kitchen. Round pedestal kitchen table and ladderback chairs with cushions in red plaid, country blue plaid, or navy blue plaid to match sink colors. Wholesale only. See your local dealer.

THE KITCHEN COLLECTION

Shenandoah Designs, Inc.
Suggested Retail Price: Kits, $2.49 to $19.49; assembled unfinished $8.49 to $28.99
Catalog No. 3400 series kits, No. 4400 series assembled/unfinished.
The Kitchen Collection consists of 1" to 1' modular cabinets that allow the builder to construct a custom kitchen to fit any dollhouse. Countertop and trim kits provide the materials needed to add the final touches. The cabinets are made of mahogany and feature raised panel doors and drawers, set off with rich brass hardware. Kits for the stove, sink and oven front add details lacking in many kitchens.

Your Listings Belong Here!
Interested in advertising in the 15th Edition of The Miniatures Catalog?

Contact Sara Benz at
1-800-558-1544,
Ext. 631
or write to;
The Miniatures Catalog
P.O. Box 1612
Waukesha, WI 53187

Miscellaneous

CUSTOM UPHOLSTERED FURNITURE

By Grace
Suggested Retail Price: $52 #BYGRQLS loveseat; $38 #BYGRQC chair
Custom upholstered furniture. Numerous styles. Large variety of fabrics. Wholesale/retail. Price list with photocopies. $1.50 plus LSASE, refundable.

ANTIQUE AND OLDER MINIATURES

Close To Your Heart
Retail list available. Artist-made items for your dollhouse or mini collection. Limited selection of older miniatures by Renewal Tootsietoy, Strombecker, Sonia Messer. Shows and mail order only. Please state what your interest is. No wholesale.

FURNITURE KITS

By Craftmark House of Miniatures
Suggested Retail Price: $3.50-$21.95
Material: Machined solid wood parts, solid brass hardware
Total of 88 furniture kits, 1/12 scale, all machined solid wood parts, solid brass hardware, detailed instructions. See your local dealer.

WROUGHT IRON TABLE WITH FOUR CHAIRS

Miniature House
Suggested Retail Price: $10.98
Catalog No. MH2397
Material: Metal with fabric cover
This set is comprised of a table and four chairs, painted white with checked tablecloth and seat covers. Also perfect for a soda or ice cream shop.

FIMO® MODELING MATERIAL

Eberhard Faber GmbH
Suggested Retail Price: See your dealer.
Catalog No. 8000
Specifications: 55 x 55 x 15 mm/65 g small block, 165 x 55 x 30 mm/350 g large block. FIMO®, the fantastic and most popular modeling material, is the leading product of its kind in Europe. It's versatile and easy to handle, and hardens in the oven at 265°F. (20 to 30 minutes). Available in 42 brilliant colors, it's ideal to create the finest decorative accessories for your dollhouse and to make exciting and imaginative objects (miniatures, figures, fashion jewelry, decorations, pictures, nameplates and a lot more).

FURNITURE

Maison des Maison
Equipales furniture, leather and reed. Various colors of leather available. Navajo sterling coffee set and oak trastero.

SOUTHWEST FURNITURE

Maison des Maisons
Southwest furniture by Joe Franek, Casa Chica and other fine artists.

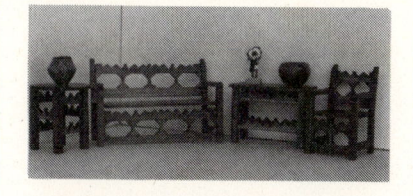

MISSION LINE FURNITURE

Taos Sun Miniatures
Suggested Retail Price: Send $2.50 for brochure and pictures.
Material: Pine and basswood
Reproductions of 17th century New Mexican furniture. Finely handcrafted in Taos, New Mexico.

'TAOS' STYLE FURNITURE

Taos Sun Miniatures
Suggested Retail Price: $2.50 for brochure and pictures
Material: pine and basswood
Each piece is hand-carved in Taos, New Mexico. "Taos" style furniture is a traditional Southwestern style but lends itself to contemporary or country settings. Three finishes available.

Furniture

THE MINIATURES CATALOG, *Fourteenth Edition*

Wicker

WINDSOR COLLECTION

Empress Arts & Crafts
Suggested Retail Price: $6 - $35
The Windsor Collection of white miniature iron-wire furniture is designed by our in-house staff. Each piece can coordinate with other pieces in the collection to make a complete room setting. Over 60 designs available. See your local miniatures dealer for these exquisite pieces.

WINDSOR COLLECTION

Empress Arts & Crafts
Suggested Retail Price: $6 - $35
The Windsor Collection of white miniature iron-wire furniture is designed by our in-house staff. Each piece can coordinate with other pieces in the collection to make a complete room setting. Over 60 designs available. See your local miniatures dealer for these exquisite pieces.

WINDSOR COLLECTION

Empress Arts & Crafts
Suggested Retail Price: $6 - $35
The Windsor Collection of white miniature iron-wire furniture is designed by our in-house staff. Each piece coordinates with others in the collection for complete room settings. Over 60 designs available.

BEADED SCREENS

KL Miniatures
Suggested Retail Price: $65-natural; $71-white + $2.50 shipping
Beaded panel screen, 6-1/4"H, completely arrangeable, reversible. Natural or white. Send LSASE for info and photo. Include $1 for full wicker brochure. IGMA artisan.

ALICE LACY'S NEW DESIGNS IN IRON WICKER

Alice Lacy, Ltd.
Catalog No. 54, 55, 53
Among our newest designs are a small low stool (cricket), a proper parlor chair, and an occasional chair to add to any room for any occasion. We think they are representative of our objective - to create handcrafted pieces which are beautiful and tough.

Interested in Becoming a Professional Miniatures Handcrafter?
Contact the Cottage Industry Miniaturists Trade Association

CIMTA
P.O. Box 5071
New Haven, CT 06525

Prices are approximate and subject to change.

BABY CARRIAGE FRAME AND ROLLING WHEELS KIT

Martha's Miniatures
Suggested Retail Price: $18.95 Ppd. (kit only). Use with your basket! Cast pewter, unpainted kit with your choice of wheels. Diameter sizes: 3/4"; 1"; 16-spoke, 1 1/4"; or 8-spoke, 1 1/4". Instructions with diagram included. Free wheel chart available. Guaranteed.

WICKER FURNITURE

Rankin's Tiny Treasures
Suggested Retail Price: $4 to $50 plus shipping. Material: Cotton cord, covered wire, wood. All pieces shown are available in three styles and in natural, white, or dark brown. Also available are baskets, plant stands, benches, swings and pet beds.

WICKER FURNITURE AND KITS

Miniatures By Sharon
Suggested Retail Price: $4 - $16 plus shipping; finished $7 - $30 plus shipping
Material: wood, linen cord, thread, cloth covered wire. Supplies available.
Many new items: kits in 1" and 1/2" scale, easy to follow instructions, finished items in 1", 1/2" and 1/4" scales, complete with cushions in your choice of color or your fabric. $1 plus LSASE (52¢) for brochure.

WICKER DOLL CARRIAGE KIT

Smallworks
Suggested Retail Price: $16 ppd., kit
Dimensions: 3"H x 3"L x 1-1/4"W
Childsize carriage holds 1-1/2" doll. Includes wire, thread, wheels plus specs for larger carriage. Uses common tools. Illustrated instructions for average skill levels.

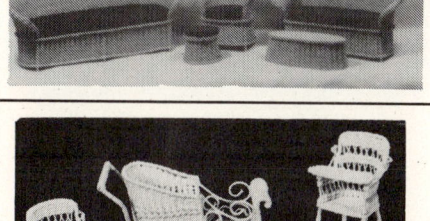

WICKER FURNITURE KITS

Omniarts of Colorado
Suggested Retail Price: $3-$15 kit
Material: Cotton cord, covered wire, wood
Designer series kits use waxed linen cord. Pieces available include: beds, vanity, stool, wall and pier mirrors, etageres, chairs, sofas, tables, plant stands, chaise, baby carriage, high chair, potty chair, conversation chair, crib, cradle, lamps, bird cages, swing, coat rack and more. New items available regularly.

RATTAN FURNITURE

Twin Palms Miniatures
Rattan furniture for any room in your house. Available finished or in economical kits. 1" and 1/2" scales. $1 and LSASE for brochure.

WARLING WICKER FURNITURE

Warling Miniatures
Suggested Retail Price: Wide range from $3-$135
Materials: Natural waxed linen cord, wood, sealed covered wires (where applicable: silk or cotton upholstery/dressing, other fabrics and hardware).
Signed, sealed and dated pieces are authentic reproductions of a bygone era to pure fantasy pieces, and encompass a broad time frame from Victorian to modern styles. Completed pieces (shown on left) or kits (shown on right) are available.

Furniture

THE MINIATURES CATALOG, Fourteenth Edition   229

Dollhouse Dolls & Accessories

Accessories

DOLL STAND
The Dollhouse Factory™
Suggested Retail Price: $1.15
Catalog No. DP041
A sturdy and fully adjustable stand that accommodates any dollhouse dolls and holds them in realistic positions. Economical and easy-to-use. All metal. See our catalog for more.

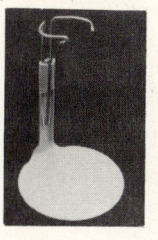

HAT STANDS
Miniature House
Suggested Retail Price: $1.80 each
Catalog No. MH2067, MH2068
These lovely hat stands are made of wood with turned bases.

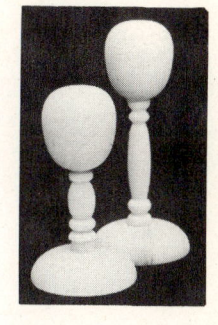

SLICKER SETS
The Doll's Cobbler
Suggested Retail Price: $33.
Three-piece set in girl's, boy's, and men's rainwear available in a variety of colors.

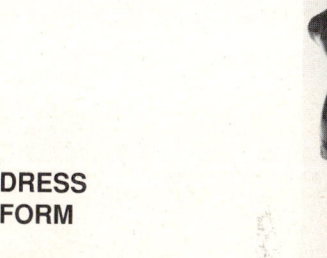

DRESS FORM
Miniature House
Suggested Retail Price: $2.39
Catalog No. MH2319
This black dress form for the sewing room is made of solid metal, perfectly proportioned.

LADIES HATS
Miniature House
Suggested Retail Price: $4.49 each
Catalog No. MH2070
Fine felt ladies feathered hats with three rosebuds. Available in burgundy, red blue and green. These quality hats fit hat stands MH2067 and MH2068.

Character Dolls

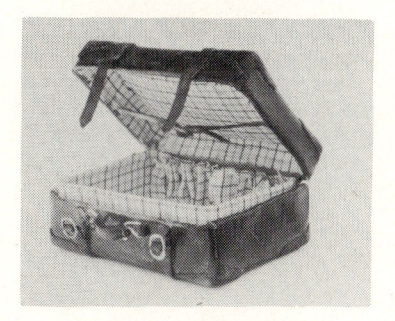

LEATHER LUGGAGE
The Doll's Cobbler
All are real working pieces with choice silk or liberty cotton linings coordinated with rich leather finishes. Six pieces now available include: A new man's tophat box, round lady's hat box, suitcase and a trunk, all $45 retail; plus a leather satchel or a Mary Poppins carpet bag at $27.

DOLLHOUSE FAMILY
Miniature House
Suggested Retail Price: $17.50
Catalog No. MH3500
Material: Bendable plastic with removable clothing
These 1" scale dollhouse dolls are more realistic and life-like than most and are priced to fit any budget. Dolls are all fully bendable.

Dollhouse Dolls & Accessories

THE MINIATURES CATALOG, *Fourteenth Edition*

GRANDPARENTS AND CHILD

Exclusive Products
Oh what a joy to visit with Grandma and Grandpa. Three piece set. Bendable arms and legs. Old time attire. #BA-20.

DOLLHOUSE CHILDREN

Miniature House
Suggested Retail Price: $8.25
Catalog No. MH3520
Material: Bendable plastic with removable clothing
These boy and girl dolls are fully bendable, life-like and very affordable. Dolls are 1" scale.

DOLLHOUSE ADULTS

Miniature House
Suggested Retail Price: $11.30
Catalog No. MH3510
Material: Bendable plastic with removable clothing
These all-plastic, bendable dolls in contemporary clothing are 1" scale.

DOLLHOUSE BABIES

Miniature House
Suggested Retail Price: $6.25
Catalog No. MH3530
Material: Bendable plastic with removable clothing
An infant and a toddler to add to your dollhouse family are 1" scale and fully bendable.

Clothing Patterns

Doll Clothing

Mary Agnes Murphy
Suggested Retail Price: Sweater $45; Cap $7.50 ppd
Material: Irish wool
Beautiful handknits in 1" scale. Authentic patterns and wools. Sweater available in pullover or cardigan style. Send SASE for color samples.

PATTERNS AND TRIM

Viv's Ribbons & Lace
We carry five lines of dollhouse doll dressing patterns for clothing, hats, shoes and accessories. Also available is six sizes of silk ribbon, bunka dyed to match, Swiss straw and embroideries, many narrow trims and braids, French and English laces both old and new, three sizes of beautiful crystal pleated laces and much more.

BABY LAYETTE

Rhonda Peden
Suggested Retail Price: See your local dealer
Sacques, kimonos and layette items in baby colors and fabrics. For contemporary and vintage nurseries. Can be worn or displayed.

DRESSES

By Teri's Mini Workshop
Suggested Retail Price: $7.50, plus $2 shipping.
Material: Mostly cottons
These dresses will fit a 1" toddler or hang on a hanger.

LOOKING FOR SOMETHING SPECIAL? CHECK WITH YOUR LOCAL MINIATURES SHOP!

Prices are approximate and subject to change.

Dollhouse Dolls

PORCELAIN BABIES

Jean Day
Suggested Retail Price: $35 plus shipping
Material: Porcelain, china painted
Solid porcelain babies in realistic poses. many styles available. Nude (sexed) or panties. Porcelain baby accessories and lamps. Original designs also available.

PORCELAIN DOLLS

Dahl's House of Miniatures
Suggested Retail Price: $36 to $215 plus shipping (completely finished)
Material: Porcelain, wire, cloth, and viscose hair.
Beautiful porcelain dolls researched for authenticity. Dressed in silk or cotton. A doll for approximately every 50 years. Send $3 for color brochure.

HALF SCALE PORCELAIN DOLLS

Dahl's House of Miniatures
Suggested Retail Price: $40-$83 plus shipping
Material: Porcelain, silk or cotton, viscose
Charming fully-jointed babies, children and adults. The 1-1/2" tall dolls pictured are 1/2" scale children or full scale dolls. Available finished or in kits, complete with porcelain material, hair and trim. Postpaid Elsie (no bear) finished $53.50, kit $39; Alice finished $59, kit $39; Shirley or Mary Mary finished $52, kit $40. Catalog $3.

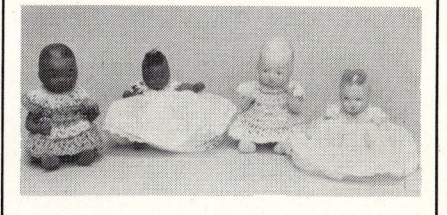

DOLLS

Garcia & Velez Co.
Porcelain babies in 1" scale. Assorted color dresses are handmade and sold separately. Several ages and sizes available.

MINI BABIES

J. Hermes
Suggested Retail Price: $1.50-$2.25 each
Material: Plastic
German imports. Full color "anatomically correct" 1" scale boy and girl babies in four positions: sitting, standing, crawling and laying. Comes dressed or undressed. Catalog #201-204.

NEW PORCELAIN DOLLS

Miniature Corner
Suggested Retail Price: See your dealer.
Material: Vinyl and fabric
Charming children and Grandma, the newest additions to our handmade German porcelain doll collection. Styles in period dress from 1700 to contemporary. Beautiful porcelain faces with fully poseable bodies. At affordable prices. Send $2 for color literature.

Dollhouse Dolls & Accessories

THE MINIATURES CATALOG, Fourteenth Edition

PLAYABLE DOLLHOUSE DOLLS

Miniature Corner
Suggested Retail Price: See your dealer.
Material: Vinyl and fabric
The finest playable dollhouse dolls made in Germany. One-piece fully bendable vinyl construction. A variety of clothing styles and periods to choose from. Clothing is removable. Shown are four-piece family and grandparents with dog.

DOLLHOUSE DOLLS

Nostalgia
Suggested Retail Price: $30 unfinished; $75 and up completely finished
D.A.G. Millie Award winner. Dressed and undressed 1" scale porcelain dolls in a full range of adults and children. We specialize in unusual costumes and designs.

Interested in Becoming a Professional Miniatures Handcrafter? Contact the Cottage Industry Miniaturists Trade Association

CIMTA
P.O. Box 5071
New Haven, CT 06525

PLAYABLE ETHNIC DOLLHOUSE DOLLS

Miniature Corner
Suggested Retail Price: See your dealer.
Material: Vinyl and fabric
Ethnic dolls for the dollhouse. New black family with proper features and skin color. Bendable, one piece construction with removable clothing. Also available: Oriental, Mexican, Indian, Eskimo and American Indian families with appropriate features, skin color and clothing.

PORCELAIN DOLLS

J. Parker
Suggested Retail Price: $65 to $175
Swallowhill dolls dressed by Joy. Elaborate Victorian and Edwardian fashions. Beautiful women, charming children. Limited editions with certificates of authenticity. Quality hand production. 100% guaranteed.

MODERN CHILDREN

Teri's Mini Workshop
Suggested Retail Price: $50 plus $2 shipping
Children of the 90's, made of porcelain. Some have dirty faces, a broken arm, a Halloween costume - all kinds of outfits. Tell me what you need.

FINE PORCELAIN DOLLHOUSE DOLLS

Petite People Plus
Suggested Price: $15 - $17 kits, $25 - $35 finished plus shipping
Dressed men, ladies, teens, toddlers and babies. Fine porcelain dolls dressed in silk and cotton with Feels-O-Fleece hair. Many popular 1" scale and 1/2" scale dolls individually china-painted to look like real people. 1" scale available in black and white. Wigs, doll kits and many accessories also available. Send $1.50 for photo and catalog.

RAG DOLLS AND STUFFED ANIMALS

Pieper Gallery
Suggested Retail Price: $49.95 + $3 S&H
Handcrafted cloth dolls for every occasion; country critters, stuffed animals, rag dolls, seasonal characters and fantasy. Each fully jointed, approximately 1-1/4" tall, 1:12 scale. Brochure available, $1. IGMA Artisan.

PORCELAIN DOLLS

Royce Piro Miniatures
Suggested Retail Price: $170-$200 (adults), $58-$65 (children), $20-$28 (kits)
Fully dressed and accessorized 1"-1' porcelain dolls, men and women. All from the artist's original sculptures. The hands are finely detailed and the heads are posable. Many fashion periods are represented, including the 1910's, 1920's and Erte. A full line of servants are also available; butler, chauffeur, cook, etc. Three-inch dressed children are available in dresses, playclothes and costumes. Doll kits of men, women and children, bald or wigged available.

PORCELAIN DOLLS

Ross' Treasure House
At last, medium priced quality porcelain dollhouse scale dolls. These are completely finished doll, not kits. Very nicely detailed hand-painted faces. Real porcelain heads, shoulders, arms, legs and feet with boots or shoes. All with bendable bodies for different positions. Synthetic or real wigs could be added to their ceramic hair. Three females and one male, dressed or undressed. Porcelain baby doll also available (2-1/2"). Baby doll is all porcelain with jointed legs and arms, dressed in blue bunting bag.

October National Dollhouse & Miniatures Month

ONE-OF-A-KIND DOLLS

Shirley Whitworth
One-of-a-kind porcelain dolls for the serious collector. The costumes are researched for the period and certificates of authenticity are given to the buyer.

Dollhouse Dolls & Accessories

THE MINIATURES CATALOG, *Fourteenth Edition* 235

Doll Kits

DOLL KITS, SWIVEL HEADS

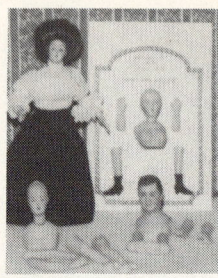

Jean Day
Suggested Retail Price: $20 plus shipping
Material: Porcelain, china painted
Kits include body pattern and directions. 60 styles available. Ladies and children have swivel heads. Toddlers and babies are all bisque with wire. Brochure is $2.

PORCELAIN DOLL KITS

J. Parker
Suggested Retail Price: $25 to $84
Swallowhill porcelain doll kits, beautifully painted, many originals. English mohair and viscose. Also silk ribbons, mini braids and trims and patterns that work! 100% guaranteed.

DOLL KITS

By Teri's Mini Workshop
Suggested Retail Price: Unpainted — $15, painted — $16, plus $2 shipping.
Material: Porcelain
Kits are available in baby boy, baby girl, toddlers or grandma and grandpa.

Dollmaking Supplies/Molds

MINIATURE DOLL MOLDS

Janna's and Karen's Molds
Suggested Retail Price: See your dealer
Material: Plaster molds
1" and 1/2" scale porcelain and 1" scale wax doll molds. Catalog $3.

FIMO® MODELING MATERIAL

Eberhard Faber GmbH
Suggested Retail Price: See your dealer.
Catalog No. 8000
Specifications: 55 x 55 x 15 mm/65 g small block, 165 x 55 x 30 mm/350 g large block. FIMO®, the fantastic and most popular modeling material, is the leading product of its kind in Europe. It's versatile and easy to handle, and hardens in the oven at 265°F. (20 to 30 minutes). Available in 42 brilliant colors, it's ideal to create the finest decorative accessories for your dollhouse and to make exciting and imaginative objects (miniatures, figures, fashion jewelry, decorations, pictures, nameplates and a lot more).

October National Dollhouse & Miniatures Month

Prices are approximate and subject to change.

1" Scale Accessories

Table of Contents

Animals	238
Bathroom Accessories	239
Bedroom Accessories	241
Bedding & Linens	242
Books & Magazines	243
Ceramic & Porcelain	244
Country	246
Dining Room Accessories	246
Doctor's Office	247
Figures	248
Fireplace	249
Foods	249
Garden & Landscaping	252
Glassware & Crystal	254
Holiday & Seasonal	254
Jewelry	259
Kitchen	259
Kits	261
Leather	262
Lighting Fixtures & Lamps	262
Living Room	264
Metalware	264
Mirrors & Screens	265
Miscellaneous	265
Musical	269
Needlework & Linens	270
Nursery	271
Paintings, Prints, Watercolors, Etchings	272
Paper Accessories	273
Period Accessories	273
Personal Items	275
Photographs	275
Plants & Flowers	276
Sculptures & Statues	278
Southwestern & Indian	285
Sports Equipment	287
Store & Shop Accessories	288
Bakery	289
General Store	290
Pet Shop	291
Specialty Shop	291
Living Room	264
Toys & Games	292
Workshop Accessories	293

THE MINIATURES CATALOG, *Fourteenth Edition*

Animals

MINI-PETS
Creative Enterprizes
Suggested Retail Price: $20 - $110 plus shipping
Material: Super Sculpey
Choose in various positions. Make a mini-home come alive. General breeds or special order your favorite pet. Individually hand sculpted.

ANIMALS
D-leprechaun
Repainted and haired Breyer horses, both 1" and 1/2". Also realistic foods and decorative hats. Information and order sheet $1. Retail and wholesale. Quality handwork.

CLOISONNE ANIMALS
Dollhouse Doll-ups
Cloisonne animals shown include an owl, elephant and bird. Also available is a horse and a quail. An exclusive of Dollhouse Doll-ups.

RING NECK PHEASANTS
Feathers N Clay
Suggested Retail Price: $35 plus shipping
Pair of 1" scale Ring Neck Pheasants. Made of clay with acrylic paint highlights. Product #1100. Many indoor varieties of birds, over 40 varieties of outdoor birds and critters. Each individually hand sculpted.

GRIZZLY'S LAST STAND
Goebel Miniatures
From the American Frontier collection. American made.

OWL-DAYLIGHT ENCOUNTER
Goebel Miniatures
From the Wildlife Series.

WINTER CARDINAL
Goebel Miniatures
From the Wildlife Series.

ORIGINAL HAND-PAINTED MINIATURE ANIMALS
Mary Hoot Miniatures
Suggested Retail Price: $20 and up
A world of animals, dogs, cats, wild animals and more. All original, all handcrafted. These are the finest quality you can find. Skillfully hand-painted on cloth forms in amazing detail. These are highly collectible, each one a work of art in miniature. 1", 1/2" and larger scales. Send SASE for list. Limited quantities.

MINI CATS
Kate's Cats
Suggested Retail Price: $17 and up
Handsculpted cats with whiskers and life like eyes. Also available, porcelain dressed cat dolls ($50 and up) and cat doll kits in three sizes with arms, legs and head ($30 and up). 1" or 1/2" scale.

Prices are approximate and subject to change.

HANDSCULPTED MINIATURES

Kitty's Kreations
Kitty's Kreations introduces a new line of original hand sculpted miniature animals. All animals are in 1" scale, intricately detailed, with glass eyes. Our selection includes cats, dogs, kittens, puppies and an assortment of barnyard animals. We also specialize in pets with children, babies, dolls and teddy bears. Please mention "The Miniatures Catalog" when sending $1 for our catalog.

RUG BUDDIES

Miniatures by Marian
Suggested Retail Price: $5 and up
Individually handcrafted bunnies, Santas, nativities, bears and clowns. Each on it's own "braided rug". Also bears of the month. Send LSASE for information.

GAIL MOREY'S "PEDIGREE" DOGS

Morey's Miniatures
1" scale, 1/2" scale, 1/4" scale. Fellow of IGMA, NAME member, AOH member.

MAMA BEAR WITH TWINS

Special Sellers
Suggested Retail Price: $10 plus shipping
Catalog No. BE 560 is featured, 3/4" high. Also available are assorted bears, bunnies and mice in adorable poses from $3 to $50. Wholesale invited.

ANIMAL FIGURES

Alice Zinn
Suggested Retail Price: $7 to $100
This is a selection of barnyard birds, wild birds and pet birds with feathers. Fuzzy cats, custom made furry dogs, a poseable monkey, rabbits, guinea pigs, mice, snakes and more are available. American made.

DRESSED CHIMPANZEES

T.K. Designs
Cowboys, clowns, ballerinas and many others available. Also undressed primates available; chimpanzees, gorillas, orangutans and capuchins. LSASE for catalog. Wholesale orders welcome.

Bathroom Accessories

1" Scale Accessories

THE MINIATURES CATALOG, *Fourteenth Edition* 239

BATHROOM SET AND NIGHTGOWN
Amoroso Originals
Velour robe and shower cap of assorted fabrics and lace trimmed, $14.50; kits, $7.50. Nightgowns are frilly see-thru with lace or organdy trim, $16.50; kits $9. Shower cap, $1.50. All items ppd.

TOWEL AND RUG SET
Amoroso Originals
Suggested Retail Price: $6 Ppd.. for set, $3.50 ppd. for towels only. Velour towels edged with beautiful laces and trims. Silk bow is finishing touch.

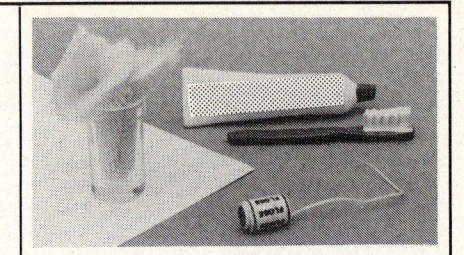

DENTAL CARE SET
Jacqueline's Wholesale
This set is sure to be approved by your family dentist. Includes dental floss, toothbrush, toothpaste, water glass and face cloth.

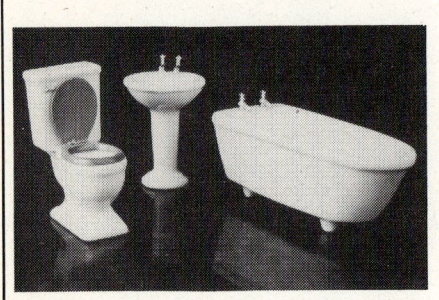

BATH SET
Houseworks
Suggested Retail Price: $35
Catalog No. 8500
Includes bathtub, sink and toilet. Each piece is genuine porcelain. Bathtub and sink feature gold plated brass fixtures and drains. Toilet features gold plated brass handle and wooden seat.

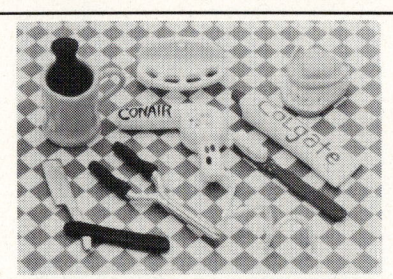

BATHROOM ACCESSORIES
Monkey Business
Finish off your bathroom with authentic necessities. Our toothbrush is available in four colors. Our hairdryer looks realistic. We also have items for older bathrooms.

BATHROOM ACCESSORIES
Jack and June's Mini-Many Things
Cherrywood washstand handcrafted by Jack. Guest towels and three-piece terry towel sets in assorted colors by June. Plumbers' helper and bowl brush in assorted colors also available.

BLUE BEDROOM TOILET SET
Lenham Pottery
Suggested Retail Price: $57.43
Material: Porcelain, white glazed, ceramic transfers
This set includes water carrier, jug, basin, potty, jardiniere and hip bath. English made.

BATHROOM FURNISHINGS
Lenham Pottery
Suggested Retail Price: $66.11
Material: Slip-cast white-glazed porcelain. These slip-cast, white-glazed porcelain baths, wash basins, and toilet kits are now available. Also available are metal plumbing castings, and gold or nickel-plated taps. Write for brochure. Made in England.

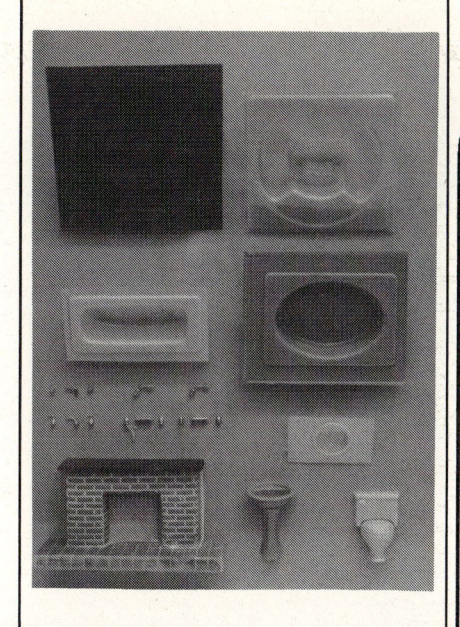

TUBS, SINKS AND TOILETS

Plastruct
Contemporary bathtubs, hot tubs, toilets and sinks in several designer colors. Standard chrome and ornate gold faucets sold separately. Fireplace kit also shown.

Plastruct... "THE" HOME IMPROVEMENT CENTER FOR MINIATURISTS

HUNDREDS OF DOLLHOUSE PRODUCTS

VOL 5   1991 SUPP

- APPLIANCES
- BATH TUBS
- FAUCETS
- FIREPLACES
- FLEXIBLE MATTINGS
- FLOORING
- HOT TUBS
- LANDSCAPING
- MICROWAVE OVENS
- PANELING
- PLUMBING HARDWARE
- REFRIGERATORS
- ROOFING
- SIDING
- SINKS
- STAINED GLASS WINDOWS
- STOVES WITH OVENS
- TOILETS
- TREES
- WASHER & DRYERS

Plastruct
SEE INDEX AND OUR LISTINGS THROUGHOUT THIS MINIATURE'S CATALOG

Bedroom Accessories

BEDROOM ACCESSORIES

Betty's Wooden Miniatures
These are some of our bedroom accessories. All are original and handmade by us in the U.S.A.

BOUDOIR ACCESSORIES- ROMANTIC ERA

Robin's Roost
Miniatures for Collectors
Suggested Retail Price: See your dealer
Band boxes (decorated hat boxes), wreaths, swan floral arrangements, decorated baskets, sets of boudoir jars, matching blankets, reminiscent of the Romantic Era. Available in many colors.

1" Scale Accessories

THE MINIATURES CATALOG, Fourteenth Edition   241

Bedding and Linens

HANDCRAFTED FURNITURE

Little Linens
Handcrafted bedroom furniture in both Classic and Contemporary design. Each style consists of a custom look dressed bed, chaise lounge, chair, hassock and skirted table. Various colors and fabrics available. All items proudly made in the USA.

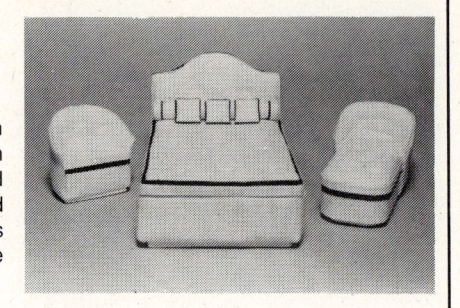

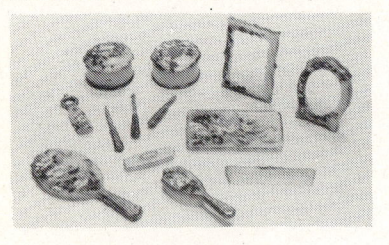

VANITY SET

Nanco Distributors
Suggest Retail Price: $27.95
Hand-painted on Chrysonbon vanity sets. Available in pink, rose, peach, yellow or custom made to order.

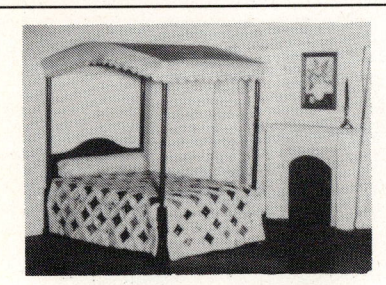

CATHEDRAL WINDOW QUILT KIT

A-Dora-Bill Miniatures
Suggested Retail Price: $10.95
Kit includes all materials. Order No. QK-1.

LINENS

Twin Palms Miniatures
Wide selection of bed linens, rug kits, finished rugs, pillows and doilies in 1" scale. $1 and LSASE for brochure.

BEDROOM ACCESSORIES

Jack and June's Mini-Many Things
Bed linens in assorted colors. Mattress and pillow sets to scale or custom made to any bed size.

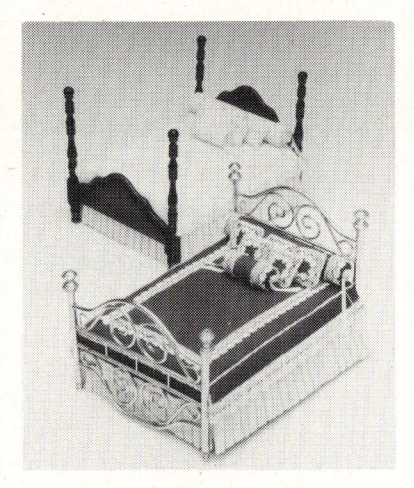

READY-MADE BEDDING

Little Linens
Suggested Retail Price: $10 - $19
Custom look bedding available in a variety of colors, mix-and-match, designed to fit any standard double or twin size bed. No glue necessary with our peel-and-stick process. Matching draperies available.

242   Prices are approximate and subject to change.

Books & Magazines

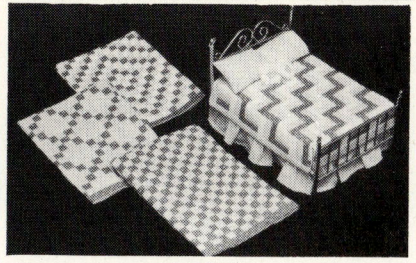

QUILTS
Vermont Home Quilts
Suggested Retail: $2.25-$50
Quilts, pillow cases, throw pillows and brass beds. Quilts available for crib, single and double beds in a variety of colors. All cotton in 1/12th scale.

UNPRINTED MAGAZINES
Aunt Ginny's
Magazines dated from 1895 to present. Also newspapers, books, sheet music, postcards, "Instant Ancestors", attic papers, yarn labels, old patterns. Catalog and sample; $2.

MINIATURE BOOKS
Houseworks
These handcrafted books are actually bound with loose pages. Packaged in assorted colors: Red, blue, green, maroon. All have gold trim on spine.

No. 5013-Size: 7/8" H x 9/16" W x 3/16" thick. 12 pieces/package, $1.95.
No. 5012-Size: 3/4" H x 1/2" W x 1/8" thick. 12 pieces/package, $1.75.

BOOKCASES
Houseworks
No. 5011-Three-unit bookcase with full shelves. Size: 9-5/16" W x 7-3/8" H x 1-3/8" D, $17.95.
No. 5010-One-unit bookcase with nonfunctional cabinet. Size: 3-3/8" W x 7-1/8" H x 1-3/8" D, $7.95.
No. 5029-Three-shelf corner cabinet with fluted and paneled front. Size: 3-3/8" W x 7-1/4" H, $10.95.
No. 5009-Three-unit bookcase with nonfunctional cabinets. Size: 9-5/16" W x 7-3/8" H x 1-3/8" D, $17.95.

READABLE BOOKS
Jacqueline's Wholesale
Readable open books with bookmarks lie flat on any table. Select from Bibles, cookbooks, children's books and classics. Realistic and irresistible.

MINIATURE PHOTOGRAPHS, ALBUMS AND FRAMING MATS
LaCasa Photos
Suggested Retail Price: $3 and up
Miniature photographs in sets, albums and other books (including 1/2" scale books), photos in folders and folder kits, stereoscopes and stereoviews, postcards (33 sets), frames, mats, paperdolls, Victorian paper goods and vintage prints. See your local dealer or send $3 for catalog and price sheet.

1" Scale Accessories

THE MINIATURES CATALOG, *Fourteenth Edition* 243

LIBRARY BOOK KITS

Miniature Corner
Suggested Retail Price: See your dealer. Complete 50 book library in each of three different sets. Authentic reproductions of English, French and German leather bound classics. Materials for complete books included. Printed in Germany.

INSTRUCTION BOOK JEWELRY MAKING IN MINIATURE

Barbara J. Raheb
Author: Barbara J. Raheb
Suggested Retail Price: $12.90 Prepaid.
Pages: 68
Softcover
For the serious dollmaker; contains clear, complete instructions with easy-to-follow black-and-white illustrations, pertinent reference information and actual projects as well as bead utilization in areas other than jewelry making. Material supply list and order form included with book.

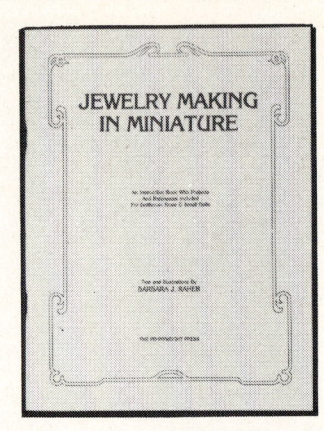

MINIATURE BOOKS

Barbara J. Raheb
Miniature books-under 1", with spines, 23K gold front-cover engravings, handsewn and bound, readable and illustrated in abridged and unabridged editions. Catalog $5. American made.

Ceramic & Porcelain

STONEWARE

Butt Hinge Pottery
Wheel-thrown stoneware miniatures capturing the spirit of traditional New England pottery for use in many dollhouse settings from the kitchen and bedroom to the garden or general store. Wholesale only. See your local dealer for further information.

CERAMIC DISHES

By Barb
Ceramic dishes and accessory sets in a large assortment of colors and designs. Can be made to order. Available in 1" and 1/2" scale. Made in the U.S.A.

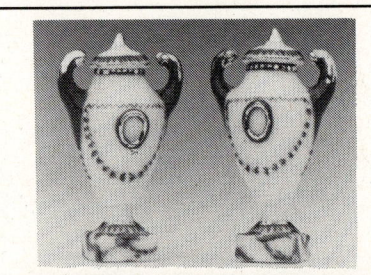

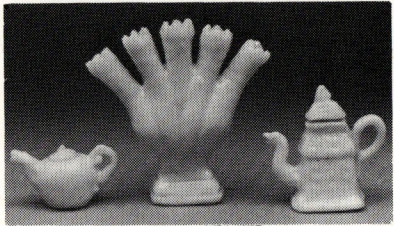

CERAMICS

Ron Benson Miniatures
Sculptures, Staffordshire teapots, Williamsburg finger vases, French urns, angels, cottages, castles and swan vase. American made.

244   Prices are approximate and subject to change.

ORIENTAL PORCELAIN
Dollhouse Doll-ups
Suggested Retail Price: $8 - $10
Oriental ginger jars in rust, green with black, pink, and white with pink design and Oriental bowl with gold trim. Made expressly for Dollhouse Doll-ups.

CERAMIC KITCHENWARE
Dollhouse Miniatures by Flo
Suggested Retail Price: $1 - $12
Dinnerware, pots, pans, canister sets, bowls. Each piece is carefully poured, handpainted and fired with a floral design. Available in white with pink, rose, yellow, light blue, or orange flowers. American made.

CERAMIC CROCKERY
"Krafts" by Betty Jean
A large assortment of styles and sizes with gray "salt-glazed" finish. Decorated with hand-painted blue designs.

WHITE CHINA
Falcon Collectible Miniatures
Suggested Retail Price: See your dealer
These exquisite white china pieces are a welcome addition to your dollhouse. They can be used in many ways and are perfect for displaying a variety of foods. Custom orders welcome. Quantity discounts available to dealers.

PORCELAIN
Lenham Pottery
This is a selection of household items in 1" scale slip-cast ceramic (porcelain). Also available is a selection of transfer printed china. Write for brochure.

PITCHER AND BOWL
Miniature House
Suggested Retail Price: $1.60
Catalog No. MH2466
White ceramic with painted flowers.

QUALITY PORCELAIN ACCESSORIES
Royal Miniatures
Suggested Retail Price: $2 - $8
Shown is a small sampling of our large line of bone china and porcelain miniatures. Wholesale only. Quantity discounts for manufacturers and distributors available.

SALT-GLAZED STONEWARE
Vernon Pottery
Suggested Retail Price: $9 - $18
Museum-quality reproductions of 19th century North American salt-glazed stoneware. Each of our 1/12 scale pots is made on the potters wheel and decorated freehand with cobalt blue clay slip. Butterchurns with walnut dashers, crocks, storage jars and preserves jars with lids, jugs and water coolers with cork stoppers, pitchers and more. Catalog $2.

Holiday themes are always so popular! Fill a miniature basket with Easter grass, then add some selected apple seeds painted with pastel shades to resemble tiny Easter eggs.

*SARAH BLOMQUIST
HOLLISTON, MA*

WHEEL-THROWN PORCELAIN
Your Local Potter
A wide range of styles in both 1" and 1/2" scales. Each piece is individually wheel-thrown and hand decorated. Reasonable prices. Brochure available.

1" Scale Accessories

Country

STONEWARE

Butt Hinge Pottery
Wheel-thrown stoneware miniatures capturing the spirit of traditional New England pottery for use in many dollhouse settings from the kitchen and bedroom to the garden or general store. Wholesale only. See your local dealer for further information.

HANDMADE MINIATURE ACCESSORIES

Betty's Wooden Miniatures
Suggested Retail Price: $2.95 to $9.95
This is just a sampling of the many original, new, handmade items we have just added to our line. American made by us.

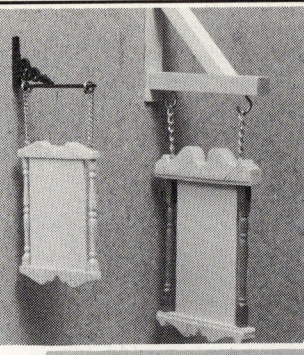

ANTIQUE NAME SIGN

Betty's Wooden Miniatures
Available in two sizes with or without brackets and post. All handcrafted. Also: crates, shelves, wall plaques, washboard, plunger, clock, tool box, scooter, breadboard, wood bin, etc. Handcrafted by us.

HANDSCULPTED MINIATURES

Kitty's Kreations
From Kitty's Kreations an assortment of barnyard animals. Shown is "Little Lost Lamb". Each item is 1" scale, made of hydrostone. Please mention "The Miniatures Catalog" when sending $1 for our catalog.

PROVINDER BASKET

Little Discoveries
Suggested Retail Price: $50 (AGB/DLX) and $25 (EC/PBX). All prices plus shipping.
Dimensions: 1-3/4" L x 6/8" W x 5/8" H
Adaptation of 1860's gathering basket handwoven using natural materials (twig bottom rests and handle). Choose empty (EC/PBX) or filled with our fresh garden vegetables (AGB/DLX).

HANDCRAFTED BASKETS

Royal Miniatures
Suggested Retail Price: $2 - $3
Shown is a small sampling from our large line of baskets. All are quality crafted and inexpensively priced. Quantity discounts available. Imported.

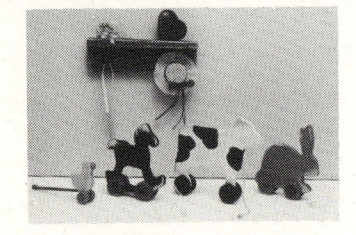

A LITTLE BIT OF COUNTRY

Wee Wonders
New country line in 1" and 1/2" scale. Shelves, benches, pull toys, hanging hearts and candles, straw hats, etc. Wholesale or retail catalog, $2.

Dining Room Accessories

Prices are approximate and subject to change.

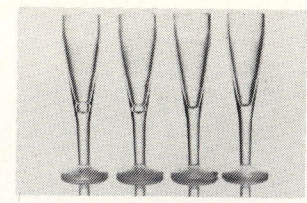

FLUTED CHAMPAGNE GLASSES

Linden Swiss Miniatures
Scale: 1", Material: Acrylic
Set of four elegant champagne glasses. Instructions for clearing glasses to have a crystal clear look included. See your local dealer. American made.

CEDAR CHEST

Our Designs Furniture Co., A Division of Henry's House of Trains and Miniatures
Suggested Retail Price: $42 prepaid or COD at extra charge
Also; complete line of miniature yard furniture in cedar as redwood. We also have an old-time console radio with working speaker and lighted dial.

FRUIT ARRANGEMENTS

Little Discoveries
Suggested Retail Price: $35 (DLX), $20 (DIN), $25 (TROP); all prices plus shipping. Handcrafted Fimo fruit in polished or painted metal bowls. Three centerpiece styles: (left-right) Deluxe (the works - apples, banana, coconut, citrus, pears, peaches, plums, berries, nectarines, grapes, pineapple); Dinner (apples, cherries, grapes and pears); Tropical (pineapple, kiwi, coconut, citrus, and banana). 36-page price list, $1.

STERLING SILVER ACCESSORIES

Maison des Maison
Art deco sterling silver designed exclusively for Maison des Maison by Jeff Wise including centerpiece bowl, candelabra, wine bucket and stand, vases, tortiere lamp and other pieces.

Doctor's Office

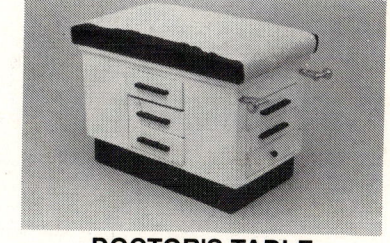

DOCTOR'S TABLE

"Krafts" by Betty Jean
Suggested Retail Price: $50
Perfect for a doctor's office, this 1" scale examination table is made by "Krafts" by Betty Jean. Other items available by special order.

FIRST AID/DOCTORS' OFFICE

Monkey Business
Our hand-painted metal miniatures are reasonably priced. The Doctor is ready for patients with our stethoscope, doctors bag, bedpan, bible, microscope and nurses hat.

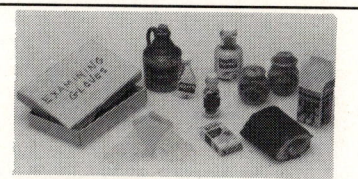

MEDICAL AND DENTAL OFFICE ACCESSORIES

"Precious Little Things" by the Fieldwood Company, Inc.
Authentically labeled medicines and medicaments for doctor, dentist, home, store, contemporary/old-time. Surgical gloves, movable hypodermic, plaster cast, enema bag, folding screen and more. Color catalog $3.50 or ask your local dealer.

DOCTOR'S OFFICE

Teri's Mini Workshop
Doctor's office supplies including doctor's bag and modern dental supplies. American made.

1" Scale Accessories

Figures

ANN FISHER'S BEARS 'N BUNNIES

Aunt Ginny's
Suggested Retail Price: SASE for complete price listing
Aunt Ginny's is the exclusive distributor for Ann Fisher's delightful Bears 'n Bunnies. Retail only.

ACCORDION BOY
Goebel Miniatures
First release of miniature M.I. Hummel, limited to 10,000. Released in 1991.

BUSY STUDENT
Goebel Miniatures
First release of miniature M.I. Hummel, limited to 10,000. Released in 1991.

MERRY WANDERER DEALER PLAQUE
Goebel Miniatures
First release of miniature M.I. Hummel, limited to 10,000. Released in 1991.

SERENADE
Goebel Miniatures
First release of miniature M.I. Hummel, limited to 10,000. Released in 1991.

WE CONGRATULATE
Goebel Miniatures
First release of miniature M.I. Hummel, limited to 10,000. Released in 1991.

FIGURES

Monkey Business
Hand-painted superior quality at low prices. We have Raggedys', Aunt Jemima, Pinocchio, soldiers and more. All hand-painted by us in the USA. Prompt shipments.

HANDSCULPTED MINIATURES

Kitty's Kreations
Kitty's Kreations introduces a new line of babies, dolls and children with pets. Each item is intricately detailed, 1" scale and made of hydrostone. Please mention "The Miniatures Catalog" when sending $1 for our catalog.

Prices are approximate and subject to change.

Fireplace

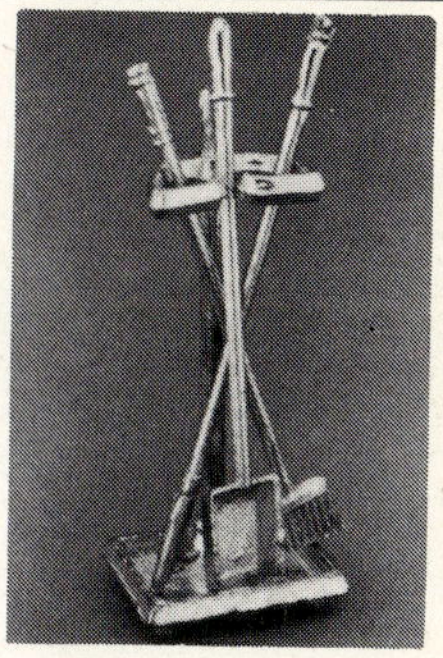

Foods

FIREPLACE TOOLS

Miniature House
Suggested Retail Price: $2.25
Catalog No. MH2401
Tools are gold-tint painted. Set has stand, brush, shovel and poker.

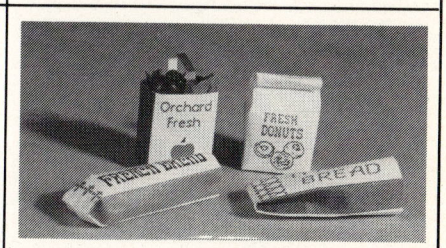

FOODS

Philip E. Bugosh
Sug: Retail Price: See your local dealer
French and Italian bread, donut bags and apple bags are part of our selection of kitchen and food items. Handcrafted.

JUDAIC FOODS

By Barb
We specialize in ethnic Judaic foods; bagels and lox, motzah, chicken soup, Sedar plates, gefilte fish, hamantashen and more. Available in 1" and 1/2" scale. Made in the U.S.A.

PIE SET

Dragonfly International
Beautifully made pie in our glazed pie plate and cover with two slices served up on matching plates and coffee-filled cups.

GOURMET GOODIES

Elliott's
Suggested Retail Price: $3 to $50
Quality miniature foods, including cornish game hens, double fudge brownies, field fresh pumpkins and oysters on the half-shell. Custom orders accepted.

ASSORTED FOODS

Cathy's Handcrafted Miniature Accessories
Crates, baskets and trays of handcrafted apples, bananas, grapes, oranges, carrots, eggplants, gourds, mushrooms, potatoes and pumpkins. Also pizza, candies, cookies, cakes and popcorn.

1" Scale Accessories

THE MINIATURES CATALOG, *Fourteenth Edition* 249

ASSORTED FOODS

Fine Food In Miniature
By Sylvia Clarke. Specializing in foods for the selective collector. Quality meals for kings and kids in 1" scale. Extensive selection includes Medieval to present, breakfasts, lunches, snacks, dinners and elaborate banquets. Custom work considered. Menu (price list) available. Canadian made.

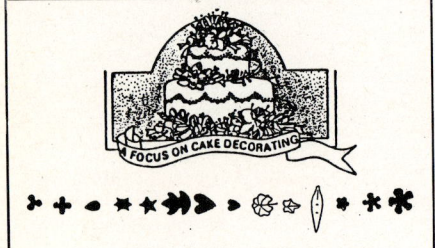

CAKES AND FLOWERS

Hanke's House
Make flowers, plants and trees with Pretty Petal Punches using tape, preserved leaves, colored or painted paper. Punches and mini cake catalog, $1.

DEVILED EGG OR VEGETABLE PLATTER

Gert's Triple "A" Minis
Suggested Retail Price: $10.60 each
Exquisitely detailed vegetable platters complete with assorted vegetables. Perfect for your mini house.

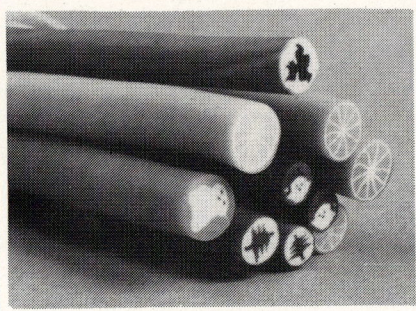

CANDY STICKS

Gert's Triple "A" Minis
Suggested Retail Price: $1.75 - $3.75 each
Colorful candy sticks available in a variety of colors and designs including starburst, Santa and other Christmas themes.

VARIOUS FOODS

The Kitchen Captive
Extensive selection of 1" and 1/2" foods and tray set ups. Basic to fancy baked goods, main course items, beverages, party servers and fancy desserts. Made of Fimo, sculpey and resin. Send LSASE for price list.

PRODUCE

Little Discoveries
Suggested Retail Price: $.50 to $50 plus shipping
Fresh fruit (apples to watermelons) and vegetables (artichokes to zucchini) sold as loose singles, gathered in containers (baskets, boxes, bowls and crates) or in stylized arrangements. All items are handcrafted in Fimo and natural materials by us. Descriptions in 36-page price list, $1.

PIES

Little Discoveries
Suggested Retail Price: $8 plus shipping
Material: Fimo in metal pie tins
Hearty homemade pies, each with ready-to-serve slice cut (or whole if you prefer). All varieties shipped in a twine-tied pastry box.

GREEN COKE BOTTLES

Miniature House
Suggested Retail Price: $1.98
Catalog No. MH2375
Six green bottles with red caps. They fit in MH2311 Coke case.

WINE BOTTLES

Miniature House
Suggested Retail Price: $2.59
Catalog No. MH2380
Six wine bottles with assorted labels.

Prices are approximate and subject to change.

QUALITY LIQUOR BOTTLES — ELEGANT COCKTAILS

Marilyn's Mini Studio
Suggested Retail Price: $2-$23
Over 55 quality liquor/wine bottles; 100 elegant cocktails, tray sets, punches and beverages for special occasions from milk to Mai Tais; bar accessories. Alka-seltzer, too. American made. Send SASE for price list.

SCALE FOODS, KITCHEN AND FIREPLACE ACCESSORIES

Our House II-Gramarye Keep
Suggested Retail Price: $.50 to $35
American made. Custom banquets a specialty. Catalogs; Period $5, Modern $5.

FOODS AND BEVERAGES

"Pannikins" by M.E.
Suggested Retail Price: $.25 to $25
Catalog/Project Booklet: $4.50
Handcrafted foods and beverages available in both 1" and 1/2" scale. Fruits, vegetables, seasonal, international, regional and period favorites, plus all supplies and "empties" for the do-it-yourselfer! Retail only.

HANDCRAFTED PRODUCE

**"Precious Little Things"
By the Fieldwood Company, Inc.**
Exceptional handcrafted produce in bulk, jars, bowls, crates or baskets, for the roadside stand, home, store, in 1" and many in 1/2" scale, assembled or in kits. Handmade baskets, garlic strands, potato and onion sacks, cement blocks, as well as table, door and mantle decorations incorporating fruit, gourds, or seasonal flowers. See our catalog or ask your local dealer. Color catalog, $3.50 Ppd., first class.

FIMO STICKS AND FOODS

Ann's Things - A Division of Mary's Miniature Mansions
Suggested Retail Price: $.50 to $25
A calendar spanning selection of decorative food and accessories (Christmas, Easter, Halloween, Valentine's Day, etc.). Handcrafted Fimo sticks to make candies, cookies, fruit, or meat trays, and candy houses. Just slice and arrange. Kits and finished products are available. Also pies, cakes, filled cookie sheets, blocks to make candy houses, garland and wreaths. Send $1 for price list. Fun for all ages!

CANDY, COOKIE & FOOD DESIGNS

Donna Smolik's Designs
Suggested Retail Price: $1.75-$4.25 each.
Candies, fruits, vegetables, meats - slice your own with a single-edged razor blade. Can be used in 1", 1/2" or 1/4" scales.

VARIOUS FOODS

Wood Products
Suggested Retail Price: See your local dealer.
All foods are beautifully handmade in the USA. We carry a wide variety of foods including turkey and ham platters, vegetable bowls and pans, meals on plates, fruits and vegetables, candy, cakes, pies and much more.

1" Scale Accessories

THE MINIATURES CATALOG, **Fourteenth Edition** 251

DECORATED ULTIMATE TREE

Doll House Shoppe
Suggested Retail Price: $10 (kit #4598) or $36 (finished, #4597)
Available made up or in kit form. Kit includes ribbon, roses and baby's breath.

HOLIDAY ACCESSORIES

Dragonfly International
Easter centerpiece with silk flowers, eggs and glazed ceramic bunny. Porcelain snowman, Santa and ceramic tree are all hand-painted and prewired to enhance your holidays.

ST. NICHOLAS

Goebel Miniatures
Part of the Night Before Christmas Series. 1-1/2" total height.

CHRISTMAS TREE KIT

Finescale Forest
Suggested Retail Price: $12 plus shipping
Durable sugar pine trunk. Stained a natural gray/brown. Foliage made from natural plants. Preserved and dyed to retain appearance, color and durability for many years. Exceptional realism. Easily assembled kit includes tree stand and assembly tool. Makes one 7" tree. Branches sturdy enough to support lights and ornaments. Trunk can be cut to make shorter tree for smaller scales.

EASTER BASKET

Gerts Triple "A" Minis
Easter basket of colored eggs with silk bowl. Also available decorated with chocolate eggs, jelly beans and candy.

HALLOWEEN TINS AND PUNCH BOWL

Gerts Triple "A" Minis
Beautifully detailed Halloween tins, available in a variety of styles. Choose from ghost cookies to assorted candies.

EIGHT TINY REINDEER

Goebel Miniatures
Sit "Up The Housetop" in the Night Before Christmas Series. 1-1/4" total height.

Prices are approximate and subject to change.

Here Comes the Bride....

The Garden Gazebo

THE PERFECT SETTING
FOR A WEDDING!
OR AN ANNIVERSARY!
OR A BIRTHDAY!
OR A SHOWER!
OR ANY PARTY!

45B BRIDAL GAZEBO - ASSEMBLED, PAINTED AND DECORATED AS SHOWN. TABLE AND CAKE ARE NOT INCLUDED, BUT ARE SOLD SEPARATELY. FURNITURE SHOWN IS ALSO AVAILABLE.
45   GAZEBO (HANDMADE AND PAINTED)
45A GAZEBO (HANDMADE, *NOT* PAINTED)
46   GAZEBO KIT (COMPLETE)

Etty's Wooden Miniatures
DIVISION OF SMITH WOOD PRODUCTS

ALL HANDMADE
OVERALL SIZE IS
15½" TALL x 10½" WIDE

HANDMADE MINIATURES / ALL 1" TO 1' SCALE
MADE IN U.S.A. / CHICAGO, IL 60631

Love is a "Mini" Splendored Thing

The Fantasy Collection

BEAUTIFUL FURNISHINGS FOR A ROMANTIC INTERLUDE

Betty's Wooden Miniatures
DIVISION OF SMITH WOOD PRODUCTS

HANDMADE MINIATURES / ALL 1" TO 1' SCALE
MADE IN U.S.A. / CHICAGO, IL 60631

White Lace & Promises

Pretty Little Keepsakes

Betty's Wooden Miniatures
DIVISION OF SMITH WOOD PRODUCTS

HANDMADE MINIATURES / ALL 1" TO 1' SCALE
MADE IN U.S.A. / CHICAGO, IL 60631

I Went to a Garden Party....
THE GARDEN COLLECTION
LOVELY INDOORS, TOO!

HANDMADE MINIATURES / ALL 1" TO 1' SCALE
MADE IN U.S.A. / CHICAGO, IL 60631

Betty's Wooden Miniatures
DIVISION OF SMITH WOOD PRODUCTS

PUNCH BOWL WITH CUPS

Gerts Triple "A" Minis
Punch bowl with cups, available in assorted styles for Christmas, Valentine's Day, St. Patrick's Day and Halloween.

YULE TREE

Goebel Miniatures
Part of the Night Before Christmas Series. 1-1/2" total height.

MAMA AND PAPA

Goebel Miniatures
Part of the Night Before Christmas Series. 1-1/4" total height.

SUGAR PLUM BOY

Goebel Miniatures
Part of the Night Before Christmas Series. 1" total height.

SUGAR PLUM GIRL

Goebel Miniatures
Part of the Night Before Christmas Series. 1" total height.

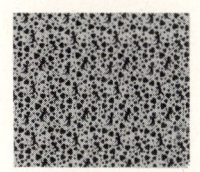

MINIATURE GIFTWRAPS

J. Hermes
Suggested Retail Price: $ .35 each
Easy-folding, full color giftwraps for all occasions. Christmas, Hanukkah, Birthday, new baby, Easter, Valentine's Day, St. Patrick's Day and Halloween. Over 100 designs available.

FINISHED GIFT SET

Linden Swiss Miniatures
Catalog No. 202. One wine bottle with two wine glasses. Displayed with gift box. American made. See your local dealer.

KIMBERLY CHRISTMAS TREE KIT

Kimberly House Miniatures
Suggested Retail Price: $16.45
Catalog No. KCT-101
Dimensions: Up to 9" high
Kit includes all materials to make the tree, plus old fashioned tree stand. Also includes materials for creating country decorations and ornaments, silver garland, material for making tree skirt, all with instructions, as well as a packet of soil for planting the tree in the yard after the holidays are over. See your dealer or write to Kimberly House.

WRAPPED PACKAGES

**Robin's Roost
Miniatures for Collectors**
Suggested Retail Price: See your dealer.
Assortments of wrapped packages for: Valentine's Day, St. Patrick's, Easter, Mother's Day, Halloween, Chanukah, Christmas, birthday, baby, over the hill and general occasion.

SEASONAL DECORATED TINS (FILLED)

**Robin's Roost
Miniatures for Collectors**
Suggested Retail Price: See your dealer.
Valentine's Day, St. Patrick's Day, Easter, Mother's Day, Halloween, Christmas and gift tins - available filled or empty. Many lavishly decorated.

1" Scale Accessories

THE MINIATURES CATALOG, Fourteenth Edition

DECORATED CHRISTMAS TREES

McCloud's
6" lycopodium trees decorated with assorted colors of pearl garland, velvet bows, packages, lace, flowers, puffs and sugarbush. Various themes also available.

CHRISTMAS TREE KITS

Robin's Roost
Miniatures for Collectors
Suggested Retail Price: See your dealer.
Size: 6" high
Basic Christmas tree kit contains: Assembled tree, garlands, bows, candy canes plus supplies to make all ornaments shown. Deluxe Christmas tree kit contains everything in basic kit plus skirt and tinsel garland kits and accessories shown.

HOLIDAY ACCESSORIES

Royal Miniatures
Suggested Retail Price: $1 - $5
Shown is a small selection from our large line of holiday accessories and decorative figurines. Customer designs welcome.

CANDY, COOKIE & FOOD DESIGNS

Donna Smolik's Designs
Suggested Retail Price: $1.75-$4.25 each. Candies, fruits, vegetables, meats - slice your own with a single-edged razor blade. Can be used in 1", 1/2" or 1/4" scales.

BRASS CHRISTMAS ACCESSORIES

Robin's Roost
Miniatures for Collectors
Suggested Retail Price: See your dealer.
Holiday hunting horn, triple candelabrum, wall sconces, Yule logholder—elegant additions to any Christmas scene plus Christmas snifter arrangement and Christmas candle arrangement (not pictured). These brass pieces complement our many other lovely Christmas accessories.

DESIGNER GINGERBREAD HOUSES

Special Sellers
Suggested Retail Price: $9 to $50 plus S&H
Collector quality gingerbread houses in more than 20 styles. Featured is GB820, a Victorian gingerbread house with gingerbread boy decorating candy house. Approximately 1" high. Wholesale invited.

ASSORTED HOLIDAYS ITEMS

Wee Wonders
Large selection of Halloween, Easter and Christmas items. Carved pumpkins, trick or treat bags, holiday decoration storage boxes, Santa's sacks and wreaths.

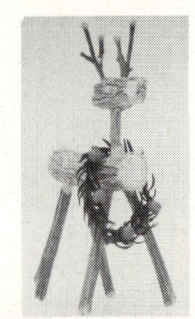

REINDEER

Wee Wonders
Suggested Retail Price: $6 plus shipping
Reindeer made from logs and twigs with wreath at neck. 1-1/2" tall. Handmade.

Jewelry

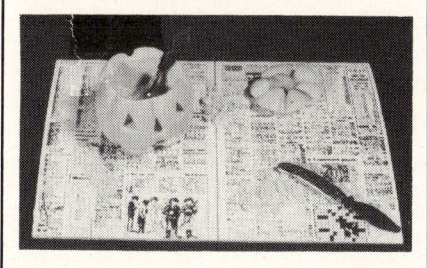

ASSORTED HOLIDAYS ITEMS

Wee Wonders
Large selection of Halloween, Easter and Christmas items. Carved pumpkins, trick or treat bags, holiday decoration storage boxes, Santa's sacks and wreaths.

CROWN JEWELS OF ENGLAND

Omniarts of Colorado
Souvenir or collector quality, coronation sets, St. Edward's, Imperial State, Prince of Wales', Queen Victoria's, Queen Mother's and British Imperial Crown of India crowns, Spencer tiara, Charles II scepter, orb, ring and bracelets. George IV diadem, Honours of Scotland, ampulla and spoon, scepter with dove. Others available.

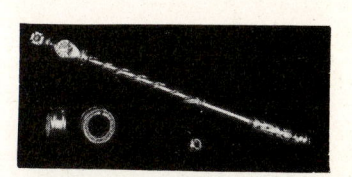

FOR FAST SERVICE, VISIT YOUR LOCAL MINIATURES SHOP

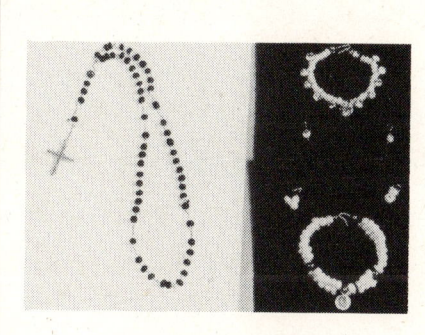

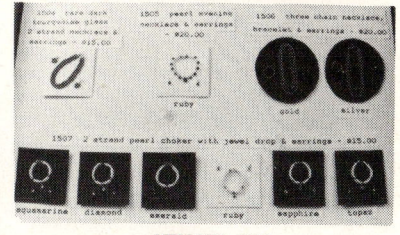

JEWELRY

Omniarts of Colorado
Suggested Retail Price: $12-$15 finished Necklaces (with earrings) that unclasp to fit on a doll. Made of tiny beads and pearls with rhinestones or genuine precious stones. Rosaries and genuine pearls also available. Many colors.

Kitchen

HOURGLASS

Clare-Bell Brass Works
Suggested Retail Price: $24.80
Catalog No. 1730100
Solid brass hourglass with white sand that actually pours through glass.

STONEWARE

Butt Hinge Pottery
Wheel-thrown stoneware miniatures capturing the spirit of traditional New England pottery for use in many dollhouse settings from the kitchen and bedroom to the garden or general store. Wholesale only. See your local dealer for further information.

1" Scale Accessories

THE MINIATURES CATALOG, Fourteenth Edition 259

KITCHEN NECESSITIES

Betty's Wooden Miniatures
Shown are some of our kitchen needs. All are original and handmade by us in the U.S.A.

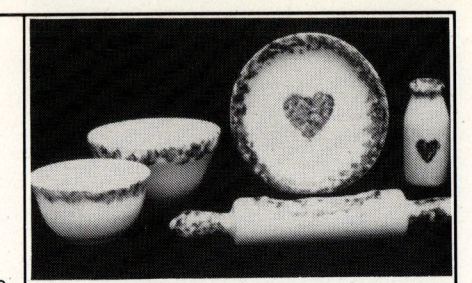

CERAMIC SPONGEWARE

"Krafts" by Betty Jean
An assortment of blue and white spongeware pieces. Special orders done in other colors.

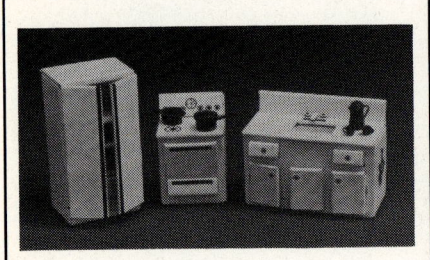

KITCHEN ACCESSORIES

Jack and June's Mini-Many Things
Metal top pastry table by Jack and also many handcrafted wooden accessories for the country kitchen. Kitchen linens available in assorted prints and colors.

KITCHEN KIT

Corri Products
Suggested Retail Price: $3.50 plus shipping
Corri kitchen kits are basic die cut forms of snowy white corrugated fiberboard and when assembled form a stove, sink and refrigerator. Sink faucets and trim are included in the kit. They are fun to put together and we furnish detailed instructions. Our other furniture kits are for bedroom, dining room, bathroom and living room. Send $2 for catalog of our complete line and local dealers.

BEER MUG

Linden Swiss Miniatures
Catalog No. 639
One mug per package. Has a frosted look. Instructions for making mug look crystal clear. See your local dealer. American made.

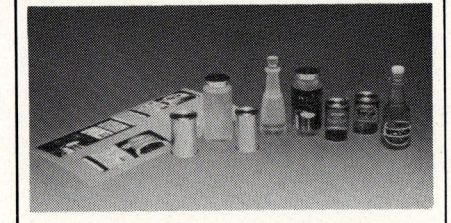

CREAMER AND SAUCES

Linden Swiss Miniatures
Catalog No. 1209. Stock your shelves with realistic cans with details such as rims and circular indentations on top. Jars are hollow. American made. Easy instructions for assembly. See your local dealer.

FINISHED CANNED GOODS

Linden Swiss Miniatures
Scale: 1", Material: Metal
Catalog No. 201
For the modern kitchen. An assortment of seven finished cans and one jar. Ready to be placed in the pantry. American made. See your local dealer.

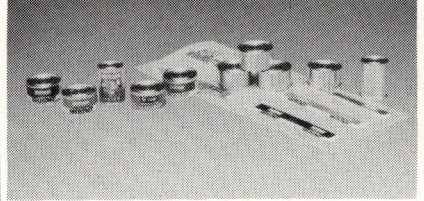

OYSTERS AND SHRIMP

Linden Swiss Miniatures
Catalog No. 1202. Food from the sea! We have twelve kits with modern canned goods to chose from. Easy instructions for assembly. All products are American made. See your local dealer.

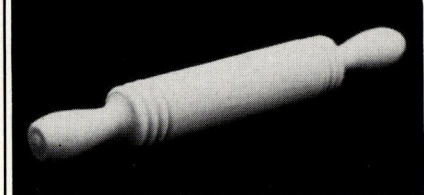

ROLLING PIN

Miniature House
Suggested Retail Price: $.50
Catalog No. MH2055
This old-fashioned rolling pin is made of wood and is true to 1" scale.

KITCHEN TOOLS

Monkey Business
Authentic accessories for your kitchen counter. From our cookie cutters, egg beater, silverware, potato and peeler, waffle iron, butter dish, etc. Send for our brochure.

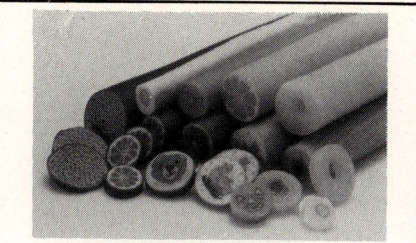

CANDY, COOKIE & FOOD DESIGNS

Donna Smolik's Designs
Suggested Retail Price: $1.75-$4.25 each. Candies, fruits, vegetables, meats - slice your own with a single-edged razor blade. Can be used in 1", 1/2" or 1/4" scales.

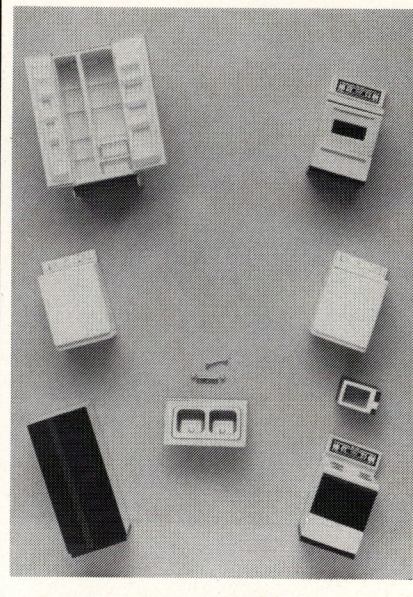

COUNTRY KITCHEN WARE

By Sir Thomas Thumb
Many beautiful hand-crafted pieces including: wooden bucket, slaw cutter, pie-board, rolling pin, carved wooden bowls, grain scoop, apple-butter paddle, etc. Catalog

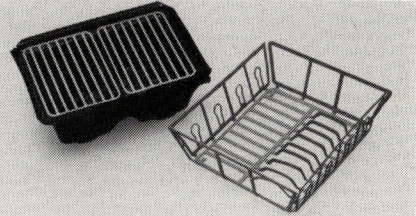

KITCHEN ACCESSORIES

Young World Studio
Dish drainer and hibachi grill in 1/12 dollhouse scale. Perfect additions to your miniature kitchen. Free catalog with order. Dish drainer; $6.50, hibachi with two utensils; $15. Add $2 S&H.

APPLIANCES

Plastruct
Contemporary appliances in three price ranges - budget refrigerator, stove, microwave, washer and dryer do-it-yourself kits; quality refrigerator, stove, washer and dryer (pictured) and collector quality refrigerator and stove with functioning doors and shelves (also pictured).

PRESERVES JARS

Vernon Pottery
Suggested Retail Price: $9/ea. + $2 S&H
Charming slip-trailed fruit made a perfect label. Our preserves jars are sweet little examples of the 19th century originals and fit neatly in your cupboard. Catalog $2.

CLEAN-UP NEEDS

Wee Wonders
Mop and bucket, dish pans with dirty dishes, laundry tubs and dog in a tub of suds.

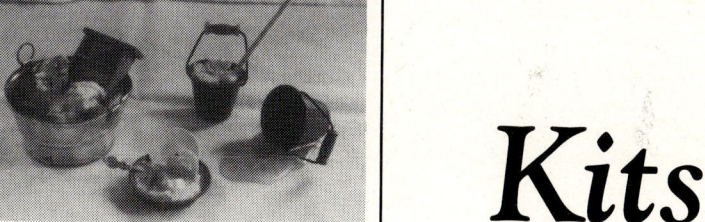

Kits

ASSORTED KITS

All Through The House, Amy Robinson
Suggested Retail Price: $2 to $8 plus S&H
Kits available for all accessories shown and more not shown. 150 more handcrafted accessories for your mini home. Send LSASE for mailer.

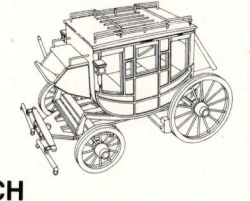

WESTERN STAGECOACH

Midwest Carriage
Suggested Retail Price: $17.95 kit
Dimensions: 9-1/2" x 6-1/4" x 4-3/4"
Authentic western stagecoach with wooden wheels. Precut plywood and hardwood pieces, steel fasteners, detailed assembly and finishing instructions included.

1" SCALE WAGON KITS

Rondel Wood Products
Specializing in making wagon and carriage kits in 1" scale. Kits include scale blueprints, instructions, pre-cut basswood patterns, hardware, wooden wheels and hubs. Shown is Peddler's Wagon #0071.

1" Scale Accessories

THE MINIATURES CATALOG, Fourteenth Edition 261

Leather

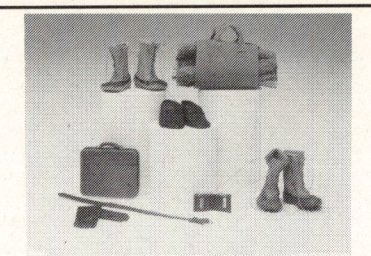

LEATHER ACCESSORIES

All Through The House, Amy Robinson
Dirty boots on paper $12, log carrier $3.75, boots $10, men's shoes $10, brief case $5, wallet $3, belt $2.50, men's gloves $2.50 and more. Send LSASE for mailer.

SHOES AND BOOTS

The Doll's Cobbler
Suggested Retail Price: $10 - $25
Colonial to Contemporary all leather, authentic and realistic by Sylvia Rountree, IGMA Fellow. Shoemaker since 1970. Some available in 1/2" scale.

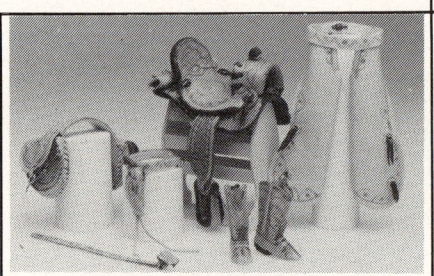

HAND-TOOLED LEATHER

Jan's Small World
Suggested Retail Price: $4 and up
Saddle, chaps, saddlebags, holster, cowboy boots and belt hand tooled from fine leather add just the right touch to your western setting. Retail and wholesale.

EQUIPALES FURNITURE

Maison des Maison
Equipales furniture, leather and reed. Various colors of leather available. Navajo sterling coffee set and oak trastero.

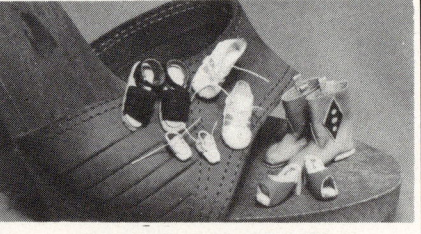

SHOES AND BOOTS

Alice Zinn
Suggested Retail Price: $3.50 to $18
Dancing shoes, ballet, toe, exercise, child and women's tap shoes, sandals, slippers, boots and saddle shoes. All sports shoes. Genuine leather. American made.

Interested in Becoming a Professional Miniatures Handcrafter? Contact the Cottage Industry Miniaturists Trade Association

CIMTA
P.O. Box 5071
New Haven, CT 06525

Lighting Fixtures & Lamps

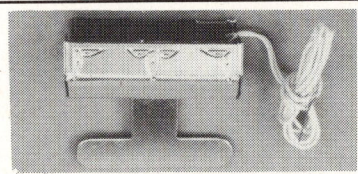

BRASS PICTURE LAMP

Cir-Kit Concepts, Inc.
Suggested Retail Price: $9.98. Catalog No. CK5003.
Dimensions: 7/8"W x 1/4"D x 5/16"H
Material: Solid brass
Decorative brass picture lamp for lighting miniature pictures and paintings. Mounts on top of frame. Connects to any 12V electrical system. 8" wires. Draws 60 ma.

262   Prices are approximate and subject to change.

3-ARM HURRICANE CHANDELIER
Clare-Bell Brass Works
Suggested Retail Price: $76.25
Catalog No. 1852120
Comes with tall clear glass chimneys. Includes ceiling plate and 2" of chain.

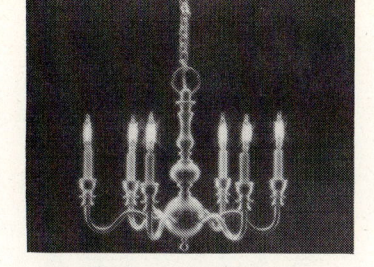

6-ARM CHANDELIER
Clare-Bell Brass Works
Suggested Retail Price: $76.25
Catalog No. 1850120
Solid brass, gold plated. Includes ceiling plate and 2" of chain. Also available in non-electric and replaceable bulbs.

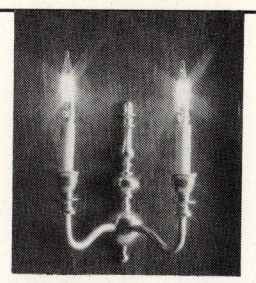

COLONIAL WALL SCONCE
Clare-Bell Brass Works
Suggested Retail Price: $31.70
Catalog No. 1853120
Solid brass. Sold singly 1" to 1' scale, gold plated. Matches the 6-arm chandelier. Replaceable bulbs available.

ELECTRIC CANDLES, HEX BASE
Clare-Bell Brass Works
Suggested Retail Price: $16.70
Catalog No. 1800123
Solid brass electric candles. Sold in pairs. Gold plated. Replaceable bulbs available.

ELECTRIC CANDLES, ROUND BASE
Clare-Bell Brass Works
Suggested Retail Price: $16.15
Catalog No. 1800121
Solid brass electric candles. Sold in pairs. Gold plated. Also available in non-electric and replaceable bulbs.

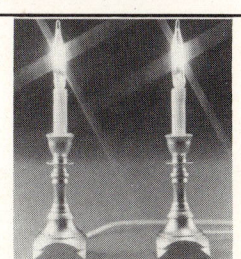

ELECTRIC CANDLES, SQUARE BASE
Clare-Bell Brass Works
Suggested Retail Price: $16.15
Catalog No. 1800123
Solid brass electric candles. Sold in pairs. Gold plated. Replaceable bulbs available.

HURRICANE WALL SCONCE
Clare-Bell Brass Works
Suggested Retail Price: $11
Catalog No. 1771120
Solid brass, gold plated, and brass non-electric round base. Sold singly.

WALL SCONCES, ROUND
Clare-Bell Brass Works
Suggested Retail Price: $15.85
Catalog No. 1770121
Solid brass. 1" to 1' scale. Replaceable bulbs available.

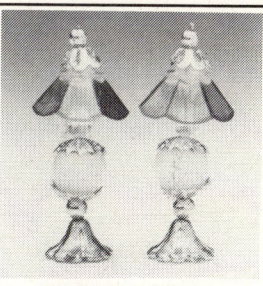

TABLE LAMPS
Miniature House
Suggested Retail Price: $3.10
Catalog No. MH613
These cute non-electric lamps come in assorted colors and styles. Two per package.

KADELI "MINIATURE WORKSHOP" KITS
JAF Miniatures
Kits teach how to easily assemble miniature chandeliers, lamps and accessories. Directions and materials included.

October National Dollhouse & Miniatures Month

1" Scale Accessories

THE MINIATURES CATALOG, Fourteenth Edition — 263

Living Room

CERAMICS

Ron Benson Miniatures
Sculptures, candlesticks, dogs, cats, animals, Staffordshire and Worcester figurines. 18th and 19th century. American made.

STERLING SILVER ACCESSORIES

Maison des Maison
Art deco sterling silver designed exclusively for Maison des Maison by Jeff Wise including centerpiece bowl, candelabra, wine bucket and stand, vases, tortiere lamp and other pieces.

LOOKING FOR SOMETHING SPECIAL? CHECK WITH YOUR LOCAL MINIATURES SHOP!

Metalware

COLLECTOR'S SHOWCASE/ORIENTAL ART

Ligia's Miniatures
Fine silver bowls and boxes Faberge style. Sterling spoons and flatware. Candlesticks with cobalt blue enamel. Oriental design rosewood screens with enamel on copper.

SILVER TRAYS

Falcon Collectible Miniatures
Suggested Retail Price: See your dealer
These beautiful trays come in a variety of sizes and styles and really dress up your table. Manufacturers will find these perfect for displaying food products. Custom orders welcome. Quantity discounts available to dealers.

HALLMARKED SILVERWARE

Ken Palmer
Suggested Retail Price: £4-£80 plus shipping
A range of hallmarked English sterling in 1" scale. Silver artifacts, silver mounted porcelain, working bracket clock and more.

Mirrors and Screens

ORIENTAL SCREENS
Dollhouse Doll-ups
Suggested Retail Price: $15 - $60
Silk embroidered screen available in two to six panels. Also glass with wood screen and small round screens with Oriental theme. Limited quantities available.

MIRRORS
Falcon Collectible Miniatures
Suggested Retail Price: See your dealer
Our line of Victorian style, 24K gold plated mirrors are available in assorted styles and sizes, very ornate to simply elegant. Make them part of your dollhouse decor today! Quantity discounts available to dealers.

MIRROR PANELS AND SKYLIGHTS
Model Builders Supply
Some of MBS's skylights are reflected in our mirror panels. They are 4" x 12" x 1mm thick, easily cut with a knife, two per package for $7.50. Skylights from $2.25 to $3.95, Canadian prices. U.S. customers, see "Plastruct".

GILDED ORNATE MIRRORS AND PICTURE FRAMES
Unique Miniatures
This wide selection provides ornate mirrors and picture frames to suit any taste. The ornate mirrors come with distortion free mirrors of unbreakable plexiglas. The picture frames are also available with mirrors. Many styles to choose from. Send $2 for complete catalog. Made in U.S.A.

Miscellaneous

STORAGE BOXES
Philip E. Bugosh
Sug: Retail Price: See your local dealer
Storage box sets come in several styles and include two sizes of multi-color boxes. Handcrafted.

1" Scale Accessories

THE MINIATURES CATALOG, *Fourteenth Edition* 265

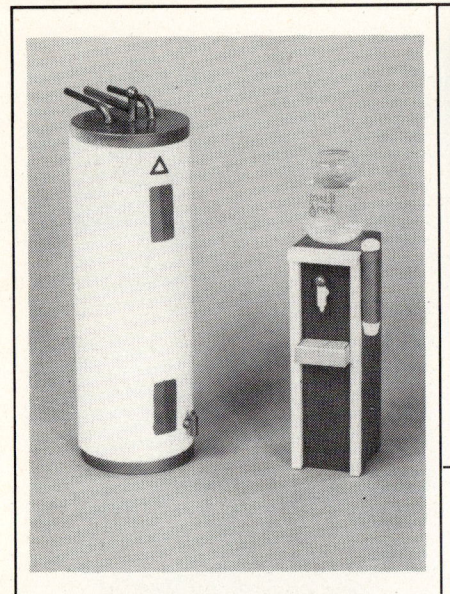

HOT WATER HEATERS
WATER COOLERS

B B Fine, Inc.
Suggested Retail Price: $20 plus shipping
Water coolers for home or office with cup holder and drip tray. One inch size has distilled water in it (also comes in 1/2" scale size). Hot water heaters are perfect for basement or laundry room for that finishing touch. Comes in both 1" and 1/2" sizes.

PICNIC BASKETS

Al Chandronnait Custom Miniatures
Suggested Retail Price: $25 - $28 Ppd.
Beautifully handcrafted picnic basket available in two scales. The 1" scale picnic basket is 2-1/4"L x 1-3/8"W, $28; the 1/2" scale basket is 1-1/8"L x 11/16"W, $25.

CLOISONNE ACCESSORIES

Dollhouse Doll-ups
Suggested Retail Price: $8 - $30
A cloisonne mirror or your favorite portrait, in an approximately 2-1/2" square frame is perfect above the fireplace in the Victorian parlor.

ORIENTAL FIGURES AND BUILDINGS

Dollhouse Doll-ups
"Mud" people and buildings with stands come from the Orient. Oriental books, bonsai trees and money trees and new topiary animals are new items being shown for the first time. An exclusive of Dollhouse Doll-ups.

ASSORTED ACCESSORIES

Cathy's Handcrafted Miniature Accessories
Handcrafted accessories for inside and outside the house. Bath mat and towel sets, laundry baskets, grocery bags, glasses, knitting, garden hoses, trimmed mailboxes, garbage cans and much more.

BASKETS

Garcia & Velez Co.
Horse hair and straw baskets handmade in Columbia, South America. 1" scale, assorted colors. Smallest - 1/8", largest - 2". We also carry hats. Imported.

PENNANTS

Jacqueline's Wholesale
Pennants for all of the major colleges and universities. Authentic colors, official designs. Ideal for den or boy's room. Many uses outside the dollhouse.

1992 CALENDARS

Jacqueline's Wholesale
Select from 30 different full-color designs: scenic spots, animals and birds, famous people and many more. A separate page for each month of the year.

ACCESSORY SAMPLING

Handcraft Designs, Inc.
Suggested Retail Price: See your dealer. Catalog Nos. from left to right and top to bottom: 2033, 6706, 2019, 2029B, 6714, H238, 6910, H250, 6934, 6985, 6986, 6957.
This sampling of accessories offered by Handcraft Designs demonstrates the range of offerings available from a line that includes both proprietary items as well as a carefully selected grouping of "open market" products. Materials range from fine handpainted ceramics through silver and gold plated items to brass, zinc die cast, naturals, pressed metals and cast resin. There are items for every room in the house and every historical period, with special emphasis on tabletop accessories and fireplace accessories.

BASEBALL CARDS

Jacqueline's Wholesale
Set of eight different full-color baseball cards. Perfect for boy's room or card collector. Colorful, inexpensive and unique.

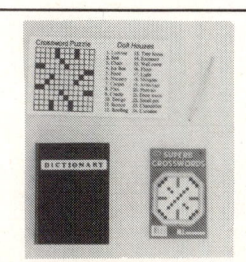

CROSSWORD PUZZLE SET

Jacqueline's Wholesale
Includes miniature crossword puzzle in which all clue words are dollhouse related. Also in the set: crossword magazine, dictionary and sharp pencil with eraser.

DECORATOR WASTEBASKETS

Jacqueline's Wholesale
Handsome in any room. Select from a dozen colorful designs. The antique map wastebasket in parchment, gold and black is elegant in the study.

MISCELLANEOUS ACCESSORIES

Jack and June's Mini-Many Things
Many handcrafted items available and orders for custom work will be considered.

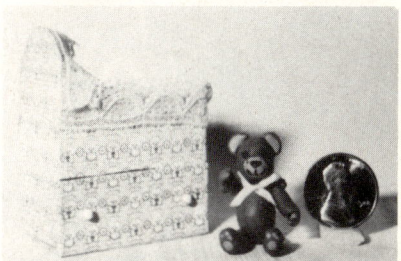

Simulated grapevine wreaths are easily formed from dark brown, waxed cord, wrapped around a large dowel or a battery. After sliding the coil off the dowel or battery it is twisted slightly then bound with a shorter length of cord as shown. To finish off add a few dried flowers and a bow of ribbon.

DIANA PUMMILL, OTTERVILLE, MO

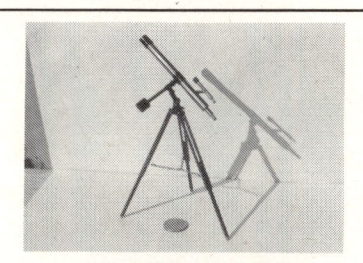

TELESCOPE AND KALEIDOSCOPES

Ligia's Miniatures
World's smallest kaleidoscope! Brass, in four styles at $32 ea. Rosewood stands, $19.50. Equatorial telescope, brass on wood tripod; $75. Beautiful replica follows any star.

KITS 'N CABOODLE

Jean's Wee Things
Catalog No. 1989
Unusual kits available: 1-1/2" dressed Raggedy Ann & Andy $15, jointed teddy bears $5, trunks for raggedy or teddy $10, Easter cake $10, Easter basket $2, ribbon candy $2.50, poinsettias $3, shell tulips $5, Christmas wreaths $3-$5, daffodils $3, and more! Brochure $1 and SASE to Kits N' Caboodle c/o Jean's Wee Things.

1" Scale Accessories

THE MINIATURES CATALOG, Fourteenth Edition 267

HANDSCULPTED MINIATURES

Kitty's Kreations
Kitty's Kreations specializes in animals, babies and children with pets. As shown in photo, each item is intricately detailed, made from hydrostone. Please mention "The Miniatures Catalog" when sending $1 for our catalog.

DECOR ITEMS

The Lawbre Company
Suggested Retail Price: $7-$55
Order Nos. 0600-0611
These items are carefully handpainted to accent inside or outside settings. Some pieces are wired and all have exquisite detail. American made.

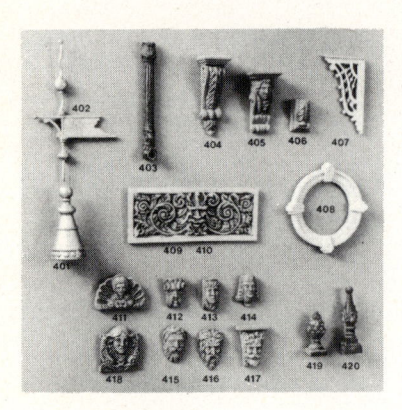

MINIATURE MONEY

The Mini Money Mint, Henry & Cheri Ackles
Suggested Retail Price: $2 for a sheet of 84 1" scale bills or 49 1/8 scale bills
Give your dolls the cash they need for all their mini-needs! Six denominations. The money is accurate, precise, double-sided and the only money copyrighted by the Copyright Office for miniaturists.

CANDY, COOKIE & FOOD DESIGNS

Donna Smolik's Designs
Suggested Retail Price: $1.75-$4.25 each.
Candies, fruits, vegetables, meats - slice your own with a single-edged razor blade. Can be used in 1", 1/2" or 1/4" scales.

DECORATIVE ARCHITECTURAL DETAILS

The Lawbre Company
Suggested Retail Price: $4-$14
Catalog Nos. 0401-0420
These are to add the finishing touch. All are cast products with various finishes appropriate for the item.

MUSEUM QUALITY WAGON MODELS

Wagonmaster Plans
Our plans are scaled from full size vehicles and are not "simplified" in any way. Every detail of construction is shown including the ironwork. Full size construction drawings are available in 1/8" and 1/2" scale. Send $1 for catalog/brochure.

FILLED GARBAGE CANS

Wee Wonders
Suggested Retail Price: $8.50
Filled trash can with curious kitty or puppy. Trash bags, spilled or upright - $4.

Prices are approximate and subject to change.

WORKING STEPLADDER

Timberbrook Wood Products
Suggested Retail Price: $6.80
Made of white pine, it's 5" high and has a movable paint tray. It comes completely assembled. See your dealer or write for more information. Order No. 3050.

COCKTAIL BAR SET

Timberbrook Wood Products
Cocktail bar: 5" with shelf and glass edge. Unpainted. Also available in 10" length. Retail $16.80. Bar rail: Brass rail compliments your cocktail bar. Retail $4.20. Also available in 10" length. Bar stools: Swivel stool. Unpainted, ready-to-decorate. Retail $4.20. Bar mirror: Glass mirror with molded, unpainted wooden frame. Retail $5.30.

ACCESSORIES

Young World Studio
Geni bottle trimmed in gold and silver with simulated ruby dot, $8. Shakespeare bust, $12. Skull on book, $15. Set of all three, $30. These are perfect for your miniature home. Add $2 shipping.

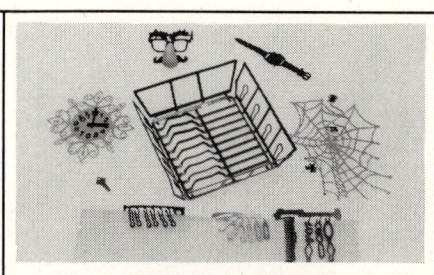

ACCESSORIES

Young World Studio
Spider web, $4.50. Dish drainer, $6.50. Bobby pins and safety pins, $4.50. Digital watch, $4.50. Keys to your house, $4. Groucho mask, $6.50. Clock, $4.50. Barrette and comb set, $4. Add $2 shipping.

SCHOOL & OFFICE SUPPLIES

Alice Zinn
Elmer's glue, Scotch tape, composition and looseleaf books, stapler set, other stationary, art and office supplies, etc.. American made.

Musical

FOR FAST SERVICE, VISIT YOUR LOCAL MINIATURES SHOP

STEREOS

Aztec Imports, Inc.
Wholesale only. Finally a realistic stereo reasonably priced! Cabinet and detached speakers are available in mahogany (T3258), oak (T4258), walnut (T6258), and white (T5258). Great for bedrooms, living rooms and dens!

KEYBOARD INSTRUMENTS

Miniatures by Carol
Suggested Retail Price: $75 to $125
Organs, pianos, harpsichords in mahogany, cherry or walnut.

1" Scale Accessories

THE MINIATURES CATALOG, Fourteenth Edition

Needlework & Linens

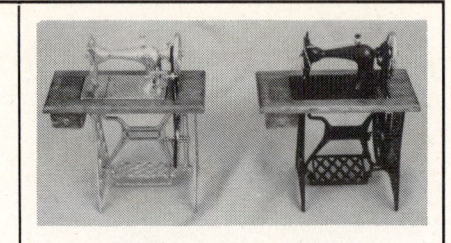

SEWING MACHINES
Aztec Imports, Inc.
Wholesale only. Made to scale!! These turn-of-the-century sewing machines are perfect for bedrooms, attics or shops. Available in silver and oak (T7999) or black and oak (T8000).

PILLOW KITS
Corner House
Suggested Retail Price: Angel and Poinsettia pillows #30 silk gauze; Log Cabin pillow #40 silk gauze - $9 plus $2 S&H Needlepoint and cross-stitch kits designed for varying skills. Large selection of needlework books, silk, cotton and organdy ribbons.

LIVING ROOM ENSEMBLE
Custom House of Needle Arts
Suggested Retail Price: $8
Catalog No. 51. Materials: Linen fabric and wool crewel yarn. Includes drapery, bell pull, sofa and chair covers adaptable to any style furniture. Also available: Bedroom ensemble which includes spread, canopy, drapery, picture, bureau scarf. Suggested Retail Price: $8. Catalog No. 39.

FRENCH KNOT RUG KITS
Renee Bowen Miniaturist
Twelve authentic patterns of New England hooked rugs. Kits include all materials, easy to follow directions and tips for creating special effects. Easy, fast, fun! Wholesale or retail inquiries invited. Brochure available.

SEWING ACCESSORIES
Dorothy's Doo-Dads
Suggested Retail Price: $5.25
Bolt of fabric, pin cushion, tape measure, buttons, ribbons, trim, embroidery floss, thread, scissors, pattern and envelope. Many other handmade items available.

CREWEL EMBROIDERY
Objects d' Art
Suggested Retail Price: $8-$14 (kits), $20-$150 (finished)
Oil paintings, crewel embroidery pictures and embroidery kits. All items in 1" scale. Catalog available.

TRANSGRAPH-X®
L J Originals, Inc.
Suggested Retail Price: $15
Catalog No. 30501
Use TRANSGRAPH-X clear plastic grid overlays to instantly convert photos or drawings into charts for miniature counted needleart. Kit includes six reusable graphs plotted 5, 11, 14, 18, 22 and 25 squares per inch; instructions and zip-lock storage bag.

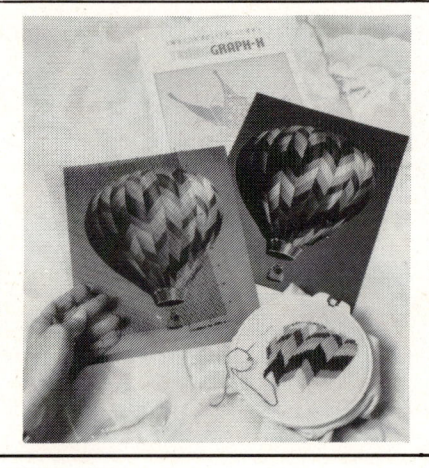

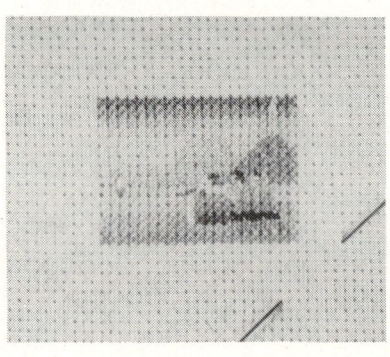

Prices are approximate and subject to change.

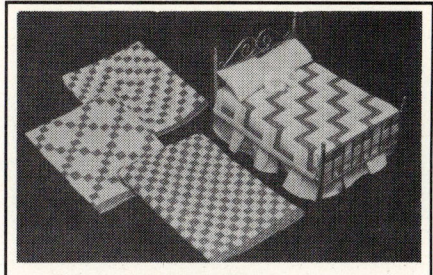

Nursery

QUILTS
Vermont Home Quilts
Suggested Retail: $2.25-$50
Quilts, pillow cases, throw pillows and brass beds. Quilts available for crib, single and double beds in a variety of colors. All cotton in 1/12th scale.

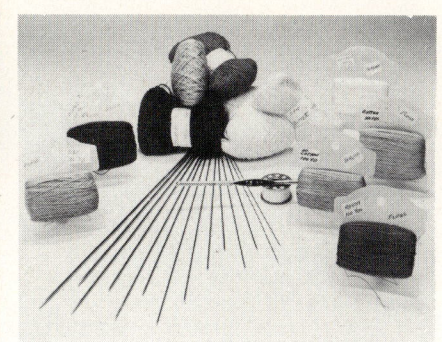

NEEDLEPOINT SUPPLIES
Wee Three
Needlework supplies for 1" to 1' scale. To create your needlework projects, here are size 2/0 to 7/0 knitting needles, small sewing and beading needles, fine yarns and threads for knitting, crocheting, sewing and tatting. Send $2 for catalog of supplies.

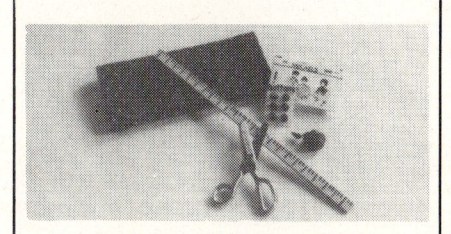

SEWING ACCESSORIES
Wee Wonders
Buttons, fabric bolts, pin cushions, patterns, yardsticks and spools of thread.

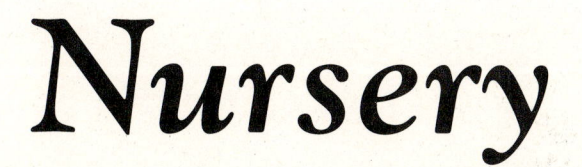

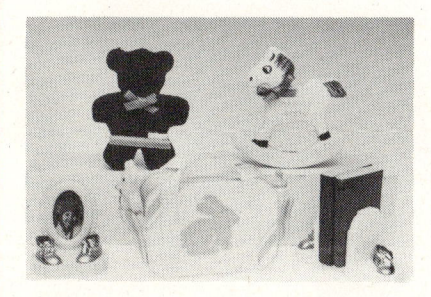

NURSERY NEEDS
Betty's Wooden Miniatures
Our baby room accessories are all original and handmade by us in the U.S.A

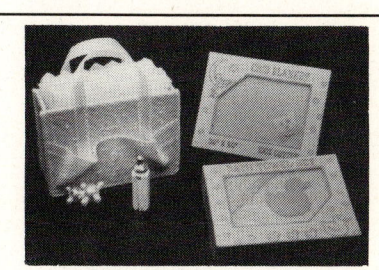

BABY ACCESSORIES
Philip E. Bugosh
Suggested Retail Price: See your local dealer.
Diaper bag with accessories and baby gift sets are available in a variety of styles and colors.

COMPLETE NURSERY LAYETTE
By Barb
Crib bumpers, quilt, pillow, receiving blanket, hooded towel, bunting, diaper bag, toys and more. Everything a new mother and baby will need. Made in the U.S.A.

BIRTH CERTIFICATE
Diminutive Specialties
Suggested Retail Price: $5, plus shipping. Birth certificate can be filled in with name, birth date, weight and length. Please use inches. The certificate comes in a white frame.

NURSERY RUGS
By Diminutive Specialties
Suggested Retail Price: $15 plus shipping. Petite point rug wtih choice of name, car, assorted bears, clown or toy train. Choice of colors.

THE MINIATURES CATALOG, Fourteenth Edition 271

1" Scale Accessories

BABY LAYETTE

Rhonda Peden
Suggested Retail Price: See your local dealer
Sacques, kimonos and layette items in baby colors and fabrics. For contemporary and vintage nurseries. Can be worn or displayed.

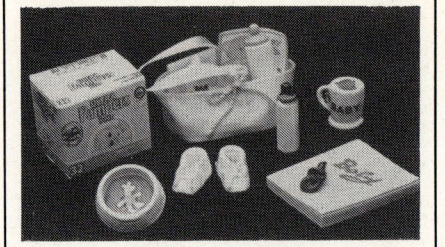

BABY SUPPLIES

Royal Miniatures
Suggested Retail Price: $1.50 - $4
Shown is a small sampling from our wide selection of baby needs. Wholesale only. Imported.

Interested in Becoming a Professional Miniatures Handcrafter?
Contact the Cottage Industry Miniaturists Trade Association

CIMTA
P.O. Box 5071
New Haven, CT 06525

Paintings, Prints, Watercolors, Etchings

ORIGINAL OILS & WATERCOLORS

Helen Joan Hairrell
Suggested Retail Price: $12.50-$35
Painted upon request - oils, watercolors, inks. Landscapes, florals, pets and birds from your photo. Send LSASE and $2 for brochure and order information. Refundable with first order.

B.K.'s Mini Frame-Up
Framed Pictures—These prints are processed to look like oil paintings. They include wood frames (some decorated). Portraits, landscapes, and still life are featured. All handmade. Suggested Retail Price: $3.00-$15.00. American made.

NEW ORLEANS ETCHINGS IN WATERCOLOR

House of Broel Miniatures
Suggested Retail Price: $15 ppd.
Original signed etchings of New Orleans in watercolor complete with 1/4" walnut finish. Wooden frame, acetate covering and matte. SASE for more information.

ORIGINAL MINIATURE PAINTINGS

"J" Designs by Phyllis "Joy" Gray
Suggested Retail Price: $15 - $150
All subjects, styles and media (including Egg Tempera), scratchboard, pastels and drawings. Framed. SASE for information.

ETCHINGS

John Anthony Miller
Suggested Retail Price: $75
John Anthony Miller original limited edition copperplate etchings and engravings. Hand-printed and hand-signed.

Prices are approximate and subject to change.

MINIATURE ARTWORK

Innovative Photography
Suggested Retail Price: $3 - $7.50
Color maps; United States, World, North American territories and three antique maps; George Washington, color; Abraham Lincoln, black/white, two sizes framed or unframed. American made.

WOOD FRAMES

Perrault Miniatures
Miniature wood frames to show off your prized miniature artwork. Frames are unpainted, you finish to your liking. 23 styles to choose from.

Paper Accessories

October National Dollhouse & Miniatures Month

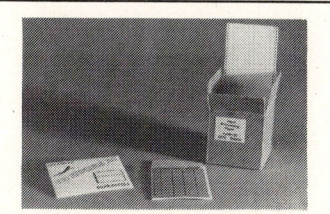

OFFICE SUPPLIES

Philip E. Bugosh
Sug: Retail Price: See your local dealer
Some of our office supplies include express mail envelopes, inter-office mail envelopes and a box of computer paper. All are handcrafted.

INKWELL WITH QUILL

Clare-Bell Brass Works
Suggested Retail Price: $9.75
Catalog No. 1728100
Brass inkwell holds genuine quill.

Period Accessories

STONEWARE

Butt Hinge Pottery
Wheel-thrown stoneware miniatures capturing the spirit of traditional New England pottery for use in many dollhouse settings from the kitchen and bedroom to the garden or general store. Wholesale only. See your local dealer for further information.

1" Scale Accessories

THE MINIATURES CATALOG, **Fourteenth Edition** 273

CERAMICS
Ron Benson Miniatures
Porcelain 17th, 18th and 19th Century reproductions, period sculptures, bowls and candlesticks. Bennington pitcher c. 1850. Staffordshire items. American made.

CERAMICS
Ron Benson Miniatures
Sevres urns c. 1760. Probably produced for Versailles, in royal rose or cobalt blue. Under 1" tall.

WALNUT WALL ACCESSORIES
The Fretworker, Kirk Ratajesak
Suggested Retail Price: $12 - $18
These ornate walnut wall accessories are handcrafted by Kirk. Furniture pieces are also available.

VICTORIAN STYLE REGISTER COVERS
Laser Tech
Suggested Retail Price: $4.95 per package of two
Made of 1/32" plexiglass. Elegant brass colored heat register covers modeled after the scrolled pattern popular in the Victorian era.

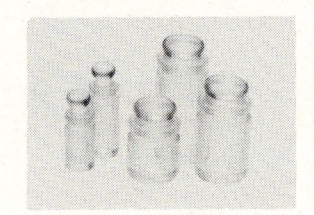

APOTHECARY JARS
Linden Swiss Miniatures
Catalog No. 600. Set of five apothecary jars, each jar a different size. American made. See your local dealer.

CANNING JARS
Linden Swiss Miniatures
Catalog No. 530.
Old fashioned canning jars. Three per package. Three quart, one quart and pint size. Each jar has simulated zinc lid. American made. See your local dealer.

FINISHED CANNED GOODS
Linden Swiss Miniatures
Scale: 1", Material: Metal
Catalog No. 200
An assortment of seven finished vintage canned goods and one jar. Ready to put on your shelf. American made. See your local dealer.

SALT-GLAZED STONEWARE
Vernon Pottery
Suggested Retail Price: $9 - $18
Museum-quality reproductions of 19th century North American salt-glazed stoneware. Each of our 1/12 scale pots is made on the potters wheel and decorated freehand with cobalt blue clay slip. Choose from over 165 historically accurate folk art designs that are collectors favorites. Butterchurns with walnut dashers, crocks, storage jars and preserves jars with lids, jugs and water coolers with cork stoppers, pitchers and more. Catalog $2.

FISH AND VEGETABLES
Linden Swiss Miniatures
Catalog No. 1107
Just one of nine kits of vintage canned goods. Instructions for easy assembly. All products are American made. See your local dealer.

STOKELY'S FINEST FRUITS
Linden Swiss Miniatures
Catalog No. 1102. We have vintage canned goods from 1933 to 1938 - Stokely brand. Comes in kit form with instructions for easy assembly. All products are American made. See your local dealer.

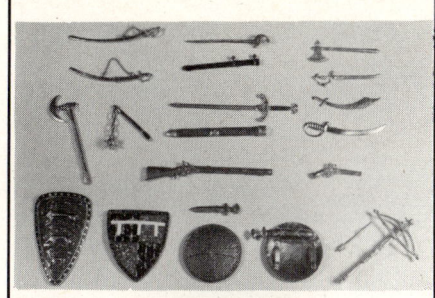

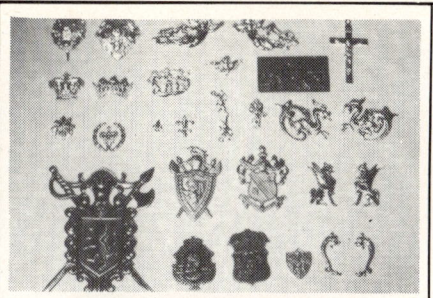

SHIELDS AND CRESTS
Omniarts of Colorado
Suggested Retail Price: Under $3
Wall and furniture trims, shields, crests, etc., objects d'art, cast candlesticks. American made.

TAPESTRIES
Omniarts of Colorado
Suggested Retail Price: $6-$10
Woven Gobelin tapestries from France, $6 each. Tapestry mounted on a decorative rod, $10 each. Imported.

ARMS AND ARMOR
Omniarts of Colorado
Suggested Retail Price: $5-$300 finished
These arms and armor are handcrafted and made of cast metal. Included in the selection are shields, weapons, cannon and suits of armor. Also available are plastic model armor kits in six styles. American made and imported.

ACCESSORIES
Alice Zinn
Contemporary shoes, hats, clothing, leather goods, toys, nursery items, stationery, bath shop, audio/visual, garden, sporting goods, outdoor birds, pets and Oriental accessories. American made.

FOR FAST SERVICE, VISIT YOUR LOCAL MINIATURES SHOP

Personal Items

HAIR CARE SET
Jacqueline's Wholesale
Hair care set helps dollhouse beauties look their best! Set includes magazine of hair styles, brush rollers with hairpins, blowdryer and Fergie-style hair bow.

Photographs

MINI PHOTOGRAPHS
Diminutive Specialties
Suggested Retail Price: $6 for color or $5 for black & white plus $1.50 shipping
Any size photograph can be miniaturized to represent the size photo you need. The mini photos range from "snapshot" size to 11" x 14" or larger if you so desire.

1" Scale Accessories

THE MINIATURES CATALOG, *Fourteenth Edition* 275

MINIATURE PHOTOGRAPHY

Jean's Wee Things
Catalog No. 1989.
Your photos miniaturized in albums or frames, in business 10 years, brochure $1 & SASE. Albums with 15 photos $10; "bronzed" baby shoes with two photos $9.

ANTIQUE PORTRAITS

Monkey Business
A selection of eight distinctive antique portraits. Each sold separately. No quantity minimum orders required. All made by us in the USA.

MINIATURE PHOTOGRAPHS

Innovative Photography
Suggested Retail Price: $2.75 - $20
Miniature photographs are unique old photos framed, in folders or in sheets, black/white or sepia. Color antique maps; Gutman babies, Arthur Eisley, Charles Burton Barber, Jesse Willson Smith prints; set of four Currier & Ives "Four Seasons". Large collection of old masters including artists Van Gogh, DaVinci, Degas, Marin, Picasso.

MINIATURE PHOTOGRAPHS

LaCasa Photos
Suggested Retail Price: $3 and up
Miniature photographs in sets, albums and other books (including 1/2" scale books), photos in folders and folder kits, stereoscopes and stereoviews, postcards (33 sets), frames, mats, paperdolls, Victorian paper goods and vintage prints. See your local dealer or send $3 for catalog and price sheet.

Plants & Flowers

PLANTS

Philip E. Bugosh
Sug: Retail Price: See your local dealer
Full realistic ferns and floor plants in 1" and 1/2". Cactus and geranium also available. Handcrafted in quality pots.

PLANTS AND FLOWERS

Cathy's Handcrafted Miniature Accessories
Handcrafted plants, flowerboxes and floral arrangements. Cattails, daffodils, ferns, hyacinths, narcissus, roses, snake plants, spider plants and zinnias.

BRIDAL BOUQUET

Doll House Shoppe
Suggested Retail Price: $18, No. 6307.
Fimo roses, silk and pearls.

FLORAL ARRANGEMENTS

Dollhouse Doll-ups
Suggested Retail Price: $2 - $30
Over 100 different flower arrangements in pots, cloisonne and porcelain vases. Flowers and leaves for bouquets, corsages and plants for your garden are available as individual items or as kits. Hand-made silk.

FLOWERS

Falcon Collectible Miniatures
Suggested Retail Price: See your dealer
Our miniature blooms make it Springtime year round. We have floral arrangements, silk plants, flower vases, window boxes and potted flowers and plant. Quantity discounts available to dealers.

SILK FLOWERS AND PLANTS

Dragonfly International
Our wonderful variety of handmade silk flower arrangements and plants has something for every room and style, inside and out.

CAKES AND FLOWERS

Hanke's House
Make flowers, plants and trees with Pretty Petal Punches using tape, preserved leaves, colored or painted paper. Punches and mini cake catalog, $1.

ASSORTED GREENERY

J. Hermes
Suggested Retail Price: $.50-$3.35
Assorted sponge and lycopodium greenery for exterior and interior use. Use for landscaping to miniature holiday Christmas decor. Assorted natural earth-tone colors, sponge greenery can be used as trees, hedges and shrubs.

TERRA COTTA POTS

Houseworks
Petite terra cotta pots $.95 each. Imported. #8001, tiny flower; #8002, small flower; #8003, urn flower; #8004, fluted flower; #8005, strawberry.

MINI HAPPY RETURNS

Kay's Kollectables
We offer over 60 beautiful florals, bridal bouquets, baskets and 12-volt electrified arrangements. Flowers are individually handmade of fine paper and treated with a pearlized luster to give them a porcelain-like finish. Pictured: Red and pink gardenias and roses in a gold vase, No. 683; medium wicker basket (F) Fall, (S) Spring and (21) mixed pinks, No. 652; bridal bouquet (white, pink, mauve), No. 533. Wholesale only, dealer inquiries welcome. Catalog $2.

1" Scale Accessories

THE MINIATURES CATALOG, Fourteenth Edition   277

BASKETS OF FLOWERS
Robin's Roost
Miniatures for Collectors
Suggested Retail Price: See your dealer
Several styles of filled flower baskets for outdoor use on your patio or in any indoor scene. From tiny ones with pansies to large assortments of flowers.

BRIDAL AND BRIDESMAID'S BOUQUETS
Robin's Roost
Miniatures for Collectors
Suggested Retail Price: See your dealer
Large and small assorted mixed bridal bouquets, small assorted mixed bridesmaid's bouquets, large and small calla lily bridal bouquets.

FLOWER ARRANGEMENTS
Robin's Roost
Miniatures for Collectors
Suggested Retail Price: See your dealer
Flower arrangements in several different color combinations in copper mugs as well as numerous types of Williamsburg arrangements in brass vases.

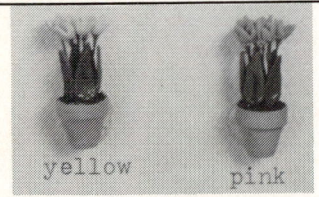

HANDCRAFTED PLANTS
Robin's Roost
Miniatures for Collectors
Suggested Retail Price: See your dealer
Black-eyed susans, yellow and purple crocuses, daffodils, white and yellow daisies, jonquils, candy striped, red, purple, yellow, pink, wine, shocking pink and white tulips in fine quality terra cotta pots.

PANSY FLAT WITH TROWEL
Robin's Roost
Miniatures for Collectors
Suggested Retail Price: See your dealer
Pansy flat with trowel and marker (also available without trowel).

October National Dollhouse & Miniatures Month

FLOWERS AND PLANTS
Wood Products
Suggested Retail Price: See your dealer
All flowers are beautifully handmade in the USA. We carry a wide variety of flowers including: violets, tulips, daffodils, daisies, poinsettias, philodendron, Boston fern, palm, cactus, crocus, roses and much more.

Sculptures & Statues

ADOBE HACIENDA DISPLAY
Goebel Miniatures
A perfect setting for all the figurines from the DeGrazia Collection. Issued in 1989.
Dimensions: 5-1/4"H x 7"W x 4"D.

AMERICAN GOLDFINCH
Goebel Miniatures
Sixth release in the Wildlife Series. Released in 1985. 5/8" high. American made.

APPLE TREE BOY
Goebel Miniatures
First release of this miniature Hummel limited to 10,000. Issued in 1989. Second release, open edition was released in 1990.

AUTUMN BLUE JAY
Goebel Miniatures
Seventh release in the Wildlife Series. Released in 1986. 3/4" high. American made.

ON THE AVENUE
Goebel Miniatures
Fourth sculpture in the Women's Series. Released in 1983. 1" high. American made.

BACKYARD FROLIC
Goebel Miniatures
Fourth release in the Children's Series. Issued in 1983. Size: 3/4". American made.

BAKER
Goebel Miniatures
First release of this miniature Hummel limited to 10,000. Issued in 1990. Second release, open edition to be released in '91.

TO THE BANDSTAND
Goebel Miniatures
Seventh release in the Americana Series. Issued in 1987. Size: 1-3/8". American made. Retired.

BLUMENKINDER "COURTING"
Goebel Miniatures
First release in the Children's Series. Issued in 1980. 3/4" high. American made.

BOTTOM OF THE SIXTH
Goebel Miniatures
Sculpt from the cover design of 1949, April 23rd issue of the *Saturday Evening Post*. Dimensions: 2"H x 1-1/2"W x 1"D. Issued in 1988. American made.

BEAUTIFUL BURDEN
Goebel Miniatures
Issued in 1989. Eleventh release in the DeGrazia Collection. Limited edition of 7500. Size: 7/8" high.

THE BLIND MEN AND THE ELEPHANT
Goebel Miniatures
Fourth release in the Oriental Series. Issued in 1986. Size 1-1/8" high. American made.

BOTTOM DRAWER
Goebel Miniatures
Sculpt from the cover design of 1956, Dec. 29th issue of the *Saturday Evening Post*. Latest addition to the Norman Rockwell Series, issued in 1989. Dimensions: 2"H x 1-1/2"W x 1"D. Dome display not included. American made.

1" Scale Accessories

THE MINIATURES CATALOG, *Fourteenth Edition* **279**

THE BRONCO BUSTER
Goebel Miniatures
One of six releases in the American Frontier Collection. Originally sculpt by Frederic Remington in 1895. Issued in 1987. Size: 1-5/8". American made.

BUILDING BLOCK CASTLE DISPLAY
Goebel Miniatures
Designed exclusively for the Children's Series. Issued in 1990. Dimensions: 5-1/4"H x 6-1/2"W x 3-1/2"D.

CHERRY PICKERS
Goebel Miniatures
From the Historical Series. American made.

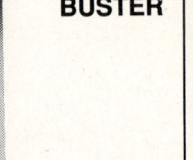

GEPPETTO/FIGARO
Goebel Miniatures
Pinocchio's "father" with Figaro the cat. One of the first five Pinocchio Series figurines. 1-3/8" high. American made.

GIDEON
Goebel Miniatures
One of the first five Pinocchio Series figurines. 3/4" high. American made.

J. W. FOULFELLOW
Goebel Miniatures
One of the first five Pinocchio Series figurines. 1-3/4" high. American made.

JIMINY CRICKET
Goebel Miniatures
One of the first five Pinocchio Series figurines. 3/4" high. American made.

KUAN YIN
Goebel Miniatures
From the Oriental Series. American made.

PINOCCHIO
Goebel Miniatures
One of the first five Pinocchio Series figurines. 15/16" high. American made.

WAITER
Goebel Miniatures
First release of this miniature Hummel limited to 10,000. Issued in 1990. Second release, open edition to be released in 1991.

CAPODIMONTE
Goebel Miniatures
The first sculpture in the Historical Series. Issued in 1980. 1" high. American made.

CARROUSEL RIDE
Goebel Miniatures
Sixth release in the Americana Series. Issued in 1986. 1-1/4" high. American made. Retired.

CENTRAL PARK SUNDAY

Goebel Miniatures
Fifth release in the Americana Series. Issued in 1985, 1" tall. American made. Retired.

CHECK-UP

Goebel Miniatures
Sculpt from the cover design of 1957, Sept. 7th issue of the *Saturday Evening Post.* Dimensions: 2"H x 1-1/2"W x 1"D. American made.

CHINESE TEMPLE LION

Goebel Miniatures
Seventh release in the Oriental Series. Issued in 1990. Size 1" high. American made.

CHIPPING SPARROW

Goebel Miniatures
First in the Wildlife Series, released in 1980. 3/4" high. American made.

CINDERELLA

Goebel Miniatures
First release of this miniature Hummel limited to 10,000. Issued in 1990. Second release, open edition to be released in 1991.

CLOWNING AROUND

Goebel Miniatures
Seventh release in the Children's Series. Issued in 1986. 1" high. American made.

COUNTRY LANDSCAPE DISPLAY

Goebel Miniatures
This display depicts the four seasons. Issued in 1989. Dimensions: 4-1/2" H x 5-1/4" W x 4" D.

DOCTOR AND DOLL

Goebel Miniatures
Sculpt from the cover design of 1929, March 9th issue of the *Saturday Evening Post.* Dimensions: 2"H x 1-1/2"W x 1"D. American made.

DOLL BATH

Goebel Miniatures
First release of this miniature Hummel, limited to 10,000. Issued in 1988. Second release, open edition was released in 1989. Total height is 13/16". American made.

Interested in Becoming a Professional Miniatures Handcrafter? Contact the Cottage Industry Miniaturists Trade Association

CIMTA
P.O. Box 5071
New Haven, CT 06525

DRESDEN DANCER

Goebel Miniatures
First release in the Women's Series. First issued in 1980. 3/4" high. American made.

EIGHT COUNT

Goebel Miniatures
One of six releases in the American Frontier Collection. Our only contemporary piece, sculpt in 1987 by Jim Pounder. Issued in 1987. 1-5/8" high. American made.

1" Scale Accessories

THE MINIATURES CATALOG, Fourteenth Edition 281

THE EMPRESS GARDEN DISPLAY
Goebel Miniatures
An enchanting display for the Oriental series. Issued in 1990. Dimensions: 5-1/4"H x 7-1/2"W x 3-3/4"D.

THE END OF THE TRAIL
Goebel Miniatures
One of six releases in the American Frontier Collection. James Earl Fraser's original was sculpt in 1894. Issued in 1987. 1-3/8" high. American made.

EYES ON THE HORIZON
Goebel Miniatures
Fourth release in the Americana Series. Issued in 1984. American made. Retired.

FARMER WITH DOVES
Goebel Miniatures
Eighth release in the Historical Series. Issued in 1989. 1-9/16" high. American made.

THE FIRST RIDE
Goebel Miniatures
One of six releases in the American Frontier Collection. Originally cast in 1888 by John Rogers. Issued in 1987. 1-1/4" high. American made.

FLORAL BOUQUET POMPADOUR
Goebel Miniatures
Fifth release in the Historical Series. Issued in 1985. 1-1/8" high. American made.

THE GEISHA
Goebel Miniatures
Second release in the Oriental Series. Issued in 1982. 3/4" high. American made.

GENTLEMAN'S FOX HUNT
Goebel Miniatures
Issued in 1990 - ninth release in the Historical Series. Size: 1-1/4" high. Companion piece to The Hunt With Hounds from the Women's Series. American made.

GRANDPA
Goebel Miniatures
Fifth release in the Children's Series. Issued in 1984. American made.

HUMMINGBIRD
Goebel Miniatures
Eleventh release in the Wildlife Series. Issued in 1990. Size 3/4" high. American made.

THE HUNT WITH HOUNDS
Goebel Miniatures
Second release in the Women's Series, released in 1981. 1" high. American made.

LITTLE FIDDLER
Goebel Miniatures
First release of this miniature Hummel, limited to 10,000. Issued in 1988. Second release, open edition was released in 1989. 7/8" high. American made.

Prices are approximate and subject to change.

LITTLE SWEEPER
Goebel Miniatures
First release of this miniature Hummel, limited to 10,000. Issued in 1988. Second release, open edition was released in 1989. 13/16" high. American made.

LITTLE BALLERINA
Goebel Miniatures
Ninth release in the Children's Series. Issued in 1988. 1-1/4". American made.

MALLARD DUCK
Goebel Miniatures
Eighth release in the Wildlife Series. Released in 1986. 3/4" high. American made.

MARBLES CHAMPION
Goebel Miniatures
Sculpt from the cover design of 1939, Sept. 2nd issue of the *Saturday Evening Post*. Issued in 1988. Dimensions: 2"H x 1-1/2"W x 1"D. American made.

MEISSEN PARROT
Goebel Miniatures
Sixth release in the Historical Series. Released in 1987. 1-3/8" high. American made.

MERRY WANDERER
Goebel Miniatures
First release of this miniature Hummel, limited to 10,000. Issued in 1988. Second release open edition was released in 1989. 13/16" high. American made.

MINTON ROOSTER
Goebel Miniatures
Seventh release in the Historical Series. Issued in 1988. 1" high. American made.

MOOR WITH SPANISH HORSE
Goebel Miniatures
Fourth release in the Historical Series. Released in 1984. American made.

THE NIGHT BEFORE CHRISTMAS SERIES
Goebel Miniatures
Available now. Display: Up To The House Top, 4-1/2" H x 5-1/2" W x 3-7/8" D. Figurines: Yule Tree, 2" high. Sugar Plum Girl, 1" high.

NO SWIMMING
Goebel Miniatures
Sculpt from the cover design of 1929, June 15th issue of the *Saturday Evening Post*. Dimensions: 2"H x 1-1/2"W x 1"D. American made.

THE PINOCCHIO SERIES
Goebel Miniatures
Available now. Display: Geppetto's Toy Shop, 7-1/2"H x 9-1/4"W x 4-3/4"D. Figurines: Geppetto/Figaro, 1-1/2" high. Gideon, 1" high.

POSTMAN
Goebel Miniatures
First release of this miniature Hummel, limited to 10,000. Issued in 1989. Second release open edition was released in 1990.

1" Scale Accessories

THE MINIATURES CATALOG, Fourteenth Edition

ROSES
Goebel Miniatures
Fifth sculpture in the Women's Series. Released in 1984. American made.

SHE SOUNDS THE DEEP
Goebel Miniatures
Third release in the Americana Series. Issued in 1983. 1" high. American made. Retired.

SNOW HOLIDAY
Goebel Miniatures
Sixth release in the Children's Series. Issued in 1985. 1/2" high. American made.

THE SNOW WHITE SERIES
Goebel Miniatures
Sold only as a complete set. Display: House in The Woods, 4-3/4" H x 7-3/4" W x 6-5/8" D. Figurines: Snow White, 1-1/2" high, dwarfs, 7/8" high. Limited edition of 19,500.

SPRING ROBIN
Goebel Miniatures
Ninth release in the Wildlife Series. Issued in 1988. Size 5/8". American made.

STORMY WEATHER
Goebel Miniatures
First release of this miniature Hummel limited to 10,000. Issued in 1988. Second release, open edition was released in 1989. Total height 15/16". American made.

TIGER HUNT
Goebel Miniatures
Sixth release in the Oriental Series. Issued in 1989. Size 1-5/16". American made.

TRIPLE SELF PORTRAIT
Goebel Miniatures
Sculpt from the cover design of 1960, Feb. 13th issue of the *Saturday Evening Post*. Dimensions: 2"H x 1-1/2"W x 1"D. American made.

VISITING AN INVALID
Goebel Miniatures
First release of this miniature Hummel limited to 10,000. Issued in 1989. Second release open edition was released in 1990.

CHINESE WATER DRAGON
Goebel Miniatures
Fifth release in the Oriental Series. Issued in 1987. Size 1" high. American made.

HOODED ORIOLE
Goebel Miniatures
Tenth release in the Wildlife Series. Issued in 1989. Size 11/16". American made.

INDIAN SCOUT AND BUFFALO
Goebel Miniatures
One of six releases in the American Frontier Collection Originally sculpt in the 1880's by Isadore Bonheur. Issued in 1987. 1-5/8" high. American made.

Prices are approximate and subject to change.

FOR FAST SERVICE, VISIT YOUR LOCAL MINIATURES SHOP

TANG HORSE
Goebel Miniatures
Third release in the Oriental Series. Issued in 1985. Size 1" high. American made.

WESTERN BLUEBIRD
Goebel Miniatures
Third release in the Wildlife Series. Released in 1982. 3/4" high. American made.

THE DEGRAZIA COLLECTION
Goebel Miniatures
From Left to Right: Flower Girl, issued 1985, size 7/8". Festival of Lights, issued in 1986, size 7/8". Wondering, issued 1985, size 3/4". Sunflower Boy, issued in 1985, size 15/16", limited 7500. My First Horse, issued 1985, size 7/8". Little Madonna, issued in 1986, size 1-1/8", limited 7500. Pima Drummer Boy, issued in 1986, size 7/8". Flower Boy, issued in 1985, size 7/8". White Dove, issued in 1985, size 5/8". Merry Little Indian, issued in 1987, size 1-1/8", limited 7500.

THE THREE LITTLE PIGS SERIES
Goebel Miniatures
Characters right out of Storybook Lane, Sticks Pig, Straw Pig, Bricks Pig and the Hungry Wolf. Pigs: 7/8" high, Wolf: 1-3/8" high.

Southwestern & Indian

INDIAN ARTS AND CRAFTS
Maison des Maisons
Native arts and crafts by Southwest Indian artists. Kachinas (figures of native dancers), story tellers and naciementos (nativities). American made.

1" Scale Accessories

THE MINIATURES CATALOG, *Fourteenth Edition* 285

SCULPTURES

The Lawbre Company
Suggested Retail Price: $18
Catalog Nos. 0651/0655
Specifications: 7/8" to 1-3/4"
Material: Antique bronze metal
These western sculptures are made from metal castings with antique bronze finish. Five different styles for a western look in decor.

RAINBOW HAND

Maison des Maisons
Authentic miniature reproductions of Indian artifacts by Rainbow Hand.

PUEBLO SCENE

Maison des Maisons
Pueblo scene of hand-cut native stone and materials showcasing pottery by Teresa Wildflower.

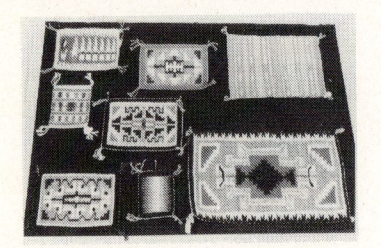

NAVAJO INDIAN RUGS

Maison des Maisons
Navajo Indian rugs by various weavers from the Southwest. Hand spun natural wool and dyes.

NATIVE ARTS AND CRAFTS

Maison des Maison
Native arts and crafts by Southwest Indian artists. Kachinas (figure of native dancers), story tellers and naciementos (nativities). American made.

PLAZA SCENES

Maison des Maisons
Suggested Retail Price: $110 - $4000.
Full plaza scenes for displaying Native American pottery and Kachinas. Made of hand-cut stones and other natural materials, complete with glass cover. One, two and three stories, various designs.

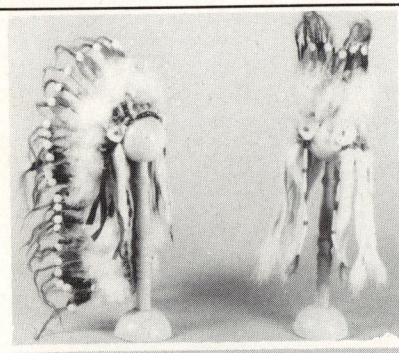

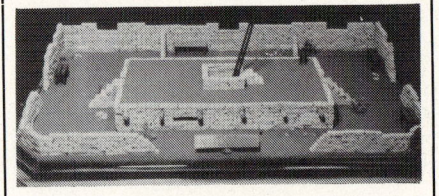

KIVA SCENES

Maison des Maisons
Suggested Retail Price: $110 and up
Various sizes available from 9" x 6" x 10" H to 30" x 18" x 14".
Kiva scenes hand-cut of native stones and various materials. Made by an American Indian - complete with dust cover.

INDIAN ARTIFACTS

Maison des Maisons
Native American Indian dresses, cradleboards, baskets and other artifacts by Tu Moonwalker, Rainbow Hand, Kay and Joe Franek and many native American artists.

AMERICAN INDIAN ARTS

Omniarts of Colorado
Suggested Retail Price: $15 and up
Offered here are superbly-crafted American Indian arts including baskets, headdresses, pottery, garments, weapons, ceremonial items by Rainbow Hand and others. American made.

NAVAJO STYLE RUGS

Olde Mountain Miniatures
Suggested Retail Price: $8.50 to $45, kits; $17.50 to $132, finished
These are some of our needlepoint rugs taken from actual Navajo rug designs. We have Two Gray Hills, Burntwater, Hubbell Revival, Chinle, Yei'i, Crystal Trading Post, Ganado and other styles. Colors vary considerably. Ask your local miniatures dealer for our kits and finished pieces.

286   Prices are approximate and subject to change.

LOOKING FOR SOMETHING SPECIAL? CHECK WITH YOUR LOCAL MINIATURES SHOP!

INDIAN POTTERY

Maison des Maison
American Indian pottery. Store tellers. Taos pueblos, seed pots and nativities. Specializing in pottery by Teresa Wildflower, Geri Naraujo, Mae Tapia, Lilly Salvador, Thomas Natseway and many more. American made.

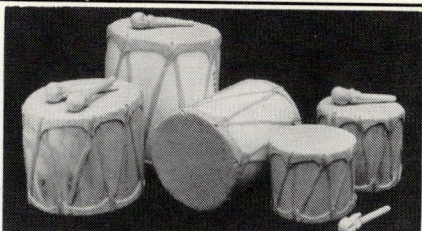

DRUMS WITH STICKS

Moreno Valley Miniatures
Suggested Retail Price: $10.50 each plus $1.50 shipping
Handcrafted Indian drums with sticks; aspen wood, leather, simulated sinew. Small 7/8"; medium 1-1/4"; large 1-3/4". 1" scale.

Sports Equipment

SPORTS EQUIPMENT

Betty's Wooden Miniatures
For the wall, our tennis rack or baseball rack with equipment. Others shown: two golf bags, clubs, Walkman, aerobics gift basket, two tennis bags, back packs. All handmade by us.

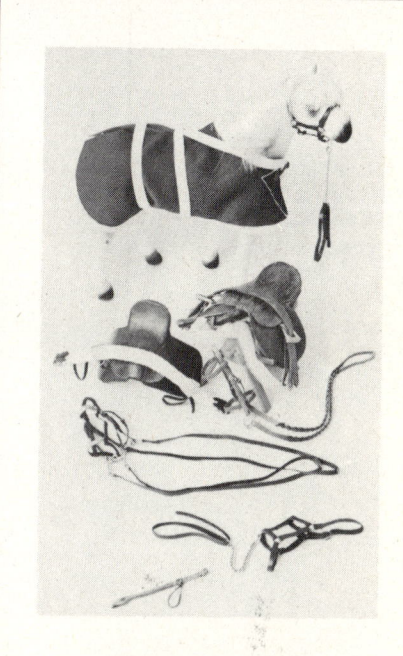

ENGLISH AND WESTERN SADDLERY

The Doll's Cobbler
Suggested Retail Price: $1.85 (riding crop), $50 (Victorian side-saddle).
Accurate to the last detail. Saddles, bridles, whips and horse collars.

HIP BOOTS AND WADERS
The Doll's Cobbler
Suggested Retail Price: $25-boots; $30-waders
Catch of the day - hip boots and overall waders for the miniature fishing enthusiast.

FISH TROPHIES
The Lawbre Company
Suggested Retail Price: $38: Nos. 725, 726, and 727; $60 No. 728.
Handpainted and mounted on walnut plaques (except sailfish). Realistic coloring and finish. American made.

SPORTING GOODS
Royal Miniatures
Suggested Retail Price: $1 - $2.50
Shown are just a few of the many sporting goods and other miniature accessories available. Customer designs are welcome.

1" Scale Accessories

THE MINIATURES CATALOG, Fourteenth Edition

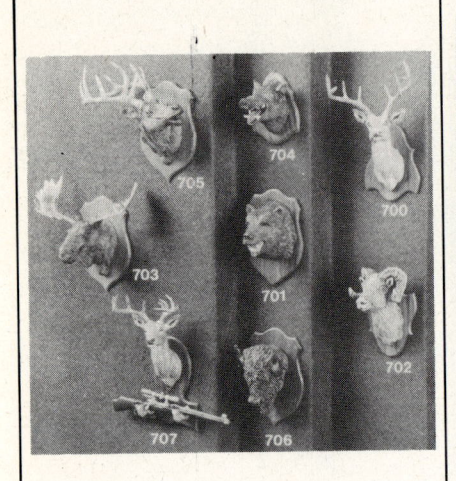

SPORTING TROPHIES

The Lawbre Company
Suggested Retail Price: $44 - $72
Catalog Nos. 0700 - 0707
These handpainted trophy heads have exquisite detail and are mounted on walnut plaques. American made.

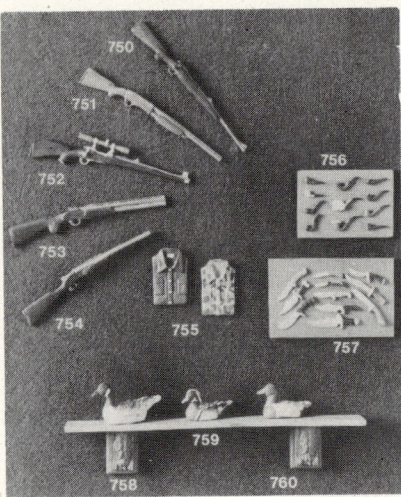

SPORTING TROPHIES

The Lawbre Company
Suggested Retail Price: $8-$30. Order Nos. 0750-0760.
These rifles, shotguns, pipe, and knife collections, shirts, and game birds are all handpainted in exquisite detail for your game room. American made.

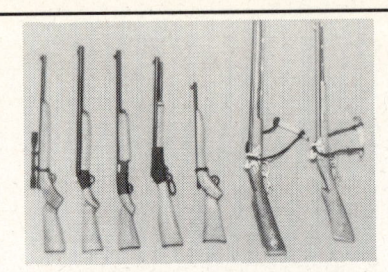

RIFLES/FISHING RODS

By Sir Thomas Thumb
Rifles antique and modern. Fishing rods. Bows/arrows. Handcarved hardwood stocks and metal barrels add authenticity to these accurately and beautifully detailed rifles. Catalog available.

SPORTS EQUIPMENT

Teri's Mini Workshop
Sports equipment from tiny golf balls to a fully equipped pool table.

1" SCALE GYM EQUIPMENT

Three Blind Mice
Suggested Retail Price: $25, five-door locker; $14, single locker; $20, weight set, $15, slant board; $10, sweat suit.

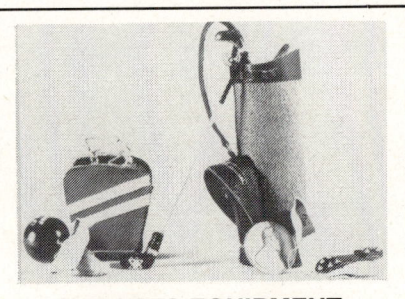

SPORTS EQUIPMENT

Alice Zinn
Tennis, baseball, hockey, basketball, golf, soccer, skiing, backpacking, rollerskating, fishing, surfing, waterskiing, etc. American made.

Store & Shop Accessories

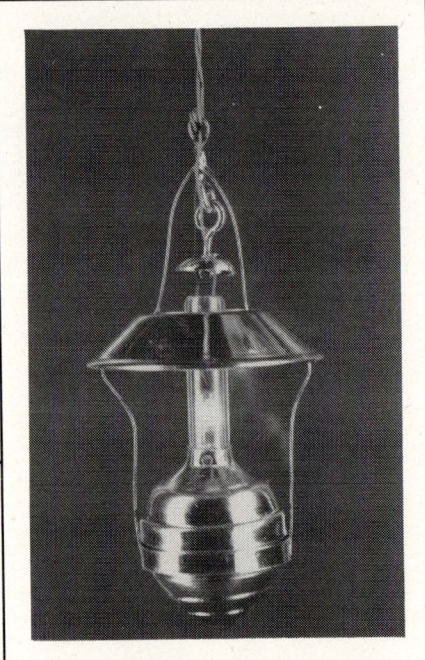

GENERAL STORE LAMP

Cir-Kit Concepts, Inc.
Suggested Retail Price: $9.95
Catalog No. CK320
This ceiling fixture may be used for lighting a general store or as a period setting. Incorporates a 12V bulb and hand-blown glass chimney. Dimensions: 3"H x 1-1/2" dia. shade. Bright brass plated.

Prices are approximate and subject to change.

Builder's Choice Landscapes
For your Miniature Home

Now you can LANDSCAPE the yard around your dollhouse in less than a 1/2 hour! And it's Easy!! The Builder's Choice Landscaping System uses pre-formed and pre-painted Landscaping Beds which you install on your house and decorate with Builder's Choice Decorative stone or wood chips, plant shrubs and bushes.

It's simple! All Builder's Choice Landscape accessories are ready to use. All you do is set them in place. The possibilities are endless. So start plans for your dream house NOW!

A COMPLETE SYSTEM

The 3000 Series Landscape Beds
*Pre-painted and finished * Wooden Base
*Easy to cut with a hobby knife to fit each Landscaping requirement
* Slips under the edge of the house to keep solid and flat
*Works with any Dollhouse * Scaled to 1"= 1 foot
*3 3/4" wide x 18" long
*Can be glued, painted or carved for custom work
*Depth allows for "planting" of shrubs and trees

The 3700 Series Plantings
*Each package contains enough for 2 planting beds
*Can be glued or custom colored

The 3500 Series Lawns
*Put anywhere - no base needed
*Pre-painted ready for grass (included)
*Can be cut, glued and custom painted
*Protects table surface
*Easily changeable for the seasons
*Heavy weight fabric lays flat and smooth

The 3600 Series Planting Bed Material
*Natural materials * Permanent Colors
*Scale size materials
*Can be glued or custom colored * Mix for variety
*Each package contains enough material to cover 2 planting beds

---

BC900	Victorian Fence	BC3602	Decorative Stone "Brown"
BC901	Victorian Gate	BC3603	Wood Chips
BC902	Colonial Fence	BC3604	Mulch
BC903	Colonial Gate	BC3605	Spring Grass
BC904	2 Victorian Posts	BC3606	Summer Grass
BC905	2 Colonial Posts	BC3607	Leaves Summer
BC3000	Brick Landscaping Bed	BC3608	Leaves Fall
BC3001	Brick Path	BC3609	Weeds
BC3002	Brick Round Tree Planting Bed Sm.	BC3610	Flowerbud Assortment
BC3004	Brick Rectangular Planting Bed	BC3611	Snow
BC3010	Timber Landscaping Bed	BC3700	Small Evergreens (2pkg)
BC3011	Timber Path	BC3701	Mugho Pine Evergreens (2 pkg)
BC3012	Timber Rectangular Planting Bed	BC3702	Foundation Shrub Assortment
BC3500	"1/4 Acre" Green Lawn(36x48)	BC3703	Tall Evergreen
BC3501	"1/2 Acre" Green Lawn (72x48)	BC3800	Trellis
BC3510	"1/4 Acre" Winter Lawn (36x48)	BC3801	Sand Box
BC3600	Decorative Stone "Marble Chips"	BC4000	Landscaping Asst. Brick
BC3601	Decorative Stone "Gray"	BC4001	Landscaping Asst. Timber

71 Hilliard St., Manchester, Ct. 06040 * Phone (203) 646-0610 * FAX(203)645-0504

New England Hobby Supply, Inc.

BUILDER'S CHIOCE PAINTS

New England Hobby Supply, Inc.
71 Hilliard St., Manchester, Ct. 06040

THE LEADER IN DOLLHOUSE PAINTS

2 Oz. Jars for exterior trim and interior work.

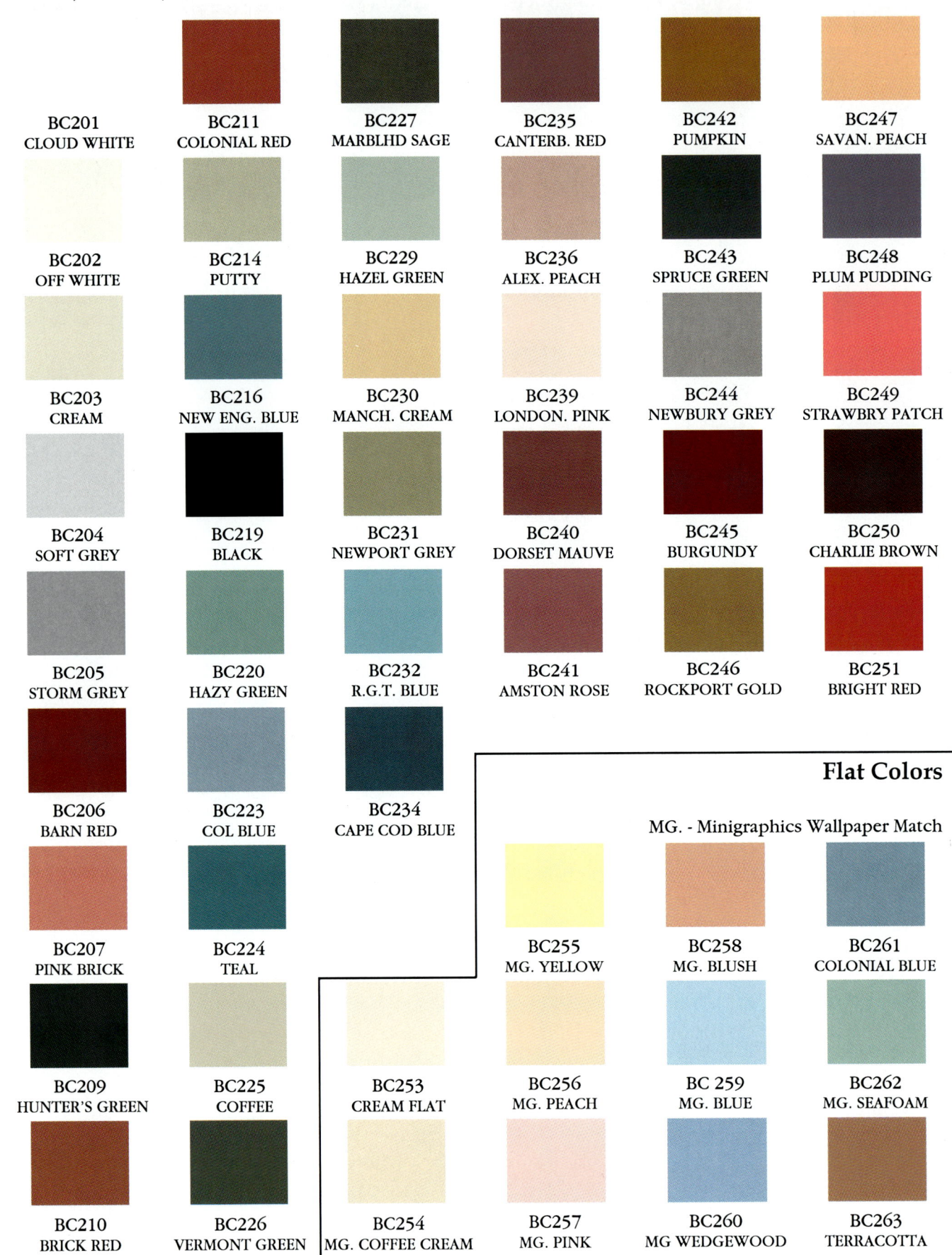

BC201 CLOUD WHITE	BC211 COLONIAL RED	BC227 MARBLHD SAGE	BC235 CANTERB. RED	BC242 PUMPKIN	BC247 SAVAN. PEACH
BC202 OFF WHITE	BC214 PUTTY	BC229 HAZEL GREEN	BC236 ALEX. PEACH	BC243 SPRUCE GREEN	BC248 PLUM PUDDING
BC203 CREAM	BC216 NEW ENG. BLUE	BC230 MANCH. CREAM	BC239 LONDON. PINK	BC244 NEWBURY GREY	BC249 STRAWBRY PATCH
BC204 SOFT GREY	BC219 BLACK	BC231 NEWPORT GREY	BC240 DORSET MAUVE	BC245 BURGUNDY	BC250 CHARLIE BROWN
BC205 STORM GREY	BC220 HAZY GREEN	BC232 R.G.T. BLUE	BC241 AMSTON ROSE	BC246 ROCKPORT GOLD	BC251 BRIGHT RED
BC206 BARN RED	BC223 COL BLUE	BC234 CAPE COD BLUE			

Flat Colors

MG. - Minigraphics Wallpaper Match

BC207 PINK BRICK	BC224 TEAL		BC255 MG. YELLOW	BC258 MG. BLUSH	BC261 COLONIAL BLUE
BC209 HUNTER'S GREEN	BC225 COFFEE	BC253 CREAM FLAT	BC256 MG. PEACH	BC 259 MG. BLUE	BC262 MG. SEAFOAM
BC210 BRICK RED	BC226 VERMONT GREEN	BC254 MG. COFFEE CREAM	BC257 MG. PINK	BC260 MG WEDGEWOOD	BC263 TERRACOTTA

These printed colors are for reference only. For exact match see color chip on paint can or color in jar.

Period and Contemporary colors! Non-Toxic Latex Paints. Great coverage - Easy Cleanup
8 oz. Cans 39 semi-gloss colors plus BC 821 Flat Ceiling White , BC 850 Black and BC 851 White Primer

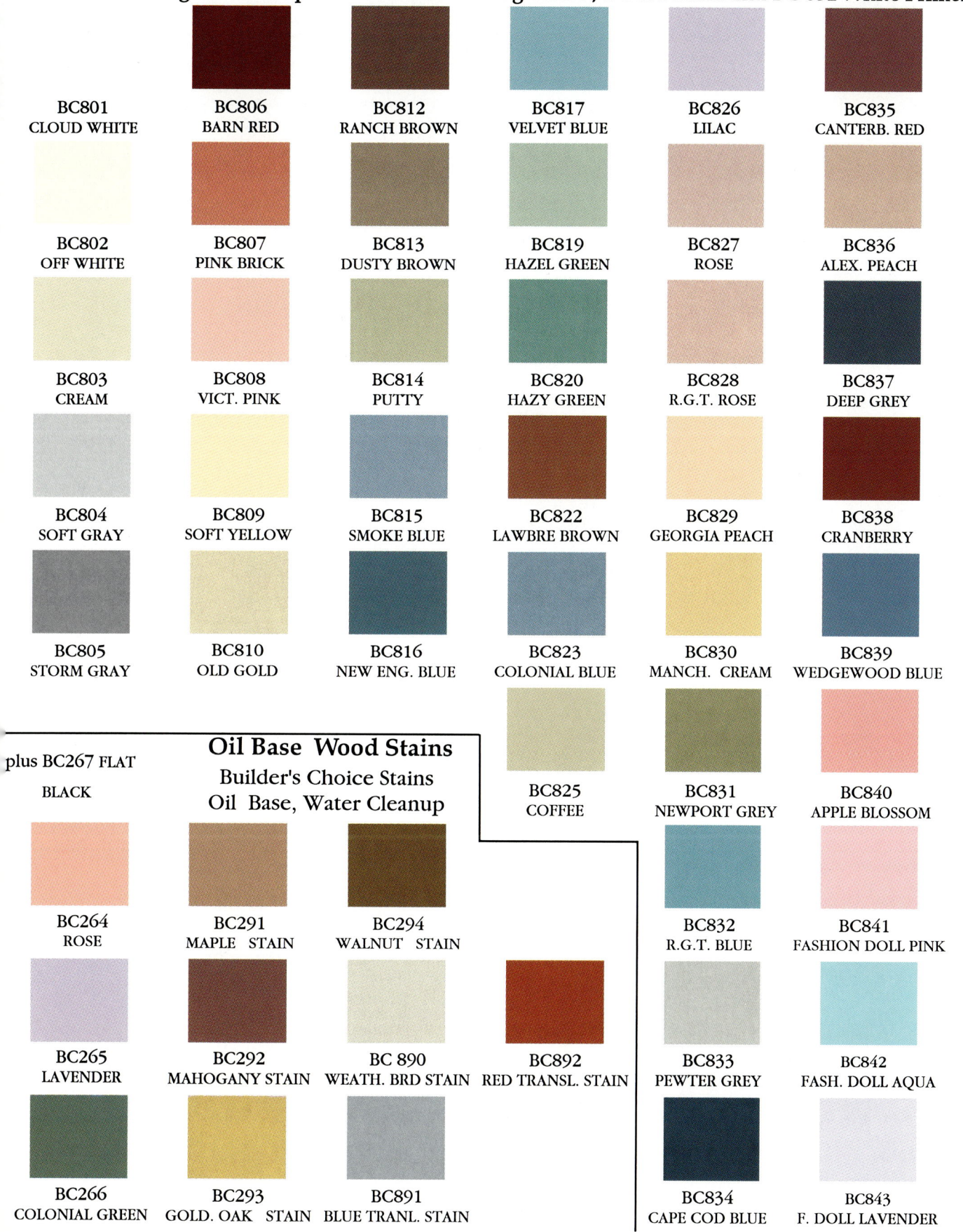

BC801 CLOUD WHITE	BC806 BARN RED	BC812 RANCH BROWN	BC817 VELVET BLUE	BC826 LILAC	BC835 CANTERB. RED
BC802 OFF WHITE	BC807 PINK BRICK	BC813 DUSTY BROWN	BC819 HAZEL GREEN	BC827 ROSE	BC836 ALEX. PEACH
BC803 CREAM	BC808 VICT. PINK	BC814 PUTTY	BC820 HAZY GREEN	BC828 R.G.T. ROSE	BC837 DEEP GREY
BC804 SOFT GRAY	BC809 SOFT YELLOW	BC815 SMOKE BLUE	BC822 LAWBRE BROWN	BC829 GEORGIA PEACH	BC838 CRANBERRY
BC805 STORM GRAY	BC810 OLD GOLD	BC816 NEW ENG. BLUE	BC823 COLONIAL BLUE	BC830 MANCH. CREAM	BC839 WEDGEWOOD BLUE

plus BC267 FLAT BLACK

Oil Base Wood Stains
Builder's Choice Stains
Oil Base, Water Cleanup

BC264 ROSE	BC291 MAPLE STAIN	BC294 WALNUT STAIN		BC825 COFFEE	BC831 NEWPORT GREY	BC840 APPLE BLOSSOM
BC265 LAVENDER	BC292 MAHOGANY STAIN	BC 890 WEATH. BRD STAIN	BC892 RED TRANSL. STAIN		BC832 R.G.T. BLUE	BC841 FASHION DOLL PINK
BC266 COLONIAL GREEN	BC293 GOLD. OAK STAIN	BC891 BLUE TRANL. STAIN			BC833 PEWTER GREY	BC842 FASH. DOLL AQUA
					BC834 CAPE COD BLUE	BC843 F. DOLL LAVENDER

These printed colors are for reference only. For exact match see color chip on paint can or color in jar.

Barbara O'Brien Miniatures
"We Get All The Curtain Calls"

All Barbara O'Brien curtains are designed for easy installation. Special ends on the curtain rods, supplied with each curtain, need only be glued to the side of the window frame. The curtain rod's length can be adjusted slightly to fit almost all of the standard windows used in dollhouses.

New England Hobby Supply, Inc.

1/2" WINDOWS

2 1/2" X 3 1/2" LONG 
BB100E-ECRU
BB100W-WHITE

1/2" PICTURE WINDOW 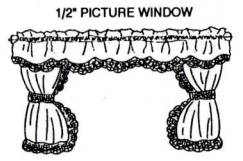
BB101E-ECRU
BB101W-WHITE

1/2" CAFE 
BB103

FLOWERED LACE SHEERS 6" LONG 
BB500W-WHITE
BB500E-ECRU

LACE PANEL 7" LONG 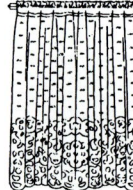
BB501W-WHITE
BB501E-ECRU

COTTAGE SET 
BB504W-WHITE
BB504E-ECRU
BB504P-PINK
BB504B-BLUE
BB504Y-YELLOW

FLOWERED LACE 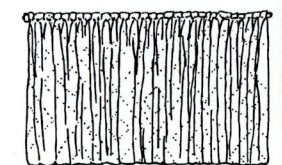
BB505E-ECRU
BB505W-WHITE

KITCHEN CURTAINS 
BB506Y-YELLOW
BB506R-RED
BB506B-BLUE
BB506W-WHITE
BB506P-PINK

EMBROIDERED TIER 
BB507W-WHITE

COUNTRY CURTAINS 7" 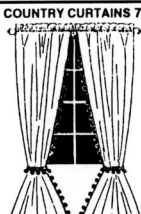
BB520E-ECRU
BB520W-WHITE

RUFFLED DOTTED SWISS TIE BACK 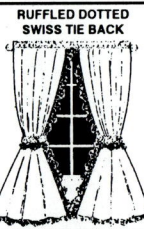
DOTTED SWISS BB521 - WHITE
PLAIN SHEERS B522W-WHITE
BB522P- PINK BB522B - BLUE
BB522Y - YELLOW

DRAPE N' CURTAIN 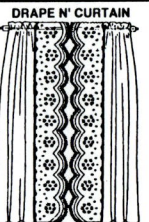
BB523C- WHITE LACE WITH CHAMPAIGN
BB523R-WHITE LACE WITH COUNTRY ROSE

RUFFLED CAPE SET 
BB524W-WHITE, BB524B-PINK
BB524Y-YELLOW-BB524B BLUE
BB524DS-WHITE DOTTED SWISS
PIC. WINDOW CAPES, 7 1/2" LONG
BB524AW-WHITE
BB524ADS-DOTTED

BAY WINDOW TIER 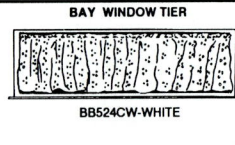
BB524CW-WHITE 
BB524B-WINDOW SWAG

VICTORIAN PRISCILLAS 3 1/2" ROD 
BB527W-WHITE
BB527E-ECRU

CABIN CURTAINS 
BB528W-WHITE
BB528E-ECRU

ATTIC CURTAIN 2" FLAT ROD 
BB529E-ECRU
BB529W-WHITE

TIFFANY RUFFLES 3 1/2" ROD 
BB530W-WHITE
BB530E-ECRU

BALLOON TOPS 4" AND 8" 
BB532B-BLUE, BB532M-MAUVE
BB532R-RED, BB532W-WHITE
BB532PW-FLORAL PERIWIG
BB532A( ) SAME COLORS 8" LONG

LACE CURTAIN W/BALLOON TOP 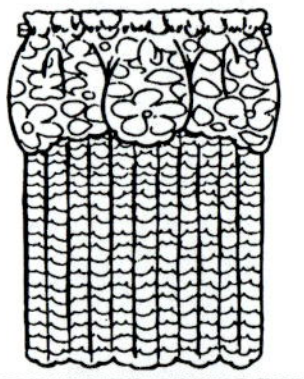
BB535W-WHITE, BB535E-ECRU
PICTURE WINDOW 7 1/2" WIDE
BB536W-WHITE BB536E-ECRU

CROCHETED LACE 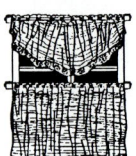
BB537W-WHITE

SIDE TIE BACK LACE 
LEFT OR RIGHT
BB538W-WHITE
BB538E-ECRU

PLAID COTTAGE 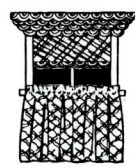
BB539B-BLUE
BB539R-RED
BB539W-WHITE

TAB CAFE 
BB540B-BLUE
BB540P-PINK
BB540W-WHITE

SHADE 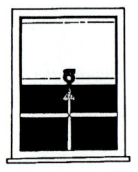
BB541E-ECRU
BB541W-WHITE
BB541A-STANDARD
BB541B-PICTURE WINDOW

TIE BACK 
BB543W-WHITE
BB543E-ECRU

NEW FASHION DOLL CURTAINS

PINK HEARTS (VELCRO BACK) — 201

EYELET WHITE (VELCRO BACK) — 202

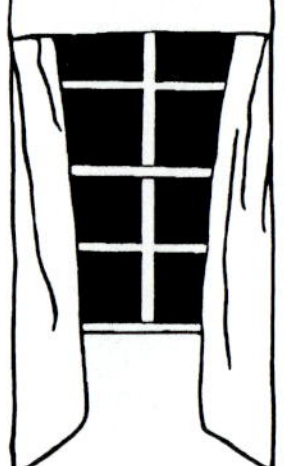

"DEMI CURTAINS" FOR MORE SUBTLE WINDOW DRESSING, ON 3 1/2" RODS

CAPE 
BBCH503 WHITE

TIE BACK 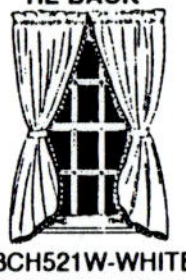
BBCH521W-WHITE
BBCH521P-PINK
BBCH521Y-YELLOW
BBCH521B-BLUE

VICTORIAN 5 1/2" LONG 
BBCH527W-WHITE
BBCH527-ECRU

SPECIAL ITEMS (NOT PICTURED)

BB502	PICTURE WINDOW LACE CURTAIN 7 1/2" ROD 6" LONG (SAME LACE AS 500)

MATCHING DISH TOWELS
FOR THE 506 SERIES KITCHEN CURTAINS

BB506TR	DISH TOWELS RED
BB506TB	DISH TOWELS BLUE
BB506TY	DISH TOWELS YELLOW
BB506TP	DISH TOWELS PINK

ACCESSORIES

BB608	9 1/2" CURTAIN RODS (pkg. of 2)
BB609	BRASS SCREW EYES (pkg. of 12)
BB610	4 1/2" CURTAIN RODS (pkg. of 3)
BB611	BEADS (pkg. of 12)

71 Hilliard St., Manchester, Ct. 06040 • Phone (203) 646-0610 • Fax (203) 645-0504

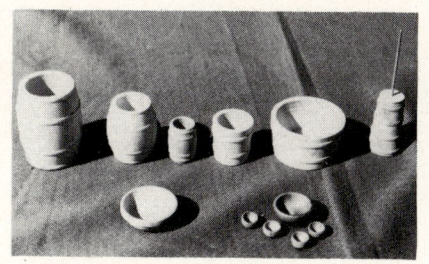

BARRELS, TUB, CHURN, AND BOWLS

Ballhagen Woodcraft
Suggested Retail Prices: Large barrel $1.60, medium barrel $1.35, keg $.95, tub $1.60, bucket $1, butterchurn $2.25, chopping bowl $1.10, and salad bowl set $2.35. Does not include shipping.
All items are birchwood and hollow. American made.

STORE SIGNS

Philip E. Bugosh
Suggested Retail Price: See your dealer. Assorted wooden signs in a variety of sizes and colors.

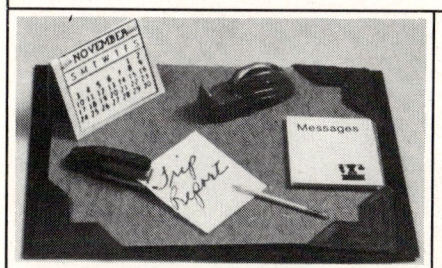

DESK PAD AND ACCESSORIES

Gert's Triple "A" Minis
Suggested Retail Price: $10.50
This desk set is perfect for your mini office. Available with a pink or green blotter.

POSTCARD RACKS

Innovative Photography
Handcrafted postcard and hanging display racks - postcards, black/white and sepia: French, Victorian and Cowboys and Indians. Color, holidays, Kewpies, scenics, foreign and assorted. Suggested retail price: $11.95/24 color cards; $9.95/24 black/white; $35 postcard rack; $25 hanging display rack. American made.

PRODUCE CONTAINERS

Little Discoveries
Suggested Retail Price: $4 empty to $24 filled, plus shipping.
Authentic reproductions of produce containers, crafted from wood and realistically weathered. Sold empty ($4 - $4.50) or filled with our fine Fimo fruits and vegetables ($6 - $24). We supply tops, wooden dividers and green tissue paper. Pictured: grape box, citrus crate, produce crate and wired crate. Price list $1.

METAL SIGNS

Nanco Distributors
Suggest Retail Price: $16
Enamel on metal advertising signs. Twelve styles available.

Bakery Shop

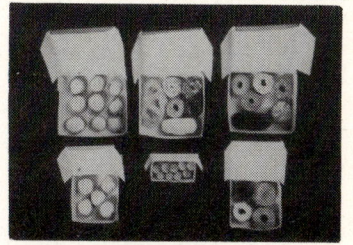

CINNAMON ROLLS AND DONUTS

Diminutive Specialties
Cinnamon rolls; large box $4, small box $2. Donuts; large box $3, small box $2. Sugared donut holes; box of 18 $3. Add shipping. Made of Fimo.

1" Scale Accessories

THE MINIATURES CATALOG, Fourteenth Edition 289

NOVELTY CAKES

Diminutive Specialties
Suggested Retail Price: $5.50 plus shipping
Each cake comes on a fancy cake board and packed in a bakery box. Ernie, Garfield, Cathy, Smurf, Rainbow Brite, Superman, clown, train, Batman and The Count. Made of Sculpey.

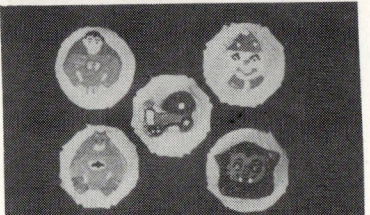

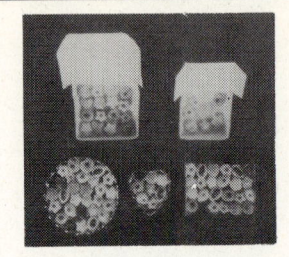

FANCY COOKIES

Diminutive Specialties
Fancy cookies; large box $4, small box $2, fancy round brass tray $8, fancy brass heart tray $2.50, rectangular brass tray $7. Add shipping. Made of Fimo.

WEDDING CAKES

Diminutive Specialties
Original limited-edition wedding cakes and reproductions of your cake. Send LSASE for ordering information.

CANDY, COOKIE & FOOD DESIGNS

Donna Smolik's Designs
Suggested Retail Price: $1.75-$4.25 each. Candies, fruits, vegetables, meats - slice your own with a single-edged razor blade. Can be used in 1", 1/2" or 1/4" scales.

General Store

FOOD STAND AND CONTAINERS

Jack and June's Mini-Many Things
Special handcrafted containers with or without food and products made to order by Jack and June.

BUSHEL BASKETS

Miniature House
Suggested Retail Price: See below
MH2011, small - $2.69
MH2012, medium - $2.79
MH2013, large - $2.79
Natural colored bushel baskets.

CANDY ROLLS

Miniature House
Suggested Retail Price: $1.19
Catalog No. MH2301
There are one dozen candy rolls in assorted bright colors.

GUMBALL MACHINE

Miniature House
Suggested Retail Price: $1.59
Catalog No. MH2315
Approximately 1" tall, this gumball machine has a painted red metal base and multi-colored gumballs.

PRODUCE BOXES

Miniature House
Suggested Retail Price: $.75 MH2009, $1.10 MH2010
Catalog No. MH2009 four slats, MH2010 eight slats
Perfect for the General Store, all wood.

STANDING GUMBALL MACHINE

Miniature House
Suggested Retail Price: $2.85
Catalog No. MH2325
A must for the General Store, this gumball machine is 3" tall and has a red painted metal base and realistic multi-colored gumballs.

GENERAL STORE ACCESSORIES

Royal Miniatures
Suggested Retail Price: $1-$3
Shown is a small selection of our general and country store miniature accessories. Wholesale only. Quantity discounts for manufacturers and distributors available.

FOOD AND ACCESSORIES

Warber's Miniatures
Here are some of the newest items, fine quality handcrafted food and accessories for the miniature dollhouse. Over 600 products. Made from Fimo. Write Warber's for more information.

Pet Shop

HANDSCULPTED MINIATURES

Kitty's Kreations
Kitty's Kreations specializes in animals, babies and children with pets. We have a large variety of cats, dogs, all in 1" scale, intricately detailed and made from hydrostone. Please mention "The Miniatures Catalog" when sending $1 for our catalog.

DOGS, CATS AND BIRDS

Alice Zinn
Custom made to your order, available in all breeds and scales. Also available are monkeys, rabbits, guinea pigs, turtles, fish, mice, parrots, hamsters, lizards, ant farms, ferrets and snakes. Accessories available include dog collars, leashes, beds, cat litter box, scratching post, pet food, toys and more. American made.

Specialty Shop

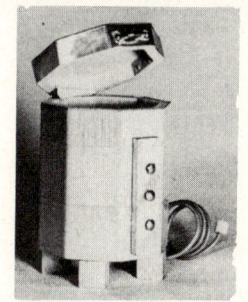

1" SCALE KILN

Three Blind Mice
Suggested Retail Price: $25

NEW FROM FARROW

To Be Tiny, Inc.
Suggested Retail Price: $3 for catalog
For that special accessory to finish your room setting, choose from the complete Farrow line available through mail order.

WICKER-LOOK FURNITURE AND HOUSEHOLD GOODS

Farrow Industries, Inc.
Suggested Retail Price: See your dealer
Licensed American made 1" scale items from Farrow Industries are shown on wicker look etagere, standing three-shelf corner what-not and end table from "Tobe Tailored" by Farrow. The shelves and table, along with the mirror and clothes hanger are solid brass and enameled. They are available in white, black or pink.

Toys and Games

GAMES
All Through The House, Amy Robinson
Darts $6.50, kite $5, jump rope $1.50, painter's palette and brush $4, backgammon $7.50, checkers $7.50, cribbage $7.50, tennis racket $8, skis (not shown) $15. Send LSASE for mailer.

BLOCKS AND BEARS IN A BOX
Philip E. Bugosh
Sug: Retail Price: See your local dealer
Block bag and assorted bears in a box. Bears come in several styles and are in multi-color windowed boxes.

MENAGERIE OF BEARS AND ANIMALS

A Grand Scale by Mary Bures
Suggested Retail Price: $50-$100 plus shipping
A complete selection of handmade Bears, Rabbits and Elephants ranging in size from 3/4" to 1-1/2". Bears and Rabbits are jointed and are available in assorted fur colors. Write for Limited Edition selections.

CALICO TEDDY BEARS

A Grand Scale by Mary Bures
Suggested Retail Price: $14-$25 plus shipping
Jointed Teddy Bears in many varieties of Calico, Gingham and Pin Dot available in sizes ranging from 1" to 2". Select from a variety of styles and holiday fabrics or customer may furnish fabric to match setting.

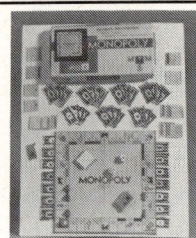

MONOPOLY GAME
Gert's Triple "A" Minis
Suggested Retail Price: $17, $19 set up
This popular game set comes complete with game pieces, houses, hotels, property cards, etc.

Prices are approximate and subject to change.

POOL TABLE

Mini Treasure House
Suggested Retail Price: $225
Material: Walnut
Finish: Tung Oil
Handcrafted by Jack Heier. This 1" scale pool table comes complete with set of numbered balls and rack, two cue sticks, leather pockets, rail sights and center spot. Truly unique!. 4-1/2" x 7-3/4".

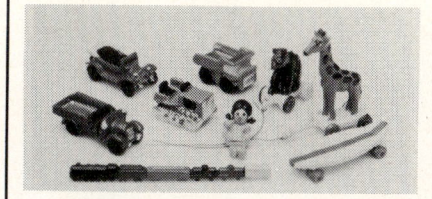

TOYS, TOYS AND MORE TOYS

Monkey Business
Our hand-painted detail is unsurpassed. Your dolls would enjoy playing with our pull toys, skateboard, cars, trucks, trains, dolls and many more.

WOODEN PULL TOY

Mary Agnes Murphy
Suggested Retail Price: $10 finished; $4.50 kit ppd
Handcrafted 1" scale pull toy available finished or in kit form. Finished bear, yellow or brown. Duck, white. Bases painted in bright nursery colors.

TOYS AND GAMES

Royal Miniatures
Suggested Retail Price: $1 - $2
Shown are just a few of the many toys and games available. Many other styles available. Customer designs are welcome.

BEARENGER BEARS

T.K. Designs
Handsewn original jointed bears. Made from synthetic "mohair" fabric. The Bearenger's have black austrian crystal eyes. LSASE for catalog. Wholesale orders welcome.

FEED FATSO GAME

Wee Wonders
Suggested Retail Price: $8 plus shipping.
Throw the balls through Fatso's mouth. 2-3/4" tall. Handmade of wood.

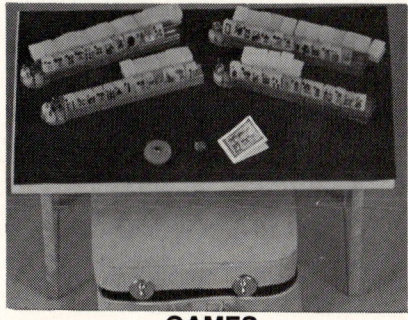

GAMES

Alice Zinn
Mah Jongg with leather case, pinball, foosball, knock hockey, Slinky, Rummy Tile and 3-D Tic-Tac-Toe. American made.

Workshop Accessories

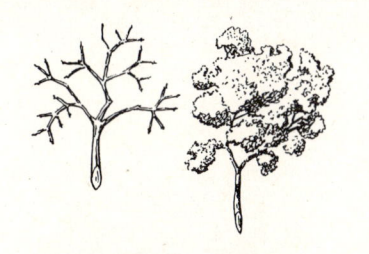

If you love grapes then you have a ready supply of the basic material necessary to create these miniature trees and shrubs. Hang the stems inverted until they have dried and then coat with glue and dip into a bag of that shredded foam available from model railroad stores. It comes in many shades of green and even fall colors. Terrie sent a nicely posed picture which shows how convincing these mini trees can be.

TERRIE DESLIPPE, S. HADLEY, MA

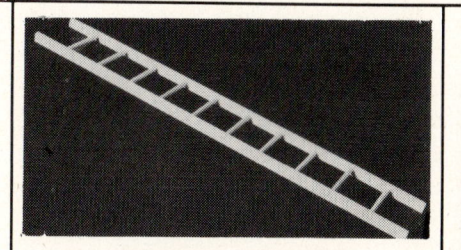

WOODEN LADDER

Alessio Miniatures
Suggested Retail Price: $ 1.50
Dimensions: 10" L x 1"W
Wooden ladder can be cut to any length for convenience. American made.

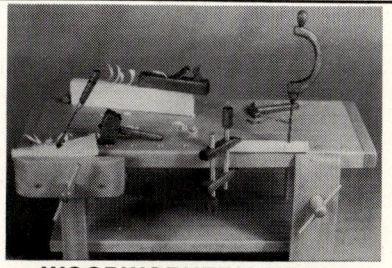

WOODWORKER'S TOOLS

Sir Thomas Thumb
Collector-quality carpenter/handyman tools, historic and modern. Workbench, shaving horse, wood planes, saws, augers, chisels, hammers and new pieces for 1991. Realism in wood and metal. Catalog available.

1" Scale Accessories

THE MINIATURES CATALOG, Fourteenth Edition 293

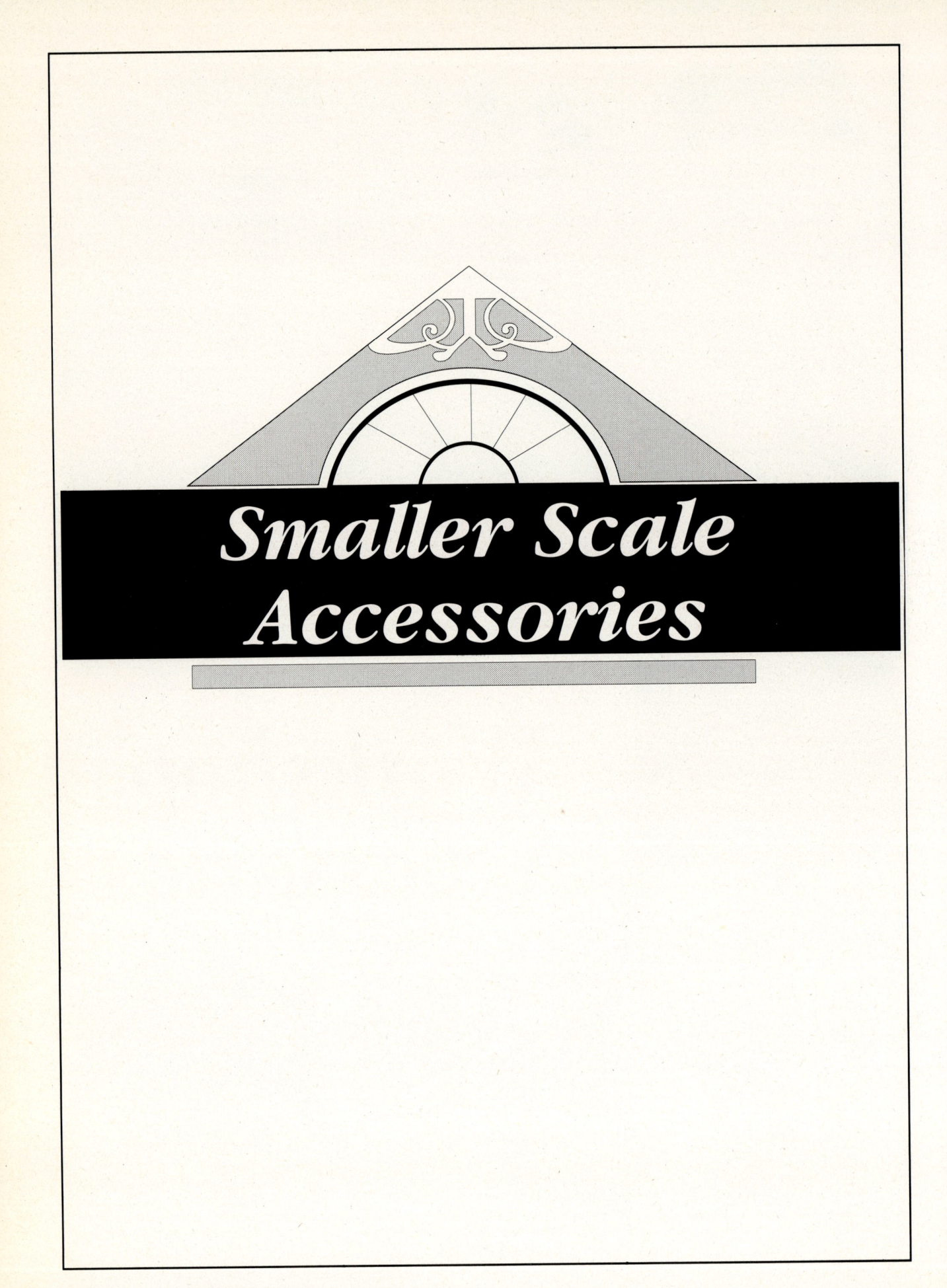

Smaller Scale Accessories

1/2" Scale Accessories

1/2" SCALE ACCESSORIES

All Through The House, Amy Robinson
Log carrier $2.50, creel $13, boots $10, indian corn $4, napkins $2, fruit bowl $5, bird feeder $5, Christmas fruit basket $7.50, tissues $1.25. Send LSASE for mailer.

TOWEL AND RUG SETS

Amoroso Originals
Suggested Retail Price: $7.50
Scale: 1/2". Material: Suede-like
Darling set of two towels and bath carpet with fringe or tiny trim and flower decorations.

1/2" SCALE ACCESSORIES

By Barb
Ceramic dish sets and accessory sets in a large variety of colors and designs. Can be made to order. Judaic foods and accessories for holidays and occasions. Lucite furniture. Made in the U.S.A.

CANDLESTICKS

Clare-Bell Brass Works
Suggested Retail Price: $5.25
Catalog No. 1270110
1/2" to 1' scale.

WOODEN PRODUCE BASKETS AND CRATES

Fantasy In Wood
Wooden produce baskets and crates in 1/2" scale. Wholesale and retail. LSASE for information.

WALNUT WALL ACCESSORIES

The Fretworker, Kirk Ratajesak
Suggested Retail Price: $5 - $18
These fine quality accessories are handcrafted by Kirk in walnut wood. Furniture pieces are also available.

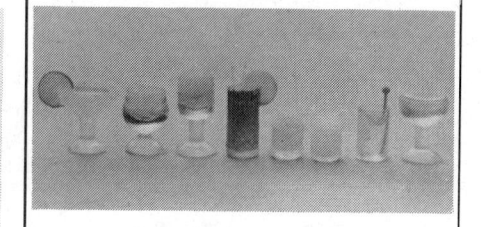

BEVERAGES

Marilyn's Mini Studio
Margarita, brandy, beer and iced tea - $3 each; orange juice, milk, gin & tonic and champagne - $2 each.

CANNING JARS

Linden Swiss Miniatures
Scale: 1/2", Material: Acrylic
Catalog No. 730
One-quart size old fashioned canning jars with simulated zinc lid. Three per package. American made. See your local dealer.

1/2" SCALE GLASSES

Linden Swiss Miniatures
Material: Acrylic
Shown is a selection of our new 1/2" scale glasses. Have frosted look. Instructions for clearing glasses to have a crystal clear look included. See your local dealer. American made.

"EVENING FOR TWO"

Linden Swiss Miniatures
Scale: 1/2", Material: Acrylic
Catalog No. 726. Includes two each: dinner and salad plates, soup bowls, water and wine goblets, one bottle of wine and candles with holders. See your local dealer. All products are American made.

VICTORIAN DOOR

Houseworks
Suggested Retail Price: $13.50
Catalog No. H6013
Exterior six panel door with low pitch hooded doorcap and scalloped transom. Size: 2-5/8" W x 4-5/8" H. Fits opening: 1-11/16" W x 4-5/32" H.

ASSORTED WINDOWS

Houseworks
No. H5043-Palladian window; nonworking French window with fan light pediment and sill. Size: 1-15/16"W x 3-5/8"H. $14.50
No. H5032-Traditional nonworking window- Self framing with six mullions and sill. Size: 1-1/2" W x 3" H $5.95.

FOR FAST SERVICE, VISIT YOUR LOCAL MINIATURES SHOP

CLASSIC FRENCH DOORS

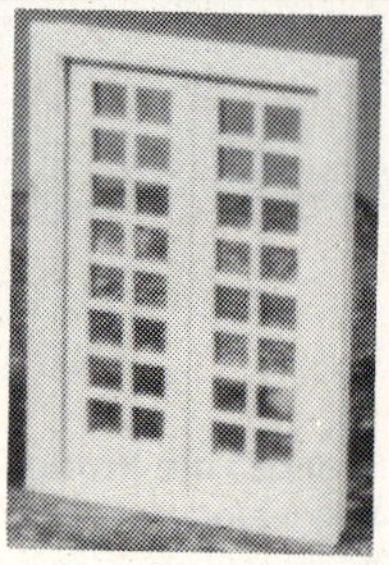

Houseworks
Suggested Retail Price: $12.50
Catalog No. H6011
Double entry doors with grids and acrylic panes. Hinged to operate separately. Size: 2-11/16" W x 3-27/32" H. Fits opening: 2-9/16" W x 3-13/16" H.

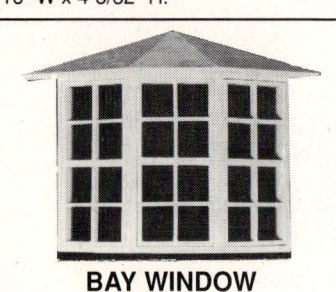

BAY WINDOW

Houseworks
Suggested Retail Price: $14.95
Catalog No. H5008
Nonworking bay features three 8-light windows with angled hood. Size: 4-15/16"W x 3-7/16"H.

VICTORIAN NONWORKING WINDOW

Houseworks
Suggested Retail Price: $10.50
Catalog No. H5042
Features low pitch hooded cap with sculpted brackets. Size: 1-15/16" W x 3-1/4" H.

DORMER

Houseworks
Suggested Retail Price: $8.95.
Catalog No. H7002
Unit includes dormer and one 4 light shutter window. Designed for 45° pitch roof. Size: 2-5/8" W x 3" H x 3-3/15" D.

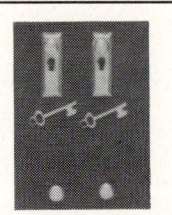

GOLD PLATED BRASS DOOR KNOB AND KNOB WITH KEYPLATE

Houseworks
Suggested Retail Price: $3 each. Catalog No. H1114 doorknob with keyplate and No. H1116 doorknob. Six pieces per package.

YORKTOWN DOOR

Houseworks
Suggested Retail Price: $9.75. Catalog No. H6014.
Exterior six panel door with sculpted door-cap and dentil moulding. Size: 2-13/16"W x 4"H. Fits opening: 1-11/16" W x 3-23/32"H.

Prices are approximate and subject to change.

Smaller Scale Accessories

1/2" SCALE LASER CUT APEX TRIMS

Laser Tech
Suggested Retail Price: (top to bottom) #AT-1001 $4.95; #AT-1002 $4.75; #AT-1003 $4.75; #AT-1005 $3.95
Made of 3/32 basswood. These 1/2" scale apex trims will accent any Victorian dollhouse. Intended for use on a 45° slope roof.

BUILDING SUPPLIES

Model Builders Supply
Some of MBS's thousands of architectural model parts. Styrene strips, 57 sizes. Stone, brick, roofing and siding sheets. 70 styles of skylights. U.S. customers, see "Plastruct".

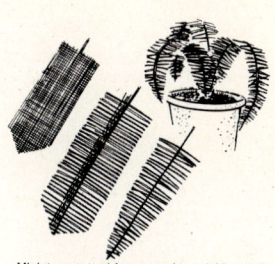

Miniature potted ferns can be quickly made from pieces of grosgrain ribbon in various shades of green. Cut to the desired length and ending in a point with the edges trimmed off, you should carefully pull out the lengthwise threads until you have only a couple left down the center of the stem. Spray the leaves with clear acrylic and bend to shape until the acrylic has set. Glue into a pot with a brown leaf or two for effect.

1/2" Scale Furniture

COUNTRY FURNITURE KITS

Inch/Foot
Suggested Retail Price: kits; $6-$18 ppd completely finished; write for prices
Material: Cherry, walnut and pine
Easy-to-assemble kits of friendly country furniture in natural and painted finishes. Kits guaranteed. Send LSASE for price list, descriptions and photos. Retail only.

WICKER FURNITURE KITS

Omniarts of Colorado
Suggested Retail Price: $2.50-$9.25 kit
Scale 1/2"-1'
Wicker furniture kits of cotton cord (white or ecru), covered wire and wood. Pieces available include: bed, vanity, stool, wall and pier mirrors, chairs, sofas, tables, decorative screen, fernery, planter, dog bed, baby carriage, high chair, crib, cradle, porch swing and more. Complete line for entire house will be available soon.

"SOUP'S ON"

The Oakridge Corporation
We offer the largest selection of quality 1/2" scale dollhouse kits, building shell kits, building components, building supplies, paints, finishes, adhesives, painting equipment, electrical, lighting, scale furniture, trees, landscaping, foundation materials, detail accessories, figures, animals, military vehicles, military and era fighting and marching figures, scale model vehicle kits, scratchbuilding and modeling tools, how-to books and unusual and hard-to-find items by many fine manufacturers.

THE MINIATURES CATALOG, *Fourteenth Edition*

1/2" FURNISHINGS

Plastruct
Home and office furnishings including bathroom, kitchen, bedroom and living room. 1/2" scale building supplies also available.

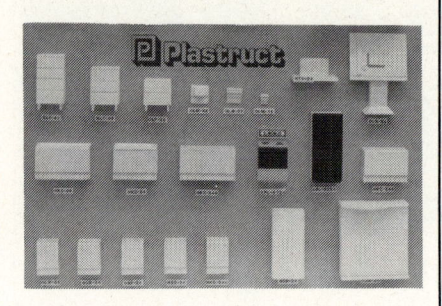

1/2" SCALE OFFICE FURNITURE AND SUPPLIES

Three Blind Mice
Suggested Retail Price: Same price for finished or unfinished. $30, desk w/typing stand; $25, desk without stand; $12, two-drawer file, $14.00, four-drawer file; $17, drafting table; $20, water cooler, $12, desk chair. Made of wood. Also available are 1/2" scale accessories shown on desk.

COLONIAL AND SHAKER FURNITURE

The Tree Trunk Studio
Suggested Retail Price: $5.50 - $79.75
Handmade Colonial and Shaker reproductions. Shown: Shaker woodbox; $26 in 1/2". Accurate scale and detailing. Custom orders.

1/2" Scale Electrical & Interior Decorating

12-VOLT "FLAME-TIP" BULB

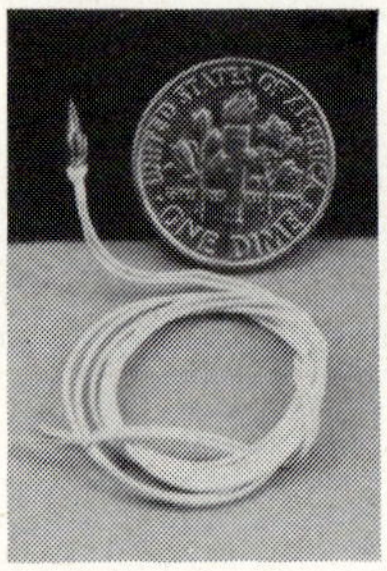

Cir-Kit Concepts, Inc.
Suggested Retail Price: $2.49
Catalog No. CK1010-11.
Smallest flame-tip bulb made. Only 0.079" in diameter. Comes with small gauge 12" wire. Works on 12 volts. Current 40 ma. Guaranteed 10,000 hours.

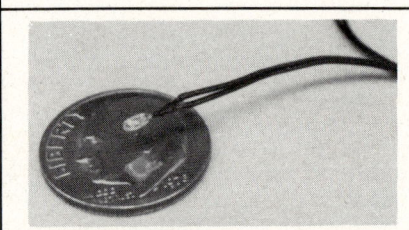

1.5 VOLT MICRO BULB WITH 8" BLACK OR WHITE WIRES

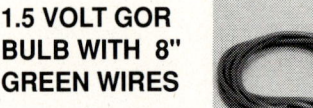

Cir-Kit Concepts, Inc.
Suggested Retail Price: $1.25. Catalog No. CK1010-13 black, No. CK1010-14 white. To our knowledge, the smallest bulb in the world; only .055" in diameter. Use with any 1.5V battery or our CK1009G 1.5V transformer. Current drain, 15 ma.

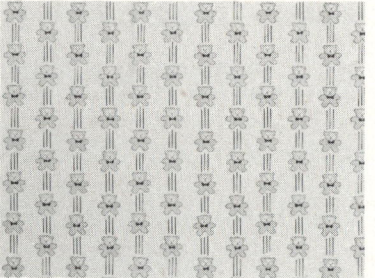

12-VOLT FLAME-TIP BULB

Cir-Kit Concepts, Inc.
Suggested Retail Price: $1.79
Catalog No. CK1010-12.
Same size and characteristics as CK1010-11. Constructed with solid wires. Use as replacement bulbs for light fixtures equipped with plug-in bulbs and receptacles.

1.5 VOLT GOR BULB WITH 8" GREEN WIRES

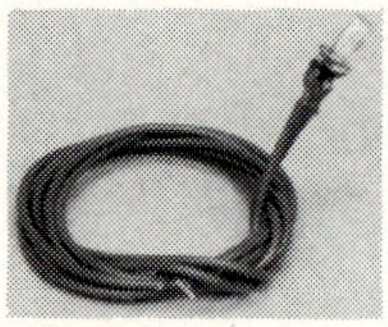

Cir-Kit Concepts, Inc.
Suggested Retail Price: $1.15
Catalog No. CK1020
Use 12 of these in series to make your own Christmas light string or use individually across a 1.5 volt source such as our CK1009G transformer. Small size makes them ideal for any scale. Each bulb consumes only 35 ma. at 1.5 volts. Approximately 3/16" long x 3/32" diameter. Also available in colors.

1/2" & 1/4" SCALE WALLPAPER

J. Hermes
Suggested Retail Price: $.35/sheet
Dimensions: 5-1/2" x 8-1/2"
Material: Printed paper
Papers for the smaller scale interior an exterior. Linoleums, flooring and wallpaper prints, bricks, siding and roofing prints. Over 300 designs and color combinations available.

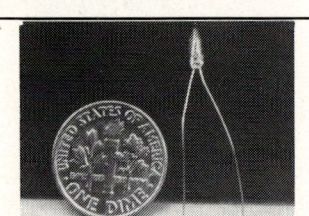

Smaller Scale Accessories

FIVE-LITE CRYSTAL CHANDELIER
The Lighting Bug
Flame bulbs and swags of tiny crystal rocailles. Order #HSZ.

FOUR-LITE BRASS CHANDELIER
The Lighting Bug
Four-lite brass chandelier with flame bulbs. Order #HSO.

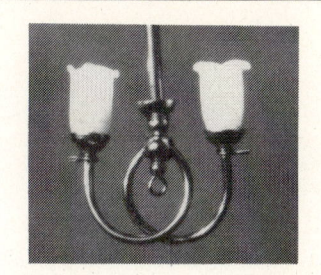

TWO-LITE BRASS CHANDELIER
The Lighting Bug
Two-lite brass chandelier with white glass shades. Order #HSJ.

Interested in a Club?
Contact the National Association of Miniature Enthusiasts for a club in your area.

N.A.M.E.
130 N. Rangeline Rd.
Carmel, IN 46032

1/2" Scale Houses, Plans & Displays

THE QUEEN ANNE ROWHOUSE 1/2"

American Craft Products
Suggested Retail Price: See your local dealer Catalog No. 108
Specifications: 11"W x 12"D x 20-1/2"H, eight rooms including spacious front entry parlor plus room-sized 2nd floor landing and hall. Divided full-size attic.
Material: 1/4" solid birch plywood
Shell kit No. 108 includes all the precision cut material necessary to build the basic house without windows, doors and trim. Optional component package No. 108-S is available providing all Carlson working windows, doors, interior stairs and exterior trim. Hinged attic side roof, two hinged side openings, fully open at rear.

THE VICTORIAN HOUSE 1/2"

American Craft Products
Suggested Retail Price: See your local dealer Catalog No. 107
Specifications: 17-1/2"W x 13-1/2"D x 20-1/2"H, six large rooms on 1st and 2nd floors plus dormer and tower areas on divided 3rd floor.
Material: birch plywood
Shell kit No. 107 includes all the precision cut material necessary to build the basic house without windows, doors and trim. Optional component package No. 107-S is available providing all Carlson working windows, doors, interior stairs and exterior trim. Fully open at rear, one hinged side opening.

HANG UP ROOM BOXES

Itty Bitty Builder
Suggested Retail Price:
#1201; 5"H x 7-1/2"W x 6"D; $34.95, finishing kit $28.70 (top)
#1203; 11"H x 11-1/4"W x 6"D; $34.95, finishing kit $24.10 (bottom)
A room box that doesn't look like a box and it can hang on the wall. Constructed of quality 1/4" plywood, comes assembled and complete with acrylic front cover. Finishing kit includes pre-cut siding, brick foundation and chimney, wood shingles, trim and moldings. Prices do not include shipping.

THE MINIATURES CATALOG, Fourteenth Edition

1/24TH SCALE COLONIAL SHELL

Houseworks
Suggested Retail Price: $90
Catalog No. H1003H
Specifications: 16-1/2"H x 8"D x 16-5/8"L
Kit includes 3/8" cabinet grade plywood, front opening designs, step-by-step instructions and a 3-in-1 Dollhouse Planbook for your reference. Write to Houseworks for information on the Houseworks Component Sets.

1/24TH SCALE GEORGIAN SHELL

Houseworks
Suggested Retail Price: $100
Catalog No. H1002H
Specifications: 16-1/2"H x 11-1/4"D x 16-5/8"L
Kit includes 3/8" cabinet grade plywood, front opening designs, step-by-step instructions and a 3-in-1 Dollhouse Planbook for your reference. Write to Houseworks for information on the Houseworks Component Sets.

1/24TH SCALE VICTORIAN SHELL

Houseworks
Suggested Retail Price: $110
Catalog No. H1001H
Kit includes 3/8" cabinet grade plywood, front opening designs, step-by-step instructions and a three-in-one Dollhouse Planbook for your reference. Write to Houseworks for information on the Houseworks Component Sets.

THE ELIZABETH ANNE

The Oakridge Corporation
Suggested Retail Price: $79.95
Catalog No. 2000H
Dimensions: 24-1/2"H x 20"H x 11-1/2"D
A truly deluxe Victorian dollhouse shell kit. Quality plywood construction. Eight large rooms plus fully accessible attic with staircase opening. Easy "tab and slot" assembly. Compatible with Houseworks components. Components, trim and siding not included.

Georgian: H1002

Victorian: H1001

Colonial: H1003

1/2" SCALE FRONT-OPENING DOLLHOUSE KITS

Real Good Toys
Suggested Retail Price: See your dealer
Catalog No. H1001 Victorian, #H1002 Georgian, #H1003 Colonial
Specifications: 16-1/2"L x 16-1/2"H x 11"D
These sturdy dollhouse kits come either as a shell or with all Houseworks components needed to create a finished dollhouse. The popular "front opening" design is just one of the unique features of these dollhouses. Created by the teamwork of Real Good Toys and Houseworks, they were originally featured in the Houseworks Dollhouse Plan Book, and are now available as a precision-cut kit that is easily assembled.

Want to list your products in the catalog next year?

To receive information on the 15th Edition of *The Miniatures Catalog*, send your name and address to: Sara Benz, *The Miniatures Catalog*, 21027 Crossroads Circle, P.O. Box 1612, Waukesha, WI 53187.

Prices are approximate and subject to change.

1/4" and Smaller Scale Miniatures

MAC GREEDY'S EMPORIUM

The Oakridge Corporation
Suggested Retail Price: $59.95
Catalog No. 3000H
Dimensions: 17"L x 17"H x 13"D
Create your own personalized version of "MacGreedy's Emporium" from the large variety of components, trims, accessories and building supplies available from the Oakridge Corporation. Quality plywood construction. Two large rooms stairway/hallway. Easy "tab and slot" assembly. Compatible with Houseworks components. Components, trim and siding not included.

THE VICTORIAN MANOR

The Oakridge Corporation
Suggested Retail Price: $112
Catalog No. 207
Dimensions: 8-1/2"H x 11"W x 8"D, Craftsman shell kit
This Victorian in 1/4" scale stands approximately 34' tall, 44' wide and 32' deep. It has a double door entryway with transom, wooden porch and steps, a single-pane, seven-panel back door, 18 8' double-hung, 8-pane windows, 40 louvered shutters, clear acetate window glass, ornate spool gable and porch trim, turned porch and balcony posts and balustrade, intricately detailed eave accents with basswood clapboard siding, scribed ceiling and floor board for porch, roof panels, eaves and trim and real cedar shakes. Wholesale and retail.

THE GREENLEAF VILLAGE FIREHOUSE AND BANDSTAND

Greenleaf Products
Suggested Retail Price: $16.25
Catalog No. 8026
Dimensions: approximately 1/4" scale, however, not true to scale
Material: 1/8" di-cut plywood, cardboard shingles and trim
The Firehouse and Bandstand can be used to expand our popular Greenleaf Village set or individually. Use them in a Winter setting for Christmas decor or as a part of your train layout. Typical of Firehouses and Bandstands in small towns across the country, this Firehouse was immortalized in a Norman Rockwell painting.

TOWN-LATTICED COVERED BRIDGE

The Oakridge Corporation
Suggested Retail Price: $37
Catalog No. 104
Dimensions: 6 1/2"H x 7"W x 12"L, Craftsman shell kit
The purpose of the covered bridge was to protect the deck and structural timbers from the elements. If a girl was lucky, her beau would pay the toll 8¢ to walk under the cool canopy on a sweltering summer's day. The bridge measures approximately 26' tall from bridge seat timber to ridge row shingles, 28' wide and 48' long. Clearance is 12' from the deck to the upper chord support beam braces. 1/4" scale kit includes walnut latticed truss work with basswood scribeboard siding, roof panels, eaves and trim, pine interior bracing and real cedar shingles. Wholesale and retail.

GREENLEAF VILLAGE

Greenleaf Products
Suggested Retail Price: $30
Catalog No. 8016
Dimensions: approximately 1/4" scale, however, not true to scale
Material: 1/8" di-cut plywood
The Greenleaf village is as cute as can be in Christmas settings, works great as individual gift boxes or display boxes and also has applicability for use with O trains. All six buildings are beautifully designed and include a church, school, carriage house, store, Tudor and scaled down Arthur dollhouse replica. charming and quaint!

Smaller Scale Accessories

THE MINIATURES CATALOG, Fourteenth Edition   305

OLD TOWNE VILLAGE

Dura-Craft, Inc.
Catalog No. OT950
Perfect for the miniature and railroad enthusiasts of all ages. HO scale (approximately 1/8"=1'). Delightful village setting. Eight pieces including barn, church, two houses, school, store, water wheel and covered bridge. Windows, trim, shakes and fencing included. All woo structures, pre-cut pieces for easy assembly. Easy to follow instructions.

HO SCALE STRUCTURE DETAILS

Grandt Line Products, Inc.
Suggested Retail Price: $1.25 - $4.
Scale: 1:87 (HO)
Material: Polystyrene plastic
Architectural and detail parts for the miniaturist in smaller scales. Items show super detail-down to wood grain on "wood" parts. Cast in adaptable styrene plastic.

1/4" SCALE ARCHITECTURAL DETAILS

Grandt Line Products, Inc.
Suggested Retail Price: $1.25 - $4.
Scale: 1/4" - 1"
Material: Polystyrene plastic
Super detailed structural parts accessories for the discriminating smaller scale miniaturist. Most castings are in gray styrene plastic...easy to adapt with a hobby knife and liquid cement. Accepts paint easily.

THE FAIRFIELD

Greenleaf Products, Inc.
Suggested Retail Price: $57
Catalog No. 8015
Scale: 1/2"
Dimensions: 20" H x 15" W x 16" D, Six rooms, attic, secret tower room, shingles included
Material: Pre-cut plywood
Picture this table center — a beautifully detailed 1/2" scale dollhouse no bigger than a placemat. Make it perfectly Victorian in every aspect, even including a tower chamber, four fireplaces, and a wrap-around porch.

Smaller Scale Accessories

GREENLEAF VILLAGE STATION AND STORE

Greenleaf Products
Suggested Retail Price: $16.25
Catalog No. 8025
Dimensions: approximately 1/4" scale, however, not true to scale
Material: 1/8" di-cut plywood
These two little charmers are perfect for Christmas decorating and in train layouts. The Village Station and Country Emporium are very easy to build and were designed to accompany our popular Greenleaf Village kit. Use individually or to expand the village.

1/4" SCALE VICTORIAN HOUSES

Parker House Miniatures
"Aunt Julia's House", Catalog No. 55, finished outside. All houses are center-split and electrified. Windows, doors and finishing materials for inside and outside are available. Made of 1/8" birch plywood throughout - available as shells or finished houses.

1/4" SCALE HOUSE/ROOM BOX

J. Hermes
Suggested Retail Price: $5-$10.
Scale: 1/4"
Material: Foam core board (1/8" thick)
Darling 1/4" scale house and breakaway box kits are inexpensive and easy-to-assemble. Ideal for workshop, class, and club projects. Uses O scale model railroad component trim. Kits can even be electrified. Instructions included. Furniture and accessories are available.

1/4" SCALE FURNITURE SET

J. Hermes
Suggested Retail Price: $8.75
Scale: 1/4"-1"
Material: Plastic
This set includes wood-tone plastic furniture for den, bedroom, bathroom, dining room and kitchen. Included is a tip sheet on "kit-bashing" these particular pieces to make different pieces. Catalog #PF-1.

THE COUNTRY CHURCH

The Oakridge Corporation
Suggested Retail Price: $56.50
Catalog No. 304
Dimensions: 7"W x 14"H x 9"D, Craftsman shell kit
On Sunday morning loud and clear you'll hear the church bells chime. The people in their Sunday best, ask the Lord to be faithfully blessed. This 1/4" scale kit contains basswood structural components, trim, a paper shingle roof, a bell and styrene windows and doors. Stained glass window material can be added as an accent or a finishing touch.

FOR FAST SERVICE, VISIT YOUR LOCAL MINIATURES SHOP

THE MINIATURES CATALOG, Fourteenth Edition

1/4" SCALE BUILDING SUPPLIES

The Oakridge Corporation
We offer the largest selection of quality 1/4" scale dollhouse kits, building shell kits, building components, building supplies, paints, finishes, adhesives, painting equipment, electrical, lighting, scale furniture, trees, landscaping, foundation materials, detail accessories, figures, animals, military vehicles, military and era fighting and marching figures, scale model vehicle kits, scratchbuilding and modeling tools, how-to books and unusual and hard-to-find items by many fine manufacturers.

Interested in Becoming a Miniatures Manufacturer?

Join the Miniatures Industry Association of America and sell products to retailers across the country.

MIAA
1100-H Brandywine Blvd.
P.O. Box 2188
Zanesville, OH 43702-3288

THE COUNTRY STORE

The Oakridge Corporation
Suggested Retail Price: $35.50.
Catalog No. 303
Dimensions: 5"W x 6"H x 10"L, Craftsman shell kit
The store that has everything including a sympathetic and flexible credit department. This 1/4" scale kit contains basswood structural components, trim siding and roof components, a paper shingle roof, stovepipe, styrene windows and doors. Can be converted into a fine miniature display piece to decorate and furnish. Wholesale and retail.

THE OLD MILL

The Oakridge Corporation
Suggested Retail Price: $54
Catalog No. 305
Scale: 1/4"
This mill comes with basswood scribed siding, real cedar shingles, a 3" waterwheel, roofing and structural components and fieldstone panels (styrene), styrene doors, windows and chimney. Available in 1/2" scale, #1305H, $159. Interior foamboard construction allows for sturdy assembly and can be converted to a dollhouse or building with an exposed interior suitable for display.

1/4" FURNISHINGS

Plastruct
Home and office furnishings including bathroom, kitchen, bedroom, living room, dining room and den. 1/4" scale building supplies also available.

"THERE GOES THE NEIGHBORHOOD"

The Oakridge Corporation
We offer the largest selection of quality 1/4" scale dollhouse kits, building shell kits, building components, building supplies, paints, finishes, adhesives, painting equipment, electrical, lighting, scale furniture, trees, landscaping, foundation materials, detail accessories, figures, animals, military vehicles, military and era fighting and marching figures, scale model vehicle kits, scratchbuilding and modeling tools, how-to books and unusual and hard-to-find items by many fine manufacturers.

Smaller Scale Accessories

Smaller Scale Miscellaneous

1/4" PLANTS AND FLOWERS
Mary Payne
From the studio of Mary Payne. Yard tree (2-1/4" tall) $15. S-L Philodendron tree (1-1/4" tall) $15. Bonsai tree (3/8" tall) $6.50. Red geraniums (1/4" tall) $5.50. Caladiums, red or white (1/2" tall) $10. Spathiphyllom (1/2" tall) $6.50. Add $1.50 shipping per order.

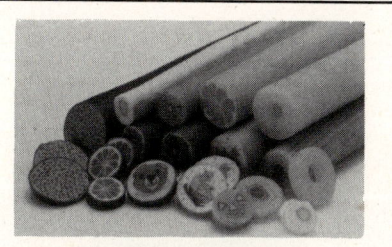

CANDY, COOKIE & FOOD DESIGNS
Donna Smolik's Designs
Suggested Retail Price: $1.75-$4.25 each. Candies, fruits, vegetables, meats - slice your own with a single-edged razor blade. Can be used in 1", 1/2" or 1/4" scales.

ANTIQUE AND OLDER MINIATURES
Close To Your Heart
Retail list available. Artist-made items for your dollhouse or mini collection. Limited selection of older miniatures by Renwal Tootsiotoy, Strombecker, Sonia Messer. Shows and mail order only. Please state what your interest is. No wholesale.

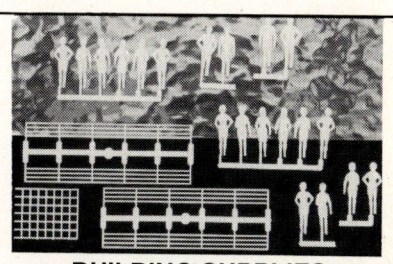

BUILDING SUPPLIES
Model Builders Supply
1/2" and 1/4" kitchen, bathroom and living room items, plus all the products shown in categories 23, 64 and 122 plus figures, trellis', steps, stairs, fences, water textures and much more. U.S. customers, see "Plastruct".

Instead of reading this, customers could be reading about your products.

To learn more about how your products can be part of the next edition of The Miniatures Catalog, contact Sara Benz, Advertising Sales Manager at (800) 558-1544, ext. 631

Or write: The Miniatures Catalog, Kalmbach Publishing Co., 21027 Crossroads Circle, P.O. Box 1612, Waukesha, WI 53187-1612

Publications & Plans

Special Services

Judy Herman Appelbaum
Appraiser of dollhouses and miniatures. Appraisals for valuation, casualty losses, insurance and contributions. Member of International Society of Appraisers.

BUTTONS AND AWARD RIBBONS FOR MINIATURISTS
Buttons By Wilson
Put your club, shop, show or statement on a pin-back button. All colors, sizes, no minimum. We also provide award ribbons, plaques and stickers for miniature events. In-stock line of buttons related to miniatures also available.

Magazines

MINIATURE QUILTS MAGAZINE
Dollhouse Doll-ups
Suggested Retail Price: $3.50
35 patterns to make your own miniature quilts. The miniature quilt kit is available for $10. Also available; punch needles, braided rug kits and supplies.

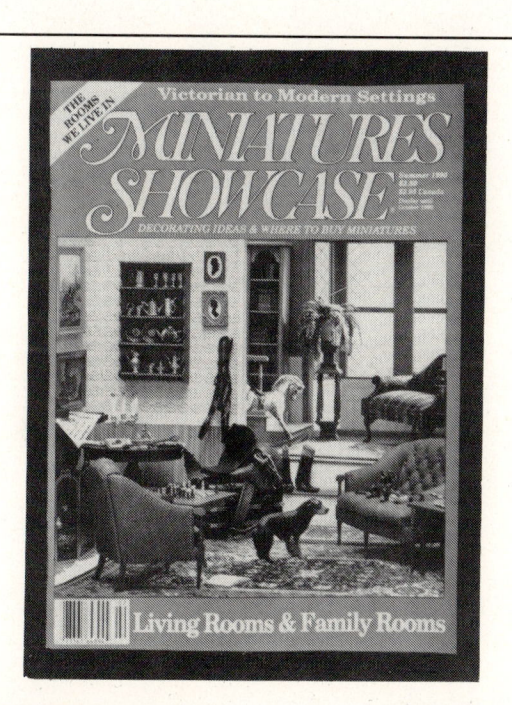

MINIATURES SHOWCASE

Kalmbach Publishing Co.
Subscription: $14.95 per year
Miniatures Showcase is a colorful full-size (8-1/4" x 11") reference guide! This magazine showcases a particular decorating period in history or a popular theme for miniatures hobbyists to enjoy in each issue. Upcoming issues for 1991-92 will include: Bed & Breakfasts, Literature and Fairytales, and Children Do the Darndest Things. Shop at home for handcrafted miniatures with this quarterly publication.

MINIATURE GAZETTE

National Association of Miniature Enthusiasts
Published by N.A.M.E., 80 pages
Membership is $20 per year, $25 foreign. Fee includes the quarterly magazine.
The *Gazette* features artists, exhibits, work projects, an extensive Calendar of Events, plus more. For information contact:
N.A.M.E.
130 N. Rangeline Rd.
Carmel, IN 46032

Publications & Plans

KIMBERLY CORNER PUBLICATION

Published by Kimberly House
Suggested Retail Price: $6 for six issues (one year), Canada $9
16 pages of fun and information, six issues a year. Inside each issue you will always find the famous *Project Insert*. *Sandy's Corner* will help you find answers to miniature problems. Nationwide product searches.

Each issue contains: *Plans* with good instructions for making miniature pieces, explained with professionally done diagrams and loaded with descriptive photos. *Artisan Corner* showing and talking about handmade pieces, accessories and components. *Product Reviews* and their applications. Many *Helpful Hints* and *How-To's*. See your dealer or write to Kimberly House.

NUTSHELL NEWS

Kalmbach Publishing Co.
Suggested Retail Price: $29 per year.
Pages: 132 average
Nutshell News is a colorful monthly magazine covering every aspect of the miniatures hobby. Coverage of major miniatures shows, work by readers, tours of collections, artisan profiles and do-it-yourself projects are included in every issue. Nutshell News is the one source you need to keep abreast of everything happening in the world of miniatures.

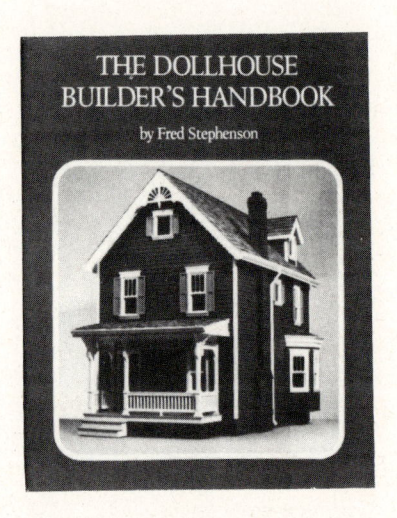

THE DOLLHOUSE BUILDER'S HANDBOOK

Design Tecnics Miniatures
Author: Fred Stephenson
Suggested Retail Price: $5.95 plus shipping
Number of Pages: 44
Softcover
Written by Fred Stephenson, the author of "The Architect's Angle" for *Nutshell News*, this thorough reference book covers all aspects of building and finishing dollhouses. The techniques apply to building a house from sheets of plywood or placing the finishing touches on a kit house, inside and out. Subjects include tools, materials, plan selection, windows, doors, siding, trim, ornaments, brick, roofing, electrification, stairs, interior finishing and much more. Profusely illustrated with photographs and excellent drawings, the information includes simple basics as well as detailed explanations where needed.

How-To Books and Plans; Houses & Shops

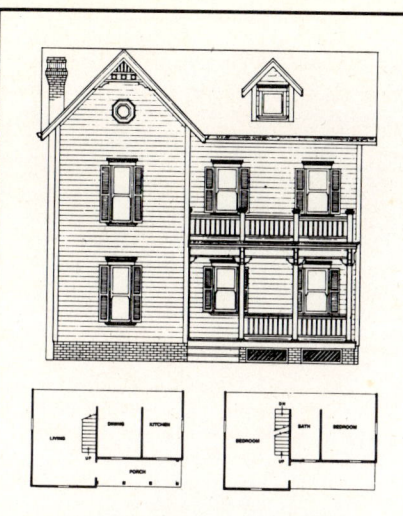

"ARCHITECT'S CHOICE" DOLLHOUSE PLANS

Design Tecnics Miniatures
Design Number 1
Author: Fred Stephenson
Suggested Retail Price: $5.95 plus shipping
Dimensions: 19-1/2" x 31-5/8" x 31" H
Design Number 1 is a roomy house with a large porch and a very convenient layout of rooms. Complete plans for building a house shell from 3/8" plywood also include suggestions and techniques for completion of siding, trim, shingles, etc.

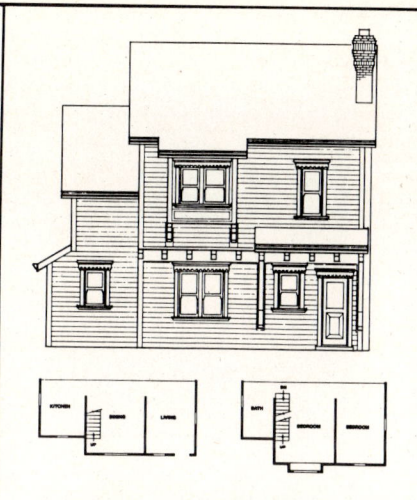

"ARCHITECT'S CHOICE" DOLLHOUSE PLANS

Design Tecnics Miniatures
Design Number 2
Author: Fred Stephenson
Suggested Retail Price: $5.95 plus shipping
Dimensions: 16-1/2" x 32-1/2" x 30-1/2" H
Design Number 2 is a picturesque house with an overhanging second floor and unique opportunities for adding bracketed trim. Complete plans for building a house shell from 3/8" plywood also include suggestions and techniques for completion of siding, trim, shingles, etc.

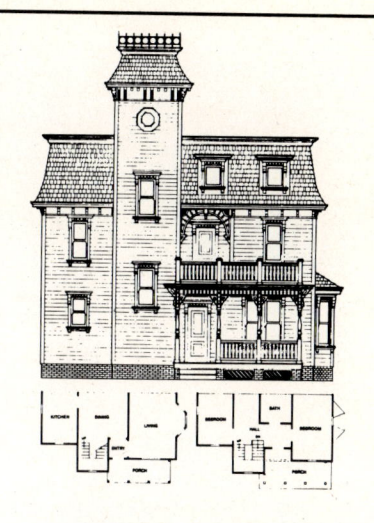

"ARCHITECT'S CHOICE" DOLLHOUSE PLANS

Design Tecnics Miniatures
Design Number 3
Author: Fred Stephenson
Suggested Retail Price: $7.95 plus shipping
Dimensions: 22-1/8" x 37-7/8" x 40-3/4" H.
Design Number 3 combines a large and serviceable floor plan with an exterior designed for the application of extensive Victorian ornamentation. Complete plans for building a house shell from 3/8" plywood also include suggestions and techniques for completion of siding, trim, shingles, etc.

"ARCHITECT'S CHOICE" DOLLHOUSE PLANS

Design Tecnics Miniatures
Design Number 4
Author: Fred Stephenson
Suggested Retail Price: $5.95 plus shipping
Dimensions: 20-3/4" x 23-1/8" x 31-7/8" H
Design Number 4 is a compact house with plenty of room for the usual living spaces. The exterior is adaptable for many different style treatments. Complete plans for building a house shell from 3/8" plywood also include suggestions and techniques for completion of siding, trim, shingles, etc.

"ARCHITECT'S CHOICE" DOLLHOUSE PLANS

Design Tecnics Miniatures
Design Number 5
Author: Fred Stephenson
Suggested Retail Price: $5.95 plus shipping
Dimensions: 20" x 36-7/8" x 33-1/4" H
Design Number 5 combines Colonial lines with a wide farmhouse porch and opportunities for adding decorative trim. Complete plans for building a house shell from 3/8" plywood also include suggestions and techniques for completion of siding, trim, shingles, etc.

"ARCHITECT'S CHOICE" DOLLHOUSE PLANS

Design Tecnics Miniatures
Design Number 6
Author: Fred Stephenson
Suggested Retail Price: $5.95 plus shipping
Dimensions: 18-1/2" x 44-1/4" x 31-15/8" H
The unique orientation of Design Number 6 contributes to a functional floor plan and plenty of places for gingerbread options. Complete plans for building a house shell from 3/8" plywood also include suggestions and techniques for completion of siding, trim, shingles, etc.

Publications & Plans

THE CATALOGUE OF DOLLHOUSES, SUPPLIES AND MINIATURES

**Published by
The Dollhouse Factory**™
Author: Robert V. Dankanics
Suggested Retail Price: $5.50
Softcover; 120 pages
This 120 page publication features over 4300 items plus helpful hints on how the professionals do it. Not only is there a vast array of products featured but also very useful information on how to use them.

THE HOUSEWORKS DOLLHOUSE PLAN BOOK

Houseworks
Author: Garth Close
Suggested Retail Price: $5.95
Catalog No. 1001
36 pages
Builds three complete houses (Georgian, Victorian and Colonial). Has over 100 step-by-step photos, diagrams, patterns and decorating tips to build three quality dollhouses. #1 Bestseller in Plan Books.

LES SHOPPES

Houseworks
Author: Garth Close
Suggested Retail Price: $5.95
Catalog No. 1002
24 pages
A European flavor is created in two separate stores and living quarters in a unique two-story corner arrangement. Highly detailed. This dollhouse is opened from the back.

DOLLHOUSES TO DREAM HOUSES, BOOK 1

Published by Greenleaf, Inc.
Now in its sixth printing.
Thirty-six pages containing 103 detailed photos and 35 step-by-step diagrams. Also included are interior decorating ideas, exterior decorating techniques, creative customizing and remodeling, easy instructions for lighting and wiring and product sources. All photographs were from our customers dollhouses at different stages of completing their Dream House.
All this and more...only $5.75
See your dealer or write Kimberly House.

DOLLHOUSES TO DREAM HOUSES, BOOK 2

Published by Greenleaf, Inc.
Suggested Retail Price: $6.25
Seventy-two page, softcover catalog containing 118 detailed photos and 75 step-by-step diagrams. Also includes information on platforms and their value, gluing chapter and chart and landscaping techniques. Different houses than Book 1. See your dealer or write Kimberly House.

"Brookwood" just one of the houses featured in this book.

Spanish House from two Coventry Cottage kits, just one of the houses featured in this book.

DOLLHOUSE PLAN BOOK

Handley House
Suggested Retail Price: $9.95
Catalog No. HH5900
Author: Al and Ethel Comunale.
Number of pages: 105
Softcover
Three completely different house plans are included in this 105-page book. Packed with helpful new hints and professional building tips, this book guides you step-by-step, using 172 photographs, illustrations, and complete easy-to-follow instructions for both the novice and master builder.

Publications & Plans

October National Dollhouse & Miniatures Month

TOWNSEND TOWERS

Houseworks
Author: Garth Close
Suggested Retail Price: $5.95
Catalog No. 1003
24 pages
Townsend Towers is a city style Brownstone that reflects the distinctive ornamental treatments popular with the late 1800's. Towers is very narrow and opens on both sides for easy play or decoration.

TUXEDO PLACE

Houseworks
Author: Garth Close
Suggested Retail Price: $5.95
Catalog No. 1005
24 pages
The charm of a formal English Tudor home is designed with an appreciation of architectural accents and proportions. Opens on both sides to expose both floors and seven rooms with an optional room if desired.

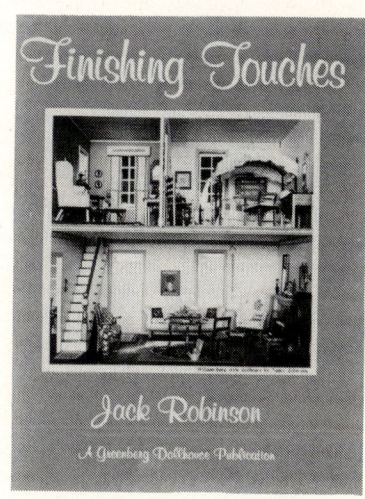

FINISHING TOUCHES

Greenberg Publishing Co., Inc.
Suggested Retail Price: $7.95 plus $3 for US shipping, $4 Canadian and Foreign
Catalog no. 10-6600
Author: Jack Robinson
8-1/2" x 11"; 64 pages
Learn how to create lightweight, realistic bricks and concrete blocks, wooden floors and simple but realistic trim to beautify and individualize any dollhouse.

How-To Books and Plans; Furniture & Furnishings

THE MINIATURES CATALOG, *Fourteenth Edition*

How-To Books and Plans; Decorative Accessories

"MINIATURES FROM BAUBLES, BANGLES AND BEADS" VOLUME 4

JAF Miniatures
Suggested Retail Price: $13.95
Softcover, 68 pages
Volume Four presents over 75 new designs utilizing jewelry findings resulting in collectible chandeliers, lamps and accessories. Clear line drawings, instructions and materials list accompany projects. Make electrified sconces with lustres, classic table lamps, pendant-laden chandeliers, simple ceiling fixtures to a tiny whale oil "Sparking Lamp", glass vase with flowers and more.

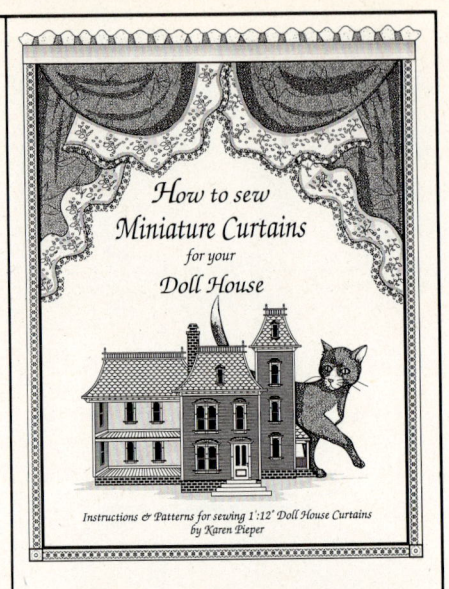

"HOW TO SEW YOUR OWN MINIATURE CURTAINS"

Pieper Gallery
Suggested Retail Price: $12.95 + $2 S&H
Sew your own miniature curtains in 1:12 scale. Patterns include; long curtain, short tiered, shirback swag, plus valances in either lace trim or fancy ruffle. Also included are instructions and tips for sewing in miniature.

How-To Books and Plans; Dolls

HOW-TO BOOKS

Dahl's House of Miniatures
New in 1991 - revised book on assembling, wigging, and interchangeable dress patterns. 41 pages with over 100 illustrations and colored pictures, $17.50 post paid. Other books available are Volume I Victorian, Volume III 1830-1877 and Volume IV Victorian. These books are $11.50 post paid.

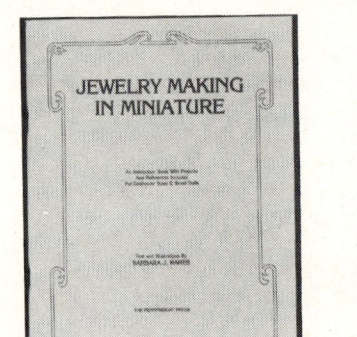

INSTRUCTION BOOK JEWELRY MAKING IN MINIATURE

Barbara J. Raheb
Author: Barbara J. Raheb
Suggested Retail Price: $12.90 Prepaid.
Pages: 68
Softcover
For the serious dollmaker; contains clear, complete instructions with easy-to-follow black-and-white illustrations, pertinent reference information and actual projects as well as bead utilization in areas other than jewelry making. Material supply list and order form included with book.

316 Prices are approximate and subject to change.

FOR FAST SERVICE, VISIT YOUR LOCAL MINIATURES SHOP

How-To Books and Plans; Miscellaneous

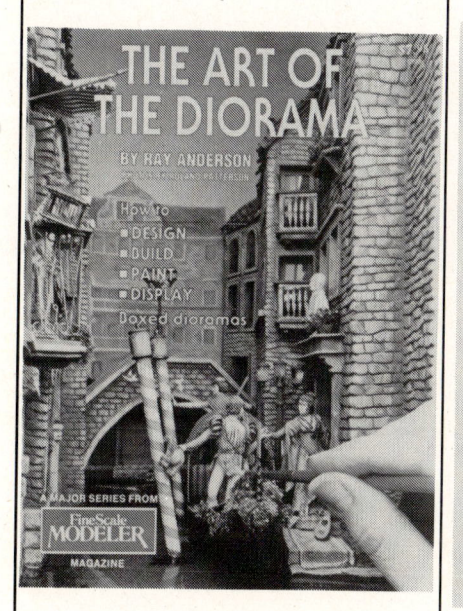

Publications & Plans

THE ART OF THE DIORAMA

Kalmbach Publishing Co.
Suggested Retail Price: $7.95 plus $3 for US shipping, $4 Canadian and Foreign
Catalog No. 12080
Every miniatures scene has a story behind it, and this 56-page book explains how to effectively design, build, paint and display that story to convey a particular message or feeling. This step-by-step guide focuses on the basic concept of the diorama - that it must have a story to tell - and then shows how to apply that concept to your miniatures scenes.

HOW TO BUILD DIORAMAS

Kalmbach Publishing Co.
Suggested Retail Price: $11.95 plus $3 for US shipping, $4 Canadian and Foreign
Catalog No. 12047
Weathering techniques, painting figures and shadow box construction are some of the topics master modeler Sheperd Paine covers in his book. He explains in 104 pages how he designs, plans and builds his dioramas from the ground up. The book includes four projects that illustrate techniques which you can use in your next miniatures project.

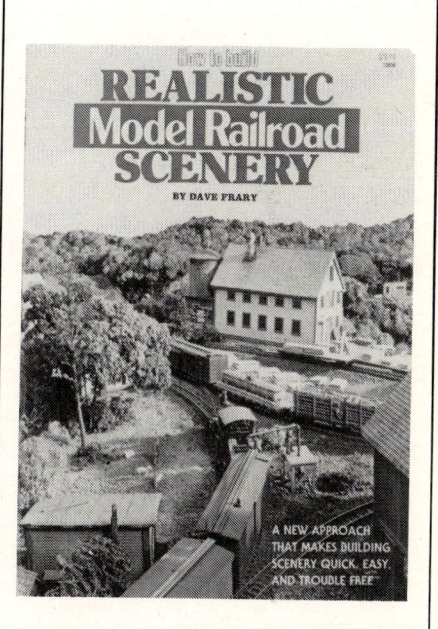

HOW TO BUILD REALISTIC MODEL RAILROAD SCENERY

Kalmbach Publishing Co.
Suggested Retail Price: $9.95 plus $3 for US shipping, $4 Canadian and Foreign
Catalog No. 12056
Add life to your miniatures by building wonderful scenes around them, regardless of your artistic ability. With hobby tips from model railroading, you can create excellent miniature settings. The author of this 100-page book tells how to build scenic forms, color and texture scenery, rocks, rubble, foliage and water and also how to create backdrops for your scenes.

THE MINIATURES CATALOG, *Fourteenth Edition* 317

HOW TO PHOTOGRAPH SCALE MODELS

Kalmbach Publishing Co.
Suggested Retail Price: $8.95 plus $3 for US shipping, $4 Canadian and Foreign
Catalog No. 12067
This 64-page book explains basic and advanced techniques for photographing miniatures in different settings. If you would like to compose and photograph your room boxes, scenes, and miniatures items with flair, the 146 photos and suggestions in this book will help improve your techniques.

PAINTING AND FINISHING SCALE MODELS

Kalmbach Publishing Co.
Suggested Retail Price: $8.95 plus $3 for US shipping, $4 Canadian and Foreign
Catalog No. 12099
After creating a miniature doll, building or any other small-scale item, there are steps necessary to take to finish the model effectively. If you need to know how to finish your miniature creations, this book offers techniques on painting, airbrushing, weathering and more. 72 pages.

SCENERY FOR MODEL RAILROADS

Kalmbach Publishing Co.
Suggested Retail Price: $7.95 plus $3 for US shipping, $4 Canadian and Foreign
Catalog No. 12008
An excellent source for ideas, this book offers 103 pages and over 300 illustrations on how to make your miniature settings appear realistic and dramatic. The author expands on many different techniques to help you create scenes with life, including zip texturing, wire-screen and hardshell techniques, model rivers, lakes and rugged rock formations.

DREAM ON WITH KIMBERLY HOUSE, BOOK ONE

Kimberly House Miniatures
Suggested Retail Price: $5.95
Author: Dennis Waldron & Sandy Thomas, authors of "Dollhouses to Dream Houses, Books 1 & 2"
Size: 8-1/2" x 11", 72 pages
A book of ideas and techniques for landscaping your dollhouse and miniature scenes. Six actual projects that can be reproduced individually or in combination. Loaded with photos in step-by-step sequence. Many definitive diagrams and illustrations. Shown is just one of the projects in this first book of the "Dream On" Striper Series.

Interested in a Club?

Contact the National Association of Miniature Enthusiasts for a club in your area.

N.A.M.E.
130 N. Rangeline Rd.
Carmel, IN 46032

SCENERY TIPS AND TECHNIQUES FROM *MODEL RAILROADER* MAGAZINE

Kalmbach Publishing Co.
Suggested Retail Price: $11.95 plus $3 for US shipping, $4 Canadian and Foreign
Catalog No. 12084
The techniques used in the model railroading hobby parallel what we do in dollhouse miniatures. In this book, authors share their ideas about scenery and many of the techniques they employ with landscaping and building materials in different miniature scales. For ideas on how to create trees and bushes, buildings, backgrounds, backdrops and more, this book can help with its 116 pages of suggestions.

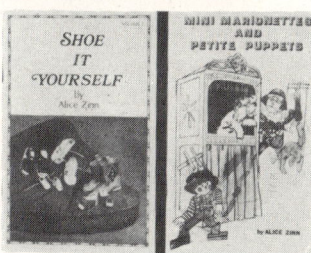

HOW-TO BOOKLETS

Published by Alice Zinn
Author: Alice Zinn
Suggested Retail Price: $5 each plus 52¢ postage for each book ordered.

Oriental Ornaments
27 pages of patterns and instructions for 1/12 scale. Kimono, Chinese pin cushion, chop sticks and more.

No Sew Clothes
24 pages to learn a new concept in miniature dressmaking. Patterns and instructions for folded shirt, leather jacket, vest and tie set and more.

Shoe It Yourself, Volume 2
19 pages of patterns and instructions for 1/12 scale. Leather boots, sandals, high-heeled clogs, tennis shoes and baby shoes. Includes patterns for two different shoe boxes.

Mini Marionettes & Petite Puppets
16 pages in all miniature settings during time periods from early history to the present. Puppets would be an appropriate form for entertainment and children's playthings. Build a puppet theater, hand puppets and marionettes.

Open Sesamini
24 pages of patterns and instructions, and diagrams to make 1/12 scale purse with checkbook, key and keycase and wallet, attache case, luggage set and sofa bed, all of which open and close.

Petite Pampered Pets
16 pages of 1/12 scale accessories for your mini furry friends include patterns and instructions for carrying case, leash, collars, toys and more.

Shoe It Yourself
Patterns and detailed instructions for making men's slippers, women's slippers, children's bunny slippers, canvas Chinese sshoes, saddle shoes and penny loafers. Includes tips on adaptations for other types of footwear.

Shoot It Yourself
Professional photographer offers 16 pages of text and photos to assist you in taking better photos of your miniatures for both fun and profit.

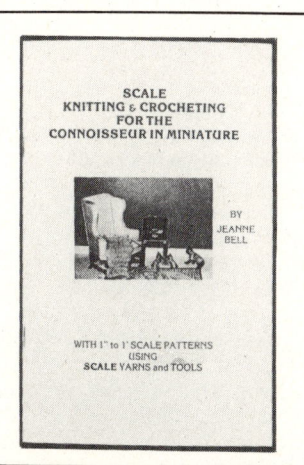

SCALE KNITTING AND CROCHETING FOR THE CONNOISSEUR IN MINIATURE

Published by Wee Three
Author: Jeanne Bell
Suggested Retail Price: $7.50
Number of Pages: 23
Expert status is certainly not required, but you should be familiar with knitting and crocheting terms to complete the patterns in this book. Included are designs for three afghans, two bedspreads, a pillow, a toy, a pullover sweater, and an infant shell sacque - all in accurate 1" to 1' scale. Supplies catalog included upon request. Postage $1.

Want to list your products in the catalog next year?

To receive information on the 15th Edition of *The Miniatures Catalog*, send your name and address to: Sara Benz, *The Miniatures Catalog*, 21027 Crossroads Circle, P.O. Box 1612, Waukesha, WI 53187.

Publications & Plans

Books and Related Products

THE MINIATURES CATALOG

Kalmbach Publishing Co.
Suggested Retail Price: $16.95 plus $3 for US shipping, $4 Canadian and Foreign, published annually, over 380 pages.
Catalog No. 12098
The Miniatures Catalog is in its 14th year of publication and is an in-depth guide to the world of dollhouse miniatures. Over 3,000 single listings offer a wide variety of dollhouses, furniture and accessories. The catalog can be purchased at miniatures shops, miniatures museums and selected independent book stores in the U.S. and Canada.

SCALE MODELING BUYERS GUIDE, 2ND EDITION

Kalmbach Publishing Co.
Suggested Retail Price: $14.95 plus $3 for US shipping, $4 Canadian and Foreign
Catalog No. 13000
8-1/4" x 10-3/4", approximately 350 pages
This handy reference guide focuses on scale modeling products, from figurines to modeling tools and equipment and also has some landscaping and diorama information relevant to the miniaturist. Available in October 1991.

1992 MINIATURES CALENDAR

Kalmbach Publishing Co.
Suggested Retail Price: $9.95 plus $3 for US shipping, $4 Canadian and Foreign
Catalog No. 68063
The 1992 Miniatures Calendar includes twelve photographs of exquisite room boxes, Americana scenes, charming antiques and more stunning work from talented miniaturists across the country. The scenes in the calendar were chosen from exhibits at the expanded Toy and Miniatures Museum of Kansas City. Available in September 1991.

Prices are approximate and subject to change.

Books for Collectors

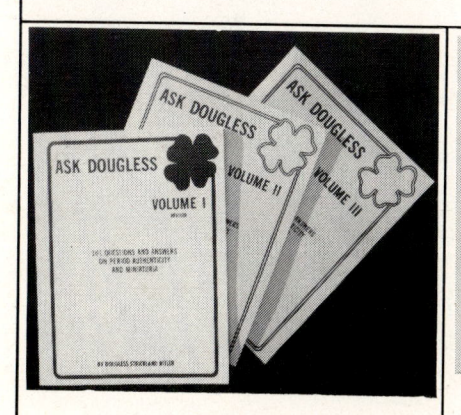

ASK DOUGLESS VOLUME I (SILVER)
ASK DOUGLESS VOLUME II (GOLD)
ASK DOUGLESS VOLUME III (COPPER)

Dougless, Ltd.
Publisher: Dee's Delights
Author: Dougless Strickland Bitler
Suggested Retail Price: $9.95 plus $2.50 postage (set of three, $33 ppd.)
Pages: 100-plus. Soft cover: 8-1/2"x11"
Nutshell News review: "Done in the same breezy style as her popular workshops and columns, entertaining as well as edifying, designed specifically for the miniaturist."
Volume I: Kitchen, bathrooms, wallpaper, windows, doors, styles, and more.
Volume II: Lighting (candle, kerosene, gas, electric), china patterns, fireplace/furnace, designs, and more.
Volume III: Illustrated Charts: Kitchens and baths (1609-1920's); Cabinet makers: Chippendale, Hepplewhite, Etc.; Architecture examples 1500-1918; much more.
Volume III Reviews: *Nutshell News:* "Hurrah! It's more of the same - invaluable reference - indexed wealth of information"; *Miniature Collector* : "facts in a social as well as historical context - leavened with Dougless' considerable good humor." Ask your dealer or order from Dougless, Ltd. Also distributed by Dee's Delights. Watch for Volume IV in the near future.

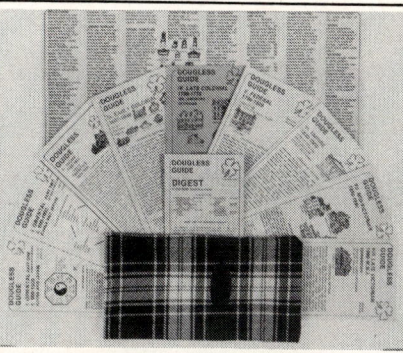

DOUGLESS GUIDES
Dougless, Ltd.
Author: Dougless Strickland Bitler.
Nutshell News review: "For a miniaturist planning an authentic setting, guides for the period are indispensible (and) proof there's nothing frivolous about your hobby." Only source for all details of North American home: 10,000 terms, 25,500 sold since 1980. First decision: Kitchen, which and when? (open hearth/iron stove/white range/wood tubs/dry sink/pump/faucets?). Thirty more categories. Guides are 8-1/2"x16" cardstock folded in eight panels. Full set (nine guides/one digest/one tartan case) $39 ($2 postage). Mention this ad and get a full set for $35 ppd. $4 each (60¢ postage), any three $12 ppd. Ask your dealer or order from Dougless, Ltd. Also distributed by Dee's Delights.
Guides available:
I. Oriental - Part One, Ten Centuries (Home and Background)
I. Oriental - Part Two, Ten Centuries (Art and Symbolism)
II. Tudor and the Twenties (16C and 20C)
III. Early Colonial, 1607-1699
    Stuart
    Puritans
    Pilgrims
IV. Late Colonial, 1700-1776
    Williamsburg
    Georgian
V. Federal, 1783-1829
VI. Empire, 1830-1860
    Greek Revival
    Antebellum
    Early Victorian
VII. Mid-Victorian 1850-1880
VIII. Late Victorian, 1880-WWI
    Edwardian

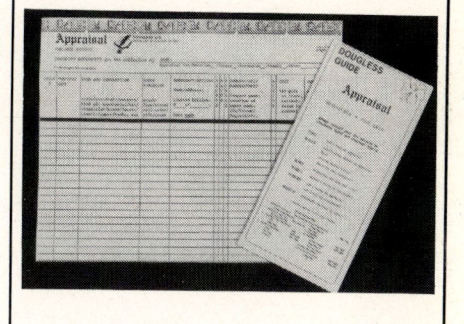

DOUGLESS GUIDE TO APPRAISAL AND RECORD-KEEPING

Dougless, Ltd.
Suggested Retail Price: $4 plus 75¢ postage
Author: Dougless Strickland Bitler
Details for keeping records, protect your heirs, How-To for Appraisals, donations, insurance, resale and more. 8"x16" cardstock, folded in eight panels, worksheet enclosed. Ask your dealer or order from Dougless, Ltd. Also distributed by Dee's Delights.

ANTIQUITIES VII CATALOG

Moreno Valley Miniatures
Suggested Retail Price: $3
Antiques, Petite Princess, Renwal, Strombecker, Tootsie Toy, Sonia Messer, assorted wood and metal collectables. Most pieces are one-of-a-kind.

Interested in Becoming a Miniatures Manufacturer?

Join the Miniatures Industry Association of America and sell products to retailers across the country.

MIAA
1100-H Brandywine Blvd.
P.O. Box 2188
Zanesville, OH 43702-3288

Publications & Plans

Ready-to-use Books

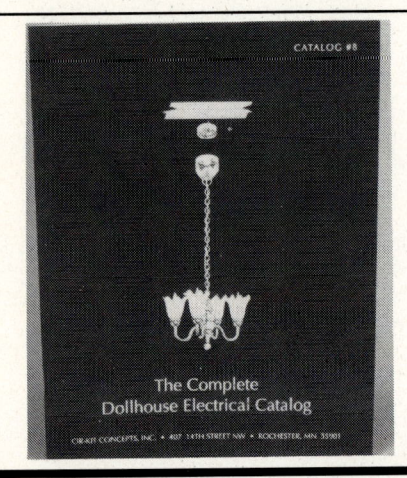

CIR-KIT CONCEPTS MINIATURE ELECTRICAL CATALOG #8

Cir-Kit Concepts, Inc.
Suggested Retail Price: $4
Shipped first class
The most extensive and detailed miniature electrical catalog ever published. Provides photos and in-depth descriptions of all Cir-Kit electrical items. Includes wide variety of hard-to-find light bulbs, miniature tools, lighting fixtures and electrical accessories. The complete reference guide for all things electrical.

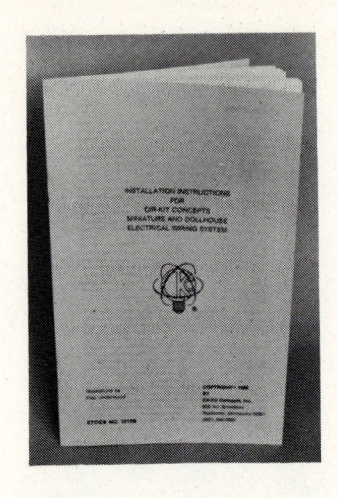

CIR-KIT CONCEPTS INSTALLATION INSTRUCTIONS

Cir-Kit Concepts, Inc.
Suggested Retail Price: Tape Wiring, CK1015, $3.95; Round Wiring, CK1015-2, $4.50, Shipped first class
These books provide detailed and concise instructions for both tape and round wiring methods. Contain master layout drawings and instructions on the installation of all electrical components. Provide many shortcuts and moneysavings ideas. Published by Cir-Kit Concepts, Inc.

Stay in front of your MINIATURES SHOWCASE back issues.

Summer 1987: Growing Up – No One Over 21 Allowed
The world of children in miniatures.

Fall 1987: Let's Celebrate!
Celebrate the holidays and special occasions in miniature.

Spring 1989: Shops and Stores
Accessories and stores for miniature collections.

Summer 1989: Miniature Kitchens and Bathrooms
Redecorate your kitchens and bathrooms: miniature stoves, ice boxes, bathtubs.

Fall 1989: Celebrate America
Discover America in miniature – quilts, Uncle Sam, Old Glory.

Winter 1990: Country Decorating
The international country look – English, French, Rustic, Victorian.

Spring 1990: Occupations and Hobbies
The things we do for fun, the things we do for money.

Summer 1990: The Rooms We Live In
Living Rooms, Family Rooms, Parlors, Drawing Rooms, Dens, Attics & Basements.

Fall 1990: Turn of the Centuries
Decorating and lifestyles, what a difference 100 years can make.

Winter 1991: Vignettes and Room Boxes
Miniature displays in tiny places.

Spring 1991: International Rooms
International decor, food, table settings, arts & crafts, museum displays.

Summer 1991: Outdoors in Miniature
Landscaping, Flowers, Gazebos, Patios, Verandas.

All copies $3.50 each

To order call toll free (800) 533-6644
(Weekdays 8:30 a.m. - 5:00 p.m. CST). Please have your credit card ready.
Or send in the coupon below.

Send to: MINIATURES SHOWCASE, Dept. 0443,
P.O. Box 1612, Waukesha, WI 53187-1612

Enclosed is my payment of $ _____ for the MINIATURES SHOWCASE back issues I've marked below.
Add for postage and handling: U.S. $3.00; Canada and foreign add 18% (minimum $4.00). Wisconsin residents add 5% sales tax. Canadian orders add 7% GST to total.

- ❑ Summer 1987 – Vol. 2, No. 3
- ❑ Fall 1987 – Vol. 2, No. 4
- ❑ Spring 1989 – Vol. 4, No. 2
- ❑ Summer 1989 – Vol. 4, No. 3
- ❑ Fall 1989 – Vol. 4, No. 4
- ❑ Winter 1990 – Vol. 5, No. 1
- ❑ Spring 1990 – Vol. 5, No. 2
- ❑ Summer 1990 – Vol. 5, No. 3
- ❑ Fall 1990 – Vol. 5, No. 4
- ❑ Winter 1991 - Vol. 6, No. 1
- ❑ Spring 1991 - Vol. 6, No. 2
- ❑ Summer 1991 - Vol. 6, No. 3

Name _____
Street _____
City, State, Zip _____
Country _____
❑ Check/money order enclosed.
❑ Charge to: ❑ MasterCard ❑ VISA
❑ American Express ($15 minimum)
Card Number _____ Exp. Date _____
Signature _____

If you don't wish to clip this coupon, copy the necessary information including department number on a separate sheet. Prices and availability subject to change. Payable in U.S. funds. Dept. 0443

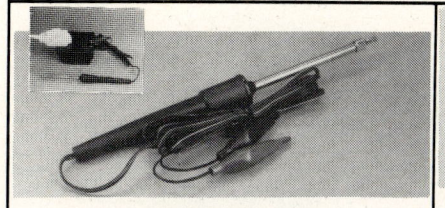

LOW-VOLTAGE SOLDERING IRON
Cir-Kit Concepts, Inc.
Suggested Retail Price: $9.95
Catalog No. CK1053
This low-voltage soldering iron works on 12 volts instead of 115 vac. Melts solder in three to four minutes. Use with 12-volt transformer or car battery.

MINI DRILL
Cir-Kit Concepts, Inc.
Suggested Retail Price: $4.95
Catalog No. CK201
This tool is a must for any miniature builder. Ideal for those areas where a power drill just won't reach. Only 4-1/2" long. High gear ratio provides a surprisingly fast turning speed. Accepts all bits in No. 60-80 range. Hollow handle for bit storage.

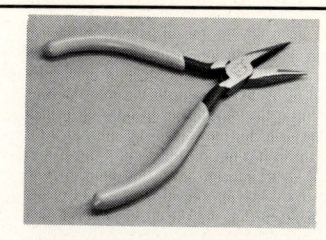

SHORT-NOSE PLIERS
By **Cir-Kit Concepts, Inc.**
Suggested Retail Price: $9.95. Catalog No. CK1042.
High-quality pliers with serrated jaws and plastic-coated, spring-loaded handles. Excellent for a multitude of miniature projects. A "must" for handling small nails and brads.

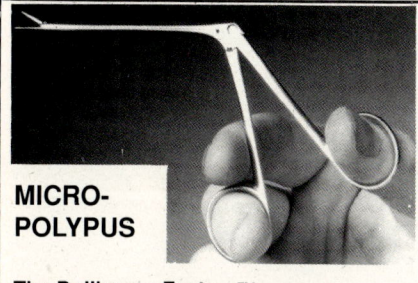

MICRO-POLYPUS
The Dollhouse Factory™
Suggested Retail Price: $19.95
A high-quality stainless steel instrument with extremely strong gripping power. Excellent for inserting small pins for electrical wiring in hard-to-reach places. See our catalog for more.

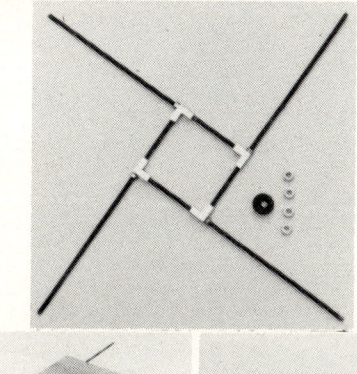

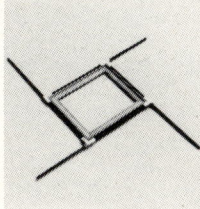

BRASS FRAMING CLAMP
Stan Gordon Enterprises
Suggested Retail Price: $10.50/quantity discounts available
The framing clamp has brass corners and holds frames, drawers, table legs, etc., during gluing. Can be partially disassembled to form two bar clamps for furniture. Comes with two sizes of nuts and a knob to aid turning the smaller nut if necessary. Maximum capacity is four inches. Detailed instructions included.

LA GUILLOTINE
Stan Gordon Enterprises
Suggested Retail Price: $29.90/quantity discounts available
La Guillotine miters miniature wood with a slicing action. The special blade cuts clean and fully vertical at any angle desired. A stop may be attached allowing exact duplication of lengths. Cuts most woods. Base is 5" x 6". Detailed instructions and two extra blades included. Additional blades available.

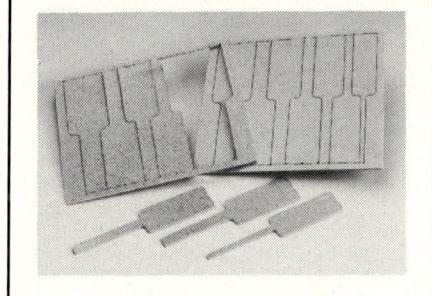

SANDING PADDLES BY GREENLEAF
Greenleaf Products, Inc.
Suggested Retail Price: $3.95 plus shipping.
Specifications: 7 two-sided paddles with 14 different size surfaces and 28 sanding surfaces; medium and fine.
Our easy to handle sanding paddles will greatly simplify the finishing of your Greenleaf dollhouse-handy for all other wood craft projects as well.

FOR FAST SERVICE, VISIT YOUR LOCAL MINIATURES SHOP

DESIGNER RIBBON SHREDDER
J. Hermes
Suggested Retail Price: $5.95
Hand held shredder instantly cuts ribbon into micro thin widths for wrapping miniature packages. Many decorative uses, too. Easy to use. Ideal for workshops and classes.

Tools & Finishing Supplies

THE MINIATURES CATALOG, *Fourteenth Edition*

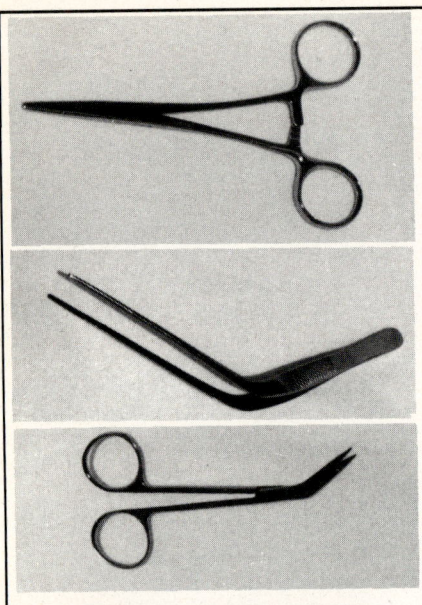

SURGICAL INSTRUMENTS

J. Hermes
Suggested Retail Price: $2.95-$21
Complete line of highest quality surgical instruments. Line includes forceps, scissors, scalpel blades and handles, tweezers in various shapes and sizes. J. Hermes is able to offer these instruments at very affordable prices. All tools are of stainless steel and are ideal for home or shop workbench.

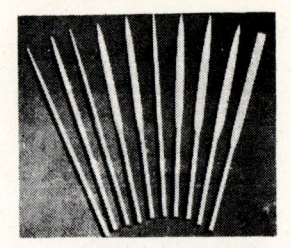

NEEDLE FILES

K & S Engineering
Suggested Retail Price: $8.95
Catalog No. 430
An assortment of ten different file styles. Perfect for miniatures and dollhouses.

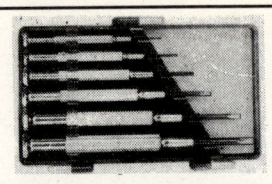

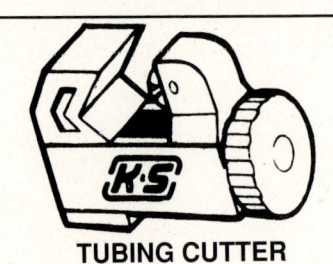

TUBING CUTTER

K & S Engineering
Suggested Retail Price: $3.95
Catalog No. 296
Nylon body makes cutting easier by reducing friction. Cuts round brass, copper and aluminum tubing. Handles sizes from 3/32" to 5/8" o.d.

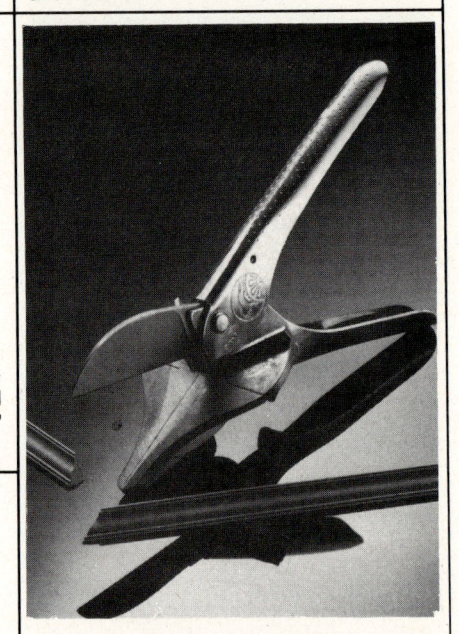

STANDARD TOOL SETS

K & S Engineering
Suggested Retail Price: $9.95 each set
Set of five nut drivers, Cat. No. 422; set of five open-end wrenches, Cat. No. 423; set of five Phillips-Allen, Cat. No. 424, set of six screwdrivers, Cat. No. 426.
Sets of K & S top quality tools with individual swivel handles. Ideal for home, workshop and field use.

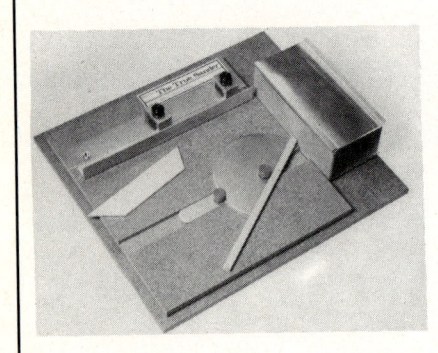

THE TRUE SANDER

Northwest Short Line
Suggested Retail Price: $26.95
Catalog No. 57-4
Speedy and accurate end finishing of model building materials for better fits and appearance. Works on wood, plastic and even (with proper abrasive sheet) metal. Square or angled ends easily handled. Sander block can hold up to four different sandpaper types at once. 7-1/2" x 7-1/2" base. See your dealer. Dealers, see your distributor or write NWSL.

MITER CUTTER

Miniature Corner
Suggested Retail Price: See your dealer.
Catalog No. 3101.
Unique cutting tool for perfect miters. Save time and mess with this easy-to-use, portable tool. Great for shingles and strips. Superb German craftsmanship, replaceable blade and five-year warranty. At better dealers or send $2 and SASE for literature.

THE CHOPPER/CHOPPER III

Northwest Short Line
Suggested Retail Price: The Chopper, $19.95; The Chopper III, $27.95
Catalog No. 49-4 and 59-4
Fast, accurate cutting to length or miter, any angle, in model building materials (wood or plastic). The easily pre-set stop makes quick duplication of exactly same size parts simple. No special blade required, uses economical single edge razor blade. Chopper III provides more space, and up to three simultaneous work setups for complex work projects and professional production. 7-1/2" x 7-1/2" and 7-1/2" x 18" bases. See your dealer.

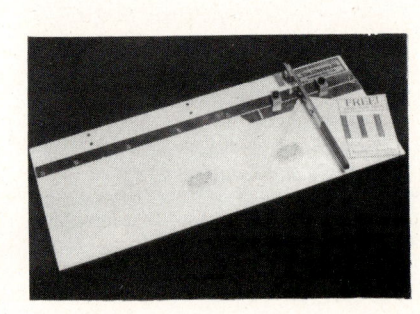

328   Prices are approximate and subject to change.

Paints & Finishes

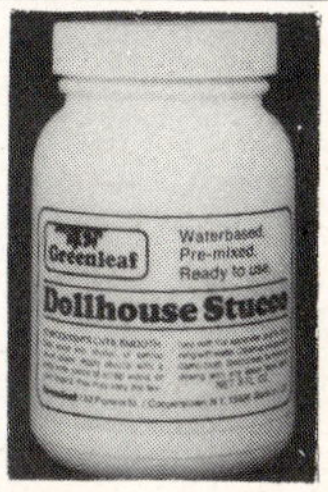

STUCCO

Greenleaf Products
Suggested Retail Price: $5.25
Catalog No. 9020
The dollhouse stucco is waterbased. It is great for foundations, chimneys or for an authentic Tudor look. Just add water and you will have mortar, stucco or textured paint depending on the amount of water that you use. It can also be tinted.

WEATHERING/ANTIQUING SOLUTIONS

A-West
Suggested Retail Price: $4.98 per 4-oz. bottle
Blacken-It for metal. Works on most metals except aluminum or stainless. Not a paint: surface conducts electricity, can be soldered.
Weather-It for wood. Ages unpainted wood models. Not a paint or stain. Can be used for old paint effects and realistic concrete from plaster.
Patina-It for copper, brass and bronze. Produces various shades of blue/green as found on exposed metal. Not a paint.

KIMBERLY PREMIXED STUCCO

Kimberly House Miniatures
Suggested Retail Price: $7.85/pint
Material: latex-base
White, Ivory, Sand or Gray (concrete)
• Ideal for ceilings, bays, interior walls or exterior. Concrete ideal for sidewalks, patio and porches.
• Covers tape wiring, woodgrain, a multitude of sins.
• One pint covers an average seven-room house.
• Clean up with soapy water.
• May be painted over.
See your dealer or write to Kimberly House.

FINISHING KIT FOR MINIATURE FURNITURE

Craftmark House of Miniatures
Kit contains one each 1 oz. bottles of Base Stain, Glaze Stain, Clear Finish and Thinner. Will finish several pieces of furniture. Available in Walnut, Catalog No. 43802; Colonial, Catalog No. 43803; or Mahogany, Catalog No. 43804. $7.95 each kit.

BUILDER'S CHOICE PAINTS

New England Hobby Supply, Inc.
Suggested Retail Price: See your dealer
Builder's Choice paints are the choice of professionals and amateurs alike. Please see the New England Hobby Supply insert between pages 288 and 289 for more information.

Want to list your products in the catalog next year?

To receive information on the 15th Edition of *The Miniatures Catalog*, send your name and address to: Sara Benz, *The Miniatures Catalog*, 21027 Crossroads Circle, P.O. Box 1612, Waukesha, WI 53187.

Detailing

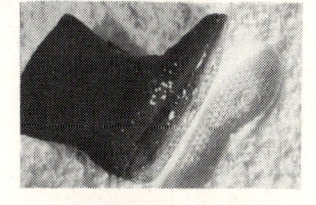

IMPAC™ SNOW

Sturm's Special Effects International
Suggested Retail Price: $4.50 plus shipping, 1 oz.
The artificial snow that imprints, packs and looks real! Excellent for close-up work. Looks like real snow. Dealer inquiries welcome.

Power Tools and Accessories

Tools & Finishing Supplies

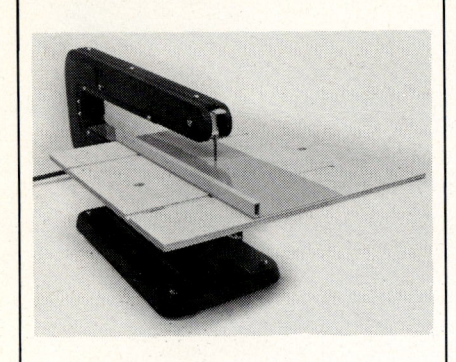

AMSI/EASY SLIDING TABLE AND RIPSAW ATTACHMENT WITH ANGLE CUTTING JIGS

AMSI Scale Model Supplies
Suggested Retail Price: $35.95 Catalog No. AMS-1, Jigs $5.95 Catalog Nos. AMS-2-3-4. Attachment permits accurate cross-cutting and ripping in use with the Dremel Scroll Saw. Make frames, decorative panels, hexagonal and octagonal table tops.
Jigs available for 45°, AMS-2; 30°/60°, AMS-3; 22 1/2°, AMS-4.

AMSI SLIDING TRAY AND MITERING TRIANGLES

AMSI Scale Model Supplies
Suggested Retail Price: $17.95
Catalog #AMS-5
New sliding tray gives precise cuts every time. Holds up to 9" widths. Tray guides slip easily into channels on Dremel Table Saw. Three angle attachments for 45°, 30°/60° or 22 1/2° cuts, $5.95 each.

ACCURA BENCHTOP COMBINATION MACHINE

Advanced Machinery Imports Ltd.
Suggested Retail Price: $1295
ACCURA Benchtop Combination Machine includes 6" table saw with carbide blade, 1/4" table router, 5" disc sander and horizontal drive (jacobs chuck). Optional miniature mortiser, lathe. Dimensions are 16"W x 16"D x 10"H.

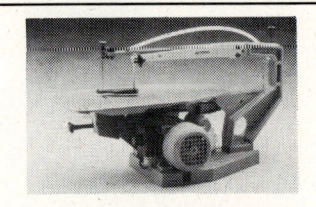

HEGNER PRECISION SCROLL SAW

Advanced Machinery Imports Ltd.
Suggested Retail Price: call for quote
HEGNER Precision Scroll Saw for on-the-spot turns to handle intricate detail in woods, plastics or metals. Eliminate sanding and vibration. Eight models available. Dimensions are 16"W x 20"D x 16"H.

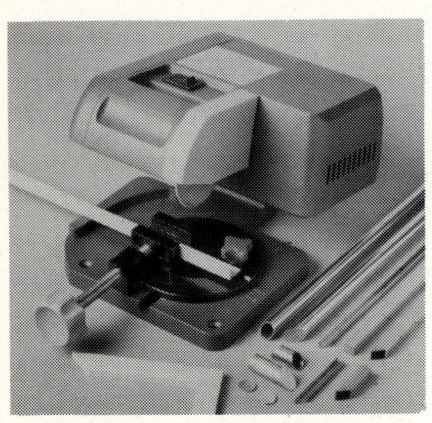

POWER MITRE/CUT-OFF SAW

The Dollhouse Factory™
Suggested Retail Price: $119.95
Catalog No. MK15218
Incredible precision saw cuts wood, steel, brass and aluminum quickly and accurately at any angle from 45° to 90°. Cuts material 3/8" thick x 3/4" wide. Just one of our many specialized hand and power tools designed for miniature work. See more in our catalogue or at our showroom.

MINIMITE

Dremel
Suggested Retail Price: $48
The Dremel MiniMite Model 750 compact cordless rotary tool is designed for precision projects. Use it anywhere precision drilling, sanding, shaping or grinding is required. The Model 750 can be used with all 1/8" and smaller shank Dremel tool bits. It comes equipped with a rechargeable, removable battery pack and its own unique plug-in battery charger. The MiniMite is compact, lightweight and designed to provide pinpoint accuracy and control when working on intricate or finely detailed projects. Order No. 750.

DREMEL 16" 2-SPEED SCROLL SAW

Dremel
Sug. Ret.: $270.00.
Dremel's new 16" 2-speed scroll saw has the power and durability for the most difficult cuts. The 1671 features induction, direct drive 1/10 h.p., and ball bearing motor. The 3/4" blade stroke cuts 890 and 1720 s.p.m., depending on motor speed. The saw uses either pin or plain or end blades and features convenient blade storage. The 12" round table made of die cast aluminum provides workers with a large workbase to complete a variety of projects. A dust blower and clear plastic guard keeps the blade free of dust and obstruction. This versatile, heavy duty scroll saw is great for making toys, puzzles, names, fretwork, and jewelry because of its' cutting capacity; it is a handy tool for do-it-yourselfers and hobby projects. The saw can be permanently mounted to a workbench or optional leg stand. Order No. 1671.

Prices are approximate and subject to change.

HEAVY DUTY FLEX-SHAFT CARVING KIT
Dremel
Sug. Ret.: $410.00.
Designed for the serious carver in mind. This powerful, high-speed (20,000 r.p.m.) quality tool will give woodcarvers tool and die makers, jewelry makers, and craftsmen an edge for getting jobs done faster, easier, with less effort and better results. Includes 1/5 horsepower heavy duty flex-shaft tool, foot speed control, 1" handpiece with quick disconnect feature. Comes with 1/4" and 1/8" collets, flex-shaft maintenance kit, wrench and lock pin, and 27 accessories that allow you to go from the roughing out stage to the finest detail. Order No. 7390.

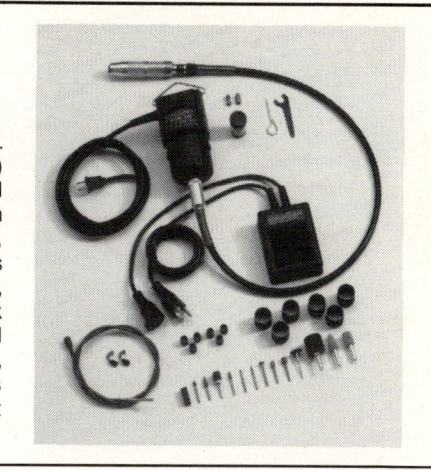

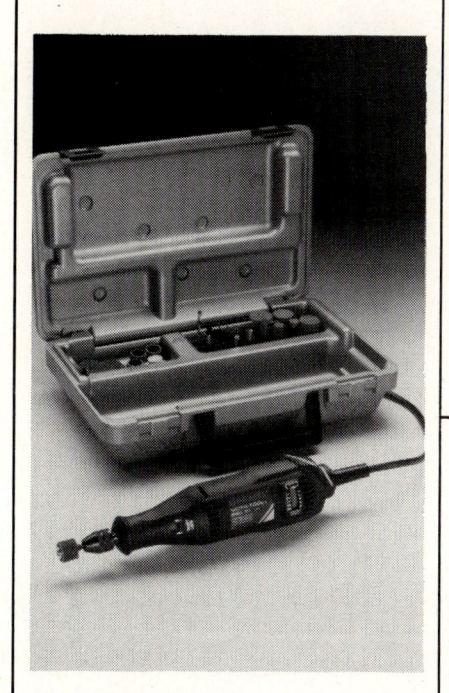

MINI-VAC/BLOWER
Mini-Vac
Suggested Retail Price: $19.95 + $3 shipping
Catalog No. MV-1
Mini-Vac vacuums up dust and particles from small delicate items and tiny, hard-to-reach places. Perfect for models of all kinds. Use as a blower to quick dry wet surfaces. Uses one 9 volt alkaline battery or A/C adapter (optional). Two wands, soft pony hair brushes and reusable dust bag.

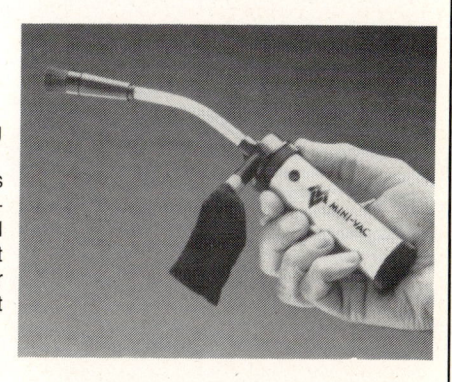

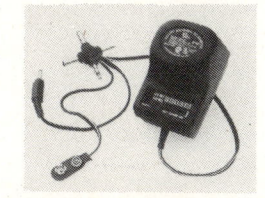

DREMEL MOTO-TOOL
Dremel
Sug. Ret.: $66.00 single speed, $98.00 two-speed, $123.00 variable speed.
The new redesigned Moto-Tools are compact, lightweight with increased speed up to 30,000 r.p.m.. Improvements include addition of keyless chuck capability for use with bits up to 1/8" and a tapered housing shape for comfortable finger-tip control. The Moto-Tool is double insulated, eliminating the need for grounding. The custom designed shatter-resistant housing fits comfortably in your hand to provide precision finger-tip control. A new thrust bearing provides greater drilling capability. Three models available are variable speed, two-speed, and single speed kits with various accessory/bit assortments. Order Nos. 2750 single speed, 2850 two-speed, 3950 variable speed.

MINI-VAC MULTI-USE A/C ADAPTER
Mini-Vac
Suggested Retail Price: See your dealer
Catalog No. MV-7
Save batteries, use an A/C adapter. Seven variable voltage output settings. Use with most all battery operated products. Six Universal plugs and LED indicator.

DREMEL DISC/BELT SANDER
Dremel
Sug. Ret.: $178.00.
Dremel Model 1731 Disc/Belt Sander is the perfect addition to workshops that require the versatility of a Disc/Belt Sander. Sharpens, sands, deburrs, polishes and finishes most woods, plastics, metals and ceramics. Smooth 7" diameter die cast aluminum table pivots 60° and locks into position for angle sanding. Includes miter gauge for angle and compound angle sanding. Removable rear platen for light finishing of curved work. Inside sanding capability of large curved surfaces. Includes one medium-grit sanding disc, one medium-grit sanding belt and miter gauge. Available June, 1990. Order No. 1731.

October National Dollhouse & Miniatures Month

Tools & Finishing Supplies

THE MINIATURES CATALOG, Fourteenth Edition

Index to Miniatures Shops

A & A Miniatures, CA 333
A Tiny Touch, NV 347
A-C's Emporium, PA 354
A.C.D. Miniatures, PA 354
Abby's Attic, AZ....333
Accent on Miniatures, CA 333
All Small, IL....340
Alley Cat Miniatures, NY 349
Angela's Miniature World, CA 334
Ann's Dollhouse Shoppe, IN 341
Barbie's Emporium, CA....334
Bearly Big Enough, CA 334
Bell's Exclusives, VA....356
Berkshire Miniatures, MA....344
Bev's World of Miniatures, IL 340
The Black Butterfly, LA 343
Camera-Craft & Hobby-
"Dollhouse Country", NJ 347
Carol's Corner, OR....353
Carolyn's Dollhouse, PA 354
Casey's Wee Littles, CA 334
Chez Riche, KY 342
Cleo's Attic Miniatures, CA 334
Colleen's Collectables, CO 337
The Company Mouse, MD....343
Cookie Jar Miniature & Doll Shop, NY....349
The Country Mouse, MI 345
Country Store Miniatures, WA 358
Crystal Brook Gift
& Miniature Shop, MA....344
Den of Antiquity, MA 344
Depot Dollhouse, MA....344
Der Sonder Haus, PA 354
Divided House of Gifts, MA....344
The Doll & Mini Nook, PA 354
Doll Faire Miniatures, CA....334
The Doll House Barn, NJ 347
Doll House Corner, FL 339
Doll House Decor, PA 354
The Dollhouse, AZ....333
The Dollhouse, AZ....333
The Dollhouse, PA 354
Dollhouse Antics, NY 349
The Dollhouse Factory, NJ 347
The Dollhouse House, MA....345
The Dollhouse Junction, NY 349
The Dollhouse Place, NY....349
The Dollhouse Treasure Shoppe, MA....345
Dollie's Dollhouse, FL 339
Donna's Dollhouse Center, IL 340
Dream House Miniatures, VA 357
Dream Houses in Miniature, NJ....348
The Elegant Dollhouse, CA 334
Enchanted Miniatures, CA....334
The Enchanting World
of Miniatures, CA 335
Exclusively Miniature, IL 341
Family Hobbies, MD 343
First Venture Gifts, WA 358
Flying "V" Miniatures, NY....350
Fred's Dollhouse
& Miniature Center, VT 356
From The Past, PA 354
Funtime Hobbies, MN 347
Gert's Miniature Towne, USA, CA....335
The Gingerbread House, NC 351
Grafton Hobby Center, VA 357
Greenhouse Miniature Shop, OH 352
Gwen's Miniatures, FL....339
Happy House Miniatures, NC 351
Harvey's Miniatures & Dollhouses, MI 346
Hobbies & Crafts Unlimited, PA 355
Hobby & Handicraft Shop, Canada....358
Hobby Craft of Madison, WI....358
Hobby House, CT 338
Hobby Palace, FL 339
Hobbys & Such, Canada....359
Holidays Dollhouse
Museum & Shop, IL 341
HolSum MiniWorld, MD....343
Hunt's Miniatures, LA....343
Jody's Small Talk Shoppe, WA 358
Judy's Collectables, ND 352
Just Miniature Scale, PA 355
Just Stuff, Inc., MD....344
Karel's Korner, FL 339
Kelley's Dollhouse, Inc., MA 345
Kimberly House Miniatures, NV 347
Kris Kringle, Ltd., CO 338
Laing's Dollhouse Shoppe, NY 350
Larrianne's Small Wonders, CA 335
Let's Play House, NJ....348
Lida-Lee Miniatures, CA 335
Lin's Corner, NJ 348
Linda's "Wee Manor", MA 345
Little Shop on the Lane, OH....352
The Little White House, DE....338
Lolly's, IL....341
Lookingglass Miniatures, OR 353
Lucille's Little House, MA....345
MacKenzie's Gifts, Canada....359
Madison Merchantile, NJ 348
Mainly Miniatures, MA....345
Manhattan Doll House, NY 350
Marietta Avenue Miniatures, PA....355
Mary Paul Miniatures, OR....353
ME & JJ's Miniatures, CA 335
Mementos Hobby Shop, ME....343
MinElaine Miniatures, AZ....333
Mini Builder, NJ 348
Mini City, UT....356
Mini Ideas, CA....335
Mini Mansions, KY 342
The Mini Mouse, AK....333
Mini Temptations, KS 342
Mini Temptations, MN 347
Mini Temptations, MO 347
Mini Things, VA....357
The Mini Treasure House, CO 338
The Miniature Attic, FL....339
Miniature Cottage Shop, CA 335
Miniature Cottage, TN....355
Miniature Designs, GA 340
Miniature Emporium, IA 342
Miniature Estates, CA 335
Miniature Maker's Workshop, MI....346
Miniature Manor, NY 350
Miniature Merchant, MN....347
Miniature Village, WI....358
Miniature World & Gifts, IA....342
Miniatures of Wilmington, NC 351
Minimae, NY 350
Miss Elaineous, NC....351
Miss Muffet's Miniatures, NC 351
Molly Brody Miniatures, CT....338
Montclair Miniatures, CA....336
More Than Miniatures, CT 338
Mostly Miniatures, IA....342
Mott Miniatures, CA 336
Mountain Miniatures, Canada....359
Ms. McPhyzz, CA....336
Ms. Peggie's Place, CA 336
Muriel's Doll House, MI 346
Muskoka Miniatures
& Keepsakes, Canada 359
My Doll's House, CA 336
My Small World, TN 356
Nana's Dollhouse
& Miniature Shop, NJ 348
Night Owl Crafts, NY....350
Old Post Miniatures, NY....350
Old Pueblo Miniatures, AZ....333
Once Upon A Time, VA....357
One Stop Miniatures, NJ....348
P & D Potpourri, IN 342
Parker True Value Miniatures, OH 352
Patowmack Toy Shop, MD....344
Pearson's Stained
Glass & Miniatures, NY....350
Peg's Dollhouse, CA 336
Petite Designs, CA....336
Petite Innovations, NJ 348
Phil's Hobbies, TX....356
Pigwidgeon's Niche, NJ 349
The Pink Dollhouse, CA....336
Pinocchio's Miniatures, MI 346
Priscilla's Dollhouse
and Bed & Breakfast, OH....352
R & N Miniatures, VA 357
Rau's Dollhouse Miniatures, MI 346
Remember When, OH 353
Rocky & His Friends, NJ....349
Rooms to Remember, FL....339
Rose's Dollhouse Goodies, NJ 349
Rosel's Miniatures/Dollhouse, MI....346
Russell Crafts, CT....338
Seahawk Miniatures, OH 353
Seedlings, MI 346
Shadow Box, MI....346
Sharon's Little Bits, CA 337
Shellie's Miniature Mania, CA 337
Shutt's Miniatures & Dolls, UT 356
Sidetrack, FL....339
The Singing Tree, England 359
Slot & Wing Hobbies, IL....341
Small Impressions, NC 352
Small Wonders, WA 358
Small World Hobbies
& Miniatures Ltd., PA 355
Smaller Scales, CA....337
Smidgen's, Inc., NY 351
Strawberry Patch, MD....344
Studio 7, CA....337
Sue's Fascination Shop, WA....358
Susan's Miniatures & Dolls, PA....355
Susie's Miniature Mansion Shoppe, OK 353
Teddy Bear Miniatures and Dolls, CA 337
Terra Toys, TX....356
Then and Now Miniature Shop, KY....343
Think Small by Rosebud, IL 341
This Olde House, ND 352
Through the Keyhole, TX....356
Tiny Dollhouse, NY 351
The Tiny Dwelling, Inc., VA 357
The Tiny Touch, RI 355
Tiny Town, IN 342
Tiny World Miniatures, FL 340
The Toy Box, FL....340
The Toy Factory, Canada....359
The Toy Parade, FL 340
"Treasures" by Paula K, NY 351
Twice Nice Shoppe, CA 337
Victoria Station, OH 353
Victorian Gardens
Miniature Shoppe, FL....340
The Victorian Pearl, OR 353
Village Emporium, VA 357
Village Miniatures, CA....337
Village of the Miniatures, IL....341
Washington Dolls' House
& Toy Museum, DC 338
Wee Creations, NC 352
The Wee Home Shoppe, PA....355
Wilma's Miniatureland, Canada 359
Wollard's Wonders, IL....341
Woodford Landing Miniatures, KY 343
The Woodhouse Shop, MA....345
The Woodworks, VA 357

332 **Prices are approximate and subject to change.**

ALASKA

The Mini Mouse, 343 W. Benson Blvd., #1, Anchorage, AK 99503. (907) 563-2778. Tues.-Fri., 10:30 a.m.-6 p.m.; Sat., 10:30 a.m.-5:30 p.m. Doll Houses, Miniatures, Gifts and Collectibles. Featuring many top artisans.

ARIZONA

Abby's Attic, 242 S. Wall St., Chandler, AZ 85224. (602) 899-6257. Mon.-Sat. 9 a.m.-5 p.m. Full line of miniatures. Photos miniaturized. Dollhouse and furniture kits. Furniture, building supplies, and accessories. Everything for building and decorating. Dolls and other collectibles.

The Dollhouse, Hilton Village, 6107 N. Scottsdale Rd., Scottsdale, AZ 85253. (602) 948-4630. Open seven days a week. Arizona's largest and most complete miniatures shop, carrying the work of national artists, local handcrafters, and manufactured items, dollhouses, and accessories.

The Dollhouse, Crossroads Festival, 4811 E. Grant Rd., Suite 125, Tucson, AZ 85712. (602) 323-8387. Open seven days a week. Tucson, Arizona's largest miniature store. Carrying a full line of furniture, accessories, dollhouses, interior decorating items, i.e. wallpaper, flooring, lights, wood trims, artist and handcrafted pieces.

MinElaine Miniatures, P.O. Box 2062, at the "Y" - Hwy. 179-89A, Sedona, AZ 86336. (602) 282-2653. Mon.-Sat., 9 a.m.-6 p.m.; Sun., 10 a.m.-5 p.m. Miniatures by Warren Dick, Gerald Crawford, Gary Larsen, Leonetta Partelow, Pete Acquisto, Judy Beals, and Ellen Blauer. Unusual selection of Indian and Southwest miniatures. See a wonderful antique doll museum free, for your added viewing.

Old Pueblo Miniatures, 3055 N. Campbell Ave., #143, Tucson, AZ 85719 (602) 322-9390. 10 a.m.-5 p.m. Mon.-Sat. Tucson's finest full-service dollhouse store. We build, paint, shingle, electrify, wallpaper and floor. Custom orders welcome. Local artisans featured. Books, kits, tools, components, furnishings. Southwest specialists.

CALIFORNIA

A&A Miniatures, 8181 Mission Gorge Rd. #G, San Diego, CA 92120. (619) 265-2010. 10 a.m.-5 p.m., closed Sun. San Diego's total miniature shop. Year round workshops. Top quality handcraft by noted artists. Full service customer oriented.

Accent on Miniatures, 23011 Moulton Pkwy., C-2, Laguna Hills, CA 92653. (714) 855-8800. 10 a.m.-5 p.m. weekdays; 12-4 p.m. Sun. Dollhouses, building supplies, furniture, handmade items, custom design, building, remodeling, and wiring. No job too small or too large.

The Mini Mouse
Doll Houses, Miniatures
Gifts and Collectables
343 W. Benson Blvd. #1
Anchorage, Alaska 99503
(907) 563-2778
Featuring many TOP ARTISANS
Hours: Tue. – Fri. 10:30-6pm
Sat. 10:30-5:30pm

abbys' attic
Dollhouses • Miniatures
Furniture • Furniture Kits • Accessories
Dolls • Teddy Bears
242 WALL STREET • CHANDLER, AZ 85224
Write or Call (602) 899-6257

For the small beginnings of wonderful dreams...
DOLLHOUSES • MINIATURES
EXCEPTIONAL DOLLS & STUFFED ANIMALS
The Doll House
Crossroads Festival (602) 323-8387
4811 E. Grant Rd., Suite 125, Tucson, AZ 85712
Open 7 Days
Across from Perkins Restaurant

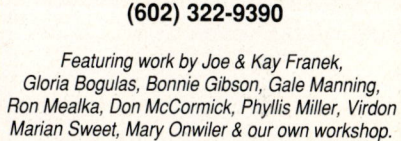

For the small beginnings of wonderful dreams...
Open 7 Days
DOLLHOUSES • MINIATURES
EXCEPTIONAL DOLLS & STUFFED ANIMALS
The Doll House
Scottsdale: Hilton Village (602) 948-4630
6107 N. Scottsdale Rd., Scottsdale, AZ 85250
Tucson: (602) 323-8387
4811 E. Grant, Suite #125, Tucson, AZ 85712

Northern Arizona's - Complete Miniature Shop - MinElaine's in Sedona
• Home of Astolat Castle
• Antique Doll Museum
Located on Beautiful "Oak Creek Canyon"
PO Box 2062 • Sedona, AZ 86336 • 602-282-2653
Hrs: Mon-Sat, 9am-6pm   Sun, 10am-5pm

OLD PUEBLO Miniatures
3055 N. Campbell Ave.
Tucson, AZ 85719
YOUR DOLLHOUSE DEPARTMENT STORE
(602) 322-9390
Featuring work by Joe & Kay Franek, Gloria Bogulas, Bonnie Gibson, Gale Manning, Ron Mealka, Don McCormick, Phyllis Miller, Virdon Marian Sweet, Mary Onwiler & our own workshop.

A & A Miniatures
8181 Mission Gorge Rd. #G
San Diego, Ca. 92120
(619) 265-2010
10 a.m. - 5 p.m. Closed Sunday
San Diego's customer oriented miniature shop-houses, tools, accessories, kits supplies. Specializing in local handcrafted items and new artists. Year round workshops at all levels

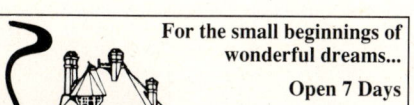

dollhouses, building materials, furniture, custom service
1/2" scale * 1" scale
ACCENT on MINIATURES
23011 Moulton Pkwy. C-2
Laguna Hills, CA 92653
LAKE FOREST EXIT I-5 FWY
(714) 855-8800
BARB GREGORY

Miniature Shops

THE MINIATURES CATALOG, Fourteenth Edition

Angela's Miniature World

The Los Angeles Area
The Quality House for
The Miniature Enthusiast

2237 Ventura Blvd.
Camarillo, CA 93010

805-482-2219

10 AM-5:30 PM
Mon. - Sat.

Barbie's Emporium

Dolls • Miniatures • Doll Supplies
Doll Houses • Related Craft Supplies
And Much More!

Fiddler Green Plaza
1269 Grass Valley Hwy. • Auburn, CA 95603
BARBIE KRAMER (916) 885-7324

BEARLY BIG ENOUGH

Miniatures • Dollhouses • Workshops
Building Supplies • Teddy Bears

"We've got what it takes to make your mini house a mini home."

Hours:
• Mon.-Sat. 10 a.m.-5:30 p.m.
• Suns./Eves. by Appt.

Susie Lim
(209) 948-2088

2314 Pacific Ave. • Stockton CA 95204

CASEY'S WEE LITTLES

1215 S. Beach Blvd.
Anaheim, CA 92804 (714) 827-7710
Mon. thru Sat. 10a.m.-6p.m.
Sun. Noon-5p.m.
Southern California's largest full service shop for collector and builder. If we don't have it, you don't need it.
Doris & Duane Casey, Managers

Angela's Miniature World, 2237 Ventura Blvd., Camarillo, CA 93010. (805) 482-2219. Mon.-Sat., 10 a.m.-5:30 p.m. The complete miniatures shop: dollhouses, unique miniatures, collectibles, and building supplies for the dedicated miniaturist. We're between Los Angeles and Santa Barbara, one block off U.S. 101 (Ventura Freeway).

Barbie's Emporium, 1265 Grass Valley Hwy., Auburn, CA 95603. (916) 885-7324. Tues.-Sat., 10 a.m.-5 p.m. A full line miniature shop. Retail/Wholesale. Doll supplies, classes and dolls.

Bearly Big Enough, 2314 Pacific Ave., Stockton, CA 95204. (209) 948-2088. Mon.-Sat., 10 a.m.-5:30 p.m.; Sun./evenings, by appointment. The largest miniature lumberyard in the valley: miniatures, dollhouses, building supplies, teddy bears, workshops, and classes.

Casey's Wee Littles, 1215 S. Beach Blvd., Anaheim, CA 92804. (714) 827-7710. Mon.-Sat., 10 a.m.-6 p.m.; Sun., 12-5 p.m. Southern California's largest full-service shop for collector and builder. If we don't have it, you don't need it.

Cleo's Attic Miniatures, 1886 S. Chester Ave., Bakersfield, CA 93304. (805) 831-9405. Tues.-Sat., 10 a.m.-5 p.m. We have a complete line of everything you need for building your dollhouse from start to finish. Mail order. We're service oriented.

Doll Faire Miniatures, 2310 Monument Blvd., Pleasant Hill, CA 94523. (415) 680-1993. Mon.-Sat. 10 a.m.-5 p.m. Sunday by appointment. Complete line of miniatures including landscaping supplies. Many custom and one-of-a-kind items from national artisans.

The Elegant Dollhouse, 1120 Fulton Ave., Sacramento, CA 95825. (916) 484-0411. Mon.-Sat., 10 a.m.-6 p.m.; most Sundays 12 noon -4 p.m. (call). Complete miniatures shop. Local handcrafters as well as all popular commercial components, kits, and supplies. Everything for the miniaturist.

Enchanted Miniatures, 2033 W. La Habra Blvd., La Habra, CA 90631. (213) 697-1460. Tues.-Sat., 10:30 a.m.-5 p.m., Sun. 1 p.m.-4 p.m. Unusual one-of-a-kind accessories and furniture. Custom handcrafted wicker, house kits, shells, and custom finishing. Extensive inventory including: Bespaq Corp., Zack Fox, Ron Benson, Nicole, and Blauer.

CLEO'S ATTIC MINIATURES

Doll Houses
Home Improvement Center

1886 S. Chester Avenue
Bakersfield, CAlif. 93304
(805) 831-9405

Doll Faire Miniatures

Complete line of miniatures including landscaping supplies. Many custom and one-of-a-kind items from national artisans.

Open Daily 10 AM-5 PM • Sun. by Appt.
(415) 680-1993
2310 Monument Blvd.
Pleasant Hill, CA 94523

THE Elegant Dollhouse

MINIATURES
ACCESSORIES

1120 FULTON AVENUE
(Between Fair Oaks and Hurley)
SACRAMENTO, CA 95825   (916)484-0411
Monday - Saturday 10-6

Enchanted MINIATURES

Unusual one of a kind accessories and furniture - custom handcrafted wicker

Featuring Bespaq • Zack Fox • Benson • Nicole • Blauer

House Kits • Shells • Custom finishing •
All building materials • Lumber • Wallcovers • Lights

2033 W. LA HABRA BLVD.
LA HABRA • 90631 • CALIF
1-213-697-1460

N. W. Corner of Beach & La Habra • VISA & MC
Hours: Tues - Sat 10:30-5 • Sun 1-4

Prices are approximate and subject to change.

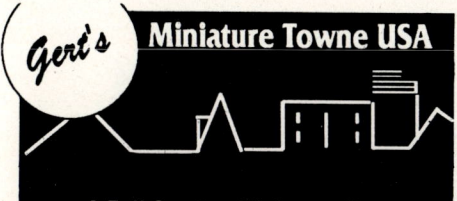

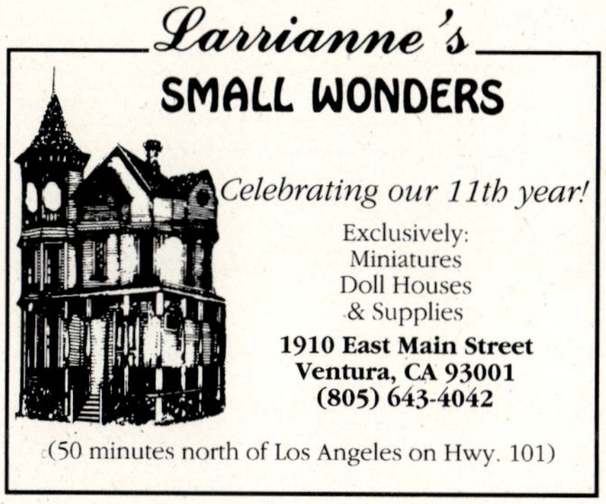

The Enchanting World of Miniatures, 2613-24th St., Sacramento, CA 95818. (916) 456-5255. Mon-Fri., 10 a.m.-5 p.m.; Sat., 10 a.m.-4:30 p.m., most Sundays, 11 a.m. -4 p.m. (call). A full service shop catering to everyone from the beginner to the collector. We carry a large selection of English miniatures at affordable prices, including dolls by Joy Dean.

Gert's Miniature Towne USA, 17624 Sherman Way, Van Nuys, CA 91406. (818) 996-3330. Gert's Miniature Towne USA. A full service shop. Quality dollhouses, kits, and a wide variety of furniture, accessories, building material, finishing and electrical supplies. Classes year round. Many collectors' items.

Larrianne's Small Wonders, 1910 E. Main St., Ventura, CA 93001. (805) 643-4042. Mon.-Sat., 10 a.m.-5 p.m. A quality well-stocked miniatures shop featuring local and national artists: Acquisto, Oldham, Partelow, Leonetta, Rainbow Hand, Jo Parker, many more. Building supplies, houses—everything. Friendly, helpful service, easy to find off 101.

Lida-Lee Miniatures, 320 Second St., Suite 1B, Eureka, CA 95501. (707) 443-5481. Mon.-Sat., 10 a.m.-5 p.m., closed Thurs. mornings. Full line shop. Miniatures for collectors and beginners. Dollhouses, building and electrical supplies.

ME & JJ's Miniatures, 1238 S. Beach Rd., Anaheim, CA 92804. (714) 761-2392. Daily, 10a.m. - 6p.m. Fully stocked including houses, doors, windows and more. Friendliness is our first priority.

Mini Ideas, 1509 Draper St., Upstairs, Kingsburg, CA 93631. (209) 897-5353. Tues.-Fri., 9 a.m.-4 p.m., Sat., 9 a.m.-1 p.m. A full line miniature shop featuring the work of local and national artisans. Unique workshops for beginners to advanced miniaturists.

Miniature Cottage Shop, 1260 Main St., Morro Bay, CA 93442. (805) 772-7858. Tues.-Fri., 10 a.m.-5 p.m.; Sat.-Sun., 10 a.m.-4 p.m. Full-line miniature shop, local artisan products. Manufacturers of custom redwood decks and hot tubs, custom room boxes and houses.

Miniature Estates, 1451 S. Robertson Blvd., Los Angeles, CA 90035. (213) 552-2200. Mon.-Sat., 10 a.m.-5 p.m.; Sun., 1 p.m.-5 p.m. One of the most complete miniatures stores in California. We carry the work of artisans and have a custom finishing shop. Mail-order worldwide.

Montclair Miniatures, 6188 Antioch St., Oakland, CA 94611. (415) 339-8021. Tues.-Sat., 10a.m.-5p.m. A complete selection of houses, furnishings, accessories, building supplies, and decorating needs.

Mott Miniatures, 8039 Beach Boulevard, Buena Park, CA 90620. (714) 527-1843. Sun.-Fri., 10 a.m.-6 p.m.; Sat., 10 a.m.-10 p.m. Summertime hours, 10 a.m.-12 midnight daily. World-famous museum and retail store since 1958. Largest miniature museum, 50 displays and houses. Featured in Guinness Book. Free passes available for shopping. Mail order catalog - $6.
See our display ad on page 358.

Ms. McPhyzz, 1486 Solano Ave., Albany, CA 94706. (415) 524-1226. Mon.-Sat., 10:30 a.m.-5:30 p.m. A full service miniatures shop, Ms. McPhyzz attracts discriminating collectors as well as beginning enthusiasts from all over the San Francisco Bay area.

Ms. Peggie's Place, 5063 Cass St., San Diego, CA 92109. (619) 483-2621. Tues.-Sat., 10 a.m.-4:30 p.m., Sun. or Mon. by appointment only. Full miniature shop. A world of miniatures in one tiny shop. No catalog available.

My Doll's House, 1218 El Prado, Ste. #136, Torrance, CA 90501. (213) 320-4828. Mon.-Sat., 10 a.m.-6 p.m., Sun., 12 noon-5 p.m., evenings by appointment. South Bay's best place to fill your dollhouse, miniature and collectible needs. Kits to custom built. Featuring workshops by local artisans.

Peg's Dollhouse, 4019 Sebastopol Rd., Santa Rosa, CA 95472. (707) 546-6137. Tues.-Thurs., 12 noon-5 p.m; Sat, 10 a.m.-4 p.m., closed Sun. and Mon. Located in an old victorian house. Each room is full of miniatures—something for every age at affordable prices.

Petite Designs, 11544 W. Pico Blvd., Los Angeles, CA 90064. (213) 477-9388. Mon.-Sat., 10:30 a.m.-5:30 p.m. A complete miniature and dollhouse emporium. Handcrafted, collector-quality items, including shipments from England. Supplies, classes, an all-service shop.

The Pink Dollhouse, 4921 E. Lansing Way, Fresno, CA 93727. (209) 291-1349. Tues.-Sat., 10a.m.-5p.m. Complete miniature shop catering to all from beginners to collectors. Featuring dollhouses, building supplies, furniture, Goebels and handcrafted items by national and local artists.

Sharon's Little Bits, 4464 California Pl., Long Beach, CA 90807. (213) 422-9779. Tues.-Sat., 10 a.m.-6 p.m. Make up houses, have furniture and accessories, building materials, collector's items. If not in stock, we'll find it.

Shellie's Miniature Mania, 178 W. 25th Ave., San Mateo, CA 94403. (415) 341-7154. Mon.-Fri., 10 a.m.-5:30 p.m.; Sat., 10:30 a.m.-4:30 p.m. We've grown! See the biggest, most varied miniature store in the San Francisco area. We've got it all–from beautiful artisan pieces to sweet stuff for kids.

Smaller Scales, 234 Main St., Pleasanton, CA 94566. (415) 846-5089. Tues.-Fri. 12 noon-5 p.m.; Thurs., 'til 8 p.m.; Sat., 9 a.m.-3 p.m. Exclusively 1/2" scale! We have an exciting selection of dollhouses, furniture, accessories, kits, building supplies and landscaping plus answers to your 1/2" scale questions. In the S.F. bay area. Catalog $2.

Studio 7, 603 San Anselmo Ave., San Anselmo, CA 94960. (415) 457-0860. Tues.-Sat., 10:30 a.m.-5 p.m. A complete miniatures shop catering to the adult collector—featuring handcrafted limited editions, quality manufactured items, wallpapers, building materials, dollhouses, and collector dolls.

Teddy Bear Miniatures and Dolls, P.O. Box 84, 583 Pine Knot Blvd., Big Bear Lake, CA 92315. (714) 866-2811. Open seven days from 10 a.m.-5 p.m. Mini real estate and all its accessories–for the collector and children. Located in beautiful Big Bear Lake Resort, high in the San Bernadino mountains.

Twice Nice Shoppe, 39106 State St., Fremont, CA 94538. (415) 792-5511. Open Tues.-Sat. Dollhouses, furniture, building and electrical supplies, kits, and accessories. Classes available.

Village Miniatures, 14938 Camden Ave., San Jose, CA 95124. (408) 377-0930. Mon.-Sat., 10 a.m.-5 p.m. Full-line miniatures shop: dollhouses, shadow boxes, furniture, electrical and building components, supplies, accessories, and handcrafted items. Classes available.

COLORADO

Colleen's Collectables, 620 Main St., Frisco, CO 80443. (800) 875-3655. Mon.-Wed., 10 a.m.-6 p.m.; Thurs.-Sat., 10 a.m.-7 p.m. Hours vary somewhat depending on the season and local activities. Feel free to call and check. I-70, Exit 201 or 203.

Doll Houses • Furnishings • Accessories
Sharon's Little Bits
4464 California Pl.
Long Beach, Ca 90807
Specially Created Shells
Building Supplies

Teddy Bear Miniatures and Dolls
Dolls ★ Teddy Bears ★ Doll Houses
Miniatures ★ Toys ★ Books ★ Gifts
583 Pine Knot Blvd
P.O. Box 84
Big Bear Lake, CA 92315
(714) 866-2811
Jerry & Gladys Schweitzer
OPEN 7 DAYS

Shellie's Miniature Mania
178 W. 25th Avenue
San Mateo, CA 94403
(415) 341-7154
Over One Hundred Miniature Room Settings Just Brimming Over With Accessories!
Only 20 minutes from San Francisco
Handmade minis by Leon Scott, Carole Spence, Karen Gibbs, Elizabeth Chambers, Betty Chapman, Bob Stevenson, Zack Fox, D. Anne Ruff, Ron Benson, and a host of others. Building and electrical supplies, dollhouses, kits and shadow boxes, plans, books, and classes.
Visit Our New Store for Collectible Dolls & Bears Next Door!

Everything for Miniaturists
Fremont's TWICE NICE SHOPPE
Dollhouses, Furniture,
Building & Electrical Supplies
Kits & Accessories
39106 State St.   Tues.-Sat.
Fremont, CA 94538   (415) 792-5511

SMALLER SCALES
"Exclusively 1/2" scale."
Catalog $2
234 Main St.
Pleasanton, CA 94566
Visa-MC
Laurel Gross   (415) 846-5089

VILLAGE Miniatures
Virginia Hecox
14938 Camden Ave.
San Jose, CA 95124
Corner of Camden & Union
Phone: (408) 377-0930

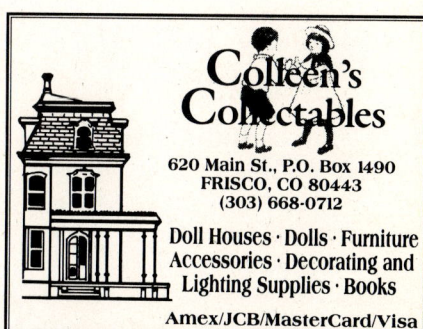

People who know miniatures know
Studio 7
DOLLHOUSE MINIATURES
603 san anselmo ave.
san anselmo, ca. 94960
(415) 457-0860 10:30am to 5:00pm

Colleen's Collectables
620 Main St., P.O. Box 1490
FRISCO, CO 80443
(303) 668-0712
Doll Houses · Dolls · Furniture
Accessories · Decorating and
Lighting Supplies · Books
Amex/JCB/MasterCard/Visa

Miniature Shops

THE MINIATURES CATALOG, *Fourteenth Edition*

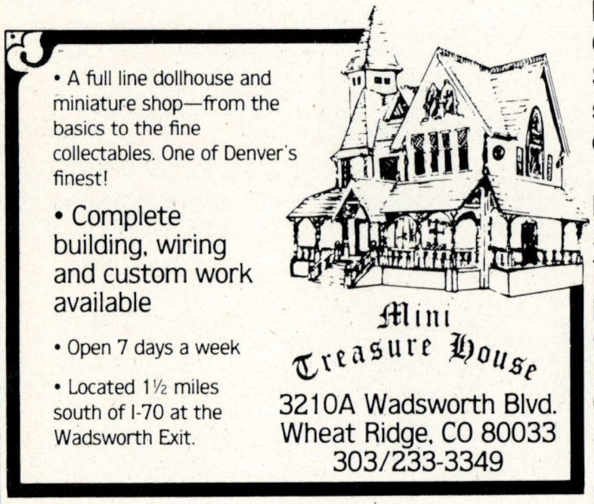

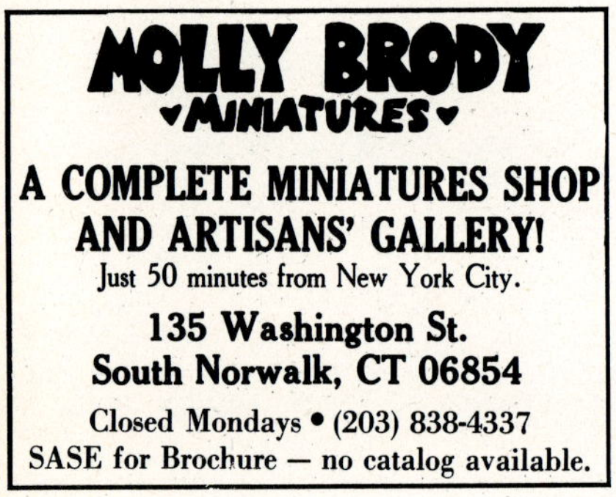

Kris Kringle Ltd., in historic "Old Colorado City", 2619 W. Colorado Ave., Colorado Springs, CO 80904. (719) 633-1210. Mon.-Sat., 10 a.m.-6 p.m.; Sun., 11-5 p.m. Everything for the "little" enthusiast. Complete line of dollhouses, building components, wallpaper, paints, lighting, accessories and furniture. Custom services available. Open seven days a week.

The Mini Treasure House, 3210-A Wadsworth Blvd., Wheat Ridge, CO 80033. (303) 233-3349. A complete dollhouse and miniature store. Fine collectibles including work by Colorado artisans. Offer full-services from repair to custom orders.

KRIS KRINGLE LTD.

in Historic "Old Colorado City"

Finest Selection in Pike's Peak Region!

2619 W. Colorado Ave.
Colorado Springs, CO 80904
(719) 633-1210

More Than Miniatures

50 Liberty St. - Rt.2
Pawcatuck, CT 06379
(203) 599-4529
open 7 days
3000 ft. of miniatures

Just take Exit 92 off of Rt. 95 & travel South on Rt. 2 approx. 2 miles.

Do a house from start to finish! The biggest and best dollhouse shop in New England.

CONNECTICUT

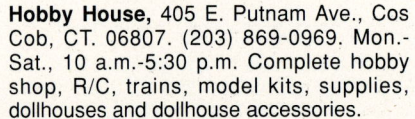

Hobby House, 405 E. Putnam Ave., Cos Cob, CT. 06807. (203) 869-0969. Mon.-Sat., 10 a.m.-5:30 p.m. Complete hobby shop, R/C, trains, model kits, supplies, dollhouses and dollhouse accessories.

Molly Brody Miniatures, 135 Washington St., S. Norwalk, CT. 06854. (203) 838-4337. Tues.-Sat., 10 a.m.-5:30 p.m.; Fri. until 7 p.m.; Sun., 12-5 p.m., closed Mon.; extended evening hours in summer. New England's largest selection of miniatures, dollhouses, construction materials, and accessories.

More Than Miniatures, 50 Liberty St., Rt. 2, Pawcatuck, CT 06379. (203) 599-4529. Mon.-Sat., 10 a.m.-5 p.m., Sun., 12 noon to 4:30 p.m., open 7 days. 3000 square feet of only dollhouse and miniature, everything needed to finish and furnish, handcrafted items in abundance, workshops available.

Russell Crafts, 481 Danbury Rd., Rt. 7, New Milford, CT 06776. (203) 354-5287. Mon.-Sat., 10 a.m.-5 p.m.; Sun., 12-5 p.m. A very large selection of dollhouses, furniture, accessories, supplies and handcrafted items. Worth a trip from anywhere.

DELAWARE

The Little White House, 1700 Newport Gap Pike, Wilmington, DE. 19808. (302) 998-6798. Tues.-Sat., 11 a.m.-5:30 p.m. Our shop offers miniature furniture, dollhouses, building and electrical supplies. We also carry Ginny dolls and clothes. Call about our classes.

DISTRICT OF COLUMBIA

Washington Dolls' House & Toy Museum, 5236 44th Street, N.W., Washington, DC 20015. (202) 244-0024. Tues.-Sat.,10 a.m.-5 p.m.; Sun., 12 noon-5 p.m.; closed Mon. Our museum shop contains a wide assortment of doll house furnishings for both beginners and collectors. Building and wiring supplies and publications. Antique dolls and toys on consignment.

- A full line dollhouse and miniature shop—from the basics to the fine collectables. One of Denver's finest!
- Complete building, wiring and custom work available
- Open 7 days a week
- Located 1½ miles south of I-70 at the Wadsworth Exit.

Mini Treasure House
3210A Wadsworth Blvd.
Wheat Ridge, CO 80033
303/233-3349

HOBBY HOUSE
10-5:30 Mon. thru Sat.
405 E. Putnam Ave.
Cos Cob, CT 06807
(203) 869-0969

MOLLY BRODY MINIATURES

A COMPLETE MINIATURES SHOP AND ARTISANS' GALLERY!

Just 50 minutes from New York City.

135 Washington St.
South Norwalk, CT 06854

Closed Mondays • (203) 838-4337
SASE for Brochure — no catalog available.

Russell Crafts

(203) 354-5287

Doll Houses —
Doll House Furniture
& Accessories

MON.-SAT. 10-5p.m., SUN. 12-5p.m.

481 Danbury Rd., Rt. 7
New Milford, CT 06776

The Little White House

Dolls • Dollhouses • Bears • Miniatures

1700 NEWPORT GAP PIKE
WILMINGTON, DE 19808
(302) 998-6798

WASHINGTON DOLLS' HOUSE & TOY MUSEUM

Tues. - Sat. 10 to 5
Sunday 12 to 5
Children under 14 $1
Adults $3

5236 44th Street, N.W.
Adjacent to Lord & Taylor,
Chevy Chase
244-0024
Flora Gill Jacobs, Director

---

338   Prices are approximate and subject to change.

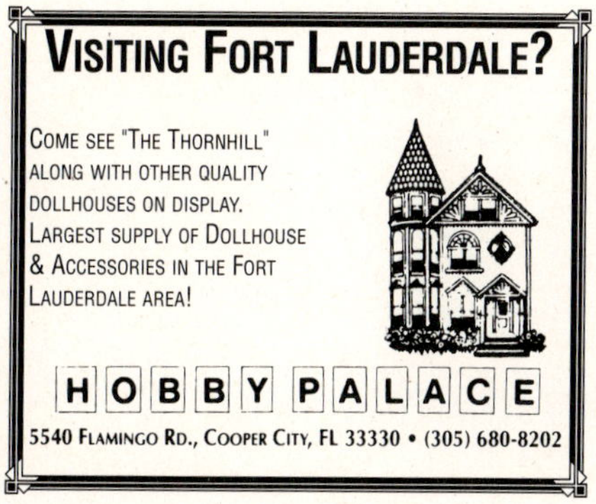

FLORIDA

Doll House Corner, 8 S.E. Fourth Ave., Delray Beach, FL 33483. (407) 272-7598. Mon.-Sat., 10 a.m.-4 p.m. Quality assembled houses and kits; lighting, building supplies, furniture, and many handmade accessories. Craft classes by well-known artisans.

Dollie's Dollhouse, 1670 Wells Rd., Orange Park, FL 32073. (904) 269-9701. Mon.-Sat., 10 a.m.-5 p.m. Located Southwest of Jacksonville, exit U.S. 21 South off I-295 South. Quality collector dolls, bears, dollhouses and miniatures for the child or the discerning collector. Retail only. You won't be disappointed.

Gwen's Miniatures, 309 Denver Ave., Stuart, FL 34994. (407) 287-4098. Tues.-Sat., 10 a.m.-5 p.m. One of the largest miniature shops in South Florida, offering complete building and electrical supplies. Custom services: construction, electrification, wallpapering, and landscaping. Locally handcrafted accessories. We also offer classes.

Hobby Palace, 5540 Flamingo Rd., Cooper City, FL 34330. (305) 680-8202. Largest supply of dollhouses and accessories in the Fort Lauderdale area. R/C and hobby supplies, dollhouses, furniture, accessories, baseball cards and collectibles.

Karel's Korner, 5300 Silver Springs Blvd., Silver Springs, FL 32688. (904) 236-2900. Mon.-Fri., 9:30 a.m.-5 p.m.; Sat., 10 a.m.-4 p.m. Two blocks west of Silver Springs and Wild Waters. Miniatures, dollhouses, dolls, supplies, furniture, and accessories for the miniatures enthusiast. Specializing in "Tomorrow's Heirlooms".

The Miniature Attic, 95 N.W. First Ave., High Springs, FL 32643. (904) 454-4300. Wed.-Sat., 10 a.m.-5 p.m.; Sun., 1 p.m.-5 p.m. Full service miniature shop. Dollhouses and components, miniature furniture (kits & finished), tools, wallpaper, rugs, accessories. Custom services include assembly, wiring and remodeling.

Rooms to Remember, 1553 Sunset Drive, Coral Gables/South Miami, FL 33143. (305) 665-9341. Tues.-Sat., 11 a.m.-5 p.m. Dollhouses, supplies, accessories, handcrafted collectors' miniatures. We specialize in weekly classes of rooms of unique design.

Sidetrack, 6908 U.S. 98 N., Lakeland, FL 33809. (813) 686-9269. Sun.-Fri., 9:30 a.m.-6 p.m, Sat., 9:30 a.m. - 5:30 p.m. A full line hobby shop. We carry a large line of miniature supplies and are willing to order out-of-stock items. Service with a smile!

COMING TO FLORIDA? DON'T MISS A VISIT TO:

DOLL HOUSE CORNER
8 S.E. FOURTH AVE.
DELRAY BEACH, FL 33483
407-272-7598
HOURS: Mon.-Sat. 10AM-4PM
Exit 42 - Atlantic Ave.-East off I-95

Dollie's Dollhouse
1670 Wells Rd.
(Next to Food Lion)
Orange Park, FL 32073
(904) 269-9701
Open 10-5 • Mon. thru Sat.

- Collector Dolls • Bears
- Dollhouses/Miniatures
- Quality Names

Located southwest of Jacksonville
Exit US-21 So. • Left on Wells Rd.

A Unique Selection Of Quality Handcrafted Miniatures

Gwen's Miniatures
309 Denver Avenue
Stuart, Florida 34994
(407) 287-4098
Dollhouses, Furnishings, Dolls, Bears, Electrical Supplies, Locally Handcrafted Items
We offer classes.
Tues.-Sat. 10:00 A.M. to 5:00 P.M.

VISITING FORT LAUDERDALE?

COME SEE "THE THORNHILL" ALONG WITH OTHER QUALITY DOLLHOUSES ON DISPLAY. LARGEST SUPPLY OF DOLLHOUSE & ACCESSORIES IN THE FORT LAUDERDALE AREA!

HOBBY PALACE
5540 FLAMINGO RD., COOPER CITY, FL 33330 • (305) 680-8202

Karel's Korner
Dolls' Houses
Miniatures
Dolls
5300 Silver Springs Blvd.
Silver Springs, FL 32688
(904) 236-2900

The Miniature Attic
95 N.W. First Avenue
High Springs, FL 32643
904-454-4333

Rooms To Remember

• Classes •
• Dollhouses & Fine Miniatures •

1553 Sunset Drive
Coral Gables/South Miami, FL 33143
(305) 665-9341

SideTrack
• TRAINS • HOBBIES • CRAFTS
6908 U.S. 98 N.   LAKELAND, FL 33809

Tiny World Miniatures

Dollhouses and Furnishings

Store Hours:
Tuesday-Saturday 10 to 5
(Closed in August)

HERB & PHYLLIS LIPSEY
6005 Highway 41, N.W.
Dade City, FL 33525

2 1/2 miles east of I-75, Exit 60
Telephone (904) 567-3820

THE TOY BOX
Dolls • Dollhouses • Steiff Bears
David Winter Cottages

(407) 632-2411
4623 South U.S. 1
Rockledge, FL 32955

Hours: 12-5 Sun
10-5 Tues-Sat
Closed Mon

Full-Line Miniatures Shop in Peddler's Village

VISITING CENTRAL FLORIDA?

Come see this area's oldest & most complete miniatures store! We're one of the largest shops in the entire southeastern United States! Take I-4 to Princeton St. Exit. Go west one mile, then 1/2 block north.

TOY PARADE
2318 Edgewater, Orlando, FL 32804
407 / 841-8042

13466 S.W. 129 St.
Miami, Florida 33186
(305) 238-6119

Victorian Gardens Miniature Shoppe

Tiny World Miniatures, 6005 Hwy. 41 N.W., Dade City, FL 33525. 2-1/2 mi. east of I-75, exit 60. (904) 567-3820. Tues.-Sat., 10 a.m.-5 p.m. Closed in August. Since 1977, the biggest little shop in Central Florida. Everything you need to build and furnish your miniature home.

The Toy Box, in Peddler's Village, 4623 South U.S. 1, Rockledge, FL 32955. (407) 632-2411. Tues.-Sat., 10 a.m.-5 p.m.; Sun., 12-5 p.m.; closed Mon. A full miniatures shop in business 10 years, same location.

The Toy Parade, 2318 Edgewater, Orlando, FL 32804. (407) 841-8042. Mon.-Sat., 9 a.m.-5:30 p.m.; extended holiday hours. Huge dollhouse selection for the beginner or serious collector. Featuring Goebels; signed artisan-made items like furniture, china, dolls; leather and brass from England; wood and ivory canes. Visa and MasterCard accepted. We ship UPS.

Victorian Gardens Miniature Shoppe, 13466 SW 129th St., Miami, FL 33186. (305) 238-6119. Tues.-Sat., 11 a.m.-6 p.m, Sun. and Mon. by appointment. A full line miniature and dollhouse shop. Large selection of handcrafted items. Large workshop area with classes given by local and nationally known artists.

GEORGIA

Miniature Designs, 470 N. Clayton St., Lawrenceville, GA 30245. (404) 339-6849. Mon.-Fri., 10 a.m.-5:30 p.m.; Sat., 10 a.m.-6 p.m.; Sun. Discounting everyday 10%-30% off retail. Dollhouse kits and ready-built, furniture, lighting, accessories and collectible pieces. Discounts apply to special orders or items mailed.

ILLINOIS

All Small, 12 Smith, The Black Smith Shoppes, Frankfort, IL 60423. (815) 469-4111. Mon.-Sat., 10 a.m.-5 p.m.; Sun., 12-5 p.m. Our selection is a fantasyland for any miniaturist, beginner or collector. Please come and see us.

Bev's World of Miniatures, 1118 E. Highway 30, Rock Falls, IL 61071. (815) 626-2665. Tues.-Sat., 10 a.m.-5 p.m. Quality dollhouse kits. A wide variety of furniture, accessories, building, and electrical supplies. Handcrafted items.

Donna's Dollhouse Center, 1029-A Burlington, Downers Grove, IL 60515. (708) 969-6150. Tues.-Fri., 10 a.m.-5:30 p.m.; Sat., 10 a.m.-5 p.m.; Sun., 12 noon-4 p.m.; closed Mon. Complete shop; doll houses, miniature building supplies and collector's box items.

MINIATURE DESIGNS
ATLANTA'S ONLY MINIATURE OUTLET STORE

ONE STOP SHOP FOR MINIATURE DOLLHOUSES AND SUPPLIES

470 N. Clayton St.
Lawerenceville, GA 30245

M-F 10-5:30
Sat. 10-6:00
404-399-6849

---

all small

12 SMITH
-THE BLACK SMITH SHOPPES-
FRANKFORT, IL 60423
815/469-4111

We have one of the largest selections of miniatures, doll houses & building supplies in the United States.

30 miles South of Chicago — Open 7 Days a Week

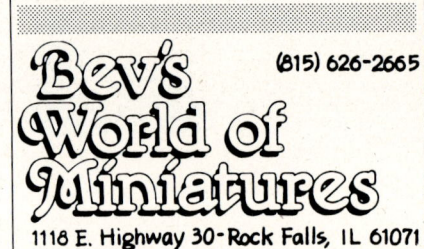

Bev's World of Miniatures
(815) 626-2665

1118 E. Highway 30 - Rock Falls, IL 61071

When in Chicagoland visit
Donna's Dollhouse Center

The shop with both the collector & hobbyist in mind

1029-A Burlington
Downers Grove, IL
60515
(708) 969-6150

New Owner:
Donna Stipcevich

Miniature Shops

Exclusively Miniature, 227 Peterson Rd. (Hwy 137), Libertyville, IL 60048. (708) 362-0818. Tues., 9 a.m.-5 p.m, Sat., 9 a.m. - 4 p.m., 9 a.m. - 5 p.m. most others. Dollhouses, kits, furniture, accessories and building supplies. We also offer in-shop miniature classes and dollhouse construction service. Call or write for information (send SASE).

Holidays Dollhouse Museum and Shop, 7644 W. Touhy, Chicago, IL 60648. (312) 774-6666. Mon. & Thurs., 1 p.m.-9 p.m.; Wed., Fri. & Sat., 10 a.m.-5 p.m.; Sun., 1 p.m.-5 p.m.; closed Tues. 108 rooms done in detail. 12 miniature houses, one for every month. Museum fee: $1.50 - adults, $1 - seniors and children. Complete line of dollhouses, furniture and supplies. Classes for adults and children.

Lolly's, 1054 Dundee Ave., Elgin, IL 60120. (708) 697-4040. Tues.-Sat., 10 a.m.-5 p.m., closed yearly Aug. 18-31. A large complete miniatures shop. 20 miles west of O'Hare Airport; six blocks south of I-90 on Rt. 25.

Slot & Wing Hobbies, 1907 W. Springfield Ave., Champaign, IL 61821. (217) 359-1909. Open daily. We carry a wide selection of dollhouse miniatures and building supplies.

Think Small by Rosebud, 3209 N. Clark St., Chicago, IL 60657. (312) 477-1920. Tues.-Fri., 10 a.m.-6 p.m.; Wed.-Thurs., 10 a.m.-8 p.m.; Sat., 10 a.m.-5 p.m.; Sun., 12-5 p.m. A full-service shop for builders and collectors. Workshop available for customers to build and finish houses and small projects. Located near Cubs Ball Park.

Village of the Miniatures, 123 N. Longwood, Rockford, IL 61107. (815) 962-1060. Mon.-Sat., 10 a.m.-4:30 p.m. We feature a large selection of miniatures including dollhouses, building supplies, accessories and more! Everything for the beginner to advanced collector. Linens, dolls, crystal and gifts.

Wollard's Wonders, 204 S. Court, Marion, IL 62959. (618) 997-4472. Mon.-Fri., 10 a.m.-6 p.m., Sat., 10 a.m.-4 p.m., Sun., 1 p.m.-5 p.m., by chance or by appointment. We feature a full line of dollhouses and accessories, plus exclusive handcrafted items.

INDIANA

Ann's Dollhouse Shoppe, 211 S. 5th St., Richmond, IN 47374. (317) 962-5317. Tues. - Sat., 10 a.m. - 5 p.m. A complete miniatures shop featuring quality assembled dollhouses and kits. A wide variety of furniture, accessories, building supplies and decorating needs.

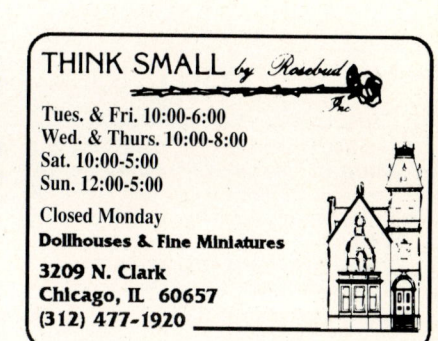

Exclusively Miniature
9-5 most days - Tue. 12-5 PM - Sat. 9-4 PM
Dollhouses - Supplies and Accessories
Dollhouse Construction & Classes
227 Peterson Road, Libertyville, IL 60048
Barbara Friddle (708) 362-0818
CALL OR SEND SASE FOR INFORMATION

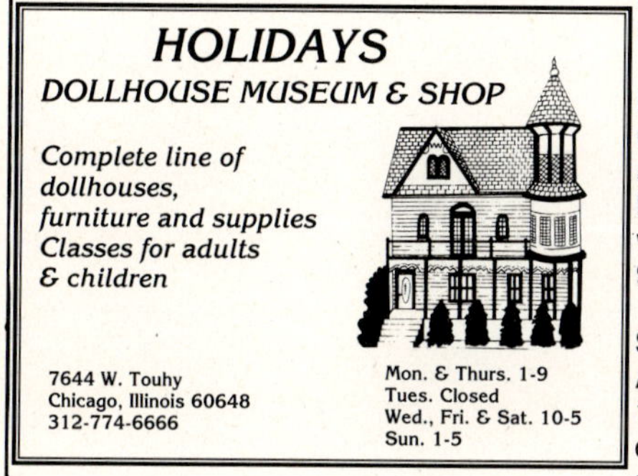

HOLIDAYS DOLLHOUSE MUSEUM & SHOP
Complete line of dollhouses, furniture and supplies
Classes for adults & children
7644 W. Touhy, Chicago, Illinois 60648
312-774-6666
Mon. & Thurs. 1-9
Tues. Closed
Wed., Fri. & Sat. 10-5
Sun. 1-5

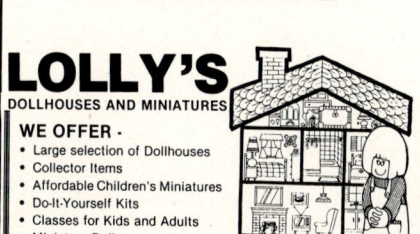

LOLLY'S DOLLHOUSES AND MINIATURES
WE OFFER -
- Large selection of Dollhouses
- Collector Items
- Affordable Children's Miniatures
- Do-It-Yourself Kits
- Classes for Kids and Adults
- Miniature Dolls

Catalog - $10.00 plus $3.00 shipping (Refundable with 1st. $50.00 mail order.)
WE ARE -
One of the Largest and Most Complete Miniature Shops!
Store Hours: Tuesday thru Saturday, 10 A.M. - 5 P.M.
closed yearly Aug. 18-31
1054 Dundee Ave., Elgin, Illinois 60120
(6 Blocks South of I-90 on Rt. 25)
708-697-4040

Dollhouse Miniatures "Slot & Wing Hobbies" Style
We carry a wide selection of dollhouse miniatures and building supplies.
OPEN DAILY
SLOT & WING HOBBIES
1907 W. Springfield Ave.
Champain, IL 61821 • (217) 359-1909

THINK SMALL by Rosebud
Tues. & Fri. 10:00-6:00
Wed. & Thurs. 10:00-8:00
Sat. 10:00-5:00
Sun. 12:00-5:00
Closed Monday
Dollhouses & Fine Miniatures
3209 N. Clark
Chicago, IL 60657
(312) 477-1920

Village of the Miniatures
We feature a large selection of miniatures. Including dollhouses, building supplies, accessories and more! Everything for the beginner to advanced collector. Linen, Dolls, Crystal and Gifts.
Store hours:
Monday to Saturday 10:00 to 4:30
123 N. Longwood, Rockford IL 61107 (815) 962-100

Wollard's Wonders
Dollhouse Building Materials, Electrical Supplies, Furniture And Accessories
Hrs. Mon.-Fri. 10-6
(Sat. 10-4, Sun. 1-5
By Appt. or Chance
(618) 997-4472
204 S. Court, Marion

ANN'S DOLLHOUSE SHOPPE
Ann C. Lee
Take Time For The Little Things
Dollhouses
Miniatures
Bears
Collector Dolls
Hours: Tues. to Sat. 10 - 5
317-962-5317
211 South 5th St. • Richmond, IN 47374

P & D Potpourri, Old Court House Shops, Crown Point, IN 46307. (219) 663-8969. Mon. - Sat., 10 a.m. - 5 p.m., Fri., 10 a.m.-7 p.m., closed Sunday. "The Dollhouse Shoppe". Largest dollhouse and miniature shop in Northwest Indiana. A full line shop with everything needed to begin and finish your dollhouse or room box. We specialize in service and are happy to special order for you. Sorry, no catalog.

Tiny Town, 205 N. Harrison, Box 456, Shipshewana, IN 46565. (219) 768-7165. Mon.-Sat., 10 a.m.-5 p.m., closed Sundays. Full line miniatures and dollhouse shop. Commercial and handcrafted furniture and accessories. Decorating and building and lighting supplies.

IOWA

Miniature Emporium, 4861 Tama St., Marion, IA 52302. (319) 373-1646. Evenings and weekends by appointment. Wallpaper, flooring, wood, furniture, kits and finished, handcrafted items, books, display/room boxes, electrical components, glues, paints and accessories. Mail order welcome. Commercial catalogs available.

Miniature World & Gifts, 130 5th St., West Des Moines, IA 50265. (515) 255-5655. Mon.-Sat., 10 a.m.-5 p.m. Complete miniatures shop with miniatures for collectors: dollhouses, handmade dolls, foods, furniture, building supplies, wallpaper, fabrics, and electrical components.

Mostly Miniatures, 450 Bluff St., Dubuque, IA 52001. (319) 588-2357. Mon.-Sat., 9 a.m.-5 p.m., Sun., 12 noon-5 p.m. A complete miniatures store for beginners and collectors. Quality dollhouses and kits, furniture, accessories, building supplies, handcrafted items. Custom assembly. Mail order.

KANSAS

Mini Temptations, Ranchmart Center, 3633 W. 95th, Overland Park, KS 66206. (913) 648-2050. Mon.-Sat. 10 a.m.-6 p.m. One of the largest selections of miniatures in the country. Dollhouses, furniture, building supplies, handcrafted items, accessories. Newest items available. Catalog $7.50. Catalogs orders call 1-800-878-8469.

KENTUCKY

Chez Riche, 1616 Grinstead Drive, Louisville, KY 40204. (502) 587-6338. Mon.-Sat., 10 a.m.-5 p.m. The only exclusively-miniatures shop in Kentuckiana. Dollhouses, dollhouse kits, lumber, lighting, furniture – all prices. We custom-build dollhouses, make drapes, dress beds, etc. Catalog $25 refundable with $100 purchase.

Mini Mansions, 401 Park Plaza Dr., Owensboro, KY 42301. (502) 926-3754. Open daily, except Wed. and Sun.; 10 a.m.-5 p.m. Handcrafted miniatures by both local and well-known artisans. Select CIMTA collectibles. Tish-Ka-Bob hand-painted country furniture, wicker, linens. A customer's delight for travelers.

P & D POTPOURRI
"The Dollhouse Shoppe"
Largest Dollhouse & Miniature Shop in Northwest Indiana...
We are a full line shop with everything needed to begin and finish your dollhouse or room box. We specialize in service and are happy to special order for you. Sorry, no catalog.
Old Courthouse Shops • Crown Point, IN 46307
(219) 663-8969
Hours: Mon - Sat: 10-5, Fri: 10-7, Closed Sunday

TINY TOWN
205 N. HARRISON BOX 456
SHIPSHEWANA, IN 46565
(219) 768-7156
LOCATED UPSTAIRS
DAVIS MERCANTILE

Miniature Emporium
Dollhouse Building Supplies and Quality Accessories
4861 Tama St.
Marion, IA 52302
(319) 373-1646
Evenings & Weekends By Appointment

Miniatures   Gifts   Dollhouses
Miniature World and Gifts
130 5th Street
West Des Moines, Iowa 50265
(515) 255-5655
Open 10-5 Mon.-Sat.   Rose McGrann

Mostly Miniatures
Doll houses & Accessories
Mon-Sat 9-5pm
Sun - 12-5pm
319-588-2357
450 Bluff
Dubuque, Iowa 52001

Mini Temptations
Ranchmart Center
3633 W. 95th
Overland Park, KS 66206
(913) 648-2050
When in Kansas City
Visit us Monday Thru Saturday:
10 a.m.-6 p.m.
Specializing in • Dollhouses
• Miniatures • Collectibles
• ©Goebel Miniatures • Pennibears™
• Wee Forest Folks

DOLLHOUSES
Only Exclusive Miniature Shop in Kentuckiana
Miniature, Dollhouses, Accessories, Lumber, Lighting
Everything to complete your dollhouse.
Open 10-5, Mon. thru Sat.
CHEZ RICHÉ
1616 Grinstead Drive
Louisville, KY 40204
(502) 587-6338
catalog available $25 refundable with $100 order

MINI MANSIONS
A Customer's Delight!
Owensboro, KY
Full line Miniature & Dollhouse Shoppe
Combined with "Kentucky Hospitality"
Large selection of fine collectibles and dollhouses. Intricate handcrafted items by local artisans. TISH-KA-BOB handpainted country furniture. Select items by other well-known artists.
**401 Park Plaza Dr. (Behind Lazarus)
Owensboro, KY 42301 (502) 926-3754**
Ruth Blakeman   Open 10 a.m.-5 p.m.
Tish Blackford   Closed Wed. & Sun.

THEN & NOW MINIATURE SHOP, INC.
400 Lexington Road
Versailles, KY 40383
606/873-9582
Open Mon.-Sat. 9:30-5:30

Most complete shop in Kentucky. Everything you need to build, decorate and furnish the house of your dreams. Y'all come!

Woodford Landing Miniatures
2632 Frankfort Avenue
Louisville, Kentucky 40206
502-893-7442
*11-5 Mon-Sat
Closed Tuesdays*

The Black Butterfly
727 Royal Street
New Orleans, La. 70116

Collectables
Miniature specialty shop •
Dolls • Dollhouses and accessories •
Classic soldiers • Limoge •
Bonnets and Dollhouse Dolls
by Rosemary Tucker

Hunt's MINIATURES
ONLY 90 MINUTES FROM NEW ORLEANS
• FURNITURE   • DOLLS
• DOLL HOUSES • ACCESSORIES
2151 WINBOURNE AVE. (504) 357-0269
BATON ROUGE, LA 70805
Daily 10:00-5:00 - Sat. 10:00-2:00

Then and Now Miniature Shop, 400 Lexington Rd., Versailles, KY 40383. (606) 873-9582. Mon. thru Sat., 9:30 a.m. - 5:30 p.m. Largest, most complete shop in Kentucky. Building and decorating assistance. 14 years experience. Custom work available.

Woodford Landing Miniatures, 2632 Frankfort Ave., Louisville, KY 40206. (502) 893-7442. Mon.-Sat., 11 a.m.-5 p.m., closed Tues. Dollhouse kits, furniture kits, accessories, building supplies, lighting, furniture, exclusive handmade items. Lessons, kit assembly, and custom houses on request.

LOUISIANA

The Black Butterfly, 727 Royal St., New Orleans, LA 70116. Mon.-Sat. 10:30 a.m.-7 p.m. Collectibles and miniatures specialty shop. Dolls, dollhouses and accessories, classic soldiers, Limoge, and Goebel. Handmade miniatures by many name artists.

Hunt's Miniatures, 2151 Winbourne Ave., Baton Rouge, LA 70805. (504) 357-0269. Full line of miniature furniture, accessories, dollhouse kits, building and decorating supplies. Take the Chippewa Exit off I-110.

MAINE

Mementos Hobby Shop, 86 Sweden St., Caribou, ME 04736. (207) 498-3711, in Maine; 1-800-248-5006. Mon.-Thurs., 9 a.m.-5:30 p.m., Fri., 9 a.m.-8 p.m., Sat., 9 a.m.-5 p.m., Sun., 11 a.m.-3 p.m. (Winter months only). We have a full-service department carrying dollhouses, accessories, furniture, wallpaper, lighting equipment, carpeting and related materials. The department continues to grow. Special orders are no problem.

MARYLAND

The Company Mouse, 4932 Elm St., Bethesda, MD 20814. (301) 654-1222. Mon.-Sat., 10 a.m.-5 p.m.; Sun., noon-4 p.m., seasonally. 127th & Coastal Hwy., Ocean City, MD 21842. (301) 250-3949. Open seven days seasonally. We are a full-service shop carrying furniture, accessories, wallpaper, carpeting, building, and electrical supplies.

Family Hobbies, 5411 East Drive, Baltimore, MD 21227. (301) 247-3239. Mon.-Wed., 10 a.m.-7 p.m.; Thurs.-Fri., 10 a.m.-8 p.m.; Sat., 10 a.m.-6:30 p.m. A full supply of dollhouses, furniture, components, accessories, balsa, base wood, tools, etc.

HolSum MiniWorld, Mountain Gate Plaza, Thurmont, MD 21788. (301) 271-4192 or (301) 271-3333. 10 a.m.-8 p.m. every day of the year except Christmas! Unique self-service miniature shop specializing in HOFCO Products. Browse, compare prices. Central cashier. Most everything 10% off! 200+ page catalog includes HOFCO collector kits and components - $6 ppd.

MEMENTOS HOBBY SHOP
86 Sweden St., Caribou, ME
498-3711

Everything for the dollhouse decorator and builder

The Company Mouse

4932 Elm St.
Bethesda, MD 20814
(301) 654-1222
Mon.-Sat.
10:00-5:00

127th & Coastal Hwy.
Ocean City, MD 21842
(301) 250-3949
Open
May-October

FAMILY HOBBIES
"His and Her Hobby Store"
*Dollhouses • Accessories • Furniture
Components • Wood • Tools*

1348 Stevens Ave.
Baltimore, MD 21227
(301) 247-3239

Hours:
M-W 10-7
Th-F 10-8
Sat 10-6:30

The Complete House of Miniatures
HolSum MiniWorld
Quality HOFCO Products

Top O' the Mountain Gate Exxon
140 Frederick Road
Thurmont, Md. Easy-off Rt. 15

Miniature Shops

THE MINIATURES CATALOG, *Fourteenth Edition* 343

Just Stuff Inc., 4505 Queensbury Rd., Riverdale, MD 20737. (301) 277-0666. Mon.-Fri., 9:30 a.m.-7 p.m.; Sat., 9:30 a.m.-5 p.m.; Sun., 12-5 p.m. Complete dollhouse accessories, supplies and miniatures. Also custom work.

Patowmack Toy Shop, 1254 Columbia Mall, Columbia, MD 21044. (301) 730-0977. Mon.-Sat., 10 a.m.-9:30 p.m.; Sun., 12 noon-5 p.m. We are a full service toy shop carrying dollhouse kits, furniture and accessories. Everything you need to assemble and furnish your very own dollhouse.

Strawberry Patch, 2809 Pulaski Hwy., Edgewood, MD 21040. (301) 538-8546. Mon.,Tues.,Thurs.,Fri.,Sat. and Sun., 1 p.m.-5 p.m., closed Wednesdays. We carry an exceptional choice of miniature furniture and accessories and articles made by Maryland miniature artisans. Dynasty Dolls.

MASSACHUSETTS

Berkshire Miniatures, 136 south St., Pittsfield, MA 01201. (413) 445-5579. Mon.-Sat., 10 a.m.-5 p.m. Western Massachusetts' most complete miniature showroom offering everything your miniature home needs. Come visit us in the beautiful Berkshire Mountains.

Crystal Brook Gift & Miniature Shop, Rt. 20, Brimfield, MA 01010. (413) 245-7647. 10 a.m.-5 p.m., 6 days a week, closed Tues. Complete selection of dollhouses, miniature furniture, accessories, kits, building supplies, and books, also 1/2", 1/4" & TBS scales. Great variety of lovable and collectible teddy bears.

Den of Antiquity, 67 High St., Danvers, MA 01923. (508) 774-7220. Tues., 10 a.m.-2 p.m.; Wed.-Fri., 10 a.m.-2:30 p.m.; Sat., 10 a.m.-3 p.m.; Sun., 12-4 p.m.; or by appointment (take Exit 23N off Rt. 128). Dollhouses, dolls, kits, miniatures, furniture, lighting, building materials, and supplies.

Depot Dollhouse, 215 Worcester Rd., Framingham, MA 01701. (617) 431-1234 or (800) 882-1162. Competitive pricing. See our display ad on inside front cover.

Divided House of Gifts, 255 Elm St., Rt. 110, Salisbury, MA 01952. (508) 462-8423. Daily, 10 a.m.-6 p.m. Custom dollhouses made on premises, clapboards machined into wood, our designs or yours. Full-line of miniatures, accessories, and building supplies. We're worth the visit!

The Doll House

ETHEL L. (DOLLY) BARNES
(508) 724-3454
WEST STREET
PETERSHAM, MA 01366

Collectible Dolls
Handcrafted Dolls
Handcrafted Teddy Bears
Doll Houses
Doll House Kits
Miniatures

All Roads Lead to
The Dollhouse Treasure Shoppe

A Full-Line Miniatures Shop

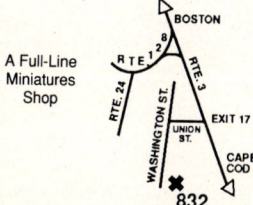

Conveniently located 1/2 mile from Rte. 3, just 15 miles south of Boston.

832 Washington Street • Braintree, MA 02184

KELLEY'S DOLLHOUSE, INC.

"We're Big in a Little Way"

84 School Street, Box 1217
West Dennis, MA 02670
(508) 394-4294

CAPE COD'S COMPLETE MINIATURES STORE

- Dollhouses/Kits or Assembled
- Furniture
- Miniatures
- Lighting
- Accessories

Free Layaway
M/C VISA

Hours: Mon. – Sat. 10-5, Sun. 12-5

Linda's "Wee Manor"
131 Front Street • Scituate, MA 02066

The Doll House, West St.-Off the Common, Petersham, MA 01366. (508) 724-3454. Wed. thru Sat., 10 a.m. - 5 p.m., Sun., 1 p.m. - 5 p.m. or by appointment. Featuring dollhouses, dollhouse kits, building supplies, furniture and miniature accessories. Also available, handcrafted dolls, teddy bears, wood pull toys and country crafts.

The Dollhouse Treasure Shoppe, 832 Washington St., Braintree, MA 02184. (617) 380-7532. Sun. - Mon., 12 noon-4 p.m.; Tues.-Sat., 10 a.m.-5 p.m., closed Sundays May through August. Complete miniature shop for beginner to collector. Specializing in unusual handcrafted items by over 50 artists. Large selection of dollhouses, furniture and finishing supplies.

Kelley's Dollhouse, Inc., 84 School St., Box 1217, West Dennis, MA 02670. (508) 394-4294. Mon.-Sat., 10 a.m.-5 p.m.; Sun., 12 noon-5 p.m. Cape Cod's complete miniatures store offering a wide selection for every budget. Experienced help is always available. Customer service is our specialty. Open year 'round.

Linda's "Wee Manor", 131 Front St., Scituate, MA 02066. (617) 545-2511/3974. Mon.-Sat., 10 a.m.-5 p.m.; Sun., 12-5 p.m. Located in Scituate Harbor. Everything to finish, furnish and accessorize your dollhouse. If you love miniatures like "Wee" do, you'll want to visit our shop.

Lucille's Little House, 1504 Hancock St., Quincy, MA 02169. (617) 479-1141. Mon.-Sat., 10-5 p.m.; Thurs. 'til 7 p.m., closed Sun. Full-line of building materials, furniture—"budget to collectible," and dollhouses. Unique selection of accessories and foods. Located just 10 minutes south of Boston in historic Quincy Center.

Mainly Miniatures, 78 Main St., Rt. 3A, Kingston, MA 02364. (617) 585-5014. Mon.-Fri., 11 a.m.-5 p.m.; Sat.-Sun., 12-5 p.m. The finest in miniatures, needlepoint, dollhouses, furniture, accessories, and building supplies for all budgets.

The Woodhouse Shop, 312 Elm St., S. Dartmouth, MA 02748. (508) 993-5014. Mon.-Sat., 9:30 a.m.-5 p.m. In the miniatures business 20 years with the largest selection in the area: Dollhouses, building components, electrical components, furniture, and accessories. Visa and MasterCard accepted.

MICHIGAN

The Country Mouse, 34836 Michigan Ave., Wayne, MI 48184. (313) 326-5766. Mon.-Sat., 10 a.m.-6 p.m.; Fri., 10 a.m.-9 p.m. A full-line miniatures shop. Dollhouses, building supplies, interior decorating supplies, furniture and accessories. Will custom build and modify house kits. Customer service our specialty.

A BIG SELECTION OF HOUSES ALL UNDER ONE ROOF

Doll Houses • Accessories • Building Materials • Dolls

Lucille's Little House
1504 Hancock St.
Quincy, MA 02169
(617) 479-1141

Hours: Mon.-Sat. 10-5, Thurs. 'til 7, Closed Sun.

MAINLY MINIATURES
"CREATE YOUR OWN HEIRLOOMS"

The finest in miniatures, needlepoint, dollhouses, furniture, accessories and building supplies for all budgets.

OPEN Mon.-Fri. 11 a.m. to 5p.m.
Sat. & Sun. 12 noon to 5p.m.

78 Main St. (Route 3A)
Kingston, MA 02364
(617) 585-5014

Heading South on Rte. 3, take Exit 9- Bear Rt for 2 miles
VISA/ MC accepted

The Woodhouse Shop

Specializing in Dollhouses and Miniatures

OPEN: Monday thru Saturday
9:30 a.m. - 5:00 p.m.

312 ELM ST.
508-993-5014
S. DARTMOUTH, MA 02748

The Country Mouse

34836 Michigan Ave.
Wayne, MI 48184
(313) 326-5766

• Monday-Saturday 10-6 •
• Friday 10-9 •

Miniature Shops

THE MINIATURES CATALOG, Fourteenth Edition 345

Harvey's Miniatures & Dollhouses, 416 Thornapple Village Plaza, Ada, MI 49301. (616) 676-3071. Tues.-Sat., 10 a.m.-5:30 p.m. Miniatures, dollhouses, hand-crafted miniatures. Over 50 percent handcrafted. Everything for the collector or dollhouse owner. If we don't have it, we can get it. Something for all ages. Gift register. Service with a smile.

Miniature Makers' Workshop, 4515 N. Woodward Ave., Royal Oak, MI 48073-6211. (313) 549-0633. Mon.-Sat., 10 a.m.-5 p.m. Retail only. Supply catalog $25 plus postage. Custom orders. One-of-a-kind furniture, accessories, scale dolls, dollhouses and dioramas. 1" and 1/2" scale. Classes and seminars.

Muriel's Doll House 824 Penniman Ave. Plymouth, MI 48170. (313) 455-8110. Mon.-Sat. 10 a.m.-5 p.m. Dollhouses, kits, and ready-built furniture. Miniature accessories and collectibles.

Pinocchio's Miniatures, 465 S. Main, Frankenmuth, MI 48734. (517) 652-2751. Daily, 10 a.m.-6 p.m.; Sun., 12-6 p.m. Handcrafted miniatures by over 200 artisans. Miniature classes. Goebel figurines. Mail order catalogs. Over 100 dollhouses and room boxes on display. Personalized shopping service available.

Rau's Dollhouse Miniatures, 656 S. Main St., Frankenmuth, MI 48734. (517) 652-8388. Daily, year around, Mon.-Sat., 10 a.m.-9 p.m.; Sun., 11 a.m.-8 p.m. Thousands of miniatures displayed in over 100 room settings.

Rosel's Miniatures/Dollhouses, 23121 Lahser Rd., Southfield, MI 48034. (313) 356-0500. Tues.-Fri., 11 a.m.- 6 p.m.; Sat., 10 a.m.-5 p.m. Quality dollhouses, furniture, accessories and lamps. Complete building, wiring, and decorating supplies. Custom construction and remodeling service.

Seedlings, 128 S. River Ave., Holland, MI 49423. (616) 392-4321. Mon.-Thurs., 9:30 a.m.-5:30 p.m.; Fri., 9:30 a.m.-9 p.m.; Sat., 10 a.m.-3 p.m.; closed Sun. Full line miniature shop located in the heart of Holland, MI, home of the Tulip Time festival. Featuring "The House That Jack Built", handcrafted in Holland.

Shadow Box, in the West Village Plaza, 2516 Henry St., Muskegon, MI 49441. (616) 737-0320. Daily, 10 a.m.-6 p.m.; Sun., 12 noon-5 p.m. Dollhouses-assembled or kits, building and decorating supplies, furniture and accessories, collector boxes and miniatures, handcrafted gifts.

Harvey's Miniatures & Dollhouses

Full line miniatures and dollhouse shop...
Handcrafted Gift Items

416 Thornapple Village
P.O. Box 359, off Ada Dr.
Ada, MI 49301
(616) 676-3071
OPEN TUES-SAT 10AM-5:30PM

Miniature Makers' Workshop
313-549-0633

4515 N. Woodward Ave.
(2 1/2 blocks south of 14 Mile Rd.)
Royal Oak, Michigan 48073-6211

Muriel's Doll House

Dollhouses
Kits and Ready-Built
Furniture
Miniature Accessories
And Collectibles

824 Penniman Ave.
Plymouth, MI 48170
(313) 455-8110

Michigan's Largest Miniatures Shop
Open 361 days a year!

REVISED 1991-92
MINIATURE & DOLLHOUSE
CATALOG
* Over 700 pages
* 350 pages in Full color
$15.00 plus $3.50 shipping &handling
Continental U.S.A. others write for shipping costs

Pinocchio's Miniatures
465 S.Main St., Frankenmuth, Mi 48734
(517) 652-2751

RAU'S Dollhouse Miniatures

See thousands of miniatures displayed in over 100 room settings. Visit us when in Michigan.
(Rau's Country Store Building)

656 S. Main Street
Frankenmuth, MI 48734

(517)652-8388 *Open 7 days year round*

Mon-Sat 10 a.m. - 9 p.m., Sun 11 a.m.-8 p.m.

ROSEL'S Miniatures & Dollhouses

Furniture, Accessories, Lamps, Kits, Dollhouses, Tools, Lumberyard, Books. We build, wire, remodel & repair.

YOUR FULL LINE MINIATURE CENTER
23121 LAHSER RD., AT W. 9 MILE RD.
SOUTHFIELD, MI 48034 TEL. 313-356-0500

Fine Miniatures & Dollhouses

Seedlings

128 S. River Avenue
Holland, MI 49423 • (616) 392-4321

SHADOW BOX
miniatures & gifts

West Village
2516 Henry
Muskegon, MI
(616) 737-0320

Open Daily 10-6, Sun. 12-5

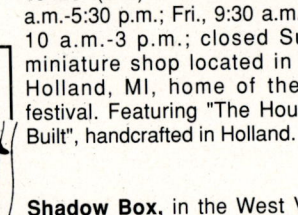

We're New!

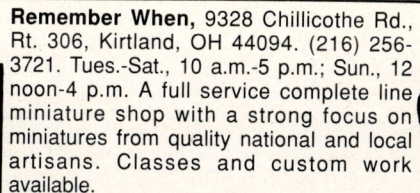

Remember When, 9328 Chillicothe Rd., Rt. 306, Kirtland, OH 44094. (216) 256-3721. Tues.-Sat., 10 a.m.-5 p.m.; Sun., 12 noon-4 p.m. A full service complete line miniature shop with a strong focus on miniatures from quality national and local artisans. Classes and custom work available.

Seahawk Miniatures, 1770 Main St., Peninsula, OH 44264. (216) 657-2716. Mon.-Sat., 10:30 a.m.-5 p.m.; Sun., 1 p.m.-5 p.m. Full-line miniatures store specializing in custom work. Nationally-known artisans' work and unique one-of-a-kind accessories. Classes available.

Victoria Station, 1905 - 4th St., N.W., Canton, OH 44708. (216) 454-9010. Mon.-Sat., 9:30 a.m.-5:30 p.m. Complete miniature shop. Commercial lines plus custom work. Featuring custom handcrafted furniture by J.G. McLoney. Hundreds of unique one-of-a-kind items, reasonably priced.

OKLAHOMA

Susie's Miniature Mansion Shoppe, 623 E. Don Tyler, Dewey, OK 74029. (918) 534-2003. Daily, 10 a.m.-5 p.m. Full line shoppe, dollhouses and kits, furniture kits, electrical supplies, lumberyard, wallpaper, carpet, flooring, handcrafted items, building supplies, custom decorating. We build, wire, remodel and repair.

OREGON

Carol's Corner, 1951 Redwood Ave., Grants Pass, OR 97527. (503) 479-8211. Tues.-Sat., 10 a.m.-4 p.m., or by appointment. House kits, shells, wiring, furniture, wallpaper, interior and exterior accessories, building materials, components, landscape materials, and handcrafted pieces. Classes and work room.

Lookingglass Miniatures, 5565 N. Stephens, P.O. Box 830, Winchester, OR 97495. (503) 673-5445. Mon.-Fri., 10:30 a.m.-5 p.m.; Sat., 10:30 a.m.-4 p.m. Everything to finish your dollhouse or room boxes. Dollhouses, furniture, lumber, kits, landscaping, dolls and doll kits. We welcome all to visit our shop.

Mary Paul Miniatures, 11511 S.W. Pacific Hwy., Portland, OR 97223. (503) 244-4490. The total miniature store. Full line of furniture, accessories, books, dolls, quilts, rugs, building components, electrical, house shells, and kits, Northwest Handcrafters' work and authentic "Heritage Colors" paint. Wholesale paint dealership information: LSASE.

The Victorian Pearl, 335 Pearl St., Eugene, OR 97401. (503) 343-1347. Mon.-Sat., 10 a.m.-5 p.m. We specialize in service, from miniature oil paintings or collector houses built from photographs, to helping you scale plans from pictures, electrifying your miniature home or create Fimo figures.

PENNSYLVANIA

A-C's Emporium, Pinebridge Mall, 1580 McLaughlin Run Rd., Pittsburgh, PA 15241. (412) 257-0340. Mon.-Sat., 10 a.m.-5 p.m., open Thursdays until 9 p.m. Dollhouses, kits, complete building center, and mini lumber department. Many handcrafted miniatures. Large selection of wallpaper and carpets. Electrical kits/food items. A complete miniature shop.

A.C.D. Miniatures, 3311 Liberty St., Erie, PA 16508. (814) 864-5959. Tues. & Wed., 10 a.m.-5 p.m.; Thurs. & Fri., 10 a.m.-6 p.m.; Sat., 10 a.m.-4 p.m., closed Sun. & Mon. Full line shop; quality houses, room boxes, building and wiring supplies and the work of local artisans.

Carolyn's Dollhouse, 1684 DeKalb Pike, Blue Bell, PA 19422. (215) 279-5099. Mon.-Sat., 10 a.m.-5 p.m., Sun. 10 a.m.-4 p.m., closed Tuesday. Full service for beginner to advanced. Dollhouses, furnishings and accessories.

Der Sonder Haus, 2574 Old Philadelphia Pike, Bird-in-Hand, PA 17505. (717) 394-3228. Mon.-Sat., 10 a.m.-5 p.m. Closed Tues. and Thurs. in Jan. and Feb. Everything you need from start to finish– from our more than 200 handcrafters and companies. We specialize in those realistic little touches that bring your scenes to life.

Doll House Decor, Rt. 100, P.O. Box 223, Village of Eagle, PA 19480. (215) 458-5669. Tues.-Sat., 10 a.m.-5 p.m.; Sun. during Nov. and Dec., 1 p.m.-4 p.m. Full-line miniatures shop, specializing in high-quality dollhouses and accessories, many handcrafted. Large variety of unusual room displays.

The Dollhouse, 223 York Rd., Warminster, PA 18974. (215) 443-7781. Mon.-Sat., 10 a.m.-5 p.m.; Fri., 10 a.m.-5 p.m.; Sun, noon-4 p.m., closed on Sun. from April through Sept. Complete selection of dollhouses, furniture, kits, accessories, dolls, handcrafted items, tools, building and electrical supplies. Custom services available.

The Doll & Mini Nook, 336 W. Broad St., Quakertown, PA 18951. (215) 536-4242. Tues.-Thurs., 10 a.m.-4 p.m.; Fri., 10 a.m.-6 p.m.; Sat., 10 a.m.-4 p.m.; closed Sun. and Mon. Dollhouse kits, large selection of furniture and accessories, electrical components, and building supplies. Full-line of collectible dolls and bears.

From The Past, Box 382, Route 73, Skippack, PA 19474. (215) 584-5842. Open seven days, 11 a.m.-5 p.m. Dollhouse kits, handmade accessories and furniture, and building supplies. Open seven days a week.

A-Cs' Emporium of Miniatures
"over 50 dollhouses on display"
(412) 257-0340
PITTSBURGH'S LARGEST MINIATURE SHOP
Pinebridge Mall
1580 McLaughlin Run Rd. • Pittsburgh PA 15241
Color Catalog of Miniatures - $2.50 (refundable)
Free Shipping within Continental U.S.

ACD MINIATURES
"We cater to your miniature needs."
3311 Liberty Street, Liberty Village
Erie, PA 16508, (814) 864-5959
Closed Sun. & Mon. • Tues.-Wed. 10-5
Thurs. & Fri. 10-6 • Sat. 10-4

CAROLYN DUDLIK'S
Dollhouses & Miniatures
Hours:
Monday to Saturday 10-5
Sunday 10-4
Closed Tuesday
1684 DeKalb Pike
Blue Bell, PA 19422
(215) 279-5099

Der Sonder Haus
in Lancaster County, PA
Visit...Relax...Browse
Take home a memory in miniature
2574 Old Philadelphia Pike
Bird-in-Hand, PA 17505
(717) 394-3228
Open Mon.-Sat., 10-5
Closed Tues. & Thurs. in Jan./Feb.

You've Got A Friend In Pennsylvania
DOLL HOUSE DECOR, INC.
Chester County's Dollhouse Center
Tues.-Sat. 10-5 (Sundays 1-4 Nov. & Dec.)
Rt. 100 - P.O. Box 223
Village of Eagle, PA 19480
(215) 458-5669

The Dollhouse
DOLLHOUSES - FURNITURE - DOLLS
MINIATURES & HANDCRAFTED ITEMS
223 York Rd., Warminster, PA 18974
(between County Line and Street Rd.)
(215) 443-7781
MON-SAT 10-5, FRI TIL 5, SUN 12-4
Closed on Sunday from April thru September

The Doll & Mini Nook
COLLECTIBLE DOLLS, DOLL RELATED ITEMS, DOLL HOUSES, MINIATURES & TEDDY BEARS
HOURS TUES. - THURS. 10-4, FRI. 10-6, SAT. 10-4, EVE. BY APPOINTMENT, CLOSED SUN. - MON.
336 W. BROAD STREET, QUAKERTOWN, PA 18951
(215) 536-4242

From The Past
Charlene & Chris
*Dollhouse Kits
*Handmade accessories
*Furniture
*Building Supplies
Route 73, Skippack, PA 19474
Open Seven Days 11-5
(215)584-5842

HOBBIES & CRAFTS U·N·L·I·M·I·T·E·D

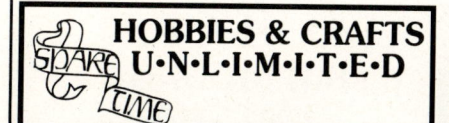

North Penn Marketplace
363 & Sunnytown Pike
Lansdale, PA 19446
215-855-8835

We specialize in value

MINIATURES
just miniature scale
Complete Miniature Shop
Photographic Reductions

100 So. Pennsylvania Ave.
Greensburg, PA 15601
412/838-0505 10-5 Mon.-Sat., 10-8 Thurs.

DOLLHOUSES

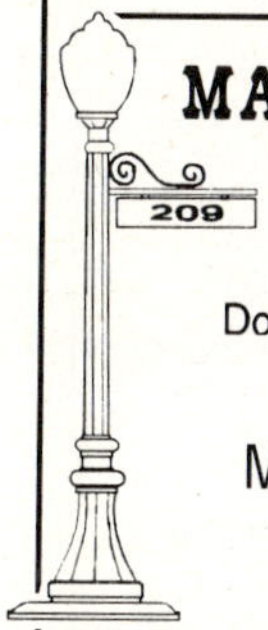

MARIETTA AVENUE MINIATURES

Doll Houses & Accessories

209 Marietta Ave.
Mount Joy, PA 17552
(717) 653-8005

Small World Hobbies and Miniatures

Mon.-Thurs. 9:30 a.m.-6 p.m.
Fri. 9:30 a.m.-9 p.m.
Sat. 9 a.m.-5:30 p.m.
Sun. 11 a.m.-4 p.m.

COMPLETE SELECTION OF MINIATURES
166 E. Lancaster Ave.
Wayne, PA 19087
215 - 687-6875

Hobbies & Crafts Unlimited, 1551 Valley Forge Rd., Lansdale, PA 19446. (215) 855-8835. Open 7 days a week. Miniatures, dollhouses, R/C cars, R/C planes, boats, trains, crafts and toys.

Just Miniature Scale, 100 S. Pennsylvania Ave., Greensburg, PA 15601. (412) 838-0505. Mon.-Sat., 10 a.m.-5 p.m.; Thurs. until 8 p.m. Large, complete miniatures shop in western Pennsylvania. Come to browse or buy—you'll enjoy! 15 minutes from either Irwin or New Stanton exit from Pennsylvania Tpke.

Marietta Avenue Miniatures, 209 Marietta Ave., Mount Joy, PA 17552. (717) 653-8005. Mon., Wed., Thurs., 10 a.m.-5 p.m.; Fri, 10 a.m.-8 p.m.; closed Sun. and Tues.; others by appointment. Dollhouses and accessories.

Small World Hobbies & Miniatures Ltd., 166 E. Lancaster Ave., Wayne, PA 19087. (215) 687-6875. Mon.-Thurs. 9:30 a.m.-6 p.m., Fri. 9:30 a.m.-9 p.m., Sat. 9 a.m.-5:30 p.m., Sun. 11 a.m.-4 p.m. Friday p.m. and Sunday during June, July and August, closed. Philadelphia area's best selection of miniatures, houses, construction supplies, lighting, and tools. No catalog.

Susan's Miniatures & Dolls, 918 N. Reading Road, Ephrata, PA 17522. (717) 733-0561. Daily, 10 a.m.-5 p.m., closed Sundays. Fine quality dollhouses, furniture, building supplies and accessories - plus - American and European dolls. We do custom work.

The Wee Home Shoppe, 279 Mill St., Danville, PA. 17821. (717) 275-6538. Tues.-Sat., 10 a.m.-4:30 p.m. Friendly, full-line shop featuring custom houses; quality house and furniture kits; building, decorating and wiring supplies; accessories—many by area artisans. Classes. Creative customer assistance. Parking in the rear.

RHODE ISLAND

The Tiny Touch, 223 County Rd., (behind Getty Gas), Rte. 114, Barrington, RI 02806. (401) 245-8820. Mon.-Sat. 10 a.m.-5:30 p.m., Thurs. 10 a.m.-8 p.m., special Christmas in Nov. and Dec. Friendly, full-line shop. Quality houses and furniture; building and wiring supplies; carpeting and wallpaper; many accessories. Helpful service

TENNESSEE

Miniature Cottage Inc., 410 E. Iris Dr., Nashville, TN 37204. (615) 298-2872. Mon.-Sat., 10 a.m.-5 p.m. Most complete miniatures speciality shop in the Southeast. Ideas and service abound! Hard-to-find tools, building supplies, accessories, and collectibles. All services available.

SUSAN'S MINIATURES & DOLLS
"meeting your mini needs"

Located Near: Historic Ephrata, Amish Country and Antique Alley at

PORCH 'N' RAIL SHOPPES
918 N. Reading Road
Ephrata, PA 17522
(717)733-0561

Open Daily 10-5 • Closed Sunday

The Wee Home Shoppe
Dollhouses for all ages

In central Pennsylvania-- only 3 miles from I-80

CREATIVE CUSTOMER ASSISTANCE

Tues-Sat 10-4:30 p.m.   279 MILL STREET
Phone: 717/275-6538   DANVILLE, PA 17821

THE TINY TOUCH
Dollhouses & Miniatures

A Full Line Miniatures Shop

223 County Rd.   Barrington, RI 02806
(Behind Getty Gas)   (Rte. 114)

(401) 245-8820

Tues-Sat, 10-5:30, Thurs 10-8, special Xmas hours

Miniature Cottage, Inc.

Most Complete
Specialty Shop
in the Southeast

Jean Flippen
(615) 298-2872

410 East Iris Drive
Nashville, TN 37204

Hours: 10-5 Mon. - Sat.
VISA - MasterCard

Miniature Shops

MY SMALL WORLD

Large selection of miniature furniture, accessories, building supplies and doll houses. Custom country collectibles available.

SALT HOUSE
127 Fox Street
Jonesborough, TN 37659
(615) 753-5113

Phil's Hobbies
Dollhouses - Furnishings
Building Supplies
Miniatures
M-F 10-7, Sat 10-6

2740 Valwood Pkwy 105
Farmers Branch, Tx
(Dallas Area) 75234
(214) 243-3603
MC / VISA / AM EX

TERRA TOYS

FULL LINE OF DOLLHOUSES
MINIATURES & FURNITURE
COLLECTIBLE DOLLS

STEIFF ANIMALS • MUSIC BOXES
COLLECTORS TOYS • BOOKS

1708 SOUTH CONGRESS, AUSTIN, TEXAS 78704
(512) 445-4489

Dallas' Largest DOLLHOUSE SHOP

THROUGH THE KEYHOLE
(THE DOLLHOUSE DEPARTMENT STORE)
OPEN 7 DAYS

102 Olla Podrida Mall
12215 Coit Rd. (So. of 635)
Dallas, TX 75251

214-387-2923

My Small World (c/o The Salt House), 127 Fox St., Jonesborough, TN 37659. (615) 753-5113. Mon.-Sat., 10 a.m.-5 p.m.; Sun., 1 p.m.-5 p.m. Complete line of miniatures for Upper East Tennessee. Shop for quality dollhouses, furniture and accessories for the beginner to collector. Custom work available.

TEXAS

Phil's Hobbies, 2740 Valwood Pkwy. #105, Farmers Branch, TX 75234. (214) 243-3603. Mon.-Fri., 10 a.m.-7 p.m., Sat., 10 a.m.-6 p.m. Dollhouses, building supplies, wallpapers and finishing supplies, furniture, miniatures and more!

Terra Toys, 1708 South Congress Ave., Austin TX 78704. (512) 445-4489. Mon.-Sat. 10 a.m.-7 p.m. Sun. Noon-6 p.m. Texas' finest toy store specializing in German imports. A great selection of miniature furniture and accessories, dollhouses and kits. Dolls of all kinds. Collectible toys. Steiff.

Through The Keyhole, 12215 Coit Rd., 102 Olla Podrida, Dallas, TX 75251. (214) 387-2923. Mon.-Sat., 10 a.m.-6 p.m.; Thurs., 10 a.m.-9 p.m.; Sun., 12 p.m.-5:30 p.m. The Complete Dollhouse Shop with the largest selection in Dallas. A dollhouse department store for all your miniatures needs.

UTAH

Mini City, 2888 So. Highland Dr., Salt Lake City, UT 84106. (801) 486-0328. Mon.-Sat., 10 a.m.-6 p.m., closed Sun. We do complete house finishing. We are also Victorian Times. Come see us when skiing in Utah, best show on Earth.

Shutt's Miniatures and Dolls, 10450 S. State St., Sandy, UT 84070. (801) 572-5991. Weekdays, 10 a.m. - 9 p.m., Sat., 10 a.m. - 7 p.m. Complete selection of dollhouse kits, plans, electrical, furniture, wallpaper, shingles, shadow boxes, building supplies and collectible dolls.

VERMONT

Fred's Dollhouse and Miniature Center, Route 7, Pittsford Village, VT 05763. (802) 483-6362. Open Tues.-Sat., 9 a.m.-5 p.m.; Sun. 10 a.m.-5 p.m. Large selection of dollhouses, kits, scaled building materials, furniture, and accessories. Fred specializes in building replicas of homes, as well as repairing, remodeling, assembling, electrifying, and custom-building dollhouses. Catalog, $4. Open year-round.

VIRGINIA

Bell's Exclusives, 4 E. Nine Mile Road, Highland Springs, VA 23075. (804) 328-0121. Tues.-Fri., 10 a.m.-3 p.m., open until 8 p.m. on Thur., also by appointment; closed Sun. and Mon. Miniatures, dolls, houses and accessories, gifts and more. Over 2,000 different minis not including furniture. If you like teeny-tiny, see our dollhouse dollhouse furniture.

MINI CITY
Retail Miniatures
Ron Clanton

We are also Victorian Times Miniature Co.

**2888 So. Highland Dr.
Salt Lake City, UT 84106
(801)486-0328**

Mon.-Sat. 10-6
Closed Sundays

**SHUTT'S MINIATURES & DOLLS
572-5991**

COMPLETE SELECTION OF
DOLL HOUSE KITS • PLANS • ELECTRICAL
FURNITURE • WALLPAPER • SHINGLES
SHADOW BOXES • BUILDING SUPPLIES
• COLLECTIBLE DOLLS

Special Orders Available • Bank Cards Welcome
10-9 WEEKDAYS/SAT 10-7

Southtowne Mall Sandy, Utah ..... **(801)572-5991**

Fred's DOLLHOUSE & MINIATURE CENTER
• Dollhouse Kits
• Building Supplies
• Furniture
• Accessories

• Custom-Built Replicas
• Remodeling
• Wiring
• Wallpapering

CARPENTER SHOP

80-page catalog $4.00

Route 7, Pittsford Village, Vermont 05763
Open Tues.- Sat. 9-5, Sun. 10-5, Closed Mon.
(802) 483-6362   Fred & Jean Harvie

Walk into a land of enchantment at
BELL'S EXCLUSIVES
4 E. Nine Mile Road
Highland Springs, VA 23075
(804) 328-0121

Miniatures, Dolls, Dollhouses & Accessories, Gifts & More

20 Min. East of Richmond. I-64 East to Highland Springs Exit. Straight to Nine Mile Rd. (stoplight) left. Straight to Holly Ave. (stoplight) right. Park & enter in rear.
Daily 10:00 am-3:00 pm. Also by appointment. Closed Sun. & Mon.

Prices are approximate and subject to change.

Dream House Miniatures

DOLLHOUSES • FURNITURE
MINIATURE ACCESSORIES

10-5 Tues., Thur., Sun.
301 COMMERCE ST.
OCCOQUAN, VA 22125
(703) 491-4664

Grafton Hobby Center

Large selection of Dollhouses and Accessories. Miniature classes and workshops available.

**110-C Dare Road
Yorktown, Virginia 23692
804-898-4184**

Monday-Friday   10 AM-8 PM
Saturday   10 AM-5 PM
Closed Wednesday & Sunday

---

mini things
"A Dollhouse & Miniature Shop"

2126 Colonial Ave. S.W.
Roanoke, VA 24015
(703) 345-HAUS

Once upon a time

120 Church Street NE
Vienna, Virginia 22180
(703) 255-3285

Full service miniature shop within a unique toy store. Dollhouse kits, building supplies, furniture, dolls, landscaping, wiring.

Mon. - Sat. 10-5 • Sun. 12 - 5 (Oct. thru May)

Dream House Miniatures 301 Commerce St., Occoquan, VA 22125. (703) 491-4664. Tues.-Sun., 10 a.m.-5 p.m. Dollhouses, accessories, furniture, lighting wallpaper, carpets and building supplies. I also special-order anything I do not have in stock and will mail-order.

Grafton Hobby Center, 110-C Dare Rd., Yorktown, VA 23692. (804) 898-4184. Mon.-Fri., 10 a.m.-8 p.m., Sat., 10 a.m.-5 p.m.; closed Wed. and Sun. Large selection of dollhouses, furniture, accessories, building supplies and tools for the hobbyist. Special orders welcome. Everything to finish a miniature mansion.

Mini Things, 2126 Colonial Ave., S.W., Roanoke, VA 24015. (703) 345-HAUS. Mon.-Sat., 10 a.m.-6 p.m. We carry Bespaq, Concord, Cullop handcrafted furniture, Glass Blowers, CirKit, Miniature House, Real Good Toys, Celerity, Houseworks and many others. We ship anywhere and do custom work. Visa, MasterCard, Amex.

Once Upon A Time, 120 Church St., N.E., Vienna, VA 22180. (703) 255-3285. Mon.-Sat., 10 a.m.-5 p.m., Sun., 12 noon-5 p.m.; Oct. through May. A full service furniture shop within a unique toy store. Dollhouses, kits, building supplies, furniture, dolls, landscaping and wiring.

R & N Miniatures, 458-C Wythe Creek Rd., Poquoson, VA 23662. (804) 868-7103. Tues.-Fri., 10 a.m.-6 p.m., Sat., 10 a.m.-4 p.m. Everything to finish and furnish your dollhouse. The most complete selection of quality kits, accessories and building supplies in Southern Virginia. Handcrafted items are our specialty. Price list - $2.

The Tiny Dwelling Inc., 1510 King St., Alexandria, VA 22314. (703) 548-1223. Tues.-Sat., 10 a.m.-5:30 p.m.; Sun., 12 p.m.-5 p.m., closed Mon. A complete dollhouse and miniatures shop.

Village Emporium, 828 Professional Place West, Chesapeake, VA 23320. (804) 547-5814. Tues.-Fri. 11 a.m.-5 p.m., Sat. 10 a.m.-3 p.m., closed Sundays. We carry dollhouses and miniatures, furniture, accessories, building materials, lumber yard, electrical supplies and needlecraft section.

The Woodworks, U.S. Rt. 13 N., Accomac, VA 23301. (804) 787-4337. Mon.-Sat. 9 a.m.-5 p.m., Sun. 1 p.m.-5 p.m. Closed Sun. and Thurs., Jan.-Mar. A full-line miniatures shop with dollhouses, kits, furniture, accessories, lamps, wiring supplies, building components, and decorating supplies. Located on Virginia's eastern shore.

R & N Miniatures

Dollhouses & Accessories
Only 5 Minutes from Interstate 64 or Rt. 17

**458-C Wythe Creek Rd.
Poquoson, VA 23662
(804) 868-7103**

Tues. - Fri. 10 - 6, Sat 10 - 4 • Price List - $2.00

The Tiny Dwelling

1510 King Street
Alexandria, VA 22314
(703) 548-1223

Dollhouses, furniture, accessories.
Something for the beginner and the advanced collector.
3 Blocks East of KING ST. METRO
Hours: Tues.-Sat. 10-5:30 • Sun. 12-5
Closed Mondays

Village Emporium, Inc.

Tidewater Virginia's largest and most complete Dollhouse and Miniature Shop.

1-1/2 miles off I-64 take exit 82 B. Follow Greenbrier Parkway to Professional Place W.

Tues.-Fri. 11-5, Sat. 10-3
Closed Sundays

828 Professional Place West
Chesapeake, VA 23320
(804) 547-5814

The Woodworks

• Dollhouses & Kits   • Accessories

EVERYTHING FROM START To FURNISH

U.S. RT. 13 N. - Accomac, VA 23301
45 Miles North of the Chesapeake Bay Bridge-Tunnel on Virginia's Eastern Shore

(804) 787-4337

"Look for the big white gazebo."

WASHINGTON

Country Store Miniatures, 813 Main St., Vancouver, WA 98660. (206) 695-1425. Mon.-Sat., 10 a.m.-5 p.m. We have small things for big ideas: plywood shells, kits, mini lumberyard, books, lights, electrical, landscaping, accessories, tools, and general store items. Also over 50 made-up models of houses and other buildings.

First Venture Gifts, 316 W. Meeker, Kent, WA 98032. (206) 859-0471. Mon.-Sat., 10 a.m.-5:30 p.m. Over 2000 square feet of miniatures, unique gifts, and classes. Custom dollhouses and fine handcrafted miniature items also available.

Jody's Small Talk Shoppe, 6825 112th St., East, Puyallup, WA 98373. (206) 848-7996. Open 7 days a week, 10 a.m.-4:30 p.m.; June, July, August, 7days, 10 a.m.-2 p.m. We carry Sir Thomas Thumb, Beth Lane dolls, Dragonfly, Houseworks, Mini-Graphics, Timberbrook, Carlson, Multi Minis. Full line miniature shoppe.

Small Wonders, East 3525 Sprague Ave., Spokane, WA 99202. (509) 535-5011. Mon.-Sat., 9:30 a.m.-5:00 p.m.; Sun., 11:30 a.m.-4 p.m. Complete supply of building materials, wallpaper, carpets, rugs and furnishings for children and collectors. Beautiful handcrafted accessories in stock.

Sue's Fascination Shop, 624 Edmonds Way, Edmonds, WA 98020. (206) 775-2017. Mon.-Sat., 9:30 a.m.-5:00 p.m.; Sun., 12 noon-4 p.m. The Pacific Northwest's largest and most complete miniature shop. Specializing in plywood shells and beveled cedar siding. Just minutes North of Seattle.

WISCONSIN

Hobby Craft of Madison, 6632 Odana Rd., Madison, WI 53179. (608) 833-4944. Mon.-Fri., 9 a.m.-9 p.m.; Sat. & Sun., 9 a.m.-6 p.m. Everything you need to finish and furnish your dollhouse! Dollhouses, furniture kits, furniture, wallpaper, lighting, mouldings, siding and more. 10% discount to N.A.M.E. group members. We ship free on all orders over $50.

Miniature Village, 1725 50 St., Kenosha, WI 53140. (800) 383-0188. Mon.-Sat., 10 a.m.-5 p.m. Customized dollhouses plus many other kits, large lumber department, furniture, electrical, and wallpaper supplies and tools. In store rebate on all purchases. The store with the mini money.

CANADA

Hobby & Handicraft Shop, 46 Queen St., South, Kitchener, Ontario, Canada N2G 1V6. (519) 744-1979. Dollhouses and accessories, miniatures, general handicraft and cake decorating supplies.

Country Store Miniatures
Many Unique Items
813 Main
Vancouver, WA 98660
(206) 695-1425
Mon.-Sat. • 10 AM-5 PM

Specializing in Miniatures
Dollhouses & Unique Gifts

Anita J. Cribb
Bill S. Cribb

FIRST VENTURE GIFTS & TOYS

316 W. Meeker   Kent, WA 98032   (206) 859-0471

The Complete Dollhouse Shop
JODY'S SMALL TALK SHOPPE
Open 7 Days A Week
10 AM-4:30PM
(206) 848-7996
6825 112th Street East
Puyallup, WA 98373
Jerry & Fran Smith

SMALL WONDERS
Miniatures
from Apples to Zebras
Museum Quality Crafted by Nationally Known Artists

East 3525 Sprague Ave.
Spokane, WA 99202
(509) 535-5011

- Dolls and Doll Houses
- Doll House Furniture
- Doll House Lighting Kits
- Miniatures

Sue's Fascination Shop
206/775-2017
624 EDMONDS WAY
EDMONDS, WA 98020

HOBBY CRAFT
in Madison, WI
Everything you need to finish and furnish your dollhouse!

Dollhouses•Furniture Kits
Furniture•Wallpaper•Lighting
Mouldings•Siding . . . and more.

10% discount to M.A.M.E. group members
We ship FREE on all orders over $50
All major credit cards accepted

6632 Odana Rd•Madison, WI 53179-1012 (608)833-4944
Hours: Mon.-Fri. 9-9, Sat. & Sun. 9-6

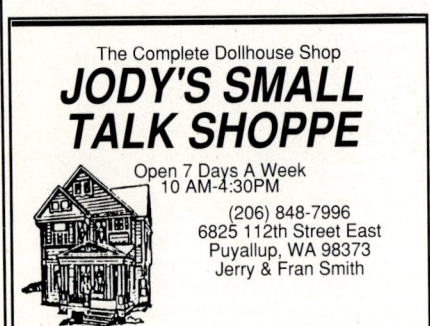

MINIATURE VILLAGE
1725- 50th St. Kenosha, WI 53140
Catalog $7.50
Refundable with $25.00 purchase
Hours: Mon.-Sat. 10-5 pm
Sundays 11-4pm
1-800-383-0188
Come see our newly expanded line of collectable dolls.

HOBBY & HANDICRAFT SHOP
46 Queen St. S., Kitchener, Ont. Canada N2G 1V6
(519) 744-1979

Dollhouses & Accessories
Miniatures • Fimo
General Handicraft & Cake Decorating Supplies

HOBBYS & Such inc.

The finest retail miniature shop in Southern Alberta

Mon.–Sat. 10-6PM • Thur. 10-8PM
F11 Heritage Plaza, 8330 Macleod Trail S.
Calgary, Alberta, Canada T2H 2V2
403-259-2888

ALWAYS A GOOD SELECTION
MINIATURE SPECIALISTS

Only complete miniature shop in area
Now in our 21st year

MacKenzies Gifts
1537 Main St. East
Hamilton, Ontairo, Canada L8K 1L4
(416) 545-2388

Now in Canada

Dollhouses * Finished Furniture & Kits
Staircases * Mouldings * Wallpaper
Doors & Windows * Siding * Lighting
and other Delightful Details

Mountain Miniatures
Box 897 • 688 Natal Road
Elkford, B.C. V0B 1H0
(604) 865-2345

Catalog available, mail orders welcome

Muskoka Miniatures and Keepsakes

(705) 687-3351
Hours Vary Seasonally

"A Full-Line Miniatures Shop for the Beginner or Advanced Collector"
• custom & local artists work
• workshops & local club
• telephone and mail orders

(send $1 for info & sample section or $5 for complete catalog)

510 Muskoka Rd. N.
Box 218
Gravenhurst, Ontario
CANADA P0C 1G0

Hobbys & Such, F11 Heritage Plaza, 8330 Macleod Trail South, Calgary, Alberta, Canada T2H 2V2. (403) 259-2888. Mon.-Sat. 10 a.m.-6 p.m., Thurs. 10 a.m.-8 p.m. Southern Alberta's finest miniature shop offering dollhouse kits, furniture and accessories, collectibles, books, tools, building materials, electrical systems and decorating supplies.

MacKenzies Gifts, 1537 Main St., East, Hamilton, Ontario, Canada L8K 1L4. (416) 545-2388. Mon.,Thurs.,Sat., 9 a.m.-5 p.m.; Fri., 9 .m.-8 p.m. Miniature specialists, large selection, complete lines, now in our 21st year.

Mountain Miniatures, P.O. Box 897, 688 Natal Rd., Elkford, B.C., Canada V0B 1HO. (604) 865-2354. Daily noon-6 p.m. Follow the ski hill signs to Natal Road. Mail order now accepted and we will ship anywhere in Canada and the US.

Muskoka Miniatures & Keepsakes, 510 Muskoka Rd. N. Box 218, Gravenhurst, Ont., Canada P0C 1G0. (705) 687-3351. Daily 10 a.m.-5 p.m.. We are firstly a full-line miniatures shop. Our hours vary seasonally. We have a year-round mail order service. Send $1 for info or $5 for complete catalogue. Sorry, only available in Canada.

The Toy Factory, 10007-80 Ave., Edmonton, Alberta, Canada T6E 1T4. (403) 433-5482. Tues.-Fri. 9 a.m.-5 p.m., Sat. 9 a.m.-3 p.m. We carry the largest selection of miniatures and supplies in Western Canada at the best prices possible.

Wilma's Miniatureland, 202 Brownlow Ave., Bldg. B, Unit G, Dartmouth, N.S., Canada B3B 1T5. (902) 468-8822, Fax (902) 468-1099. Mon.-Fri., 10 a.m.-5 .m.; Sat., 10 a.m.-2 p.m. Large selection of miniature furniture, accessories, building supplies and dollhouses.

ENGLAND

The Singing Tree, 69 New Kings Rd., London SW6. 01-736-4527. Mon.-Sat., 10 a.m.-5:30 p.m. One of London's leading shops specializing in new and old dolls houses. Exclusive collection of miniatures. Mail order catalogue £3 (inc. P&P) Europe, £5 or U.S $10 in bills (inc. P&P) U.S.A., Australia, South Africa and Japan.

TOY FACTORY

MINIATURES & DOLL HOUSES

• Building Supplies
• Wiring & Fixtures
• Wallpaper
• Furniture
• Paint
• Accessories

THE TOY FACTORY
10007 80 Avenue - Edmonton, Alberta T6E 1T4 (403) 433-5482

Wilma's Miniatureland

Visit our Shop at
202 Brownlow Ave., Bldg. B, Unit G
Burnside Industrial Park
Dartmouth, Nova Scotia B3B 1T5

Large selection of miniature furniture, accessories, building supplies and doll houses.

Ph. (902) 468-8822 • Fax (902) 468-1099

THE SINGING TREE

Dolls Houses & Miniatures
We are one of the leading specialists in Dolls Houses and their furnishings. Most pieces exclusive to us.
MAIL ORDER CATALOGUE: £2.50 (inc. P&P) U.K., £3.00 (inc. P&P) Europe, £5.00 or US $10 in bills (inc. P&P) USA, Australia, S. Africa & Japan.
Shop open Monday to Saturday 10.00 to 5.30. Visa, Access, and American Express accepted. 69 New Kings Rd., London SW6. Tel: 011-736 4527

Cover Story:

Who killed
Sir Reginald K. Davver?

Since anything is possible in miniatures, the editors of *The Miniatures Catalog* would like you to solve this "who-dun-it" caper.

MOTT MINIATURES

The home of the worlds first and largest miniature museum is also home to the first full-time miniature store. And we intend to make it the best. In business at the same location for over 33 years. Where N.A.M.E. began.

World Famous Museum Open Free To The Public...

Since 1958 when the Mott Miniatures first came to Knott's Berry Farm, America's Oldest Themed Amusement Park, millions of people each year have had the opportunity to see the Mott Miniatures World Famous Museum on permanent display since 1958. Over 50 houses and displays depicting the history of American living and the American merchant. See us in the Guinness Book. But there is a way you can see and shop at the Mott Miniatures without having to pay that admission fee. You can obtain a shopping pass at the Guest Relations Window to the Right of the Entrance to the park. FREE PARKING is available. Call (714) 527-1843 for more details. OPEN 7 Days

MAIL ORDER CATALOG

This all new "From Our House for Your House" catalog for 1991 is available now. The 1991-92 version sports over 700 pages with 1/2 in *full-color*. Comes complete with price book. Our catalog does require a deposit to cover the cost of printing and mailing but your deposit is <u>fully refundable</u> with your first purchase. Plus as an added bonus, we will send you a sheet of coupons good for hundreds of dollars in FREE and discounted merchandise.

Order your catalog today...

$23.00 if purchased in our store

$25.00 postage paid all U.S.

$28.00 postage paid to Canada

DEPOSIT IS FULLY REFUNDABLE WITH FIRST ORDER

We carry Greenleaf, Real Good Toys/New Concept and Hofco Houses also

TOLL FREE ORDERING...

Now you can place your $25.00 minimum credit card order and your call is absolutely FREE. You can order from any of our catalogs or from a current or recent issue of the Dee's Delights "From Our House for Your House" catalog. Our toll free number is good anywhere in the United States. For our customers in Canada, please let us know if you would use an 800 number if one were made available to you. To place credit card orders under $25.00 or to make inquiries or obtain more information please call (714) 527-1843. FAX (714) 527-5204

1-800-874-6222 Call now and place your $25.00 minimum credit card order.

MOTT MINIATURES MUSEUM AND STORE, *since* **1958**
8039 Beach Blvd., Buena Park, California 90620-9985

Prices are approximate and subject to change.

October National Dollhouse & Miniatures Month

MINIATURA

BRITAIN'S INTERNATIONALLY RENOWNED SHOW FOR DOLLS' HOUSE ENTHUSIASTS

Our BIRMINGHAM (ENGLAND) shows have approximately 150 dealers, and usually include some from abroad. There is also a TRADE-ONLY section.

They are held at THE NATIONAL MOTORCYCLE MUSEUM by Birmingham Airport.

"MINIATURA" AUTUMN 1991
Sat., September 28th (Limited Entry by Advance Postal Booking Only)
Sun., September 29th (Pay at the Door.....Advance booking Optional)

"MINIATURA" SPRING 1992
Sat., March 21st (Limited Entry by Advance Postal Booking Only)
Sun., March 22nd (Pay at the Door.....Advance booking Optional)

"MINIATURA" AUTUMN 1992
Sat., September 12th (Limited Entry by Advance Postal Booking Only)
Sun., September 13th (Pay at the Door.....Advance booking Optional)

For details of times and admission charges, and advance ticket booking system, see our advertisements in the specialist magazines . . . or send $2 (bills) for inclusion on our mailing list for 1992.

Our GLASGOW (SCOTLAND) show, introduced in 1991, has about 60 dealers and is growing. It takes place at the new GLASGOW ROYAL CONCERT HALL.

"THE SCOTTISH MINIATURA"
Sun., June 21st, 1992 (Open to all - pay at the door) • Watch the press for further info. and developments.

ENQUIRIES
BOB and MURIEL HOPWOOD • "MINIATURA"
41 Eastbourne Avenue, Hodge Hill • Birmingham B34 6AR, England
Tel. (UK) 021 783 2070

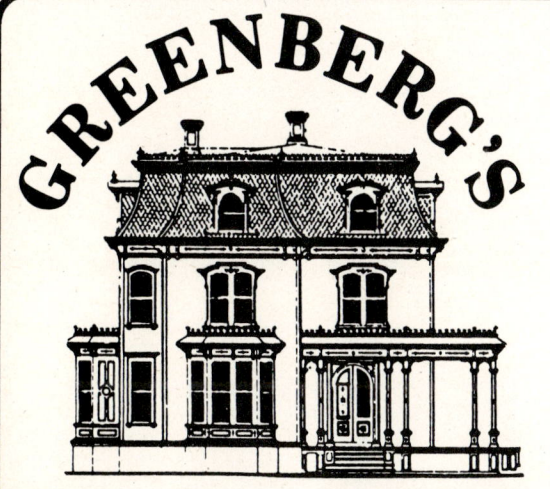

GREENBERG'S

GREAT TRAIN, DOLLHOUSE & TOY SHOW

Each show features magnificent dollhouses, helpful demonstrations on: electricity, wallpaper, brick, etc. Large marketplace offers miniatures, dollhouses, toy trains and accessories, and collectible toys. Wide selection - competitive prices. Contact us to confirm a show date or request schedule with detailed directions

Admission: $5.00;   Hours: 11a.m. - 5p.m.
children under 12, free with adult.

GREENBERG SHOWS, INC.   7566 Main Street
Sykesville, MD 21784   **(301)795-7447**

PHILADELPHIA, PA: Aug. 3-4 and   Dec. 14-15, 1991
Philadelphia Civic Center, Hall B. 3400 Civic Center Boulevard.
Special Admission $6.00 - includes parking.

HUNTINGTON, WV: August 10-11, 1991
Huntington Civic Center. Free parking. In cooperation with NRHS.

NEW ORLEANS, LA: August 17-18, 1991
Pontchartrain Center. I-10, north on Williams Blvd. Free parking.

CHATTANOOGA, TN: September 14-15, 1991
Chattanooga Civic Center. Free parking.

HEMPSTEAD, L.I., NY   September 28-29, 1991
Hofstra University, Physical Fitness Center. Free parking.

RICHMOND, VA: October 26-27, 1991
Richmond Fairgrounds, Better Living Center. Free parking.

EDISON, NJ: Nov. 2-3, 1991   1/25-26/92
Raritan Center Exposition Hall, Raritan Plaza. Free Parking.

CHERRY HILL, NJ: November 9-10, 1991
Garden State Park, Grandstand Building, on Route 70.

PITTSBURGH, PA: Nov. 16-17, '91   2/22-23 & 7/18-19/92
Pittsburgh Expo Mart at Monroeville. Free parking.

WILMINGTON, MASS: Nov. 30-Dec. 1, 1991   4/4-5/92
Shriner's Auditorium, 99 Fordham Road. I- 93, Exit 39. Free parking.

TIMONIUM, MD: Dec. 7-8, 1991   3/21-22/92
Timonium Fairgrounds, Exhibition Hall, York Road. Free parking.

TAMPA, FL: 1/4-5/92
Florida State Fairgrounds, FL Living Center. I-4 at U.S. Hwy. 301.

VIRGINIA BEACH, VA: 1/4-5/92
Virginia Beach Pavillion & Convention Center. Free parking.

POMPANO BEACH, FL: 1/11-12/92
Broward Community College - North Campus. Free parking.

HACKENSACK, NJ: 3/28-29/92
Fairleigh Dickinson University, Rothman Center. Free parking.

TOWSON, MD: *Towson State University*   7/11-12/92

THE MINIATURES CATALOG, Fourteenth Edition

CALENDAR

1991 AUGUST

August 10-11—Philadelphia, PA. Greenberg's Great Train, Dollhouse & Toy Show. 11 a.m.-5 p.m. $5 adults, children under 12 free with adult. Philadelphia Civic Center. Workshops, demonstrations, exhibits, door prizes. Greenberg Shows, Inc., 7566 Main St., Sykesville, MD 21784. (301) 795-7447.

August 17-18—Lincoln City, OR. Seventh Annual Lincoln City Dollhouse & Miniature Show & Sale. Sat., 11 a.m.-4 p.m., Sun., 12 p.m.-4 p.m. $1. Elks Lodge, 2020 N.E. 22 St. Demonstrations, exhibits, door prizes. Vicki Williams, P.O. Box 83, Otis, OR 97368. (503) 994-9796.

August 18—Cleveland, OH. C.M.S. Fair. 10 a.m.-5 p.m. $3. Holiday Inn, Strongsville, OH. Workshops, exhibits, door prizes. Preview Aug. 17, 1:30 p.m.-5 p.m. $8. Cleveland Miniaturia Society, P.O. Box 1043, Cleveland, OH 44120. (216) 751-5963.

August 17-18—Hyannis, MA. CCMS Twelfth 1991 Dollhouse & Miniature Show. 10 a.m.-5 p.m. Sheraton Hyannis. Workshops, exhibits, door prizes. Cape Cod Miniature Society, P.O. Box 1541, Sandwich, MA 02563. (508) 477-5121 or (508) 564-4500.

August 24-Glendale, CA Happy Dolling's Miniature Mansions. 10 a.m.-4 p.m. $4. Glendale Civic Auditorium, 1401 Vendugo Rd., Glendale, CA 91208. Workshops, door prizes. Barbara Kouri, P.O. Box 6806, Burbank, CA 91510-6806. (818)767-4172 (Pacific time).

August 24—Bellingham, WA. Bellingham Miniature Show. 10 a.m.- 5 p.m. $3. Nendels, 714 Lakeway Dr. Demonstrations, exhibits. Eastside Miniature Show, 18120 Bothell Way, N.E., #A6, Bothell, WA 98011. (206) 486-0988.

August 25—Mystic, CT. Mystic Summer Festival of Miniatures & Dollhouses. Sunday, 10 a.m.-4 p.m. Adults $3.50. Sr's/Child (5-12) $2.50. Ramada Inn, I-95 & Rt. 27 (Greenmanville Ave.), Mystic, CT. Door prizes. Mainly Miniatures, LTD., P.O. Box 1187, Westerly, R.I. 02891. (401)596-9218.

SEPTEMBER

September 7-8—San Rafael, CA. Marin Miniature Shows. 10 a.m.-5 p.m.; 11 a.m.-4 p.m. $4 adults, $2 under 12. Marin Center - Exhibit Hall; Civic Center Drive. Demonstrations, exhibits, door prizes. Marin Miniature Shows, 20 Truman Drive, Novato, CA 94947 (415) 897-9585 0r 897-6228.

September 7-8—Akron, OH. Miniature Fair and Doll Show. 10 a.m.-5 p.m.; 11 a.m.-5 p.m. $3 adults, $1.50 children 6-12. Stan Hywet Carriage House and Manor Auditorium. Exhibits. Stan Hywet Hall and Gardens, 714 N. Portage Path, Akron, OH 44303-1399. (216) 836-5533.

September 15—Morgantown, PA. Seventh Annual Reading Area Dollhouse Miniature Show & Sale. 10 a.m.-5 p.m.; 11 a.m.-4 p.m. $3 adults, $1 children under 12. Wilson World Hotel-Mom Outlet Mall, Exit 22, PA Turnpike. Door prizes. Diane Fogel, 3313 Pruss Hill Road, Pottstown, PA 19464. (215)323-9289.

September 21-22—Denver, CO. 10 a.m.-5 p.m. $3.50 adults, $1.50 children. Workshops, demonstrations, exhibits, door prizes. Preview night September 20, 7:30 p.m.-10 p.m. The Denver Museum of Miniatures, Dolls & Toys, 1880 Gaylord, Denver, CO 80206. (303) 322-1053.

September 21-22—Omaha, NE. Midlands Miniature Showcase "Music, Music, Music" Sat. 9 a.m.-5 p.m.; Sun., 9 a.m.-4:30 p.m. $3 adults, $1.50 children. Red Lion Inn, 16th and Dodge St. Workshops, exhibits. Preview night Sept. 20, 7 p.m.-10 p.m. $60 pre-registered. Omaha/Council Bluffs Miniature Guild. Edna Perkins, 806 Hogan Dr., Papillion, NE 68046. (402) 339-5071.

September 22—Fort Wayne, IN. Summit City Dollhouse & Miniatures Show & Sale. 10 a.m.-4:30 p.m. $4.00 adults, $1.50 children. Marriott Inn, I-69 at Exit 112A. Exhibits, door prizes hourly. Bright Star Promotions, Inc., Valerie Rogers, 3428 Hillvale Road, Louisville, KY. (502) 432-STAR.

September 22—Framingtham, MA. Doll, Bear, Miniature Show & Sale. 10 a.m.-3:00 p.m. $3.00 adults, children under 12 FREE. Sheraton Tara Rte 9. Exhibits, door prizes. Rainbow Bazaar Show, Cindy Amburgey, 47 Jackson Ave., Fitchburg, MA 01420. (508) 345-1993 or 342-8292.

September 22—Westwood, MA. Miniature Show & Sale. 10 a.m.-5:00 p.m. $1.50 adults, $.50 teens. Thurston Jr. High, Westwood, Rte#109. Exhibits, door prizes. Aaron Guild Chapter, NSDAR. Mrs. Stanley Cottrell, 76 Winter St., Norwood, MA 02062. (617) 769-0955.

September 22—Newark, NJ. World of Mini Mania Doll Show - Fall Frolic. 10 a.m.-4:30 p.m. $5 adults, $4.50 seniors, $2.50 children under 12. Vista International Hotel at Newark Airport (Route 1 South - Service lane). Workshops, demonstrations, door prizes. Preview 9 a.m.-10 a.m. $7. Victorian Vintage, 64 Mae Belle Dr., Clark, NJ. 07066 (908) 382-2135.

September 22—Niagara Falls, NY. Seventh Annual Doll, Toy & Miniature Show & Sale. 10 a.m.-4:00 p.m. $2 adults, $.50 children under 12. Niagara #1 Fire Hall, 6010 Lockport Road. Exhibits, door prizes. Rainbow Dollmakers of Niagara County. Doris Wilkins, 2930 Birch Ave., Niagara Falls, NY 14305. (716)284-8985.

September 28-29—Birmingham, England. "Miniatura". Sat. 11 a.m.-6 p.m. (limited nos., advanced booking only), £6 (in advance by post only); Sun. 10 a.m.-4:00 p.m. (unlimited), £2.80 (at door), £2.50 (by post). The National Motorcycle Museum, Birmingham, England. Demonstrations, exhibits. "Miniatura", (Bob and Murial Hopwood), 41 Eastbourne Avenue, Hodge Hill, Birmingham B34 GAR, England. (UK) 021-783-2070.

September 28-29—West Des Moines, IA. Tiny Treasures Charity Miniature & Dollhouse Show. Sat. 10 a.m.-5:00 p.m.; Sun. 11 a.m.-4 p.m. $3 adults, $1.50 children. Super 8 Lodge - Westmark, I-80 & Ashworth Rd., West Des Moines. Workshops, exhibits, door prizes, raffle. Very Important Partners - Polk County Juvenile Court, 120 Second Ave., Des Moines, IA. (515) 286-2047.

September 28-29—Hempstead, L.I., N.Y. Greenberg's Great Train, Dollhouse & Toy Show. 11 a.m.-5:00 p.m. $5 adults, free children under 12 with adult admission. Hofstra University. Demonstrations, exhibits, door prizes. Greenberg Shows, Inc., 7566 Main Street, Sykesville, MD 21784. (301) 795-7447.

September 29—East Windsor, CT. Collector's Showcase Shows of Bears, Dolls, Miniatures and Accessories. 10 a.m.-4:00 p.m. $4. Ramada Inn. Special attraction: Doll hospital and appraisal clinic. Kitty Osker, 32 Wallace St., Stamford, CT 06902. (203)327-1936.

OCTOBER

October 5—Bloomington, Minnesota. Minneapolis/St. Paul Dollhouse Miniatures Show & Sale. 10 a.m.-5 p.m. $4 adults, $1.50 children. Best Western Thunderbird, 2201 East 78th St., Bloomington, MN. 55420. Workshops. Preview October 4, 7 p.m.-9:30 p.m. $8. Tom Bishop Productions, Inc. P.O. Box 8571 Coral Springs, FL. 33075. (305)755-0373.

October 5-6—Portland, OR. The Portland Miniature Show. Sat., 10 a.m.-5 p.m., Sun., 11 a.m.-4 p.m. $4. Montgomery Park, 2701 N.W. Vaughn St. Workshops, exhibits, silent auction to benefit Oregon food bank. Kay Fisher, 13757 Upper Cow Creek Rd., Azalea, OR 97410. (503) 837-3743.

October 6—Greenwich, CT. Collectors Showcase Show of Bears, Dolls, Miniatures & Accessories. 10 a.m.-4 p.m. $4. Greenwich Civic Center, Exit 5, I-95. Kitty Osker, 32 Wallace St., Stamford, CT 06902. (203) 327-1936.

October 6—Wilmington, DE. Fourteenth Wilmington Dollhouse & Miniature Show. 10 a.m.-5 p.m. $4 adults, $3 seniors, $1.50 children. Hotel Du Pont. Door prizes. Philadelphia Miniature Enthusiasts. Gloria Hinkel, 2410 High Rd., Huntingdon Valley, PA 19006. (215) 947-6030.

October 6—St. Albans, VT. Second Annual Fall Foliage Miniature Show & Sale. Sun. 10 a.m.-4 p.m. $1 adult, Free children under 12, with adult. St. Albans Town Central School, Route 7. Exhibits, door prizes. St. Albans Dollhouse & Miniature Club, Sandy Laferriere, Rd #3, Box 300A, St. Albans, VT 05478. (802) 524-6877.

October 11-12—Riverview, NB, Canada. It's A Small World. Fri., 12 p.m.-9 p.m., Sat., 10 a.m.-5 p.m. NA. Moncton Miniature & Doll Enthusiasts. Mrs. Jean MacArthur, 687 Coverdale Rd., Riverview, NB, Canada E1B 3K7. (506) 386-6808.

October 11-13—Hanover, MA. Dollhouse & Miniatures Show & Sale. Fri./Sat. 9:30 a.m.-9:30 p.m., Sun.12-6 p.m. Free. The Hanover Mall (Route 3 to Exit 13). Held in celebration of National Dollhouse & Miniatures Month. Kelley's Dollhouse, Inc. (508) 394-4294. Dealer inquiries welcomed.

October 12—Rochester, N.Y. 29th Annual Dolls, Miniatures and Dollhouse Show & Sale. 10 a.m.-5 p.m. $3. Minch Hall, East Henrietta and Calkins Rds., Thruway Exit 46. Exhibits, door prizes. Patricia Kohlman Finnerty, 101 Flynnwood Dr., Rochester, N.Y. 14612. (716) 723-1535.

October 12-13—Tucson, AZ. "Miniature Gourmet" Fourteenth Annual Show & Sale. 11 a.m.-5 p.m. $3 adults, $1.50 children. 6245 E. Bellevue. Exhibits, door prizes. The Tucson Miniature Society proceeds go to Comstock Children's Foundation. Show Chairman, Nina Skopp, 5942 E. 20th Street, Tucson, AZ 85711. (602) 790-1242.

October 12-13—Atlanta, GA. Atlanta Miniature Society 12th Annual Show & Sale. Sat. 10 a.m.-5 p.m., Sun. 11 a.m.-4 p.m. $4. Sheraton Century

Show Calendar

Center Hotel, I-85 at Clairmont Rd. Exhibits. Atlanta Miniature Society, 4320 Colony East Dr., Stone Mtn., GA 30083. (404) 284-5666.

October 12-13—Amarillo, TX. Magic Moments in Miniature. 12 noon-5 p.m. $2 adults, $1 children under 12. Amarillo Garden Center, 1400 Street. Workshops, exhibits, door prizes. Mini Casade Amarillo and Merry Mini Makers, Billie Love, 4224 W. 38th Ave., Amarillo, TX 79109. (806) 352-3451.

October 12-18—Ashland, OR. The College of Miniature Knowledge. 8 a.m.-5 p.m. and 7:30 p.m.-9:30 p.m. daily. Contact for admission price. Ashland Hills Inn, 2525 Ashland St. Workshops pre-registered. Kay Fisher, 13757 Upper Cow Creek Rd., Azaleo, OR 97410. (503) 837-3743.

October 13—Owensboro, KY. Owensboro "River City Days" Dollhouse Show & Sale. 10 a.m.-4:30 p.m. $4 adults, $1.50 children. Executive Inn on Ohio Riverfront. Demonstrations, exhibits, hourly door prizes. Bright Star Promotions, Inc., Valerie Rogers, 3428 Hillvale Road, Louisville, KY 40241. (502) 423-STAR.

October 13-14—Rockford, IL. Dreams Come True Dollhouse Miniatures Show. Sun. 10 a.m.-5 p.m., Mon. 11 a.m.-4 p.m. Adults $4, 2-day $6; children $2. Clock Tower Resort (Wallingford Center). Workshops, exhibits, door prizes. Karin Skupien, 10337 Ellsworth Dr., Roscoe, IL 61073. (815) 623-2011.

October 16-20—St. Louis, MO. St. Louis Fall Home Show. St. Louis Convention Center. Wed. thru Sun. Demonstrations, exhibit, raffle. Home Builders Association. For more information call: Alice (314) 726-1162 or Marian (314) 394-9576.

October 18-19—Riverview. N.B., Canada. It's A Small World. Fri. 12-9 p.m., Sat. 10 a.m.-5 p.m. $1 adults, $.50 children. Riverview Kinsmen Center, 145 Lakeside Dr., Riverview. Door prizes. Moncton Miniature & Doll Enthusiasts, Mrs. Jean MacArthur, 687 Coverdale Rd., Riverview. N.B. E1B3K7, Canada.

October 19-20—Ft. Lauderdale, FL. Florida Fall Showcase of Dollhouse Miniatures Show & Sale. Sat. 10 a.m.-5 p.m., Sun. 12-4 p.m. $4 adults, $1.50 children. Holiday Inn - Ft. Lauderdale North, 4900 Powerline Rd., Ft. Lauderdale, FL 33309. Tom Bishop Productions, Inc., P.O. Box 8571, Coral Springs, FL 33075. (305) 755-0373.

October 19-20—Greensburg, PA. 13th Annual Dollhouse & Miniature Show. Sat. 10 a.m.-5 p.m., Sun. 11a.m.-5 p.m. $3 adults, $1.00 children. Mt. View Inn, Route 30 East of Greensburg, PA. Western Pennsylvania's largest show - free parking - dining room facilities. Door prizes. Unit 10 Westmoreland Hospital Auxiliary, c/o Eileen Durbin, 419 Ridge Road, Greensburg, PA 15601. (412) 834-2738 or Betty Davis, 536 Santone Drive, Greensburg, PA 15601. (412) 834-4742.

October 20—Lyndhurst, Hampshire, England. New Forest Dolls' House & Miniatures Fair. 10 a.m.-4:30 p.m. Ticket only. Preview (10:00-12 noon) £2.50, Afternoon £1.75. Lyndhurst Park Hotel, Lyndhurst. June Stowe, 147 Wilton Road, Shirley, Southampton, Hampshire, England (0703) 771995.

October 20—Hudson, Ohio. Greater Cleveland Area Dollhouse & Mini Show. 10 a.m.-4:30 p.m. $4 adults, $1.50 children. Holiday Inn - Hudson. Demonstrations, exhibits, hourly door prizes. Bright Star Promotions, Valerie Rogers, 3428 Hillvale Road, Louisville, KY 40241. (502) 423-STAR.

October 20—Nashua, N.H. Doll, Bear, Miniature Show & Sale. 10 a.m.-3 p.m. $3 adults, Free children under 10. Sheraton Tara exit 1, rte 3, Nashua, N.H. Exhibits, door prizes. Rainbow Bazaar Shows, Cindy Amburgey, 47 Jackson Ave., Fitchburg, MA 01420. (508) 345-1993 or 342-8292.

October 26—Williamsburg, VA. Williamsburg, VA Dollhouse Miniatures Show & Sale. 10 a.m.-5 p.m. $4 adults, $1.50 children. Holiday Inn - Patriot, 3032 Richmond Rd., Williamsburg, VA 23185. Workshops. Preview Oct. 25, 7 p.m.-9:30 p.m. $8. Tom Bishop Productions, Inc., P.O. Box 8571, Coral Springs, FL 33075. (305) 755-0373.

October 26-27—St. Louis, MO. Gateway Miniature Fair. Sat. 10 a.m.-5 p.m., Sun. 11 a.m.-4 p.m. $4 adults, $2 children. Holiday Inn North, 4545 N. Lindbergh Blvd., Bridgeton, MO. Exhibits, door prizes. Miniature Museum of Greater St. Louis, Joanne Mart, 324 George; Kirkwood, MO 63122. (413) 822-7322.

October 26-27—Richmond, VA. Greenberg's Great Train, Dollhouse & Toy Show. Sat. 11a.m.-5 p.m., Sun. 11 a.m.-4 p.m. $5 adults, Free children under 12 with adult admission. Easy Living Center, Richmond Fairgrounds. Demonstrations, exhibits, door prizes. Greenberg Shows, Inc., 7566 Main Street, Sykesville, Maryland 21784. (301) 795-7447.

October 27—Honolulu, HI. Waikiki & Mini. 10a.m.-5 p.m. $3. Hilton Hawaiian Village, Honolulu, HI. Workshops. Teri's Mini Workshop, Box 387, Goldenrod, FL 32733.

October 27—Elmont, N.Y. St. Vincent DePaul's Famous Model Train-Toy & Doll Show. 10a.m.-4 p.m. $4. 1510 DePaul Street, Elmont, N.Y. 11003. Exhibits. St. Vincent DePaul Parish, 1500 DePaul St., Elmont, N.Y. 11003. (516) 352-2127.

October 28—Lahaina, HI. Maui & Mini. 6 p.m.-10 p.m. $3. Embassy Suites, 104 Kaanapali Shores Place, Lahaina, Maui, HI. Workshops. Teri's Mini Workshop, Box 387, Goldenrod, FL 32733.

NOVEMBER

November 2—Plainview, N.Y. Long Island, N.Y. Dollhouse Miniatures Show & Sale. 10 a.m.-4 p.m. $4 adults, $1.50 children. Plainview Plaza Hotel, 150 Sunnyside Blvd., Plainview, L.I., N.Y. 11803. Workshops. Preview Nov. 1 7 p.m.-9:30 p.m. $8. Tom Bishop Productions, Inc., P.O. Box 8571, Coral Springs, FL 33075. (305) 755-0373.

November 2-3—Edison, N.J. Greenberg's Great Train, Dollhouse & Toy Show. 11 a.m.-5 p.m. $5 adults, Free children under 12 with adult admission. Raritan Center Expo Hall. Demonstrations, exhibits, door prizes. Greenberg Shows, Inc., 7566 Main Street, Sykesville, MD 21784. (301) 795-7447.

November 2-3—Albuquerque, NM. Albuquerque Doll, Miniature, Old Toy Show. Sat., 9 a.m.-6 p.m.; Sun., 10 a.m.-5 p.m. $1.50 adults, $1 children. Creative Arts Bldg., State Fair Grounds. Exhibits. Collector's Showcase, Virginia Miller, 7512 Sky Ct. Cr. NE, Albuquerque, NM 87110. (505) 883-6986.

November 3—Hamilton, Ontario, Canada. Ninth Annual Dollhouse & Miniature Show & Sale. 10 a.m.-4 p.m. $2 adults, $1 seniors and children under 12. Mohawk College (Student Center), Fennell Campus, Fennell Ave. W. Demonstrations, exhibits, door prizes. Hamilton & Area Mini-Crafters, 80 Albany Ave. OT 27 East 44th St., Hamilton, Ontario, Canada. (416) 544-9857 or 383-8530.

November 3—Danbury, CT. Collectors Showcase Show of Bears, Dolls, Miniatures & Accessories. 10 a.m.-4 p.m. $4. Ethan Allen Inn, Exit 4 I-84. Kitty Osker, 32 Wallace Street, Stamford, CT 06902. (203) 327-1936.

November 3—Frederick, MD. Frederick Dollhouse & Miniature Sale. 11 a.m.-5 p.m. $3. Holiday Inn at Rt. 85 and Interstate 270. Workshops, demonstrations, Preview Nov. 3, 9 a.m.-11 a.m., $10. Sally R. Hofelt, 17524 Longstreet Cr., Sharpsburg, MD 21782. (301) 432-5628.

November 3—Auckland, New Zealand. Kiwi's & Minis. 10 a.m.-5 p.m. $3. TOA. Workshops. Teri's Mini Workshop, Box 387, Goldenrod, FL 32733.

November 4 thru December 9—St. Louis, MO. Miniatures Through Time. 10:30 a.m.-4:30 p.m. House tours and Lunch Nov. 4, 12-2 p.m. Exhibited at Campbell House, Eugene Field House, Hawken House, and Sappington House museums. Raffle. For more information call: Alice (314) 726-1162 or (314) 394-9576.

November 9—Busbane, Australia. Mickey & Mini Down Under. 10 a.m.-5 p.m. $3. TOA. Workshops. Teri's Mini Workshop, Box 387, Goldenrod, FL 32733.

November 9-10—Santa Barbara, CA. Calm's Small World. Sat., 10 a.m.-5 p.m., Sun., 11 a.m.-4 p.m. $3 adults, $2 seniors and children. Earl Warren Showgrounds, Hwy. 101 and Las Positas. Workshops, demonstrations, exhibits. Child Abuse Listening and Mediation, April Thede, 235 Canon Dr., Santa Barbara, CA 93105. (805) 687-7023.

November 9-10—Largo, FL. SEMTA - Dollhouse & Miniature Show & Sale. Sat. 10 a.m.-5 p.m., Sun. 11 a.m.-4p.m. $4 adults, $3.50 seniors, $1 children under 12. Honeywell Minn-REG Building - 6340 126th Ave. N., Largo, FL. Exhibits, door prizes. Barbara Godfrey, 2112 Bonita Way S., St. Petersburg, FL 33712. (813) 867-4723.

November 9-10—King of Prussia, PA. Philadelphia Miniaturia. Sat. 10 a.m.-5 p.m., Sun. 11 a.m.-5 p.m. $5. Valley Forge Convention Center. Workshops, door prizes. Preview Nov. 8, 6 -9:30 p.m. $12. Frank Moroz and Pat Bauder, P.O. Box 518, Langhorne, PA 19047.

November 9-10—Cherry Hill, N.J. Greenberg's Great Train, Dollhouse & Toy Show. 11 a.m.-5 p.m. $5 adults, Free children under 12 with adult admission. Garden State Park. Demonstrations, exhibits, door prizes. Greenberg Shows, Inc., 7566 Main Street, Sykesville, MD 21784. (301) 795-7447.

November 10—Jordan, Ontario, Canada. G.N.O.M.E. Show & Sale of Miniatures. 10 a.m.-5 p.m. $3 adults, $2 seniors and children. Beacon Motor Inn. Pat Ostovar, 8th Avenue Louth, RR #1, Jordan, Ontario, Canada, LOR 150. (416) 562-4963.

November 10—Jordan, Ontario, Canada. Canada's Sixth Annual Juried Show of Miniatures. 11 a.m.-5 p.m. $3 adults, $2 seniors and children. Beacon Motor Inn. Pat Stonham, 960 Metler Rd., Fenwick, Ontario, Canada LOS 1CO. (416) 892-3718.

November 16-17—Columbus, OH. Columbus Miniature Society Dollhouse & Miniature Show & Sale. Sat. 10 a.m.-5 p.m., Sun. 11 a.m.-4 p.m. $3 adults, $1 children under 12. Aladdin Temple, 3850 Stelzer Rd., Columbus. Columbus Miniature Society, c/o Jan Danley, 1300 Millington Ct., Columbus, OH 43220. (614) 459-0725.

November 16-17—Pittsburgh, PA. Greenberg's Great Train, Dollhouse & Toy Show. 11 a.m.-5 p.m. $5 adults, Free children under 12 with adult admission. Pittsburgh Expo Mart. Demonstrations, exhibits, door prizes. Greenberg Shows, Inc., 7566 Main Street, Sykesville, MD 21784. (301) 795-7447.

November 23—Augusta, GA. Christmas in Miniature. 10 a.m.-2 p.m. $3 adults, $1 children

THE MINIATURES CATALOG, Fourteenth Edition

under 12. Good Shepherd Church, 2230 Walton Way. Workshops, demonstrations, exhibits, door prizes. Friends of The Symphony & Augusta Miniature Society, Sue Alexanderson, 1103 Milledge Rd., Augusta, GA 30904. (404) 738-7527.

November 23-24—Salisbury, MD. Eleventh Annual Doll, Miniature & Toy Show & Sale. Sat., 11 a.m.-6 p.m., Sun., 12 p.m.-5 p.m. Admission price. Wicomico Youth & Civic Center. Exhibits, door prizes. Soroptimist International of Salisbury. Lou Elin Sheller, 627 N. Pinehurst Ave., Salisbury, MD 21801. (301) 742-7277.

November 24—Parsippany, NJ. World of Mini Mania. 10 a.m.-4:30 p.m. $5 adults, $2.50 children under 12. Embassy Suites Hotel, Parsippany Blvd. (Route 202). Workshops, demonstrations, door prizes. Victorian Vintage, 64 Mae Belle Dr., Clark, NJ. (201) 382-2135.

November 24—Reading, PA. Reading Dollhouse Miniature Show & Sale. 10 a.m.-5 p.m. $3 adults, $1 children 10 and under. The Inn at Reading. Door prizes. Diane Fogel, 3313 Pruss Hill Road, Pottstown, PA 19464. (215) 323-9289.

November 30—Baintree, MA. Dollhouse & Miniatures Show & Sale. 9:30 a.m.-4 p.m. $3 adults. Sheraton Tara Hotel (Rt. 128 to exit 6). Kelley's Dollhouse, Inc. (508) 394-4294. Dealer inquiries welcomed.

November 30-December 1—Wilmington, MA. Greenberg's Great Train, Dollhouse & Toy Show. 11 a.m.-5 p.m. $5 adults, Free children under 12 with adult admission. Shriner's Auditorium. Greenberg Shows, Inc., 7566 Main Street, Sykesville, MD 21784. (301) 795-7447.

November TBA-Atlanta, GA. Christmastime in Dixie. 10 a.m.-4 p.m. $4 adults, $1.50 children. Marriott Inn Northwest, I-75 at Windy Hills exit. Demonstrations, exhibits, hourly door prizes. Bright Star Promotions, Inc., Valerie Rogers, 3428 Hillvale Road, Louisville, KY 40241. (502) 423-STAR.

DECEMBER

December 1—Newark, NJ. World of Mini Mania. 10 a.m.-4:30 p.m. $5 adults, $4.50 seniors, $2.50 children under 12. Vista International Hotel at Newark airport, Rt. 1 South - Service Lane). Workshops, demonstrations, exhibits, door prizes. Preview 9-10 a.m. $7. Victorian Vintage, 64 Mae Belle Dr., Clark, NJ. 07066. (908) 382-2135.

December 1—Elmont, N.Y. St. Vincent DePaul's Famous Model Train-Toy & Doll Show. 10 a.m-4 p.m. $4. 1510 DePaul Street, Elmont, N.Y. 11003. Exhibits. St. Vincent DePaul Parish, 1500 DePaul St., Elmont, N.Y. 11003. (516) 352-2127.

December 7-8—Timonium, MD. Greenberg's Great Train, Dollhouse & Toy Show. 11 a.m-5 p.m. $5 adults, Free children under 12 with adult admission. Timonium Fairgrounds. Demonstrations, exhibits, door prizes. Greenberg Shows, Inc., 7566 Main Street, Sykesville, MD 21784. (301) 795-7447.

1992 JANUARY

January 4-5—Tampa, FL. Greenberg's Great Train, Dollhouse & Toy Show. 11 a.m-5 p.m. $5 adults, Free children under 12 with adult admission. Florida State Fairgrounds. Demonstrations, exhibits, door prizes. Greenberg Shows, Inc., 7566 Main Street, Sykesville, MD 21784. (301) 795-7447.

January 4-5—Virginia Beach, VA. Greenberg's Great Train, Dollhouse & Toy Show. 11 a.m-5 p.m. $5 adults, Free children under 12 with adult admission. Virginia Beach Convention Center. Demonstrations, exhibits, door prizes. Greenberg Shows, Inc., 7566 Main Street, Sykesville, MD 21784. (301) 795-7447.

January 11-12—Pompano Beach, FL. Greenberg's Great Train, Dollhouse & Toy Show. 11 a.m-5 p.m. $5 adults, Free children under 12 with adult admission. Broward Community College-North Campus. Demonstrations, exhibits, door prizes. Greenberg Shows, Inc., 7566 Main Street, Sykesville, MD 21784. (301) 795-7447.

January 12—Elmont, N.Y. St. Vincent DePaul's Famous Model Train-Toy & Doll Show. 10 a.m-4 p.m. $4. 1510 DePaul Street, Elmont, N.Y. 11003. Exhibits. St. Vincent DePaul Parish, 1500 DePaul St., Elmont, N.Y. 11003. (516) 352-2127.

January 18-19—Jacksonville, FL. Second Annual Jacksonville Miniature Show. Sat. 10 a.m-5 p.m., Sun. 11 a.m.-4 p.m. $3 adults, $2 children. Holiday Inn Conference Center, Arlington Expressway. Workshops, exhibits, door prizes. First Coast Miniature Show, Beverly Harvey, 5370 Contina Ave., Jacksonville, FL 32211. (904) 743-5764.

January 18-19—Palm Beach Gardens, FL. SEMT - Dollhouse & Miniature Show & Sale. Sat. 10 a.m-5 p.m., Sun. 11 a.m.-4 p.m. $4 adults, $3.50 seniors, $1 children under 12. MacArthurs Holiday Inn, 4431 PGA Blvd. at I-95, Palm Beach Gardens, FL. Door prizes. Barbara Godfrey - SEMTA, 2112 Bonita Way S., St. Petersburg, FL. 33712. (813) 867-4723.

January 19—Brooklyn Center, MN. Twelveth Annual Dolls in Winter. 10 a.m-4 p.m. $3. Earle Brown Heritage Center. Door prizes. Carol's Doll House, 10617 University Ave. NE, Blaine, MN 55433. (612) 755-7475.

January 25-26—Anaheim, CA. Southern California Dollhouse Miniatures Show & Sale. 10 a.m-5 p.m. $4 adults, $1.50 children. Anaheim Plaza Resort Hotel, 1700 S. Harbor Blvd., Anaheim, CA 92802. Workshops. Preview Jan. 24, 7-9:30 p.m. $8. Tom Bishop Productions, Inc., P.O. Box 8571, Coral Springs, FL 33075. (305) 755-0373.

January 25-26—Gainsville, FL. SEMT - Dollhouse & Miniature Show & Sale. Sat. 10 a.m-5 p.m., Sun. 11 a.m.-4 p.m. $4 adults, $3.50 seniors, $1 children under 12. Holiday Inn University Center, 1250 W. University Ave., Gainsville, FL. Exhibits, door prizes. Barbara Godfrey - SEMTA, 2112 Bonita Way S., St. Petersburg, FL. 33712. (813) 867-4723.

January 25-26—Edison, NJ. Greenberg's Great Train, Dollhouse & Toy Show. 11 a.m-5 p.m. $5 adults, Free children under 12 with adult admission. Raritan Center Expo Hall. Demonstrations, exhibits, door prizes. Greenberg Shows, Inc., 7566 Main Street, Sykesville, MD 21784. (301) 795-7447.

January 25-26—Portland, OR. Fifteenth Annual Miniature Show & Sale. 10 a.m-5 p.m. $3 adults, $2 children 6-12. Red Lion Inn/Lloyd Center, Exhibit Hall, 1000 N.E. Multnomah, Portland, OR. D & K Enterprises, Karla Smith, P.O. Box 5916, Vancouver, WA 98668. (206) 693-7629.

January 26—Newark Airport, NJ. World of Mini Mania. 10 a.m-4:30 p.m. $5. The Marriott Hotel at Newark Airport. Workshops, demonstrations, exhibits, door prizes. Preview 9-10 a.m. $7. Victorian Vintage, 64 Mae Belle Drive, Clark, NJ 07066.

FEBRUARY

February 1-2—Daytona Beach, FL. Collector's Showcase Show of Miniatures & Doll House Accessories. 10 a.m-4 p.m. $4. Ramada Resort Hotel, Exit 88, I-95. Note: there are NO dolls or bears in this show. Kitty Osker, 32 Wallace Street, Stamford, CT 06902. (203) 327-1936.

February 1-2—Janesville, WI. Fantasy Faire. Sat. 10 a.m-5:30 p.m., Sun. 12-5 p.m. Free. Janesville Mall. Demonstrations, exhibits. Jan Shereck, 402 Lincoln Street, Janesville, WI 53545.

February 8-9—Culver City, CA. Miniatures West Sixth Annual Miniature Fantasy Show & Sale. Sat. 10 a.m-5 p.m., Sun. 11 a.m.-4 p.m. $5, $4 with name card, $2 children. Veteran's Memorial Auditorium, 4117 Overland (at Culver Blvd.). Workshops, exhibits, door prizes. Miniatures West Club, Judy Lancaster, 5711 Owensmouth #117, Woodland Hills, CA 91367. (818) 340-5291.

February 8-9—Ft. Lauderdale, FL. Fourteenth Annual South Florida Dollhouse Miniatures Show & Sale. Sat. 10 a.m-5 p.m., Sun. 11 a.m.-4 p.m. $4 adults, $1.50 children. Sterling Suites Hotel, 555 NW 62nd St., Ft. Lauderdale, FL 33309. Workshops, exhibits. Preview Feb. 7, 7-9:30 p.m. $10. Tom Bishop and Rita Demarco, P.O. Box 8571, Coral Springs, FL 33075. (305) 755-0373 or (404) 745-5849.

February 9—Ft. Old Greenwich, CT. Collector's Showcase Show of Bears, Dolls, Miniatures & Accessories. 10 a.m-4 p.m. $4. Greenwich Civic Center, Exit 5, I-95. Kitty Osker, 32 Wallace Street, Stamford, CT 06902. (203) 327-1936.

February 15—Kissimmee, FL. Orlando Dollhouse Miniatures Show & Sale. 10 a.m-5 p.m. $4 adults, $1.50 children. Ramada Resort Maingate at the Parkway, 2900 Parkway Blvd., Kissimmee, FL 34746. Workshops. Preview Feb. 14, 7-9:30 p.m. $8. Tom Bishop Productions, Inc., P.O. Box 8571, Coral Springs, FL 33075. (305) 755-0373.

February 22—Atlanta, GA. Atlanta's "Heart of Dixie" Dollhouse Miniatures Show & Sale. 10 a.m-5 p.m. $4 adults, $1.50 children. Dunwoody Hotel and Conference Center, 1850 Cotillon Dr., Atlanta, GA 30338. Workshops. Preview Feb. 21, 7-9:30 p.m. $8. Tom Bishop Productions, Inc., P.O. Box 8571, Coral Springs, FL 33075. (305) 755-0373.

February 22—Atlanta, GA. Atlanta's "Heart of Dixie" Dollhouse Miniatures Show & Sale. 10 a.m-5 p.m. $4 adults, $1.50 children. Dunwoody Hotel and Conference Center, 1850 Cotillon Dr., Atlanta, GA 30338. Workshops. Preview Feb. 21, 7-9:30 p.m. $8. Tom Bishop Productions, Inc., P.O. Box 8571, Coral Springs, FL 33075. (305) 755-0373.

February 22-23—Monroeville, PA. Greenberg's Great Train, Dollhouse & Toy Show. 11 a.m-5 p.m. $5 adults, children under 12 free with adult. Pittsburgh Expo Mart. Demonstrations, exhibits, door prizes. Greenberg Shows, Inc., 7566 Main St., Sykesville, MD 21784. (301) 795-7447.

February 29—Enfield, CT. Enfield Lions Club Dollhouse & Miniatures Show & Sale. Sat. 9:30 a.m.-4 p.m. $2.50. Enfield Street School. Exhibits, door prizes. Enfield Lions Club, 26 Mathewson Ave, Enfield, CT 06082. (203) 745-2835.

February 29-March 1—Eugene, OR. Eugene Miniature Club Show & Sale. Sat. 10 a.m-5 p.m., Sun. 12-4 p.m. $1.50 name members, seniors, $2 general public. Irving Grange Hall, 1011 Irvington Dr. Exhibits, door prizes. Eugene Miniature Club, 2824 Stark St., Eugene, OR 97404. (503) 688-6821.

February '92-Ft. Mitchell, KY. Cincinnati - Northern Kentucky Dollhouse & Miniatures Show & Sale. 10 a.m.-4:30 p.m. $4 adults, $1.50 children. Drawbridge Inn, I-75 at Buttermilk Pike. Demonstrations, exhibits, hourly door prizes. Bright

Star Promotions, Inc., Valerie Rogers, 3428 Hillvale Road, Louisville, KY 40241. (502) 423-STAR.

MARCH

March 1-Danbury, CT. Collector's Showcase Show of Dolls, Bears, Miniatures and Accessories. 10 a.m.-4:p.m. $4. Ethan Allen Inn, Exit 4, I-84. Kitty Osker, 32 Wallace Street, Stamford, CT 06902. (203) 327-1936.

March 7-8-Houston, TX. Houston Dollhouse Miniatures Show & Sale. Sat. 10 a.m.-5:p.m., Sun. Noon-4 p.m. $4 adults, $1.50 children. Holiday Inn - Medical Center, 6701 So. Main St., Houston, TX 77030. Workshops, exhibits. Preview Mar. 6, 7-9:30 p.m. $8. Tom Bishop Productions, Inc., P.O. Box 8571, Coral Springs, FL 33075. (305) 755-0373.

March 15-Frederick, MD. Frederick Dollhouse & Miniature Sale. 11 a.m.-5:p.m. $3. Holiday Inn, Exit 31A at Rt. 85 off of Interstate 270. Workshops, demonstrations. Preview Mar. 15, 9-11 a.m. $10. Sally R. Hofelt, 17524 Longstreet Circle, Sharpsburg, MD 21782. (301) 432-5628.

March 21-Ft. Myers, FL. Thirteenth Southwest Florida Miniature & Dollhouse Show & Sale. 10 a.m.-4:30 p.m. $3 adults, $1 under 12. Arabia Temple, 2010 Hanson St. Exhibits, door prizes. Mini-De-Lights Miniature Club, P.O. Box 07336, Ft. Myers, FL 33919. Ann Schluessler, (813) 489-0228

March 21-22-Birmingham, England. Miniatura. Sat. 11 a.m. - 5 p.m., Sun. 10 a.m. - 4 p.m. The National Motorcycle Museum, Birmingham, England. Demonstrations, exhibits. Bob & Muriel Hopwood, 41 Eastbourne Avenue, Hodge Hill, Birmingham B34 6AR England. 021 783 2070.

March 21-22-Timonium, MD. Greenberg's Great Train, Dollhouse & Toy Show. 11 a.m. - 5 p.m. $5 adults, free under 12 w/adult admission. Timonium Fairgrounds. Demonstrations, exhibits, door prizes. Greenberg Shows, Inc., 7566 Main Street, Sykesville, MD 21784. (301) 795-7447.

March 21-22-Kansas City, MO. Miniature Fantasies. Sat. 10 a/m/ - 5 p.m., Sun. 11 a.m. - 4 p.m. Workshops, exhibits, door prizes. Preview Night March 20, 7-9 p.m. Miniature Fantasies, Inc., 5118 NW 59th Ter, Kansas City, MO 64151. Barbara Griggs, (816) 587-2350.

March 28-29-Hackensack, NJ. Greenberg's Great Train, Dollhouse & Toy Show. 11 a.m. - 5 p.m. $5 adults, free under 12 w/adult admission. Rothman Center, Fairleigh Dickinson University. Demonstrations, exhibits, door prizes. Greenberg Show, Inc., 7566 Main Street, Sykesville, MD 21784. (301) 795-7447.

March 29-Duluth, GA. N.A.M.E. Region E-3 Houseparty - "Georgia On My Mind". 11 a.m. - 4 p.m. $4 adults, $1.50 children under 12. Atlanta Marriott Gwinnett Place. Exhibits. National Association of Miniature Enthusiasts, 5645 Nottingham Drive, Lilburn, GA 30247. Carol Friedrichsen, (404) 921-5064.

March '92-Evansville, IN. River City Dollhouse & Miniature Show & Sale. 10 a.m. - 4:30 p.m. $4 adults, $1.50 children. Radisson Inn at the Airport. Demonstrations, exhibits, door prizes hourly. Bright Star Promotions, Inc., 3428 Hillvale Road, Louisville, KY 40241. Valerie Rogers, (502) 423-STAR.

APRIL

April 4- Nashua, NH. New England's Masters of the Miniature Arts Show & Sale. 10 a.m. - 5 p.m. $4 adults, $1.50 children. Holiday Inn - Nashua, 9 Northeastern Blvd. Workshops. Preview, April 3, 7-9:30 a.m. Tom Bishop Productions, Inc., P.O. Box 8571 Coral Springs, FL 33075. (305) 755-0373.

April 4-5-Phillipsburg, NJ. Eggsibit '92. Noon - 5 p.m. $3. Firth Youth Center, 108 Anderson St. Demonstrations, exhibits, door prizes. Firth Youth Center, 525-419 Fisher Ave, Phillipsburg, NJ 08865. Kit Stansbury, (908) 859-4496.

April 4-5-Wilmington MA. Greenberg's great Train, Dollhouse & Toy Show. 11 a.m. - 5 p.m. $5 adults, free children under 12 w/adult admission. Shriner's Auditorium. Demonstrations, exhibits, door prizes. Greenberg Shows, Inc., 7566 Main Street, Sykesville, MD 21784. (301) 795-7447.

April 5-Cincinnati, OH. Dollhouse & Miniature Show & Sale. 10 a.m. - 5 p.m. $10. Cincinnati Convention Center. Workshops, demonstrations, exhibits, door prizes. Preview night, April 4, 5-9 p.m. $7. The Miniature Society of Cincinnati, 1350 Observatory Drive, Cincinnati, OH 45208. James R. Minor, (513) 321-9516.

April 5-Elmont, NY. St. Vincent DePaul's Famous Model Train, Toy & Doll Show. 10 a.m. - 4 p.m. $4. 1510 DePaul St. Exhibits. St. Vincent DePaul Parish, 1500 DePaul St., Elmont, NY 11003. (516) 352-2127.

April 11-Rochester, NY. 30th Annual Dolls, Miniatures and Dollhouse Show & Sale. 10 a.m. - 5 p.m. $3. Minch Hall, East Henrietta and Calkins Rds., Exit 46. Exhibits, door prizes. Patricia Kohlman Finnerty, 101 Flynwood Dr., Rochester, NY 14612.

April 11-12-Arlington Heights, IL. Chicago's Masters of the Miniature Arts Show & Sale. Sat. 10 a.m. - 5 p.m., Sun. 11 a.m. - 4 p.m. $4 adults, $1.50 children. Radisson Hotel, 75 W. Algonquin Rd. Workshops. Preview night, April 10, 7-9:30 p.m. $8. Tom Bishop Productions, Inc., P.O. Box 8571 Coral Springs, FL 33075. (305) 755-0373.

April 11-12-San Rafael, CA. Marin Miniature Shows. Sat., 10 a.m. - 5 p.m., Sun. 11 a.m. - 4 p.m. $4 adults, $2 under 12. Marin Center- Exhibit Hall, Civic Center Dr. Demonstrations, exhibits, door prizes. Marin Miniature Shows, 20 Truman Dr., Novato, CA 94947. (415) 897-9585 or (415) 897-6228.

April 12-August 23-Mystic, CT. Spring Festival of Miniatures - Mystic's Summer Festival of Miniatures & Dollhouses. 10 a.m. - 4 p.m. $3.50 adult, $2.50 seniors and children 5-12. Ramada Inn, Mystic, CT., I-95 & Rt. 27. Door prizes. Mainly Miniatures, Ltd., P.O. Box 1187, Westerly, RI, 02891. (401) 596-9218.

April 26-Wilmington, DE. First State Mini Club Show & Sale. 10 a.m. - 4 p.m. $3.50 adults, $3 seniors, $2.50 under 12. Brandywine Terrace, 3416 Philadelphia Pike. Exhibits, door prizes. First State Mini Club, 113 Downs Drive, Wilmington, DE 19807. (302) 992-9065.

April '92-Atlanta, GA. Springtime in Dixie. 10 a.m. - 4:30 p.m. $4 adults $1.50 children. Marriott In Norcross. Demonstrations, exhibits, door prizes hourly. Bright Star Promotions, Inc., 3428 Hillvale Rd., Louisville, KY 40241. Valerie Roger, (502) 423-STAR.

April '92-Louisville, KY. Derbytown Dollhouse & Miniature Show & Sale. 10 a.m. - 4:30 p.m. $4 adults, $1.50 children. Holiday Inn East - Hurstbourne & I-64. Exhibits, door prizes hourly. Bright Star Promotions, Inc., 3428 Hillvale Rd., Louisville, KY 40241. Valerie Rogers, (502) 423-STAR.

April '92-Nashville, TN. Music City Dollhouse & Miniature Show & Sale. 10 a.m. - 4:30 p.m. $4 adult, $1.50 children. Holiday Inn - Briley Pkwy off I-65 & I-40. Demonstrations, exhibits, door prizes hourly. Bright Star Promotions, Inc., 3428 Hillvale Rd., Louisville, KY 40241. Valerie Rogers, (502) 423-STAR.

MAY

May 2-3-Boise, ID. Through The Keyhole. 10 a.m. - 5 p.m., 1 p.m. - 5 p.m. $2. Idaho State Museum - Julia Davis Park. Exhibits, door prizes. Mini Les Bois Miniature Club, P.O. Box 4482, Boise, ID 83711-4482.

May 3-Reading, PA. Reading Dollhouse Miniature Show & Sale. 10 a.m. - 5 p.m. $3 adults, $1 under 12. The Inn at Reading. Door prizes. Dian Fogel, 3313 Pruss Hill Rd., Pottstown, PA 19464. (215) 323 9289.

May 8-9-Riverview N.B. Canada. It's A Small World. Fri., noon - 9 p.m., Sat., 10 a.m. - 5 p.m. Riverview Kinsmen Center, 145 Lakeside Dr. Door prizes. Moncton Miniature & Doll Enthusiasts, 687 Coverdale Rd., Riverview, N.B. E1B 3K7 Canada. Mrs. Jean MacArthur.

May 8-9-St. Louis, MO. Gateway Miniature Show. May 8, 7 p.m. - 10:30 p.m., May 9, 10 a.m. - 5 p.m. $4. Exhibits, door prizes. Miniature Museum of Greater St. Louis, 746 Henry Ave., Ballwain, MO 63011. Louise Levitt, (314) 227-3300.

May 9-11-London, England. The London Dollhouse Festival. Kensington Town Hall, Hornton Street, W.8. Mrs. Caroline Hamilton, 25 Priory Road, Kew Green, Richmond, TW9 #DQ England. 081-948 1893.

May 16-Arlington, WA. Marysville Mini-Makers Miniature Show & Sale. 10 a.m. - 4 p.m. $2 adults, $1 seniors & children. Stillaguamish Senior Center, 18308 35th Ave. N.E. Demonstrations, workshops, door prizes. Mrs. Dorothy R. Morrill, 16600 25th Ave. N.E., SP-158, Arlington, WA 98223. (206) 652-7346.

May '92-Perrysburg, OH. Greater Toledo Area Dollhouse & Miniature Show & Sale. 10 a.m. - 4:30 p.m. $4 adult, $1.50 children. Holiday Inn French Quarter. Demonstrations, Exhibits, door prizes hourly Bright Star Promotions, Inc., 3428 Hillvale Rd. Louisville, KY 40241. Valerie Rogers, (502) 423-STAR.

JUNE

June 7-Gaithersburg, MD. The World of Teeny, Tiny Things. 11 a.m. - 5 p.m. $1. Casey Community Center. Demonstrations, exhibits, door prizes. City of Gaithersburg, Dept. of Parks & Recreation, 810 S. Frederick Avenue, Gaithersburg, MD 20877. (301) 258-6366.

June 7-Newark Airport, NJ. World of Mini Mania. 10 a.m. - 4:30 p.m. $5. Vista International Hotel at Newark Airport, Route 1 South-Service Lane. Workshops, demonstrations, exhibits, door prizes. Preview hour, 9-10 a.m. $7. Victorian Vintage, 64 Mae Belle Drive, Clark NJ 07066. (908)382-2135.

June 21-Glasgow, Scotland. The Scottish Miniatura. 10:30 a.m. - 4:30 p.m. Strathclyde Suite, Royal Concert Hall Exhibits. Bob & Muriel Hopwood, 41 Eastbourne Ave, Hodge Hill, Birmingham B34 6AR England. 021-783 2070.

JULY

July 11-12-Towson, MD. Greenberg's Great Train, Dollhouse & Toy Show. 11 a.m. - 5 p.m. $5 adults, under 12 free w/adult admission. Towson Center, Towson State University. Demonstrations, exhibits, door prizes. Greenberg Shows, Inc., 7566 Main St., Sykesville, MD 21784. (301) 795-7447.

July 12-Belleville, IL. Eighth Belleville Dollhouse & Miniature Show & Sale. 10 a.m. - 4 p.m. $3. Belle-Clair Expo Building. Exhibits. Kay Kieber, 300 Ross Lane, Belleville, IL. (618) 233-0940.

July 12-Brooklyn Center, MN. Ninth Annual Dolls in Summer. 10 a.m. - 4 p.m. $3. Earle Brown Heritage Center. Door prizes. Carol's Doll House, 10617 University Ave. N.E., Blaine, MN 55433. (612) 755-7475

July 18-19-Monroeville, PA. Greenberg's Great Train, Dollhouse & Toy Show. 11 a.m. - 5 p.m. $5 adults, under 12 free w/ adult admission. Pittsburgh Expo Mart. Demonstrations, exhibits, door prizes. Greenberg Shows, Inc., 7566 Main St., Sykesville, MD 21784. (301) 795-7447.

July 25-26-Lakeland, FL. Seventh Annual Lakeland Miniature Guild Mid-Summer Dollhouse & Miniature Show & Sale. Sat. 10 a.m. - 5 p.m., Sun. 11 a.m. - 4 p.m. $3 adults, $1 children. Lakeland Miniature Guild, P.O. Box 1486, Lakeland, FL 33802-1486. (813) 644-2819.

July 26-Pittsfield, MA. A Festival of Miniatures. 10 a.m. - 4 p.m. $3.50 adults, $2.50 seniors & children 5-12. Berkshire Hilton, Berkshire Commons, Rt. 7. Exhibits, door prizes. Berkshire Miniatures, 136 South St., Pittsfield, MA 01201. Susan Coelho, (413) 445-5579.

AUGUST

August 1-2-Dayton, OH. Three Blind Mice. Sat. 10 a.m. - 5 p.m., Sun. 11 a.m. - 5 p.m. $3 adults, $2 seniors. Hara Conference & Exhibition Center. Exhibits. Peg Busker & Deb Scherack, 740 W. Dorothy Lane, Kettering, OH 45459. (513) 296-0985 or (513) 438-8578.

August 1-2-Philadelphia, PA. Greenberg's Great Train, Dollhouse & Toy Show. 11 a.m. - 5 p.m. $6 adults including. parking, under 12 free w/ adult admission. Philadelphia Civic Center. Demonstrations, exhibits, door prizes. Greenberg Shows, Inc., 7566 Main St., Sykesville, MD 21784. (301) 795-7447.

August 2-Elmont, NY. St. Vincent DePaul's Famous Model Train, Toy and Doll Show. 10 a.m. - 4 p.m. $4. 1510 DePaul St. St. Vincent DePaul Parish, 1500 DePaul St., Elmont, NY 11003. (516) 352-2127.

August 12-13-Birmingham, England. Miniatura. The National Motorcycle Museum. Demonstrations, exhibits. Bob & Muriel Hopwood, 41 Eastbourne Ave, Hodge Hill, Birmingham B34 6AR England. 021-783 2070.

August 15-16-Lincoln City, OR. Eighth Annual Lincoln City Dollhouse & Miniature Show & Sale. Sat. 10 a.m. - 4 p.m., Sun. noon - 4 p.m. $1. Elks Lodge, 2020 N.E. 22nd St. Demonstrations, exhibits, door prizes. Vicki Williams, P.O. Box 83, Otis, OR 97368. (503) 994-9796.

August 22-Glendale, CA. Happy Dolling's Miniature Mansions. 10 a.m. - 4 p.m. $4. Glendale Civic Auditorium, 1401 Verdugo Blvd. Barbara Kouri, P.O. Box 68061, Burbank, CA 91510-6806.

(818)767-4172 evenings.

August 23-Strongsville, OH. Cleveland Miniatureia Society Fair. 10 a.m. - 5 p.m. $3 adults & children. Holiday Inn. Workshops, exhibits, door prizes. Preview, August 22, 1:30-5 p.m. $8. (216) 468-0174.

SEPTEMBER

September 12-13-San Rafael, CA. Marin Miniature Shows. Sat. 10 a.m. - 5 p.m., Sun. 11 a.m. - 4 p.m. $4 adults, $2 children under 12. Marin Center Exhibit Hall, Civic Center Drive. Demonstration, exhibits, door prizes. Marin Miniature Shows, 20 Truman Dr., Novato, CA 94947. (415) 897-9585 or (415) 897-6228.

September 20-Newark Airport, NJ. World of Mini Mania. 10 a.m. - 4:30 p.m. $5. Vista International Hotel at Newark Airport. Route 1 South Service Lane. Workshops, demonstrations, exhibits, door prizes. Preview hour, Sept. 20, 9-10 a.m. $7. Victorian Vintage, 64 Mae Belle Dr., Clark, NJ 07066. (908) 382-2135.

September 26-27-West Des Moines, IA. Tiny Treasures Charity Miniature & Dollhouse Show. Sept. 26, 10 a.m. - 5 p.m., Sept. 27th, 11 a.m. - 4 p.m. Supper 8 Lodge - Westmark, I-80 & Ashworth Rd., Exit 121. Workshops, exhibits, door prizes, raffle. Very Important Partners - Polk County Juvenile Court, 120 Second Ave., Des Moines, IA. (515) 286-2047.

September '92-Morgantown, PA. Eighth Annual Reading Area Dollhouse Miniature Show & Sale. 10 a.m. - 5 p.m. Wilson World Hotel - Mom Outlet, Exit 22, PA Turnpike. Door prizes. Diane Fogel, 3313 Pruss Hill Rd., Pottstown, Pa 19464. (215) 323-9289.

OCTOBER

October 4-St. Albans, VT. Third Annual Fall Foliage Miniature Show & Sale. 10 a.m. - 4 p.m. $1 adults, under 12 free w/adult. St. Albans Town Central School, Route 7. Exhibits, door prizes. St. Albans Dollhouse & Miniature Club. Sandy Laferriere, RD #3, Box 300A, St. Albans, VT 05478. (802) 524-6877.

October 10-Rochester, NY. 30th Annual Dolls, Miniatures and Dollhouse Show & Sale. 10 a.m. - 5 p.m. $3. Minch Hall, East Henrietta and Calkins Rds., Exit 46. Exhibits, door prizes. Patricia Kohlman Finnerty, 101 Flynwood, Dr., Rochester, NY 14612.

October 11-Rockford, IL. Dreams Come True Dollhouse Miniatures Show. Sun. 10 a.m. - 5 p.m. $4 adults, 2 day $6, $2 children. Clock Tower Resort (Wallingford Center) Workshops, exhibits, door prizes. Karin Skupien, 10337 Ellsworth Dr., Roscoe, IL 61073. (815) 623-2011.

October 11-12-Amarillo, TX. Magic Moments in Miniature. Noon - 5 p.m. $2 adults, $1 children. 1400 Street - Amarillo Garden Center. Workshops, exhibits, door prizes. Mini Casa de Amarillo and Merry Mini Makers, 4224, W. 38th Ave., Amarillo, TX 79109. (806) 352-3451.

October 10-11-St. Louis, MO. Gateway Miniature Show & Sale. Oct. 24, 10 a.m. - 5 p.m., Oct 25, 11 a.m. - 4 p.m.. $4. Harley Hotel of St. Louis, I-270 & I-170. Workshops, exhibits, door prizes. Miniature Museum of Greater St. Louis, 324 George,

Kirkwood, MO 63122. Joanne Martin, (314) 822-7322.

October 25-Elmont, NY. St. Vincent DePaul's Famous Model Train, Toy and Doll Show. 10 a.m. - 4 p.m. $4. 1510 DePaul St. Exhibits. St. Vincent De Paul Parish, 1500 DePaul St., Elmont, NY 11003. (516) 352-2127.

NOVEMBER

November 1-Hamilton, Ontario, Canada. Hamilton & Area Mini Crafters - 10th Annual Dollhouse & Miniature Show & Sale. 10 a.m. - 4 p.m. $2. Mohawk College Students Centre, Fennell Campus, Fennel Ave. West. Demonstrations, exhibits, door prizes. Hamilton & Area Mini Crafters, 80 Albany Ave. or 27 East 44th St., Hamilton, Ontario, Canada. (416) 544-9857 or (416) 383-8530.

November 7-8-King of Prussia, PA. Philadelphia Miniaturia. Sat. 10 a.m. - 5 p.m., Sun. 11 a.m. - 5 p.m. $5. Valley Forge Convention Center. Workshops, door prizes. Preview night, Nov. 6, 6-9:30 p.m. $12. Frank Moroz or Pat Bauder, P.O. Box 518, Langhorne, PA 19047.

November 8-Jordan, Ontario, Canada. G.N.O.M.E. Show & Sale of Miniatures. 10 a.m. - 5 p.m. $3 adults, $2 seniors & children. Beacon Motor Inn. Pat Ostovar, 8th Ave. Louth, RR#1, Jordan, Ontario, Canada LOR 150 (416) 562-4963.

November 8-Jordan, Ontario, Canada. Canada's 7th Annual Juried Show of Miniatures. 11 a.m. - 5 p.m. $3 adults, $2 seniors and children. Beacon Motor Inn. Exhibits. Pat Stonham, 960 Metler Rd., Fenwick, Ontario, Canada Los 1C0. (416) 892-3718.

November 14-15-Columbus, OH Columbus Miniature Society Dollhouse & Miniature Show & Sale. Sat. 10 a.m. - 5 p.m., Sun. 11 a.m. - 4 p.m. $3 adults, $1 children under 12. Aladdin Temple, 3850 Stelzer Rd. Workshops, demonstrations, exhibits, door prizes. Columbus Miniature Society, 1300 Millington Ct., Columbus, OH 43220. Jan Danley, (614) 459-0725.

November 14-15-Santa Barbara, CA. CALM's Small World. Nov. 14, 10 a.m. - 5 p.m., Nov 15, 11 a.m. - 4 p.m. Earl Warren Showgrounds. Workshops, demonstrations, exhibits. Child Abuse Listening Mediation, 235 Canon Dr., Santa Barbara, CA 93105. (805) 687-7023.

November 21-Augusta, GA. Christmas in Miniature. 10 a.m. - 4 p.m. $3 adults, $1 children. Church of the Good Shepherd, 2230 Walton Way. Workshops, demonstrations, exhibits, door prizes. Friends of the Symphony, 1103 Milledge Rd., Augusta, GA 30904. Sue Alexanderson.

November 29-Newark Airport, NJ. World of Mini Mania. 10 a.m. - 4:30 p.m. $5. Vista International Hotel at Newark Airport, Route 1 South Service Lane. Workshops, demonstrations, exhibits, door prizes. Preview hour, Nov. 29, 9-10 a.m. $7. Victorian Vintage, 64 Mae Belle Dr., Clark, NJ 07066. (908) 382-2135.

DECEMBER

December 6-Elmont, NY. St. Vincent DePaul's Famous Model Train, Toy and Doll Show. 10 a.m. - 4 p.m. $4. 1510 DePaul St. Exhibits. St. Vincent DePaul Parish, 1500 DePaul St., Elmont, NY 11003. (516) 352-2127.

Index of Miniature Museums

ARIZONA

Phoenix Art Museum, 1625 N. Central Ave., Phoenix, AZ 85004; (602) 257-1222. Tues-Sat., 10 a.m.-5 p.m.; Wed., 10 a.m.-9 p.m.; Sun., 12 p.m.-5 p.m. Closed Mondays and Holidays. $3 adults, $1.50 students, $2.50 seniors, free children under 6. Miniatures.

CALIFORNIA

Angel's Attic (Angels for Autistic Children), 516 Colorado Ave., Santa Monica, CA 90401; (213) 394-8331. Thurs.-Sun., 12:30 p.m.-4:30 p.m. $4 adults, $3 seniors, $2 children under 12. Miniatures, antique dolls/toys, antique dollhouses.

Hobby City Doll Museum, 1238 S. Beach Blvd., Anaheim, CA 92804; (714) 527-2323. Open daily 10 a.m.-6 p.m. $1 adults, 50¢ children, seniors. Miniatures, antique dolls/toys, antique dollhouses.

Maynard Manor at Miniature Mart, 1807 Octavia St., San Francisco, CA 94109; (415) 563-7436. Open Mon.-Fri., 10:30 a.m.-3:30 p.m by appointment only. 42-room castle "Maynard Manor" $3 admission.

Motts Miniatures, Knotts Berry Farm, Buena Park, CA 90620; (714) 527-1843. Open Oct.-May: Mon.-Fri., 10 a.m.-6 p.m., Sat., 10 a.m.-10 p.m., Sun., 10 a.m. - 7 p.m.; June: gradual increase in hours; July-mid-Sept.: Sun.-Fri., 9 a.m.-12 midnight, Sat., 9 a.m.-1 a.m. Antique dolls/toys, antique dollhouses.

CONNECTICUT

Crafty Owl Shop, 470 Washington Ave., North Haven, CT 06473, (203) 239-9793; Mon.-Thurs., 10 a.m.-5 p.m.; Fri.-Sat., 10 a.m.-4:30 p.m.; Sun., noon-4 p.m.; Summer closed on Sun. Shop with exhibit of dollhouses and miniatures.

Historical Museum of the Gunn Memorial Library, Route 47 & Wykeham Rd., Washington, CT 06793; (203) 868-7756. Thurs., Fri. and Sat., 12-4pm. Dollhouses, dolls, antique dolls/toys, antique dollhouses.

Wilton Heritage Museum, 249 Danbury Rd., Wilton, CT 06897; (203) 762-7257. Tues.-Thurs., and selected Sundays. 10 a.m.-4:30 p.m. Dec. and Jan. every Sun., 2-4 p.m. Antique dolls/toys antique dollhouses mostly. Special Christmas exhibit in December and January.

COLORADO

Denver Art Museum, 100 West 14th Ave. Parkway, Denver, CO 80204; (303) 575-2793. Tues.-Sat., 10 a.m.-5 p.m.; Sun., noon-5 p.m. $3 adults, $1.50 students and seniors, free for children 5 and under w/adult. Sat. free. Miniatures, antique dolls/toys, antique dollhouses.

The Denver Museum of Miniatures, Dolls and Toys, 1880 Gaylord St., Denver, CO; (303) 322-3704. Wed.-Sat., 10 a.m.-4 p.m.; Sun., 1-4 p.m. $2.50 adults, $2 seniors, $1.50 children. Miniatures, dollhouses, dolls, antique dolls/toys, antique dollhouses.

WASHINGTON, D.C.

National Museum of American History, 14th St. & Constitution Ave., N.W., Washington, D.C. 20560; (202) 357-1300. Seven days, 10 a.m.-5:30 p.m. Free. Antique dolls/toys, antique dollhouses.

Washington Dolls' House & Toy Museum, 5236 44th St., N.W., Washington, D.C. 20015; (202) 244-0024. Tues.-Sat., 10 a.m.-5 p.m.; Sun., noon-5 p.m. $3 adults, $1 children under 14. Antique dolls/toys, antique dollhouses.

FLORIDA

Henry Morrison Flagler Museum, Whitehall Way, P.O. Box 969, Palm Beach, FL 33480; (407) 655-2833. Tues.-Sat., 10 a.m.-5 p.m.; Sun., noon-5 p.m. $5 adults, $2 children 6-12. Miniatures, antique dolls/toys, antique dollhouses.

ILLINOIS

Art Institute of Chicago, Michigan Ave. & Adams St., Chicago, IL 60603; (312) 443-3600. Mon.-Fri., 10:30 a.m.-4:30 p.m.; Tues., 10:30 a.m.-8 p.m.; Sat., 10 a.m.-5 p.m.; Sun., noon-5 p.m. Suggested donation: $6 adults, $3 students, seniors, and children 6-14; Tues., free. Ten Thorne Rooms in Junior Museum.

Museum of Science & Industry, 57th St. & Lake Shore Dr., Chicago, IL 60637; (312) 684-1414. Open daily 9:30 a.m. 4 p.m. 9:30 a.m.-5:30 p.m. holidays and weekends. Admission & parking free. Colleen Moore's *Fairy Castle*; Louise Gardner doll collection.

INDIANA

Children's Museum of Indianapolis, 3000 N. Meridan, Indianapolis, IN 46208; (317) 924-5437. Mon.-Sat., 10 a.m.-5 p.m.; Sun., noon-5 p.m.; Thurs., until 8 p.m. Labor Day-May 21. $4 adults, $3 seniors, children 2-17 1 year youth pass. Antique dolls/toys, antique dollhouses.

IOWA

Museum of Amana History, P.O. Box 81, Amana, IA 52203; (319) 622-3567. Located on Main Street. Mon.-Sat., 10 a.m.-5 p.m.; Sun., noon-5 p.m.; closed Nov. 15-Apr. 15. $2.50 adults, $1 children. Antique dolls/toys (10 dolls, 100 toys), six antique dollhouses.

The Barn Museum, Two blocks north of Hwy. 6, South Amana, IA 52334, (319) 622-3058. Daily, 9 a.m.-5 p.m., Apr.1-Oct. 31. $2.50 adults, 50¢ children 6-12. Over 175 buildings in 1" scale depicting history of farming and rural life, created by Henry Moore.

MASSACHUSETTS

The Children's Museum, 300 Congress St., Boston, MA 02210; (617) 426-6500. Summer: June-Labor Day, seven days, 10 a.m.-5 p.m.; Fri., 10 a.m.-9 p.m. Winter: Labor Day-May 31, Tues.-Sun., 10 a.m.-5 p.m.; Fri., 10 a.m.-9 p.m.; Mon., closed. $6 adults, $5 seniors and children 2-15, $2 children 1-2. Fri. 5-9 p.m., admission $1. Miniatures, antique dolls/toys, antique dollhouses.

Children's Museum, 276 Gulf Rd., South Dartmouth, MA 02748; (508) 993-3361. Tues.-Sat., 10 a.m.-5 p.m.; Sun., 1 p.m.-5 p.m. $3 admission. Miniatures, antique dolls/toys.

Essex Institute, 132 Essex St., Salem, MA 01970; (508) 744-3390. Nov. - May, Tues.-Sat., 10 a.m. - 5 p.m., Sun. and Holidays, 12-5 p.m. June - Oct., Mon. 10 a.m. - 5 p.m., Thurs., 10 a.m. - 9 p.m. $6 adults, $5 seniors, $3.50 children 6-16. Miniatures antique dolls/toys, antique dollhouses.

Old Sturbridge Village, Rt. 20 West, Sturbridge, MA 01566; (508) 347-3362. Nov.-May, Tues.-Sun., 10 a.m.-4 p.m. May-Oct. Mon.-Sun. 9 a.m.-5 p.m. $14 adults, $7 children 6-15. Antique dolls/toys.

Wenham Museum, 132 Main St., Wenham, MA 01984; (508) 468-2377. Mon.-Fri., 11 a.m.-4 p.m.; Sat., 1 p.m.-4 p.m.; Sun., 2 p.m.-5 p.m. $3 adult, $1 children 6-14, $2.50 seniors & groups by reservation. Antique dolls/toys, antique dollhouses, 17th century house w/period furnishings.

Yesteryears Museum Assn. Inc., Main & River St., Sandwich, Cape Cod, MA 02563; (508) 888-1711. May 15-Oct. 31, Mon.-Sat., 10 a.m.-4 p.m.; Closed Sundays. $2.50 adults, $2 seniors, $1.50 children under 12. Group rates. Antique dolls/toys, antique dollhouses.

MICHIGAN

Children's Museum, 67 East Kirby, Detroit, MI 48202; (313) 494-1210. Mon.-Fri. 1 p.m.-4 p.m, Sat. 9 a.m.-4 p.m. May-Oct. closed Sat. Free.

Henry Ford Museum, 20900 Oakwood Blvd., Dearborn, MI 48121; (313) 271-1620. Daily 9 a.m.-5 p.m. $10.50 adults, $9.50 seniors over 62, $5.25 children 5-12. Antique dollhouses.

MISSOURI

Toy and Miniature Museum of Kansas City, 5235 Oak St., Kansas City, MO 64112; (816) 333-2055. Wed.-Sat., 10 a.m.-4 p.m.; Sun., 1 p.m.-4 p.m. $3 adults, $2.50 students and seniors, special tour/group rates with reservations. Miniatures, antique dolls/toys, antique dollhouses.

Missouri Historical Society, Lindell & DeBalivier St., St. Louis, MO 63112; (314) 361-1424. Tues.-Sun., 9:30 a.m.-4:45 p.m. Free Admission. Antique dolls/toys, antique dollhouses, history of Missouri.

NEBRASKA

Louis B. May Museum, 1643 N. Nye Ave., Fremont, NE 68025; (402) 721-4515. Apr.-Dec., Wed.-Sun., 1:30 p.m.-4:30 p.m. $2 adults, 50¢ children under 12. Antique dolls/toys, dollhouses.

NEW JERSEY

Monmouth County Historical Assoc., 70 Court St., Freehold, NJ 07728; (908) 462-1466. Tues.-Sat., 10 a.m.-4 p.m.; Sun., 1 p.m.-4 p.m. $2 adults, $1.50 seniors, $1 children 6-18, members and children under 6 free. Antique dolls/toys, antique dollhouses.

NEW MEXICO

Museum of International Folk Art, 706 Camino Lejo, Santa Fe, NM 87504; (505) 827-6350. Mailing address, P.O. Box 2087. Mon.-Sun. 10 a.m.-5 p.m. $3.50 adults, children under 17 free. Dolls.

NEW YORK

New York Historical Society, 170 Central Park West, New York, NY 10024; (212) 873-3400. Tues.-Sun., 10 a.m.-5 p.m. $4.50 adults, $3 seniors, $1 children under 12. Miniatures, dollhouses, antique toys.

Museum of the City of New York, 5th Ave. & 103rd St., New York, NY 10029; (212) 534-1672. Free admission, suggested donations, $4 adults, $3 children, students, seniors, $6 family. Wed.-Sat., 10 a.m.-5 p.m.; Sun., 1 p.m.-5 p.m. Closed Mon. Antique dolls/toys, antique dollhouses.

Aunt Len's Doll & Toy House, 6 Hamilton Terrace, New York, NY 10031; (212) 281-4143. By appointment only. Miniatures, dollhouses, dolls, antique dolls/toys, antique dollhouses.

Shaker Museum, Shaker Museum Rd., Old Chatham, NY 12136; (518) 794-9100. May - Oct., daily, 10 a.m.-5 p.m. $6 adults, $5 seniors, $3 children 8-17, $14 families. Museum food service, County picnic buffet. Miniatures rooms, antique dollhouse.

Margaret Woodbury Strong Museum, 1 Manhattan Square, Rochester, NY 14607; (716) 263-2700. Mon.-Sat., 10 a.m.-5 p.m.; Sun., 1 p.m.-5 p.m. $3 adults, $2.25 seniors and students, $1 children 3-16. Miniatures antique dolls/toys, antique dollhouses.

The Museum at Stony Brook, 1208 Rt. 25A, Stoney Brook, NY 11790; (516) 751-0066. Wed.-Sat., 10 a.m.-5 p.m., Sun., Noon - 5 p.m. $6 adults, $4 seniors and students, $3 children 6-12, children under 6 free. Sun., noon-5 p.m. Miniatures, antique dolls/toys, 15 miniature period rooms.

Yorktown Museum, 1974 Commerce St., Yorktown Heights, NY 10598; (914) 962-2970. Tues.-Fri., 9:30 a.m.-4:30 p.m.; Sat.-Sun., 1 p.m.-4 p.m. Suggested donation. Dollhouses, dolls, antique dolls/toys, antique dollhouses.

OHIO

Western Reserve Historical Society, 10825 East Blvd., Cleveland, OH 44106; (216) 721-5722. Tues.-Sat., 10 a.m.-5 p.m.; Sun., noon -5 p.m. $4 adults, $2 seniors and students, children under 6 free. Miniatures, antique dolls/toys antique dollhouses.

Rutherford B. Hayes State Memorial, 1337 Hayes Ave., Fremont, OH 43420; (419) 332-2081. Mon.-Sat., 9 a.m.-5 p.m.; Sun., noon-5 p.m. $3 adults, $2.50 seniors, $1 children 7-12. Antique dolls/toys, antique dollhouses.

Allen Co. Historical Society, 620 W. Market St., Lima, OH 45801. Antique dolls/toys, antique dollhouse replica of Mt. Vernon.

OKLAHOMA

Eliza Cruce Doll Museum (Ardmore Public Library), 320 E Street Northwest, Ardimore, OK 73401; (405) 223-8290. Mon.-Thurs., 10 a.m.-8:30 p.m.; Fri., Sat., 10 a.m.-4 p.m. Free. Miniatures, antique dolls.

PENNSYLVANIA

Chester County Historical Society, 225 N. High St., West Chester, PA 19380; (215) 692-4800. Tues.-Sat., 10 a.m.-4 p.m.; Wed., 1 p.m.-8 p.m.; Closed Sun. Museum, $2.50 adults, $1.50 under 18. Library, $4.50 adult, $2.50 student. Admission to library allows entry to museum. Antique dollhouses.

Mary Merritt Doll Museum, RT 422, Douglasville, PA 19518; (215) 385-3809. Mon.-Sat., 10 a.m.-4:30 p.m.; Sun., 1 p.m.-5 p.m. $2 adults, $1 children, under 5 free. Miniatures, antique dolls/toys; antique dollhouses.

RHODE ISLAND

Newport Historical Society, 82 Touro St., Newport, RI 02840; (401) 846-0813. Tues.-Fri., 9:30 a.m.-4:30 p.m.; Sat. 9:30 a.m.-noon, (9;30 a.m. - 4:30 p.m., June 15-Labor Day. Miniatures, Antique dolls/toys (Christmas only).

VERMONT

Shelbourne Museum, U.S. Rt. 7, Shelbourne, VT 05482; (802) 985-3344. Mid May-mid Oct., open daily 9 a.m.-5 p.m. $14 adults, $6 children 6-14. Miniatures, antique dolls/toys, antique dollhouses.

WISCONSIN

House on the Rock Inc., Spring Green, WI 53588; (608) 935-3639. Open 7 days a week. Ticket sales 8 a.m.-4 p.m., Viewing 8 a.m.-6:45 p.m. $13 adults, $8 children 7-12, $3 children 4-6. Miniatures, antique dolls/toys, antique dollhouses.

Milwaukee Public Museum, 800 W. Wells St., Milwaukee, WI 53202; (414) 278-2702. Open daily, 9 a.m. - 5 p.m. $4.50 adults, $2.50 children 4-17, $3 Milwaukee County seniors and students. Free to Milwaukee County residents Mon. Antique dolls/toys, antique dollhouses.

Milwaukee County Historical Society, 910 N. Old World Third St., Milwaukee, WI 53203; (414) 273-8288. Free. Mon.-Fri., 9:30 a.m.-5 p.m.; Sat., 10 a.m.-5 p.m.; Sun., 1 p.m.-5 p.m. Antique dolls/toys, antique dollhouses.

*Museum listings are printed **free of charge**. Additions, deletions, and corrections should be sent in writing to: Kalmbach Publishing Co., The Miniatures Catalog, Museums, 21027 Crossroads Circle, P.O. Box 1612, Waukesha, WI 53187.*

Index of Manufacturers, Artisans and Suppliers

A

AMSI Scale Model Supplies, 4234 Petaluma Blvd. North, P.O. Box 750638, Petaluma, CA 94975. Wholesale only. Manufacturer. Price list available; see your local miniatures dealer. Manufacturers of AMSI landscape materials for all scales. Catalog and information sheets, upon request. pp. 112, 213, 330

A-West, P.O. Box 1144, Woodstock, GA 30188. Retail, wholesale and manufacturer. SASE for brochure. Weathering/antiquing solutions: Age shingles and wood, make plaster "concrete," blacken most metals, give copper/brass/bronze that old blue/green look. Stainless needlepoint applicator bottles. pp. 326, 329

A-Dora-Bill Miniatures, 401 Rosewood Lane, Sprague River, OR 97639. Manufacturer. Brochure and price list, LSASE. Curtain rods, towel bars, tissue holders and tissue, drapery rods, furniture and quilt kits, dollhouse plans, glue jigs, diamond plastic for windows, ceiling paper, and our new crib kits and 1/2 size glue jigs. pp. 224, 242, 326

A Grand Scale, 8910 W. 178th St., Tinley Park, IL 60477. Artisan, retail and wholesale. Price list and photos available, LSASE + $1. Many varieties of calico and furry Teddy Bears and other animals ranging in size from 3/4" to 2". Hours by appointment. p. 292

Advanced Machinery Imports Ltd., P.O. Box 312, 2 McCollough Drive, New Castle, DE 19720. Retailer, wholesaler and importer. Catalog and price list available free. Exclusive source for fine European machines offering complete service and technical assistance. Critically acclaimed HEGNER products include eight scroll saws, blades and accessories, plus the ACCURA benchtop workstation. Optional accessories also available. p. 330

Afton Classics, 37 Commerce St., Chatham, NJ 07928. Manufacturer since 1966. 1/12 scale dollhouses of fine quality and reasonable price. We use 3/8" cabinet grade plywood almost exclusively. Colonial, Victorian, Federal and Southern styles. Includes windows, doors and stairs. Easy to assemble. pp. 22, 30, 35, 46, 49, 50

All Through the House—Amy Robinson, 5 Paquatanee Pl., Biddeford, ME 04005. Retailer, wholesaler and artisan. LSASE for brochure. 1" and 1/2" handcrafted accessories and kits. Always adding new items to make your house more "homey". 150 handmade (by me) items to choose from. Kits are great for club projects and in-store workshops. Reasonably priced. pp. 261, 262, 292, 295

Alessio Miniatures, 13 Everest Ct., Huntington Station, NY 11746. Wholesale only. Catalog and information sheets, free. pp. 18, 19, 103, 104, 106, 110, 293

American Craft Products Inc., 1530 N. Old Rand Rd., Wauconda, IL 60084. Manufacturer. Catalog, $2; price list available; see your local miniatures dealer. American manufacturers of collector-quality miniature houses, Carlson Components, the finest line in the industry, and Carlson Display Kits. House kits are available in shell kit form with optional component package that includes Carlson Components. All products made in America. Quality and satisfaction guaranteed. pp. 19, 22, 30, 41, 47, 50-52, 64, 65, 79, 84, 86-88, 110, 112, 114, 115, 121, 168, 296, 303

American Victorians by Clell Boyce, P.O. Box 65126, Vancouver, WA 98665. Retail, wholesale, manufacturer and artisan. Write for brochure. $1. Assembled Victorian period house shells and components in 1" scale. pp. 51, 75

Amoroso Originals, 3117 Yukon Ave., Costa Mesa, CA 92626. Retail, wholesale, manufacturer and artisan. Brochure, $3. Beautiful dressed beds, brass day beds, dressing table sets, furniture, accessories for bed and bath rooms, hat boxes, roses, bouquets, trims and silk ribbons. Distributor for Sloman Glue Products. pp. 207, 240, 295, 326

Ann's Things (A Division of Mary's Miniature Mansions), 6111 Harmon Place, Springfield, VA 22152. Retail, wholesale and artisan. Price list available for $1. Handcrafted Fimo sticks to make candies, cookies, fruit, or meat trays and candy houses. Also pies, cakes, garlands and wreaths. Kits and finished products are available. Dealer inquiries are welcome.

Judy Herman Appelbaum, 148 W. 23rd St., New York, NY 10011. Appraiser of dollhouses and miniatures. p. 311

Architecturally Designed Dollhouses, P.O. Box 129, Lakeview Dr., North Salem, NY 10560. Artisan of finished buildings, retail only. We build collector quality custom houses and shops in 1" scale. We are also a fully stocked miniature shop. Richard Charles Pfeiffer, architect and emeritus professor of architecture also designs his own. pp. 30, 35, 39, 41, 52, 53

Artply, Inc., See Dee's Delights, Inc. pp. 23, 25, 26, 31, 39, 52, 53, 205, 213, 224

Aunt Ginny's, 5813 Irving Ave., N., Brooklyn Center, MN 55430. Retailer, wholesaler and artisan. Wood and plexiglass display shapes. Magazine covers from 1895 - 1991, books, sheet music, attic papers, cards, photos. Catalog and sample; $2. Bears, bunnies and food by Ann Fisher. Baskets, wreaths and other accessories. (Mail order and miniature shows only). pp. 67, 243, 248

Aztec Imports, Inc., 6345 Norwalk Rd., Medina, OH 44256. Wholesale only.

Catalog available, $10. Miniature furniture and accessories. pp. 37, 38, 148, 149, 162, 195, 202, 207, 214, 218, 222, 224, 269, 270 See our display ad on the outside back cover.

B

B&B Etching Products, Inc., 18700 N. 107th Ave. #3, Sun City, AZ 85373. Retail, wholesale, and manufacturer. Price list available. Brochure $1. "Gravila" - Electric 2 g. engraving tool for plastic, plexiglas, glass, metal and mirror. Writes like a pen. "Etching Creme" - glass and mirror etching (non-acid) cream liquid. p. 326

B.B. Fine, Inc., 650 San Pablo Ave., Casselberry, FL 32707. Retail, wholesale and manufacturer. Price list, $3. Five different display units for home or store. Injection moulded in kit form or fully finished. Hot water heaters or water coolers in 1" or 1/2" scale. pp. 218, 219, 266

B.H. Miniatures, 20805 N. 19th Ave., Suite #5, Phoenix, AZ 85027. Wholesale, retail, manufacturer and artisan. Mail order catalog available, $3. Precut, ready-to-assemble basswood furniture kits and handcrafted finished pieces. "Victoriana Collection", "Country Collection II" and "Tommy's Room". Large selection of prepasted wallpaper with coordinating fabric and velvet carpeting. Selection of display boxes. pp. 70, 169, 172, 197-199, 201-203, 207

B.K.'s Mini Frame-Up, 504 Love Dr., Prospect Heights, IL 60070. Wholesale only. Catalog $4 (non-refundable). Framed pictures and mirrors. CIMTA member. p. 272

Ballhagen Woodcraft, Route 5, Box 332, Lebanon, MO 65536. Retail, wholesale, manufacturer and distributor. Catalog, $2.50 retail; see your local miniatures dealer. Specializing in miniature stores and commercial buildings, fixtures and accessories, including gas station items, gas pumps and cart kits. Four sizes of room boxes (not shown). Dealer inquiries invited. pp. 41, 42, 289

Ron Benson Miniatures, P.O. Box 5231, Richmond, VA 23220. Retail and wholesale. Catalog, $2. Porcelain miniatures of 18th and 19th century antiques including sculptures, bowls, cachepots and vases. All limited editions of 250. pp. 244, 254, 264, 274

Betty's Hobbies, 6201 Jackie Terrace, Ft. Worth, TX 76148. Prize list available, send SASE. Retail and manufacturer. Dollhouse kits, custom designs and building. All types of finishing equipment and supplies. Mail order. p. 54

Betty's Wooden Miniatures, Div. Smith Wood Products, 6150 Northwest Hwy., Chicago, IL 60631. Wholesale and retail; mail order. 22-page, full-color wholesale catalog, free to dealers. Individuals may send $4 for copy of 22-page, full-color catalog, a retail mail-order source, and a list of stores in your area that sell our miniatures. Manufacturers of quality, handcrafted furniture, accessories, and building components for dollhouses and displays in 1" scale. We also make gazebos, display boxes, a line of petite shelves for displaying miniatures and 165 bridal miniatures. pp. 37, 67, 70, 71, 75, 106, 149, 208, 209, 214, 220, 225, 241, 246, 254, 260, 271
See our insert between pages 256-257.

Renee Bowen, 28 York St., Kennebunk, ME 04043. Artisan, retail and wholesale, mail order or by appointment. Send LSASE for rug flier. For illustrated brochure of Shaker and Country, furniture, accessories, games and toys, please send $1. pp. 199, 270

Philip E. Bugosh, 15841 Beech Daly, Redford, MI 48239. Wholesale only. See your local dealer. Handcrafted 1", 1/2", 1/4" and 1/44 scale room boxes and a wide variety of accessories. Dealer information available. CIMTA member. pp. 71, 249, 252, 255, 265, 271, 273, 276, 289, 292

Butt Hinge Pottery, 1 Butt Hinge Rd., Chelmsford, MA 01824. Wholesale only, artisan. For catalog, see your local miniatures dealer. We offer a large variety of wheel-thrown stoneware miniatures capturing the spirit of traditional New England pottery. The pieces lend themselves to use in many dollhouse settings from the kitchen and bedroom to the garden or general store. Well-fitted lids, finely thrown spouts, and unusual handles enhance many of the pieces. pp. 244, 246, 259, 273

Buttons by Wilson, 215 Chestnut St., Florence, MA 01060. Retailer, wholesaler and manufacturer. Special products and services, assistance to miniature stores and clubs. Price list available at no charge. We manufacture pinback buttons, award ribbons, award plaques and other advertising items with the logo of a club or show. p. 311

By Barb, 7 Aron Court, Bethpage, NY 11714. Artisan. Catalog, $3.50. Barb handcrafts contemporary miniature accessories in 1" and 1/2" scale. Scout sets, sleeping bags, school supplies, scuba gear, rain slickers and bean bag chairs are just some of the accessories in her line. Barb also handcrafts lucite furniture and an extensive array of reasonably priced ceramic dishes and accessory pieces. She has been specializing in making unique Judaic miniatures for the collector since 1978. Barb has a new addition...a complete nursery layette. pp. 209, 244, 249, 255, 271, 295

By Grace, 105 Guffey Terrace, Lynchburg, VA 24502. Retailer, wholesaler, manufacturer and artisan. Price list with photocopies, $1.50 plus LSASE. Unique "one of a kind" customized beds (country, Victorian, contemporary and traditional). Wood or brass finish, with our designer linens. Matching or coordinated upholstered loveseats, chairs, chaise lounges and slipper chairs for the bedroom or other living spaces. Curtains available on special request. Priced according to selection and detail. pp. 196, 200, 203, 209, 220, 227,

C

Carlson (see American Craft Products), 1530 N. Old Rand Rd., Wauconda, IL 60084. Manufacturer. Catalog, $2; price list available; see your local miniatures dealer. A division of American Craft Products American manufacturers of Carlson Components, the finest line in the industry, and Carlson Display Kits. All products made in America. Quality and satisfaction guaranteed.

Cathy's Handcrafted Miniature Accessories, 57-08 157 St., Flushing, NY 11355. Artisan and manufacturer, wholesale. LSASE for price list. Handcrafted plants, flowerboxes, floral arrangements, fruits, vegetables, foods, candies, holiday items and assorted accessories for inside and outside the house. Dealer inquiries welcome. Member CIMTA, MIAA. p. 276

Cathy's Original Miniatures, 735 Lacock Ave., Rural Hall, NC 27045. Retailer, wholesaler and artisan. Send SASE for free price list, add $2 for color photos. Handcrafted miniature treasures featuring miniature chenille Christmas trees, both decorated and undecorated and accessories. Most items are of original design, which include three sizes of trees, two for use in dollhouses and one for display inside a glass dome. Various ornaments such as beaded garland, cross-stitched tree skirts, hand-woven paper stars, cross-stitched ornaments, Santa faces and beaded ornaments. Kits available. pp. 249, 255, 266

Celerity Miniature Homes, 8635 267th St. W., Farmington, MN 55024. Manufacturer, wholesale only, see your local miniatures dealer. Catalog $2.50. Collector quality wooden dollhouses, sold in kits, assembled shells or assembled with beautiful, unique hand-finished exteriors. We are known for our fine collection of Victorian homes. pp. 19, 23, 26, 27, 31, 42, 43, 47, 53-55, 65

Al Chandronnait Custom Miniatures, 19 Winnhaven Dr., Dept. MC, Hudson, NH 03051. Artisan, retail and wholesale. Catalog free with LSASE. Handcrafted 1" scale accessories. p. 266

Chrysnbon Inc. see Dee's Delights. p. 205

Chrysolite, Inc., 1711 West "G" Ave., Kalamazoo, MI 49007. Retailer, wholesaler and manufacturer. Catalog, free with LSASE. Over 40 chandeliers, table lamps and wall lamps for 12V systems. Distinctive hand-blown glass. This line has preserved authenticity, precise detailing and scale and is priced moderately. p. 127

Cir-Kit Concepts, Inc., 407 14th St., N.W., Rochester, MN 55901. Catalog, $4. Manufacturer of tape wiring systems for dollhouses, including "to scale" outlets, plugs and switches. pp. 127, 128, 137-140, 146, 147, 150, 157, 162, 255, 262, 288, 302, 322, 326, 327

Clare-Bell Brass Works, P.O. Box 218, 26 Christian Hill Rd., Lovell, ME 04051. Manufacturer. Catalog, $1.50. Solid brass miniatures—1" to 1' scale. Brass beds, electric lamps and lighting fixtures, weathervanes, household items, accessories, etc. pp. 84, 106, 107, 148-150, 162, 196, 203, 260, 263, 273, 295 See our display ad on page 1.

Close to Your Heart, P.O. Box 37549, Denver, CO 80237. Retail. Price list available, SASE requested. Artist made items for your dollhouse or mini collection. Shows and mail order. Limited selection of older miniatures. Renwal, Marx, Tootsie Toy, Strombecker and Sonia Messer. pp. 227, 309

Compass Miniature Industries, Inc., 3180 Ryan Lane, Little Canada, MN 55117. Manufacturer, wholesale. Catalog and price list available free. See your local miniatures dealer for retail prices. A complete line of dollhouse kits from elegant Victorians to unique Contemporary houses. Handcrafted from 3/8" 7-ply birch plywood. Models are available in kit form, assembled shell and with professionally finished exteriors. Complete interior wiring is available on assembled shells and decorated models. pp. 25, 28, 31, 43, 46, 47, 52, 56, 59, 60

Concord Miniatures, Division of Cardinal, Inc., 400 Markley St., P.O. Box 99, Port Reading, NJ 07064. Wholesaler. Catalog available, $5. 1" to 1' scale furniture and accessories. pp. 200, 203, 225

Corner House, 4005 Spyglass Lane, Bethany, OK 73008. Artisan. Catalog $1. Cross-stitch and needlepoint kits. Supplies for needlework, ribbons, bunka, etc. p. 270

Corri Products, 710 Oak St., P.O. Box 128, Fort Atkinson, WI 53538. Wholesale only. Catalog, $2. The Corri kits are die cut from white corrugated fiberboard including suggestions for finishes and detailed instructions. Satisfaction and price are attained by children and adults in completing these miniature kits. pp. 71, 260

Craftmark House of Miniatures, 147 Lake St., Delaware, OH 43015. Miniature furniture kits, pre-finished furniture, accessories, glues, stains and finishes. Distributed by better wholesalers throughout the U.S. and abroad. pp. 93, 176, 194, 227, 329

Creative Enterprizes, 1203 Murray Dr., Dept. M, Tecumseh, MI 49286. Artisan. Brochure, 50¢ and SASE. I sculpt animals and people from Super Sculpey. Each piece is individually sculpted. I use no molds. I do special orders of people's pets; also general breeds. I work mainly in 1" scale but can do 1/2" if requested. p. 238

Custom House of Needle Arts, 2 Main St., P.O. Box 1128, Norwich, VT 05055. Mail order retail only. $1.50 catalog, full line of crewel full size. SASE for miniature information sheet. Embroidery (crewel) kits, miniature kits for living room and bedroom ensembles to cover any style miniature furniture. p. 270

D

D-leprechaun, 3108 Superior Lane, MC-5, Bowie, MD 20715. Artisan, retail and wholesale. Price list, $1. Handcrafted items in 1" and 1/2" scale. All kinds of foods, lavish hats, repainted and haired Breyer horses. p. 238

Dan-Dy Crafts, P.O. Box 148, East Templeton, MA 01438. Wholesale, manufacturer. Catalog, $2, refundable with order. Handcrafted colonial furniture available in unfinished, light and dark stains, uniform blue, gloss white and richtone black. pp. 196, 225

Dahl House of Miniatures, 10320 Toledo Circle, Bloomington, MN 55437. Retail, wholesale, manufacturer and artisan. Catalog, $3. Charming porcelain dolls by Beverly Dahl, pattern books, hats, silk fans, bow makers, ribbon, doll dressing supplies including viscose hair, kits (including 1-1/2" tall half-scale children, silk rose, straw hat, small silk hat, fan, silk bonnet and doll head jewelry). pp. 233, 316

Jean Day, 3969 Larchwood Dr., Victoria, BC V8N 3P4 Canada. Artisan, wholesale and retail. Brochure, $2. China-painted, swivel-headed, poseable porcelain people and kits. Babies and dressed doll's dolls, china-painted plates and baby toys and doll stands are also available. pp. 233, 236

Dee's Delights Inc., 3150 State Line Rd., North Bend, Cincinnati, OH 45052. Wholesale only. Catalog, 700 pages and over 24,000 different items, $25 (refundable with $200 order). Information sheets available. Complete miniature lines of furniture, furniture kits, accessories, building components, flooring, lighting, dolls, paints, glues, dollhouses, room boxes, hobby books and FIMO modeling compound. pp. 55, 79, 103, 210

Delicate Draperies by Donna Smith, 17F Village Way, Norton, MA 02766 Manufacturer, see your local dealer for prices. Specializing in elegant, handcrafted curtains and draperies. p. 173

Design Tecnics Miniatures, 6420 West 95th St., Suite 201, Overland Park, KS 66212. Retailer, wholesaler, manufacturer, artisan and publisher. See your local dealer. Send SASE for free price list. Author Fred Stephenson designs and builds custom dollhouses as well as the six "Architect's Choice" dollhouses as shells or completely finished houses, retail and wholesale. Published materials are distributed by Miniature Lumber Shoppe, Dee's Delights and New England Hobby Supply. pp. 32, 43, 56, 71, 312, 313

Diminutive Specialities, 10337 Ellsworth Dr., Dept. MC, Roscoe, IL 61073. Retail only, no wholesale. Catalog, $5; brochure, LSASE. Nite-lite boxes, miniature photos, accessories, bake shop items, room boxes. Mail order, shop (call for appointment), classes and shows. pp. 71, 255, 271, 275, 289, 290

Doll House Shoppe, 9831 S. 78th Ave., Unit B, Hickory Hills, IL 60457. Manufacturer. Catalog $2 (dealers only). See your local dealer. A complete line of handcrafted miniature accessories, holiday miniatures, plants, flowers and toys as well as a line of handmade German dollhouse dolls. pp. 256, 277

The Doll's Cobbler, Sylvia Rountree, P.O. Box 906, Berlin, MD 21811. Retail, wholesale, manufacturer and artisan. Newly revised catalog, $3.75. Leather miniatures: shoes, boots, saddlery, luggage, rainwear and fishing gear. All are authentic in design and historically correct by I.G.M.A. Fellow since 1981. Shoemaker since 1970. pp. 231, 262, 287

Dollhouse Doll-ups, P.O. Box 1935-280, Woodland, CA 95695. Importer, artisan. Retail, wholesale and mail order. LSASE and $1 for price list/catalog. All items are exclusive of Dollhouse Doll-ups. Products available include accessories form the Orient. Specially made items include cloisonne vases, silk flowers for arrangements and gardens, "mud" people, buildings, stands, Bonsai trees, money trees, Oriental books, screens, cloisonne lamps, silk brocade fabric, Oriental rugs of Bokhara design and quilt kits. pp. 150, 161, 169, 238, 245, 265, 266, 277, 311

The Dollhouse Factory, 157 Main St., Lebanon, NJ 08833. Retail, wholesale, manufacturer, artisan and mail order. Catalog, $5.50. One of the oldest and most experienced companies specializing in dollhouses, miniatures, supplies, tools and professional information. "The Complete Dollhouse Center" in 1", 1/2", and 1/4" scales. pp. 28, 55, 65, 97, 204, 231, 314, 327, 330
See our display ad on page 4.

Dollhouse Miniatures By Flo, P.O. Box 863713, Plano, TX 75086. Retail and wholesale. Catalog, $3; information sheets, 50¢. Hand-painted bathroom sets and ceramic miniatures for every room in your dollhouse! pp. 223, 245

Dorothy's Doo-Dads, P.O. Box 241, Bothell, WA 98041. Retail and wholesale and manufacturer. Send SASE for price list. Handmade accessories for your sewing, knitting and craftrooms. Knitted and crocheted items. Counted cross-stitch kits. Quilt frames. p. 270

Dougless Ltd., 150 North Ave., #303, Dept. K, Tallmadge, OH 44278. Retail and wholesale. See your local dealer or order from Dougless Ltd. Send SASE for complete details. 1. *Dougless Guides*: (30 categories for each American period). 2. (Book) *Ask Dougless Vol. I* (a must for miniaturists). 3. (Book) *Ask Dougless Vol. II* (more information for miniaturists). 4. (Book) *Ask Dougless Vol. III* (illustrated charts: kitchen, bath, architecture, cabinet makers, more). 5. Lecture-Workshops; programs; Symposiums. 6. Guide to Appraisals and Record-Keeping. Also distributed by Dee's Delights. p. 321

Dragonfly International, 6643 32nd St., #106, N. Highlands, CA 95660. Wholesaler and manufacturer. See your local miniatures dealer. Ceramic and porcelain dishes, mugs, holiday accessories, silk plants, flowers and landscaping. pp. 249, 255, 256, 277

Dremel, 4915 21st St., Racine, WI 53406. Manufacturer. Catalog and price list available. Compact power tools: MiniMite, Moto-Tool, high speed rotary tool; Freewheeler Cordless Moto-tool; Heavy Duty Flex Shaft Carving Kit; Scroll Saw; Belt and Disc-Belt Sander; Table Saw; Router Attachment; Flexible Shaft Attachment; accessories and bits. pp. 330, 331

Dura-Craft Inc., P.O. Box 438, Newberg, OR 97132. Manufacturer, wholesale only. Free price list, brochure and line drawings. Manufacturer of quality dollhouse kits, furniture kits and shakes. Product warranty. pp. 28, 29, 32, 45, 48, 55-58, 107, 198, 214, 221, 223, 306

E

Elect-A-Lite Inc., Retail and wholesale, color sheets free. Original manufacturer of Made in USA copper tape and wiring kits for dollhouses. Service and full warranty. Line of 23 of the most popular imported miniature lighting fixtures. pp. 128, 129, 140, 141, 147, 148, 150, 157

The Elfworks, 9 Cardinal Drive, Stevens, PA 17578. Artisan, retail and manufacturer. Pictures available. If you can dream it, we can build it. Finely crafted miniatures homes. Choose one of our styles or we will custom build your home or building of your choice. Finished outside shell or move-in condition. Finely crafted oak or cherry room boxes, handcrafted fireplaces. For more information call or write. p. 18

Elliott's, 2707 Beaver Ave., Simi Valley, CA 93065. Retail, wholesale and artisan. Price list available, send SASE. Unusual, quality gourmet foods made from Fimo and Cernit. Variety of foods from holiday menu to backyard cookout. Custom orders accepted. p. 249

Empress Arts & Crafts, 971 Commonwealth Ave., Boston, MA 02215. Wholesale only. Specializing in unique handmade gifts, folk art and miniatures from around the world. Our new Windsor Collection features over 50 designs of miniature white, iron-wire furniture including gazebos, flower carts, rocking chairs, nursery furniture and much more. Available from your local miniatures dealer. p. 228

Exclusive Products Co., 8940 Ellis Ave., Los Angeles, CA 90034. Wholesale only. Catalog, free. One-stop source for over 500 pieces of miniature furniture and accessories. Fast delivery! pp. 162, 196, 204, 218, 232

F

Eberhard Faber GmbH, P.O. Box 1220, EFA Strasse 1, D-8430 Neumarkt/Opf., Germany. Manufacturer. See your local dealer. Modeling compounds to create miniatures and fashion jewelry. pp. 99, 168, 227, 236, 324

Falcon Collectible Miniatures, P.O. Box 3663, Gardena, CA 90247. Manufacturer, wholesale. We specialize in porcelain tea sets, dinner sets, floral arrangements, silk plants, flatware, sterling silver, flower vases, bathroom sets, garden furniture and much more. Dealers, send for our free catalog. pp. 214, 223, 245

Fantasy In Wood, P.O. Box 1055, Bandera, TX 78003. Retail, wholesale, manufacturer and artisan. Price list available, LSASE. Wooden produce baskets, crates, containers in 1" and 1/2" scale. pp. 252, 295

Farrow Industries, Inc., P.O. Box 561, Saunderstown, RI 02874. Wholesaler and manufacturer. See your local dealer. The finest in American-made licensed miniature accessories. The complete line includes over 500 finished items including name brand reproductions along with brass or pewter hand-painted and gold-plated accessories. Over 100 kits are also available. p. 292

Feathers-N-Clay, 295-A Bordeaux Court, Chico, CA 95926. Retail, wholesale and artisan. Price list available, send LSASE. Add $2 for color photos. Over 50 varieties of birds. Accessories include perches, nests, play boards and birdhouse kits. Custom work welcome. Will do any variety in 1", 1/2" or 1/4" scale. Also miscellaneous critters, i.e. hamster, white mice, turtles, snakes, lizards and more. Each bird and critter is hand sculpted of clay. Accessories are handmade. p. 238

Fine Food in Miniature, by Sylvia Clarke, 1203-2020 Jasmine Cr., Gloucester, Ontario, Canada K1J 8K5. Retail, wholesale, manufacturer and artisan. Price list available, $2. Foods for the selective collector. Quality meals for kings and kids in 1" scale. Selection includes medieval to present, breakfasts, lunches, snacks, dinners and elaborate banquets. Canadian made. Also, table accessories made in England. Custom work considered. p. 250

Finescale Forest/Bragdon Enterprises, 2960 Garden Tower Lane, Georgetown, CA 95634. Retail, wholesale, manufacturer and artisan. Price list available; see your local miniatures dealer. We manufacture evergreen landscape and Christmas tree kits. Finished trees are available by custom order. We also offer a variety of bulk natural landscape materials. p. 256

The Fretworker, Kirk Ratajesak, P.O. Box 397M, Clinton, WI 53525. Artisan, retail and wholesale. Send LSASE for price list. Scrollwork, wall accessories and furniture pieces. All items are personally cut out by myself. Available in 1" and 1/2" scale. Some kits available. pp. 76, 274, 295, 296

G

G.E.L. Products, 19 Grove St., Rockville, CT 06066. Wholesale and manufacturer. Brochure, 50¢. Manufacturers of dollhouse kits and accessories. G.E.L. houses have realistic clapboard siding machined into wood itself through our unique routing process. Sample and brochure upon request. pp. 31, 56

Garcia & Velez Co., 37 Cypress Blvd., E., Homosassa, FL 32646. Wholesale only. Catalog $1. Information sheets free. Handmade dollhouse accessories including dolls, baskets and natural materials (horse hair and Ivory nut, a specialty). pp. 233, 266

Gary Plastic Packaging Corp., 770 Garrison Ave., Bronx, NY 10474. Manufacturer. Free catalog. Manufacturers of rigid plastic boxes and foam inserts for packaging. p. 65

Gert's Minis, 718 Meadow St., Sanford, FL 32773. We have a nice selection of party platters, candy sticks, games and assorted household accessories. LSASE for price list. pp. 250, 256, 257, 289

Goebel Miniatures, 4820 Adohr Lane, Camarillo, CA 93010. Wholesale and manufacturer. Literature and price list available. Miniature figurines—cast in bronze. Hand painted. Some limited edition. pp. 68, 69, 238, 248, 256, 257, 278-285

Carl Goldberg Models, 4734 W. Chicago Ave., Chicago, IL 60651. Manufacturer of adhesives, epoxies and adhesive accessories. pp. 324, 325

Stan Gordon Enterprises, P.O. Box 5482, Sherman Oaks, CA 91413. Retail and manufacturer. Brochure, LSASE. Manufacturers of La Guillotine, a mitering device, and the Brass Framing Clamp, for clamping frames, furniture etc. p. 327

Grandt Line Products Inc., 1040 B Shary Court, Concord, CA 94518. Retail, wholesale and manufacturer. Catalog, $4.50, ask for miniatures; Price list available. Detailed structural components and accessories in 1/2" scale and smaller. Most pieces cast in gray polystyrene: windows, doors, railings, chimneys, hardware, figures, wheels, stairs and more. pp. 296, 297, 306

Greenberg Publishing Co., Inc., 7566 Main St., Sykesville, MD 21784. Publisher. Free catalog. Leading specialty publisher of books on miniatures, toy collectibles and toy trains. p. 315

Greenleaf Products Inc., P.O. Box 388, 58 N. Main St., Honeoye Falls, NY 14472. Retail and wholesale. Include $2 when requesting catalog. Color sheet available free. Line art available to dealers. Manufacturing dollhouses and dollhouse accessories featuring exceptional style and design, easy assembly and affordable prices. Elect-a-Lite dollhouse wiring kits and fixtures. pp. 24, 26, 29, 37, 44, 45, 49, 57-59, 93, 107, 164, 201, 305-307, 314, 327, 329

See our display ad on the inside front cover.

H

Helen Joan Hairrell, 2901 N. 51st Lane, Phoenix, AZ 85031. Artist and miniaturist. Brochure, LSASE and $2 fee refundable with first order. Paintings—oils, watercolors and ink sketches, signed and dated. Landscapes and still-life florals in oil on canvas. Birds and sketches framed behind poly sheeting. Personal construction and finishing of wood frames. Calendars. All in 1" scale. p. 272

Handcraft Designs, Inc., 63 E. Broad St., Hatfield, PA 19440. Wholesale only (except mail-order where unavailable locally). Catalog, $3.50. Proprietary, historically authentic furniture and accessories in fine scale for most periods; wallpaper, rugs, *Mini-Hold, E-Z Hold, Cernit* modeling compound; carefully chosen selection of popularly-priced, open-market accessories and furnishings. pp. 66, 103, 162, 169, 196, 204, 210, 215, 221, 225, 267, 325

Handley House, Two locations: P.O. Box 8658, Ft. Worth, TX 76124 and 2 Fourth St., Wheeling, WV 26003. Wholesale distributor and manufacturer with over 13,500 miniature items. Every type of item available is represented in our selection, from dollhouse kits to anything necessary to build, finish, decorate and furnish them. pp. 75, 80, 116, 117, 142, 164-166, 215, 227, 297, 315, 325

Hanke's House, 215 No. Galbraith, Blue Earth, MN 56013. Retailer. Make flowers, plants and trees with pretty petal punches using tape, preserved leaves, and colored or painted paper. Punches and mini cake catalog, $1. pp. 250, 277

The Happy Unicorn, 901 Ellynwood Dr., Glen Ellyn, IL 60137. Retail and wholesale. Catalog, $4.50. Phyllis S. Tucker crystal chandeliers, kits and accessories. p. 134

Hartman's Miniature Glass Works, 27 Lewis St., P.O. Box 168, Dryden, NY 13053. Artisan, retail and wholesale. For all those miniature glass needs, give us a try! Over 100 stock items plus we will endeavor to match any item you have or do a new item for you. We have the capability to do large orders at discount. Our 12th year in business. Send SASE for free brochure and price list. p. 254

J. Hermes, P.O. Box 4023, El Monte, CA 91734. Retail and wholesale. Catalog, $3. Information sheets, 25¢. Manufacturers of 1", 1/2", and 1/4" scale wallpapers, giftwraps, and linoleums. Distributor of unique accessories, tools, adhesives, kits and more. pp. 71, 125, 146, 166, 169, 172, 222, 233, 257, 277, 302, 307, 325, 327, 328

Hill's Dollhouse Workshop, 9 Mayhew Dr., Fairfield, NJ 07006. Wholesale only. Catalog and information sheets, SASE. Wood sample on request. Manufacturers of birch type, 3/8" plywood, dollhouse kits. Room boxes, special order, your size. House parts dadoed for easy assembly. Openings fit Houseworks components. Custom openings to your order. All porch railings and interior stair and stairwell hole railings are Timberbrooks'. All houses now have 1-1/2" foundations. pp. 49, 59

Homestead Homes, 5769 Cottonwood Rd., Bozeman, MT 59715. Artisan, wholesale, retail and manufacturer. Brochure, $1. Handcrafted reproductions of log cabins built during the 1800's. Appropriate cabin accessories and furnishings. Outhouses. Corrugated aluminum roofing/siding. pp. 28, 39, 107

Mary Hoot Miniatures, 8396 Winding Trail, Mason, OH 45040. Artisan. Wholesale and retail. Send SASE for product list. Original handmade and handpainted animals. MasterCard and Visa accepted. p. 238

House of Broel Miniatures, 2220 St. Charles Ave., New Orleans, LA 70130. Retail. Price list available. Original etchings. p. 272

Houseworks Ltd., 2388 Pleasantdale Rd., Atlanta, GA 30340. Manufacturer. Catalog, $3. Price list available to dealers. We provide the highest quality miniature dollhouse components. We specialize in windows, doors, hardware, bricks, fireplaces, siding, shingles, electrical items, lighting, Laseretch® plexiglass inserts for windows and doors, and many other accessories. We also provide high-end dollhouse shell kits and component sets. pp. 23, 25, 46, 60, 76, 78-80, 85, 88-90, 93, 94, 99, 100, 104, 107, 108, 110-112, 115-118, 121-123, 129, 142, 143, 157, 162, 163, 166, 173, 240, 243, 277, 297-300, 304, 314, 315

I

Inch/Foot—Jean L. Mattox, 2991 Woodcrest Dr., Napa, CA 94558. Retailer. LSASE for price list with photos and descriptions. Wooden kits for country scenes; settles, rockers, picnic tables, children's chairs, rocking horses and whatever else catches my fancy! pp. 198, 301

Innovative Photography, 1724 N.W. 36th, Lincoln City, OR 97367. Retail and wholesale. Catalog $2.50. Specialize in handmade miniature photographs artistically framed, in folder or sheets. Victorians, old masters, babies and children, animals, wedding and birth certificates, photo albums. Postcards, postcard racks and hanging display racks. pp. 273, 276, 289

Itsy-Bitsy Realty, 10591 Kyte Rd., Rt. 4, Rochelle, IL 61098. Manufacturer, artisan. LSASE for details and information. Custom-made dollhouses of your home or building to your specifications. Custom-made roomboxes of your favorite room or design of your choice. p. 26

Itty Bitty Builder, 405 Kirby Ct., Suite C, Walnut Creek, CA 94598. Wholesale, retail and manufacturer. Brochure, SASE; two stamps for shops brochure, one stamp for hang up room boxes brochure. Hang up room boxes that look like a house in 1" and 1/2". Wild West Saloon and Classic shops available in one-story and two-story models. Custom work also available. pp. 43, 44, 72, 303

J

"J" Designs—Phyllis "Joy" Gray, 8636 Colbath Ave., Panorama City, CA 91402. Artisan. Price sheet available; send SASE. Original paintings, drawings, scratchboard etchings, furniture, door decorations, personalized welcome mats, hand-painted ceramic dogs and cats. Wardrobe trunks and carved boxes, sculptures. p. 272

JAF Miniatures, R.R. 3, Osceola, MO 64776. Retail and wholesale. Catalog, $5. Over 1600 brass jewelry findings, Swarovski Austrian full lead crystal beads, glassware for chandeliers and accessories "Selected Especially for the Miniaturist". Instruction book - New Volume 4: "Miniatures from Baubles, Bangles and Beads." Kadeli Kits and Kadeli Miniature Workshop Kits for chandeliers. Accessories. pp. 129, 263, 316

Jack and June's Mini-Many Things, P.O. Box 865, Lincoln City, OR 97367. Retail, wholesale, manufacturer and artisan. SASE for price list. Special handcrafted crates and baskets with or without fresh produce for your general store or kitchen, miscellaneous country items and linens. Products made to order. pp. 240, 242, 252, 260, 267, 290

Jacqueline's Wholesale, P.O. Box 23464, Oakland, CA 94623. Retail and wholesale. Dealers write for color and prices on your letterhead, include LSASE. pp. 240, 243, 266, 267, 275

Jan's Small World, 3146 Myrtle, Billings, MT 59102. Retail, wholesale, manufacturer. Retail catalog $5, refundable. Wholesale catalog $3. I carry a cabin, carriage house, school, church, and new this year a barn house. These are all made in Montana. I also have over 300 handcrafted items, furniture and accessories to enhance your settings. Retail catalog also has dozens of other manufacturer's merchandise. pp. 29, 38, 39, 107, 199, 262

Janna's and Karen's Molds, P.O. Box 3013, Walnut Creek, CA 94598. Artisan, wholesale, retail and manufacturer. Catalog, $3; price list free of charge. 1" and 1/2" miniature doll molds and "how-to" publications for making and dressing miniature dolls. p. 236

Jean's Wee Things, 157 Glen St., Rowley, MA 01969. Artisan. Brochure, $1 plus SASE. Personal miniature photographs from your personal photos!!! Albums and frames. Kits 'n Caboodle, unusual kits available including 1-1/2" dressed Raggedy Ann & Andy. pp. 267, 276

Joshua's Wholesale, 2020 Ave. G, Suite 1002, Plano, TX 75074. $5 for color catalog refundable with first order. Order toll-free 1-800-527-5943. Large inventory of original printer's type and reproduction cases. 2000 miniature collectibles. Fax # (214) 422-2358. p. 272

K

K&S Engineering, 6917 W. 59th St., Chicago, IL 60638. Wholesale only. Catalog and information sheets free. Brass tubing, squares, rods, angles, channels, strips, sheets, rectangles and hexagons. Aluminum tubing and sheets. Music wire. pp. 85, 328

Kalmbach Publishing Co., 21027 Crossroads Circle, P.O. Box 1612, Waukesha, WI 53187. Publisher of Miniatures Showcase, Nutshell News, Miniatures Dealer, The Miniatures Catalog and other quality hobby books and calendars. Free catalog. pp. 311, 312, 317, 318, 319, 320

Kate's Cats, Rt. 1, Box 51A, Eddy, TX 76524. Artisan, retail, wholesale and manufacturer. Catalog $2. Sculpey cats, hand sculpted with whiskers and life like eyes. Porcelain cat dolls - dressed; also cat doll kits (four paws and head) - dolls and kits available in three sizes. p. 238

The Keshishian Collection, P.O. Box 3002, San Clemente, CA 92672. Brochure $3. Oriental rugs and classic tapestries replicated in detail in miniature. Custom modifications. p. 170

Kay's Kollectables, 2557 N. 41st St., Milwaukee, WI 53210. Artisan, wholesale only. Catalog $2. Over 60 handcrafted floral arrangements, bridal bouquets, Christmas flowers and 12-volt electrified candle arrangements. Dealer inquiries welcome. pp. 277

Kimberly House Miniatures, 3867 S. Valley View #12, Las Vegas, NV 89103. Retail, wholesale and manufacturer. Catalog $4, refundable with first order. Kimberly masonry, slate, Italian tile, and kitchen/patio tile; Kimberly tree and shrubbery kits; complete landscaping supplies; premixed stucco; staircase kits and store fixture kits. Full line of miniature houses, furniture and accessories. "Dollhouses to Dream Houses" informative Book 1 and Book 2, "Dream On with Kimberly House, Book 1" and the popular "Kimberly Corner" publication. pp. 80, 81, 113, 167, 172, 215-217, 219, 220, 257, 312, 318, 329

The Kitchen Captive, 414 E. Chapel Ave., Cherry Hill, NJ 08034. American handcrafted foods and beverages in 1" and 1/2" scale. Some Williamsburg accessories and holiday foods and decorations. Basic to fancy foods and trays. Send LSASE for price sheet. p. 250

Kitty's Kreations, P.O. Box 4069, Elmira, NY 14904. Artisan, retail and wholesale. Catalog $1. Kitty's Kreations is your premier place to purchase quality handcrafted, 1" scale, hydrostone animals, children and baby dolls. We supply over 50 detailed products, including cats, kittens, dogs, farm animals, children with pets, baby dolls and teddy bears. All items are originally designed by artisan Catherine Jacobs. pp. 239, 246, 248, 268, 291

KL Miniatures, 25670 Lehmann Blvd., Lake Villa, IL 60046. Artisan, retail. Send LSASE and $1 for price list and brochure. I make wicker furniture and petit point pillows, rugs and more. I carry dogs, ceramic bathsets, tiles, postcard cottages (IGMA artisan for wicker and needlepoint). Beatrix Potter figures. p. 228

"Krafts" by Betty Jean, 215 West 11th St., Cherokee, OK 73728. Manufacturer, retail. Send LSASE and $2 for catalog. Ceramic crockery, vases, flower pots, holiday items (lighted), needlework by Angie and other accessories. Doctor's table by special order. pp. 245, 247, 260

KriStan Prepasted Wallpaper & Floor Covering, 27575 Flamingo, Spring Grove, IL 60081. Wholesale only. 230 prepasted wallpapers with some matching fabrics and borders. Also, 35 selections of KriStan floor covering. Sample package available for $5, refundable with first $50 order. pp. 161, 169, 172

L

L J Originals, Inc., 516 Sumac Place, DeSoto, TX 75115. Brochure, $1 (refundable with purchase). Manufacturer of Transgraph-X Design-Your-Own Needleart kits. Great for reproducing art into needleart miniatures. Retail, wholesale and distributor pricing. Dealer inquiries are welcomed. p. 270

La Casa Photos, P.O. Box 36035, San Jose, CA 95158. Retail, wholesale and manufacturer. Catalog and price list, $3; see your local miniatures dealer. Vintage and contemporary photographs, books, postcards, stereos, etc. pp. 243, 276

Alice Lacy Ltd., 411 Front St., Bath, ME 04530. Wholesale and designer. Brochure, SASE; price list available to dealers. Handcrafted iron wire wicker furniture with a graceful, delicate appearance. Each piece is festooned with loops, braids and decorative scrolls. Fine needlework cushions and handpieced quilts complement the wicker. Original designs by Alice Lacy. pp. 221, 228

Laser Tech, 6669-G Peachtree Industrial Blvd., Norcross, GA 30092. Manufacturer. Catalog price; $1.75. Manufacturer of laser dollhouse components ranging from trims and grilles to Victorian screen doors and engraved door inserts with the finest laser detail that is available. Send for our catalog showing our complete line of components. pp. 76, 86, 90, 105, 174, 274, 300, 301

The Lawbre Company, 888 Tower Rd., Unit J, Mundelein, IL 60060. Mail-order and wholesale. Catalog, $4, refundable. Period designed miniature houses, custom designs or reproductions of existing homes, staircases, fireplaces and architectural castings. Also, trophy items, garden statues, fountains, and decorative pieces. pp. 32, 35, 38, 43, 45-48, 59-61, 72, 75, 82, 113, 148, 163, 167, 252-254, 268, 286-288 See our display on page 7.

Le' Petite Architect, P.O. Box 55815, Sherman Oaks, CA 91413. Manufacturer, retail and wholesale. Catalog price; $2, includes color chart. LSASE for price list. Manufacturer of specialized contemporary dollhouse accessories. Easy to assemble, marble finish bathroom kits, flooring tiles, lighting units and furniture. pp. 129, 157, 167, 223

Lenham Pottery, 215 Wroxham Rd., Norwich, NR7 8AQ Norfolk, England. Retail and wholesale. Specialists in own design 1" scale slip-cast ceramic porcelain bathroom fittings and taps, kitchen sinks and utensils, with colored decals. Horses at 1/8", 1/10", 1/12", 1/16" scales. Brochures: model horse and harness $3; dollhouse china $3. Information sheets: fashions and patterns $4; horse harnessing, to scale $4. Checks accepted. pp. 240, 245

The Lighting Bug, Ltd., P.O. Box 39, Clarendon Hills, IL 60514-0039. Completely assembled line of electrified floor, table, ceiling, hanging and chandelier lites for your entire dollhouse. Heirloom quality reproductions of full size lighting fixtures assure authenticity. Available in 1" and 1/2" scale. Some available with replaceable bulbs. handcrafted in the USA. 15 years of exacting workmanship. Wholesale and retail. Send LSASE and $5 for brochure #8 with supplements A & B, 1/2" scale picture sheet and pricelist. pp. 135, 150, 151, 303

Ligia's Miniatures, 2315 Caracas St., La Creseenta, CA 91214. Artisan, retail, wholesale and manufacturer. Send $1 and SASE for price list. Fine quality accessories on silver or copper enameled (glass on metal) with emphasis on the Faberge style enamels on silver. Also Oriental cloisonne on copper for some furniture pieces. pp. 264, 267

Lil-Crafts, P.O. Box 275, North Reading, MA 01864. Retail and wholesale. Catalog free. Information sheets LSASE. pp. 81, 82, 108, 163, 164

Linden Swiss Miniatures, P.O. Box 571, 41400 Terwilliger Road, Anza, CA 92306. Retail, wholesale and manufacturer. Brochure, LSASE; price list available. See your local miniatures dealer. Glasslike items: glasses, bottles and jars. Wine bottles with labels. Metal cans with labels. Our product comes in kit-form. We do have a few finished items. All items are made in America. pp. 247, 257, 260, 274, 295

Little Discoveries, P.O. Box 404, W. Somerville, MA 02144. Retailer, manufacturer and artisan. 36-page price list, $1. We create "farm fresh" produce in 1" scale—sold loose, singly, gathered in our own manufactured containers or mixed in stylized arrangements. We offer a variety of bakery goods, including customized wedding, anniversary and birthday cakes. And you can satisfy your mini sweet tooth with any of our forty types of handcrafted candies. pp. 246, 247, 250, 289

Little Linens, 130 Annadale Rd., Staten Island, NY 10312. Manufacturer, wholesaler. See your local miniatures dealer. Custom look bedding available in a variety of colors and patterns—mix and match-designed to fit any standard size double or twin size bed. No glue necessary with our new peel-and-stick process. Ready to hang custom look drapes-available in a variety of colors and styles. Handcrafted bedroom furniture in Classic and Contemporary styles consists of custom look dressed bed, chaise lounge, chair, hassock and skirted table. Various colors and fabrics available. All items proudly made in the USA. pp. 174, 210, 242

Little Things by Jody, P.O. Box 639,Midvale, UT 84047. Retail and wholesale. Handmade braided rugs. Assorted colors and sizes. Custom rugs made to match unique decor or special room size. Sample rug $4 plus LSASE. Price list available at no charge. p. 169

M

Maison des Maisons, 23 Sedgwick Dr., Englewood, CO 80110. Retail only; price list available, SASE. $4 for pictures. By appointment only. Native American artifacts including room boxes, furniture, pottery, baskets, paintings, kachinas, dolls, kivas, plaza scenes and related items. Also fine art in miniature including silver by Acquisto, Quintenar Fisher and Keuker. pp. 66, 67, 69, 171, 209, 227, 247, 262, 264, 285-287

Marilyn's Mini Studio, P.O. Box 34717, Los Angeles, CA 90034. Retail, wholesale and artisan. Price list available, send SASE. Quality liquor bottles, elegant cocktails, punches, tray sets and beverages for all holiday occasions; bar accessories. pp. 251, 295

Martha's Miniatures, 6440 McCullom Lake Rd., Wonder Lake, IL 60097. Retail, wholesale and manufacturer. Catalog, SASE with two stamps. Manufacturer of superior quality, unpainted cast pewter items: baby carriage frame, thread spools, thimbles, garden items, lanterns, television, stereo items, fishing and hobby tools, kitchen faucets, shower faucet set, books, toys, animals, frames, wheels, etc. New items! Free frame chart and wheel chart, SASE. Visa accepted. pp. 211, 229

Mary's Miniature Mansions, 6111 Harmon Pl., Springfield, VA 22152. Artisan. Color photos, $10. ($9 refundable when photos are returned). Beautifully carved Victorian furniture in 1" and 1/2" scale. Custom work welcomed. pp. 204, 251

McCloud's, 1555 Overbrook Rd., Williamsport, PA 17701. Mini trees, wreaths and door decorations. Send $2 for price list. CIMTA and MIAA member. p. 258

Sonia Messer Imports Inc., 4811 Glencairn Rd., Los Angeles, CA 90027. Very fine period furniture exquisitely carved. Some kitchen, bathroom items. Importer. Price list available. p. 194

Index of Manufacturers, Artisans & Suppliers

THE MINIATURES CATALOG, *Fourteenth Edition* 375

Midwest Carriage, 7472 Goldenrod Dr., Mentor-Lake, OH 44060. Artisan, retail and wholesale. Price list and brochure available, send $2. Specializing in authentic horse-drawn vehicles and accessories. 1/12", 1/24" and 1/16" scale kits. Chuck wagon, connestoga wagon, stagecoach, circus wagon, milkwagon and publications. 15 different kits in all. p. 261

John Anthony Miller, 461 E. Main St., Suite C, El Jardin Building, Ventura, CA 93001. Artisan. Detailed original limited edition copperplate etchings and engravings. All hand-printing and hand-signed by John Anthony Miller. p. 272

Mini-Graphics Inc, 2975 Exon Ave., Cincinnati, OH 45241. Retail and wholesale. Catalog, $5. Interior decorating for miniatures including wallpaper, matching and coordinated fabric, wall-to-wall carpeting, area rugs, wallpaper paste, pillows, video workshops on two-hour tapes, kits to accompany tapes. p. 211

Mini Mansions, 10, The Hawthorns, Great Ayton, Middlesbrough, Cleveland, England TS9 6BA. Manufacturer, retail and wholesale. Brochure $2. Electronic flickering fire unit suitable to integrate into 12 volt system. For fire grates or kitchen range. Suitable all scales. p. 143

Mini-Minerals, 2932 Avalee St., Walkertown, NC 27051. Retail, wholesale, manufacturer and artisan. Price list available. The Sakura line of Mini-Minerals. Japanese room and furnishings - 1" scale. p. 40

The Mini-Money-Mint, 89 E. Benson Way, Sandy, UT 84070-2662. Wholesale and retail. Send letter of request for wholesale terms. Manufacturer of miniature money for dollhouse dwellers. A division of Henry's House of Trains & Miniatures. p. 268

Mini Treasure House, Jack Heier, 3210A Wadsworth Blvd., Wheat Ridge, CO 80033. Retail and dealer consideration. Handcrafted pool tables and genuine slate shingles. pp. 109, 293

Mini-Vac, 217 S. Orange St., Suite #4, Glendale, CA 91204. Manufacturer, wholesale and retail. Brochure 10¢. Mini-Vac holds the patent for the original miniature hand-held vacuum. We also market 9 volt alkaline batteries and A/C adapters. The Mini-Vac/Blower is a tool with 100 uses from models and miniatures to computers and cameras. The Mini-Vac/Blower gets the job done. One year limited warranty. p. 331

Miniature Corner, 303 Clay Ave., Jeannette, PA 15644. Barbara Elster. Wholesale only. Catalog, $5. Importers of unusual, high-quality dollhouse related products from Germany. Furniture, accessories, dollhouse dolls, carpets, landscape supplies and children's dollhouses. Many are handmade by skilled artisans in the Bavarian Cottage Industry. pp. 171, 201, 204, 205, 207, 223, 233, 234, 244, 253, 328

Miniatures Dealer, 21027 Crossroads Circle, P.O. Box 1612, Waukesha, WI 53187. The only trade magazine for the miniatures industry. Subscription price: $24 per year. Subsidiary of Kalmbach Publishing Co. pp. 193

Miniature House, c/o Handley House, P.O. Box 8658, Ft. Worth, TX 76124. Manufacturer/importer of dollhouse lighting, components, building supplies, brick, shingles, siding, doll families and furniture/accessories. Over 300 items. pp. 77, 82, 83, 90-92, 94-96, 100, 101, 105, 108-113, 117-120, 122-125, 129-133, 143-145, 147-149, 151-154, 156, 158, 163, 166, 167, 197, 211, 212, 217, 221-223, 226, 231, 232, 245, 249, 250, 261, 263, 290, 291, 325

Miniature Lumber Shoppe, 812 Main St., Grandview, MO 64030. Manufacturer, wholesale and retail. Catalog prices: $2 - 1" scale wood products; $2.50 1/4" small scale. Retail store and manufacturer of wood moldings, stripwood and sheetwood in basswood and many hardwoods. Our 1" scale product line includes unique doors, windows, building components and dollhouses. Nationally known for a complete line of 1/4" scale building components, furniture, house kits and accessories. pp. 101, 104

Miniature Manors, 1673 Litchfield Turnpike, Woodbridge, CT 06525. Manufacturer. Information sheets, $1. Assembled and finished mini-homes. Also kits, house plans, shingles and components in 1" and 1/2" scales. Manufacturers of a complete line of split cedar shingles and basswood dollhouse trims. pp. 78, 106, 109, 168
See our display ad on the inside back cover.

Miniature Towne, USA, 17624 Sherman Way, Van Nuys, CA 91406. Quality dollhouses, kits, and a wide variety of furniture, accessories, building material finishing, and electrical supplies. Classes year round. Many collectors' items. p. 200

Miniature Rugs by Joan Adams, 2706 Sheridan Dr., Sarasota, FL 34239. Catalog $2.75. 1/12th sheared punchneedle rug catalog of over 40 designs. Graphs, transparency graphs, completed rugs, canvas, punchneedles and embroidery scissors available. p. 171

Miniatures by Carol, 870 Thacker St., Des Plaines, IL 60016. Artisan, retail. Contemporary furniture for living room, den, bedroom, dining room, kitchen, stove, refrigerator, keyboard instruments, organs, pianos and harpsichords. Price list available free with LSASE. pp. 212, 226, 269

Miniatures by Marian, 749 Sommerdale Ct., Rural Hall, NC 27045. Artisan, retail and mail order. Colorful Fimo miniatures of clowns, bunnies, bears, Santas, nativities and more. Also Moravian-type trays featuring Bible, candlestick, star, bun and coffee. Price list available free with LSASE. p. 239

Miniatures Showcase, 21027 Crossroads Circle, P.O. Box 1612, Waukesha, WI 53187. A colorful, full-size reference magazine for miniature hobbyists. Subscription price: $14.95 per year. Subsidiary of Kalmbach Publishing Co. pp. 311

Miniatures Unlimited, 1275 E. 85th St., Brooklyn, NY 11236. Wholesale only. Manufacturer and artisan. Catalog, $3.25. A unique line of handcrafted treasures. Furniture, accessories, patio furniture, lawn gliders, cellar doors, bunk beds, trundle beds, book shelves, toy chests, office furniture, bath shelves, hampers, wooden folding clothes dryers and much, much more! pp. 212, 219

Miniaturelite, P.O. Box 164, Hinsdale, IL 60522-0164. Completely assembled, affordable, attractive line of electrified lites in 1" scale for dollhouses and miniature rooms. Handcrafted in the USA. Packaged on peg boards with see-through blishters. Wholesale and retail. For literature, send LSASE and $4. Discover Miniaturelite.

Model Builders Supply, 40 Engelhard Drive, Unit #11, Aurora, Ontario, Canada L4G 3V2. Wholesale and manufacturer. 108-page catalog, $6 with prices, in Canada, for U.S., see Plastruct. MBS manufactures 112 patterns of textured plastic sheet for brick, stone, block sidings, roofs, glass blocks, etc. in all scales. Also trusses, skylights, mirror plastic, rippled water, plastic sheets, trees, shrubs, grass mats, foliage, modern appliances and bathroom items. Adhesives, tools and lots more. pp. 76, 83, 103, 108, 111, 167, 215, 224-226, 265, 301, 309

Monkey Business, 7745 Evergreen Terrace, Burlington, WI 53105. Retail, wholesale and manufacturer. Retail catalog, $3; wholesale catalog, free. Entire product line featured in full-color brochure. We manufacture high-quality, hand-painted metal miniatures. We offer a variety of accessories, figurines, toys, trophies, shoes, office items, portraits, tools, colonial items, kitchen items, animals, etc. Quality guaranteed. pp. 240, 247, 248, 261, 276, 293

Moreno Valley Miniatures, P.O. Drawer 977, Angel Fire, NM 87710. Retail only, shows or by appointment. Over 50 artists represented. Early American, Shaker and

Southwest. Only antiques and collectables are cataloged: Antiquities VII catalog - $3. pp. 287, 321

Morey's Miniatures, Rd. 2, 38-C, Unadilla, NY 13849. Retail only. Information sheets, $1. Handsculpted pedigree dogs in 1" and 1/2" scale—many in a playful mischievous way. Sixty different breeds in stock. p. 239

Mother Muck's Minis, 755 Lacey Way, North Salt Lake, UT 84054. Retail, wholesale and artisan. Brochure, $3. Quality handcrafted miniatures in 1" and 1/2" scales. Expanding line of plants, flowers, foods, decorative accessories, holiday and southwestern items. p. 296

Mary Agnes Murphy, 527 Cherry St., Fall River, MA 02720. Artisan. Price list, SASE. Limited editions of American and Irish country furniture in 1" and 1/2" scale. Handcrafted toys and accessories, oil paintings, and Christmas items. Hand-knit Irish sweaters, baby sets, mittens and caps. Miniature clothing items including red longjohns and bridal gowns. pp. 232, 293

N

Nanco Distributors Corp., 776 Bloomfield Ave., Verona, NJ 07044. Wholesale only. Complete line of miniatures–quality dollhouses, furniture, kits, accessories, full line of building supplies, flooring, lighting, paints and glues. pp. 171, 242, 289

National Association of Miniature Enthusiasts—NAME, 130 N. Rangeline Rd., Carmel, IN 46032. National group of hobbyists who hold regional houseparties for members. Publisher of the *Miniature Gazette*. p. 311

Nellie Originals, 6001 Edgewater Dr., Corpus Christi, TX 78412. Retail, wholesale, and artisan. Brochure free with LSASE. Fine 1" scale, hand-crafted furniture modeled from historical sites and other originals by Nelson Lewis. Beds dressed, pillows, towels by Louise. Custom orders welcome. p.197

New England Hobby Supply, 71 Hilliard St., Manchester, CT 06040. Wholesale, manufacturer. See your local miniatures dealer. Complete miniature distributor also manufactures The Builder's Choice paints, Builder's Choice landscaping and Bell Helpers, tools and accessories for miniatures. pp. 168, 173, 217, 329
See our insert between pages 288-289.

Ni-Glo® Lamps by Nicole, 5684 Sterling Rd., Hamburg, NY 14075. Retail, wholesale and manufacturer. Color photo $5. Free brochure. Original intricately handcrafted lamps. Meticulously free-hand china painted designs. Fired in electric kiln several times to insure permanent color. Decals are not used on our fine line of porcelain pieces. All lamps have replaceable 12 volt lights. Tiffany-style lamp is casted in solid bronze with antique finish. Porcelain lamps have brass component parts. State when ordering choice of floral or bird design you would like on your Contemporary, Victorian or Colonial lamp. Bone china dinnersets with matching floral arrangements, vases and umbrella stands also available. p. 155

Noonmark, 1150 N.E. 130th St., P.O. Box 75585, Dept. MC14, Seattle, WA 98125. Manufacturer and artisan. Retail and wholesale. Brochure, $1 (refundable) and LSASE. Fine quality etched glass and related products. pp. 77, 86, 93, 125

Norm's Originals, 16520 Densmore Ave. North, Seattle, WA 98133. Artisan, retail, wholesale and manufacturer. Send LSASE for price list. I make a limited line of hardwood furniture kits which have been proven in weekend workshops in my home. Most kits are replicas of full size furniture taken from catalogs, resource books and antique stores. Upon request, I also do finished furniture and custom work. p. 207

Northeastern Scale Models, 99 Cross St., P.O. Box 727, Methuen, MA 01844. Manufacturer. Catalog, $1; price list available. See your local miniatures dealer. Fine quality wood moldings, siding, strips, sheets, laser cut trims. Also custom laser cutting services. pp. 40, 96-98, 102, 111
See our insert between pages 80-81.

Northwest Short Line, P.O. Box 423, Seattle, WA 98111. Manufacturer and wholesale. Information sheets, $1. Model building tools, gears and motors. p. 328

Nostalgia, 147A Nottingham Rd. Eastwood, Nottingham, England NG16-3GJ. Manufacturer, artisan and retailer. Catalog, $2. Millie Aware winning dressed and undressed dolls. p. 234

Nutshell News, 21027 Crossroads Circle, P.O. Box 1612, Waukesha, WI 53187. A colorful monthly magazine for the miniatures hobby. Subscription price: $29 per year. Subsidiary of Kalmbach Publishing Co. pp. 312

O

The Oakridge Corporation, P.O. Box 247, Dept. 14MC, Lemont, IL 60439. Distributor, wholesale, retail and manufacturer. 180-page 1/4" and 1/2" scale catalog, $4; 180-page 1" scale "121" catalog, $4. We offer the largest selection of quality 1/4", 1/2" and 1" scale dollhouse kits, building shell kits, building components, building supplies, paints, finishes, adhesives, painting equipment, electrical, lighting, scale furniture, trees, landscaping, foundation materials, detail accessories, figures, animals, military vehicles, military and era fighting and marching figures, scale model vehicle kits, scratchbuilding and modeling tools, how-to books and unusual and hard-to-find items by many fine manufacturers. Recognized as the industry leader in 1/4" and 1/2" scale dollhouse miniatures. pp. 300, 301, 304, 305, 307, 308

Objects d' Art, C. P. 324, Quebec, QC G1R 4P8. Artisan, wholesale and retail. Price list and catalog available. Oil paintings, crewel embroidery pictures and embroidery kits. All items are 1" scale. p. 270

Olde Mountain Miniatures, RD 3, Box 163-A, Fort Plain, NY 13339. Retail, wholesale, manufacturer and artisan. Catalog, $2. Our line is completely handcrafted by us, collector quality. We have leaded, stained windows, Southwestern, Oriental and Colonial room boxes, pre-Revolutionary furniture, post and beam structures, needlepoint rugs, Harmony Forge pewter hardware and fireplace accessories. Most items in both kits and finished form. Member CIMTA, IGMA and MIAA. pp. 73, 96, 125, 195, 286

Omniarts of Colorado, 498 S. High St., Denver, CO 80209. Artisan, manufacturer,, wholesale and retail. Catalog $3.50. Specializing in items for castles, palaces and museums. Complete line of original wicker furniture kits in 1" and 1/2" scales. Fantasy items. American Indian arts. Fine jewelry. English artisans. Member CIMTA, CASTLE, IGMA, NAME and SAM. pp. 176, 220, 229, 259, 275, 286, 296, 301

Our Designs Furniture Company, a division of Henry's House of Trains & Miniatures, 89 E. Benson Way, Sandy, UT 84070. Retail, wholesale, manufacturer and artisan. Catalog, free; price list available. Custom make furniture on request. Carried by Dee's Delights. p. 247

Our House II—Gramarye Keep, 2132 Baxter St., Los Angeles, CA 90039. Retail, wholesale, manufacturer and artisan. Two types of catalogs, $5 each. I make scale foods; a stock selection in the catalogs and certain items on request. 1", 1/2" and some fashion doll items are stock—other scales are custom. I work in periods from Roman to modern, including a lot of medieval. I also carry accessories (a few made by me) for the kitchen and dining room by Reynolds, Royal, Farrow, Hermes and some Getzan items. p. 251

P

Ken Palmer, Artist Craftsman in Silver, 124 Willmott Rd., Sutton Coldfield, West Mids., England B75 5NW. Artisan. Send LSASE for information, $5 for brochure. A range of hallmarked English sterling silver artifacts, silver mounted porcelain, working bracket clock and more. 1" scale. p. 264

"Pannikins" by M.E. (Mary Eccher), Harbor Pl., South Salem, NY 10590. Retailer and artisan. Catalog/project booklet, $4.50. Handcrafted foods and beverages including international, regional and period food dishes; also, supplies and "empties" for the do-it-yourselfer. pp. 103, 251

J. Parker, Box 34, Midland, Ontario, Canada L4R 4K6. Retailer and artisan. Catalog, $3. Porcelain doll kits in 1/12 and 1/24 scale. Original patterns, English mohair. pp. 234, 236

Parker House Miniatures, 5448 Briggs Ave., La Crescenta, CA 91214. Jane and Norm Parker, Artisans. Catalog $2.50. Quarter-inch scale, handcrafted, signed, dated Victorian houses and furniture. Houses are available electrified, decorated, and furnished, or electrified shell only. p. 307

Paul's Specialties, 3880 Grape Vine Rd., Huntington, WV 25701. Manufacturer of electric and non-electric collector's turntables and glass domes. pp. 66, 67

Mary Payne, P.O. Box 52173, Atlanta, GA 30355. Photo brochure available. Complete line of plant and flower kits in 1", 1/2" and 1/4" scale for house and garden. Rubber trees, hanging baskets, caladiums, iris, orchids, roses, bonsai trees, topiary trees, geraniums, Christmas cactus, wreaths, swags, holly and pointsettias. Over 80 kits. Easy to follow instructions, color photo, and the finest materials available insure satisfaction. For complete list send LSASE. Dealer inquiries invited. p. 309

Rhonda Peden, P.O. Box 1546, Myrtle Creek, OR 97457. Artisan, wholesaler. Price list available from your local dealer. Baby clothes and linens in 1" scale. Made in traditional fabrics and four baby colors. For dressing dolls and nursery display. pp. 232, 272

Derek Perkins, 14811-D Clark Ave., Hacienda Heights, CA 91745. Retail and small dealer consideration. Catalog $2, refundable. Finely detailed architectural components, fireplaces and complete walls. Easily used by kitchen table miniaturists or professionals. The details are worth looking at. pp. 78, 92, 164

Don Perkins Miniatures, 1708 - 59th St., Des Moines, IA 50322. Artisan selling retail by mail and at miniature shows. No wholesale. Price list and brochure available for $1. Furniture, accessories and needlepoint replicate early period American pieces. A variety of adult and child chairs, rockers and stools with rush seats are offered as kits. All materials are included. pp. 120, 197, 212

Perrault Miniatures, 27609 Loyola Ave., Hayward, CA 94545. Manufacturer, wholesale and retail. Price list available free of charge. Send for descriptive price list. Retail at shows. 23 sizes or styles to choose from. Mail order. Dealer inquiries welcome. p. 273

Petite People Plus, 16 Teed St., Huntington Station, NY 11746. Artisan, retail and wholesale. Catalog and photo $1.50. Price list available. Fine porcelain handpainted dollhouse dolls in 1" and 1/2" scale. We handcraft black and white porcelain dolls dressed or in kit form that look like real people. Other handcrafted items by us are landscaping, ceramics, sterling silver, clothes and foods. Look for us at shows. p. 234

Pieper Gallery, 533 Main St., Box 582, Dennis, MA 02638. IGMA Artisan, wholesale and retail. Doll brochure; $1, book and wreath/hat information; SASE. Handcrafted cloth dolls; country critters, stuffed animals, rag dolls, seasonal characters and fantasy. Also dried flower wreaths and hats, as well as instruction and pattern booklet on "How To Sew Your Own Miniature Curtains". pp. 235, 316

Royce Piro Miniatures, 2871 Dusty Stone Ct., Santa Rosa, CA 95405. Artisan, retailer. Brochure free with SASE. Fully dressed porcelain dolls - men, women, children and doll kits. p. 235

Pitty Pat Miniatures Inc., 1500 Old Deerfield Rd., Highland Park, IL 60035. Manufacturer. See your local miniatures dealer. We are manufacturers of fully coordinated furniture, accessories, ceramic bathroom sets, complete modern kitchen sets, wallpaper, electrified lamps, carpeting, and cornices with drapes for every room in your dollhouse. Complete licensed Disney, Raggedy Ann & Andy and Beatrix Potter lines plus our new, exclusive Binkee division. pp. 212, 222, 226
See our display ad on page 2.

Plastruct, 1020 S. Wallace Pl., City of Industry, CA 91748. Manufacturer, wholesaler and mail order. Catalog, $7. Plastruct manufactures and distributes nearly 2500 different model parts in all scales. Included are plastic strips, shapes, sheet and tubing; wood strips and sheet; over 200 landscaping products; over 100 different plastic patterned sheets of roofing, flooring, siding, etc.; plastic figures and vehicles. Product categories are building foundation, construction, finishing, landscaping, scale representation, interiors, accents, 1:12 dollhouse, 1:24 dollhouse, 1:48 dollhouse, engineering, crafts/miscellaneous, tools and accessories, kits, plans and books. In Canada, contact MBS, 40 Englehard Drive #11, Aurora, Ontario L4G 3V2. pp. 78, 82, 111, 120, 168, 218, 241, 261, 302, 308
See our display ad on page 241.

Precious Little Things, P.O. Box 6, Dept. BC, Chester, VT 05143. Retail and wholesale. Mail order and shows only. Catalog, $3.50 (1st class); information sheets SASE (on kits, handblown glass, medicines, and medical items, piano and harp only. All other items in catalog only). We specialize in handcrafted furniture and accessories. Our Mason jars, produce, roadside stands, baskets, medical, holiday items and "Confidence Creator" kits (both in 1" and 1/2" scale) being particularly popular. pp. 40, 247, 251

Q

Quad Company, 12 Grove St., Ballston Spa, NY 12020. Wholesale, retail and manufacturer. Send LSASE for brochure and order form. We manufacture "tiny turnings" line of finely detailed, easy-to-assemble wooden furniture kits and spindles. pp. 36, 101, 206

R

Barbara J. Raheb, 30132 Elizabeth Court, Agoura Hills, CA 91301. Retail, wholesale and artisan. Catalog, $5, catalog of miniature books (retail and wholesale). How-to instruction book: Jewelry Making in Miniature, $12.90 ppd. pp. 244, 316

Rankin's Tiny Treasures, Route 6, Dogwood Hills #9, Harrison, AR 72601. Retail, wholesale and artisan. Brochure, SASE plus $1, refundable with order. Handcrafted wicker furniture and accessories, redwood and adirondack outdoor furniture and custom upholstered Victorian and country furniture. 400 fabric samples available for upholstery pieces. Items available in 1" and 1/2" scale. p. 229

Real Good Toys Inc., 10 Quarry Hill, Barre, VT 05641. Manufacturer. Catalog, $4. See your local miniatures dealer. Wholesale only. We produce the broadest range of dollhouse kit designs available anywhere in the world. Only the finest quality materials are used and every kit is handcrafted with care by Vermont craftspeople. pp. 20, 24, 29, 32-34, 36, 38, 44, 46, 61, 62, 304

Robin's Roost–Miniatures for Collectors, P.O. Box 186, Grayslake, IL 60030. Manufacturer. Dealers, please request color catalog and price list on your letterhead. Fine hand-crafted plants, flower arrangements, bridal bouquets, holiday and seasonal accessories, wrapped packages, boudoir accessories, seasonal tins (filled and empty), Christmas tree kits, miniature accessories plus 1/2" scale plants. pp. 241, 257, 258, 278

Rondel Wood Products, 2679 Washington Rd., N. Waldoboro, ME 04572. Retail, wholesale and manufacturer. Catalog $2. 1/12 scale wagon kits. p. 261

Ross' Treasure House, Ltd., 823 West 1st St., North Vancouver, British Columbia, Canada V7P 1A4. Wholesale and manufacturer. Catalog available. Miniatures, dollhouses, dolls, hobby supplies, gifts, collectables. Importers. pp. 212, 235

Rossco Products Inc., 1195 E. 347th St., Eastlake, OH 44095. Retail and wholesale. Information sheets available. Urethane slate roofs. Brick sheets, elastomeric patio brick sheets, welcome mats. Vinyl printed wood flooring, school, kits. pp. 40, 83, 84, 109

Royal Miniatures, 15025 Califa St., Van Nuys, CA 91411. Wholesale. Catalog $3. Over 1000 quality miniature accessories, including glassware, brassware, baskets, porcelain, spatterware, country, sports, children's accessories and much more. Bulk packaging and terms for manufacturers, distributors, etc. pp. 213, 245, 246, 253, 254, 258, 272, 287, 291, 293, 296

d. Anne Ruff Miniatures, 1100 Vagabond Lane, Plymouth, MN 55447. Retail, wholesale, manufacturer and artisan. Brochure with fabric swatches, $3 refundable; price list available. Upholstered 1" and 1/2" furniture, draperies and curtains, Pretty Pleaters, Pretti Point rug kits, accessory kits and patterns, display boxes. pp. 66, 171, 174

Russell Crafts, 481 Danbury Rd., Rte. 7, New Milford, CT 06776. Manufacturer, retail and wholesale. Manufacturer of solid wood dollhouses, kits, assembled and finished - small cottages, shops, room boxes, colonials, schoolhouses, firehouses, stables, gazebos, barns and custom houses. Send $2 for brochure. pp. 24, 35, 38

Sharon E. Russell-Miniatures by Sharon, P.O. Box 2124, Chino, CA 91708-2124. Retailer, manufacturer, artisan. Brochure and price list $1.50 plus LSASE (52¢). Wicker furniture and kits in 1", 1/2" and 1/4" scales. Easy-to-follow instructions. Finished items are all handmade in 1", 1/2" and 1/4" scales. Cushions included, choice of color or your fabric. Watch *Nutshell News* for new address. p. 229

Pat Russo Miniatures, 314 Commercial St., Weymouth, MA 02188. Wholesaler and artisan. Price list available. See your local miniatures dealer. Handmade Fimo characters, ultra suede baby pram and wicker trunk with doll or bear. Featuring a handmade bedroom set with handpainted scenes on the fronts of the hutch and bureau. All items intricately detailed and personalized by Pat Russo. p. 213

S

Scientific Models Inc., 340 NS Snyder Ave., Berkeley Heights, NJ 07922. Catalog $1. Miniature furniture kits and accessories. pp. 97, 199, 200, 202, 206

Shenandoah Designs Inc., P.O. Box 313, Brookfield, CT 06804. Manufacturer, wholesale only. Send $1 for complete literature. 1" scale furniture kits, assembled furniture, kitchen kits and assembled units. Porch & Patio kits and assembled pieces. Porcelain doll kits. Some 1/2" scale items available. pp. 195, 218, 226

Sir Thomas Thumb, 1398 E. Oregon Rd., Leola, PA 17540. Retail, mail order and wholesale. Catalog, $1 plus LSASE. Exquisitely handcrafted collector-quality reproductions of early American pieces is our speciality. Country kitchen accessories, antique painted country furniture, farm and garden tools, antique and modern woodworker/handyman tools, flintlock and modern rifles, bows and arrows. You will be delighted! pp. 200, 253, 261, 288, 293

Small Time Operators, Wavecrest A-206, Star Route 155, Kaunakakai, HI 96748. Artisan. Handcrafted light fixtures and hand-painted Faberge flower arrangements. Wholesale. No catalog. pp. 136, 159

Smallworks, 10465 NW Lee Ct., Portland, OR 97229. Retail, wholesale and manufacturer. Original wicker designs and original dolls by artisan Melinda Small Paterson. Price list available, send LSASE + $1. pp. 202, 229

Donna Smolik's Designs, P.O. Box 4994, Englewood, CO 80155 Artisan. Brochure, $1, refundable with order. Candy, cookie and food designs, intricately detailed. Slice your own with a single edged razor blade. Can be used to create foods or Christmas decorations, fantasy creations, garnishes, etc. pp. 251, 258, 261, 268, 289, 296, 309

Special Sellers, 5826 Macinness Dr., Memphis, TN 38119. Manufacturer and artisan. Price list free with SASE. Designer gingerbread candy cottages in more than 20 styles including a gingerbread village of five candy houses for fireplace mantle. Collector quality Fimo panorama egg scenes, dime-size mini scenes and storybook characters. Also, assorted Fimo bears, bunnies and mice in loveable poses and scenes. pp. 239, 258

Sturm's Special Effects International, Inc., P.O. Box 691, Lake Geneva, WI 53147. Manufacturer of artificial snow for miniature work. Price list available. p. 329

T

T.K. Designs, 5730 Elder Place, Madison, WI 53705. Artisan, retail and wholesale. LSASE for catalog. Handmade original 1" scale primate figures; chimpanzees, gorillas, orangutans and capuchins. Handsewn jointed Bearenger Bears. Original sculpted one-of-a-kind fantasy troll and Cloverton (Hobbit type) figures. pp. 239, 293

Taos Sun Miniatures, P.O. Box 2907, Taos, NM 87571. Retail, wholesale, manufacturer and artisan. Brochure $2.50, refundable. Our line is completely handcrafted by us. Collector quality in 1" scale. "Pueblo" style room boxes complete or partially-finished kits. pp. 73, 227

Teri's Mini Workshop, Box 387, Goldenrod, FL 32733. Retail, wholesale, manufacturer and artisan. Catalog, $1 and LSASE. Handcrafted sporting goods, medical supplies, nursery items, contemporary dolls, pet supplies, beauty parlor pieces. pp. 219, 222, 232, 234, 236, 247, 288

Three Blind Mice, 6715 Cedar Cove Dr., Centerville, OH 45459. Retail only. For information, send SASE. pp. 219, 288, 291, 302

Timberbrook Wood Products, Hovey Lane, South New Berlin, NY 13843. Retail and wholesale. Catalog $2. Miniature building components including windows, doors and stairs. Specialities: bi-fold doors, disappearing attic stairs, slate, Tudor casement windows, basement windows and hardware. pp. 40, 79, 114, 269

To Be Tiny, P.O. Box 1492, North Kingston, RI 02852. Retail mail order only. Send $3 for complete Farrow Industries and Tobe Tailored colored brochures and price list. p. 291

Tree Trunk Studio—Jenifer K. Johnson, P.O. Box 312, Dayton, OH 45406. Artisan,

Index of Manufacturers, Artisans & Suppliers

THE MINIATURES CATALOG, Fourteenth Edition

wholesale and retail. Catalog, $1 refundable. Handcrafted colonial and shaker reproductions in 1" and 1/2" scales. Constructed of select hardwoods with careful detailing and beautiful finishes. Special orders welcomed. pp. 200, 302

Twin Palms Miniatures, P.O. Box 263295, Escondido, CA 92026. Retail, wholesale, manufacturer and artisan. Rattan furniture in finished (limited production) and kit form in 1" and 1/2" scales. Contemporary needlepoint rug kits. pp. 229, 242

U

Unique Miniatures, Route 1, Box 463A, Cambridge, MN 55008. Retail and wholesale. Catalog $2. Architectural castings of several styles and of many items. pp. 78, 86, 105, 164, 265

V

Vermont Home Quilts, P.O. Box 757C, Lyndonville, VT 05851. Retail, wholesale, artisan and mail-order. Brochure $1 plus LSASE. Quilts are made from cotton, using suitable prints for 1" scale and are fully lined. Accessories are available in coordinating colors. Custom colors available for additional charges. Wholesale inquiries are invited. pp. 243, 271

Vernon Pottery, 441 Bethune Dr., Virginia Beach, VA 23452. Retail, wholesale and artisan. Catalog, $2. Museum-quality reproductions of 19th century North American salt-glazed stoneware. All of our 1" scale pots are handmade on the potters wheel and decorated free hand with cobalt blue clay slip. Choose from over 165 folk art designs. Butterchurns with walnut dashers, crocks, jars with lids, jugs and water coolers with cork stoppers, pitchers and more. I.G.M.A. artisans. pp. 245, 261, 274

Viv's Ribbons & Lace, 212 Virginia Hill Dr., Martinez, CA 94553. Retail and wholesale. Catalog $3.50. Many narrow trims and braids including soutache, tiny picot, six sizes of silk ribbon with bunka dyed to match. Old and new English and French cotton laces, beautiful Swiss embroideries and hat straw, three sizes of tiny pleated laces. many dollhouse doll dressing books and patterns. Also available are glues and special mini glue dispensers, pleaters, dollhair, books and patterns for doll house patchwork quilts. pp. 161, 232

W

Wagonmaster Plans, P.O. Box 1757, Mammoth Lakes, CA 93546. Retailer. Catalog, $1. Museum quality wagon models can be made from these plans, scaled from full-size vehicles, which include every detail down to the last nut and bolt. p. 268

Walmer Dollhouses, 2100 Jefferson Davis Hwy., Alexandria, VA 22301. Manufacturer. Wholesale only. Quality wooden dollhouses from the child's toy to the adult's collectible–finished dollhouses and beautiful kits that fit–featuring many architectural styles and designs and the best combination of price, quality and service anywhere! pp. 20-24, 34, 44, 45, 47, 48, 62, 73

Warber's Miniatures, 626 E. State St., Geneva, IL 60134. Handcrafted items available. All items made from Fimo. Write to us for more information. p. 291

Warling Miniatures, 22453 Covello St., West Hills, CA 91307. Artisan. For price list and brochure send $1 and LSASE. Our specialty is Victorian to modern wicker furniture and accessories in 1" and 1/2" scales, available completely finished or in kit form. Sealed, signed and dated pieces are available in natural or white and are upholstered and/or dressed the color of your choice. Wicker kits contain natural color waxed linen cord that can be left natural or sprayed white when completed. p. 229

Wee Three, 53 Miller Rd., Bethany, CT 06525. Retail only. Catalog $2. Fine needlework supplies. p. 293, 319

Wee Wonders, 222 7th St., Seal Beach, CA 90740. Artisan, retail, wholesale and manufacturer. Catalog $2. Handmade miniature accessories including toys, holiday decorations, food, sewing items and country folk art. Exquisitely done in 1" and 1/2" scale. Over 200 items to choose from. pp. 246, 253, 258, 259, 261, 268, 271, 296

Shirley Whitworth, 86 Pigeon Rd., Willimantic, CT 06226. IGMA artisan specializing in one-of-a-kind porcelain dolls for the serious collector. The costumes are researched for the period and certificates of authenticity are given to the buyer. The rugs are also to scale and are in "hooked" and Oriental designs. My work may be seen at shows or by appointment. Limited accessories also available. p. 235

What's Next?, 1000 Cedar Ave., Scranton, PA 18505. Retail, wholesale and artisan. Catalog $1. Exquisite porcelain bathroom set. Textured asphalt shingles, roll roofing, landscaping material, cedar shakes and tile floors. Dealer inquiries welcome. pp. 109, 110, 168, 224

Wilshire Miniatures, RD #1, Box B7, Mount Upton, NY 13809. Retailer and artisan. Send LSASE for brochure. Specializing in horse oriented miniatures including stable tools, tack, Breyer horses, cats and dogs (Otterbourne and Stone Mountain), tack room furniture and tin roofing. p. 40

Wood Products, 1456 Andrew S.E., Kentwood, MI 49508. Manufacturer. See your local dealer. Specializing in handmade foods and flowers. pp.. 251, 278

Woodcraft Specialties, 70 Cherry St., Locust Valley, NY 11560. Retail, manufacturer and artisan. We specialize in custom-built room boxes and one-of-a-kind precision built high quality dollhouses. For more information on our Harlingen House or custom building send a LSASE with your requirements. p. 62

Y

YLI Corporation, P.O. Box 109, Provo, UT 84603. Retail and wholesale. Catalog $2.50. 100% silk ribbon, spark organdy ribbon, synthetic silk ribbon, fancy ribbon. YLI also has silk thread in 215 colors and many more unique hard-to-find products including bunka to match silk ribbon. p. 161

Young World Studio, 228 Green Valley Rd., East Meadow, NY 11554. Retailer. Incredible American 1" scale miniature accessories. Spider webs, can openers, sculptures, hibachis, genie bottles and much more. Send $3 for more information and sample gifts. p. 261, 269

Your Local Potter, 3092 Woodmanor Ct., Ann Arbor, MI 48108. Artisan. Send LSASE for brochure. Wheel thrown, hand decorated porcelain in a variety of styles ranging from spongeware to delicate polychrome vases and lidded jars. Available at shows and via mail order. p. 245

Z

Alice Zinn, 23286-A S.W. 54th Way, Boca Raton, FL 33433. Retail, wholesale and artisan. Catalog, $2 plus double stamped long envelope. Custom-made animals, pets and pet accessories, wild birds and woodland animals, shoes, clothes, hats, leather goods, kid's stuff, stationery, bath items, audio/visual equipment, Oriental accessories, Chinese food, sporting goods, garden and patio accessories, custom work and workshops. pp. 237, 250, 251, 260, 267, 273, 286, 289, 291, 317

PRODUCT INDEX

A

Accessories—Decorative 1", 237-293
Accessories—1/2" Scale, 295-296
Accessories—Doll, 231
Adhesives & Glues, 324-325
Adobe Mix, 80
Andirons, 162
Animals, 238-239
Antique Shop, 42
Apex Trim, 76-77, 79
Apothecary Accessories, 274
Appliances—Kitchen, 226, 260-261
Applicator Bottle, 326
Arbor Kits, 37
Arch, 78
Architectural Components, 75-78
Armor—Medieval, 275
Awl, 326

B

Baby Buggy, 220, 229
Bakery Shop Accessories, 289-290
Bakery Display Case, 219
Balloons, 255
Balusters, 99-100
Bar Set, 269
Barbeque Grill, 253
Barn, 38
Barrels, 289
Baseball Cards, 267
Baskets, 246, 252, 254, 256, 266, 278, 290
Bathroom Accessories, 223-224, 239-241
Bathroom Furniture, 222-224
Bathroom Towels, 240
Battery Holders, 137, 138, 139, 142, 146
Bay Windows, 78-79, 298
Beauty Parlor, 219
Bedding, 242
Bedroom Accessories, 241-242
Beds—also see Furniture, 195-198, 202-204, 206-212
Beer Mug, 260
Bell—Door, 135, 142
Bicycles, 287
Bird Baths, 253
Bird Feeders, 253
Birdhouses, 214, 253
Birds, 291
Birth Certificates, 271
Blacken-It, 329
Blinds—Window, 173
Blocks—Corner, 100
Books & Related Products, 320
Books—Ready-to-Use, 322
Books for Collectors, 321
Bookcase, 212, 218, 243
Bowling Accessories, 288
Bowls—Soup, 245
Box—Battery, 145
Boxes—Produce, 289-290, 295
Brackets, 77
Brass Hinges, 93-94
Brick & Stone Supplies, 79-84
Brick—1/2", 299
Bridal Accessories, 277-278, also see the insert between pp.256-257
Brief Case, 262
Brownstone, 47, 80-81
Building Components & Supplies, 76-125
Building Supplies—1/2" Scale, 296-301
Bulb Extractor, 326
Bungalow, 48
Bunk Beds, 212
Butter Churns, 289

C

Cabin Furniture, 199
Cabins & Cottages, 26-29
Cakes, 255, 290
Calendar of Shows, 362-366
Calendar—1991 Miniatures, 320
Calendars, 266
Candies, 250-251, 257-259, 261, 268, 290, 309
Candles—Electric, 153
Candlesticks, 150
Candlesticks—1/2", 295
Canned Food Kits, 260, 274
Canopy Beds, 206-207
Cape Cod Houses, 18
Carpeting & Rugs, 169-171, 270-271
Carriage House & Stable, 39
Castles & Forts, 18-19
Catalogs, 78
Cats, 238
Cedar Chest, 247
Ceiling Fans, 128, 130
Ceiling Fixtures, 127-136, 155
Ceramic & Porcelain Accessories, 233-235, 244-245, 274
Chairs, 176, 196-197
Chair Rails, 77
Champagne Glasses, 247
Chandeliers, 127-136, 155, 263
Character Dolls, 231-232
Charcoal, 253
Checkerboard, 293
Chess, 293
Chests, 194-195, 247
Children's Houses, 19-22
Chimneys, 75-76, 83, 108
Chimneys—Glass, 143-144
Chimneys—1/2", 297
Chimneys—1/4", 306
Chimpanzees, 239
China, 245
Christmas Lights, 144, 147, 255
Christmas Tree, 255-258
Christmas Wreath, 140
Church, 39, 307
Churn—Butter, 289
Clamps, 327
Clapboard, 111
Clocks, 176, 194
Clocks—Grandfather, 176
Clothing Patterns, 232
Clothing—Doll, 232
Coach Lamps, 148-149
Cocktail Bar Set, 269
Collector's Boxes & Printer's Trays, 70
Colonial & Federal Furniture Kit, 176, 194-195
Colonial & Federal Furniture, 195-197
Colonial Houses, 22-24
Colonial, Southern & Georgian Houses, 45-45
Columns, 78
Contemporary Furniture, 207-213
Contemporary Houses, 25-26
Control Panel—Lighting, 139
Cookstoves, 204-205
Corner Blocks, 100
Corner Posts, 101, 300
Cottages & Cabins, 26-29

Product Index

Country Accessories, 246-247
Country Furniture, 197-200
Country Store, 43
Cradle, 222
Crates, 295
Crib, 221-222
Crown Molding, 104
Crowns—Jeweled, 259
Crystal & Glassware Accessories, 247, 254
Cupolas, 75
Curtains & Rods, 173-174, also see the insert between pp. 288-289
Cutter—Mitre, 328

D

Darts, 293
Day Beds, 207
Deck, 37
Decorations—Holiday, 254-259
Decorations—Party, 255
Dental Care Set, 240
Desks, 194, 219
Desk Accessories, 288-289
Desk Lamps, 150, 153-154, 156
Detailing, 329
Dining Room Accessories, 247
Dinnerware—1/2", 295
Dishes—see Ceramic & Porcelain
Displays for Miniatures, 63-73
Display Cabinets, Boxes, & Lamps, 64-66, 219
Display Case—Bakery, 219
Display Racks, 219
Doctor's Office Accessories, 247
Dog, 239
Doll Accessories, 231
Dolls—Character, 231-232
Dolls—Dollhouse, 233-235
Doll Clothing & Patterns, 232
Doll Kits, 236
Doll Stand, 231
Dollmaking Supplies/Molds, 236
Dollhouse Dollhouses, 40, also see the insert between pp. 80-81
Dollhouse Turntables, 66
Door Accessories—1/2", 296-300
Door Bells, 135, 142
Door Kits & Parts, 84-86
Door Knobs & Keyplates, 84, 93
Door Knockers, 84, 94
Door Locks, 94-95
Door Mat, 252
Door Panes, 85
Door Pulls, 94
Doors—1/2", 296-300
Doors—1/4", 306
Doors—Working, 86-93
Donuts, 289
Dormer, 76-77, 107, 114
Dormer—1/2", 298
Draperies, 173-174
Drapery Rods, 173
Drawer Pulls, 94-95
Dress Forms, 231
Dressers, 194-196, 198, 202, 204, 208
Dressing Tables Set, 207
Drills, 327

Drums, 287

E

Electrical & Interior Decorating—1/2" Scale, 302-303
Electrical Systems & Accessories, 126-159
Electrical Parts & Accessories, 137-145
Electrical Systems, 145-147
Electrification—Miscellaneous, 147
Etched Door Glass, 86
European Furniture, 176
Extension Cords, 143
Eyelets, 138

F

Fabric & Trim, 161
Farmhouses, 30-34
Federal Style Houses, 35-36
Federal & Colonial Furniture Kit, 176, 194-197
Federal & Colonial Furniture, 169, 170
Fencing, 76, 82, 100, 254, also see the insert between pp. 288-289
Figures, 248
Fimo, 99, 103, 168, 227, 236, 251, 324
Finishing Kit, 329
Finishing Supplies & Tools, 323-331
Firehouse, 45
Fireplace Accessories, 162, 249
Fireplaces, 162-164
Fireplace Flickering Lights, 162
Fireplace Screens, 162
Fishing Gear, 287-288
Fixtures—Ceiling, 127-136, 155
Fixtures—Wall, 157-159
Flag, 94
Flickering Lights—Fireplace, 140, 142-144, 162
Floor & Table Lamps, 149-156
Flooring—1/2", 297
Flooring, 164-168
Flooring Tiles, 164, 166-168
Flower Pots, 253, 277
Flowers & Plants, 276-278
Foods, 249-252
Foods—1/2", 295-296
Foods—Holiday, 255-257
Foods-Judaic, 249
Forceps, 330, 326
Forts & Castles, 18, 19
Fountains—Outdoor, 252-253
Fountains—Wall, 252
Frames, 265
Framing Clamp, 327
Freezer, 219
French Doors, 84, 88-90
Fruits, 247, 250, 274
Furniture, 175-176, 194-229
  European, 176
  Colonial & Federal, 176, 194-197
  Country, 197-200
  Victorian, 201-205
  20th Century, 205-207
  1930-Contemporary, 207-213

  Outdoor, 213-218
  Store & Office, 218-220
  Nursery, 220-222
  Bathroom, 222-224
  Kitchen, 224-226
  Wicker, 228-229
  Miscellaneous, 227
Furniture—1/2" scale, 301-302
Furniture—1/4", 307-308
Furniture—Wicker, 228-229, 301
Fuses, 142, 144

G

Games & Toys, 292-293
Garage, 40
Garden & Landscaping Accessories, 252-254
Garden Lamp, 216
Gas Station, 42
Gates, 254
Gazebos, 36-38
General Store, 41-42, 44
General Store Accessories, 290-291
Geni Bottle, 269
Georgian & Southern Colonial Houses, 45-46
Gift Baskets, 254
Giftwrap—Holiday, 257
Gingerbread House, 258
Glass Chimneys, 143-144
Glass Stock—Thin, 77
Glass Domes & Showcases, 66-67
Glassware & Crystal Accessories, 247, 254
Glassware—1/2", 295
Glues & Adhesives, 324-325
Glue—Elmers, 325
Glue Jigs, 326
Glue Sticks, 325
Golf Accessories, 287-288
Grandfather Clocks, 176
Grape Arbor Kit, 215
Gravila, 326
Greenery, 277
Greenhouses, Gazebos & Garden Buildings, 36-38
Grill—Barbeque, 253
Grommets, 142
Guillotine Cutter, 327
Gumball Machines, 290-291
Gutter, 104
Gym Equipment, 288

H

Hair Care Set, 275
Hammers, 326
Hand Tools, 326-328
Handrails, 98
Hardware & Metal Parts, 93-97
Hat, 231
Hat Salon, 201
Hat Stand, 231
Haunted House, 39
Hedge Clippers, 253
High Chair, 221
Hinges, 94-96

Holiday & Seasonal Accessories, 254-259
Holiday Decorations, 254-259
Holster, 262
Horse Stable, 40
Hose—Garden, 253, 266
Hot Tub, 37
Hourglass, 259
Houses, Plans & Displays—1/2" Scale, 303-305
Houses & Buildings, 18-62
Houses—1/4", 305-308
How-To: see Plans & How-To
Hurricane Lamp, 150, 153

I

Icebox, 198, 200, 206, 210
Indian & Southwestern Accessories, 285-287
Inkwell With Quill, 273
Interior Decorating Materials, 160-174

J

Japanese Tea Room, 40
Jewelry Accessories, 259
Jewelry Findings, 129
Judaic Foods, 249

K

Kaleidoscopes, 267
Keyboard—Electric, 269
Kiln, 291
Kitchen Accessories, 259-261
Kitchen Furniture, 224-226
Kites, 292
Kits—Wagon, 261
Kiva Scenes, 67

L

Ladders, 252, 269, 293
Lamps, Table & Floor, 149-15
Lamp—Hurricane, 150, 153
Lamp—Picture, 157
Lamps—Coach, 157
Lamps—Tiffany, 155-156
Landscaping & Garden Accessories, 252-254, also see insert between pp. 288-289
Landscaping Material—see also Outdoor, 206-209
Lantern, 129, 153
Lattices, 75, 101
Laundry Machines, 210
Leather Accessories, 262
Light Bulbs, 138-139, 144-145
Light Sets, 139, 146
Light Switches, 138, 141
Lighting Fixtures & Lamps, 262-263
Lighting Control Panel, 139
Lighting—Outdoor, 148-149
Lights—Christmas, 144, 147, 255
Linens, Needlework & Sewing Accessories, 270-271

Linens—Bed, 242
Liquor Bottles, 251
Living Room Accessories, 264
Log Cabins, 28-29
Luggage, 231
Lumber Supplies, 97-98

M

Magazines, 311
Mah Jongg, 293
Mailboxes, 214, 245
Mansion, 45
Maps, 273
Medicines, 247
Merchantile, 44
Metalware Accessories, 247, 264
Metal Parts & Hardware, 93-97
Microwave, 261
Millwork, 92-96
Millwork—1/2", 297
Miniatures Shops, 334-359
Mirrors & Screens, 265
Mirror Panels, 262
Miscellaneous Accessories—1", 265-269
Miscellaneous Buildings, 38-40
Mitre Cutter, 328
Modeling Compounds, 103
Molds & Dollmaking Supplies, 236
Moldings, 102-105
Money, 268
Mops, 261
Mortar, 80-81
Museums of Interest To Miniaturists, 367-368
Musical Instruments & Accessories, 269

N

Nails, 94, 96
Needle Files, 328
Needlework, Linen & Sewing Accessories, 270-271
Newel Posts, 99-101
Newel Posts—1/2", 299
Nightgown, 240
Nite-lite Box, 71
Novelty Displays, 67-69
Nursery Accessories, 271-272
Nursery Furniture, 220-222

O

Office & Shop Buildings, 41-45
Office & Store Furniture, 218-220
Organ, 269
Oriental Room Box, 73
Oriental Screens, 265
Outdoor Lighting, 148-149
Outdoor Furniture & Landscaping Materials, 206-209
Outlet, 137
Outlet Cover, 139
Oysters, 260

P

Paintings, Prints, Watercolors, Etchings, 272-273
Paints & Finishes, 329, also see insert between pp. 288-289
Paneling & Trim for Walls & Ceilings, 102, 168
Paper Accessories, 273
Park Bench, 213
Party Decorations, 255
Patina-It, 329
Patio Furniture—see Outdoor Furniture 215, 218
Pennants, 266
Period Accessories, 273-275
Personal Items—1" Accessories, 275
Pet Bed, 291
Pet Shop Accessories, 291
Pheasants, 238
Photographs, 243, 275-276
Piano, 269
Picket Fence, 214-215
Picnic baskets, 266
Picture Lamp, 262
Picture Window, 120
Pinball, 293
Pitcher, 245
Plans & How-To: Furniture & Furnishings, 315
Plans & How-To: Decorative Accessories, 316
Plans & How-To: Dolls, 316
Plans & How-To: Houses & Shops, 312-315
Plans & How-To: Miscellaneous, 317-319
Plant Stand, 206
Plantation, 45-46
Planters, 174
Plants & Flowers, 276-278
Plastic Boxes, 65
Plastic Sheets, 82-83, 108, 111, 167-168
Playpen, 221
Playscale Houses, 20
Pliers, 327
Plugs, 137, 139, 144
Plunger, 246
Pool Table, 293
Popcorn, 291
Porcelain & Ceramic, 233-235
Porch, 73
Porch Fence, 100
Porch Posts, 101
Porch Railings, 76, 98-99
Porch Spindles, 99
Porch Swing, 216
Porch Trim, 99
Postcards, 289
Post Lamps, 149
Posts, 99-100
Posts—1/2", 299
Posts—Corner, 101, 300
Posts—Newel, 99-101
Posts—Newel—1/2", 299
Posts—Porch, 101
Pots—Flower, 253, 277
Potty Chair, 221

Power Tools & Accessories, 329-331
Power Strips, 144
Preserves Jars, 261
Printer's Trays & Collector Boxes, 70
Produce Boxes, 289-290, 295
Publications & Plans, 310-322
Pumpkins, 255
Punch Bowls, 256-257

Q

Quilts, 243, 271

R

Racks—Display, 219
Railings, 76-77, 98-99, 113
Rainwear, 231
Ready-to-Use Books, 322
Receptacles—Electrical, 145
Refrigerator, 198, 200, 206, 210
Reindeer, 258
Resin, 96
Ribbon Shredder, 327
Ribbons, 161
Rifles, 288
Rolling Pin, 260
Roofing Materials, 107-110
Roofing—Slate, 109
Room Boxes & Vignettes, 65, 70-73
Rug—1/2", 295
Rugs & Carpeting, 169-171, 270, 271

S

S Hooks, 94
Saddlery, 287
Saloon, 43
Sanders, 328, 331
Sanding Paddles, 327
Saws, 330
Saws—Table, 330
Sceptre—Jeweled, 259
School House, 38-40
School Supplies, 269
Sconces, 157-159, 263
Screens & Mirrors, 265
Screens, 228, 265, also see the insert between pp. 80-81
Screens—Fireplace, 162
Screwdriver Set, 326
Scrollwork, 76
Sculptures & Statues, 278-285
Seasonal & Holiday Accessories, 254-259
Sewing, Needlework & Linen Accessories, 270-271
Sewing Accessories, 270-271
Shades—Glass, 127-128
Shades—Lamp, 138
Shades—Window, 173
Shelves, 67
Shingles, 106-109
Shingles—1/2", 299
Shoes, 262
Shop & Office Buildings, 41-45
Shovels, 253
Show Calendar, 362-366

Shrink Tubes, 138, 141
Shrubbery, 216
Shutters, 110
Shutters—1/2", 299
Siding Materials, 111
Signs, 289
Silverware—see also Metalware, 247, 264
Sinks, 222, 226, 241
Skylights, 265
Sled, 287
Smaller Scale Accessories, 295-309
Smaller Scale Miniatures, 305-309
Smaller Scale Miscellaneous, 309
Snow, 329
Sockets, 139
Sofa, 202-203, 210-211
Solder, 326
Soldering Iron, 327
Soup Bowls, 245
Southern Colonial & Georgian Houses, 45-46
Southwestern & Indian Accessories, 285-287
Specialty Shop Accessories, 291-292
Special Services, 311
Spindles, 99, 101
Spindles—Porch, 99
Spindles—Staircase, 101
Spinning Wheel, 204
Splicing Material, 141
Sport Accessories, 287-288
Sprinkler, 253
Stable, 40
Stained Glass, 120, 125
Staircases, 112-114
Stairs—1/2", 299
Stand—Doll, 231
Stereo, 269
Stone & Brick Supplies, 79-84
Stonewear, 244-246, 259, 273-274
Storage Boxes, 265
Store & Office Furniture, 218-220
Store—General, 41-42, 44
Store & Shop Accessories, 288-289
Stove, 198, 200, 206, 210
Stucco, 80, 172, 329
Surgical Instruments, 328
Swing—Porch, 216
Switch—Covers, 139
Switches, 138

T

Table & Floor Lamps, 149-156, 263
Table Saws, 330
Tape Wire, 137
Tapestries, 170, 275
Teddy Bears, 292
Telescope, 267
Televisions, 208
Tennis Accessories, 287-288
Terminal Blocks, 139
Test Probes, 139
Tiara, 259
Tinwear—Kitchen, 265
Toilet, 240-241
Tool Box, 246, 252
Tools, 293, 328

Tools—Fireplace, 154, 241
Tools—Power & Accessories, 329-331
Tools & Finishing Supplies, 323-331
Tools—Hand, 326-328
Topiary Trees, 217
Towel Bar, 95
Towels—Bath, 240
Townhouses, 47-48, 60
Toys & Games—1", 292-293, also see insert between pp. 80-81
Transformer, 137-139
Trashcans, 267
Tree—Christmas, 255-258
Trees, 213, 216
Trim—Apex, 76-77, 90, 301
Trims, 97-98, 105-106, also see insert between pp. 80-81
Trim & Paneling for Walls & Ceilings, 102, 168
Trophies—Sporting, 287-288
Tubs, 223, 240-241
Tudor Houses, 48-49
Turnings, 101, 300
Turntables, 66

V

Vanity Set, 242
Vases, 252
Vegetables, 250
Venetian Blinds, 173
Victorian Houses, 49-62
Victorian Furniture Kit, 201-202
Victorian Furniture, 202-205
Vignettes & Room Boxes, 65, 70-73

W

Wagons, 261, 268
Wainscotting, 168
Wall Fixtures, 157-159
Wall Coverings, 172
Wallpaper, 161, 172
Wallpaper—1/2", 302
Washboard, 246
Weather-It, 329
Weathering Liquids, 329
Weathervanes, 106-107
Welcome Mats, 252
Wheelbarrow, 252-253
Wheels—1/2", 297
Wicker Furniture, 228-229
Windows—Working, 120-125
Windows—Non-working, 114-120
Window Blinds & Shades, 173
Windows—Bay, 78-79, 298
Window Stock Parts & Kits, 125
Window—Dormer, 76-77, 107, 114
Window Treatments, 173
Windows—1/2", 296-300
Windows—1/4", 306, 308
Windows—Stained Glass, 115, 120
Wine, 250
Wiring, 138, 145-147
Wood Turnings, 97
Workshop Accessories—1", 293
Wreath—Christmas, 140